EFFECTIVE SCHOOL INTERVENTIONS

ALSO AVAILABLE

Effective
School
Interventions

THIRD EDITION

Evidence-Based
Strategies for Improving
Student Outcomes

Matthew K. Burns
T. Chris Riley-Tillman
Natalie Rathvon

THE GUILFORD PRESS
New York   London

Library of Congress Cataloging-in-Publication Data

Names: Burns, Matthew K., author. | Riley-Tillman, T. Chris., author. |
  Rathvon, Natalie, author.
Title: Effective school interventions : evidence-based strategies for
  improving student outcomes / Matthew K. Burns, T. Chris Riley-Tillman,
  Natalie Rathvon.
Description: Third Edition. | New York : The Guilford Press, [2017] | Natalie
  Rathvon appears as sole author on first (1999) and second (2008) editions'
  title pages. | Includes bibliographical references and index.
Identifiers: LCCN 2017028511 | ISBN 9781462526147 (hardcover : acid-free
  paper)
Subjects: LCSH: Inclusive education—United States. | Classroom
  management—United States. | Behavior modification—United States. |
  Academic achievement—United States. | Social skills—Study and
  teaching—United States.
Classification: LCC LC1201 .R38 2017 | DDC 371.9/046—dc23
LC record available at *https://lccn.loc.gov/2017028511*

About the Authors

Matthew K. Burns, PhD, is Associate Dean for Research and Professor of School Psychology in the College of Education at the University of Missouri–Columbia. He is a past editor of *School Psychology Review* and *Assessment for Effective Intervention.* His research focuses on the use of assessment data to determine individual or small-group interventions. Dr. Burns served on the faculty of the University of Minnesota for 10 years and Central Michigan University for 5 years. He has published over 175 articles, book chapters, and books, most related to response to intervention, academic interventions, and facilitating problem-solving teams.

T. Chris Riley-Tillman, PhD, is Professor and Chair of the Department of Educational, School and Counseling Psychology at the University of Missouri–Columbia. He is a senior advisor for the National Center on Intensive Intervention and the creator and lead developer of the Evidence Based Intervention Network, a nonprofit website that features evidence-based intervention and assessment resources for educational professionals. Dr. Riley-Tillman has published over 100 articles and 6 books focusing on evidence-based practice in schools and is editor of The Guilford Practical Interventions in the Schools Series. He is a Fellow of Division 16 (School Psychology) of the American Psychological Association and a member of the Society for the Study of School Psychology.

Natalie Rathvon, PhD, now retired, was Assistant Clinical Professor of Psychology at The George Washington University, where she supervised graduate students in school-based placements. A former teacher, guidance director, counselor educator, and psychologist in private practice, she has provided consultation and professional development to schools and agencies in assessment and accountability, reading, problem-solving teams, and school interventions. Dr. Rathvon has published several books for professionals and parents.

Preface

The first edition of this book was published in 1999 and the second in 2008; much has changed since then. The mandates of the No Child Left Behind Act (NCLB) of 2001, the Every Student Succeeds Act (ESSA) of 2015, and the Individuals with Disabilities Education Improvement Act (IDEIA) of 2004 require that school personnel support students in general education with scientifically based instructional practices. Schools are now explicitly charged with implementing scientifically based interventions and evaluating their effectiveness to increase the likelihood that all students will reach the proficiency standards set forth in NCLB.

There has been an unparalleled growth in the knowledge base of empirically validated interventions since the publication of this book's first edition, due in part to intervention research grants from the Institute of Education Sciences of the U.S. Department of Education, and the What Works Clearinghouse's mechanism for distributing the results (e.g., practice guides). The National Center on Intensive Intervention's "tools charts" has also supported the distribution of interventions by reviewing interventions and related assessment methods (*www.intensiveintervention.org/resources/tools-charts*). The Internet has allowed wide distribution of intervention resources that are available for free to practitioners (e.g., *www.ebi.missouri.edu*; *www.interventioncentral.org*; *www.gosbr.net*). Finally, many schools across the country are implementing multi-tiered systems of support (MTSS) to systematically identify and intervene in order to improve academic and behavior deficits.

Today's school consultants need more than a few isolated strategies that target single low-performing or ineffectively behaving students. They need to be knowledgeable about a broad range of strategies that enhance teachers' capacity to create orderly, productive learning environments and students' capacity to benefit from instruction. In particular, they need to be knowledgeable about interventions that can improve the outcomes for an entire classroom while still accommodating diverse learners. Moreover, busy practitioners have limited time to sift through the ever-expanding array of intervention-oriented journals, books, and web-based resources to locate a strategy that matches the problem they are trying to address. Even if practitioners are able to locate an intervention targeting the referral problem, other barriers to implementation remain. Because of space limitations in journals and books, interventions are seldom described in sufficient detail to permit accurate and effective implementation. Many interventions described in the literature or available from commercial publishers are too costly, time-consuming, and/or complex to be implemented by regular classroom teachers. Consultants seeking to assist teachers of struggling students must first identify a suitable strategy for the identified problem within the limits of their resources and then attempt to adapt it to the exigencies of the classroom environment. Given these constraints, it is a small wonder that even when prereferral interventions are attempted, consultants tend to rely on a narrow range of strategies, and teachers often report that the referral problem remains unsolved.

PURPOSE

This book bridges the gap between research and the practical realities of consulting in today's schools by providing a compendium of empirically validated interventions that have been translated from the original source or sources and adapted for implementation in the regular classroom environment. Each of the 83 interventions is presented in a standardized format that provides step-by-step implementation procedures to facilitate treatment integrity and successful outcomes. Designed specifically for use within a consultation framework, the format has been developed and refined in the context of numerous consultations, *in vivo* coaching sessions, intervention assistance team meetings, and professional development programs. To meet the increasing demand for accountability and data-driven decision making in educational programming, each intervention includes an evaluation component that describes several different methods of assessing its effects on the targeted area of concern. This book is also a resource guide to the rapidly expanding field of evidence-based school interventions. In addition to the citations for each intervention, each chapter includes an annotated list of print- and web-based resources to assist consultants in locating other useful materials.

AUDIENCE

This book is written for practitioners in school psychology, child and adolescent clinical psychology, regular and special education, counseling, educational administration, and school social work and for graduate or preservice students in those disciplines. It should be especially useful to school psychologists, consultants, special education coordinators, regular and special education teachers, and other practitioners involved in intervention-based service delivery. It is also intended to serve as a resource for practitioners who conduct psychological and psychoeducational assessments with school-age children. Using this book, they can locate strategies targeting a wide variety of referral problems and include them in the recommendation sections of their reports to help link assessment results to intervention. Examples of this application are provided in Chapter 2.

NEW TO THIS EDITION

The book retains the same basic structure as the first two editions, but we made substantial revisions based on reader feedback and to incorporate recent research and developments in the field of school-based interventions. Other changes designed to reflect best practices and enhance usability follow.

- Of the 83 interventions, 20 are new to this edition. In the field of school-based interventions, *recent* is not always synonymous with *efficacious* and *usable*, but the interventions are based on current research or seminal studies that are still relevant to today's schools.

- The chapters have been organized according to intervention topics to facilitate easy use. Interventions are now classified as academic (general, reading, mathematics, writing, and content areas), behavioral (academic behaviors, group, individuals, and other settings), and preschool.

- The intervention briefs include a section about intervention intensity. Practitioners implementing a response-to-intervention (RTI) or MTSS framework often ask whether interventions are appropriate for Tier 1, Tier 2, or Tier 3. We are hesitant to classify interventions in such a way because interventions may work for multiple tiers, and it is too simplistic to conceptualize interventions in such a way. Therefore, we describe the intervention intensity based on the amount of resources needed to implement them and the appropriate target (whole class, small groups, or individual students).

ORGANIZATION OF THE TEXT

The text consists of two parts. In Part I, Chapter 1 reviews the context for the evidence-based-intervention movement and its evolution into RTI and MTSS frameworks. Chapter 2 contextualizes interventions within the intervention assistance team (IAT) process, discusses systems to implement them, and considers relevant ethical and legal codes. Chapter 3 outlines the skills that interventionists need to be successful beyond implementing individual interventions, including selecting interventions, consulting with teachers in a problem-solving framework, assessing student skills, and analyzing data.

Part II presents the 83 interventions. Chapter 4 includes 41 interventions designed to improve academic performance. Chapter 5 includes 35 intervention briefs for behavior difficulties, organized according to academic behavior and as group interventions, individual interventions, and interventions for settings other than classrooms. Finally, Chapter 6 presents 7 interventions for preschoolers, but many of the interventions presented in the other two chapters are also appropriate for children in preschool.

A NOTE OF THANKS

We again express our appreciation to the many readers and field-test participants who have provided feedback on the first two editions of this book. We welcome your suggestions for improving future editions of *Effective School Interventions: Evidence-Based Strategies for Improving Student Outcomes* and invite you to contact us at *burnsmk@missouri.edu, rileytillmant@missouri.edu,* or *JNRathv88@aol.com.*

Matthew Burns and Chris Riley-Tillman also thank Natalie Rathvon for including us in the third edition of the book. We both used and recommended her first two editions because they were outstanding resources. We are honored to be included in this version.

We greatly appreciate the efforts of Kristy Warmbold-Brann, who helped organize and support our writing, and of The Guilford Press team, especially Natalie Graham, for their support. We also gratefully acknowledge the giants on whose shoulders we stand. These include such people as Ed Shapiro, Irwin Hyman, Stan Deno, and Ken Merrell, whom we have lost as friends and trusted mentors, and Jim Ysseldyke, Sylvia Rosenfield, Tom Kratochwill, and others who created the path we now walk but who have retired from the daily profession.

Finally, Matthew and Chris gratefully acknowledge the loving support of their families—Mary, Matthew, Kate, Erin, and Luke.

Prologue

NATALIE RATHVON

This book began with a question. In the early 1990s, I was teaching a seminar on school consultation to a group of psychology interns who were providing assessment and intervention services in the local schools. Each week I would give a short presentation on various aspects of consultation, including models, ethics, listening skills, and so on, after which the interns would present cases for discussion. I was also conducting research on consultation and writing up cases from my own work in the schools with the idea of preparing a book on the subject. One morning, as my supervisees were practicing listening skills in pairs and I was congratulating myself on how well the session was going, an intern who had been struggling with an especially difficult classroom situation suddenly leaned across the conference table and wailed plaintively, "But what do I do after I'm done listening to the teacher?" As the entire class looked expectantly at me, I realized that I was poorly prepared to answer that question. Like many other educators at that time, I had a "bag of tricks" consisting of strategies borrowed from other teachers, garnered from workshops and professional journals, or created on the spur of the moment, but nothing that I could pass on in an organized, easy-to-use format. It was a watershed moment, not only for the seminar but also for the direction that my own research would take. I promptly abandoned the notion of writing a school consultation book and began scouring the professional literature for practical, evidence-based strategies that I could share with the class, as well as use in my own consultation work.

As I searched for practical interventions, the school ecologies in which the interns and I were working, as well as my experiences as a teacher, counselor, and psychologist, shaped the selection criteria. Many of the handbooks of classroom strategies for teachers or consultants then available offered few or no data supporting their effectiveness with students beyond the authors' reassurances. In contrast, the professional literature regularly reported strategies with documented effectiveness in helping students with learning or behavior challenges, but those interventions were often impractical for busy educators. For example, they relied on additional resources not available in the regular classroom, involved major alterations in teacher routines, or required teachers to participate in lengthy training programs in order to learn the strategy and implement it effectively. As a consultant working primarily in underresourced urban settings, I needed interventions that could be quickly and easily taught to teachers or trainees with a minimum of extra resources, classroom disruption, or training time. As part of that effort, I began experimenting with a standardized, step-by-step intervention format that was suitable for individual or group teacher consultation, student support team meetings, and professional development sessions. This aspect of the field testing was one of the most useful and rewarding aspects of preparing the book. The teachers in the schools to which I was consulting were dedicated, hard-working professionals who cared deeply about their students, and they were eager to share their successes, as well as their struggles. Moreover, they were not reticent in offering unvarnished feedback on what I was presenting and how I was presenting it, and they were quick to let me know if a particular strategy was too time-consuming, complex, or intrusive.

Another factor shaping the intervention format was the increasing demand for accountability in education. As the intervention-assistance and collaborative-teaming movements gathered momentum, teachers and administrators were being asked for data to determine whether the instructional practices and strategies being implemented were effective, but they needed uncomplicated, classroom-friendly evaluation tools, not elaborate measures that only a researcher with a team of graduate students could employ. I therefore provided in each intervention a choice of several evaluation tools that adhered as closely as possible to the methodology in the original study but that were capable of being implemented by classroom teachers, student support team members, or consultants.

The interns in the agency in which I was working were also clamoring for help in developing recommendations to include in the assessments they were conducting. After hours of parent and teacher interviewing, classroom observations, and diagnostic testing in school or clinic, they would prepare lengthy reports detailing the students' academic or behavioral problems. Like many other assessors, including me, however, they lacked access to an easy-to-use guide to empirically based strategies to address the needs that had been identified. In that era, student evaluations tended to focus on classification for placement in special education rather than on providing information for improving classroom performance. In contrast, the question foremost in the minds of the teachers and parents who had been waiting for weeks or even months for the results was: "Now that we know this, what can we do to help the student become more successful?" In fact, as I sat in test-informing sessions with my trainees, I would often observe parents and educators flip rapidly through the pages of the report they had just received in the hope of finding some concrete strategies they could put immediately into practice. So I began having the trainees include, in the recommendation sections of their assessment reports, information on interventions being used in consultation settings to target the needs that had been identified. This application was field-tested for several years with George Washington University clinical psychology predoctoral students conducting clinic- and school-based assessments as part of their training.

It took 4 years to research, field-test, and finalize the interventions. As I worked, the knowledge base of empirically based interventions grew exponentially, prompting numerous updates and rewrites in addition to the revisions I was constantly making in light of field-testing results. *Effective School Interventions: Strategies for Enhancing Academic Achievement and Social Competence (ESI)* appeared in 1999, with 76 interventions in three basic categories: proactive, academic, and behavioral. The book that had begun as a practical guide that I could use in my own work turned out to be useful to other educators, and I was delighted to hear how others found it helpful in their classrooms and schools. I was especially gratified to hear from educators involved in graduate training programs, as *ESI* had been developed in that context. I also benefited greatly from the feedback I was receiving on *ESI*, including the specific interventions, format, and evaluation tools, and began using the data to prepare a second edition.

I was diverted, however, by another question or, rather, a set of questions. During the time I had been writing *ESI,* I had heard with increasing frequency the following questions, this time from parents as well as school personnel: "Why are so many young children having trouble learning to read? How can we identify at-risk students early in their school careers before it's too late for them to catch up?" At that time, there was a widespread notion that children in the early primary grades were too young to be assessed for reading problems. If they could read only a few words or couldn't read at all, how could their reading skills be tested? By the time struggling readers were identified using typical testing instruments and methodologies, they had often fallen so far behind that they had little chance of catching up, even if they began receiving special assistance. Now, a growing body of research was demonstrating that at-risk children in the early primary grades could be accurately identified by means of recently developed scientifically based assessments and, moreover, that early intervention was much more effective in helping them become successful readers. So I began exploring the burgeoning array of early reading tools and field-testing them with young poor readers in the schools to which I was consulting. The result was *Early Reading Assessment: A Practitioner's Handbook (ERA),* published in 2004.

I then returned to preparing a second edition of *ESI.* By this time, the evidence-based intervention and practice movement had evolved, with the development of response-to-intervention and multi-tiered student support models and an even greater emphasis on data-based decision making. To reflect these and other changes in the field, the second edition was a major revision, with 42 new interventions and enhanced coverage of best practices in evaluation, legal issues and ethics, positive behavior support, and other topics especially relevant for collaborative intervention planning. Also new was a chapter devoted to strategies for preschoolers, the impetus for which arose from field-testing the instruments later included in *ERA.* Based on field testing and feedback from the first edition, intervention procedures were also clarified and expanded, with a total of 70 interventions in the same basic categories. *Effective School Interventions, Second Edition: Evidence-Based Strategies for Improving Student Outcomes* appeared in 2008.

Now, in 2017, nearly two decades after the appearance of the first edition of *ESI,* I am delighted and honored that Chris Riley-Tillman and Matt Burns, who have contributed enormously to the field, have brought the book into its next phase. My hope is that it will continue to serve as a useful resource for teachers, administrators, graduate students, and all those engaged in the effort to support students and their families. Once again, I wish to acknowledge the warmth and generosity of the teachers and administrators involved in the field testing who welcomed me into their classrooms and schools and were willing to try something different to help their students. I would also like to express my appreciation to the staff of The Guilford Press, with whom I have been happily associated for more than 20 years, especially Natalie Graham, in whose expert and benevolent hands this edition has taken shape. My love and gratitude, as always, to my husband, James, my dearest collaborator in all of my life's endeavors.

Contents

CHAPTER FIVE   Interventions to Improve Social Behavior   219

Purchasers of this book can download
and print select figures at
www.guilford.com/burns3-forms
for personal use or use with students
(see copyright page for details).

EFFECTIVE SCHOOL INTERVENTIONS

PART I

The Intervention Assistance Approach to Improving Student Outcomes

CHAPTER ONE

Introduction

Some teachers reading this book might find this hard to believe, but education in this country has never been better. More students attend school to completion than ever before, instruction in all states is now directed by challenging content standards in the core academic subjects, schools are systematically using data to drive instruction and intervention efforts, teachers frequently function within high-performing teams that focus on improving student outcomes, and technology has become a common tool to enhance student learning in many schools, and in many cases it is working! Scores on the National Assessment of Educational Progress (NAEP) have consistently gone up over the past 25 years for all students and for students from every ethnicity group. The gap between white and black students in reading and mathematics has gone down substantially, but it still exists, and reducing it further has become a national priority. The graduation rate in this country has reached an all-time high of 81%. The data clearly indicate that teachers, administrators, school psychologists, school counselors, and other educational professionals should be proud of their profession and the positive impact they have on children and youth.

Despite the preponderance of effective practices and positive outcomes in most states, every teacher and school-based professional reading this book can easily identify students who are not achieving success:

Tom, the third grader who seems so good at mathematics but almost refuses to read and write.

Wayne, the fifth grader with a positive attitude who tries so hard but just does not remember what he learned yesterday.

Tina, the sixth grader who tells you that she "hates math."

Greg, the eighth grader who will not sit still in class.

Jim, the tenth grader who seems to have given up entirely and who everyone is sure has started experimenting with drugs.

Each of these students has two things in common. First, every teacher, school psychologist, counselor, and speech and language pathologist sees potential in each of these students. Second, school-based personnel are frustrated that they cannot do more to help them.

The last few decades have also seen a dramatic rise in the diversity and intensity of student needs, coupled with greater demands for accountability and a school curriculum linking student performance to high-stakes testing. America's classrooms are now home to a highly diverse student population in terms of achievement levels, ethnic and linguistic backgrounds, socioeconomic status (SES), and disability status, including an increasing number of students from families living below the poverty level and/or from homes in which English is not the primary language. In 2012, the percentage of white students in public K–12 schools fell below 50% for the first time in this country's history, and almost 10% of children and youth in public schools do not speak English as the first language (National Center for Education Statistics [NCES], 2015).

Federal legislation, such as the No Child Left Behind Act (NCLB) and its successor, the Every Student Succeeds Act (ESSA), mandated scientifically validated practices in schools. At the same time, there has been a growing recognition of the critical influence of school experiences on children's long-term outcomes, especially for children from high-poverty and diverse backgrounds (Hamre & Pianta, 2001; Klingner & Artiles, 2006; Rimm-Kaufman, Fan, Chiu, & You, 2007). To meet these challenges, education professionals will need expertise in helping teachers create classroom environments that promote academic productivity and appropriate social behavior for an increasingly diverse student population. In particular, they will need information about a broad range of strategies that are not only effective in enhancing outcomes for individual students but that can also be applied on a group basis to help all the students in a classroom become successful learners. Education professionals will also need information about the evidence-based-practice approach to intervention, which is the process of designing, implementing, and evaluating interventions, regardless of whether that process is implemented by an individual or within a team-based framework.

THE EVIDENCE-BASED-INTERVENTION AND -PRACTICE MOVEMENT

In the not-too-distant past, education professionals tended to rely on interventions based primarily on familiarity, but schools are now mandated to use evidence-based practices according to ESSA. There have also been numerous calls in the field urging school psychologists to implement evidence-based strategies and practices at the classroom and building levels to assist students with learning and behavioral problems (e.g., Forman et al., 2013; Kratochwill & Shernoff, 2004; Kratochwill & Stoiber, 2000; Stoiber & Kratochwill, 2000). In 1998, Division 16 of the American Psychological Association and the Society for the Study of School Psychology collaborated to form the Task Force on Evidence-Based Interventions in School Psychology with the mission of bridging the research-to-practice gap by identifying prevention and intervention programs, using rigorous criteria to review them, and providing ratings reflecting that review (Kratochwill & Stoiber, 2000; Stoiber & Kratochwill, 2000); Division 16 later formed the Working Group on Translating Science to Practice (Forman et al., 2013). In a related effort, the Institute of Education Sciences (IES) at the U.S. Department of Education established the What Works Clearing House (*www.whatworks.org*) in 2002 to develop standards for reviewing and synthesizing educational research and to provide educators, policymakers, researchers, and the public with a central independent source of scientific evidence of effective educational interventions.

Evidence-based interventions (EBIs) are strategies, practices, and programs with available research documenting their effectiveness and data suggesting that they are enhancing student outcomes. ESSA refers on numerous occasions to evidence-based practices, but it offers no specific definition as to what constitutes an evidence-based intervention or practice. The act does define what represents strong evidence, which includes at least one randomized experimental study, and moderate evidence, which includes a quasi-experimental study.

Intervention Assistance Teams and EBIs

Although EBIs have been a popular concept of late, they are not new. Many of the current ideas in EBI can be linked back to the early consultation literature (Bergan & Kratochwill, 1990) or data-based program modification (DBPM; Deno & Mirkin, 1977). Many schools implemented consultation-based approaches to identifying EBIs such as DBPM through an intervention assistance team (IAT), which was a multidisciplinary collaboration to identify, analyze, and suggest interventions in order to increase teacher effectiveness and support students experiencing difficulties (Graden, Casey, & Christenson, 1985). Federal special education guidelines required interventions before students could be referred for an evaluation to identify a disability, but they did not outline what that prereferral should entail. Thus, many schools implemented IATs but did so in a wide variety of ways across and within states. As Buck, Polloway, Smith-Thomas, and Cook (2003) observed, "pre-referral is one of the most inconsistently applied processes in education" (p. 350). Meta-analytic research found large effects for IATs, but differences in effectiveness were found and attributed to the implementation integrity of those teams (Burns & Symington, 2002). Moreover, the only direct assessment of the effect that implementation of a prereferral IAT process had on student outcomes was conducted with the Pennsylvania Instructional Support Team model (Kovaleski, Tucker, & Stevens, 1996), which found that teams with high implementation had stronger outcomes and that low implementation led to outcomes similar to those of a control group (Kovaleski, Gickling, Morrow, & Swank, 1999).

In addition to implementation integrity, IATs experienced several other difficulties. First, the interventions provided by IATs were often simplistic and low quality (Flugum & Reschly, 1994; Telzrow, McNamara, & Hollinger, 2000). Rather than targeting the classroom environment and making recommendations that required teachers to make substantive changes in their instructional or behavior management practices, IATs tended to emphasize recommendations that focused on factors outside of the classroom, such as counseling and after-school tutoring (McNamara & Hollinger, 2003; Meyers, Valentino, Meyers, Boretti, & Brent, 1996).

Second, IATs were often unable to assist teachers in solving the referral problem, especially in the case of students with behavioral difficulties. Teams rarely considered the function of ineffective behavior or the influence of classroom environmental factors on student behavior and tended to select punitive and exclusionary strategies rather than strategies that helped students learn acceptable replacement behaviors (Scott et al., 2005). Under these circumstances, the likelihood of a successful outcome was greatly diminished.

Third, teachers often made little or no effort to implement team recommendations, especially at the secondary level (Rubinson, 2002). As Sindelar, Griffin, Smith, and Watanabe (1992) aptly observed, "Regardless of the quality of the plan that the team develops, its implementation by the classroom teacher remains the most crucial step of the process" (p. 255). Teachers' failure to implement recommendations was related to the frequent failure by teams to provide adequate follow-up and support to teachers after recommending interventions (Bahr, Whitten, Dieker, Kocarek, & Manson, 1999; Doll et al., 2005), as well as to teachers' perception that teams ignore or devalue their input during the problem-solving process (Slonski-Fowler & Truscott, 2004).

Fourth, IATs often failed to implement a systematic data collection and progress monitoring system to generate information for problem solving or to assess intervention effectiveness (Truscott, Cosgrove, Meyers, & Eidle-Barkman, 2000). Teams typically devoted too little time to gathering and reviewing information to help define problems and moved too rapidly to discussing intervention alternatives (Meyers et al., 1996). Once interventions had been implemented, teams and teachers alike often failed to employ objective evaluation procedures to determine whether the intervention had been implemented as planned (i.e., to assess treatment integrity) or to assess changes in student performance (Bahr et al., 1999; Flugum & Reschly, 1994; Meyers et al., 1996). Even when some form of follow-up was provided, teams seldom used direct measures of student outcomes, such as curriculum-based assessments or classroom behavioral observations. Instead, teams typically relied on verbal contacts for follow-up and teacher judgment for evaluating intervention effectiveness (Bahr et al., 1999; Truscott et al., 2000). Data-based evaluation methods, such as graphing intervention results, comparing pre- and postintervention data, and conducting systematic classroom observations, were rarely used (Bahr et al., 1999). Without collecting and analyzing data to document intervention effects, however, consultants and teachers cannot determine which, if any, strategies result in improved student performance.

Fifth, there was a lack of knowledge of EBIs and effective problem-solving processes by team members. Over 90% of school psychologists who responded to a survey indicated a need for more training in interventions (Nelson & Machek, 2007), and a large majority of special education teachers reported that they continued to use interventions for which there was a questionable research base (Burns & Ysseldyke, 2009). Similarly, despite evidence that students who are referred to teams that include special educators are significantly less likely to be retained or referred for special education evaluations (Burns, 1999), educational specialists, such as reading teachers or speech–language pathologists, are often not included on teams, limiting teams' ability to design effective interventions, especially strategies targeting academic performance (Slonski-Fowler & Truscott, 2004; Truscott et al., 2000).

Finally, the IAT process was not contextualized within a larger intervention framework and often operated independently of instructional practice. Consider a school with 500 students. On average, 20% of students need additional support despite effective instructional practices (Burns, Appleton, & Stehouwer, 2005), which suggests that in a school of 500 students, 100 of them will need additional support. Many schools would attempt to meet and conduct an IAT for 100 students. Needless to say, there cannot be an effective intervention process when schools are gathering five to eight professionals, collecting all relevant data about students, engaging in in-depth analyses, and selecting research-based interventions that address the underlying function of behavior for 100 students. First, schools need a systemic approach that addresses the needs of most of these 100 students, leaving only approximately 5% (25 in our fictitious school of 500). Second, school personnel should examine the core instruction and classwide disciplinary practices to make sure that they are research based and implemented with fidelity. Thus effective team intervention has to be more systematic and systemic.

Multi-Tiered Systems of Support and EBIs

The Individuals with Disabilities Education Improvement Act (IDEIA, 2004) incorporated a system intervention-oriented approach to service delivery by focusing on intervention services rather than on traditional assessments to identify students' needs and to monitor progress. IDEIA permits local education agencies to use up to 15% of federal funds for early intervening services for students in grades K–12, with a special focus on students in grades K–3 who have not been identified as needing special education or related services but who require additional academic and behavioral support to succeed in a general education environment (20 U.S.C. § 1413[f][1]). In addition, IDEIA permits local education agencies to identify children with specific learning disabilities by means of a process that measures response to scientific, research-based interventions as a substitute for or supplement to ability–achievement discrepancy models of eligibility determination (20 U.S.C. 1414 [b][6]; 34

C.F.R. 300.307[a][2]). Although the term is not specifically used in IDEIA, this process is referred to as *response to intervention* (RTI).

RTI is a proactive approach designed to identify students with academic or behavioral difficulties as soon as they begin to struggle (Yell, Shriner, & Katsiyannis, 2006). In RTI models, students receive evidence-based instructional practices and interventions, with the level of service matched to their level of need and frequent monitoring to determine response. Progress monitoring results are used to make decisions about the need for additional interventions or levels and types of services in general and/or special education. Although there are several variations of the RTI approach, they all have several components in common: (1) the use of increasingly intensive levels ("tiers") of intervention, (2) a reliance on research-based instruction and interventions, (3) a problem-solving approach for matching interventions to student needs and making educational decisions, and (4) systematic data collection and monitoring to determine whether students are making sufficient progress.

RTI is most often implemented within a multi-tiered system of support (MTSS), which uses a three-tiered model to address academic and behavioral difficulties. Data are used to analyze problems at three levels within an MTSS, which then directs interventions. Tier 1 of a three-tiered MTSS consists of universal screening, quality core instruction, and effective behavior management for all students in the general education program. Students who fail to make adequate progress in Tier 1 receive a second level of support in Tier 2 that is often delivered in small-group settings, in addition to the regular classroom practices. Students for whom the Tier 2 intervention was not effective are then usually referred for Tier 3 services, which often involve bringing in a problem-solving team. Interventions delivered at Tier 3 are often intensive and delivered in a one-on-one or one-on-two format.

Although there are multiple intervention components that differentiate Tier 1 from Tier 2 and Tier 2 from Tier 3, the level of problem analysis needed to identify the appropriate intervention is likely the essential attribute of each tier. Students receiving a Tier 3 intervention usually do so in a one-on-one format, but it is not unusual to group two or three students together who are getting the same intervention within Tier 3. It is also not unusual to deliver an intervention within Tier 2 to an individual student or a group of two. However, Tier 1 analysis at Tier 2 will reduce intervention effectiveness, and Tier 3 level of analysis is not sustainable for Tiers 1 or 2. We discuss problem analysis across the tiers next.

Problem Analysis

One of the primary reasons that IAT models were not effective was that the IATs did not engage in appropriate problem analysis. As we have discussed elsewhere (e.g., Burns & Gibbons, 2013; Burns, Riley-Tillman, & VanDerHeyden, 2012), there are specific problem-analysis questions that can guide school personnel decisions at each tier. The primary problem-analysis question addressed at Tier 1 is, "Is there a classwide need?" Data are used to determine whether the student difficulties are the result of systemic issues that require changes in core instruction. The primary problem-analysis question at Tier 2 is, "What is the category of the problem?" Data are collected at Tier 2 to determine the broad area of deficit for individual students. For example, does the student lack decoding skills? Is the student motivated by positive attention from an adult? Does the student know the basic multiplication facts? Data suggest the category of the deficit, and students are grouped based on the data in order to receive interventions that target that deficit. Finally, the primary problem-analysis question for Tier 3 is, "What is the causal/functional variable?" Analyses at Tier 3 are often quite complex and may examine variables such as using more errorless and salient stimuli to support initial acquisition, increased repetition to support retention, and others, and they are often identified through a brief experimental analysis of student behavior.

It would go beyond the scope of this chapter to adequately discuss how to use data to answer the three questions above. Generally speaking, questions about classwide needs are addressed by examining universal screening data. For example, if a school used curriculum-based measures of reading (CBM-R) as a seasonal benchmark assessment, then school personnel would compute the median score for each classroom and compare it with the seasonal benchmark. If the median is below the criterion, then there is a classwide need, and an intervention is implemented. Previous research has consistently shown that providing classwide interventions has led to significant student growth in reading (Burns, Pulles, Helman, & McComas, 2016; Burns et al., 2015; Mathes, Howard, Allen, & Fuchs, 1998) and mathematics (VanDerHeyden & Burns, 2005; VanDerHeyden, McLaughlin, Algina, & Snyder, 2012). Categorical decisions are made with assessments of individual skills such as decoding, reading fluency, comprehension, multiplication, and functional assessments of behavior difficulties. Those data are then used to target intervention decisions. Finally, data used to analyze problems within Tier 3 could come from any number of assessments but should be a multidimensional, direct measure of the problem that is repeatable in order to document change (Hosp, 2008). Examining the types of data described here would likely improve decisions made by school-based teams.

Professional Learning Communities or Problem-Solving Teams?

As stated above, one of the difficulties with IATs was that they were not contextualized within a larger intervention framework and often operated independently of instructional practice. Many schools currently use problem-solving teams (PSTs) as an extension of the IAT concept in which professionals from different disciplines meet to systematically analyze data to suggest interventions for individual students. The PST process is often more systematic than its predecessors but still is not well contextualized within a broader system. Moreover, given that questions raised within an MTSS often address classroom practices and building policies, classroom teachers should be involved in the decisions.

Professional learning communities (PLCs) are groups of teachers and school personnel who collaborate to enhance learning for students (DuFour, Eaker, & DuFour, 2005). Effective PLCs work collectively toward shared goals, implement best practice for student achievement, and utilize a cycle of inquiry to promote continuing improvement (DuFour & Eaker, 1998). Effective MTSS implementation is usually guided by an effective PLC. For example, PLCs should be the groups examining screening data to identify classwide interventions and students who need additional support, using additional diagnostic data to target Tier 2 interventions, and reviewing measures of student progress to determine whether students are adequately improving with intervention. Having the PLC involved in these decisions links classroom teachers and supplemental supports, core instruction and intervention, and student outcomes and MTSS implementation.

The school's PST or IAT enters the MTSS process at Tier 3. An effective IAT model or PST will always be a component of an effective intervention framework, but that is a resource that should be reserved for students with the most intense needs. Consider a school with 750 students. In all likelihood, probably at least 150 (20%) of the students in the school will need additional support. Imagine trying to convene a PST to talk about 150 students in one school year! If the team met each week and talked about 2 students each time, that would be a total of approximately 70 students. A strong Tier 1 intervention and Tier 2 framework are likely needed to get that number down to 35 to 40 students, which is a number that would enable much more successful intervention efforts by a PST.

Unfortunately, many teachers do not have the prerequisite skill to successfully function within a PLC or PST, and many PLCs struggle to identify common assessments, criteria with which to judge student proficiency, and a process to collaboratively analyze data and improve student learning (DuFour et al., 2005; Love, 2009). Therefore, data analysis within a PLC needs to be systematic and examined with specific guiding protocols. Moreover, members of PLCs and PSTs need to be knowledgeable about what makes an intervention effective and how to select appropriate interventions. We discuss these points next.

WHAT MAKES A GOOD INTERVENTION?

The interventions included in this text were located by searching online databases, peer-reviewed journals, and books in the consultation, behavioral sciences, and teacher effectiveness literatures. The strategies have been adapted from the original sources as needed to facilitate implementation in general education settings. In cases in which an intervention has been modified and validated in one or more subsequent studies, two or more sources have been cited, and the most effective and practical features of each version have been retained. In several cases, the components evaluated in two or more studies have been combined to create a single intervention (e.g., *Delivering Effective Reprimands; Delivering Effective Commands: The Precision Request Program*). The eight criteria used to select interventions for inclusion in this book are described here.

Criterion 1: Documented Evidence of Effectiveness

Only interventions with empirical evidence of effectiveness in improving the behaviors they were designed to address were considered for inclusion. In analyzing experimental and quasi-experimental research to determine which interventions are effective, researchers commonly use the method of meta-analysis. In a meta-analysis, the results from each study are converted into a common unit of measurement called an effect size (ES) that expresses the difference in outcomes between the experimental (intervention) group and the control (nonintervention) group in standard deviation units. The results of several studies evaluating the same intervention or instructional practice can then be combined to determine the average effect of that strategy. A positive ES indicates that the intervention groups outperformed the control groups, whereas a negative ES indicates that the intervention groups performed less well than the comparison groups. In addition to determining the average overall ES for an intervention, researchers can use statistical analyses to determine whether greater ESs are associated with various characteristics of the students receiving the intervention (e.g., grade, initial vocabulary skills, behavior) and/or various forms or intensities of the intervention (e.g., researcher- vs. teacher-delivered, less vs. more intensive, individual vs. small-group format).

In the most common method of deriving ES, termed *d,* the mean of the control group is subtracted from the mean of the experimental group. The mean difference between groups is then divided by the pooled (average) standard deviation (*SD*) of the two groups ([SD_1 + SD_2]/2) to obtain a common *SD* that represents the difference between the measurements. The actual formula uses the square root of the average variance for the two studies (variance equals the *SD* squared), but the *SD* works well for most studies. For example, an ES of 0.50 means that students in the experimental group scored, on average, one-half of an *SD* higher on the outcome measure than did students in the control group (Cooper, Valentine, & Charlton, 2000).

Cohen's (1988) guidelines are commonly used to interpret effect size, with an ES of 0.20 indicating a small or mild effect, an ES of 0.50 indicating a medium or moderate effect, and an ES of 0.80 indicating a large or strong effect. According to the What Works Clearinghouse Intervention Rating Scheme (*www.whatworks.ed.gov/reviewprocess/essig.pdf*), a minimum

ES of 0.25 is the smallest positive value at which the effect is "substantively important." ESs can also be translated into percentile gains for use in interpreting the impact of an intervention. For example, an ES of 0.25 represents a percentile gain of 10 points for the average student in the intervention group, meaning that the typical treated student scored higher than 60% of untreated students. An ES of 0.80 (large effect) indicates that the typical student in the intervention group scored higher than 79% of untreated students.

Interventions included in this book either were included in meta-analytic research and had strong effects or had multiple studies that demonstrated effectiveness. The original source had to include some systematic, objective method of documenting observable changes in student performance. Many studies employed single-subject designs, such as A-B-A-B, withdrawal, reversal, alternating treatments, or multiple baseline methods, that used data from observations of classroom behavior; or academic measures, such as percent-correct scores on classroom tasks. A sizable number of the interventions have been validated across different grades, academic subjects, settings (e.g., resource room, inclusive classroom, general education classroom), formats (e.g., individual, small-group, whole-class), and student populations (students without identified disabilities, students with disabilities, English language learners, etc.), providing additional evidence of their effectiveness in improving student outcomes.

Criterion 2: Consistent with an Ecological Perspective

Focusing on internal deficits in the child as the sole cause of a student's school problems provides little information or direction for designing school-based interventions. In contrast, an ecological approach views student problems as arising not only from child characteristics but also from mismatches between student needs and environmental variables, including classroom management and instructional practices. Adopting an ecological perspective to academic and behavior problems not only expands the analysis of factors that may be contributing to those problems but also yields a broader range of targets for school-based interventions (Barnett, Bell, & Carey, 2002; Truscott et al., 2000). Also in keeping with an ecological perspective, the interventions are designed to be minimally intrusive so that they can be implemented in general classroom settings without singling out individual students or unduly disrupting teachers' typical instructional and behavior management systems. Interventions that require major alterations in classroom ecologies are unlikely to become integrated into teachers' routines or to have the desired effects on student performance (Elliott, Witt, Kratochwill, & Stoiber, 2002; Lentz, Allen, & Ehrhardt, 1996). Several interventions designed for parent delivery are also included, but these too require minimal training and supervision by school personnel and minimal alterations in family routines.

Criterion 3: Alignment with the Function of the Problem (Causal Variable)

Interventions also had to align with the function of the problem, which we refer to as the *causal variable*. In other words, we avoid comprehensive interventions in favor of those that target specific problems. Our research (e.g., Burns et al., 2016) has consistently shown that it is preferable to use data to select interventions based on student need than to deliver a comprehensive intervention. Many people reading this book could likely identify a student for whom they attempted a research-based intervention that had worked well for a previous student but did not work well for the current student. The reason that happens is often that the intervention does not address the correct problem for the student. Using repeated reading will likely result in positive outcomes for a student who struggles with reading fluency, but the results will be much more disappointing if the student struggles to decode words or does not have adequate phonemic awareness.

In addition to matching the skill area, interventions should match the phase of learning. Haring and Eaton (1978) outlined a learning hierarchy through which skills progress as they are learned. People start in the acquisition phase, in which performance is slow and inaccurate and instructional efforts should focus on modeling, explicit instruction, and immediate feedback on accuracy. Once the student can perform the task with sufficient accuracy (probably around 90%), then he or she moves to the proficiency phase, which is accurate but slow performance and in which instruction should focus on increasing the speed with which the student completes the task. Some might question whether the speed with which a task is completed really matters, but according to learning hierarchy, it does, because performing the task with sufficiency and accuracy and speed enhances the student's ability to generalize the skill. Generalization does not occur unless the skill is automatized, but a student must first be accurate and then demonstrate sufficient speed. Students in the generalization phase can demonstrate the skill in different contexts. Lastly, once a student can generalize the skill, then he or she can modify it to solve problems in novel situations. An intervention should be designed to teach the skill initially (through modeling, explicit instruction, and corrective feedback) for students in the acquisition phase, *or* to build proficiency (through repeated practice and feedback on speed), *or* to enhance generalization. There is considerable research that demonstrates the effectiveness of matching the instructional task to the phase of the student (Burns, Codding, Boice, & Lukito, 2010; Chafouleas, Martens, Dobson, Weinstein, & Gardner, 2004).

Criterion 4: Emphasis on a Proactive Approach to the Problem

Priority has been placed on strategies that help teachers create learning environments that prevent problem behavior from occurring rather than on strategies that are applied after problem behavior has already occurred. Many of the classroom interventions that have appeared in the literature are *contingency-based,* that is, they involve manipulating *consequences* to shape behavior. In contrast, proactive strategies emphasize manipulating *antecedents,* that is, modifying the classroom environment to promote high levels of student engagement and thus prevent academic failure and disruptive behavior.

Criterion 5: Capable of Classwide Application

Traditional intervention assistance approaches directed at a single low-performing or ineffectively behaving student are of limited utility in helping teachers become more effective instructional managers or behavioral problem solvers. On the contrary, given the growing needs and diversity of the student population and federal mandates for improving outcomes for all students, teachers need strategies that can enhance the academic performance and social competence of all of the students in a classroom. Moreover, when a teacher refers an individual student because of some learning or behavior problem, consultants often discover that the problem extends beyond the referred child to several students or to the class as a whole. Although the teacher is focusing on one student, the referred child's dysfunctional behavior is embedded within an ineffective organizational, instructional, or behavior management system that is interfering with the optimal performance of several or all of the students in that classroom. In keeping with this universal perspective, interventions have been selected that were either originally designed to be implemented on a classwide basis or that could be readily adapted to that format while at the same time accommodating students with special needs within that group.

   This edition also includes several behavioral interventions that were originally designed to be implemented on a schoolwide basis. Schoolwide interventions are increasingly being used to improve behavior and social competence for an entire student body and are especially valuable in targeting problem behaviors that occur in nonclassroom settings, such as hallways, cafeterias, and the playground (Sugai, Horner, & Gresham, 2002).

Criterion 6: Capable of Being Easily Taught through a Consultation Format

Interventions that place high demands on consultant or teacher time to ensure accurate implementation are unlikely to find their way into consultants' repertoires or teachers' routines, regardless of their documented effectiveness in solving the target problem (Boardman, Argüelles, Vaughn, Hughes, & Klingner, 2005; Gersten, Chard, & Baker, 2000). For this reason, only interventions that can be easily taught to educators in individual or group-oriented consultative settings have been included. Similarly, strategies with complex implementation or evaluation procedures as presented in the original sources have been modified to increase their practicality and to facilitate a high degree of treatment integrity. The standardized format used for all of the assessments and interventions in this book has been designed specifically for use in consultation settings, including consultant–teacher sessions and professional development programs. Strategies that were judged to be so complex that modifications to accommodate the realities of the regular classroom would have reduced intervention effectiveness were excluded from consideration.

Criterion 7: Capable of Implementation Using Regular Classroom Resources

This criterion reflects the goal of enhancing the capacity of general education teachers to meet the needs of diverse learners rather than relying on special education programming. All the interventions in this book can be delivered using resources that are already present in the typical classroom or can be prepared or obtained with minimal cost and effort. Interventions have been selected that capitalize on the human and material resources already present in general education settings, including teachers, peers, the regular curriculum, and typically available classroom resources. Strategies requiring substantial additional human or material resources, such as extra staff, special services personnel, supplementary curricular materials, and special equipment, or that require the removal of students from the regular classroom, were either modified or excluded from consideration. This eliminated individual and small-group social skills training or counseling programs, as well as the ever-increasing array of commercially published curricula targeting academic performance or social competence. For similar reasons, most interventions with a home-based component had to be excluded. Although numerous strategies involving parents as intervention agents have appeared in the literature, the majority require a substantial investment of teacher, consultant, and/or parent time for accurate implementation, target a single student or a small group, and even then sometimes fail to achieve meaningful changes in student achievement or behavior (e.g., Callahan, Rademacher, & Hildreth, 1998; Kahle & Kelley, 1994). Here, only the simplest school–home interventions that require minimal parent training and teacher or consultant involvement and that can be applied to an entire classroom group have been selected.

Criterion 8: Capable of Being Evaluated by Reliable, Valid, and Practical Methods

Consistent with the evidence-based intervention movement, federal mandates, and ethical practice (American Psychological Association [APA], 2010; National Association of School

Psychologists [NASP], 2010), the interventions in this book target concrete, observable student behaviors that can be objectively measured over time. In addition to the evaluation procedures described in Chapter 2 and the curriculum-based measurement (CBM) procedures presented in Chapter 4, each intervention includes at least two and as many as four methods of gathering information on preintervention performance and evaluating performance changes subsequent to intervention. Observational and evaluation measures are designed to be as practical as possible so that they can be easily implemented by regular classroom teachers, consultants, or other school personnel. Although efforts have been made to match the methodology of the original sources, evaluation procedures have been modified for many interventions to accommodate the exigencies of the regular classroom setting and to approximate more closely the typical data collection methods of classroom teachers and school-based consultants. Moreover, because many of the interventions originally targeted only one student or a small group of students, observational and evaluation methods suitable for classwide application have been substituted for or added to the original individually focused procedures.

ETHICS FOR INTERVENTION EFFORTS

Careful attention to legal and ethical issues relative to selecting, implementing, and evaluating interventions is a key component of the intervention assistance process. Practitioners must ensure that the interventions they recommend through IATs, case-centered consultation, professional development, and other forms of service delivery are aligned with federal and state laws and regulations, district guidelines, and the ethical principles and practice standards of professional groups, including the APA (2010) and NASP (2010). The major issues in this area include (1) intervention targets, (2) intervention effectiveness, (3) possible undesirable side effects and outcomes, (4) parent involvement, (5) student involvement, (6) documentation, (7) evaluation, (8) consultant competence, and (9) provisions for referral for additional services if interventions are unsuccessful.

Intervention Targets

Ethical practice mandates that interventions focus on enhancing academic and social competencies rather than on reducing unwanted behavior, or what Conoley and Conoley (1992) have termed "dead-person targets"—that is, behaviors best performed by dead people, such as sitting still and being quiet. Moreover, an ecological perspective requires that intervention targets include not only student behaviors but also environmental variables that may be influencing student performance. The sequence of interventions in this book—beginning with strategies targeting the classroom environment, followed by interventions designed to enhance academic performance and, finally, interventions designed to reduce inappropriate behavior and improve social competence—is intended to emphasize the order in which targets should be considered. One promising approach to intervention target selection is to focus on *keystone behaviors* (Barnett, Bauer, Ehrhardt, Lentz, & Stollar, 1996; Barnett et al., 1999), defined as behaviors that are likely to have the greatest impact in terms of the desired outcomes and/or that lay the foundation for improved functioning in the student's current or future environment. For example, cooperation and self-regulation, which have been repeatedly identified as keystone behaviors for children (Barnett et al., 1999; Pelco & Reed-Victor, 2007), constitute the primary or secondary targets of many of the proactive and behavioral interventions in this text.

Strategies that teach positive alternative behaviors and enhance students' capacity to manage their own behavior are preferable to strategies that merely impose negative consequences for undesired behavior. Under IDEIA, school teams must consider positive behavioral interventions and supports in developing plans to address the problem behavior of students with disabilities (34 C.F.R. § 300.324[a][2][i]).

Intervention Effectiveness

Early in the history of school interventions, consultants had limited access to resources on empirically validated strategies and often relied on their own subjective judgment or personal repertoire of interventions. Given the growing database of empirically validated interventions, however, and the mandates of ESSA to implement evidence-based practices, consultants have a responsibility to recommend strategies with demonstrated effectiveness in addressing the referral problem, that is, strategies "that the profession considers to be responsible, research-based practice" (NASP Principles for Professional Ethics [NASP-PPE], 2010, II.3.9, p. 8). Indeed, part of their ethical responsibility is to keep informed about interventions that have empirical support for effectiveness and relevance for their student populations (NASP-PPE, 2010, II.1.4). All of the interventions in this book have a research base documenting their effectiveness in addressing the referral problem. In addition, each intervention includes at least two and as many as four measures for monitoring progress so that intervention plans can be modified when data indicate that the student is not responding to the intervention or that the response is insufficient to achieve the specified goal.

Possible Undesirable Side Effects and Outcomes

Consultants are ethically obligated to select procedures that maintain the dignity of students and minimize the risk of adverse side effects (NASP-PPE, 2010, Principle I). Many of the interventions in this book include interdependent group contingencies, in which access to reinforcement depends on some aspect of performance for the entire group. Although group contingencies can have powerful effects on student behavior and performance (Stage & Quiroz, 1997) and are much more efficient than individually based contingency programs, consultants should be aware of the potentially negative social consequences that may occur under these systems. Although interdependent group contingencies are designed to capitalize on positive peer pressure, with group members encouraging each other to work toward the reward, peer harassment can occur if students perceive that some individuals are performing poorly or are deliberately trying to sabotage the group's chances of earning the reward. Consultants who recommend strategies involving interdependent group contingencies should therefore advise teachers of this possibility and help them take preventive measures, such as modeling appropriate behavior if the group fails to earn the reward for a particular intervention period, selecting interventions with built-in opportunities to earn back lost points, and placing uncooperative students in a separate group so that their behavior does not reduce their classmates' chances to obtain reinforcement. Observations during initial implementation can also help detect any undesirable side effects or negative outcomes that may not have been anticipated during the planning process.

Partnering with Parents

Partnering with parents in the intervention assistance process is not only an essential component of best practice but also an integral aspect of an ecological approach to problem solving. Regardless of the level of commitment and dedication among consultants and IAT members, no one is more invested in the child's success than the parent. The parent should be contacted by the classroom teacher as soon as a concern has been identified, rather than waiting until a referral for intervention assistance is imminent. That is, when parents learn that their child is being referred to an IAT, communications between the referring teacher and parents, including efforts to resolve the problem, should have already taken place, so that the referral simply constitutes another phase in the intervention assistance process. Once the referral has been made, parental involvement can take many forms, including sharing information during problem identification and analysis, helping to develop the intervention plan, and helping to monitor the student's response to the intervention. One effective but underutilized form of parent involvement consists of training parents in the same academic or behavioral strategies being implemented by the teacher in the classroom. Many of the interventions in this text can be taught to parents in one-to-one training sessions or as part of group-oriented parent education programs.

Involving parents as collaborative partners throughout the intervention assistance process is consistent not only with ethical standards requiring consultants to encourage parental participation in designing services for their children—including "linking interventions between home and school, tailoring parental involvement to the skills of the family, and helping parents gain the skills needed to help their children" (NASP-PPE, 2010, II.3.10, p. 8)—but also with IDEIA mandates to inform parents about the strategies designed to increase their child's rate of learning (34 C.F.R. § 300.311[a][7]), receive progress monitoring data (34 C.F.R. § 300.309[b][2]), and participate in meetings relating to their child's identification, evaluation, and placement (34 C.F.R. § 300.501). In designing intervention plans, consultants should also be mindful that they are ethically obligated to offer alternatives regarding the services to be provided that take into account parental values and capabilities and show respect for the family's ethnic/cultural values (NASP-PPE, 2010, II.3.10). Moreover, if parents object to school-based services, consultants are ethically bound to respect those wishes and direct parents to alternative resources in the community (NASP-PPE, 2010, I.1.5).

With the widespread implementation of IATs, most school districts have developed policies requiring parental notification for referrals to team-based IATs, although formal policies relating to the need for notification in the case of individual consultants are less common. When the consultant is a regular school employee, such as a school psychologist, written parental permission is generally not necessary to consult with teachers regarding strategies for enhancing a student's opportunities to learn in the regular classroom setting, as long as those strategies do not involve unusual or out-of-classroom treatments. When a nonschool employee, such as an external consultant, will be providing consultation or intervention assistance services, however, parents should be notified in writing. Moreover, when the consultant is not a school employee, written parental permission must be obtained for school staff to provide the consultant with personally identifying student information. Parental permission is generally not required for interventions that affect all students in a class equally unless those interventions involve some unusual contingency or departure from daily routines, such as a field trip occurring off school grounds. Written parental consent should *always* be obtained for assessments and interventions that involve providing additional services to an individual student, such as a behavioral assessment, individual or small-group social skills training, or a major change in the student's educational program, especially if it involves removing the student from the classroom or treating the student differently from his or her classmates in some way. Even with classwide interventions, informing parents and inviting their input and support can enhance both acceptability and effectiveness (Brantley & Webster, 1993).

Student Involvement

At a minimum, students should be informed about the nature of a planned intervention, the intervention agents involved, and the anticipated outcomes (NASP-PPE, 2010, I.1.3).

Explaining the essential components of an intervention plan to the target student and soliciting assent can be an empowering experience that encourages investment by the key stakeholder in the intervention assistance process. Although many students in the upper elementary grades and above can benefit from participating in consultation sessions and IAT meetings, the degree of benefit and the optimal level of involvement depend on several factors, including the nature of the referral problem, the student's capacity to participate positively in the problem-solving process, and the parents' views regarding the desirability of their child's involvement. Although there is virtually no research on the nature, extent, and results of student participation in IATs, there is some evidence that student monitoring of RTI is as effective as teacher monitoring, if not more so (Bahr, Fuchs, Fuchs, Fernstrom, & Stecker, 1993). Field testing indicates that involving the referred student in analyzing the problem, generating possible solutions, affirming intervention goals and strategies, and evaluating progress can be essential to the success of the plan, especially in the case of chronic lack of productivity and/or problem behavior. Of course, consultants must take care that the discussions in meetings attended by the student focus on developing solutions and affirming the student's capacity to participate positively in the intervention assistance process rather than on rehearsing the student's deficits. Finally, in strategies that involve another student as an intervention agent, such as peer tutoring or peer behavior monitoring, and that will not be implemented on a classwide basis, permission for the peer intervention agent to participate should be obtained in writing from his or her parents, as well as assent from the peer agent.

Intervention Assistance Documentation

Documenting the intervention assistance process is important not only for monitoring the progress of the students being served but also in order to provide accountability data regarding the intervention assistance activities (Kovaleski, 2002). Intervention plans for individual students should be documented in the students' school records. If interventions are delivered through a team-based format, they should also be documented in team records. One advantage of maintaining a master set of IAT records is that all the data are together and readily available for use in program evaluation. Consultants and IAT members should bear in mind that under the 1974 Family Educational Rights and Privacy Act (FERPA; Public Law 93-380), also known as the Buckley Amendment, parents have access to essentially all of their child's school records, including records of classroom observations, intervention-related assessments, consultations, and intervention plans, as well as the right to challenge the accuracy of those records and the right to a hearing regarding their accuracy (34 C.F.R. § 99.10). Exempted from this requirement are so-called sole possession notes, defined in FERPA as "records that are kept in the sole possession of the maker, are used only as a personal memory aid, and are not accessible or revealed to any other person except a temporary substitute for the maker of the record" (34 C.F.R. § 99.3). If consultants share their notes with others, such as teachers, administrators, or IAT members, however, these notes are reclassified as educational records and become accessible to parents. Moreover, under IDEIA's procedural safeguards, parents have the right to examine any records that have been collected as part of the special education decision-making process for their child (34 C.F.R. § 300.501).

If interventions target an entire class of students and do not involve major changes in educational programming or single out any students for differential treatment, documentation in IAT records is sufficient, although providing written notification to parents is recommended.

Evaluating Intervention Effectiveness

Ethical practice requires that consultants provide targeted, data-based interventions and "modify or terminate the treatment plan when data indicate the desired outcomes are not being attained" (NASP-PPE, 2010, II.2.2, p. 7). Although consultants and teachers alike often fail systematically to collect accountability data in the intervention assistance process, especially data directly related to student outcomes (Bahr et al., 1999; Doll et al., 2005), failure to do so means that there is no objective basis for determining the effectiveness of the interventions that have been implemented. As noted above, plans should specify the time period for evaluating students' RTIs, as well as the specific measures that will be used for progress monitoring. Frequent progress monitoring helps to ensure that interventions that are inappropriate, inadequate in intensity, or less than optimal in some other way can be modified in a timely manner so that students are not deprived of the right to learn (Hixson, Christ, & Bruni, 2014). To facilitate progress monitoring and accountability, all the interventions in this book include at least two and as many as four methods for evaluating their effectiveness, ranging from measures already in place in regular education classrooms, such as homework completion rates and report card grades, to direct observational methods for measuring the productivity or behavior of an entire classroom group.

Consultant Competence

Consultants are ethically obligated to be aware of the limits of their own competence and to offer services only within those boundaries (NASP-PPE, 2010, II.1.1; APA *Ethical Principles of Psychologists and Code of Conduct* [APA-EP], 2010, 2.01a). Given an increasingly diverse student population and legislative mandates for evidence-based practices and data-based decision making, demands on consultant competence are greater than ever. In practice, it can be difficult for consultants to determine the degree to which they possess an acceptable level of competency in each of the many domains in which they are providing services (intervention design, team-based consultation, professional development, data collection and analysis, etc.). As part of the process of evaluating their own competence, consultants involved in IATs should ask themselves the following questions:

"Am I offering a broad enough range of research-based interventions to intervention agents and consumers?"

"Do I understand the theoretical basis, rationale, and the likely outcomes for the interventions I recommend?"

"Am I aware of the amount and quality of the evidence base for the interventions in terms of the target student population?"

"Can I provide a comprehensive written description of intervention procedures?"

"Can I demonstrate the strategies to intervention agents and provide them with hands-on technical assistance so that they can implement them with fidelity?"

"Can I help intervention agents to evaluate the effectiveness of the strategies in the setting(s) in which they will be implemented?"

"Do I understand the possible side effects or potential negative consequences of the strategies with the target student population?"

As the student population becomes increasing diverse, consultants must continually evaluate their competence to provide services to students and families from culturally diverse backgrounds, a task complicated by the paucity of empirically based intervention studies with students from ethnic and linguistic minorities. As stated in the most recent APA guidelines, psychologists are required "to consider client characteristics such as cultural background, disability, native language, or other diversity factors when assessing their own competence to provide services" (APA-EP, 2010, 2.01b). Similarly, NASP guidelines underscore the fact that consultants are ethically obligated to provide to students and families services that respect cultural diversity and family ethical and cultural values (NASP-PPE, 2010, I.3.2). A collaborative approach to problem solving can help to meet this standard and is aligned with ethical guidelines requiring practitioners to "enlist the assistance of other specialists in supervisory, consultative, or referral roles as appropriate in providing effective services" (NASP-PPE, 2010, II.1.1, p. 6). Moreover, consultants are required to maintain and enhance their competence by participating in professional development experiences that enhance their knowledge and skills (NASP-PPE, 2010, II.1.4). Keeping abreast of ethical and legal issues in school-based consultation and IATs is a challenging but critical aspect of continuing professional development for consultants.

Provisions for Referral

Consultants must ensure that the problem-solving process does not abrogate parents' rights under IDEIA. The intervention assistance process described above includes provisions for referring students for special education evaluations or other services if interventions are unsuccessful or if the student's response is insufficient. Documenting interventions is important not only for assessing the student's response to scientifically based interventions but also for maintaining a record of the strategies that have been implemented prior to referral for additional services. Because, under IDEIA, parents have the right to request that their child be evaluated at any time if they suspect the presence of a disability (34 C.F.R. § 300.301[b]), consultants should inform parents of their right to a free comprehensive evaluation for their child while also informing them of the benefits potentially available through the intervention assistance process. A review of district and state procedural manuals for IATs reveals a wide variation in guidelines for the time period during which interventions are attempted before teams move to a referral for special education services. Kovaleski (2002) suggested that a period of 50 school days, from the initial referral by a parent or teacher to the completion of the IAT process, is sufficient to ensure that an intervention has had time to work without unduly delaying an assessment. Including parents as collaborators from the beginning of the intervention assistance process, including analyzing the problem, planning strategies, and assessing intervention effectiveness, not only facilitates home–school communication about the student's response or the lack thereof but also ensures that parents are cognizant of each aspect of the problem-solving process in the event that an individual evaluation is recommended at a later date.

INTERVENTION FORMAT

The intervention briefs in this book are grouped into three chapters that present academic, behavioral, and preschool strategies, in that order. Each intervention brief has a standardized format designed to be as succinct and nontechnical as possible while still including sufficient detail for accurate implementation and reliable evaluation. Samples of materials required for implementation, such as charts and student handouts, are included for many of the interventions. The format is designed to facilitate the intervention assistance process in individual and group-oriented consultative settings and has been extensively field-tested in professional development workshops, individual and group consultations with teachers, school psychologists, and other school personnel. The 10 sections of the intervention briefs are described below. Where appropriate, we added sections to some briefs and may have not included some sections in others, but all follow this standard outline to some degree.

Overview

The overview provides a brief description of the intervention, its target, a rationale for its use, and a summary of the anticipated results. Also included is information about the original setting and student participants and the results obtained in the original study or studies. For schoolwide strategies, a brief description of school demographics and other relevant characteristics of the original intervention site is included.

Goal

This section presents the specific purpose or purposes of the intervention in terms of concrete, observable student academic and/or social behaviors and the function of those behaviors. We also discuss whether the intervention teaches skills (acquisition), allows for practice (fluency), builds retention (maintenance), or enhances generalization.

Intervention Intensity

Many schools are currently implementing MTSS for academic and behavioral difficulties. Most utilize a three-tiered approach in which Tier 1 consists of core instruction, Tier 2 comprises targeted small-group interventions, and Tier 3 consists of intensive intervention for individual students with the most severe needs. This section discusses for what level of intervention intensity each intervention is appropriate. Many interventions can be used across tiers, so we avoid classifying them by tier but instead discuss different levels of intensity that the intervention can address.

Materials

This section lists all of the materials required for successful implementation. Many interventions require minimal materials, such as posterboard for charts, and some require no material resources at all. For contingency-based strategies, suggestions for tangible, activity, or social reinforcers are included in this section.

Options to Monitor Progress

The final phase of any intervention model is to monitor the effects of the intervention. Even the most well-researched intervention may not work for individual students. Thus this section presents methods for assessing the target behavior(s) in order to determine whether the intervention results in improved student performance. For each intervention, at least two and as many as four different data-gathering strategies are included, varying along a continuum of complexity, from naturally occurring classroom assessments, such as grades on tests and quizzes, to observational methods using special recording forms. Although we emphasize measures that gather information about target behaviors for an entire classroom, methods for documenting the behavior of a single student or a small group of students are also included for most interventions.

Intervention Steps

This section provides comprehensive step-by-step implementation procedures. In many cases, procedures have been amplified or modified from those presented in the original studies for the sake of clarity and practicality. Every effort has been made to accommodate the realities of the regular classroom environment without sacrificing effectiveness and fidelity to the original strategy. Because teaching students a specific set of procedures is a key component of many of the strategies, two subsections—*Introduction and Training* and *Implementation*—have been added to those interventions to enhance usability. Similarly, a *Preparation* subsection has been added for several strategies requiring additional planning steps prior to implementation.

Variations

This component describes one or more intervention variations. Some of these variations were developed during field testing, whereas others are derived from additional experiments presented in the original article or from other studies implementing modifications of the original intervention. By providing additional intervention alternatives for consultants to offer to teachers, these variations increase the likelihood that teachers will find some of the suggested strategies acceptable and implement them with fidelity.

Notes

The notes component presents additional information designed to enhance implementation, such as tips on training students in the procedures. We also discuss any implementation issues and problems that are reported by the original authors or observed during field testing, along with suggestions for overcoming those problems.

Sources

The sources section provides a complete citation for the article(s) or book(s) from which the intervention was adapted. In the case of interventions drawing on more than one source, all of the relevant references are cited.

Additional Resources

This additional section, which is included for several strategies, describes print and electronic resources that can facilitate implementation, such as commercially available versions of the intervention or websites with relevant materials.

HOW TO USE THIS BOOK

From the perspective of this book, school-based interventions should focus on enhancing students' academic and social competence rather than on simply reducing unwanted behavior. Moreover, interventions should target the learning context within which inappropriate behavior is occurring. Readers may use the table of contents and index to locate strategies for specific targets, such as homework completion, reading vocabulary, or disruptive behavior in nonclassroom situations.

Cautions

As school consultants know only too well, no intervention is equally effective with every student, with every teacher, or in every situation. Intervention selection should be a collaborative effort between consultant and teacher, or among team members and referring teachers. Parent involvement is also a critical element in enhancing intervention effectiveness. In contrast to traditional school–home communications that simply provide parents with information, often negative, about children's performance, the intervention assistance approach actively encourages parents' participation in analyzing and solving their children's school problems. Finally, whether consultants are working with individual teachers, school-based teams, or parents, they can enhance their own effectiveness by offering a variety of empirically based intervention alternatives for consideration and facilitating the decision-making process rather than advocating a particular strategy.

WEBSITE RESOURCES

National Center on Intensive Intervention
www.intensiveintervention.org

The website for the National Center on Intensive Intervention (NCII) provides resources on academic and behavior interventions with a focus on children with intensive needs. The NCII also has resources on progress monitoring for both academic and behavioral outcomes.

National Center for Learning Disabilities
www.ncld.org

The website for the National Center for Learning Disabilities provides numerous resources on RTI, including a parent advocacy brief with case examples of two students (both with early reading problems) illustrating the RTI implementation process.

National Research Center on Learning Disabilities
www.nrcld.org

The National Research Center on Learning Disabilities conducts research designed to help the learning disabilities field understand policies, practices, and prevalence of learning disabilities, as well as to identify best practices for their intervention components. Among the resources offered on the website is a learning disabilities toolkit to assist practitioners in understanding changes related to specific learning disabilities determination and RTI.

Evidence-Based Intervention Network
http://ebi.missouri.edu

The Evidence-Based Intervention Network (EBIN) was developed with a partnership among the University of Missouri, East Carolina University, and Indiana University to develop and provide guidance in selecting and implementing classroom interventions that have convincing research to support their effectiveness. It is developed around the four phases of the learning hierarchy and provides free intervention protocols.

Scientifically Based Research: A Link from Research to Practice
http://gosbr.net

Go SBR is a free website developed and maintained by iSTEEP (*www.isteep.com*) on which interventions are published and are free to use in schools. The interventions may be used by educational professionals in their schools without charge but cannot be sold or distributed.

Promising Practices Network for Children, Families and Communities
www.promisingpractices.net

Sponsored by the RAND Corporation, this website features summaries of programs and practices that have been empirically demonstrated to improve outcomes for children, youth, and families. Program information can be viewed according to four major outcome areas: (1) healthy and safe children, (2) strong families, (3) children ready for school, and (4) children succeeding in school.

Intervention Central
www.interventioncentral.org

Created by Jim Wright, a school psychologist from Syracuse, New York, this website offers a wealth of free tools for promoting positive classroom behavior and effective learning.

What Works Clearinghouse
www.whatworks.ed.gov

Established in 2002 and sponsored by the U.S. Department of Education, the What Works Clearinghouse (WWC) is designed to provide educators, policymakers, and the public with an independent source of scientific evidence of effective educational programs and practices. The frequently updated site provides intervention and topic reports for strategies targeting elementary, middle, and high school students. Among the new features is an "intervention finder" to assist users in locating WWC-reviewed interventions based on topic and rating.

Institute of Education Sciences Publications and Products
http://ies.ed.gov/ncee/wwc/Publication

The website provides several free resources. There are 19 practice guides that summarize research for practitioners about important topics and include recommendations for practice. There are also hundreds of intervention reports that describe the research on various interventions. The website is searchable so that practitioners can find interventions for particular topics.

CHAPTER TWO

Using Evidence-Based Interventions to Enhance Student Outcomes

Whereas the primary function of this book is to provide educational professionals with many intervention options, it takes a larger process to select the correct intervention, implement the intervention effectively, assess core outcomes related to the interventions, and finally make decisions about what to do next. The purpose of this chapter is to outline the core steps in the problem-solving process with a focus on intervention selection, implementation, and analysis. We do not expect readers to adopt this system, as most schools have some problem-solving process in place. Rather, we outline the core steps of effective problem solving so that a school process can be reviewed to consider what might need to be added or aspects that could be removed.

KEY STEPS IN THE INTERVENTION ASSISTANCE PROCESS

The 10-step intervention assistance process described below is based on procedures developed during field testing, our experiences with problem-solving teams (PSTs), and resources in the literature (Barnett et al., 1999; Burns, Peters, & Noell, 2008; Burns, Riley-Tillman, & VanDerHayden, 2012; Shapiro, 2011). The process is intended to apply to intervention-oriented assistance provided by individual consultants, grade-level teams, professional learning communities (PLCs), and PSTs. Throughout this chapter we refer to PSTs as *intervention assistance teams* (IATs). This term is considered to be an umbrella for all of the different names that PSTs have in schools. We believe it is important to consider "intervention" and "assistance," as many "problem-solving" teams in schools often do not focus on individual child or small-group intervention assistance. For example, teams that focus on schoolwide, grade, or classroom problems may not have time to focus on the individual or small-group levels. It is our belief that it is critical to have a team or teams (e.g., grade-level teams) in schools who spend considerable time focusing on individual and small-group interventions.

Stage 1: Problem Definition

Step 1: Initial Referral

The intervention assistance process begins with a request for assistance from a teacher to the consultant or a referral from a teacher, faculty member, or parent to the IAT. In the case of IATs, referrals are reviewed by the system coordinator (team leader or chair) to determine whether all the necessary information has been included. Teachers and staff members who have relevant information about the referred student are asked to complete a data collection form prior to the meeting so that their input can be considered even if they are unable to attend the meeting. Field testing indicates that it is extremely helpful if the consultant or a team member conducts an observation in the classroom or problem setting prior to the first meeting to "see what the teacher is seeing" and help identify the nature of the problem.

A record is maintained of the initial referral and subsequent parent contacts, consultation sessions, and/or IAT meetings. In the case of a referral by a teacher, the teacher should have contacted the parent prior to the referral to review the concerns, obtain the parent's perception of the problem, and engage in informal problem solving. At this point, the team chairperson contacts the parent to inform him or her of the referral and invites the parent (and the student, if appropriate) to participate in a meeting to discuss the problem and generate solutions. Written notification of the referral is also sent to the parent at this time.

Step 2: Clarifying the Problem

The second step in the intervention process is for a small number of professionals to meet to define the problem in observable and measurable terms. Consultants meet with the referring teacher to better understand the problem. Within an IAT process, it is often more efficient and effective to have one representative of the team serve as a consultant and meet with the referring teacher before the IAT meets. After agreeing on how to define the problem, the consultant and teacher document the definition and refine the referral information for clarity. Focusing on only one or two target behaviors at a time is strongly recommended to avoid overwhelming the teacher and team members alike. Defining the problem in observable behavioral terms also helps the team identify methods of assessing the student's current level of performance.

Step 3: Obtaining Baseline Data

The referring teacher, consultant, and/or IAT members obtain additional direct measures of the target behaviors to identify preintervention performance levels and help clarify the discrepancy between the student's current and desired levels of performance. Data gathering may include classroom observations by the consultant or an IAT member, teacher observations of the student, parent and student interviews, and/or direct assessments (i.e., curriculum-based measurements in the target area).

Stage 2: Problem Analysis

Step 4: Conducting an Ecological Analysis of the Problem

The IAT meeting begins with a brief review of the referral information and the strategies the teacher has previously tried to resolve the problem. Members then reach a consensus regarding the nature of the problem, the specific skills the student needs to acquire or use in order to be successful, and the desired outcomes of intervention. A case manager is assigned at this point to serve as the major resource for the referring teacher for the remainder of the process and to assist with implementation and progress monitoring. A staff member may also be assigned to serve as an advocate for the parent and/or student and to support the parent and student during IAT meetings.

The teacher and consultant and/or IAT members review the data that have been collected to identify the factors that may be contributing to the problem, including student, peer group, classroom, curriculum, and home variables. Parents are also involved in analyzing the problem, as are students, as developmentally appropriate. Field testing indicates that data obtained from parent and student interviews, especially for students beyond the early primary grades, and from classroom observations can be critical in developing hypotheses about factors contributing to problems, especially chronic disruptive behavior and lack of academic productivity. The purpose of this step in the intervention process is to hypothesize the reason for the problem behavior. As such, it is important to focus on why the problem behavior makes sense considering the environment rather than focusing heavily on variables that cannot be changed.

Step 5: Exploring Alternative Intervention Strategies

The teacher and consultant and/or IAT members discuss intervention strategies that may help reduce the discrepancy between the current and the desired performance. Building on the last step, it is important to consider the likely reason for the problem behavior. For example, if in Step 4 the team hypothesizes that the student is engaging in problem behavior to gain attention, intervention strategies explored should be validated to address this situation. Students and parents are also involved in generating possible school- and home-based interventions. Strategies are evaluated for acceptability, effectiveness, cost in terms of human and material resources, feasibility in terms of the skills and styles of intervention agents, and closeness of match to classroom and home ecologies.

Step 6: Selecting Interventions

One or more strategies are selected. Final intervention selection rests with the teacher(s) and/ or parent who will be responsible for implementing the strategies. In a team situation, several team members or other personnel may be implementing strategies.

Step 7: Developing the Intervention Plan

A written intervention plan is developed that describes the selected strategy or strategies and timelines for implementation. The plan also clarifies the roles and responsibilities of the individuals involved in implementation, including teacher, parent, and/or student roles; assistance to be provided by the consultant, IAT members, and/or school staff; and strategies for monitoring progress. The plan includes a date for reviewing the effectiveness of the plan in reducing the discrepancy between the current and the desired performance. Ideally, the interval between initial implementation and plan review should be based on data generalized from published studies of the intervention. Field testing indicates that the time period between initial implementation and plan review should be no more than 2 weeks for behavior problems (and considerably less if problems are severe). For academic problems, a time period of 6–8 weeks or a full grading period is often necessary to evaluate students' response to supplementary instruction or other interventions.

Stage 3: Plan Implementation

Step 8: Implementing the Intervention Plan

The teacher or other intervention agent implements the agreed-upon plan with the support of the consultant or IAT case manager. Support for teachers may include in-class coaching, demonstrations, modeling, and performance feedback, depending on the complexity of the intervention, teacher skills and experience, and the severity of the problem. Support for parents may include direct training, indirect training (i.e., didactic training), follow-up telephone contacts and conferences, and other means of assistance. Within an IAT process, a consultant from the team should meet with the implementing teacher within 2 weeks to discuss unforeseen difficulties. Progress is monitored by the intervention agent with the assistance of the consultant or IAT case manager. Another classroom observation occurs at this point to assess treatment integrity and provide feedback and support for the teacher.

Stage 4: Plan Evaluation

Step 9: Evaluating Intervention Plan Effectiveness

The teacher and consultant and/or IAT analyze the student's rate of progress and performance relative to the goals specified in Step 7. Additional evaluation data are obtained from the parent and student (as appropriate) for use in comparing baseline and current performance. If the student is making insufficient progress toward the goals defined in the plan in Step 7, the parent and student (as appropriate) are invited to another meeting to collaborate in identifying barriers to progress and modifying the intervention plan. If the student is making sufficient progress toward meeting the goals defined in the plan, the strategies are continued, with periodic reviews to monitor progress. If the goals of the plan have been achieved and no further assistance is needed, the case is closed, with follow-up consultation as needed. Records are kept to document outcomes and provide information for evaluating the effectiveness of the IAT.

Step 10: Continued Problem Solving, Plan Revision, and Possible Referral

If the student has not made sufficient progress toward achieving the goals in the plan, additional data for use in understanding and solving the problem may be obtained and a revised plan developed. When the teacher and consultant or IAT members agree that the interventions have been appropriate and that the problem is still not solved, the student is referred for a special education evaluation or other, more individualized and intensive, forms of assistance. Data obtained from Stages 1 through 4 should be used in the special education eligibility determination process, and, if the student is found eligible for services, to develop the individualized education plan (IEP).

EVALUATING INTERVENTION EFFECTIVENESS

The importance of documenting changes in student outcomes during the intervention assistance process cannot be overemphasized. After intervention implementation, consultants may hear teachers report, "I tried what you [or the team] recommended, and it didn't work," only to discover that no objective assessment of the effects of the intervention on student performance has been conducted. Systematically evaluating changes in performance or behavior not only provides information for assessing intervention effectiveness so that strategies can be modified as needed but also contributes to teachers' maintenance of interventions by demonstrating that positive change is indeed occurring. Specifying objective measures of changes in student performance is even more critical for interventions targeting social behavior than for strategies targeting academic achievement. Because grades and measures of academic productivity, such as homework completion rates, are part of the regular data-gathering process in classrooms, teachers can readily monitor changes in academic performance. In contrast, teachers are much less likely to use objective methods of monitoring social behaviors, such as checklists documenting the frequency of desired and undesired target behaviors, and thus may fail to detect small positive changes and abandon an intervention prematurely.

Barriers to Evaluation in the IAT Process

Despite the increasing emphasis on data-based decision making in education and frequent calls in the professional literature to document intervention effects (e.g., Brown-Chidsey, Steege, & Mace, 2008; Shapiro & Gebhardt, 2012), evaluation continues to be the most neglected aspect of the intervention assistance process. In a national survey of school psychologists (Bramlett, Murphy, Johnson, Wallingford, & Hall, 2002), only 40% of respondents reported that they conducted some type of evaluation to assess the effectiveness of their consultation and intervention practice. Moreover, when evaluations were conducted, teacher verbal report was the most common form (55%). Similarly, studies of IATs have consistently reported that teams fail to conduct adequate assessments of target behaviors prior to intervention and changes in those behaviors after implementation and that the data typically collected are subjective in nature (Burns et al., 2008; Flugum & Reschly, 1994; Kovaleski, 2002; Wilkinson, 2005).

Several factors contribute to the frequent failure of participants in the intervention assistance process to evaluate intervention effects. First, given the constraints on consultant and teacher time, the pressure to create changes in the performance of a low-performing or disruptive student or classroom group often takes precedence over systematically evaluating student response to those efforts. As a result, teacher and consultant time tends to be allocated to implementation rather than to evaluation, and evaluation often consists of the subjective impressions of the teacher and consultant, which may not coincide with each other or with observable changes in student behavior. Teachers' resistance to evaluation is also related to the increased demands placed on them by the intervention assistance process. Teachers who refer students to IATs are typically asked first to provide data on the student's current level of performance, then to alter their instructional and/or management routines by implementing one or more interventions, and then to collect additional data documenting the student's response to the interventions. If the interventions appear to be successful in solving the referral problem from the teacher's perspective, documenting changes in student outcomes may seem even less of a priority. On the other hand, if student achievement or behavior does not appear to be improving, teachers may become discouraged or frustrated with the intervention assistance process and may fail to collect data systematically, especially if the evaluation methods do not fit into the classroom ecology.

Finally, lack of training plays a major role in practitioners' failure to evaluate intervention effectiveness, with school-based teams reporting that they lack training in monitoring student progress and evaluating the effectiveness of intervention plans (McDougal, Moody Clonan, & Martens, 2000; Telzrow et al., 2000). This is not a surprising finding, given that many consultants and educators received their training before the current emphasis on data-based decision making, which requires a broad range of technical skills and competencies in areas such as observational recording, curriculum-based measurement, functional behavioral assessment, and data analysis. Moreover, because many states leave IAT training to local districts, the quantity and quality of the training that consultants and participants receive varies considerably (Buck et al., 2003).

The Rationale for Evaluating Intervention Effectiveness

Despite these obstacles, integrating accountability into the intervention assistance process is an essential aspect of best practice for several reasons. First, evaluation is needed to assess changes in the target behavior of referred individual students or classroom groups. Without systematic accountability methods, consultants and teachers will be unable to determine which interventions are effective with which types of problems and with which types of student populations, and interventions will continue to be delivered primarily on the basis of familiarity or ease of implementation rather than effectiveness. Second, accountability data can encourage participants to remain engaged in the intervention assistance process (Slonski-Fowler & Truscott, 2004). When teachers and team members have objective data indicating that a student is responding positively to an intervention, they are more likely to be supportive of that strategy and the intervention assistance process in general. Feedback to students is probably the most neglected aspect of the evaluation process, despite accumulating evidence that providing students with explicit information about their own progress can significantly enhance their performance (Hattie, 2009). Many of the interventions in this book include student-focused feedback components, such as public posting (e.g., *Classwide Peer Tutoring, Red Light/Green Light*), contingent teacher praise (e.g., *Delivering Effective Praise*), and systematic error correction (e.g., *Using Response Cards to Increase Academic Engagement and Achievement*). Moreover, several strategies involve training students to monitor their own performance (e.g., *Self-Monitoring of Academic Productivity*; *Three Steps to Self-Managed Behavior*). Finally, as noted above, ethical practice requires that consultants assess the effectiveness of planned interventions in terms of student outcomes. Conducting a systematic evaluation of intervention effectiveness may be time-consuming, but it is essential to ensure that IATs will achieve the purpose for which they have been developed: enhancing the quality of education for all students.

Selecting Evaluation Measures

Researchers have used a wide variety of measures to assess intervention effectiveness, ranging from a single-item scale rating the behavior of one student on a 10-point continuum (Christ, Riley-Tillman, Chafouleas, & Jaffery, 2011) to computer-facilitated observational systems that can record information about dozens of teacher and student variables (Greenwood, Carta, Kamps, Terry, & Delquadri, 1994). In this book, evaluation of changes in student performance is an integral component of every strategy, but pre- and postintervention measures have been designed from an ecological perspective. That is, the focus is on assessing changes in target behaviors in the context of the regular classroom environment, using measures designed to be as unobtrusive and practical as possible without sacrificing reliability and validity. Just as importantly, measurement targets and data collected must be directly related to observable student behaviors rather than to perceptions of other stakeholders, such as teachers or parents. Although teacher and parent judgments of changes in student performance and behavior provide valuable consumer satisfaction data, evaluation measures must also include direct assessments of student behavior, because the ultimate goal of school-based interventions is improvement in student functioning.

The observation–evaluation component of each intervention in this book describes several assessment strategies for documenting changes in classroom environmental variables, academic performance, or behavior. In keeping with the group-oriented nature of the interventions, evaluation measures are primarily designed to assess aspects of student engagement, academic achievement, or social behavior for an entire classroom, but most can be easily adapted for use with individual students or small groups of target students. To encourage the regular collection of accountability data, many evaluation measures rely on naturally gathered information, such as report card grades, scores on quizzes and tests, or homework accuracy rates. Naturalistic evaluation procedures that fit readily into current classroom routines are not only less ecologically intrusive but are also more acceptable to teachers, who typically bear the dual responsibilities of intervention implementation and progress monitoring.

Evaluating Changes in Academic Performance

Assessing changes in academic achievement is especially important because students' success is defined by the degree to which they are able to master the "business" of school: learning. Evaluation strategies for many of the academic interventions rely on *curriculum-based measurement* (CBM), a method of direct assessment that can be used to measure student growth over time with any type of instructional method or curriculum. Because CBMs can be administered frequently, they yield a pattern of scores that indicate whether the student is making adequate progress relative to intervention goals, to classroom peers, and/or to grade-level expectations. Moreover, CBMs in mathematics, spelling, written expression, and the content areas can easily be administered to groups. Chapter 3 presents an overview of this type of assessment and provides step-by-step procedures for conducting CBMs in reading, mathematics, spelling, writing, and the content areas.

BEST PRACTICES FOR MAXIMIZING STUDENT OUTCOMES

Best Practice 1: Understand Teachers' Perspectives on Classroom Problems

Much has been written about teacher resistance to consultation in general and to classroom-based interventions in particular (e.g., Berger et al., 2014; Hylander, 2012). Dealing effectively with so-called teacher resistance begins with understanding teachers' perspectives on student problems and their experiences with special education service delivery. Despite abundant evidence that classroom variables, such as the nature and pacing of instruction, teachers' management and relational styles, and behavioral contingencies, have a powerful effect on students' academic achievement and social behavior (Barth, Dunlap, Dane, Lochman, & Wells, 2004; Perry, Donohue, & Weinstein, 2007), teachers tend to attribute student problems to internal dispositional causes or home factors over which they believe they have no control, especially in the case of behavior problems (Athanasiou, Geil, Hazel, & Copeland, 2002; Goyette, Dore, & Dion, 2000; Truscott et al., 2000). Although this approach is not productive, it is understandable. Focusing on the home or child rather than on variables that the teacher controls removes responsibility for the student's success from the teacher. If teachers view problems as arising from the characteristics of the student or the student's home environment, they have little incentive to modify their instructional or behavior management practices in an effort to improve the student's chances for success. Instead, it is more logical from the teacher's perspective to seek assistance in removing the "sick" student from the "healthy" classroom. Teachers are therefore likely to refer students with the goal of removing them from the classroom or accessing treatments delivered outside of the classroom, such as tutoring and counseling, rather than implementing interventions that require alterations in their own routines.

A second factor contributing to teacher resistance to the intervention assistance process relates to teachers' expectations based on traditional special education service delivery. Prior to the inclusion movement and special education law's emphasis on serving students in the least restrictive environment, teachers developed the expectation that the vast majority of the students they referred would be tested, found eligible for services, and placed in special education programs for some or all of the school day. Pragmatically, from the view of the general education teacher, the process was to remove the child rather than to find a solution for the problem. Despite the widespread implementation of IATs, many teachers continue to view them from a *prereferral* perspective, that is, as a time-consuming step on the way to obtaining special services for students (Klingner & Harry, 2006; Slonski-Fowler & Truscott, 2004). It is also important to remember that when teachers refer a student to a consultant or an IAT, they are likely to feel that they have already tried everything possible to help that student. As a result, they may resist implementing strategies requiring them to modify their current instructional or management practices, or they may fail to implement the strategies as planned and then declare them unsuccessful (Gutkin & Curtis, 1999). In addition, because of school psychologists' traditional role as assessors of individual students, teachers tend to view them as the gatekeepers for special education services. If consultants offer classroom-based interventions rather than individual psychoeducational evaluations as possible solutions to student problems, teachers may regard the intervention assistance process as preventing students from accessing needed services, at least initially (Doll et al., 2005; Rubinson, 2002; Truscott et al., 2000).

Consultants may also inadvertently contribute to teacher resistance by failing to acknowledge teachers' previous efforts to support struggling students. Armed with information about evidence-based interventions (EBIs) and the desire to be helpful, consultants may initiate the problem-solving process too soon, making recommendations prematurely to overwhelmed teachers and unwittingly increasing their feelings of ineffectiveness. This is especially likely to occur in the context of an IAT meeting, during which referring teachers must discuss their inability to help a student succeed academically or behaviorally in front of their own colleagues (Doll et al., 2005). Such an experience can be humbling for any teacher, but it can be particularly difficult for experienced teachers, who are accustomed to being able to solve their own problems without assistance from others. Sometimes listening empathically to a frustrated teacher's concerns and validating the teacher's attempts to help a low-performing or misbehaving student is the most helpful intervention that consultants can offer.

There are two key strategies for addressing teacher resistance to an intervention-oriented approach to student problems. First, all referrals to IATs should be done in a systematic manner and should come from a grade-level team. Each referring teacher would complete a referral form, but then that form should be signed off on by a regularly meeting team such as a grade-level or a department (e.g., English) team at a high school. That way each referring teacher would discuss the student's difficulty with some group of colleagues to initially brainstorm and to discuss the need to refer to the IAT. Second, teachers and other stakeholders, including administrators and parents, should be educated about the purpose of IATs and the manner in which they function, a process that is likely to extend over the first several years of implementation. Before teachers can fully invest in the intervention assistance process, they are likely to have to experience its effectiveness in increasing their capacity to help their own students. Because success reduces resistance, consultants participating in IATs should make every effort to work first with teachers who request assistance and to focus on problems that appear solvable. Teachers who have positive results with IATs are likely to share their experiences with their fellow teachers, thus increasing program acceptability. On the other hand, no news spreads faster than a failed consultation, and even a single failure can solidify teacher resistance.

Despite the obstacles to teacher acceptance of IATs, adopting an ecological approach to student problems can be empowering for consultants and teachers alike. When problems are ascribed not solely to the student's characteristics but to mismatches between the student's needs and the characteristics of the learning environment, the consultant's role is no longer that of helping an ineffective teacher obtain an out-of-class placement for a dysfunctional child with a teacher with greater expertise (i.e., the special education teacher). Instead, the consultant's task is to enhance the referring teacher's professional skills by helping that teacher create a more effective learning environment, not only for the target student but for all of the students in the classroom.

Best Practice 2: Be Creative in Finding Time for Consultation

Finding time to consult with teachers is a perennial problem for practitioners (Burns et al., 2012; Doll et al., 2005; Erchul & Martens, 2002). In many elementary schools, teachers do not have daily planning periods in which they are free from the responsibility of supervising students. More often, teachers have several free periods a week on different days while their students participate in physical education, art, or other "specials." Finding time to consult with teachers at the middle and high school levels can be even more difficult. Although most secondary-level teachers have one regular planning period per day, it can take days or even weeks to find a time when all of the staff responsible for a particular student or, at a minimum, all those who have concerns about a student can meet. Although many teams schedule their activities at the end of the school day when teachers do not have classroom duties, teachers often have other responsibilities, such as attending other meetings and sponsoring after-school activities. Nevertheless, finding a regular time for team meetings and sticking to it is critical to team functioning and effectiveness. The more regular team meetings can be, the more likely the team is to become integrated into the school culture (Burns, Wiley, & Viglietta, 2008).

Collaborating with administrators to find time for teacher consultation is essential to the success of individual consultants and team-based IATs alike. If a teacher is experiencing problems with a student or classroom group, however, the building administrator also has a problem. Principals are often willing to arrange for support staff to cover classes or to cover classes themselves to permit teachers to meet with a consultant. Eating lunch with teachers can create opportunities for consultation, but problems of confidentiality arise if conversations about students can be overheard by other staff or pupils. Arranging to join teachers for lunch in their classrooms on a day when they do not have cafeteria duty is a better alternative and can help create an informal collegial atmosphere conducive to problem solving. Groups of teachers who are having difficulty with a particular class or student are often willing and eager to meet during their lunch period to discuss the problem, especially if they believe that the consultant will be available for follow-up assistance.

Another approach is to use grade-level teams as the basis for the IATs. Most elementary schools have teams of teachers who meet on a regular basis, often as PLCs. High schools may have teams that are composed of teachers from a single department. The advantages of these teams are abundant—they meet regularly, and the team has considerable knowledge about the child and environment and about typical academic and behavior performance in that school for their grade. Obviously, using grade-level or department teams also poses some challenges. School-based teams are unlikely to have members with expertise in the core IAT process. Grade-level teams also have a number of other responsibilities. Nevertheless, with some creativity this team has the potential to be the first stage in the problem-solving process. By adding an administrator and an intervention-focused specialist to grade-level teams once a week, over time they can develop into an effective IAT.

Another strategy might be doubling classes to free teachers for consultation time. For example, paraprofessionals or substitute teachers can cover classes so that teachers can meet with the consultant or attend IAT meetings. In some schools, principals arrange for a permanent substitute 1 day a week throughout the year who rotates through classes so that teachers can join the IAT. Effective consultation takes time—time to observe in classrooms, to talk with teachers, to design intervention plans, to assist with implementation and progress monitoring, and to provide follow-up support. Regardless of the time constraints that beset all consultants, their personal receptiveness and availability to help teachers are crucial to the success of the intervention assistance process. Consultants who appear overly busy or preoccupied may inadvertently communicate the message that they are not genuinely interested in listening to teachers' concerns and are therefore unlikely to be approached for assistance. Similarly, consultants who merely suggest strategies without taking time to provide concrete help with implementation can undermine teachers' sense of self-efficacy, contribute to teacher resistance, and reinforce the notion that only "experts" can deal with difficult-to-teach students.

On the other hand, teachers can be tremendously creative in carving out time from a busy school day to talk with a consultant who appears to be genuinely interested in helping them solve classroom problems. Provided that the teacher and the consultant can talk together without being overheard, productive consultations can be conducted on the playground, in the hall during class changes and restroom breaks, outside of the building at dismissal time, and in the classroom while students are having snack breaks, resting, doing independent seatwork, or working in cooperative learning groups. When teachers and administrators believe that consultation is valuable, they will find time to consult where no time seemed available before.

Best Practice 3: Offer Interventions That Are Evidence-Based for the Current Case

One of the features of EBIs that is often ignored is that the interventions are only evidence-based for specific problems. As such, one of the most critical tasks of a consultant is to help a teacher identify the nature of the problem (typically referred to in the behavioral literature as "function") and match interventions appropriately. We believe the most sound approach is to use the instructional hierarchy (Haring & Eaton, 1978) as the primary framework for matching interventions to a child's skill proficiency to produce the strongest gains for the student. Regardless of the skill being learned (e.g., reading, math computation, social skills), the process is consistent, starting with *acquisition* and then building higher and higher levels of *fluency*, then *generalizing* and *adapting* the skill to other situations. If we know the stage of learning, we understand the core approach necessary for a successful intervention. This approach has clear applications for academic issues, but it can also be applied to social behavior problems (Burns et al., 2012). On the most basic level, any behavior (walking in line or sight-word reading) proceeds through the stages of learning. It is critical to know whether a child has not learned the appropriate behavior or is not fluent in it when selecting an intervention.

Acquisition—Academic

The goal of this stage is to teach the skill and focus on accuracy. Interventions at this stage focus on modeling correct responding, providing cues and more intensive prompts to facilitate correct responding, and providing immediate corrective feedback. It is important to note that independent practice at this stage is unproductive (and can be harmful) as the child will have a high error rate.

Acquisition—Behavior

Consistent with academic skills, the goal of behavior instruction in this phase is to teach the child to know when the behavior is correctly exhibited and when it is not. Interventions in this stage should be based on direct instruction with immediate feedback when the behavior is incorrect or used at the wrong time.

Fluency—Academic

After a child has acquired a skill and can accurately use it, the next step is to facilitate rapid or automatic responding that remains accurate (Binder, 1996). At this stage, interventions will focus on providing many opportunities to respond with delayed corrective feedback. Assuming a lower error rate, it can be unproductive to interrupt a child's response, as it can reduce opportunities to respond.

Fluency—Behavior

As with academic skills, fluency building of social behavior is the logical goal after a child can accurately display the desired target behavior. At this stage, interventions are selected by focusing on two questions. First, *What is a child getting from not exhibiting the correct behavior?* Often an inappropriate behavior is reinforced, resulting in that behavior being used rather than the appropriate behavior. Second, *Is the child getting out of some task when he or she misbehaves?* If misbehavior results in avoiding something the child does not like to do, then she or he will misbehave when that task is presented. In this case, there is often a task demand that the child is not able to do without frustration; therefore, one should consider whether the child can't do the task demand or is deciding not to do it.

Generalization and Adaptation

Once the student responds fluently when presented with the task under conditions that are identical to training conditions, the student is ready for generalization training. The goal of learning at the generalization stage is to facilitate skill performance under slightly different task demands (slightly different conditions, settings, problem presentations). Productive instructional strategies that facilitate generalization include providing the student with the opportunity to practice responding in different settings, different contexts, and with slightly variable tasks (Stokes & Baer, 1977). Many of the strategies that were helpful at the acquisition stage of learning will be helpful at this stage, too, including using cues and providing corrective feedback to guide and then reinforce correct generalization.

Generalization and Adaptation—Behavior

When a child can fluently exhibit a behavior skill in the classroom, the goal of intervention shifts to support the use of that skill in different environments or the adaptation of that skill to solving new problems or challenges that the student might encounter. Technically, the goal of behavior intervention at the generalization stage is to increase the likelihood that a trained behavior is presented across time, setting, and/or target in the absence of the conditions that promoted its acquisition (Stokes & Baer, 1977). As with the fluency-building stage, intervention in the generalization programming stage is focused primarily on adapting the target environment (where you desire the child to exhibit the target behavior) to increase the likelihood of presentation.

Best Practice 4: Offer Interventions That Balance Treatment Effectiveness with Treatment Acceptability

Although consultants are ethically bound to offer evidence-based strategies, even an intervention with a documented history of effectiveness in solving the referral problem will be unsuccessful in improving student functioning unless the teacher implements it. Assessing treatment acceptability is, therefore, an important aspect of intervention selection. *Treatment acceptability* refers to judgments made by intervention consumers, such as teachers, students, and parents, regarding the degree to which they believe a planned intervention is reasonable, appropriate, and likely to be effective (Eckert & Hintze, 2000). There is considerable evidence that teachers do not select interventions based on whether or not the strategies have been empirically validated but instead on whether they themselves believe that the strategies can enhance learning for all students and are feasible and easy to implement (Boardman et al., 2005). Although acceptability is positively related to implementation accuracy and intervention effectiveness (Allinder & Oats, 1997; Eckert & Hintze, 2000), it is important to note that teacher satisfaction with interventions is not sufficient to ensure accurate implementation or successful outcomes (Cowan & Sheridan, 2003). Moreover, even when interventions are effective in improving the target behavior, teachers often discontinue them after the researchers have departed (Hawkins, & Heflin, 2010), indicating that other factors are critical to maintenance.

In general, positive strategies, such as praise, differential reinforcement, and token economies, are more acceptable to teachers and other intervention consumers than reductive strategies, such as ignoring, response cost, and time-out (Turan & Erbaş, 2010). Not surprisingly, teachers tend to prefer interventions that are less complex and less time-consuming and that fit easily into the classroom ecology (Elliott et al., 2002). There is also an inverse relationship between treatment acceptability and years of teaching experience, such that more experienced teachers rate *all* interventions as less acceptable than do less experienced teachers (Ghaith & Yaghi, 1997). On the other hand, the more severe a student's problem is, the more likely it is that any intervention will be considered acceptable, especially if teachers are able to access on-site technical assistance (Eckert & Hintze, 2000).

Assessing Intervention Acceptability

In matching interventions to teacher preferences and classroom ecological systems, consultants may wish to assess intervention acceptability using a formal measure. Several scales have been developed for this purpose, including the Behavior Intervention Rating Scale (BIRS; Von Brock & Elliott, 1987), a 24-item, 6-point Likert scale assessing teacher or parent perceptions of intervention acceptability and effectiveness. The BIRS has been used frequently to assess intervention acceptability in analogue investigations and treatment programs. Consultants may also wish to measure students' reactions to school-based interventions. The most widely used measure of children's judgments of intervention acceptability is the Children's Intervention Rating Profile (CIRP; Witt & Elliott, 1985). Written at a fifth-grade readability level, the CIRP is a 7-item, 6-point Likert scale assessing children's perceptions of the acceptability of behavioral interventions. The CIRP has been validated on more than 1,000 students in grades 5–10 and used in numerous investigations of behavioral treatments (Elliott, Turco, & Gresham, 1987; Lane, Mahdavi, & Borthwick-Duffy, 2003; Turco & Elliott, 1986). Both the BIRS and the CIRP are reproduced in Elliott et al. (2002).

One more recent development is the Usage Rating Profile—Intervention, Revised (URP-IR), which was developed to assess factors related to intervention implementation (Chafouleas, Briesch, Neugebauer, & Riley-Tillman, 2011). The URP-IR measures teachers' (or other interventionists') ability to accept the intervention, how feasible they believe the intervention is, their understanding of the intervention, and whether they view the system as supportive of intervention. This measure results in a broader view of social validity that allows consultants to address the reasons for concerns more specifically. For example, if a teacher indicates that he or she does not feel confident in his or her understanding of the intervention, that can be addressed.

In addition to using these generic scales, consultants can develop and administer intervention-specific acceptability scales for teachers or students prior to implementation, to evaluate acceptability, or after implementation, as consumer satisfaction surveys. Figure 2.1 presents an example of a student intervention acceptability scale designed to measure student reaction to the *Good Behavior Game Plus Merit*, a team-based intervention targeting disruptive behavior. This version is intended for use with elementary school students, but it can be modified for use with older students by including additional items and/or increasing the number of ratings from 3 to 5 (i.e., from *strongly disagree* to *strongly agree*) to enhance measurement sensitivity.

Strategies for Enhancing Intervention Acceptability

Because ecological intrusiveness is a major factor in teacher resistance to interventions, consultants can enhance acceptability by matching interventions to teachers' current classroom routines and procedures as closely as possible (Lentz et al., 1996). For overwhelmed teachers, interventions should be as simple as possible and require minimal modifications in instructional and behavior management routines. Suggesting that a teacher with severe classroom management problems begin by implementing *Collaborative Strategic Reading*, an intervention that involves dividing the class into groups that engage in a sequence of self-managed reading and writing activities, is likely to increase rather than solve those problems, at least initially. Moreover, the teacher would be likely to resist such a recommendation out of fear of

How I feel about the *Good Behavior Game Plus Merit*	Yes	Not Sure	No
1. I liked playing the *Good Behavior Game Plus Merit*.			
2. The *Good Behavior Game Plus Merit* was fair for everyone.			
3. The *Good Behavior Game Plus Merit* helped our class follow the rules and behave better.			
4. Other teachers should use the *Good Behavior Game Plus Merit*.			
5. I would tell my friends to participate in the *Good Behavior Game Plus Merit*.			

FIGURE 2.1. Student Intervention Acceptability Scale for the *Good Behavior Game Plus Merit*.

losing control of the class. Consultants can also increase the acceptability of an intervention by taking the time to explain not just the procedures for implementation but also the rationale for the strategy, its theoretical basis, and the anticipated outcomes. The more knowledge teachers have regarding the purpose of an intervention and its potential effect on student learning and behavior, the more likely they are to implement interventions as planned and to sustain them over time (Klingner et al., 1999).

Best Practice 5: Emphasize Strategies That Enhance the Functioning of the Entire Classroom Group Rather Than Merely the Target Student

Although teachers typically refer individual students, rather than groups of students, for intervention assistance, consultants following up a referral with a classroom observation often discover that some, many, or all of the other students in the classroom have similar problems. This is especially likely to be true for referrals for inappropriate behavior. If more than one or two students in a classroom exhibit the same difficulty, then the environment, not the students, needs to change. Even when a single student is the focus of intervention, priority should be given to strategies that can be implemented with the entire class rather than just with the target individual. Group-focused strategies have many advantages over interventions that target a single student. First, they are efficient in terms of time and labor, especially in classrooms with more than one low-performing or ineffectively behaving student. Second, they avoid the problem of singling out individual students, which may be embarrassing for students, especially those beyond the early primary grades. Third, classwide strategies are more acceptable to teachers, who often complain that it is unfair to allocate special attention to one student at the expense of others (Gersten, Fuchs, Williams, & Baker, 2001). Fourth, shifting the focus of intervention assistance from one low-performing or misbehaving student to the classroom system as a whole has the potential to have a positive impact on the functioning of the other students in that system (Elliott et al., 2002). Finally, research has consistently shown the effects of classwide interventions on student skills in reading (Burns et al., 2015; Burns et al., 2016), math (VanDerHeyden, McLaughlin, Algina, & Snyder, 2012) and behavior (Chafouleas, Hagemoser Sanetti, Jaffery, & Fallon, 2012).

Best Practice 6: Be Prepared to Support Teachers throughout the Intervention Assistance Process

Until quite recently, consultants primarily depended on oral instructions as the primary vehicle for change within the consultation framework. Contrary to this "talk and hope" strategy, there is abundant evidence that verbal instructions are insufficient to ensure that teachers will implement an intervention accurately or continue it after consultation contacts have ended (e.g., Hagermoser Sanetti, Luiselli, & Handler, 2007). On the contrary, it is now clear that teachers require much more training and support than was previously thought if they are to implement the interventions to which they have agreed and maintain them accurately over time (Sterling-Turner, Watson, Wildmon, Watkins, & Little, 2001).

During the initial implementation phase, consultants should be available to provide hands-on assistance in the form of modeling, coaching, and performance feedback. Classroom-based technical assistance, such as in vivo modeling and coaching, is especially important for interventions that involve major changes in classroom organizational and instructional structures, such as collaborative learning formats (e.g., classwide peer tutoring, reciprocal peer tutoring) and strategies that require misbehaving students to move to a different location (e.g., *Sit and Watch: Teaching Prosocial Behaviors*). In-class assistance also ensures that consultants are available to provide support with behavior management if it is needed. Research (e.g., Klingner, Ahwee, Pilonieta, & Menendez, 2003) and field testing alike attest that low levels of treatment integrity or failure to sustain an intervention are often related to classroom management issues rather than to dissatisfaction with the intervention.

Although classroom-based technical assistance may be a new role for some practitioners, it is an essential competency for today's school consultants. An increasing body of research documents the importance of providing in vivo technical assistance as an integral part of professional development and the process of introducing evidence-based practices into classrooms (Becker, Bradshaw, Domitrovich, & Ialongo, 2013; Dunst & Raab, 2010). Not only does classroom-based support increase intervention acceptability and enhance the consultant's credibility with teachers, but it also provides an opportunity to obtain valuable insights about the classroom ecology, including teacher–student and student–student interactions, teachers' behavior management skills, and the nature and pacing of instruction. It is also a powerful relationship-building practice. A teacher who observes a consultant struggling to implement *Sit and Watch: Teaching Prosocial Behaviors* (a strategy that requires a misbehaving child to sit quietly in a chair at the classroom periphery and watch his or her classmates engaging in an activity from which he or she has just been removed) with a very oppositional student is likely to feel supported in an entirely different way than would a teacher who receives only a verbal or written description of the same intervention. Just as importantly, classroom-based assistance increases the consultant's ability to empathize with the teacher and understand the teacher's perspective regarding the nature of the problem and the possible barriers to successful implementation.

Consultants should also be available to help teachers collect and analyze data for use in monitoring students' response to interventions (RTI). Although the observation and evaluation methods for the interventions in this book have been designed to be as simple as possible without sacrificing reliability and validity, even the simplest observation can be more easily performed by someone other than the teacher, who must be continually responding to the demands of daily classroom life. For this reason, consultants are encouraged to offer assistance in gathering baseline data, monitoring student progress, and evaluating intervention effectiveness, especially when initiating a consultative relationship.

Best Practice 7: Assess and Maximize Treatment Integrity

Treatment integrity is a generally considered to be the extent to which an intervention was correctly implemented (Hagermoser Sanetti & DiGennaro Reed, 2012), but it is a multidimensional construct (Southam-Gerow & McLeod, 2013). Treatment integrity, also referred to as treatment fidelity, is affected by a wide range of factors, including (1) the complexity of the intervention, (2) the time and materials required for implementation, (3) the number of intervention agents needed to implement the intervention, (4) efficacy (actual and as perceived by the intervention agents and stakeholders), and (5) the motivation of those implementing the intervention (Gresham, MacMillan, Beebe-Frankenberger, & Bocian, 2000; Hagermoser Sanetti & DiGennaro Reed, 2012). It is essential to assess treatment integrity in order to help distinguish interventions that are ineffective from those that are potentially effective but are inaccurately implemented (Hagermoser Sanetti, Gritter, & Dobey, 2011). Meta-analytic research found that treatment integrity for classroom interventions deteriorates rapidly over time, with teachers typically implementing interventions with high fidelity for a few days, after which they gradually fail to implement them accurately or discontinue using them altogether (Solomon, Klein, & Polityło, 2012). Although 100% treatment integrity is not necessary to produce successful results (Harn, Parisi, & Stoolmiller, 2013), most studies have found a positive relationship between treatment integrity and intervention effectiveness (Polanin & Espelage, 2015).

Although treatment integrity is important, consultants and IAT members often fail to assess it, and measures are often confined to teacher verbal reports when it is assessed. Comparisons between direct observations and teacher self-reports of intervention integrity often yielded conflicting results (Allen & Blackston, 2003; Little, Hudson, & Wilks, 2002). Teachers reported that they implemented an intervention for disruptive behavior with fidelity 54% of the time, whereas direct observation found that teachers implemented the intervention as planned only 4% of the time (Wickstrom, Jones, LaFleur, & Witt, 1998)!

Treatment integrity can be assessed using a variety of methods, including direct observation, teacher self-reports, teacher and student interviews, examining permanent products (e.g., score cards for a math intervention or a poster listing strategy steps for a writing intervention), or self-completed checklists documenting the completion of each intervention component or step (see Figure 2.2). As shown above, direct observations and teacher self-reports can be inconsistent. Moreover, a comparison between direct observation, teacher self-reports, and permanent products from the interventions indicated better agreement between teacher self-reports and observations, but permanent products did not accurately reflect integrity (Begeny, Upright, Easton, Ehrenbock, & Tunstall, 2013). Therefore, it is likely important to use a combination of methods to assess treatment fidelity.

Strategies for Maximizing Treatment Integrity

Following is a list of recommendations for maximizing treatment integrity that are drawn from observations made during field testing and from the literature as noted.

1. Avoid complex and ecologically intrusive strategies that disrupt current instructional and behavior management routines. The goal of any intervention is to increase teachers' professional effectiveness in meeting student needs, not to increase their burden in the classroom.
2. Develop a written intervention plan that outlines implementation procedures, responsibilities for each intervention agent, strategies for monitoring progress, and dates for reviewing the plan. Detailed descriptions of interventions should also be provided within the plan and reviewed with intervention agents to ensure that they understand the intervention goals, procedures, and desired outcomes.
3. Provide direct training in intervention procedures, including modeling, guided practice, coaching, and performance feedback (Sterling-Turner et al., 2001). Direct training should involve demonstrations of intervention procedures not only in the intervention setting (e.g., classroom, hallway, playground) but also outside of the target context so that the consultant can help the teacher integrate the strategy into established classroom routines.
4. Include a follow-up observation component in the intervention plan. Follow-up observations provide an opportunity to assess treatment integrity, modify the intervention as needed, and evaluate the effectiveness of the intervention plan. Data from follow-up observations should be in writing so that the consultant can review the information with the teacher and/or the IAT and later document that the intervention and follow-up meeting occurred. Implementation checklists are one type of measure that can be used in the follow-up process (see Figure 2.2).

Class/student name: _____   Teacher: _____

Activity observed: _____   Observer: _____

Observation time: _____ to _____

Check to indicate completed intervention components.

Date of observation:	____	____	____	____	____
Sit and Watch component 1. The teacher describes the student's inappropriate behavior.					
2. The teacher identifies acceptable replacement behavior(s) for the situation.					
3. The teacher escorts the student to the Sit and Watch chair.					
4. The teacher directs the student to observe the appropriate behaviors of other students.					
5. After the student has been sitting quietly for 1 minute, the teacher asks the student if he or she is ready to rejoin the activity and display the appropriate behavior.					
6. If the student responds positively, the teacher permits the student to return to the activity. If the student responds negatively, the teacher tells the student to continue to sit and watch and then asks again in a few minutes.					
7. When the student returns to the group, the teacher provides positive attention for appropriate behavior as soon as possible.					
Quiet Place component 1. If the student continues to be disruptive, the teacher escorts the student to the classroom Quiet Place and indicates the reason for the removal.					
2. When the student is calm and sitting quietly, the teacher asks the student if he or she is ready to sit quietly and watch in the Sit and Watch chair.					
3. If the student responds positively, the teacher returns the student to the Sit and Watch chair and continues from Step 4. If the student responds negatively, the teacher tells the student to continue to sit and watch in the Quiet Place and then asks again in a few minutes.					
4. When the student returns to the group, the teacher provides positive attention for appropriate behavior.					
Number of procedures accurately implemented (total of seven for *Sit and Watch* only; total of 11 with Quiet Place backup)	___ /7 ___ /11	___ /7 ___ /11	___ /7 ___ /11	___ /7 ___ /11	___ /7 ___ /11

FIGURE 2.2. Sample implementation checklist.

Best Practice 8: Use a Variety of Training Formats to Expand Teachers' and Team Members' Knowledge of Interventions and the Intervention Assistance Process

Lack of training for teachers and team members in effective interventions has been repeatedly identified as a major barrier to successful implementation of school-based problem-solving teams (McDougal et al., 2000; Truscott et al., 2000). Given the time constraints of typical consultation sessions and IAT meetings, consultants need to examine a variety of formats for helping teachers and team members learn about EBIs for solving common referral problems, as well as effective procedures and processes related to the intervention assistance process. For teacher training, options include preservice and inservice professional development programs, small-group workshops, and individual consultation. Training during preservice days is a particularly good alternative because teachers have not yet established classroom routines and behavioral expectations. Workshops that include small-group activities not only provide opportunities for teachers to share effective strategies for enhancing student achievement and behavior with their colleagues but can also increase staff cohesion and encourage a collaborative approach to problem solving. Providing opportunities for collaboration among regular and special education personnel is especially important because their schedules often give them little time to interact during the school day.

Field testing indicates that preservice training in a core group of keystone interventions that aim at critical management targets is much more effective than attempting to train teachers in a large repertoire of alternative strategies for managing behavior. Moreover, implementing the same strategies across classrooms and nonclassroom settings (e.g., hallways, the lunchroom) can have a powerful positive effect on schoolwide student behavior and overall school climate. At the same time, however, follow-up training is essential once school has begun, with beginning teachers especially likely to need additional in vivo technical assistance. The full complement of professional development components, including initial training, guided practice, and follow-up observations and feedback, should be provided to all faculty and staff involved in implementation. For example, for an intervention targeting transitions in a classroom that regularly includes aides or assistants, all classroom staff should participate in training and receive periodic performance feedback. Similarly, for interventions that potentially involve other teaching or office staff, including all intervention agents in all aspects of training is crucial to success. Of course, for schoolwide interventions, training and follow-up technical assistance should be provided to all faculty and staff with implementation responsibilities, not just classroom teachers.

Peer mentoring is an effective but often neglected training format for expanding teachers' knowledge and use of evidence-based practices. A teacher who has mastered an intervention could provide direct assistance and support to another teacher in using the same strategy. Although peer observations take time and effort to arrange, the opportunity to watch a colleague implementing an intervention is a powerful learning tool and can diminish resistance to a particular strategy. Peer mentoring has been successful in expanding the use of research-based interventions in schools and is much preferred by teachers to traditional professional development formats (Vaughn & Coleman, 2004). Moreover, teachers are more likely to sustain innovative instructional practices if they have an opportunity to interact with their fellow teachers who are also implementing those practices (Klingner et al., 1999).

When IATs serve as the delivery system for intervention assistance programs, the consultant's role in professional development becomes more complex. The consultant can meet with the team to provide information about a variety of interventions targeting common referral problems, demonstrate specific strategies, and conduct workshops on topics identified by the team as priorities based on student and teacher needs. Training for team members in team-based consultation practices, including observations, data collection and analysis, the problem-solving process, team building, and outcome evaluation, will also need to be provided. Although comprehensive training for all team members in the technical skills and competencies required in the intervention assistance process is optimal, it may be very difficult for every member to participate in the full range of professional development activities provided at the building, district, and/or state levels. One approach is to provide comprehensive training in one or more specific areas or skills (e.g., data collection and analysis, consultation, intervention design) to a single team member, who can then train the other team members or serve as the resident expert on that team in those areas (Doll et al., 2005; McDougal et al., 2000).

Another set of challenges concerns finding effective and practical forums for training parents when parents serve as the primary intervention agents or participate in interventions with a home component. Training can be provided on an individual basis, through group-oriented parent education programs, or through parent participation on an IAT. When students receive psychological or psychoeducational assessments as part of the problem-solving process or for special education eligibility determination, information on specific interventions can be provided to parents and teachers in the recommendations sections of the reports, as described below.

Best Practice 9: Foster Relationships with Key Participants in the Intervention Assistance Process

The intervention assistance process is embedded in a set of complex relationships involving consultants, teachers, team members, administrators, students, and parents. Because consultation is an indirect service delivery model, its ultimate success depends upon the cooperation of the consultee in implementing the agreed-upon intervention (Sheridan, Rispoli, & Holmes, 2014). In other words, the most carefully designed intervention plan will not enhance a student's chances for success unless the teacher or parent takes action. Because school consultants rarely have direct line authority over teachers, consultants' ability to build trusting relationships with teachers is fundamental to teachers' investment in the intervention assistance process and the extent to which they implement the interventions to which they have agreed (Erchul & Martens, 2002). If teachers believe that their input is not valued or that they have not received sufficient follow-up and support after implementation, they are likely to disengage from the intervention assistance process by failing to implement the recommended strategies or failing to refer other students (Slonski-Fowler & Truscott, 2004).

The Role of the Principal in IAT Success

Research has consistently identified administrator support as critical to the success of consultation in general and of IATs in particular (Burns, Wiley, & Viglietta, 2008). In a study by Kruger, Struzziero, Watts, and Vacca (1995), administrator support accounted for more than 50% of the variance in teacher satisfaction with school-based teams. Although it is not clear whether direct participation by administrators in team meetings is essential to the success of school-based teams or whether more general support is sufficient, a national survey of teams in 200 elementary schools (four teams per state) found that 75% of teams included general education administrators as regular members (Truscott et al., 2005). Principals play a crucial role in supporting the intervention assistance process by helping to ensure that team members and faculty receive sufficient training for effective participation, allocating resources to support evidence-based practices recommended by IATs, and conveying to teachers the message that they are responsible for implementing classroom interventions with integrity and monitoring students' response to intervention before special education services can be considered (Burns, Wiley, & Viglietta, 2008). Administrator involvement is also necessary to schedule space and times for meetings, facilitate contacts with other teams and specialists within the building and district, and integrate IATs with other projects and initiatives being simultaneously implemented at the building and district levels. Just as importantly, principals play an indirect but vital role in creating a school culture that values a collaborative, intervention-oriented approach to student problems and in which IATs are likely to succeed. In schools in which principals are uninvolved in or resistant to IATs, failure is virtually inevitable.

Consultants should make every effort to encourage the building principal to participate in IAT planning and to become a regular member of the school-based team. Thus principals should participate in IAT-related professional development, especially during initial implementation of a school-based PST, and should be active participants during meetings. Consultants can also promote administrators' investment in IATs by expanding their role in intervention delivery. Involving the principal as an intervention agent not only capitalizes on the influence of the most powerful individual in the school but can also increase administrator commitment to IATs by providing opportunities for the principal to encourage positive student behavior rather than merely to impose consequences for problem behavior.

It is possible for the principal to convey support of the IAT process without actually attending meetings. The principal can have a designee who attends meetings, but the designee must make it clear that she or he is there to represent the principal and should meet with the principal shortly after the meeting to summarize the proceedings. Teams are likely more effective if the principal is an active member of the team, but it would be preferable to have a designee than to not have any administrative support at all or to have the principal attend the meeting while being an inactive participant (e.g., checking e-mail while the team meets).

Building Collaborative Relationships with Parents

Collaborating with parents is one of the most neglected aspects of IATs. Although there is considerable evidence that interventions that involve both parents and teachers can significantly enhance children's academic performance and school-related behavior (Jeynes, 2012), very few studies have evaluated the extent or effects of parent participation in IATs. Level of parent involvement is moderated by how the meetings are organized, relationships with IAT members, communication, problem-solving processes, and parent emotions (Esquivel, Ryan, & Bonner, 2008). Parent report of home support for interventions was a significant predictor of goal attainment, however, supporting the inclusion of parents in the intervention assistance process. Unfortunately, parent participation in the intervention assistance process is typically minimal. In a national survey of school-based PSTs (Truscott et al., 2005), less than a third (28%) of surveyed teams included parents as members. Moreover, only about 9% of reported interventions involved working with parents or increasing communication between school and home, and only 4% of the interventions were designed to be delivered by parents.

The failure to promote the meaningful participation of parents in the intervention assistance process is especially ironic in view of the fact that teachers and team members overwhelmingly attribute the source of student problems to within-student or within-family factors (Rubinson, 2002; Truscott et al., 2000). It has been our experience that many interventions fail because parents are not involved or only nominally involved in the problem-solving process. Chronic behavior problems and lack of academic productivity are especially resistant to classroom interventions without some meaningful form of home–school collaboration. Although involving parents in the intervention assistance process can be difficult because of cultural or linguistic differences, family stressors, work and health issues, and a host of other factors, school consultants must make every effort to solicit the assistance of the individuals who have the greatest investment in the referred student and his or her success. Many interventions in this book can be delivered by parents who receive training in the procedures and follow-up support.

Best Practice 10: Be Sensitive to Cultural Diversity in the Consultation and Intervention Assistance Process

Given the rapidly changing demographics in the United States, one of the greatest challenges facing today's consultants and educators is designing interventions that are acceptable and effective across different cultural and linguistic groups. Despite the current emphasis on providing EBIs in the regular classroom to improve student outcomes and reduce unnecessary referrals to special education, there is still a dearth of empirical data on the relative acceptability or effectiveness of school-based interventions with students from culturally and linguistically diverse backgrounds (Lindo, 2006). Similarly, despite the widespread implementation of school-based PSTs, there is virtually no research specifically evaluating the effectiveness of IATs with students from diverse backgrounds. In the absence of a well-defined research base, two research-based consultative frameworks can be especially useful to practitioners as they strive to develop and maintain a culturally and linguistically responsive intervention assistance process: (1) an ecological perspective and (2) an ethnic validity model.

An ecological approach is important in problem analysis and intervention design for all students, but it is especially important in the case of culturally and linguistically diverse learners. When considering factors contributing to problems displayed by students from culturally and linguistically diverse backgrounds, consultants and educators must be sensitive to the ways in which cultural and linguistic factors influence learning and behavior at school (Ortiz, Wilkinson, Robertson-Courtney, & Kushner, 2006). Data obtained during the problem-solving process must be interpreted in the context of the student's cultural, linguistic, and racial/ethnic background in order to distinguish between background differences that may be contributing to school problems and learning or behavior deficits that warrant intervention (Wilkinson, Ortiz, Robertson, & Kushner, 2006). Childrearing and socialization practices, communication styles, norms for behavior, and attitudes toward education are all embedded in a cultural context (Sheridan, 2000). In the case of English language learners, differentiating between genuine disabilities and problems related to limited English proficiency and educational histories characterized by frequent disruptions of schooling and inadequate instructional opportunities can be especially difficult (Figueroa & Newsome, 2006).

A second framework that can assist consultants in considering the effects of cultural differences on the intervention assistance process and evaluating the appropriateness of interventions with students from diverse backgrounds is the ethnic validity model (Barnett et al., 1995). An extension of the concept of social validity, *ethnic validity* refers to the degree to which intervention goals, assistance processes, and outcomes are acceptable to intervention recipients and stakeholders with respect to their cultural/ethnic beliefs and value systems. In the context of a problem-solving model, three key components are involved in establishing ethnic validity: (1) the problem-solving process, (2) intervention acceptability, and (3) teaming strategies. During the problem-solving process, consultants must consider the possible impact of cultural and linguistic differences on the tasks involved in each stage. For example, individuals from different ethnic groups may view student problems from very different perspectives. Cultural differences also have an influence on the acceptability of interventions. For example, interventions that provide tangible rewards for academic performance or positive behavior may be unacceptable to individuals from certain cultures. Consultants must be especially sensitive to cultural beliefs and value systems in designing home-based interventions or interventions with a parent component. In the absence of this sensitivity, intervention failure or low levels of treatment integrity may reflect a mismatch between intervention design and family values (Sheridan, 2000). To enhance ethnic validity, consultants can design interventions that are sensitive to the values of students and their families and offer a range of interventions from which to choose.

Consultants can also increase ethnic validity through teaming strategies by adopting a collaborative approach to problem solving that respects the family's cultural values and norms. One way of enhancing ethnic validity relative to this component is to include school staff or community residents from the same cultural/ethnic/linguistic background as the referred student in the intervention assistance process (Barnett et al., 1999). Ethnically valid teaming also requires taking the time to establish rapport and build trust rather than moving rapidly to discussing interventions. It is important to listen respectfully to the parents' perspective on the nature and origin of the problem, their past efforts to deal with the problem, and their perspectives on the most appropriate interventions. Including family members throughout the problem-solving process is essential to help distinguish between behaviors that reflect academic or social competence deficits and behaviors that are appropriate in light of students' cultural and linguistic backgrounds (Ortiz et al., 2006).

Bias in the Intervention Assistance Process

Awareness of one's own cultural values and biases and those of others involved in the intervention assistance process is especially important in view of evidence that students' racial/ ethnic and/or linguistic backgrounds may influence teachers' referral patterns, the assessment process, eligibility decisions made by teams, and the interventions that students receive. In a recent synthesis of the research literature on referral rates for assessment or intervention for three racial groups (African American, European American, and Hispanic), Hosp and Reschly (2004) found that African American students were significantly more likely to be referred than European American students. Research also indicates that special education eligibility teams often fail to consider the potential impact of contextual factors, such as prior schooling, language proficiency, and home variables, on learning or behavior problems and have difficulty distinguishing between cultural and linguistic differences and specific disabilities (Figueroa & Newsome, 2006; Ortiz et al., 2006). In a study by Wilkinson and colleagues (2006) examining the eligibility decisions for 21 Spanish-speaking English language learners identified by school multidisciplinary teams as having reading-related learning disabilities, determinations by an expert panel differed significantly from those of the school teams. Although the panel agreed that 5 of the 21 students had reading-related learning disabilities, they questioned whether that was the appropriate classification for 6 other students and judged that the achievement problems of the remaining 10 students were attributable to factors other than specific disabilities, such as interrupted schooling or lack of prereferral interventions.

Students' racial and linguistic backgrounds may also have an influence on the intervention assistance process and the types of interventions students receive. When English language learners are referred for academic or behavioral difficulties, teams often give only perfunctory attention to prereferral strategies and move rapidly to recommend testing for special education services (Klingner & Harry, 2006). Moreover, when English language learners are identified with disabilities, they are pulled from general education classrooms for more time than their English-speaking peers, but they are not as often placed in the most restrictive environments (Sullivan, 2011). Teachers' intervention preferences also vary by racial/ethnic group in that students from ethnic minority groups are two to three times more likely to be sent to the office for behavior infractions than their European American peers and more likely to be expelled (Skiba et al., 2011).

If IATs are to serve as effective delivery systems for improving the performance of diverse students, consultants must ensure that the intervention assistance process is culturally and linguistically responsive. By maintaining an awareness of their own cultural and ethnic values and encouraging an open dialogue throughout the problem-solving stages, consultants will be better prepared to adjust the intervention assistance process, intervention plans, and specific strategies to address the needs of culturally diverse students and their families. As part of this effort, consultants can help to organize professional development activities to increase their own knowledge of culturally competent practices and that of others involved in IATs, but developing cultural competency is a lifelong process.

INTERVENTION CASE EXAMPLES

Although in some cases a single intervention will be sufficient to solve a classroom problem, consultants often discover that individual students and classroom groups referred to IATs have not one but multiple problems that interfere with their ability to benefit from instruction. In such cases, implementing an *intervention package* consisting of several strategies that target the set of problem behaviors enhances the likelihood of success. The following case examples illustrate the use of intervention packages to improve student outcomes, the first for an individual student and the second for an entire class.

Case Example 1: Aggressive and Noncompliant Preschooler

Four-year-old Kelvin was a constant disruption in his prekindergarten classroom. He frequently grabbed toys from other children, had difficulty completing activities without the constant support of the teacher or classroom assistant, and often failed to comply with adult directions. His behavior was especially problematic during transitions. He had trouble waiting in line and would push or bother the children standing near him. When his teacher or the classroom assistant would attempt to redirect or correct him, he would put his hands over his ears, pull away from them, or attempt to kick or hit them. Screening measures indicated that his receptive and expressive language skills were in the average range, but he had so much difficulty attending to instructional activities that his early literacy skills were beginning to lag behind those of his classmates. Although his teacher had talked with Kelvin about his behavior and offered numerous incentives for positive behavior, these strategies were only occasionally effective, and Kelvin's aggressive and noncompliant behaviors were increasing as the school year continued.

Intervention Targets and Components

Results of a functional behavioral assessment (FBA) that included several classroom observations and interviews with Kelvin's teacher and mother suggested that adult and peer attention for inappropriate behavior, along with the desire to escape from less preferred activities, might be fueling the problem behavior. Moreover, during the FBA interview, Kelvin's mother noted that because of her work situation, he spent much of his time outside of school with her own mother, who set few limits on Kelvin's behavior. Intervention targets were as follows: (1) increasing compliance with adult directions, (2) reducing aggressive behavior and increasing cooperative behavior, and (3) encouraging use of verbal rather than physical means to communicate needs. The team selected an intervention package that consisted of three strategies. To address Kelvin's noncompliant and aggressive behavior, *Delivering Effective Commands: The Precision Request Program*, which integrates several dimensions of effective reprimands into a structured instructional sequence, was implemented. A second intervention, *Sit and Watch,* which combines a classroom time-out with contingent observation and incidental teaching, was implemented to help Kelvin acquire more socially appropriate behaviors. Because transitions were the most frequent settings for aggressive behavior, *Promoting Independent In-Class Transitions with Self-Assessment and Contingent Praise* was also applied, an intervention that teaches children to monitor their own transition behaviors.

Interventions were taught via a series of professional development workshops attended by the entire prekindergarten faculty, followed by classroom-based technical assistance. In vivo support included modeling, guided practice, and performance feedback, with the consultant prompting and providing direct assistance to the teacher and classroom assistant in using the strategies as they were needed. For example, if Kelvin failed to comply with teacher instructions and the teacher did not immediately take action, the consultant would quietly prompt the teacher to follow through to ensure that inappropriate behavior was given consistent consequences. Similarly, if Kelvin resisted going to the *Sit and Watch* chair, the consultant would demonstrate the procedures and provide support as needed. All three of the interventions were implemented on a classwide basis.

Although implementation of these strategies was associated with decreases in disruptive and aggressive behavior, Kelvin's teacher did not feel that his response to the intervention package sufficiently reduced the discrepancy between his behavior and her behavioral expectations for the class. Therefore, *Banking Time*—a strategy in which a teacher provides brief sessions of nondirective, relationship-building interactions to target students—was added to the package. After group and individualized training, the teacher began providing 5-minute *Banking Time* sessions for Kelvin three times a week at the beginning of nap time. Not only did the sessions help Kelvin relax prior to what was often a difficult period for him, but they also provided an opportunity for him and his teacher to relate to each other in a new and more rewarding way. Kelvin's mother attended a *Banking Time* session to observe the procedures and agreed to implement the strategy at home several times a week. By the end of the year, Kelvin's behavior had improved dramatically, and his teacher and mother were hopeful that he would be able to transition successfully to kindergarten.

Case Example 2: Unproductive and Disruptive Sixth-Grade Social Studies Class

The teacher of this sixth-grade social studies class was in her second year at an inner-city middle school in which the majority of students were from ethnically diverse and low-income backgrounds. Although she experienced management problems with most of her classes, her social studies class was especially disruptive and unproductive. The students also had very diverse academic skills. Results of schoolwide language and reading screening assessments indicated that many students also had low vocabulary and comprehension skills, making it difficult for them to understand their textbooks or to follow ongoing classroom instruction. At the time that consultation was initiated, more than half the class had failing grades, and the teacher and principal were extremely concerned.

Intervention Targets and Components

A series of classroom observations revealed that most students were displaying low levels of academic engagement and high rates of off-task and disruptive behavior and that the teacher was failing to scan the entire room on a regular basis. During one observation, the teacher was so focused on interacting with a student seated on one side of the room that she failed to notice when two other students sitting on the other side of the room got up and wandered out into the hall. Interventions were taught by means of a year-long schoolwide professional development program focusing on proactive classroom management and reading enhancement for middle school students, supplemented by classroom observations, individual teacher consultations, and in-class coaching. Because of concerns about poor student achievement and recurring discipline problems across all three grades, the school also initiated an IAT that met twice a month to provide consultative help to teachers and to design professional development activities targeting common problems. Intervention targets included the following: (1) increasing opportunities to respond to academic material, (2) increasing classwork and homework completion rates, (3) building comprehension skills in the context of content-area instruction, and (4) encouraging more positive attitudes toward learning. Because reviews of students' grades and screening data indicated that the most inattentive and disruptive students also had the most severe reading problems, emphasis was placed on enhancing vocabulary and comprehension while simultaneously increasing opportunities to respond to academic material.

A package consisting of four interventions was implemented. First, to increase available instructional time and to reduce opportunities for off-task and disruptive behavior, the teacher implemented *Active Teaching of Classroom Rules,* which provides direct instruction in classroom procedures and contingent teacher praise for following the rules. For students with chronic disruptive behavior, *Debriefing: Helping Students Solve Their Own Behavior Problems,* a strategy that helps students cope more effectively with situations that have been the setting for inappropriate behavior, was implemented with the support of the assistant principal. This intervention was implemented on a schoolwide basis to promote consistency across settings. To encourage peer support for following classroom rules, the teacher also implemented the *Good Behavior Game Plus Merit,* a team-based strategy that provides rewards for appropriate behavior. Field testing has demonstrated that this and other interventions that divide students into teams that compete to earn rewards based on prosocial behaviors are particularly helpful in combating negative peer group attitudes and behaviors. In this case, the variation that provides bonuses for academic productivity was implemented (see Chapter 5). As disruptive behavior diminished, *Admirals and Generals: Improving Content-Area Performance with Strategy Instruction and Peer Tutoring,* which is an intervention in which pairs of students work together to read and summarize textual material, was added twice a week.

As the semester continued, the frequency and intensity of disruptive behavior diminished. Students also became more actively engaged in class discussions and their academic tasks and looked forward to the opportunity to work with a partner for part of the class period. Two of the students with the most serious behavior problems were referred to the school's IAT and began receiving intensive individualized assistance that included targeted reading assessments, after-school tutoring, and regular conferences that included family members and the school counselor. At the end of the semester, most of the students' grades and attitudes had improved substantially, and the teacher reported that although she had considered not returning to the school the following year, she now looked forward to continuing in her current position.

PRINT RESOURCES

Jacob, S., & Decker, D. M. (2010). *Ethics and law for school psychologists* (5th ed.). New York: Wiley.

This comprehensive sourcebook on ethics, law, and professional standards is specifically designed for school psychologists. Two chapters with particular relevance to IATs review ethical and legal issues in school counseling and therapeutic interventions and in teacher and parent collaboration. Numerous case examples—some from case law, some fictitious—illustrate core principles.

National Association of School Psychologists. (2010). *Principles for professional ethics*. Bethesda, MD: Author. Available at *www.nasponline.org/Documents/Standards%20and%20Certification/Standards/1_%20Ethical%20Principles.pdf*

This publication contains the NASP ethical guidelines, which are frequently reviewed to ensure that the principles and standards reflect current conditions. The manual is available for free download.

WEBSITE RESOURCES

National Center for Culturally Responsive Educational Systems
www.nccrest.org

Funded by the U.S. Department of Education's Office of Special Education Programs, the National Center for Culturally Responsive Educational Systems (NCCRESt) provides technical assistance and professional development to close the achievement gap between students from culturally and linguistically diverse backgrounds and their peers and to reduce inappropriate referrals to special education. The site offers an extensive library of practitioner briefs, assessment tools, and research reports in the areas of culturally responsive practices, early intervention, literacy, and positive behavior support.

Wrightslaw
www.wrightslaw.com

The Wrightslaw website includes thousands of articles and resources about special education and advocacy, including the full text of IDEIA 2004 and documents comparing IDEA 1997 and IDEIA 2004. Available for purchase is the second edition of *Special Education Law* by Peter Wright and Pamela Wright, which includes the full text of IDEIA 2004, IDEIA 2004 regulations, the full text of the Family Educational Rights and Privacy Act (FERPA), and other federal statutes, with analysis and commentary.

CHAPTER THREE

Important Skills for Intervention Success

As noted throughout Chapters 1 and 2, for an evidence-based intervention (EBI) to help a child in need, you need more than just the intervention. In this chapter, we present many of the skills that are essential to design and implement an intervention, as well as to assess and analyze the effectiveness of the intervention. These skills are presented in three different sections. In the "Intervention Skills" section, we present skills related to the selection, design, and implementation of an intervention. In this section, we also include skills related to working with teachers in a problem-solving framework. In the "Assessment Skills" section, we present a number of brief covering methods of evidence-based assessment. Finally, in the "Analysis" section, we focus on skills needed to present and analyze data to evaluate student progress. To help link these skills to specific interventions, skills that are useful for particular interventions are noted in the intervention brief. For example, curriculum-based measurement (CBM) for reading is noted as an ideal assessment method for which to monitor progress in an intervention brief focused on increasing oral reading fluency.

Intervention Skills

COACHING: A KEY TRAINING TOOL FOR INTERVENTION SUCCESS

Coaching is commonly implemented in K–12 schools and involves teachers learning effective professional development practices to support and "assist with implementation challenges" in teaching (Killion, 2009, p. 9). Coaching can also be used to support the intervention process by having a consultant provide direct assistance to a teacher in learning a specific intervention or using the intervention as planned. Effective coaching includes modeling, observations, and immediate performance feedback, which can enhance treatment integrity and positive outcomes for interventions (DiGennaro-Reed, Codding, Catania, & Maguire, 2010).

The first step in the intervention process may be to model the intervention by demonstrating it for the teachers before they implement it independently. This can take several forms, including demonstrating it with the student with whom the intervention will be implemented in the same setting, demonstrating it with a different teacher in a more controlled setting, or providing a video model that the teachers watch before implementation but also when questions arise. Teachers favorably rate in-class demonstrations of interventions proposed by problem-solving teams (PSTs; Lane et al., 2003). Moreover, video modeling led to increased implementation of interventions (DiGennaro-Reed et al., 2010) and problem-solving processes to identify interventions (Collins, Higbee, Salzberg, & Carr, 2009).

Once the teachers can independently implement the intervention, then the coach observes the intervention being implemented in order to provide feedback. Research has consistently recognized the importance of observing the new practice being learned (Kretlow, Cooke, & Wood, 2012). Immediate performance feedback is perhaps the most important aspect of effective coaching. Although modeling is important, adding verbal feedback increased intervention integrity to 100% (DiGennaro-Reed et al., 2010). The least intrusive method of feedback is to have the consultant observe from the back of the classroom (or some other convenient place) and signal to the teacher to take an action when it is needed. A high-tech version of this method involves a wireless transmitter system that permits the coach to prompt or provide immediate corrective feedback to the teacher without interrupting instruction. Teacher training programs have successfully used this "bug-in-the-ear" (BIE) technology to improve teacher use of appropriate instructional practices (Scheeler & Lee, 2002), and for within-service teachers in cotaught classrooms (Scheeler, Congdon, & Stansbery, 2010). In the absence of this technology, the consultant can simply walk up to the teacher and give a quiet prompt that cannot be heard by nearby students. Coaching that includes direct observation with immediate performance feedback and, if necessary, additional in vivo modeling and support is especially important in helping teachers to implement interventions targeting disruptive behavior.

INTERVENTION SCRIPTS AND IMPLEMENTATION CHECKLISTS: TOOLS FOR PROMOTING AND ASSESSING TREATMENT INTEGRITY

An *intervention script* consists of a set of guidelines or prompts outlining each step of a strategy or set of strategies (i.e., an intervention package) in observable terms (Allen & Blackston, 2003), and it can provide step-by-step directions for implementing an intervention (Hawkins, Morrison, Musti-Rao, & Hawkins, 2008). Written in the language of the intervention agent, scripts promote treatment integrity by ensuring that teachers and other intervention agents, such as parents, have access to complete descriptions of implementation procedures. Scripts are especially helpful in enhancing treatment integrity when interventions will be implemented in more than one setting or by more than one agent, such as in several classrooms, in the classroom and on the playground, or at home and at school. The Intervention Steps component of the strategies in this book has been specifically designed to serve as a script to increase teachers' ability to implement the planned intervention with integrity and consultants' ability to support teachers in the implementation process.

Scripts are also valuable tools in the technical assistance process. The consultant can use the script to role-play the intervention with the teacher to anticipate implementation problems and clarify any misunderstandings. After the consultant has role-played the entire intervention, the consultant and the teacher can collaborate to modify the script as needed. Similarly, scripts serve as supports for in vivo demonstrations during which the consultant implements the intervention in the target setting while the teacher follows along with the script. The use of scripts with teachers as intervention agents is associated with high levels of treatment integrity and positive outcomes for students (Allen & Blackston, 2003; Hawkins et al., 2008). Moreover, teachers rate intervention scripts as highly acceptable, especially when scripts are developed collaboratively (Hawkins et al., 2008).

An intervention script can be converted into an *implementation checklist* for use in assessing treatment integrity and providing performance feedback to teachers. Also called a *procedural checklist* or *treatment integrity checklist,* an implementation checklist is a direct observation recording form that documents the completion of each intervention step. Implementation checklists can be completed by teachers, consultants, or intervention assistance team members during initial implementation or at periodic intervals to monitor treatment integrity over time.

INTERVENTION-ORIENTED TEST REPORTS

Until quite recently, psychological and psychoeducational evaluations tended to focus on classification for categorical decision making rather than on providing clinically and instructionally relevant information to improve children's functioning. Test reports should provide useful information to teachers, interventionists, and parents and should be written to do so. Following are specific recommendations to make reports more intervention-oriented or to help write an intervention report.

1. Organize the report around steps in the intervention/problem-solving process. Include a section each on problem identification, problem analysis, the intervention plan, and the plan to evaluate effects. If implementing the intervention is part of the assessment process, such as in a response-to-intervention (RTI) model, then include a section on the effects of the intervention.
2. Provide descriptions of skills that students successfully completed and those with which they struggled.
3. Describe skills rather than underlying processes. There is a tendency to try to impress parents and school-based professionals with technical terms, but they tend to confuse rather than clarify or impress. Just say what the student did and did not do.
4. Avoid discussing what students are capable of doing and just state what they did or did not do. The tester does not know what students are capable of doing; he or she only knows what the student did and should not assume that the sample of behavior generalizes beyond that sample. Moreover, it sends a very different message to teacher and parents to say that a student did not complete a particular task than to say that the student is not capable of performing the task.
5. Provide descriptions of test scores rather than just reporting the scores.
6. Present progress monitoring data with graphs that are easily understood.
7. Describe the context for the academic or behavioral problems.
8. Provide explicit recommendations that are realistic for the given context.

The following examples illustrate how the interventions in this book can be included in the recommendation sections of test reports to help teachers and parents implement evidence-based strategies targeting the areas of need that have been identified by the evaluation. The examples, based on data from actual test reports, are grouped according to the target domain.

Recommendations for Improving Academic Productivity and Homework

1. To encourage Juanita to complete her class assignments in a timely manner, have her monitor her own attentiveness and task completion using *Self-Monitoring of Academic Productivity*. This involves having her record her academic behaviors on a 10-item form

for her teacher to review. The intervention can be implemented on a classwide basis if her teacher so desires. A sample of the self-monitoring form is attached to this report.

2. To promote independent work habits and task persistence, Renaldo's teacher may wish to use the *Coupon System,* in which a predetermined number of coupons are taped on Renaldo's desk and removed for unnecessary requests for help. If Renaldo has at least one coupon left at the end of the designated period, he earns a reward. This strategy can also be used on a whole-class basis.

3. Marcia would benefit from direct instruction in effective homework strategies, using *Project Best: Seven Steps to Homework Completion.* In this intervention, students learn a seven-step strategy for managing homework assignments, as well as a set of effective study habits.

Recommendations for Improving Reading

1. To build Antonio's decoding skills, use the *Word Building* strategy. In the word building activity, students learn letter–sound relationships by changing a single letter in a target word to form a new word. A sample word building sequence is attached to this report.

2. Rich would benefit from additional opportunities to read aloud and receive immediate feedback for oral reading errors. In the easy-to-use *Paired Reading* procedure, parent and child read aloud together until the child indicates that he or she is ready to read independently, after which the parent provides support with any mistakes. Rich's parents are encouraged to use *Paired Reading* for 10–15 minutes four times a week. His teacher will be able to recommend reading material at an appropriate level.

3. LaTayntsha should be taught strategies for organizing and remembering the material in her textbooks, such as using *Critical Thinking Maps,* which provide a visual framework for organizing text. She can complete maps during or after reading to enhance her learning and then use the completed maps as study aids. An example of a critical thinking map is attached to this report.

Recommendations for Improving Mathematics

1. Given Jim's difficulty retaining and applying basic multiplication facts, he could be taught his facts with *Incremental Rehearsal,* which is a flashcard intervention that teaches new facts by practicing them, interspersed with known facts, at a ratio of 8 known to 1 unknown. The intervention is usually implemented one-on-one but could be facilitated with technology.

2. Wayne struggles to understand the basic concept of addition. Therefore, he could participate in the *Part–Part–Whole* intervention, which uses colored chips to teach the numbers that are represented in number sentences.

Recommendations for Improving Written Language

1. Greg would benefit from *Peer Editing,* an intervention that teaches students a structured procedure for revising their written productions within a peer tutoring format. Peer editing can be conducted during writers' workshop or as part of the language arts period.

2. To increase Tom's spelling skills, use *Word Boxes,* an activity that teaches students to make connections among the sounds and letters in a word. Word box activities can be conducted on a one-to-one basis, during small-group reading instruction, or with the entire class. A sample word box sequence is attached to this report.

Recommendations for Improving Behavior and Social Competence

1. To encourage Abby to follow teacher directions promptly, *Precision Requests and a Time-Out Procedure* is recommended. This strategy combines a structured request sequence with incentives for compliance. At the beginning of each activity, Mr. Shafer could give Abby a happy face sticker, which she can wear as long as she follows directions. If she still has the sticker at the end of the activity, then Mr. Shafer would give her a small reward or put a sticker on a Good Behavior Chart. Using precision requests at home as well as at school enhances the effectiveness of the strategy.

2. Ryan would benefit from the opportunity to monitor his own classroom productivity and behavior using the *Three Steps to Self-Managed Behavior* intervention. In this strategy, Ryan records his behavior on a checklist that is reviewed by his teacher at the end of each period. His teacher awards points for accurate self-ratings and positive behavior and talks briefly with him about acceptable alternative behaviors, if needed. When Ryan earns a specific number of points on 4 out of 5 days, he receives a reward. Ryan should take his checklist home every day so that his parents can encourage his efforts to work productively.

USING REWARDS EFFECTIVELY

The use of rewards in school settings to promote student performance and motivation has long been a controversial issue among researchers and educators alike. Despite the numerous studies attesting to the effectiveness of rewarding students for academic achievement and appropriate behavior (Hattie, 2009), including the voluminous literature on functional behavioral analysis (Horner, Sugai, & Anderson, 2010), many teachers see rewards and praise as contradictory to their training (Bear, 2013). Contrary to this contention, empirical studies evaluating the effects of rewards on performance and motivation (Cameron, Pierce, Banko, & Gear, 2005; Mitchell, Tingstrom, Dufrene, Ford, & Sterling, 2015), including meta-analyses of nearly 100 studies of intrinsic motivation (Cameron & Pierce, 1994; Henderlong & Lepper, 2002), have consistently found that extrinsic rewards not only do not undermine performance or motivation but actually increase task interest and engagement, especially if delivered well. In these studies, negative effects are confined to situations in which external rewards are offered simply for engaging in a task and without regard to task completion or performance quality, and even in these cases the impact on intrinsic motivation is minimal. Moreover, many of today's students lack the motivational resources needed to sustain effort on their school assignments, and even the most effective classrooms include some activities, such as drill-and-practice tasks, that students often find boring. Finally, the strategies in this book that incorporate incentives as intervention components have been empirically demonstrated to be effective in enhancing academic productivity, achievement, and/or social behavior.

Noncontingent Reinforcement as an Intervention for Challenging Behavior

Among reward-based interventions, *noncontingent reinforcement* (NCR), also called *fixed-time reinforcement* or *timed positives,* has been reported as an effective treatment for challenging behavior among individuals with developmental disabilities. Most frequently implemented by trained therapists in controlled settings, NCR involves delivering reinforcement on a fixed-time schedule independent of the target individual's behavior (for reviews, see Carr, Severtson, & Lepper, 2009). The stimulus delivered is typically the stimulus that has been demonstrated by functional analysis to be maintaining the problem behavior, such as attention or access to preferred tangible items. For example, a child exhibiting severe tantrums might receive teacher attention every 30 seconds, regardless of his or her behavior during the interval. After the tantrums have been reduced, the schedule of reinforcement is gradually faded to a level that is more ecologically viable. Because NCR does not result in increases in appropriate alternative behaviors, it is often combined with educationally oriented interventions to promote the development of positive skills (Doughty & Anderson, 2006; Phillips & Mudford, 2011).

Potential Pitfalls of Contingency-Based Strategies

Despite the efficacy of rewards in promoting academic productivity and appropriate social behavior, consultants should be aware of several potential pitfalls in implementing contingency-based interventions. These include (1) teacher resistance to the use of rewards, (2) reward satiation, and (3) delivery in situations in which only a subset of students in a classroom earns the reward.

Dealing with Teacher Resistance to Rewards

Although teachers have long used social reinforcers such as public recognition and praise to encourage academic productivity and appropriate behavior, some teachers are reluctant to implement interventions that involve delivering material rewards in the belief that such rewards constitute bribes for behaviors that students should exhibit naturally. Resistance is especially likely if teachers are asked to implement strategies that offer incentives to only one or a few unproductive or disruptive students while their appropriately behaving classmates have no access to the reward. The interventions in this book avoid this problem, because all the strategies are designed to be applied to an entire classroom group rather than to one student or to a small group. Even for interventions that create intraclass team competitions, the procedures permit all teams to win and obtain the reward. Another concern frequently expressed by teachers regarding the use of material reinforcers is the amount of time and effort required to dispense rewards. To address this concern, the reinforcement procedures for the interventions in this book were either originally designed or have been adapted to permit maximum ease of delivery and minimum disruption to ongoing instruction. In addition, a variety of tangible, social, and activity-based rewards are suggested for contingency-based strategies, permitting teachers to select reinforcers that best match their own preferences and classroom ecologies.

Reducing Satiation Effects

A second potential pitfall for contingency-based interventions is reward satiation, which refers to a situation in which rewards lose their ability to motivate behavior with continued use. There are several strategies that can reduce satiation effects. First, students can be involved in selecting the rewards or privileges. Many of the contingency-based strategies in this book include the use of a *reinforcement menu*—a list of possible rewards—to assess student preferences. In view of evidence that students may favor different kinds of rewards than those preferred by teachers, parents, and administrators (Berkowitz & Martens, 2001; Gray, Gutkin, & Riley, 2001), involving students in reward selection can be critical to intervention success. Moreover, because reinforcement surveys may be more accurate in identifying rewards that lack motivating properties for students than those that can enhance performance (Northup, 2000), developing a reinforcement menu that identifies as many rewards as possible that are not only appealing to students but also acceptable to teachers is highly recommended (see Figure 3.1 for an example).

Reward satiation can also be mitigated by incorporating unpredictability into the reinforcement structure. For example, the teacher can invite students to draw from a grab bag or "surprise box" containing a variety of small rewards, such as colorful pencils and erasers, inexpensive toys, and wrapped candy. A popular reward in this format is the "homework pass," a note exempting the student from homework in a particular subject for that day. The surprise box can also contain numbered slips of paper, with each number designating a reward listed on the reinforcement menu. Another strategy involves conducting a classroom raffle, with eligibility to participate in the raffle based on satisfactory performance of the target behaviors. At the end of the day or week, the names of all students achieving the criterion are placed in a box, one name is drawn, and the student whose

Directions: Here is a list of possible rewards our class could earn. Please put a check in the column that matches your level of interest in each reward. Your ratings will be used to help select the rewards for our class.

	Level of interest		
Possible reward	**Low**	**Medium**	**High**
30 minutes of computer time			
Class video or DVD			
Visit another grade to read aloud to students			
10 minutes of classroom basketball			
15 minutes of card or board games			
Permission to take the class pet home for the weekend			
15 minutes of silent ball			
10 minutes extra lunch time			
15 minutes of a math computer game			
Trip to computer lab			
One game of fruit-basket turnover			
Homework pass			
10 minutes of extra recess			
10 minutes of music			
Class field trip			
Class party			
Group games in gym			
Free time			
15 minutes of reading with a classmate			
Good note home			

FIGURE 3.1. Sample Reinforcement Menu.

name is drawn receives the reward. This strategy not only limits expenditures on rewards but also is especially appropriate for incentives that involve reducing academic tasks, such as homework passes, because teachers are usually reluctant to permit large groups of students to skip assignments. The *Response Cost Raffle* in Chapter 5 is based on this type of contingency system.

A growing body of research indicates that making the rewards in contingency-based interventions unpredictable can significantly enhance the power of the contingency. The *Mystery Motivator* strategy involves displaying an envelope containing a reward or description of a reward in a prominent place in the classroom. Viewing a concealed and uncertain reward, as with a wrapped gift, increases anticipation and the motivating capacity of the reward. Another strategy is to randomize reinforcement criteria so that students cannot predict which set of performance standards will be applied to the target behaviors. Interventions randomizing group contingency components can produce immediate and dramatic improvement in student outcomes (Theodore, Bray, Kehle, & Jenson, 2001).

Finally, using social reinforcers such as public recognition and positive teacher attention rather than tangible rewards can help minimize satiation. Many of the interventions in this book include public recognition of academic performance or positive social behavior as a motivational component. Relationship-based rewards that provide opportunities for students to interact with valued adults or peers are also likely to be less subject to satiation effects. These rewards can include eating lunch with the teacher, reading to other students, participating in school service projects, or coming early or staying after school to help the teacher with a special project.

Managing Reinforcement Delivery

Because all of the interventions in this book have been designed or adapted for use with entire classes rather than individual students, all students have an equal opportunity to earn rewards under the contingency-based strategies. As a result, most of the problems associated with delivering a reward to a few students while others remain unrewarded have been eliminated. Even with classwide interventions, however, reinforcement delivery problems can occur with interventions that involve competition among teams. In some investigations of team-based strategies, nonwinning teams were required to continue performing school tasks, often in the same classroom as their victorious peers. Field testing and research alike (e.g., Wolfe, Boyd, & Wolfe, 1983) indicate that students may become disgruntled and disruptive if they must watch their classmates enjoy a reward or privilege they have failed to earn. Supervising a group of unrewarded students under these circumstances can be especially problematic for teachers with poor classroom management skills and can increase resistance to the intervention assistance process. Although the team-based interventions in this book permit all students to win and receive the reward if each team meets the criterion, not every team may meet the criterion on a particular day or on enough days to earn a weekly reward. Moreover, teachers may occasionally wish to use a contingency-based intervention with a single student or a small group of students rather than with the entire class.

There are several methods of managing reinforcement delivery when some students in the classroom will not receive a reward. One strategy is to send the students who have earned the reward to another teacher or staff member to receive the reinforcement. For example, the reward can consist of viewing a video or DVD in another classroom or extra time in the gym, media center, or computer lab. Teachers implementing the same intervention can collaborate in supervising students, with winners from the two classrooms going to one room to receive the reward, while students who did not earn the reward go to the other room to continue working on their assignments or to participate in some less preferred activity. A second strategy is to replace activity rewards with small, tangible rewards that can be delivered unobtrusively to individual students, such as positive school–home notes, stickers, or miniature candy bars. Delivering these reinforcers at the very end of the school day minimizes opportunities for disruptive and unproductive behavior among students not receiving the rewards (see the *Response Cost Raffle* in Chapter 5). Third, reinforcement for appropriate academic or social behavior can be provided at home rather than in the classroom. Teachers and consultants can collaborate with parents and students to develop home-based social or material incentives for academic or behavior goals.

Issues in Selecting and Delivering Reinforcers

For many low-performing and disruptive students, the usual rewards available in the classroom environment, such as grades and teacher praise, are insufficient to maintain appropriate behavior. As a result, many of the interventions in this book are *contingency-based,* that is, they include some form of incentive to encourage academic productivity and prosocial behavior, such as public recognition, opportunities to participate in team-based competitions, and material and activity rewards. Although these contingency-based strategies have been documented to have positive effects on the target behaviors, the use of external rewards in schools continues to be a matter of controversy. In recent years, the growth of schoolwide incentive programs that offer tokens or "dollars" for positive academic and/or social behavior that can be redeemed for items in a school store has fueled the long-running debate as to whether external rewards undermine motivation and achievement (e.g., Martens & Witt, 2004; Witzel & Mercer, 2003).

Assessment Skills

Effective assessment is critical to effective intervention, and there are entire journals dedicated to assessment (e.g., *Assessment for Effective Intervention*). However, it is important to ask not only whether the assessment practice is evidence-based but whether the data are validated for the purpose for which they are being used. From an intervention perspective, data are usually used for screening, diagnosis, and monitoring student progress. There are entire books about each of these ideas (e.g., Briesch, Chafouleas, Riley-Tillman & Contributors, 2016; Chafouleas, Riley-Tillman, & Sugai, 2007; Kettler, Glover, Albers, & Feeney-Kettler, 2014; Riley-Tillman, Burns, & Gibbons, 2013), so we focus on diagnosis and monitoring student progress in this section.

PROBLEM ANALYSIS AND DIAGNOSIS

After a student is identified as at risk for failure, interventionists then conduct a diagnostic assessment to better analyze the problem and target intervention efforts. Diagnostic assessments provide data that are crucial for instruction, but most school personnel do not use effective assessment practices to analyze reading problems as part of the intervention process. In this section we discuss two approaches to diagnostic assessments: curriculum-based assessment for instructional design and brief experimental analyses.

Curriculum-Based Assessment for Instructional Design

In 1977 Ed Gickling coined the phrase *curriculum-based assessment* (Coulter, 1988) to refer to an assessment model that examined student skill within the existing course content in order to improve student learning (Gickling, Shane, & Croskery, 1989, pp. 344–345). The name has evolved; it is now called *curriculum-based assessment for instructional design* (CBA-ID; Burns & Parker, 2014), and it represents an assessment model that is specifically designed to analyze student problems. The data are used to assess an instructional level. Assessment procedures for reading essentially require the student to read for 1 minute from classroom reading material (e.g., basal reader, chapter book, content-area book) while the assessor records number of words read correctly. This number is then divided by the total number of words in the sample to create a percentage of words read correctly. The percentage is then compared with an instructional-level criterion of 93–97%.

Research has consistently demonstrated that using CBA-ID data to determine a student's instructional level led to increased reading fluency (Burns, 2007; Roberts & Shapiro, 1996), math skills (Burns, 2002), and student time on task (Gickling & Armstrong, 1978; Treptow, Burns, & McComas, 2007). There has also been considerable research regarding the reliability of CBA-ID data (Burns, Tucker, Frame, Foley, & Hauser, 2000; Burns, VanDerHeyden, & Jiban, 2006; Parker, McMaster, & Burns, 2011) and the validity of resulting decisions (Burns, 2007; Burns & Mosack, 2005).

Assessment Procedures

Administration procedures closely match those of CBM, discussed shortly. Students read for 1 minute while an assessor records errors. However, there are two fundamental differences. First, the assessment material is not standardized but instead consists of whatever material is used for reading instruction (e.g., reading basal, leveled books, reading sheets). The assessment occurs by having the student read directly from the instructional material while the assessor follows along on a photocopy. Second, the data are converted to a percentage and interpreted relative to an instructional level. The total number of words read correctly is divided by the total number of words (Words Read Correctly + Errors) and multiplied by 100 to get a percentage of words read correctly. The percentage is then compared with the criterion of 93–97% correct. Those scores that fall within that range represent an instructional level. However, scores that are below 93% represent a frustration level in which the material is too difficult, and those above 97% are an independent level and mean that the material is too easy.

CBA-ID for math also closely follows CBM (discussed shortly) but only focuses on one specific skill (e.g., single-digit multiplication, division of a double-digit number by a single-digit number, or multidigit subtraction with regrouping). CBA-ID for math is not assessed with percentage of items correct, as is reading, but instead is scored in digits correct per minute (DCPM). In order to determine DCPM, the total number of digits correct in the probe is divided by the length of the administration (e.g., 60 digits correct in a 4-minute administration would result in 15 DCPM). The data are then compared with fluency criteria for an instructional level of 14–31 DCPM for 2nd and 3rd graders and 24–49 DCPM for older students (Burns et al., 2006). Scores below the lowest end of the instructional-level range fall within the frustration level and suggest that the skill is too difficult for the child, and those that exceed the highest score of the instructional level range fall within the independent range.

Intervention

CBA-ID was developed to be used with students with disabilities, and much of the research was conducted with that most vulnerable population. Special education teachers often have the flexibility to use different reading material for individual students in order to ensure an instructional level (93–97%). Alternatively, interventionists can preteach the unknown words to "elevate the passage to an instructional level" (Gravois & Gickling, 2002, p. 895). Previewing reading material before completing an assigned task has consistently led to better reading fluency and comprehension among children with and without disabilities (Burns, Hodgson, Parker, & Fremont, 2011).

CBA-ID can be used for math interventions as well by creating single-skill assessments of the objectives used within any given curriculum. Each assessment would be administered, using procedures described for CBM for math (discussed later in the chapter), until the highest skill in the sequence at which the student scores in the instructional level (14–31 digits correct per minute for second and third graders, and 24 to 49 digits correct per minute for fourth and fifth graders) is identified. Afterward, the students could be grouped to receive an intervention for that skill.

Finally, *Incremental Rehearsal* (IR; Tucker, 1989) is an intervention that is based on the principles of CBA-ID. It has frequently been researched both as a stand-alone intervention (Codding, Archer, & Connell, 2010; Nist & Joseph, 2008; Volpe, Burns, DuBois, & Zaslofsky, 2011), and within a CBA-ID assessment-to-intervention model (Burns, 2007). IR is specifically discussed in two briefs in Chapter 4.

Brief Experimental Analysis

Brief experimental analysis (BEA) is an assessment technology that uses CBM to identify effective strategies for academic problems, especially reading problems. An experimental form of functional assessment, BEA directly tests the effects of several interventions within a short time frame by comparing baseline performance on CBMs in reading (R-CBM), with R-CBM performance subsequent to the introduction of one or more interventions. Interventions are selected based on hypotheses regarding the factors that may be contributing to poor performance, such as lack of motivation, low skill levels, insufficient practice, or a mismatch between student skills and instructional materials (Daly, Andersen, Gortmaker, & Turner, 2006).

Current approaches to BEA include three different methods. In the first approach, intervention components are applied and evaluated one by one, beginning with the easiest and least complex (Daly, Martens, Dool, & Hintze, 1998; Jones & Wickstrom, 2002). For example, contingent rewards, repeated reading, and listening previewing are introduced sequentially, performance under each intervention condition is compared with the baseline, and the most effective intervention is selected. In the second approach, an intervention is introduced, after which additional strategies are implemented one by one until the desired results are obtained (Daly, Martens, Hamler, Dool, & Eckert, 1999). In the third approach, an intervention "package" consisting of several components is applied simultaneously, after which the package is dismantled one component at a time until the simplest intervention capable of producing the desired results is identified (Daly, Persampieri, McCurdy, & Gortmaker, 2005). Although this approach requires more resources initially than the first two approaches, it may ultimately enhance usability because a simpler intervention can be selected if it produces the same results as the package (Daly et al., 2006).

A growing body of research documents BEA's utility in selecting effective interventions for students with reading problems (Burns & Wagner, 2008; Jones et al., 2009; Schreder, Hupp, Everett, & Krohn, 2012), including early literacy (Petursdottir et al., 2009). BEA has also been validated for use in selecting components for parent–child tutoring interventions (Persampieri, Gortmaker, Daly, Sheridan, & McCurdy, 2006; Evans, Valleley, & Allen, 2002).

MONITORING STUDENT PROGRESS

The final phase of the intervention process is to monitor the effects of the intervention and to make adjustments as needed (Shapiro, 2011). The term *progress monitoring* refers to the process of frequently assessing student academic and behavioral performance in order to evaluate the effects of an intervention or instruction (McLane, n.d.). There are several ways to monitor progress, but CBM is ideally suited to monitoring the progress of individual students with academic deficits, and Direct Behavior Ratings (DBR) are suitable for behavior problems.

Developed by Deno, Mirkin, and their colleagues at the University of Minnesota Institute for Research on Learning Disabilities (e.g., Deno, 1985, 1986; Deno & Mirkin, 1977), CBM is a set of standardized, fluency-based measurement procedures that can be used to index academic performance and progress toward intervention goals or grade-level standards. CBM is ideally suited for monitoring the progress of students receiving academic interventions because the measures are brief (1–5 minutes) and can be administered frequently. A voluminous body of evidence demonstrates that CBM procedures are reliable and valid methods of identifying students at risk for academic failure, monitoring progress, and evaluating the effectiveness of school-based interventions (see Wayman, Wallace, Wiley, Tichá, & Espin, 2007, for a review).

CBM in Reading

CBM in reading consists of a set of brief, standardized procedures assessing reading fluency using a student's own curricular materials or generic grade-level materials. There are two types of CBMs in reading: oral reading fluency and maze fluency. In oral reading fluency (hereafter referred to as R-CBM), the student reads aloud for 1 minute in a passage selected to be at an end-of-year competency level (termed an oral reading probe), and the score is the number of words read correctly. In maze fluency, the student reads silently for a specified time (2.5–3 minutes) in a passage in which every seventh word has been deleted and replaced with three choices, and the score is the number of correct replacements. Maze fluency measures are more efficient because they can be administered to groups of students or delivered by computer (e.g., Shin, Deno, & Espin, 2000), but there is some evidence that maze fluency performance is less sensitive to reading growth and a poorer predictor of reading proficiency than R-CBM (Ardoin, Witt, Suldo, & Connell, 2004).

Although oral reading probes were originally taken from materials in students' own curricula, most practitioners now conduct R-CBM using generic probes, such as the passages in the Dynamic Indicators of Basic Early Literacy Skills (DIBELS; Good & Kaminski, 2002). Research has demonstrated that R-CBM can lead to valid decisions even when the reading probes are not drawn from the student's own curriculum (Fuchs & Deno, 1994) and that generic passages have less measurement error than passages randomly selected from graded readers (Hintze & Christ, 2004). Moreover, literature-based and trade-book probes are likely to underestimate performance levels compared with passages constructed from traditional basal reading materials or generic passages and are less sensitive to individual differences (Bradley-Klug, Shapiro, Lutz, & DuPaul, 1998). For these reasons, and because today's classroom reading materials vary widely in difficulty level, R-CBMs for students instructed in literature-based or trade-book materials should be conducted using probes from a comparable basal series or from generic passages controlled for readability.

Numerous studies have demonstrated that R-CBM is a reliable, valid method of monitoring the progress of both proficient and poor readers (Fuchs, Fuchs, Hosp, & Jenkins, 2001), predicting reading outcomes and performance on high-stakes assessments (McGlinchey & Hixson, 2004), and evaluating the effectiveness of reading interventions (Stoner, Scarpati,

Phaneuf, & Hintze, 2002). R-CBM has also been successfully used to assess the progress of English language learners in early identification and intervention programs (Haager & Windmueller, 2001).

Early Reading Skills with CBM

Because beginning readers have limited ability to access text, R-CBM is not sensitive to individual differences in oral reading skills until the second semester of first grade or even later for less proficient readers (Kaminski & Good, 1996). To bridge this gap, Good and Kaminski (2002) included a downward extension in DIBELS for preliterate children consisting of four fluency-based measures of phonemic awareness and alphabet knowledge. A growing body of evidence documents that the DIBELS prereading measures are reliable and valid predictors of future reading performance and can be used to identify children at risk for reading failure and to assess response to reading interventions. The DIBELS measures and two additional CBM-type early reading measures are described next.

INITIAL SOUND FLUENCY

The examiner asks the child to identify the one of four pictures that begins with a target sound. The child is also asked to produce the beginning sound of an orally presented word matching one of the pictures. The score is the number of initial sounds correct per minute for a set of four picture probes, obtained by multiplying the number of correct responses by 60 and dividing that product by the number of seconds needed to complete the task.

LETTER-NAMING FLUENCY

The child names upper- and lowercase letters displayed in random order. The score is the number of letters correctly named in 1 minute.

PHONEME SEGMENTATION FLUENCY

The child segments three- and four-phoneme words spoken by the examiner into individual phonemes. Credit is given for each correct sound segment, and the score is the number of correct sound segments per minute.

NONSENSE-WORD FLUENCY

The child pronounces two- and three-phoneme pseudowords presented on a page. The child may pronounce the individual sounds or read the whole word. The score is the number of correct letter sounds per minute.

LETTER-SOUND FLUENCY

The child identifies the sounds of lowercase letters displayed in random order. The score is the number of letter sounds correctly identified in 1 minute.

WORD IDENTIFICATION FLUENCY

The child reads as many words as possible from a graded word list with 50 words. The score is the number of words correctly read in 1 minute.

The first four measures described above are available from the DIBELS website (*http://dibels.uoregon.edu*). AIMSweb (*www.aimsweb.com*) offers a slightly different set of four early literacy assessments, consisting of letter-name, letter-sound, phoneme segmentation, and nonsense-word fluency measures, as well as a set of five early literacy assessments for Spanish speakers (letter-name, letter-sound, syllable segmentation, syllable reading, and syllable- and word-reading fluency). Letter-sound fluency and word identification fluency (WIF) materials are also available at Edcheckup (*www.edcheckup.com*) and Project AIM (Alternative Identification Models; *www.glue.umn.edu/%7Edlspeece/cbmreading/index.html*). WIF materials in English and Spanish are available at Intervention Central (*www.interventioncentral.org*). Finally, readers are referred to FastBridge Learning (*www.fastbridge.org*) for another set of CBM materials that were developed from considerable research and psychometric considerations.

Administration of CBM in Reading

For screening/benchmarking, select three reading passages, either from the student's current materials or, preferably, from a generic set of passages set at end-of-year competency levels. If materials are taken from the student's own text, select a passage from the beginning, middle, and end of the book and administer them in that order. For progress monitoring, select one passage. Two copies of each passage are required: one for the student to read and the other for the examiner to use to score the student's oral reading.

Preprimer- and primer-level passages should be brief (less than 50 words). Passages should be approximately 150 words for grades 1–3 and approximately 250 words for grades 4–8. Passages should be prose text rather than poetry or plays, should not contain too much dialogue, should have no more than a single illustration, and need not be limited to the beginning of stories.

To assess comprehension, prepare five to eight comprehension questions for each passage. Questions should include both literal (Who?, What?, When?, Where?) and inferential questions (How?, Why?).

ASSESSMENT STEPS: ORAL READING

1. Give the student the copy of the first reading passage and give the following directions:

   "When I say 'Begin,' begin reading aloud at the top of this page. Read across the page. Try to read each word. If you come to a word you don't know, I'll tell it to you. You will have 1 minute. Be sure to do your best reading. Are there any questions? Begin."

2. Follow along on a copy of the reading passage and place a slash over words read incorrectly, as indicated below. At the end of 1 minute, say "Stop!" and place a vertical line on your copy of the passage after the last word read.

3. For screening/benchmarking, administer two more passages. For progress monitoring, only one passage is usually administered.

ADMINISTRATION: READING FLUENCY AND COMPREHENSION

1. Randomly select one of the three passages for the comprehension screening. Administer two probes as described above but give these directions for the third:

   "When I say 'Begin,' begin reading aloud at the top of this page. Read across the page. Try to read each word. If you come to a word you don't know, I'll tell it to you. I will be asking you a few questions afterward. Be sure to do your best reading. Are there any questions? Begin."

2. Allow the student to finish reading the entire passage, but mark where he or she is at the end of each minute.
3. Permit the student to look at the passage while you are asking the comprehension questions.

SCORING ORAL READING

1. Mark errors as follows:
   a. *Mispronunciations.* If the student mispronounces a word, provide the correct word and count it as an error. If the student makes the same error several times, count it as an error each time unless it is a proper noun. If the error involves a proper noun, count it as an error the first time but not subsequently.
   b. *Omissions.* If the student leaves out an entire word, count it as an error but do not supply the word.
   c. *Substitutions:* If the student says the wrong word, provide the correct word and count it as an error.
   d. *Insertions:* If the student adds a word or words, count it as an error.
   e. *Hesitations.* If the student pauses for 3 seconds, supply the word and count it as an error.
   f. Repetitions, self-corrections, dialectical substitutions (e.g., *ax* for *ask*), and dialectical suffix deletions (e.g., *walk* for *walked*) are not counted as errors.
   g. If the student skips a line or loses his or her place, stop timing and redirect the student to the appropriate place in the text, but do not count it as an error. Then resume timing.
2. To determine words read correctly per minute (WCPM), count the number of words the student read correctly in 1 minute. If the student reads for more than 1 minute, as when comprehension questions are administered, multiply the total number of words read correctly by 60 and then divide that product by the number of seconds needed to read the passage, as follows:

$$\frac{\text{Number of words read correctly} \times 60}{\text{Total reading time in seconds}} = \text{Words read correctly per minute}$$

INTERPRETATION

1. For screening/benchmarking, score each of the three probes as described above. The student's score on that book or set of probes is the *median* (middle) WCPM score on the three probes and the comprehension score (if used). The median score is used rather than the mean score to control for the effects of difficulty. For progress monitoring, score the probe as described above to determine WCPM.
2. Compare WCPM scores with published national norms (e.g., *https://dibels.uoregon.edu/docs/DIBELSNextFormerBenchmarkGoals.pdf*), local norms, or R-CBM benchmarks related to success on district or state assessments, if available.
3. If desired, graph WCPM scores for use in determining whether the student is making adequate progress toward end-of-year expectations or whether instructional modifications are needed.

NOTES

1. Procedures for constructing oral reading probes from students' regular curriculum or alternative basal materials are presented in Rathvon (1999) and Shapiro (2011).
2. Practitioners should note that most generic passages are calibrated for the goal level of reading for each grade level, that is, they are set at a year-end competency level.
3. R-CBM is most appropriate for students in grades 1–6. For younger students, CBM-type pre-reading measures are available from several sources, as noted above. To assess reading skills in older students, *Vocabulary Matching*—a metric described in the Content Area section of this chapter—is recommended.
4. Administering only one oral reading probe may be sufficient for screening/benchmark purposes (Ardoin et al., 2004).

SOURCES

Hosp, M. K., Hosp, J. L., & Howell, K. W. (2016). *The ABCs of CBM: A practical guide to curriculum-based measurement* (2nd ed.). New York: Guilford Press.

Shapiro, E. S. (2011). *Academic skills problems: Direct assessment and intervention* (4th ed.). New York: Guilford Press.

ADDITIONAL RESOURCES

Generic reading passages, including a Spanish DIBELS version, are available free of charge at the DIBELS home page (*http://dibels.uoregon.edu*) and at Intervention Central (*www.interventioncentral.org*). A commercial version of the DIBELS measures is available from Sopris West (*www.sopriswest.com*). Other sets of generic reading passages are offered at Edcheckup (*www.edcheckup.com*) and AIMSweb (*www.aimsweb.com*). Web-based graphing and data management systems are available from the same sources.

CBM in Mathematics

Curriculum-based measurement in mathematics (M-CBM) consists of a set of brief, fluency-based standardized procedures that can be used to measure mathematics competence and progress toward grade-level standards. There are two basic types of M-CBM problem sets, termed *math probes*—(1) computation probes and (2) concepts and application probes—each of which can consist of single-skill probes sampling only one type of problem (e.g., addition, subtraction, money problems) or multiple-skill probes sampling several different types of computation or concept problems. Like R-CBM, M-CBM can be used in screening/benchmarking programs and in monitoring student progress toward intervention goals or end-of-year objectives. Math probes can be constructed to align with the student's own curriculum or a general mathematics scope and sequence (see Shapiro, 2011), but the process is very time-consuming and offers little control over variability in difficulty or content. Generic math probes, which are available from a variety of sources, are therefore recommended.

When used for screening/benchmarking or progress monitoring purposes, each M-CBM probe has the same number of items sampling the problems covered in the entire year's curriculum. For computation probes, the student is presented with 25 items sampling the problems covered in the annual curriculum and given 2 minutes to answer as many items as possible. Answers are scored in terms of correct digits written in 2 minutes. For concepts and applications probes, the student is presented with 18–25 items covering topics such as number concepts, money, measurement, graphs and charts, and problem solving. The student has 5–10 minutes, depending on grade level, and the score is the number of correct answers. As with R-CBM, results can be graphed and analyzed to determine whether student progress is sufficient to meet intervention goals and/or end-of-year expectations and whether the instructional program should be modified. Teachers' implementation of M-CBM has been associated with accelerated growth in mathematics for elementary school students (Allinder & Oats, 1997; Fuchs, Fuchs, Karns, Hamlett, & Katzaroff, 1999; VanDerHeyden & Burns, 2005). M-CBM is also a moderate to strong predictor of performance on criterion measures, such as norm-referenced and end-of-year achievement tests, although the correlations are lower than those for R-CBM (Shapiro, Keller, Lutz, Santoro, & Hintze, 2006). Moreover, low interscorer agreement for digits correct has been reported, even for trained scorers (Thurber, Shinn, & Smolkowski, 2002), and many teachers are unfamiliar with that scoring procedure. For that reason, problems-correct is included as an optional scoring metric for computation probes in the following discussion.

Assessing Early Math Skills with M-CBM

Although CBM-type measures assessing the emergent literacy skills of prereaders were developed over a decade ago, no comparable measures of foundational math skills for identifying young students at risk for early math failure or monitoring progress in early math skills were available until quite recently. Clarke and Shinn (2004) have developed a set of four early math measures that index young children's informal number sense development, including the ability to understand the meaning of numbers and discriminate relationships among numbers. Preliminary evidence of reliability, concurrent and predictive validity, and sensitivity to growth over time has been documented in a small sample of grade 1 students (Clarke & Shinn, 2004). Preliminary evidence of concurrent and predictive validity is also available for kindergarten students (Chard et al., 2005). The four measures are available as the *Test of Early Numeracy* at AIMSweb (*http://aimsweb.com*), along with user norms and rate of improvement statistics for fall, winter, and spring for kindergarten and grade 1. Variations of three of the measures (excluding Oral Counting) and an additional measure are available for free download at the Research Institute of Progress Monitoring website (*www.progress-monitoring.org*. The five measures are:

ORAL COUNTING

The student counts orally, beginning with 1. The score is the number of numbers correctly counted in 1 minute.

NUMBER IDENTIFICATION

The student identifies numerals between 0 and 20 randomly presented on a sheet of paper. The score is the number of numerals correctly identified in 1 minute.

QUANTITY DISCRIMINATION

The student identifies the larger of two numbers presented in a grid of boxes on a sheet of paper. Each box contains two randomly sampled numbers from 0 to 20. The score is the number of correctly identified larger numbers in 1 minute.

MISSING NUMBER

The student is presented with a series of boxes containing a string of three numbers between 0 and 20 in a pattern (e.g., counting by 2's) displayed on a sheet of paper. The first, middle, or last number of the string is missing, and the student is asked to state the number that is missing. The score is the number of missing numbers correctly identified in 1 minute.

QUANTITY ARRAY

The student identifies the number of dots in a series of boxes presented on a sheet of paper. The score is the number of correctly counted dots per box in 1 minute.

Overview

M-CBM consists of a set of fluency-based standardized procedures that are used to index students' performance in math and monitor progress over time. In M-CBM screening/ benchmarking and progress monitoring programs, each probe is designed to sample all of the curriculum objectives for that grade, and the results are used to identify students at risk for math failure or to evaluate students' progress toward intervention goals or end-of-grade expectations. M-CBM probes can be designed to index competency in two basic areas: (1) computation and (2) concepts/applications. Because M-CBM math probes yield information on fluency as well as accuracy, they are especially helpful for identifying students who have learned basic computational skills but cannot perform them fast enough to keep up with the pace of classroom instruction or achieve at grade-level expectations. Math probes can be administered to individuals or groups of students. Although the digits-correct scoring method is more sensitive to individual growth, many teachers and consultants are unfamiliar with this procedure, and it is much more time-consuming. A problems-correct metric is therefore included as a scoring option. Because many of the items on concepts/applications probes have multiple-part answers, they must be scored on a blanks-correct basis.

Materials

1. Stopwatch or timer.
2. Pencils with erasers, two per student.
3. Equal-interval graph paper or graphing program (optional).

Computation Probes

For each student, two or three sheets of math problems, 25 problems per probe.

Concepts and Application Probes

For each student, two or three sheets of math problems, 18–25 problems per probe.

Assessment Steps

1. Distribute the worksheets, give each student two pencils with erasers, and give the following instructions:

Directions for Single-Skill Probes

"The sheets on your desk have math facts/math problems on them. All the problems are [addition or subtraction or multiplication or division] [measurement, money, graphing, etc.] problems. When I say 'Begin,' turn the sheets over and begin answering the problems. Start with the first problem on the left on the top row [point]. Work across and then go to the next row. If you can't answer the problem, make an X on it and go on to the next one. If you finish one sheet, go on to the next. Are there any questions? Begin!"

Directions for Multiple-Skill and Concept/Applications Probes

"The sheets on your desk are math facts/math problems. There are several types of problems on the sheets. Look at each problem carefully before you answer it. Some problems may have more than one blank. Try to fill in as many blanks as you can because you will get credit for each blank you answer. When I say 'Begin,' turn the sheets over and begin answering the problems. Start with the first problem on the left on the top row [point]. Work across and then go to the next row. If you can't answer the problem, make an X on it and go on to the next one. If you finish one sheet, go on to the next. Are there any questions? Begin!"

2. At the end of 2 minutes, say, "Stop! Put your pencils down."
3. For screening/benchmarking, administer three M-CBMs probes and use the median score of the three probes for interpretive purposes. For progress monitoring, administer a single probe.
4. If desired, graph digits-correct scores for use in determining whether the student is making adequate progress toward intervention goals or end-of-year expectations or whether instructional modifications are needed.

Scoring and Interpretation

OPTION 1: DIGITS-CORRECT SCORING METHOD (COMPUTATION PROBLEMS)

1. Count the separate correct digits in an answer. For all problems except division, only digits below the answer line are counted. When scoring multiplication problems, however, score digits as correct if the addition operations are performed correctly, even if the answer is incorrect. That is, do not penalize students twice for a single error.
2. When scoring division problems, count digits as incorrect if the incorrect operation is performed or if incorrect place values are used.
3. If the student completes the worksheets before the time is up, divide the number of correctly written digits in the answer by the total number of seconds and multiply by 120 to obtain an estimate of the digits-correct score.
4. Count omitted problems as errors.
5. Count reversed digits as correct, with the exception of 6's and 9's.
6. Compare digits-correct scores with local norms, web-based norms, or end-of-year goals.

OPTION 2: PROBLEMS-CORRECT SCORING METHOD (CONCEPTS/APPLICATIONS PROBLEMS AND/OR COMPUTATION PROBLEMS)

1. Give credit for each correct answer. For multiple-answer problems, award one point for each correct blank. Score omitted problems as errors. The score is the number of correct problems/blanks within the time limit. If desired, divide the number of correct problems/blanks by the total number of problems/blanks to obtain a percent-correct score.

2. Compare problems-correct or percent-correct scores with local norms, web-based norms, or end-of-year goals.
3. If desired, graph digits-correct, problems-correct, or percent-correct scores for use in determining whether the student is making adequate progress toward end-of-year expectations or whether instructional modifications are needed.

NOTES

1. M-CBM can also be used in *survey-level assessment* to determine students' math instructional level (see Burns & Parker, 2014). Burns, VanDerHeyden, and Jiban (2006) provide instructional-level criteria, but only for only two grade ranges (grades 2–3 and 4–5).
2. Very few normative data are currently available for interpreting the results of concepts/applications probes. For practitioners interested in developing local norms, see the procedures described in Stewart and Silberglitt (2008).
3. Benchmark (end-of-year) goals and norms for weekly M-CBM growth rates for students in grades 1–6 in computation and grades 2–6 in concepts and applications are available in Stecker, Fuchs, and Fuchs (2005, p. 64) and on the AIMSweb site (*www.AIMSweb.com*).
4. M-CBM is most appropriate for students in grades 1–6. For younger students, CBM-type early numeracy measures are available from several web-based sources.

SOURCES

Hosp, M. K., Hosp, J. L., & Howell, K. W. (2016). *The ABCs of CBM: A practical guide to curriculum-based measurement* (2nd ed.). New York: Guilford Press.
Shapiro, E. S. (2011). *Academic skills problems: Direct assessment and intervention* (4th ed.). New York: Guilford Press.

ADDITIONAL RESOURCES

Burns, M. K., & Parker, D. C. (2014). *Curriculum-based assessment for instructional design: Using data to individualize instruction.* New York: Guilford Press.

   M-CBM sheets are available free of charge at Intervention Central (*www.interventioncentral.org*). The fee-based AIMSweb (*www.aimsweb.com*) offers M-CBM benchmarking and progress monitoring sets for grades 1–6. Web-based graphing and data management systems are available from the same sources. Several websites permit users to create customized M-CBM sheets, including *www.aplusmath.com* and *www.school-housetech.com*.

CBM in Writing

Curriculum-based measurement in writing (W-CBM) consists of a standardized set of procedures requiring students to write for 3 minutes in response to an instructional-level story starter or essay prompt. Because the utility of W-CBM scoring methods varies by grade level, separate versions are presented for early primary grade students, elementary students, and secondary-level students. For students in the elementary grades, the number of words written, number of words spelled correctly, and number of correct word sequences produced during writing probes are strongly correlated with standardized measures of written expression and teacher ratings of writing skill (Gansle, Noell, VanDerHeyden, Naquin, & Slider, 2002) and can differentiate between students with learning disabilities and typically achieving students (Watkinson & Lee, 1992). At the secondary level, however, where the writing process is more complex, words written and words spelled correctly are not sensitive to individual differences and are only weakly or moderately correlated with criterion measures. Instead, more complex metrics, such as the number of correct word sequences or the number of correct word sequences minus incorrect word sequences, are better predictors of writing proficiency (Jewell & Malecki, 2005; Malecki & Jewell, 2003). Similarly, for students in the early primary grades, who are just beginning to develop written production skills, the standard W-CBM procedure is of limited utility in monitoring writing progress or evaluating the effectiveness of writing interventions because of *floor effects* (i.e., many students obtain very low scores). At this stage of writing development, W-CBM probes consisting of dictated words or sentences are highly correlated with teacher ratings of writing ability and other global judgments of writing performance (Lembke, Deno, & Hall, 2003).

Overview

In W-CBM, students are provided with story starters or writing prompts and asked to write for 3 minutes. The number of words written, the number of words spelled correctly, and the number of correct word sequences during these writing probes are strongly correlated with standardized measures of written expression, teacher ratings of students' writing skills, and other measures of general writing proficiency. Moreover, W-CBM can reliably differentiate between students with learning disabilities and their normally achieving peers, as well as among students enrolled in basic, regular, and enriched levels of English class, and is sensitive to changes in writing performance over time. Because the predictive power of W-CBM tasks and metrics varies across grade levels, three versions of W-CBM are presented: (1) one for early primary grade students that substitutes word or sentence dictation tasks for story starters; (2) one for elementary school students; and (3) one for middle and high school students. Each version includes several validated scoring options, ranging from simple to more complex. Writing probes may be administered to students individually, in small groups, or in whole-class settings. Student performance can be evaluated by means of local norms, intrastudent comparisons, and, for certain metrics, web-based norms.

Materials

1. Pencils with erasers, two per student (early primary grade students); pencils with erasers or pens, two per student (elementary and secondary students).
2. Stopwatch or timer.
3. Equal-interval graph paper or graphing program (optional).

ADDITIONAL MATERIALS FOR EARLY PRIMARY GRADE STUDENTS

1. Sheets of lined paper, one per student.
2. Lists of high-frequency words, 30 words per list (word dictation task) and/or lists of 12 sentences, each consisting of 5–7 words (sentence dictation task).

ADDITIONAL MATERIALS FOR ELEMENTARY AND SECONDARY STUDENTS

1. Sheets of lined paper with a writing prompt printed at the top, one per student, with additional sheets of lined paper.
2. Story starters or topic sentences, such as:
   a. When Marcus woke up that morning, he knew that his life was about to change.
   b. It was a dark and stormy night.
   c. I will never forget the first time I met my best friend.
   d. Describe the clothing that students in your school wear.
   e. Explain why local school boards should include a student representative.

Assessment Steps: Early Primary Grade Students (Grades 1–2)

1. Give each student a sheet of lined paper and two pencils. Word dictation is recommended for first-semester first graders and lower performing students. Either word or sentence dictation may be used for second-semester first graders, second graders, and higher performing early primary grade students. Give the following directions:

   "I want you to write some words (sentences). I am going to read each word (sentence) twice and then I want you to write it. If you don't know how to spell a word, do your best to write it anyway. Are there any questions?"

2. Dictate each word (sentence) twice and then pause for students to write. After students have finished the current word (sentence) or have paused for 5 (10) seconds, move on to the next word (sentence).

3. Continue dictating words or sentences for 3 minutes. After 3 minutes, say "Stop and put your pencils down."

Scoring and Interpretation: Early Primary Grade Students

OPTION 1: WORDS WRITTEN (WW)

1. Count the number of written words. A *word* is defined as a sequence of letters that can be recognized, even if it is misspelled. Do not count numerals as words.

2. Compare the WW score with local norms or students' previous scores.

OPTION 2: WORDS SPELLED CORRECTLY (WSC)

1. Count the number of words spelled correctly. A *correctly spelled word* is defined as a recognizable, correctly spelled word. Do not award credit to words containing reversals.

2. Compare the WSC score with local norms or students' previous scores.

OPTION 3: CORRECT LETTER SEQUENCES (CLS; WORD DICTATION TASK ONLY)

1. Count the number of correct letter sequences. A *correct letter sequence* is defined as two adjacent letters that are correctly placed in a word.

2. Compare the CLS score with local norms or students' previous scores.

OPTION 4: CORRECT WORD SEQUENCES (CWS; SENTENCE DICTATION TASK ONLY)

1. Count the number of correct word sequences. A *correct word sequence* is defined as two adjacent correctly spelled words that are semantically and syntactically acceptable within the context of the sentence. Beginning and ending punctuation are counted in the sequences. Give credit for capitalization on the first word of a sentence and appropriate punctuation at the end of a sentence, and do not award credit if appropriate capitalization and end punctuation are omitted.

2. Compare the CWS score to local norms or students' previous scores.

OPTION 5: CORRECT MINUS INCORRECT WORD SEQUENCES (C-IWS; SENTENCE DICTATION TASK ONLY)

1. Count the number of correct word sequences as described above. Then count the number of incorrect word sequences. An *incorrect word sequence* is defined as two adjacent

words, one or both of which is syntactically incorrect, grammatically incorrect, incorrectly spelled, incorrectly capitalized if it occurs at the beginning of a sentence, and/or incorrectly punctuated if it occurs at the end of the sentence.

2. Calculate the number of correct minus incorrect word sequences by subtracting the number of incorrect word sequences from the number of correct word sequences.
3. Compare the C-IWS score with local norms, students' previous scores, or web-based norms.

Assessment Steps: Elementary Grade Students (Grades 1–6)

1. Give each student a sheet of lined paper with a story starter printed across the top, an extra sheet of lined paper, and two pencils or pens. Give the following directions:

> "I want you to write a story. I am going to read a sentence to you first, and then I want you to write a short story about what happens. You will have 1 minute to think about the story you will write and then have 3 minutes to write it. Do your best work. If you don't know how to spell a word, you should guess. Use the sentence I read as your first sentence but don't write that sentence again. Are there any questions? For the next minute, think about . . . [read story starter]."

2. After 1 minute, say, "Begin writing."
3. After 3 minutes, say, "Stop and put your pencils/pens down."

Scoring and Interpretation: Elementary Grade Students

OPTION 1: WORDS WRITTEN (WW)

1. Count the number of written words. A *written word* is defined as a word that can be recognized, even if it is misspelled. If the student writes a title, include the title in the scoring. Do not count dates or numerals (e.g., 2007, 3) as words.
2. If a student stops writing before the 3 minutes are up, divide the number of correctly written words by the number of seconds spent writing and multiply by 180 to obtain the words-written-correctly rate per 3 minutes.
3. If the student writes the story starter as part of the story, include the words in the starter as part of the total word count.
4. Compare the WW score with local norms, students' previous scores, or web-based norms.

OPTION 2: WORDS SPELLED CORRECTLY (WSC; SEE ABOVE)

OPTION 3: CORRECT LETTER SEQUENCES (CLS; SEE ABOVE)

OPTION 4: CORRECT WORD SEQUENCES (CWS)

Score as above. Compare the CWS score to local norms, students' previous scores, or web-based norms.

OPTION 5: QUALITY EVALUATION OF WRITING MECHANICS

Based on writing mechanics such as capitalization, spelling, punctuation, sentence construction, and paragraph construction, as well as the overall appearance of the written product, assign a quality rating from 1 to 5 (1 = poor; 2 = fair; 3 = average; 4 = good; 5 = very good).

Assessment Steps: Middle and High School Students (Grades 6 or 7–12)

1. Give each student a sheet of lined paper with a story starter (topic sentence) printed across the top, an extra sheet of lined paper, and two pencils or pens. Give the following directions:

   > "I want you to write a short story (essay). I am going to read a sentence to you first, and then I want you to write a short story about what happens (a short essay about that topic). You will have 1 minute to think about the story (essay) you will write and then have 3 minutes to write it. Do your best work. If you don't know how to spell a word, you should guess. Use the sentence I read as your first sentence but don't write that sentence again. Are there any questions? For the next minute, think about . . . [read writing prompt]."

2. After 1 minute, say, "Begin writing."
3. After 3 minutes, say, "Stop and put your pencils/pens down."

Scoring and Interpretation: Middle and High School Students

OPTION 1: CORRECT WORD SEQUENCES (CWS; SEE ABOVE)

OPTION 2: CORRECT MINUS INCORRECT WORD SEQUENCES (C-IWS; SEE ABOVE)

OPTION 3: SENTENCES WRITTEN (SW)

1. Count the number of sentences written. A *sentence* is defined as any string of words separated from another group of words by a period, question mark, or exclamation point. Sentences do not have to be complete or grammatically correct to receive credit.
2. Compare the SW score with local norms or students' previous scores.

NOTES

1. Guidelines for developing local writing norms are provided below.
2. High-frequency words for word dictation and sentence dictation tasks can be found in Harris and Jacobson (1972) or on one of the many Dolch word list websites (e.g., *http://reading. indiana.edu/ieo/bibs/dolchwordlist.html*). Examples of narrative story starters can be found in Shapiro (2011) and Hosp et al. (2016).

SOURCES

Lembke, E., Deno, S. L., & Hall, K. (2003). Identifying an indicator of growth in early writing proficiency for elementary school students. *Assessment for Effective Intervention, 28,* 23–36.

Shapiro, E. S. (2011). *Academic skills problems: Direct assessment and intervention* (4th ed.). New York: Guilford Press.

Weissenburger, J. W., & Espin, C. (2005). Curriculum-based measures of writing across grade levels. *Journal of School Psychology, 43,* 153–169.

ADDITIONAL RESOURCES

Intervention Central (*www.interventioncentral.org*) offers W-CBM administration and scoring sheets for total words, correctly spelled words, and correct word sequences. AIMSweb (*www. aimsweb.com*) provides fall, winter, and spring norms for correct word sequences and total words written for students in grades 1–8, as well as web-based data management and graphing.

CBM in Spelling

Curriculum-based measurement in spelling (S-CBM) is a set of brief, fluency-based standardized procedures used to index spelling performance and progress toward grade-level expectations in spelling. As with R-CBM and M-CBM, S-CBM can be used for universal screening/benchmarking programs, in which sets of three spelling probes are administered to all students three or four times a year, and for more frequent monitoring of student progress toward intervention goals or end-of-year objectives for at-risk students. Each spelling probe consists of 12–17 words randomly sampled from the pool of words students are expected to master during the year and dictated for 2 minutes. If students are taught from a grade-based spelling textbook, spelling probes can be constructed using the classroom curricular materials. As noted above, however, most school districts have replaced textbook-based spelling instruction with instruction integrated within language arts and content-area subjects, so that words for spelling instruction and assessments are drawn from a variety of sources. When this is the case, graded word lists controlled for difficulty should be used.

Two options are included for scoring S-CBMs: (1) correct letter sequences (CLS), defined as an adjacent pair of correctly spelled letters, and (2) number of words spelled correctly. Although the CLS method is more sensitive to differences among students and small changes in student performance, it is also more complex and time-consuming. Moreover, because improving skills in spelling whole words is the ultimate goal, the number of words spelled correctly should be monitored at periodic intervals (Fuchs, Fuchs, Hamlett, Walz, & Germann, 1993). Studies have documented that both metrics are highly correlated with standardized measures of spelling and that spelling CBMs can reliably distinguish among students with disabilities, students receiving Title I services, and regular education students, regardless of which of the two scoring methods is used (Shinn, Ysseldyke, Deno, & Tindal, 1986). Moreover, higher spelling achievement is associated with teacher use of skills analysis based on S-CBM performance (Fuchs, Fuchs, Hamlett, & Allinder, 1991).

Overview

In spelling, all students in a classroom are usually placed in the same level of the curriculum regardless of their skill development. For that reason, the results of S-CBM are not generally used to make decisions about moving students to a different level of the curriculum. Instead, spelling probes are conducted to identify students who would benefit from supplementary targeted instruction and to indicate the degree to which students are acquiring spelling skills relative to their classmates and end-of-year expectations. In S-CBM screening/benchmarking, measures are administered in fall, winter, and spring to index spelling achievement and identify at-risk students. S-CBM progress monitoring is conducted at more frequent intervals to measure students' response to spelling interventions and/or progress toward end-of-year standards. S-CBM results can also be analyzed to provide information for instructional planning based on the types of errors frequently made by students. Research has demonstrated that S-CBM is a reliable and valid predictor of performance on norm- and criterion-referenced spelling measures and that it can differentiate between students with and without disabilities. Two scoring options are presented: (1) the number of correct letter sequences (pairs of adjacent letters) spelled correctly and (2) the number of words spelled correctly. S-CBMs may be administered to students individually or in groups.

S-CBM performance can be evaluated by means of local norms, intrastudent comparisons, and, for correct letter sequences, web-based user norms.

Purpose

1. To identify students in need of supplementary instruction in spelling.
2. To monitor students' progress toward intervention or end-of-year spelling goals.
3. To evaluate the effectiveness of spelling interventions and instructional practices.
4. To provide information for instructional planning and program improvement.

Materials

1. Spelling lists of words randomly sampled from the spelling textbook or, preferably, grade-level curriculum-independent lists; for students in grades 1 and 2, use 12-word lists; for students in grades 3 and up, use 17-word lists.
2. Pencils with erasers, two per student.
3. Sheets of lined paper, two per student, or spelling notebooks, one per student.
4. Stopwatch or timer.
5. Equal-interval graph paper or graphing program (optional).

Assessment Steps

1. Distribute the writing materials and give the following directions:

   "I am going to read some words to you. I want you to write the words on the sheet in front of you. Write the first word on the first line, the second word on the second line, and so on. I'll give you 7 seconds (10 seconds for students in grades 1 and 2) to spell each word. When I say the next word, try to write it, even if you haven't finished the last one. Are there any questions? Begin!"

2. Dictate each word in order at the appropriate interval, repeating each word twice. If a word is a homonym, use it in a short sentence.
3. At the end of 2 minutes, say, "Stop! Put your pencils down." If students have nearly completed a word and the time has expired, permit them to finish writing that final word.
4. For screening/benchmarking, administer two more lists. For progress monitoring, administer one list.

Scoring and Interpretation

OPTION 1: CORRECT LETTER SEQUENCES (CLS)

1. For scoring purposes, each word has an extra character placed before and after it and one more letter sequence than the number of letters in the word. For example, the six-letter word *BUTTER* has seven possible letter sequences (*B, BU, UT, TT, TE, ER,* and *R*).
2. Count the number of correct letter sequences. For example:
   a. *BUTTER* has seven letter sequences correct.
   b. *BUTTAR* has five letter sequences correct.
   c. *BUTER* has five letter sequences correct.
   d. *BATTAR* has three letter sequences correct.
3. For screening/benchmarking, score each of the three probes as described above and use the median score for interpretative purposes. For progress monitoring, score the probe as described above.
4. Compare the CLS rate with intrastudent norms, local norms, or web-based norms.

OPTION 2: WORDS SPELLED CORRECTLY (WSC)

1. Count the number of words spelled correctly to obtain a words-spelled-correctly rate (WSC).
2. For screening/benchmarking, score each of the three probes as described above and use the median score for interpretative purposes. For progress monitoring, score the probe as described above.
3. Compare the WCS rate with intrastudent norms, local norms, or web-based norms.

NOTES

1. Lists can be generated by writing grade-level words on index cards or entering them in a word processing program and then randomly selecting sets. If CLS will be used as the metric, each list should include the same number of three-, four-, five-, (and more) letter words.
2. To evaluate S-CBM performance using a whole-word metric, local norms at the classroom, school, or district level can be developed, using guidelines described in Stewart and Silberglitt (2008).
3. Having students respond to S-CBMs in their spelling notebooks permits both teachers and students to assess progress over time.

SOURCES

Hosp, M. K., Hosp, J. L., & Howell, K. W. (2016). *The ABCs of CBM: A practical guide to curriculum-based measurement* (2nd ed.). New York: Guilford Press.
Shapiro, E. S. (2011). *Academic skills problems: Direct assessment and intervention* (4th ed.). New York: Guilford Press.

ADDITIONAL RESOURCES

AIMSweb (*www.aimsweb.com*) offers sets of 3 benchmarking lists and 30 progress monitoring lists for each of grades 1–8 based on seven commonly used spelling series and reading word lists. Also available are fall, winter, and spring norms for correct letter sequences for students in grades 1–8.

Evaluating the Effectiveness of Social Studies and Science Interventions

Methods for assessing the effectiveness of the strategies in this section include quiz and test grades, classwide percentages of students with low grades, classwide academic engagement rates, and comprehension-based measures, such as the number of important elements included in summaries and self-reports of strategy use. In addition to the evaluation procedures provided for each intervention, directions for constructing and administering *vocabulary-matching probes*, a form of CBM in the content areas, are provided below.

Although CBM methods have been used since the 1980s to monitor student progress in reading, mathematics, spelling, and writing, researchers have only recently extended CBM technology to content-area learning. A series of studies by Espin and her colleagues have demonstrated that a 5-minute vocabulary-matching measure, consisting of 20 terms and 22 definitions (including two distractors) drawn from students' own texts, is a reliable and valid indicator of performance and growth in content-area learning for middle school and high school students (Busch & Espin, 2003; Espin, Shin, & Busch, 2005). Results of vocabulary-matching probes can be interpreted by means of intraclass comparisons (i.e., comparing an individual student's score with the class mean or median) and by creating expectancy tables that incorporate scores on end-of-year examinations or high-stakes assessments (Espin & Tindal, 1998).

Content Areas: Vocabulary Matching

For many middle and high school students, limited vocabulary knowledge, poor decoding skills, and impaired fluency interfere with their ability to read and understand their content-area texts, putting them at risk for failure in those classes. *Vocabulary matching*, a 5-minute assessment tapping these three critical skills, uses curriculum-based procedures to monitor student progress in content-area classes. A growing body of research demonstrates that vocabulary matching is a reliable and valid indicator of student performance on content-area tasks, including standardized tests, grades, and tests of subject-area knowledge, and is sensitive to individual differences in growth. Moreover, scores on vocabulary-matching probes reliably differentiate between students with and without learning disabilities. Data from vocabulary-matching probes can be used to identify students at risk for failure in content-area classes early in the school year and to evaluate the appropriateness of content-area classes for students with disabilities. After the initial benchmark assessment, vocabulary-matching probes can be administered on a weekly or biweekly basis to target students to monitor learning and determine the need for additional interventions. The probes can be administered on an individual, small-group, or whole-class basis.

Materials

1. Create a pool of vocabulary terms with their definitions from the content to be covered during the semester or school year. For performance-level (benchmark) testing, a pool of 100–150 terms is sufficient. For progress monitoring, a larger pool is needed, depending on the frequency of assessment. Select terms from the textbook glossary, teacher lectures and notes, or a combination. Develop a short definition (fewer than 15 words) for each term, using the textbook glossary, teacher notes or lectures, or a student dictionary.
2. For each probe, randomly select 20 terms with their definitions and two additional definitions not matching any of the 20 terms. List the terms alphabetically down the left side of the page and the definitions on the right side of the page with a blank next to each definition. For benchmark testing, create three probes. For progress monitoring, generate a weekly or biweekly probe.
3. Stopwatch or timer.
4. Pencils with erasers, one or two per student.
5. Equal-interval graph paper or graphing program (optional).

Assessment Steps

1. Give each student a vocabulary-matching probe and give the following directions:

    "Here is a list of terms and definitions from this course. When I say 'Begin,' match as many definitions with their terms as you can by writing the number of the definition in the blank next to the correct term. You will have 5 minutes. You will see terms we have not covered yet, so don't worry if you don't know all of the words. Are there any questions? Ready? Begin."

2. At the end of 5 minutes, say, "Stop!" and collect the probes.
3. For benchmark testing, administer two more probes. For progress monitoring, administer only one probe.

Scoring

1. Award one point for each correct match. Sum the number of correct matches to obtain a percent-correct score.
2. For benchmark testing, use the median (middle) score on the three probes to control for the effects of difficulty across probes.
3. For greater reliability in progress monitoring, administer two probes weekly and record the mean score of each pair of adjacent probes.

Interpretation

1. For benchmark testing, rank student results from highest to lowest and calculate a class mean and median. Students whose performance is very discrepant from that of their average peers are likely to need additional interventions to be successful in the content-area class from which the vocabulary terms are drawn.
2. For progress monitoring, graph or have students graph their weekly or biweekly scores. Compare the results with end-of-semester or end-of-year goals you set collaboratively with the students. If progress monitoring data indicate that students are making limited progress, modify or intensify content-area interventions.

NOTES

1. To reduce preparation time, use a word processing program to create a master list of vocabulary terms and definitions and generate probes.
2. Local norms can be developed for use in predicting performance on end-of-year examinations or high-stakes assessments. Create an expectancy table by recording student scores on vocabulary probes, along with their scores on final examinations or high-stakes assessments. The following year, use the data in the table to estimate the likelihood that students with specific vocabulary scores will have difficulty achieving success in the content-area classes or passing high-stakes examinations (Espin & Tindal, 1998).

SOURCES

Espin, C. A., Busch, T. W., Shin, J., & Kruschwitz, R. (2001). Curriculum-based measurement in the content areas: Validity of vocabulary-matching as an indicator of performance in social studies. *Learning Disabilities Research and Practice, 16,* 142–151.

Espin, C. A., Shin, J., & Busch, T. W. (2005). Curriculum-based measurement in the content areas: Vocabulary matching as an indicator of progress in social studies learning. *Journal of Learning Disabilities, 38,* 353–363.

Monitoring Progress for Behavior

Event recording methods, which monitor discrete behaviors, are also relatively easy for classroom teachers to use. Momentary time-sampling methods, which involve rating student behavior several times per minute, are more feasible for an observer other than the teacher. Although the quality of the data (evidence base) is critical, consultants should also involve teachers in selecting observational methods and data collection procedures. Collaborating with teachers in selecting data collection measures, as well as interventions, not only conveys respect for teachers' perspectives but also affirms teachers as active participants in documenting improvement in students' academic or social competence. In addition, consultants should be prepared to demonstrate the selected methods, to observe the teacher using them, and to help analyze and interpret the results. Finally, consultants should be prepared to conduct some of the observations themselves. Although the observation and evaluation methods for the interventions in this book have been designed to be as simple as possible without sacrificing reliability and validity, even the simplest observation can be more easily performed by someone other than the teacher, who must be continually responding to the demands of daily classroom life. Assisting with data collection not only supports teachers in the intervention assistance process, it also provides consultants with invaluable information regarding the classroom environment that can be used to design and modify interventions.

Observational Recording Methods

Many of the observation strategies make use of one or more of four observational coding methods: (1) group event recording, (2) group interval recording, (3) classwide scanning, and (4) group time sampling. These four methods are versions of two basic observational procedures: (1) event recording and (2) momentary time sampling.

Event recording consists of tallying the number of times one or more target behaviors occurs. The *Group Event Recording Form* (see Figure 3.2) is designed to monitor the frequency of occurrence of one to five positive and/or negative target behaviors for an entire class for up to 7 days or observation periods. *Discrete behaviors*—behaviors with identifiable beginnings and endings, such as call-outs, out-of-seats, or hand raises—are most appropriate for monitoring with event recording. The data yielded by this method are frequency counts of the target behaviors displayed by a class or group.

Momentary time sampling consists of observing a student at predetermined intervals and recording whether or not the student is exhibiting a target behavior at the moment of observation. The *Group Interval Recording Form* is designed for consecutively recording the behavior of every student in a class or group at predetermined intervals, such as every 5, 10, or 15 seconds (see Figure 3.3). The observer records whether each student is displaying one of several mutually exclusive behaviors, such as on-task, off-task, or disruptive behavior, at the moment of observation. The data collected by this method are classwide or group-wide rates of each of the target behavior categories. Because observation is continuous, this method must be conducted by some individual other than the classroom teacher, at least while the teacher is delivering instruction. Although the emphasis in this book is on classwide observation methods, the *Group Event Recording Form* and the *Group Interval Recording Form* can also be used to monitor the behavior of an individual student or a small group of target students.

Classwide scanning, a version of momentary time sampling, involves rapidly surveying an entire class and tallying the number of students in each of several mutually exclusive behavior categories at the moment of observation. Classwide scanning differs from the standard momentary time-sampling procedure in that student behavior is monitored at longer intervals rather than coded sequentially every few seconds. Using the *Classwide Scanning Form,* the observer records whether students are on task, off task, or disruptive at predetermined intervals, such as every 3, 5, 10, or 15 minutes (see Figure 3.4). Although shorter intervals yield more reliable data, longer intervals permit teachers to monitor student behavior systematically without unduly interrupting ongoing instruction. When classwide scanning is conducted by individuals not involved in delivering instruction, shorter intervals can be used. The data collected by classwide scanning consist of the percentages of students falling into each of the behavior categories.

In *quadrant sampling,* a variation of classwide scanning, the observer divides the class into four groups by eye and sequentially records the behavior of each quadrant as either on task or off task in an all-or-nothing judgment. If all of the students in the group being

Teacher: _____ School: _____

Description of class or group: _____

Number of students in class or group: _____

Dates of observation: _____ Time(s) of observation: _____

Observer: _____ Class activity: _____

Directions: Select one or more target behaviors (desired or undesired) to monitor and list them in the first column. Place a check or tally in the box for each occurrence of each target behavior during the observation session or day.

Target behavior	Session 1	Session 2	Session 3	Session 4	Session 5	Session 6	Session 7

Behavior 1 occurrences: _____

Behavior 2 occurrences: _____

Behavior 3 occurrences: _____

Behavior 4 occurrences: _____

Behavior 5 occurrences: _____

FIGURE 3.2. Sample Group Event Recording Form.

observed are on task, the interval is scored as on task, whereas if one or more students in the group are off task, the interval is scored as off task. The *Group Time-Sampling Form* (see Figure 3.5) is designed to sample student behavior at predetermined intervals, such as every 3 or 5 minutes. Because student groups are identified on the form by number, the observer can determine whether some groups are more off task than others and use that information to modify classroom organization and instructional routines.

Assessing the Reliability of Direct Behavioral Observations

Given the realities of the typical school environment, a single individual will conduct classroom observations in most cases. Using two or more observers yields more reliable information, however, and is necessary to obtain interrater reliability data. The two observers can consist of the referring teacher and the consultant, two IAT members, or pairs of trained student interns or paraprofessionals. A common formula for calculating interrater reliability for two observers that can be used for event recording and time sampling procedures is as follows:

$$\text{Interobserver agreement} = \frac{\text{Number of agreements}}{\text{Number of agreements} + \text{Number of disagreements}} \times 100\%$$

The percentage agreement index represents the percentage of occasions on which two observers agree that a behavior did or did not occur. Interobserver percentage agreement should be 80% or higher in order to conclude that measurements of behavior are reliable and valid.

Behavior: Direct Behavior Ratings

Direct Behavior Ratings (DBR) are another approach to monitoring student progress from behavior interventions with a strong research base. DBR were developed by combing the strengths of behavior rating scales (ease of collection) and direct observation (close proximity of data collection to the time and place of the behavior of interest; Chafouleas, Christ, Riley-Tillman, Briesch, & Chanese, 2007; Christ, Riley-Tillman, & Chafouleas, 2009; Riley-Tillman, Chafouleas, & Briesch, 2007) to provide an assessment approach that is both highly feasible (efficient, easy, repeatable) and flexible (can be used for many behaviors in a variety of settings).

The name of DBR outlines the method's core features: DBR is <u>D</u>irect. DBR ratings are collected immediately after the observation period. As a result, the level of inference is lower than ratings collected days, weeks, or months after the target behavior. DBR targets <u>B</u>ehavior. The targets of DBR are behaviors that are accessible for observation and evaluation by the rater. As such, target behaviors should be defined, resulting in a number of individual DBRs (e.g., Academic Engagement, Disruptive Behavior, and Respectful). DBR involves <u>R</u>ating. Finally, DBRs are ratings in that they were developed to be based on the rater's perception of the target behavior. In this manner they are akin to behavior rating scales. Although this can be viewed as a negative aspect of the assessment, perception is a critical aspect of documenting a response to intervention. Specifically, DBR allows for ratings that can address constructs such as appropriateness to context (e.g., meeting expectations, working with peers appropriately).

For an example of a DBR, see Figure 3.6. The steps to completing a DBR are as follows on page 84:

Teacher: _____ School: _____

Description of class or group: _____

Number of students in class or group: _____ Class activity: _____

Date of observation: _____ Time of observation: _____ to ____

Observer: _____ Length of observation interval: _____

Directions: Beginning at the left side of the room, glance at each student at the designated interval (e.g., 5, 10, or 15 seconds) and code that student's behavior as on-task (+), off-task (−), or disruptive (×) at the moment of observation. Record behavior for each student in turn and then begin again with the first student.

1	2	3	4	5	6	7	8	9	10	11	12	13	14	15	16	17	18	19	20
21	22	23	24	25	26	27	28	29	30	31	32	33	34	35	36	37	38	39	40
41	42	43	44	45	46	47	48	49	50	51	52	53	54	55	56	57	58	59	60
61	62	63	64	65	66	67	68	69	70	71	72	73	74	75	76	77	78	79	80
81	82	83	84	85	86	87	88	89	90	91	92	93	94	95	96	97	98	99	100
101	102	103	104	105	106	107	108	109	110	111	112	113	114	115	116	117	118	119	120
121	122	123	124	125	126	127	128	129	130	131	132	133	134	135	136	137	138	139	140
141	142	143	144	145	146	147	148	149	150	151	152	153	154	155	156	157	158	159	160
161	162	163	164	165	166	167	168	169	170	171	172	173	174	175	176	177	178	179	180

$$\text{Percentage of target behavior} = \frac{\text{Number of intervals per category}}{\text{Total number of observation intervals}} \times 100$$

Percentage of on-task behavior   = _____

Percentage of off-task behavior   = _____

Percentage of disruptive behavior   = _____

FIGURE 3.3. Sample Group Interval Recording Form.

Teacher: _____ School: _____

Description of class or group: _____

Number of students in class or group: _____ Class activity: _____

Date of observation: _____ Time of observation: _____ to _____

Observer: _____ Length of observation interval: _____

Directions: Scan the class at the designated interval (e.g., every 3, 5, 10, or 15 minutes) and tally the number of students in each behavior category. Tally marks for each interval should sum to the number of students in the entire group. Sum the tallies for each behavior category and divide by the number of intervals coded times the total number of students to obtain the percentage of students in each category.

Interval	On-Task	Off-Task	Disruptive	Totals
1				
2				
3				
4				
5				
6				
7				
8				
9				
10				
11				
12				

Percentage of students per category = $\dfrac{\text{Total number of students per category}}{\text{Number of intervals} \times \text{total number of students}} \times 100$

Percentage of on-task students　　=　_____

Percentage of off-task students　　=　_____

Percentage of disruptive students　=　_____

FIGURE 3.4. Sample Classwide Scanning Form.

Teacher: _____ School: _____

Description of class or group: _____

Number of students in class or group: _____ Class activity: _____

Date of observation: _____ Time of observation: _____ to _____

Observer: _____ Length of observation interval: _____

Directions: With your eye, divide the class into four groups of approximately equal numbers of students. If desired, write the names of the students in each group in the corresponding blanks at the bottom of the form. Beginning at the left side of the room, glance at each quadrant at the selected interval (1-, 3-, or 5-minute interval). If all of the students in the group are on-task at the moment of observation, record a plus (+) for the observed quadrant. If any of the students in the quadrant being observed are not on task, record a minus (–). During the next interval, observe the next group, and so forth until you have observed all of the groups. Then begin again with the first group.

Group 1	Group 2	Group 3	Group 4	Group 1	Group 2	Group 3	Group 4
Group 1	Group 2	Group 3	Group 4	Group 1	Group 2	Group 3	Group 4
Group 1	Group 2	Group 3	Group 4	Group 1	Group 2	Group 3	Group 4
Group 1	Group 2	Group 3	Group 4	Group 1	Group 2	Group 3	Group 4

Group percentage
of on-task intervals = $\dfrac{\text{Number of plus intervals per group}}{\text{Number of intervals per group}}$ × 100

Classwide percentage
of on-task intervals = $\dfrac{\text{Total number of plus intervals}}{\text{Total number of observation intervals}}$ × 100

Group 1 percentage of on-task behavior = ____% Students: _____

Group 2 percentage of on-task behavior = ____% Students: _____

Group 3 percentage of on-task behavior = ____% Students: _____

Group 4 percentage of on-task behavior = ____% Students: _____

Classwide percentage of on-task behavior = ____%

FIGURE 3.5. Sample Group Time-Sampling Form.

- Step 1: Complete the top of the DBR form (e.g., Date, Student, Day of Week).
- Step 2: Define the observation rating period (e.g., 9:00 A.M.–9:45 A.M.) and activity (e.g., independent work).
- Step 3: Select the behaviors to be rated.
- Step 4: Immediately following the observation period, rate the student's behavior (e.g., percentage of time displayed, total number of times displayed).

A great deal of research has accumulated in regard to DBR scales, with more than 50 DBR-related publications. There have been several studies supporting the fact that DBR is efficient and acceptable to educational professionals (Chafouleas, Riley-Tillman, & Sassu, 2006; Miller, Chafouleas, Riley-Tillman, & Fabiano, 2014; Riley-Tillman, Chafouleas, & Eckert, 2008). Studies have also demonstrated that DBR can be used in universal screening (Chafouleas, Jaffery, Riley-Tillman, Christ, & Sen, 2013; Kilgus et al., 2012; Kilgus, Riley-Tillman, Chafouleas, Christ, & Welsh, 2014; Miller et al., 2015). Finally, research documented an evidence base for the use of DBR in monitoring student progress (Briesch, Chafouleas, & Riley-Tillman, 2010; Chafouleas, Briesch, Riley-Tillman, Christ, & Kilgus, 2010; Chafouleas, Kilgus, Riley-Tillman, Jaffery, & Harrison, 2012; Harrison, Riley-Tillman, & Chafouleas, 2014; Riley-Tillman, Methe, & Weegar, 2009). This research base resulted in DBR for Academic Engagement and Disruptive Behavior being rated by the National Center for Intensive Intervention as valid, reliable, and sensitive to change. For more information on DBR, see *http://dbr.education.uconn.edu.*

Analysis

GRAPHING: AN ESSENTIAL TOOL FOR EVALUATING INTERVENTION EFFECTIVENESS

Detecting changes in student performance or behavior can be difficult and time-consuming when reviewing lists of numbers, a series of observational forms or anecdotal records, and other types of data. Graphs provide a way of organizing data collected during baseline and intervention phases into easy-to-read visual displays that permit teachers, team members, parents, students, and others involved in the intervention process to determine whether the intervention plan is having the desired effect on the target behavior. The graph most commonly used to analyze behavioral data is a *time-series graph,* which depicts changes in one or more target behaviors over time. Frequency, percent score, or some other metric is plotted on the vertical axis (*y* axis), and time is plotted on the horizontal axis (*x* axis). A line connects the individual data points, creating a path that reveals the pattern and trend of the target behavior. To denote the change from baseline to intervention phase or from one intervention to another, a *condition line*—a vertical line drawn parallel to the *y* axis and separating the data points in the various phases—can be added.

Graphs also serve as key tools in demonstrating the need for special services in response-to-intervention eligibility decision-making frameworks. Graphs can be used to display not only the student's response to intervention but also the intensity of the intervention supports that have been implemented, such as the frequency of teacher contacts. Moreover, by plotting comparison peer performance on the same graph, the discrepancy between the performance of the referred student and that of typical students in the same educational context can be easily evaluated (Barnett, Daly, Jones, & Lentz, 2004).

Date: M T W Th F	Student:	Activity Description:
	Rater:	

Observation Time:	Behavior Descriptions:
Start: _____ End: _____ ☐ Check if no observation today	**Academically engaged** is defined as actively or passively participating in the classroom activity. For example: writing, raising hand, answering a question, talking about a lesson, listening to the teacher, reading silently, or looking at instructional materials. **Respectful** is defined as compliant and polite behavior in response to adult direction and/or interactions with peers and adults. For example: follows teacher's direction, prosocial interaction with peers, positive response to adult request, verbal or physical disruption without a negative tone/connotation. **Disruptive** is defined as student action that interrupts regular school or classroom activity. For example: out of seat, fidgeting, playing with objects, acting aggressively, talking/yelling about things that are unrelated to classroom instruction.

Directions: Place a mark along the line that best reflects *the percentage of total time* the student exhibited each target behavior. Note that the percentages do not need to total 100% across behaviors, since some behaviors may co-occur.

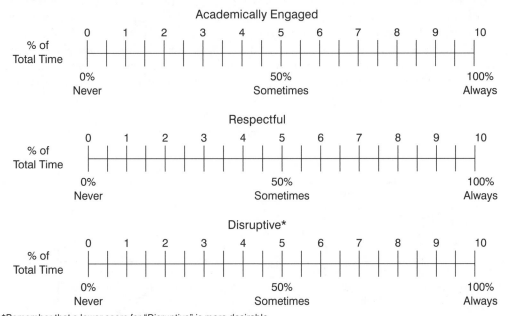

*Remember that a lower score for "Disruptive" is more desirable.

FIGURE 3.6. Example of a Direct Behavior Rating form. From Chafouleas, Riley-Tillman, Christ, and Sugai (2009). Copyright © 2009 the University of Connecticut. All rights reserved. Permission is granted to duplicate for personal and educational use as long as the names of the creators and the full copyright notice are included in all copies.

Reprinted in *Effective School Interventions: Evidence-Based Strategies for Improving Student Outcomes, Third Edition,* by Matthew K. Burns, T. Chris Riley-Tillman, and Natalie Rathvon (The Guilford Press, 2017). Purchasers can download enlarged versions of this figure (see the box at the end of the table of contents).

Figure 3.7 displays baseline and intervention conditions for Anthony, a kindergarten student referred for high rates of aggressive behavior, including pushing, hitting, and throwing toys and other objects. Also plotted on the graph are median aggressive behaviors for three typical classroom peers selected by the teacher. An inspection of the graph reveals not only that the frequency of Anthony's aggressive behaviors has decreased markedly during the intervention phase compared with baseline but also that his aggressive behavior has stabilized at approximately the level of typical classroom peers.

Graphing resources are available on the Intervention Central website (*www.interventioncentral.org*), including ChartDog, an online application for generating time-series graphs for academic performance data, and a link to a site permitting users to create Excel time-series graphs for common academic measures (CBM and DIBELS) and behavioral measures (frequency, time on task, and the *Behavioral Observation of Students in Schools*).

Evaluating IAT Outcomes

In addition to evaluating changes in the performance of individual students and groups of students, school-based teams should assess the overall effectiveness of their IATs. Frequently used measures of IAT effectiveness include the following: (1) number of students referred for special education who are actually placed in special education programs (i.e., appropriate referrals for special education services); (2) proportion of students from minority backgrounds placed in special education programs (i.e., checks for the disproportionate placement of students from certain racial/ethnic/linguistic minority groups); (3) changes in the achievement and behavior of referred students; (4) teacher, parent, and student satisfaction with IAT activities and interventions; (5) changes in teachers' instructional and behavior management practices; and (6) number of requests for intervention assistance. Gathering information on outcomes of referred students is essential not only for data-based decision

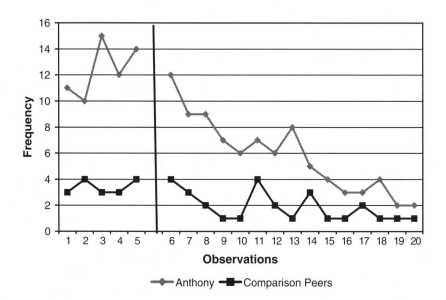

FIGURE 3.7. Frequency of aggressive behaviors during baseline and intervention phases for Anthony and three comparison peers.

making but also for evaluating overall team effectiveness. Moreover, student outcomes should be evaluated not only in terms of whether or not referred students have met the goals specified in their intervention assistance plans but also in terms of the degree to which the discrepancy between their level of performance and grade-level standards has been reduced. Data for discrepancy-based evaluation methods can be gathered from norm-referenced and criterion-referenced achievement tests, curriculum-based measures, report card grades, office disciplinary referrals, behavior rating scales, and other objective measures. For example, a review of IAT data may reveal that 85% of students referred for academic problems attained their individual goals, but that only 50% were reading on grade level at the end of the intervention period, as measured by criterion-referenced reading assessments, or scored within the average range on end-of-year standardized tests.

Self-evaluation of team procedures and processes is also a critical accountability component for team-based IATs. Bahr and colleagues (1999) developed a 10-item scale to assess the effectiveness of school-based intervention teams from the perspective of the team members themselves (see Figure 3.8). The scale has evidence of content validity, based on judgments by school consultation experts; has an overall reliability of .95; and has been used in several large-scale IAT evaluation studies (Bahr et al., 1999; Bahr et al., 2006). Scales for evaluating IAT effectiveness from the perspective of intervention consumers, including teachers and parents, are available on numerous district and state department of education websites and at Intervention Central (*www.interventioncentral.org*).

Interpreting Graphs

There are a number of methods to consider when using graphed data to determine whether a student responded to the intervention. Visual analysis allows documentation of change in a number of manners as appropriate for each specific case. Specifically, the core methods are examining (1) level, (2) trend, (3) variability, and (4) immediacy. Each of these methods will have varied appropriateness for each case. For example, *trend* would be more useful for most academic intervention, but *immediacy* and *level* will likely be best for behavioral difficulties.

Change in Level

The first method to examine in considering intervention outcome data is the level, which typically involves comparing the mean or median in the baseline phase with the intervention phase. For example, in Figure 3.9, the intervention reduced calling-out behavior from 11.4 to 2.4. These same data could be considered in terms of the median in each phase (baseline phase: 13, intervention phase: 2). It is advantageous to use the median score when there are some outlier data in either phase.

Change in Trend

For interventions that focus on learned behavior (e.g. reading or social skills), the trend can be a useful metric for describing the rate of learning. Outcome data in a phase are generally increasing, decreasing, or stable. Interventions should increase the rate of learning, and the rate of learning should be higher in the intervention phase than in the baseline phase for a successful intervention. Interventionists can compute a trend with the Slope function in MS Excel, which provides a specific rate of how the target behavior changed over a period of time.

1. Our team develops appropriate interventions regarding the student's needs.						
Strongly Agree						Strongly Disagree
1	2	3	4	5	6	7

2. Our team develops manageable interventions for teachers and students.						
Strongly Agree						Strongly Disagree
1	2	3	4	5	6	7

3. Our team uses a shared decision-making process.						
Strongly Agree						Strongly Disagree
1	2	3	4	5	6	7

4. Our team clearly defines the role every member has in working on a specific student concern.						
Strongly Agree						Strongly Disagree
1	2	3	4	5	6	7

5. I encourage fellow educators to use our team when they have a specific student concern.						
Strongly Agree						Strongly Disagree
1	2	3	4	5	6	7

6. I am satisfied with our intervention team process.						
Strongly Agree						Strongly Disagree
1	2	3	4	5	6	7

7. Our team is effective in meeting the needs of the problem identifier (e.g., teacher).						
Strongly Agree						Strongly Disagree
1	2	3	4	5	6	7

8. Our team is effective in meeting the needs of the student.						
Strongly Agree						Strongly Disagree
1	2	3	4	5	6	7

9. Team members communicate clearly with one another.						
Strongly Agree						Strongly Disagree
1	2	3	4	5	6	7

10. Overall, I think our team is effective.						
Strongly Agree						Strongly Disagree
1	2	3	4	5	6	7

FIGURE 3.8. Sample Team Effectiveness Scale. Adapted from Bahr, Whitten, Dieker, Kocarek, and Manson (1999, p. 72). Copyright © 1999 the Council for Exceptional Children. Adapted by permission.

Change in Variability

In some cases, the goal is to remove variability of the target behavior, which is defined as the range of data in a phase. For example, some students can display a range of behavior from very good to quite problematic in a short period of time. See Figure 3.10 for an example of a classwide intervention targeted at decreasing students' "out of seat" behavior to illustrate the importance of variability. In this case, there is a great deal of variability preintervention (2–16 instances of out-of-seat behavior). After the intervention, the range is decreased to 0–5. Although still present, the really problematic days have been removed since the intervention began.

Immediacy/Latency of Change

In some cases, it is expected that behavior will change slowly (e.g., many academic interventions), but for behavior interventions it is often predicted that the change will occur rapidly. In such cases, it is critical to document how quickly the behavior changes, which is referred to as immediacy. A rapid change after implementing the intervention increases the likelihood that the change occurred as a result of the intervention and not some other factor.

Numerical Interpretation of Level and Growth

Many interventions are interpreted by graphing the data and comparing treatment data to baseline, but baseline data are not always collected. For example, a student receiving a Tier 2 intervention in a multi-tiered system of support would likely start the intervention with-

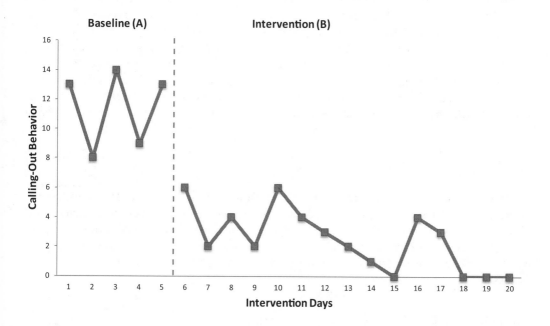

FIGURE 3.9. Sample intervention graph: Level change. From Riley-Tillman, Burns, and Gibbons (2013). Copyright © 2013 The Guilford Press. Reprinted by permission.

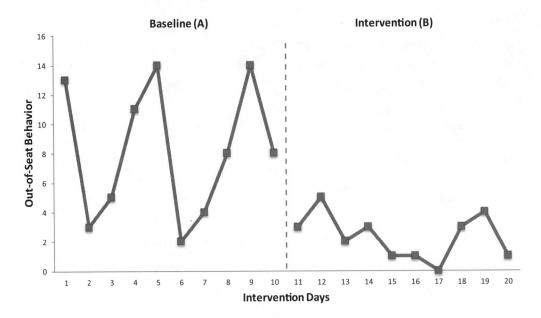

FIGURE 3.10. Sample intervention graph: Decreased variability. From Riley-Tillman, Burns, and Gibbons (2013). Copyright © 2013 The Guilford Press. Reprinted by permission.

out adequate baseline data having been collected. Thus intervention data without baseline are often interpreted with a dual-discrepancy (DD) model (Burns & Senesac, 2005; Fuchs 2003). Students who are discrepant from expectations for both postintervention level *and* growth are described as dually discrepant, and the intervention is judged to be ineffective. If the postintervention fluency scores meet or exceed standards, then the student is considered a proficient reader who no longer needs intervention. If the student is meeting expectations for growth but has yet to meet standards for level (e.g., seasonal benchmark criteria), then the intervention is leading to sufficient growth and should be continued. However, if the data suggest that the student is not making sufficient growth and has yet to meet level expectations, then the intervention is not working and needs to be changed.

Level Criteria

Of the two components of a DD, level is the most straightforward and easy to interpret. Discrepancies in postintervention level consist of any scores that fall below the given standard. Some schools use performance below the 25th percentile. Other schools compare postintervention scores with criterion-referenced standards such as estimates of risk published by DIBELS (see *https://dibels.uoregon.edu/docs/DIBELSNextFormerBenchmark-Goals.pdf*).

Growth Criteria

Growth within a DD framework is usually examined by computing slope with the intervention data and weeks of intervention using ordinary least squares (OLS). There are pub-

· lished standards for growth based on research for reading (Deno, Fuchs, Marston, & Shin, 2001; Fuchs, Fuchs, & Speece, 2002) or national norms (Aimsweb, 2010; Hasbrouck & Tindal, 2006). A more recently developed and commonly used approach is to base growth standards on rates of growth according to benchmark standards. For example, standards associated with DIBELS suggest that proficient readers in second grade should read at least 52 words correctly per minute in the fall, 72 in the winter, and 87 in the spring. If the data are collected in the 2nd, 18th, and 34th weeks of the school year, which is somewhat typical, then the weekly growth rate of those three target scores would be 1.09 words read correctly per minute per week. In other words, students would need to increase their scores by 1.09 words per minute each week in order to maintain a level of growth that matched benchmark expectations for proficiency. Slope scores for student data that fell below 1.09 suggest a discrepancy from expectations for growth, and those that are at or above 1.09 suggest adequate growth.

CONCLUSION

Effective interventionists must have skills other than selecting effective interventions. They need to know how to select interventions and how to match them to student needs while ensuring adequate implementation integrity, how to assess student skills to determine need and to monitor progress, and how to interpret the data that they collect. In other words, interventionists need to understand EBIs, evidence-based assessments, and evidence-based analyses. The combination of these three skills are likely to ensure success.

PART II

Evidence-Based School Interventions

CHAPTER FOUR

Interventions to Improve Academic Performance

The majority of referrals to school psychologists involve students with academic problems (Bramlett et al., 2002). Given the increasing diversity of students being served in regular classrooms, including children of poverty, non-native English speakers, and students with disabilities, helping teachers implement instructional practices that can enhance the academic performance of groups of students as well as individual students is a priority for today's consultants. In particular, consultants need information about group-oriented interventions that promote academic productivity and achievement and can be implemented using regular curricular materials. Moreover, without appropriate early intervention, students who struggle with academic skills in early elementary school are likely to struggle academically throughout their school careers (Darney, Reinke, Herman, Stormont, & Ialongo, 2013).

Interventions that improve academic achievement are crucial not only to assisting students in meeting learning standards but also to promoting positive social outcomes. Academic achievement is strongly associated with social competence, beginning in the early primary grades (Reinke, Lewis-Palmer, & Merrell, 2008). The relationship between academic achievement and social competence is especially strong for reading, with mounting evidence that interventions that enhance reading skills can also have positive effects on behavior (Beck, Burns, & Lau, 2009; Lane, O'Shaughnessy, Lambros, Gresham, & Beebe-Frankenberger, 2001; Treptow et al., 2007).

Academically focused interventions have the potential to reduce disruptive behavior by creating a classroom ecology within which all students are productively engaged. The less "down time" there is, the fewer the opportunities are for off-task behavior to escalate into disruption. Moreover, strategies that increase students' ability to respond correctly to instruction are likely to reduce inappropriate behavior arising from students' effort to escape from tasks that they perceive as too difficult (Gunter, Hummel, & Conroy, 1998).

This chapter presents several interventions that consultants can use to improve the reading, writing, and mathematics skills of students in all grades. In addition, several interventions can be used with or adapted for small groups or even classwide efforts.

General Interventions to Improve Academic Performance

USING RESPONSE CARDS TO INCREASE
ACADEMIC ENGAGEMENT AND ACHIEVEMENT

Overview

Students learn and remember more when they actively respond during instruction. All too often, however, lesson formats fail to provide for sufficient participation, and students become passive observers of instruction. For low-performing students, this passivity compounds their problems because they lose opportunities to receive teacher feedback and improve their knowledge and skills. In this intervention, students write short answers on laminated boards in response to teacher questions during whole-class instruction. Response card lesson formats not only increase students' opportunities to respond but also effectively enhance instructional effectiveness by permitting teachers to conduct ongoing assessments of student performance, provide immediate feedback, and modify instruction until all students demonstrate understanding (Horn, 2010).

Response card instruction has been shown to enhance participation rates, on-task behavior, and academic achievement across a wide range of grade levels and subjects for students in general education, as well as for students with disabilities and English language learners (Christie & Schuster, 2003). Moreover, students enjoy the novelty of the strategy and prefer using response cards to raising their hands. First developed for use in social studies and science classes, response card instruction can be implemented in any subject and is especially effective as a review strategy during the last 5 or 10 minutes of an instructional period. A variation with a preprinted card format appropriate for younger students is also presented.

Goal

Response cards improve participation and learning by providing frequent opportunities for active student responding and immediate teacher feedback. Response cards fall into the category of a proficiency intervention because they are designed to facilitate practice after the skill has been initially taught.

Intervention Intensity

Response cards are most often used as a classwide intervention but could be easily adapted for small groups. It is likely not intense enough to be appropriate for individual interventions, but it could be modified for individual students.

Materials

1. Stopwatch or watch with second hand.
2. Weekly quiz, one quiz per student.
3. White laminated tileboards (9″ × 12″) or manila folders, cut in half and placed inside plastic sheet protectors, one per student.
4. Dry erase black markers, one per student.
5. Felt squares (about 4″ square), paper towels, or dry erasers, one per student.
6. 3″ × 5″ index cards with preprinted responses on either side (*Yes/No* or *True/False*), one per student; printing should be large enough to be easily read from the front of the room; alternately, use color-coded cards, with contrasting colors on either side of a

single card (e.g., red for *Yes*, blue for *No*) or two differently colored cards (optional; see Variation).

Options to Monitor Progress

1. Calculate the class average on weekly quizzes and/or chapter tests for a selected subject for the previous month by summing individual student scores and dividing by the total number of students.
2. Using a sheet of paper with a list of student names or a copy of a seating chart attached to a clipboard, record the number of times one or more target students respond to a question by hand raising during a selected instructional period for 4–7 days.
3. Calculate the percentage of students with grades of D or F in a selected subject for the current grading period or for the school year thus far.

Intervention Steps

Introduction and Training

1. Explain to the students that they will be learning a new and more interesting way to participate in class. Distribute the tileboard cards, markers, and erasers and conduct a 10- to 15-minute training session using the procedures described below.
2. Tell students to answer your questions by printing their answers in one or two words on their response cards. Pose a question and say, "Write your answer" to cue the students to begin writing. After 5 seconds, say "Cards up." Remind students to hold their cards above their heads so that you can see all responses.
3. Quickly scan all student responses and provide feedback as described below.
4. Say "Cards down" to signal students to lower their cards, erase the previous response, and prepare for the next response.

Implementation

1. During the lesson, present information for the first 15 or 20 minutes. After you present each new fact or concept, ask a question about it and have students respond by writing one- or two-word answers on their cards or folders and holding them up.
2. After visually scanning all of the response cards, provide praise for correct answers or corrective feedback for incorrect answers, as follows:
   a. If everyone has written the right answer, give the feedback to the whole class:

   "Good, class, I see that everyone wrote *gas*. Water vapor is a *gas*."

   b. If some students show incorrect answers, acknowledge that some have answered correctly and also provide the correct answer:

   "I see that many of you have *gas* as the answer. That is correct, water vapor is a *gas*."

   c. If no students have the correct answer, indicate this and provide the correct answer:

   "I do not see any correct answers. The correct answer is *gas*. Water vapor in the atmosphere is a *gas*."

3. Later in the lesson, ask a series of review questions related to the newly presented facts and concepts. Be sure to repeat any questions that were missed by a majority of students earlier in the lesson to ensure that students have understood their errors.
4. Praise students for using the response cards promptly and provide corrective feedback as needed.

Variation: Preprinted Response Card Format

Distribute preprinted cards at the beginning of each lesson. Teach students to respond to questions by displaying the side of the card with the answer toward you. Pose a question and say "Cards up." After you scan the cards, say "Cards down." Provide praise for correct answers and error feedback for incorrect answers. Conduct additional demonstrations and practice sessions if students are inadvertently displaying the wrong side of the card. For young students, use two differently colored cards.

NOTES

1. For self-contained classes, have students keep response card materials at their desks. For departmentalized classes, collect response card materials at the end of each period and distribute them prior to instruction.
2. To prevent doodling, tell students that you will give them 2 minutes (or some other amount of time) at the end of the period to draw on their cards, provided that they write only answers to teacher questions on their cards during instruction.
3. Although preprinted response cards are easier for teachers to see than write-on response cards, they are more time-consuming to prepare and limit responses to predetermined recognition-type responses. Write-on cards slow student responses and instructional pacing because more time is needed for writing and erasing answers and for teacher inspection, but they permit a much wider range of responses.

SOURCES

Christie, C. A., & Schuster, J. W. (2003). The effects of using response cards on student participation, academic achievement, and on-task behavior during whole-class, math instruction. *Journal of Behavioral Education, 12,* 147–165.

Horn, C. (2010). Response cards: An effective intervention for students with disabilities. *Education and Training in Autism and Developmental Disabilities, 45*(1), 116–123.

INCREMENTAL REHEARSAL FOR WORDS, MATH FACTS, AND LETTER SOUNDS

Overview

Incremental Rehearsal (IR; Tucker, 1989) is a flashcard technique that can be used with students with varying difficulties, for different age groups, and for various skills. IR presents a small percentage of new material within a high percentage of known items at a ratio of 1 unknown to 7, 8, or 9 knowns and rehearses the new item while incrementally increasing the number of knowns presented each time (e.g., first unknown, first known, first unknown, first known, second known, first unknown, first known, second known, third known, first unknown, second known, third known, fourth known . . . eighth and final known). Research has consistently shown that IR increases retention and generalization for word recognition, math facts, vocabulary, letter sounds, and many other skills (Burns, Zaslofsky, Kanive, & Parker, 2012). In fact, IR is the most frequently researched flashcard approach and has consistently been shown to be more effective than any other. Although the intervention uses flashcards, it can also be done with any presentation venue, such as pointing to stimuli, using pictures, or presenting known and unknowns within a computer program.

IR is an intensive intervention and should only be used for students who really struggle with retaining and using newly learned information. It is generally used after a skill or stimulus has been initially taught. For example, IR could be used for math facts after the student understands the concept of the operation or for letter sounds after they have been taught what sound the letter makes in context. The intervention is described here for use with word recognition, math facts, and letter sounds, but IR could be used for almost any material that requires rote memorization.

Goal

The goal of IR is to increase how well students retain newly learned information. It can assist students in remembering any basic fact, such as math facts, sight words, letter sounds, vocabulary words, and so forth. It is designed to increase retention. Thus IR is a maintenance intervention.

Intervention Intensity

IR is intended to be an intensive intervention. It is usually delivered one-on-one and is for students for whom other, less intensive interventions did not work.

Materials

1. A list of known and unknown items.
2. 3" × 5" index cards on which to write knowns and unknowns.

Options to Monitor Progress

1. Perhaps the best and quickest way to monitor progress is to show the card that was taught 1, 2, or 7 days earlier and ask the student to provide the correct answer. Record the number (and percentage) of items correctly answered within 2 seconds.
2. Provide the student with examples of each stimulus in a generalized context—for example, taught letter sounds in words, taught words in sentences, and word problems for taught math facts. Record the number and percentage of correctly generalized stimuli.

Intervention Steps

Introduction and Training

1. Begin by assessing what the student knows and does not know.
2. Individually present each potential unknown stimulus to the student in random order to assess whether it is known or unknown. Stimuli correctly identified (e.g., words read, sound given for a letter, correct answer to a math fact) by the student within 2 seconds of presentation are considered known, and those not correctly identified within 2 seconds are unknown. The time limit of 2 seconds is oftentimes used to assess known words, but 3 seconds could be used for English language learners to accommodate for dialectical and pronunciation issues.
3. Write each unknown item horizontally on a 3" × 5" index card. Also write down 8–10 known items on an index card that the student can read within 1 second of presentation. The latter items will be used as known words.

Steps for Reading Words

1. Present the first unknown word to the student while verbally providing the correct pronunciation. Next, ask the student to orally restate the word.
2. Ask the student to use the word in a sentence. If the word is used grammatically and semantically correctly, even if the sentence is simplistic, then reinforce the child and move to Step 5. If the word is not correctly used, then provide a short definition or synonym and use the word in a sentence. Next, ask the child to make up a different sentence with the word in it and move to the next step if he or she does so correctly. Words not used correctly at this point should be removed and instructed in more depth.
3. Rehearse the unknown word with the following sequence and ask the student to state the word every time it is presented:
   a. Present the first unknown word and the first known word.
   b. Present the first unknown word, the first known word, and the second known word.
   c. Present the first unknown word, the first known word, the second known word, and the third known word.
   d. Present the first unknown word, the first known word, the second known word, the third known word, and the fourth known word.
   e. Present the first unknown word, the first known word, the second known word, the third known word, the fourth known word, and the fifth known word.
   f. Present the first unknown word, the first known word, the second known word, the third known word, the fourth known word, the fifth known word, and the sixth known word.
   g. Present the first unknown word, the first known word, the second known word, the third known word, the fourth known word, the fifth known word, the sixth known word, and the seventh known word.
   h. Present the first unknown word, the first known word, the second known word, the third known word, the fourth known word, the fifth known word, the sixth known word, the seventh known word, and the eighth known word.
4. After completing the rehearsal sequence with the first word, that first unknown word is then treated as the first known, the previous eighth known is removed, and a new unknown word is introduced. Thus the number of cards always remains nine.
5. Continue individually rehearsing unknown words until three errors occur while rehearsing one word. Errors need not occur only on the word currently being rehearsed. Any inability to state a word correctly within 3 seconds counts as an error, even if that error occurs on a previously rehearsed word or a word that was known before the sequence began.

Steps for Math Facts

1. Present the first unknown fact to the student while verbally providing the correct pronunciation. Next, ask the student to orally restate the fact. For example, say, "Three times six is eighteen. What is three times six?" If the child responds, "Eighteen," then say, "Three times six is eighteen. Please say the correct answer when you see this problem."
2. Rehearse the unknown fact with the following sequence and ask the student to state the fact every time it is presented:
   a. Present the first unknown fact and the first known fact.
   b. Present the first unknown fact, the first known fact, and the second known fact.
   c. Present the first unknown fact, the first known fact, the second known fact, and the third known fact.

    d. Present the first unknown fact, the first known fact, the second known fact, the third known fact, and the fourth known fact.

    e. Present the first unknown fact, the first known fact, the second known fact, the third known fact, the fourth known fact, and the fifth known fact.

    f. Present the first unknown fact, the first known fact, the second known fact, the third known fact, the fourth known fact, the fifth known fact, and the sixth known fact.

    g. Present the first unknown fact, the first known fact, the second known fact, the third known fact, the fourth known fact, the fifth known fact, the sixth known fact, and the seventh known fact.

    h. Present the first unknown fact, the first known fact, the second known fact, the third known fact, the fourth known fact, the fifth known fact, the sixth known fact, the seventh known fact, and the eighth known fact.

3. After completing the rehearsal sequence with the first fact, that first unknown fact is then treated as the first known, the previous eighth known is removed, and a new unknown fact is introduced. Thus the number of cards always remains nine.

4. Continue individually rehearsing unknown facts until three errors occur while rehearsing one fact. Errors need not occur only on the fact currently being rehearsed. Any inability to state a fact correctly within 3 seconds counts as an error, even if that error occurs on a previously rehearsed fact or a fact that was known before the sequence began.

Steps for Letter Sounds

1. Present the first unknown letter to the student while verbally providing the correct pronunciation. Next, ask the student to orally restate the letter and sound.

2. Ask the student to think of a word that starts with the given sound. If the student provides a correct word that starts with the sound, then reinforce the child and move to Step 3. If the word is not correct or if the student does not provide a word, then provide a word for him or her that starts with the sound and ask him or her to provide a different word. If the student still does not provide a correct word that starts with the sound, then proceed, but the student may need additional support with phonemic awareness.

3. Rehearse the unknown letter with the following sequence and ask the student to state the letter sound every time the letter it is presented:

    a. Present the first unknown letter and the first known letter.

    b. Present the first unknown letter, the first known letter, and the second known letter.

    c. Present the first unknown letter, the first known letter, the second known letter, and the third known letter.

    d. Present the first unknown letter, the first known letter, the second known letter, the third known letter, and the fourth known letter.

    e. Present the first unknown letter, the first known letter, the second known letter, the third known letter, the fourth known letter, and the fifth known letter.

    f. Present the first unknown letter, the first known letter, the second known letter, the third known letter, the fourth known letter, the fifth known letter, and the sixth known letter.

    g. Present the first unknown letter, the first known letter, the second known letter, the third known letter, the fourth known letter, the fifth known letter, the sixth known letter, and the seventh known letter.

    h. Present the first unknown letter, the first known letter, the second known letter, the third known letter, the fourth known letter, the fifth known letter, the sixth known letter, the seventh known letter, and the eighth known letter.

4. After completing the rehearsal sequence with the first letter, that first unknown letter is then treated as the first known, the previous eighth known is removed, and a new unknown letter is introduced. Thus the number of cards always remains nine.

5. Continue individually rehearsing unknown letters until three errors occur while rehearsing one letter. Errors need not occur only on the letter currently being rehearsed. Any inability to state a letter sound correctly within 2 seconds counts as an error, even if that error occurs on a previously rehearsed letter or a letter that was known before the sequence began.

6. If the student is in kindergarten or first grade, then consider using only five knowns to keep the intervention session shorter. It may also be appropriate to use different stimuli as knowns. For example, letter sounds can be taught using picture cards or shapes as knowns, and the student would merely name the picture or shape when the card is presented.

SOURCES

Burns, M. K., Riley-Tillman, T. C., & VanDerHeyden, A. M. (2012). *RTI applications: Vol. 1. Academic and behavioral interventions.* New York: Guilford Press.

Burns, M. K., Zaslofsky, A. F., Kanive, R., & Parker, D. C. (2012). Meta-analysis of incremental rehearsal using phi coefficients to compare single-case and group designs. *Journal of Behavioral Education, 21,* 185–202.

Tucker, J. A. (1988). *Basic flashcard technique when vocabulary is the goal.* Unpublished teaching materials, School of Education, University of Chattanooga. Chattanooga, TN.

ADDITIONAL RESOURCES

The link from the Evidence-Based Intervention Network (*http://ebi.missouri.edu/?s=incremental*) includes a description of procedures, video models, and summaries of research. The following articles examine the use of IR with various stimuli and include implementation procedures.

Bunn, R., Burns, M. K., Hoffman, H. H., & Newman, C. L. (2005). Using incremental rehearsal to teach letter identification with a preschool-aged child. *Journal of Evidence Based Practice for Schools, 6,* 124–134.

Burns, M. K., Dean, V. J., & Foley, S. (2004). Preteaching unknown key words with incremental rehearsal to improve reading fluency and comprehension with children identified as reading disabled. *Journal of School Psychology, 42,* 303–314.

Codding, R. S., Archer, J., & Connell, J. (2010). A systematic replication and extension of using incremental rehearsal to improve multiplication skills: An investigation of generalization. *Journal of Behavioral Education, 19,* 93–105.

Volpe, R. J., Burns, M. K., DuBois, M., & Zaslofsky, A. F. (2011). Computer-assisted tutoring: Teaching letter sounds to kindergarten students using incremental rehearsal. *Psychology in the Schools, 48,* 332–342.

COVER, COPY, AND COMPARE:
INCREASING ACADEMIC PERFORMANCE WITH SELF-MANAGEMENT

Overview

The Cover, Copy, and Compare (CCC) strategy is a self-managed intervention that can be used to enhance accuracy and fluency in a variety of academic skill domains. Students look at an academic stimulus (such as a multiplication problem for CCC Mathematics or a spelling word for CCC Spelling), cover it, copy it, and evaluate their response by comparing it to the original model. If an error is made, the student engages in a brief error correction procedure before proceeding to the next item. CCC combines several empirically based intervention components, including self-instruction, increased opportunities to respond to academic material, and immediate corrective feedback. CCC has been successful in improving academic engagement and achievement for students with and without disabilities in elementary, middle school, and high school classrooms across a wide variety of subjects, including mathematics, science, geography, spelling, and word recognition (Conley, Derby, Roberts-Gwinn, Weber, & McLaughlin, 2004; Skinner, McLaughlin, & Logan, 1997). High in usability, it requires little student training or teacher time, other than worksheet preparation. CCC can be implemented as a whole-class activity or as part of an independent seatwork period while the teacher works with individual students or small groups. Procedures for a generic CCC version and for CCC in four academic subjects are presented. Two variations designed to enhance motivation during CCC sessions by means of group contingencies and public posting are also included.

Goal

CCC improves accuracy and fluency in basic academic skills by teaching students a self-management procedure that provides increased opportunities to respond to academic material. Given that CCC increases accuracy, it is an acquisition intervention. However, it should not be used as a means to first teach a skill, but only to practice it in a way that increases accuracy among students who do not respond accurately.

Intervention Intensity

CCC is most appropriate for small groups of students who require additional support completing skills with accuracy. It could be modified for classroom applications, but it does not provide sufficient support to be an intensive intervention for individual students. Interventionists should consider a more intensive intervention such as IR if a more intensive intervention is needed or if CCC is not successful.

Materials for CCC in Any Subject

1. Worksheets with 10–15 problems or items in the target subject; problems should be listed on the left side of the paper with space at the right for copying and correction, one to three worksheets per student.
2. 3″ × 5″ index cards, one per student (optional; see Note 2).
3. Overhead projector and transparency with sample worksheet (optional).
4. Stopwatch, timer, or watch with second hand.
5. Folders containing sheets of lined paper or graph paper, one per student.
6. Posterboard chart for displaying the class average number of correctly completed problems during timed tests (optional; see Variation 2).

Additional Materials for CCC Mathematics

Math worksheets, with computation problems and the answers listed on the left side of the sheet and the same problems on the right, unsolved, one to three worksheets per student.

Additional Materials for CCC Spelling

Spelling worksheets, with 10–15 spelling words (5–10 words for early primary grade students) listed on the left side of the sheet and blank lines on the right for writing each word, including space for corrections, one to three worksheets per student. For classrooms using differentiated spelling instruction, prepare one set of worksheets per spelling group.

Additional Materials for CCC Vocabulary

Vocabulary worksheet, with 10–15 vocabulary words and their definitions listed on the left side of the sheet and blank lines on the right for writing each word and a definition for that word, one per student. For classrooms using differentiated reading instruction, prepare one set of worksheets per reading group.

Additional Materials for CCC Word Identification

Word list worksheet, divided into three vertical sections, with a list of 10–15 words (5–10 words for early primary grade students) in the left-hand section, the words written again in dashed lines in the middle section, and blank lines for writing each word in the right-hand section, one per student. For classrooms using differentiated reading instruction, prepare one set of worksheets per reading group.

Options to Monitor Progress

1. Calculate percent-correct scores on daily classwork, quizzes, or tests in a selected subject for 5–10 days for the entire class or a target group of students.
2. Administer curriculum-based measurement probes in the selected subject to the entire class or a target group of students.

Intervention Steps

Introduction and Training

1. Tell the students that they will be learning a new method of improving their performance in the selected subject called Cover, Copy, and Compare, or CCC.
2. Give each student a copy of a CCC worksheet in the target subject. Demonstrate the use of the CCC procedure as described below, using your own copy of the worksheet or a transparency displayed on an overhead projector.
3. After the demonstration, conduct a classwide practice in which students complete one or more worksheets or item sets. Remind students that they will not benefit from the CCC strategy if they simply copy the correct item from the model rather than attempting to solve or study it first. Provide corrective feedback as needed and praise the students for managing their own learning.

CCC MATHEMATICS

1. Silently read the first problem and the answer on the left side of the paper.
2. Cover the problem and answer with an index card or your nonwriting hand.
3. Write the problem and answer from memory in the space on the right side of the paper.

4. Uncover the problem and answer on the left side to check your response.
5. Evaluate your response. If the problem is written incorrectly and/or the answer is incorrect, repeat the procedure with that item before proceeding to the next item.

CCC SPELLING

1. Silently read the first word on the list on the left side of the paper.
2. Cover the word with an index card or your nonwriting hand and write it again from memory on the blank line on the right side of the paper.
3. Uncover the word on the left and compare it with your spelling of the word.
4. Evaluate your response. If your spelling is incorrect, repeat the procedure with that word before proceeding to the next word.

CCC VOCABULARY

1. Silently read the first word on the list and its definition on the left side of the paper.
2. Cover the word with an index card or your nonwriting hand and write both the word and its definition on the blank line on the right side of the paper.
3. Uncover the word on the left and compare your definition with the model.
4. Evaluate your response. If the definition is inaccurate or incomplete, repeat the procedure with that word before proceeding to the next word.

Implementation

1. Implement the CCC procedure several times a week in the target subject. Because CCC can become tedious if it is implemented too often and for too long a period, use it primarily as a review at the end of a lesson or as one of several activities during independent seatwork.
2. For instructional periods during which all students are simultaneously participating in CCC, set a fixed amount of time for the CCC session (5–15 minutes), signal students to begin, and have them complete as many trials as possible during that time.
3. When students reach mastery level (90% or above accuracy) on one set of problems or items, provide them with another set. For CCC Spelling and Vocabulary, include two or three words from prior lists on the new list to promote retention.
4. Once a week, administer a worksheet based on the material that has been practiced during the CCC period as a timed 3-minute assessment. For CCC Spelling, dictate spelling words for 3 minutes. Have students exchange papers, score them under your direction, and graph the number of items completed correctly in 3 minutes or spelled correctly on the spelling assessment in their subject-area folders.

Variations

VARIATION 1: CCC WITH CLASSWIDE INCENTIVES FOR BEHAVIOR

During CCC sessions, record bonus points on the chalkboard for appropriate CCC behaviors and deduct points if you observe students copying the answers without going through the entire procedure. When the class has accumulated a specified number of points, deliver an activity-based reward, such as extra recess, music time, or an in-class game.

VARIATION 2: CCC WITH CLASSWIDE INCENTIVES FOR PERFORMANCE

Record the total number of problems completed correctly on the weekly timed CCC assessments on the chalkboard or chart. When the number reaches a specified goal (e.g., 300 correctly completed math problems), celebrate with a classwide reward, such as a pizza, popcorn, or ice cream party.

NOTES

1. As students become proficient in using the CCC procedure in one subject, add CCC in another subject in which basic skills practice is needed.
2. Using index cards as covers may slow some students down and make the procedure more cumbersome (Skinner et al., 1997). Alternately, have students fold their worksheets in half lengthwise, so that the answers appear on one side and the blank lines or problems without solutions appear on the other side. For each item, have students look at the model and then fold the sheet over to the right side, covering the model with the correct answer, before responding.
3. Preparing worksheets with a larger number of problems or items (20–30) eliminates the need for several sets of sheets per session.

SOURCES

Conley, C. M., Derby, K. M., Roberts-Gwinn, M., Weber, K. P., & McLaughlin, T. F. (2004). An analysis of initial acquisition and maintenance of sight words following picture matching and Copy, Cover, and Compare teaching methods. *Journal of Applied Behavior Analysis, 37,* 339–350.

Skinner, C. H., McLaughlin, T. F., & Logan, P. (1997). Cover, Copy, and Compare: A self-managed academic intervention effective across skills, students, and settings. *Journal of Behavioral Education, 7,* 295–306.

ADDITIONAL RESOURCES

The link from the Intervention Central website (*www.interventioncentral.org/tools.php*) is to a math worksheet generator, which creates worksheets for the four basic math operations in a CCC format.

    The link from the Evidence-Based Intervention Network (*http://ebi.missouri.edu/?cat= 36&paged=2*) includes a form for the technique, a video modeling it, and a brief of the evidence.

CLASSWIDE PEER TUTORING

Overview

Classwide Peer Tutoring (CWPT) is a low-cost, efficient instructional intervention that enhances student achievement by increasing opportunities for active responding and immediate feedback. Unlike traditional peer tutoring, which is designed to remediate the deficiencies of individual pupils by pairing them with higher achieving students, CWPT was developed specifically to provide additional academic practice for every student in a classroom. Moreover, because peer tutors are provided with the correct answers for tutoring tasks, the strategy permits immediate error correction. In CWPT, students practice basic academic skills four times a week, with each student serving as tutor and tutee during a 30-minute tutoring period. On Fridays, students are tested on the material presented during the week and are pretested on the material for the upcoming week. CWPT includes both competitive and collaborative structures, with tutoring pairs organized into teams that earn points for accurate performance and appropriate tutoring behavior.

CWPT has been successful in improving academic achievement, productivity, and attitudes toward learning in a wide variety of subjects and in regular, inclusive, and special education settings (Bowman-Perrott et al., 2013). Moreover, longitudinal studies indicate that students participating in CWPT show higher levels of academic engagement and achievement and are less likely to need special education services and to drop out of school, compared with students not receiving CWPT (Burks, 2004). In addition to general CWPT procedures, specific procedures for implementing CWPT in oral reading, word identification, and spelling are presented, including two adaptations for English language learners (Greenwood, Arreaga-Mayer, Utley, Gavin, & Terry, 2001).

Goal

CWPT is used to improve academic productivity and achievement by increasing opportunities for students to respond and receive immediate feedback without increasing the amount of instructional time. CWPT can be used for a variety of academic skills, but is designed to help students become more proficient.

Intervention Intensity

CWPT is explicitly designed for classroom applications. It has strong potential to address potential difficulties within core instruction and could be applied to small groups as well.

Materials for CWPT in Any Subject

1. Box containing red and blue slips of construction paper, with an equal number of each color and summing to the number of students in the class.
2. Curricular materials appropriate for basic skills practice, one set per student pair.
3. Point sheets, consisting of sheets of paper or index cards with a list of consecutive numbers, one per student.
4. Kitchen timer with bell, stopwatch with audible signal, or watch.
5. "Team Points Chart," consisting of a posterboard chart or section of the chalkboard listing team names, with columns for posting team point totals and daily and weekly winning teams.
6. Adhesive stars or stickers.

Additional Materials for CWPT in Vocabulary

1. Vocabulary flashcards (bilingual cards for the English language learner adaptation).
2. "Smiley faces" and question marks, about 5 inches in height, made of colored construction paper (English language learner adaptation).
3. Overhead projector and transparencies with lists of vocabulary words or colored chalk (English language learner adaptation).

Additional Materials for CWPT in Spelling

1. List of spelling words or regular spelling materials, one per student pair.

2. Notebooks or folders with sheets of ruled paper, one per student (see Implementation section).
3. Overhead projector and transparencies or SMART Board with lists of spelling words or colored chalk (English language learner adaptation).

Additional Materials for CWPT in Mathematics

Math flashcards or worksheets with math problems.

Additional Materials for CWPT in Social Studies, Science, Language Arts, or Other Subject Areas

Workbook pages or textbook-based reproducible skill sheets, one uncompleted page and one correctly completed page per student pair.

Options to Monitor Progress

1. Calculate percent-correct scores on daily classwork, quizzes, or end-of-unit tests for the entire class or a group of target students in the selected subject for 5–10 days or for the current grading period.
2. Using a *Group Interval Recording Form* with a 15-second interval, begin at the left side of the room and glance at each student in turn. Record a plus (+) if the student is on task for the duration of the interval and a minus (–) if the student is off task at any time during the interval. When you have rated each student, begin again at the left side of the room.
   a. *On-task behavior* is defined as looking at the teacher or an appropriately participating peer, answering teacher-delivered questions, working on lesson materials, and any other task-related behavior.
   b. *Off-task behavior* is defined as being out of seat, talking without permission, playing with nonlesson materials, and any other behavior interfering with task completion for oneself or others.
   c. Conduct these observations for 30–45 minutes during the selected instructional period for 4–7 days.
3. Administer curriculum-based measurement probes in the selected subject to a group of target students or to the entire class.

Intervention Steps

Introduction and Training

1. Explain to the students that they will be learning an enjoyable new way of working together to get more out of their lessons.
2. Demonstrate the tutoring procedures as described below, with yourself as tutor and a student as tutee. Then select two more students and guide them through the procedures, while the other students observe, and provide praise and corrective feedback as needed. Conduct two more brief demonstrations with other student pairs and then guide students through a classwide tutoring session. As part of the training, teach students to talk only during tutoring sessions, speak only to their tutoring partners, and use "inside" voices.
3. On Fridays, have students draw names from the box for assignment to one of two teams for the coming week. Within each team, form random pairs in subjects in which tutors can use a master sheet with the correct answers for checking tutees' responses, such as

spelling, vocabulary, mathematics, and the content areas. For tutoring in oral reading, pair students with similar skill levels. For CWPT with English language learners, pair low-achieving with average-achieving students and average-achieving with high-achieving students, based on level of English proficiency and past progress in reading. Pair students new to the United States with bilingual students, if possible. Then assign each pair of students to one of two teams. Change tutoring pairs and team assignments each week.

Implementation

1. The entire CWPT procedure requires 30 minutes, during which each student tutors for 10 minutes and receives tutoring for 10 minutes. An additional 5–10 minutes is needed to sum and post individual and team points. For students in grades 1 and 2, shorten tutoring times from 10 minutes to 5 minutes per student.
2. Begin the session by asking students to move to their tutoring stations (paired desks or some other arrangement). Designate one partner in each pair as the first tutor and distribute point sheets and CWPT tutoring materials.
3. Set the timer for 10 minutes. The tutor presents the items one at a time (e.g., math flashcards, vocabulary or spelling words, social studies questions), and the tutee responds orally for oral reading or vocabulary and in writing for other subjects.
4. If the answer is correct, the tutor awards 2 points on the tutee's point sheet. If the answer is incorrect, the tutor provides the correct response, asks the tutee to write or say the correct answer three times, and then awards 1 point for the correction. Tutors present the reading passage, word or spelling list, flashcards, or set of items as many times as possible during the 10 minutes.
5. After 10 minutes, students switch roles and repeat the procedures for another 10 minutes.
6. During CWPT time, monitor tutoring by moving around the classroom, answering questions, giving corrective feedback, and awarding bonus points (1 point per pair per session) for correct tutoring procedures and cooperative behavior.
7. When the timer rings at the end of the next 10 minutes, have each pair of students report the total points earned (or their individual points; see below). Sum the points for each team and record the total score for each team on the Team Points Chart.
8. Lead the class in applauding the winning team for the day and place a star or sticker next to the team name. Also lead a round of applause for the losing team for its efforts.
9. On Friday, administer a test on the materials students have practiced. Have team pairs exchange papers, correct each other's answers, and award 5–10 points for each correct response. Enter these scores on the Team Points Chart and determine a weekly team winner. If desired, also administer a pretest of the material to be covered in the coming week. Have students exchange papers and correct them. Use these scores to help determine student pairs for the coming week.
10. Also on Friday, lead the class in applauding the winning team of the week. If desired, award a privilege to winning team members, such as lining up first for lunch. The losing team is also applauded for good effort and sportsmanship.

CWPT IN WORD IDENTIFICATION

1. Give each student pair a set of reading flashcards and two point sheets. The tutor shows the first flashcard to the tutee. If the tutee pronounces the word correctly, the tutor places the flashcard back in the pack and awards 2 points.
2. If the tutee does not pronounce the word correctly, the tutor supplies the correct word. The tutee then pronounces the word once and receives 1 point. If neither student in the pair knows the word, the students raise their hands to request teacher assistance.

3. Following the tutee's correct response, the tutor places the flashcard to the side for additional practice during the session.
4. After 10 minutes, students reverse roles and repeat the procedures.

CWPT IN WORD IDENTIFICATION: ADAPTATION FOR ENGLISH LANGUAGE LEARNERS (SPANISH EXAMPLE)

1. Prior to the CWPT session, introduce the new set of words in a whole-class format using bilingual flashcards, as described below.
   a. First pronounce each word in Spanish and have students repeat the word in Spanish. Then pronounce each word in English and have students repeat the word in English.
   b. Verbally spell each word in English and have students verbally spell the words in English.
2. Pair students as described above for English language learners and then follow the CWPT word identification procedures.

CWPT IN SPELLING

1. Give each student pair the weekly spelling list for the entire class or their spelling group and two lined sheets of paper.
2. The tutor presents the first spelling word. The tutee pronounces the word and spells it aloud while writing it on the sheet of paper.
3. If the word is correct, the tutor says, "Correct, give yourself 2 points!" and the tutee marks a "2" beside the word on the practice sheet.
4. If the word is incorrect, the tutor points to, pronounces, and spells the missed word. The tutee must write the missed word correctly three times before receiving the next word.
5. If the tutee writes it correctly three times, the tutor awards 1 point. If any of the three practice words were spelled incorrectly, the tutee receives 0 points.
6. After 10 minutes, students switch roles.

CWPT IN SPELLING: ADAPTATION FOR ENGLISH LANGUAGE LEARNERS (SPANISH EXAMPLE)

1. Prior to the CWPT session, present the new spelling words on the chalkboard or using an overhead projector, with each word spelled in Spanish and English.
2. English words should be divided into syllables of different colors, with prefixes identified by the color red and suffixes by the color blue.
3. Pair students as described above for English language learners and then follow the CWPT spelling procedures.

NOTES

1. Training takes two 30- to 45-minute sessions. During the first session, explain the partner and team formats, the process of awarding points, and tutoring procedures. During the second training session, review transitioning to and from CWPT sessions and provide additional practice in the tutoring procedures.
2. Creating a permanent classroom arrangement of paired desks greatly facilitates implementation and reduces downtime while students reposition their desks.
3. Field testing indicates that beginning with a highly structured subject, such as spelling or math-

ematics computation, facilitates implementation. When students have mastered the procedures, introduce CWPT in another area, such as word identification or oral reading.

4. Teachers considering CWPT sometimes express concern that the intervention will lead to increased noise levels and will diminish their control over student behavior. An orderly environment can be maintained by continually monitoring during CWPT (vs. grading papers or performing other administrative tasks), awarding bonus points for following the rules, and administering brief time-outs from the opportunity to earn points by having students put their pencils down for 15–30 seconds if classroom noise becomes excessive.

5. Although the standard version of CWPT does not include any contingencies other than teacher praise and public recognition, field testing indicates that awarding a small privilege to members of the daily and weekly winning team, such as lining up first for lunch, specials, or dismissal, enhances motivation.

SOURCES

Bowman-Perrott, L., Davis, H., Vannest, K., Williams, L., Greenwood, C., & Parker, R. (2013). Academic benefits of peer tutoring: A meta-analytic review of single-case research. *School Psychology Review, 42,* 39–55.

Burks, M. (2004). Effects of Classwide Peer Tutoring on the number of words spelled correctly by students with LD. *Intervention in School and Clinic, 39,* 301–304.

Greenwood, C. R., Arreaga-Mayer, C., Utley, C. A., Gavin, K. M., & Terry, B. J. (2001). Classwide Peer Tutoring Learning Management System: Applications with elementary-level English language learners. *Remedial and Special Education, 22,* 34–47.

ADDITIONAL RESOURCES

Greenwood, C. R., Delquadri, J., & Hall, R. V. (1997). *Together we can: Classwide Peer Tutoring for basic academic skills.* Longmont, CO: Sopris West.

The Juniper Gardens website (*www.jgcp.ku.edu*) provides information about CWPT, including the Classwide Peer Tutoring Learning Management System (CWPT-LMS), a computerized teacher support program for managing student progress in CWPT instruction and program implementation. Included are a formative evaluation system, a CWPT advisor and teacher mentor, and the capability to create data and performance graphics.

SELF-MONITORING OF ACADEMIC PRODUCTIVITY

Overview

Teachers often feel that they must waste valuable instructional time reminding students to begin and complete classroom tasks in a timely manner. In this simple, cost-effective strategy, students learn to monitor and rate themselves on a set of behaviors that enhance the likelihood of academic success, including attending to directions, beginning assignments promptly, and asking appropriately for help when needed. Self-monitoring interventions are especially appropriate for targeting academic productivity because they shift the responsibility for managing academic assignments and task-related behaviors from teachers to students. When used on a classwide basis, they not only help students become more independent learners, but they also give teachers more time for instruction.

The intervention can be used to promote on-task behavior and academic productivity in any instructional format, including whole-class instruction, small-group instruction, and independent seatwork. In the original study, implemented in language arts, reading, and computer classes with four at-risk middle school students, self-monitoring produced immediate increases in on-task behavior and improvement in academic performance for all four target students across all three classroom settings (Wood, Murdock, Cronin, Dawson, & Kirby, 1998). More recent research found that self-monitoring increased academic engagement, decreased problem behavior, and increased productivity and accuracy of school work with students with disabilities (Rock, 2005). Three variations are presented: one for use with an individual student or small group, one for multisubject implementation, and one with an interdependent group contingency to encourage productivity and accurate self-evaluation.

Goal

Self-monitoring increases academic productivity by teaching students to monitor their own behaviors while performing daily classwork assignments. It should only be used with students who can successfully complete the task. Monitoring frustration will have a negative impact on students. Therefore, self-monitoring falls within the proficiency category of interventions because it is designed to help students complete work more quickly while being more productive.

Intervention Intensity

Self-monitoring can be added to most interventions. It is likely not feasible for a classroom but could be used for small groups or with individual students who need intensive support.

Materials

1. Self-monitoring forms, one per student (see Figure 4.1).
2. Posterboard chart and gold adhesive stars (optional; see Variation 3).

Options to Monitor Progress

1. Select an instructional period during which students are especially off task and unproductive. Using a *Classwide Scanning Form* with a 5-minute interval, scan the room at the end of each interval, starting with the front of the room and ending with the back, and tally the number of students in each of the following behavior categories:
   a. *On-task behavior,* defined as working on the assigned task, asking or answering teacher-delivered questions, following teacher directions, and performing other behaviors relevant to the lesson.
   b. *Off-task behavior,* defined as sitting without having appropriate materials at hand, gazing around the room or at classmates, or any other unengaged behavior.
   c. *Disruptive behavior,* defined as making noises, calling out, getting out of seat, arguing with peers, or any other behavior that interferes with ongoing instruction.
   Conduct these observations for 30–45 minutes a day for 4–7 days.
2. Calculate percent-correct scores on daily classwork assignments in a selected subject for a group of target students or the entire class for 5–10 days or the previous grading period. If desired, calculate the class average percent-correct score for daily classwork assignments by summing percent-correct scores for each student and dividing by the number of students in the class.
3. Calculate the number of daily classwork assignments completed with 80% accuracy or above in the selected subject for a group of target students or the entire class for 5–10 days.

Name: _____ Date: _____ Subject: _____

1. I was ready to begin working at the start of class.	_____ Yes	_____ No
2. I began working as soon as I could.	_____ Yes	_____ No
3. I worked hard.	_____ Yes	_____ No
4. I did everything that I was supposed to.	_____ Yes	_____ No
5. I raised my hand and talked during class.	_____ Yes	_____ No
6. I paid attention.	_____ Yes	_____ No
7. I asked for help when I needed it by raising my hand.	_____ Yes	_____ No
8. I got the assignment done.	_____ Yes	_____ No
9. I looked over my paper before I turned it in.	_____ Yes	_____ No
10. I turned in my assignment.	_____ Yes	_____ No

FIGURE 4.1. Sample self-monitoring sheet: Checklist for Success. From Wood, Murdock, Cronin, Dawson, and Kirby (1998, pp. 266–268). Copyright 1998 by Springer Science and Business Media. Adapted by permission.

Intervention Steps

Introduction and Training

1. Explain to the class that they will be learning how to improve their grades in the selected subject by monitoring their own behavior during classwork time.
2. Lead a discussion about behaviors that facilitate successful completion of daily assignments (e.g., listening to directions, beginning promptly, and completing the entire assignment) and those that interfere with success (e.g., failing to pay attention to directions, not asking for help when needed, and not working hard until the task is completed).
3. Give each student a copy of the self-monitoring forms and review the behaviors that students will be observing and evaluating. Demonstrate examples of productive and unproductive behavior during classwork time and have students use their self-monitoring forms to rate your behavior. Circulate to review student responses, and provide assistance and feedback as needed.
4. Tell students that you will give them a few minutes each day at the end of the period to ask themselves if they have performed the target behaviors and to complete the self-monitoring forms. After they have completed the forms, you will walk around the room to review everyone's response.

Implementation

1. Distribute the self-monitoring forms at the beginning of the period.
2. Five minutes before the end of the period, instruct students to complete the forms. After students have had time to rate their behaviors, circulate and scan each form as you move around the room. If you observe that a student has been inaccurate in his or her self-evaluations, provide brief private feedback. If many students are inaccurate, conduct an additional review of the procedures.

Variations

VARIATION 1: SELF-MONITORING WITH ONE STUDENT OR A SMALL GROUP
OF TARGET STUDENTS

To implement with one or a small group of target students, provide training on an individual basis and tailor the items on the form to the specific problem behaviors. Review the form privately with the students at the end of the period. If desired, have students take their forms home to be signed by parents and returned the following day.

VARIATION 2: SELF-MONITORING IN MULTIPLE SUBJECTS

For implementation in more than one subject, have students use one form per subject and keep the forms in their subject-area folder or notebook. Conduct periodic spot checks of self-monitoring accuracy and provide praise and corrective feedback as needed.

VARIATION 3: SELF-MONITORING WITH A GROUP CONTINGENCY

Each day that at least 80% of the students have 80% success or more on their self-monitoring sheets (or some other criterion) and you agree with those ratings, select a student to put a gold star on the chart. If the class accumulates four stars during the week, provide a group activity reward on Friday, such as extra recess, game time, or music time. Gradually raise the criterion as student productivity increases.

SOURCES

Rock, M. L. (2005). Use of strategic self-monitoring to enhance academic engagement, productivity, and accuracy of students with and without exceptionalities. *Journal of Positive Behavior Interventions, 7*, 3–17.
Wood, S. J., Murdock, J. Y., Cronin, M. E., Dawson, N. M., & Kirby, P. C. (1998). Effects of self-monitoring on on-task behaviors of at-risk middle school students. *Journal of Behavioral Education, 8*, 263–279.

Interventions to Improve Reading Performance

Reading difficulties are by far the most common reason for referral to intervention teams (Bramlett et al., 2002), and a specific learning disability in reading is by far the most commonly identified special education disability (National Center for Education Statistics, 2016). Poor reading skills are closely linked to increased likelihood of dropping out of high school (Bridgeland, Dilulio, & Morison, 2006), and severe reading difficulties can impede a student's ability to find and keep a job after high school (Wagner, Newman, Cameto, Garza, & Levine, 2005).

School personnel appear to be considerably more knowledgeable about reading than in previous years, due in large part to the National Reading Panel (NRP; 2000) and its various reports. The NRP presented reading as consisting of three major components: alphabetics (phonemic awareness and phonics instruction), reading fluency, and comprehension (including vocabulary and comprehension instruction). Subsequent research has shown that reading interventions can be targeted to students' needs within the NRP framework to enhance the likelihood of success (Burns et al., 2016). Quality instruction should address all NRP areas, but it is likely that early elementary-age children demonstrate more deficits related to phonemic awareness and phonetic decoding (Snow, Burns, & Griffin, 1998) and would require interventions that target those skills, but older students need support with reading fluency and comprehension (Alvermann & Earle, 2003).

This section presents interventions for all aspects of reading proficiency. Interventions designed for phonemic awareness (e.g., *"The Ship Is Loaded with . . . "*) are appropriate for younger children, whereas those for comprehension (e.g., *Strategies for Inferential Comprehension*) are most likely suited for older students. However, most of the interventions presented in this section are appropriate across age groups and can be implemented with various degrees of intensity (e.g., classwide for core instruction, small groups, or individual students).

PHONEMIC AWARENESS: ELKONIN BOXES

Overview

Many readers of this book will be familiar with Elkonin boxes, because they are a powerful tool to teach that words are made of sounds. Phonemic awareness is the knowledge that words are made of sounds and that those sounds can be manipulated to make words. Elkonin (1973) first demonstrated the boxes, and subsequent research has supported their effectiveness. Joseph (2000a) used the boxes to practice sounds within words, which led to increased phonemic awareness and decoding skills. A later adaptation of the word boxes included practicing on a mobile device. Both the paper and electronic versions of the intervention led to increased skills among three struggling readers in first grade, two of whom were English language learners (Larabee, Burns, & McComas, 2014).

Goal

Elkonin boxes are used initially to teach that words are made up of sounds and to have the student practice breaking words into sounds. This intervention is most appropriate for young children or somewhat older students (e.g., first or second grade) who struggle with the most basic foundations of reading. The intervention focuses on initially teaching phonemic awareness, which makes it an acquisition intervention.

Intervention Intensity

The intervention could be used for individuals who need intensive support in learning phonemic awareness. However, the intervention could be modified to initially teach phonemic awareness to a larger group or as part of a small-group intervention.

Materials

1. A small personal whiteboard.
2. A dry-erase marker to make the three boxes on the board, as shown in Figure 4.2.
3. A small magnetic token.
4. A list of words that contain the target number of sounds (e.g., three).
5. Reinforcers as needed.

Options to Monitor Progress

Phonemic awareness is difficult to assess. One option would be to use curriculum-based measures that assess phonemic awareness. Phoneme segmentation fluency seems especially relevant to this intervention, but initial sound fluency could be used, too.

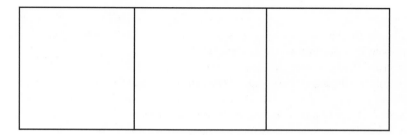

FIGURE 4.2. Elkonin boxes.

Implementation

1. Hold up the whiteboard with the three boxes drawn on it.
2. Explain to the student that there are three boxes, the first one (point to the first square on your left), the second one (point to the middle square), and the third one (point to the third square or the one on the farthest right).
3. Next slowly say a word with three sounds in it (e.g., d/o/g) and say, "I hear three sounds in this word, /d/ /o/ /g/," being careful to pronounce each sound correctly. For example, *d* is not pronounced "duh," and *g* is not pronounced "guh."
4. Take the token in your hand and explain that you are going to say the word slowly and, when you hear the first sound, you will place the token in the first box, and when you hear the second sound, you will put the token in the second box, and when you hear the third sound, you will slide the token to the third box.
5. Next, model it by saying the word slowly and sliding the token over for each sound. Conclude by saying the word normally while sliding your finger under the boxes quickly as you say the word.
6. Have the student then take the token and slide it along from the first to third box as you say the first to third sounds. Praise and give corrective feedback as needed.
7. After the student successfully performs the task with minimal support, practice by verbally saying three to five more words and having the student move the token into the appropriate boxes. Be sure to have the student say the whole word after sliding the token into the third box.

NOTES

1. In order for this intervention to work, the interventionist must clearly model the process and the correspondence between the sound in the word and the correct box.
2. Magnetic letters and whiteboards work quite well, and students tend to enjoy using them.
3. It is likely beneficial to include the corresponding letters in the boxes. Thus the intervention can be implemented exactly as described above, but simply write the letters in the appropriate boxes, using small letters so that the student does not erase them as she or he moves the token from box to box. Including the written letters starts to build letter–sound correspondence while working on phonemic awareness.

SOURCES

Elkonin, D. B. (1973). U.S.S.R. In J. Downing (Ed.), *Comparative reading* (pp. 551–579). New York: Macmillan.

Joseph, L. M. (2000a). Developing first graders' phonemic awareness, word identification, and spelling: A comparison of two contemporary phonic instructional approaches. *Reading Research and Instruction, 39,* 160–169.

Larabee, K. M., Burns, M. K., & McComas, J. J. (2014). Effects of an iPad-supported phonics intervention on decoding performance and time on-task. *Journal of Behavioral Education, 23,* 449–469.

PHONEMIC AWARENESS: "THE SHIP IS LOADED WITH . . . " INTERVENTION

Overview

Phonemic awareness is the most basic building block on which reading is built. It consists of knowledge that words are made up of individual sounds and that those sounds can be manipulated to make words. "The Ship Is Loaded with . . . " game is an easy way to have students practice manipulating sounds. This activity requires a small group of students who sit in a circle, toss a small soft object (e.g., beanbag), and practice rhyming words.

Goal

The goal of the game is to enhance the phonemic awareness of students by having them practice manipulating sounds. This intervention is for students who struggle with the most basic foundations of reading. It is likely most appropriate for young children. The intervention focuses on practicing the use of sounds to make words, which makes it a proficiency intervention.

Intervention Intensity

The intervention has to be implemented with a group. Therefore, it is appropriate as part of an instructional approach with a classroom or as part of a small-group intervention. It could be used as part of an intervention program with an individual student if implemented with other students who could serve as models for the target student.

Materials

1. A small Nerf ball or soft object (e.g., beanbag) that can be tossed around a circle. Stopwatches or watches with second hands, one per student pair.
2. Target words to start the activity.

Options to Monitor Progress

1. Phonemic awareness is difficult to assess. One option would be to use curriculum-based measures that assess phonemic awareness, such as initial sound fluency or phoneme segmentation fluency.
2. Measures of rhyming words can help show progress with phonemic awareness. Intervention Steps.

Implementation

1. Have four or five students sit in a circle on the floor.
2. The teacher begins by explaining the game and the rules.

3. The teacher then says, "The ship is loaded with . . . " and selects a single-syllable word with the target sound. For example, *balls* could be used, but it does not need to be a word that is exactly semantically correct (*holes, mats,* etc., would be fine).

4. Next, the teacher gently tosses the ball to one of the students who then restates the sentence "The ship is loaded with . . . " and then finishes the sentence with a different word that rhymes (e.g., *halls*).

5. If the word rhymes, then praise the student by saying "Yes, [word] rhymes with *balls.*" If the word is incorrect, then provide positively worded corrective feedback. The word does not have to be semantically correct or even be a real word to count.

6. The student then tosses the object to a different student, who states the starting sentence and provides a different ending word that rhymes with the pattern word. Praise each correct response.

7. Continue the game until each student takes a correct turn.

NOTES

1. This game is designed to build phonemic awareness fluency. Thus the students should understand the idea of rhyming and be able to do it with some proficiency.

2. It is very important that this activity be treated as a game with positive feedback and praise and that the students be allowed to have fun with it.

SOURCE

Adams, M. J., Foorman, B. R., Lundberg, I., & Beeler, T. (1998). *Phonemic awareness in young children: A classroom curriculum.* Baltimore: Brookes.

THREE STEPS TO BETTER DECODING WITH WORD BOXES

Overview

Word Boxes—drawn rectangles divided into sections corresponding to the number of phonemes in words—provide a visual structure for analyzing the sounds of spoken words. When used to target decoding, word box activities help students make connections among the sounds in a word, the letters matching the sounds, and the orthographic pattern of the word. This strategy presents a three-part word box activity consisting of sound segmentation, letter-to-sound matching, and spelling. As the teacher articulates each sound in a word, students first move counters into the boxes, then move letters into the boxes, and finally write letters in the boxes. Typically implemented in one-to-one or small-group settings, word box instruction has also been validated in a whole-class format. Compared with students receiving traditional phonics instruction, students receiving word box instruction display better word identification and spelling skills on taught words, as well as on words not taught (Joseph, 2000b). Two variations are presented: (1) a peer-mediated version that increases students' opportunities to respond in a whole-class format and (2) a version suitable for classrooms using a differentiated spelling instructional model.

Goal

Word Boxes help students attend to the phonological and orthographic features of words using a visual decoding framework and a guided interactive procedure. Thus word boxes are interventions for students who struggle with decoding or spelling and are designed to help build proficiency with the skill.

Intervention Intensity

The intervention could be used as part of instruction with a classroom or small group but is best implemented one-on-one or two-on-one. Word Boxes could be part of an intensive intervention program for individual students who struggle with decoding.

Materials

1. 9″ × 12″ dry-erase boards, each with a drawn rectangle divided into boxes according to the number of sounds in the target words (e.g., three boxes for consonant–vowel–consonant words), one per student.
2. Dry-erase markers, one per student.
3. Dry-erasers or felt squares, one per student.
4. Two to four colored chips (the number corresponding to the number of phonemes in the target words), one set per student.
5. Two to four plastic or tile letters (the number corresponding to the number of letters in the taught words), one set per student.
6. Plastic ziplock bags, each containing a set of the five items listed above, one bag per student.
7. Pictures for target words (optional; see Note).
8. List of spelling words for the week, one copy per student pair (optional; see Variation 1).

Options to Monitor Progress

1. Create a spelling test of 20 words based on the phonograms (consonant–vowel–consonant patterns) that have been introduced. Administer the test and calculate percent-correct scores for each student in the class or a target group of students.
2. Calculate percent-correct scores on weekly spelling tests for the entire class or a group of target students for several weeks or the previous month.
3. Calculate the percentage of students in the entire class with grades of B or better in spelling for the previous grading period.

Intervention Steps

Introduction and Training

1. Tell the class that they are going to play a game called Word Boxes to help everyone become better spellers. Distribute the boards, markers, erasers, and ziplock bags with chips (counters) and letters.
2. Using the procedures presented below, model the Word Box activity step by step on the chalkboard. Then, using the same target word, have all of the students complete the Word Box activity independently and circulate to provide corrective feedback as needed. Provide additional practice with other words until students are familiar with the procedures.

STEP 1: SEGMENTING SOUNDS

1. Ask the students to take out their counters and place them beneath each section of the divided box.
2. As you slowly articulate a word (e.g., "mmmm-aaaa-nnnn" for *man*), have them place

the counters sequentially in the respective sections of the box. Move around the room to check students' responses and provide encouragement and feedback as needed.

3. For additional practice, have the students replace the counters beneath each section of the box and then chorally say the word slowly as they simultaneously move the counters one at a time into each section of the box.

STEP 2: LETTER-TO-SOUND MATCHING

1. Have students remove the counters and take out the letters.
2. Have students chorally articulate the word slowly as they place the letters in the appropriate sections of the box.

STEP 3: SPELLING

1. Have students put away the letters, take out their markers, and write the letters of the word in the respective divided sections of the boxes as they slowly pronounce each sound in the word.
2. Have students hold up their boards for you to inspect or move around the room and give corrective feedback as needed.
3. After you have checked students' responses, have them wipe the letters off their boards. At this point, they may need to redraw the divided rectangles on their boards.
4. Repeat all three steps for each of the target words in the lesson.

Implementation

1. Conduct word box activities for 15–20 minutes per session, presenting between 6 and 10 words per session, depending on students' literacy development. A new word family can be presented about once a week. Be sure to review previously taught words in subsequent sessions.
2. As students become more proficient in the Word Box procedure, they can work in pairs or small groups, as described in the variations.

Variations

VARIATION 1: PEER TUTORING FORMAT

Review the target words by writing them on the chalkboard and having students chorally pronounce each word. Divide the class into pairs of students. Give each pair a copy of the spelling list and a set of Word Box materials (omitting the counters). Have students take turns administering the list of spelling words to their partners and performing the Word Box activity. Have students check off each correctly spelled word on the list. If time permits, have students readminister any misspelled words to each other.

VARIATION 2: DIFFERENTIATED INSTRUCTIONAL FORMAT

After initial classwide training, give students a copy of the list for their spelling group. Review the words for the first group by writing them on a dry-erase board and having students chorally pronounce the words. Then pair students as described in Variation 1 above and have them practice while you move on to the next group.

NOTE

For younger children or English language learners, display pictures of the target words and have students chorally name and discuss their meaning prior to the Word Box activity.

SOURCES

Burns, M. K., Riley-Tillman, T. C., & VanDerHeyden, A. M. (2012). *RTI applications: Vol. 1. Academic and behavioral interventions.* New York: Guilford Press.

Joseph, L. M. (2000b). Using word boxes as a large group phonics approach in a first grade classroom. *Reading Horizons, 41,* 117–127.

WORD BUILDING

Overview

Teachers are all too familiar with so-called "partial decoders"—poor readers who can decode the initial grapheme of a novel word but have difficulty applying sound–symbol knowledge to other letter positions within words. This intervention assists students in fully decoding words by systematically directing their attention to each grapheme position within a word. Using letter cards, students form a chain of words that differ by a single grapheme at the beginning, middle, or end of the word in an activity called *progressive minimal contrasts.* Focusing attention on each individual letter–sound unit in a word is critical in promoting the formation of more accurate and fully specified representations of printed words in memory. After each transformation, students decode the new word. To integrate decoding with text reading, students conclude each lesson by reading "silly sentences" that contain a high proportion of the new words. In the original study, implemented in an after-school tutoring program with 24 poor readers ages 7–10, participants showed significantly greater improvement in decoding for all grapheme positions, as well as greater gains on standardized measures of decoding, reading comprehension, and phonological awareness, compared with a control group (McCandliss, Beck, Sandak, & Perfetti, 2003). In this adaptation, a peer-mediated format has been substituted for the one-to-one tutoring setting to facilitate classwide implementation. The one-to-one original version, which is also suitable for delivery in a small-group format, is presented as a variation.

Goal

Word Building can be used to build decoding skills with an activity that transforms one word into another by changing a grapheme at the beginning, middle, or end of the word. Word Building addresses multiple issues. First, it is a decoding intervention that helps students with code-based issues. Second, it is a proficiency intervention that allows students to practice letter sounds, but it also facilitates generalization into words and sentences.

Intervention Intensity

The intervention could be used as part of instruction with a classroom or small group, but it is best implemented one-on-one or two-on-one. Word building could be part of an intensive intervention program for individual students who struggle with decoding.

Materials for Each Intervention Session or Lesson

1. 5–16 letter cards, one set per student.
2. "Smiley faces" and question marks, about 5" in height, made of colored construction paper.
3. Overhead projector and transparencies (optional).
4. Plastic ziplock bags, one per student (optional; see Note 3).
5. 8–10 sentences consisting primarily of words formed in the lesson.
6. Flashcards for each word formed in the lesson or index cards, one set per student pair or instructional group (optional; see Variation).
7. Small whiteboard and whiteboard markers (optional; see Variation).

Options to Monitor Progress

1. Construct a list of 20 one-syllable pseudowords by taking words from students' current reading material and recombining onset and rime units (e.g., *nan, vot, gip, glom*). Administer the list to a group of target students or the entire class and calculate a percent-correct score for each student.
2. Calculate average grades in reading for a group of target students or the entire class for the previous month or marking period.
3. Using students' regular reading materials, administer curriculum-based oral reading probes (R-CBM) with the comprehension option to a group of target students or the entire class.

Intervention Steps

Preparation

Divide the class into pairs, based on reading group or skill level. Change student pairs every 2 or 3 weeks, but match skill levels in each pair as much as possible. For each lesson, proceed as indicated below.

Part 1: Word Building

1. Give each student a set of letter cards and conduct a brief review of those letter sounds.
2. Pronounce a word containing the letter–sound units for the lesson (e.g., *sat*) and ask students to use their cards to "build" the word. After students form the word, write the word on the chalkboard or transparency and have students modify their constructions as needed. Then have students chorally read the word.
3. Tell the students to insert, delete, or exchange a specific letter card to transform the current word into the next word in the lesson (e.g., *sat* to *sap*; see Figure 4.3). Sequences of letter changes should draw attention to each position within a word (e.g., initial consonant, second consonant within a consonant cluster, medial vowel, final consonant) and ensure that the same letters appearing in the initial position also appear in other positions. After each new word is formed, have students read it chorally.
4. Use the following error correction procedures:
   a. If students have difficulty pronouncing a word after forming it, avoid pronouncing the word for them. Instead, encourage an attempt based on the letter sounds. If students have trouble combining letter sounds, guide them through the process of progressively blending the sounds together.
   b. If students mistake the word for a similarly spelled word, write out the target word

	c	a	t
	c	a	p
	t	a	p
	t	i	p
	r	i	p
t	r	i	p
d	r	i	p
d	r	o	p

FIGURE 4.3. Sample progression of word transformations for *Word Building*. The new grapheme card in each trial is shaded to illustrate how each successive transformation directs attention to different grapheme positions by holding constant the other letters from the previous word.

and the error word on the chalkboard or transparency and help them analyze the differences between the two words in terms of letter–sound units.

Part 2: Peer Tutoring

1. After students have completed the Word Building sequence, have them move to their tutoring stations (pairs of adjacent desks). Give each student pair a set of flashcards and designate one student to begin as tutor.
2. The tutor shows the first flashcard to the tutee. If the tutee pronounces the word correctly, the tutor places the flashcard on the smiley face.
3. If the tutee cannot read the word, the tutor supplies it and places the flashcard on the question mark for additional practice. If neither of the students can read the word, they raise their hands to request teacher assistance.
4. After the tutee reads the missed word correctly, the tutor places the flashcard to the side for additional practice. After 5 minutes, students reverse roles and repeat the procedures.
5. During the tutoring session, circulate to provide assistance and corrective feedback. If most of the students can read at least 80% of the lesson words correctly, move on to the next lesson. If the accuracy criterion is not met, conduct more Word Building activities using the same set of words.

Part 3: Sentence Reading

1. Using the chalkboard or a transparency, display a set of sentences containing a high proportion of words that students have just decoded and others that can be decoded based on the material taught to that point. Make the sentences silly and fun to read—for example: "Did Tip sip and slip?"; "Hot Spot does not sit on a pot."

2. Call on students to read the sentences aloud and provide help as needed using the proce-dures described above. For words containing phonics features that students have not yet mastered, encourage students' attempts to read the words, but pronounce the words if necessary.
3. After students have successfully read the sentences, conduct a playful discussion about the meaning of the sentences.

Variation: Individualized or Differentiated Instructional Format

At the beginning of each unit, select a set of words from the unit lessons (e.g., vowel digraphs). If the target student(s) can read at least 90% of the words, skip that unit and proceed to the next unit pretest. Provide additional instruction based on the letter–sound correspondences in the skipped unit for students who did not reach the accuracy criterion.

    At the end of each unit, administer a posttest of words drawn from the unit lessons. If the student(s) can read at least 90% of the lesson words, move to the next unit pretest. If the accuracy criterion is not met, provide additional activities based on the letter–sound units in the previous unit.

NOTES

1. This intervention is appropriate for students who have completed grade 1 and have received instruction in the basic letter sounds.
2. In the original study, students participated in 77 lessons, grouped into 23 units containing 4–7 lessons each, as follows: (1) units 1–10, short vowels; (2) units 11–15, long vowel sounds con-trolled by silent *e*; (3) units 16–19, vowel digraphs (*ae, ee, oa, ow, oy*); and (4) units 20–23, changes in vowel pronunciation in different phonetic environments (e.g., *r*-controlled vowels).
3. To increase usability, have students create their own flashcards by writing the words to be studied on index cards. Have them store their cards in ziplock bags.

SOURCE

McCandliss, B., Beck, I. L., Sandak, R., & Perfetti, C. (2003). Focusing attention on decoding for children with poor reading skills: Design and preliminary tests of the word building interven-tion. *Scientific Studies of Reading, 7,* 75–104.

GRAPHOSYLLABIC ANALYSIS: FIVE STEPS TO DECODING COMPLEX WORDS

Overview

Syllabication, segmenting a multisyllabic word into its constituent syllables, is an important strategy for word reading, especially as students progress through school and encounter more complex vocabulary in their textbooks and reading materials. Unfortunately, all too many students fail to reach the full alphabetic phase of reading, in which readers are able to decode multisyllable words by forming complete connections between the spellings and pronunciations of syllabic units. In this intervention, students learn a strategy for analyzing words into their constituent parts as they practice reading a set of multisyllabic words over several trials. Only one syllabication rule is taught, the need to create a separate syllable for each vowel. In the original study, conducted with 60 students in sixth through ninth grades who were reading at third- to fifth-grade levels, the intervention group demonstrated greater improvement in spelling and reading unfamiliar real words and pseudowords than a no-treatment group and a group of struggling readers who practiced reading the same words as wholes, with the strongest effects for the poorest readers (Bhattacharya & Ehri, 2004). More recent research also saw greater gains in decoding, fluency, and comprehension among middle school students in comparison with a control group (Diliberto, Beattie, Flowers, & Algozzine, 2008). In this adaptation, a response card format is used to facilitate classwide implementation, with the original one-to-one format included as a variation.

Goal

Graphosyllabic Analysis improves decoding skills by teaching students a five-step syllable segmentation strategy. The intervention is designed to increase decoding skills by increasing the accuracy with which students sound out multisyllabic words. Thus it is an acquisition intervention that should be accompanied with modeling and immediate corrective feedback.

Intervention Intensity

The intervention could be used as part of instruction with a classroom or small group, but it is best implemented one-on-one or two-on-one. Thus graphosyllabic analysis could be part of an intensive intervention program for individual students who struggle with decoding.

Materials

1. Word cards, consisting of four sets of 25 multisyllabic words written on 3″ × 5″ index cards, one set per student.
2. Sheets of paper listing the words in each set, one sheet each per student (optional; see Note 2).
3. 9″ × 12″ whiteboards, dry-erase markers, and erasers, one each per student.
4. Index cards or a 9″ × 12″ whiteboard, dry-erase markers, and erasers (optional; see Variation).

Options to Monitor Progress

1. Administer a 20-item word list corresponding to the current grade placement or estimated reading level of a group of target students or the entire class. Continue to administer easier or more difficult word lists until you determine each student's instructional level, defined as the highest list on which a student can read 15 out of 20 words.
2. Using students' regular reading materials in a literature or content-area class, administer curriculum-based measurement of oral reading fluency with the comprehension option to a group of target students.

Intervention Steps

1. Tell students that you are going to teach them a strategy for reading complex and unfamiliar words by dividing words into syllables.
2. Using the chalkboard or an overhead transparency, demonstrate the five-step syllable analysis as follows:

Step 1: Read the Word Aloud.

Display a sample multisyllabic word (e.g., finish) on the chalkboard or a transparency and pronounce it:

"*Finish.*"

Step 2: Explain the Word's Meaning.

Ask the students to give the word's meaning(s) and provide corrective feedback if needed:

"That's right, *finish* means 'to complete a task.'"

Step 3: Orally Divide the Word into Syllables.

1. Pronounce each syllable aloud while raising one finger at a time to count the syllables:

   "There are two syllables in the word *finish*. I'll read it again—*fin-ish.*"

2. Explain the one-vowel, one-syllable rule:

   "Every syllable contains a vowel. Vowels are usually spelled with the letters *a, e, i, o, u, y,* or certain combinations of these letters, such as *ea, ee,* or *ai*. The word *finish* has one vowel in each syllable—/i/ in *fin* and /i/ in *ish*."

3. Explain how to distinguish incorrect from correct segmentations:

   "Each letter can go in only one syllable. For example, I can't divide the word *finish* as *fin-nish*. I have to put the letter *n* in only one syllable—*fin-ish.*"

4. Explain that the sounds in the syllables must match sounds in the whole word:

   "The sounds in the syllables should be as close as possible to the sounds in the whole word. We don't say *fine-ish* because we don't hear *fine* and *ish* in *finish*. We don't say *fin-ush* because we don't hear *fin* and *ush* in *finish*. We say *fin-ish* because we hear *fin* and *ish* in *fin-ish.*"

Step 4: Match the Pronounced Form of Each Syllable to Its Spelling

Pronounce each syllable aloud while you use your thumbs or a pointer to expose each syllable in turn while covering the other letters: "Fin–ish."

Step 5: Blend the Syllables to Say the Whole Word.

1. Moving your finger or pointer from left to right, slowly blend the syllables to pronounce the whole word.

   "Finally, I put the syllables together and read the whole word—*finish.*"

2. Present another, slightly more complex example (e.g., *violinist*) and guide students through each step. Have students write the sample word on their whiteboards and practice pronouncing and exposing one syllable at a time while you circulate to provide help as needed. For Step 4, accept different ways of dividing words into syllables as long as each syllable contains only one vowel sound, the letters students expose match the sounds they pronounce, each letter is included in only one syllable, and the combination of letters forms a legal pronunciation (e.g., *fi-nish* but not *fini-sh*).

3. Divide the class into pairs of students with similar reading skills, give each pair the first set of words, and have them apply the five steps to read each word. Circulate to provide corrective feedback as needed.
4. Have the pairs repeat the steps three or four times for each set to help secure the words in memory.

Variation: Individual or Small-Group Format

For delivery in an individual or small-group format, use index cards or a small whiteboard to demonstrate the strategy steps.

NOTES

1. In the original study, target words were selected from *Basic Elementary Reading Vocabularies* (Harris & Jacobson, 1972).
2. To increase usability, distribute sheets of paper listing the four word sets and have students copy the words on index cards. Have them store each word set in a separate ziplock bag.

SOURCES

Bhattacharya, A., & Ehri, L. C. (2004). Graphosyllabic analysis helps adolescent struggling readers read and spell words. *Journal of Learning Disabilities, 37,* 331–348.

Diliberto, J. A., Beattie, J. R., Flowers, C. P., & Algozzine, R. F. (2008). Effects of teaching syllable skills instruction on reading achievement in struggling middle school readers. *Literacy Research and Instruction, 48,* 14–27.

DUET READING

Overview

The Duet Reading (DR) procedure is an assisted intervention in which an interventionist reads a passage jointly with a student by orally reading every other word. Thus DR specifically targets reading accuracy by modeling correct reading of words in the passage. In order for this intervention to work, the interventionist must clearly model each word. She or he must also model fluent reading. It is easy to fall into word-by-word robotic-sounding phrasing unless the interventionist moves the pace at a comfortable yet relatively rapid rate. Moreover, this intervention is used only until accuracy improves, at which time DR ends and a different intervention in which prosodic reading is modeled begins. Previous research found that the intervention increased reading accuracy so that students could better participate in fluency-building activities (Parker & Burns, 2014).

Goal

DR is designed to increase the accuracy with which students read connected text. DR is appropriate for students who have adequate phonetic skills but who struggle applying those skills to reading text. Students who would likely respond best to DR are those who accurately read substantially less than 93% of the words from grade-level text. However, it is worth noting again that fluency should be the appropriate intervention target, not phonetics. The intervention increases accuracy, which makes it an acquisition intervention.

Intervention Intensity

The intervention is best implemented one-on-one and can be somewhat time- and resource-intensive. Therefore, it is likely an intensive intervention for students who struggle with reading fluency.

Materials

One copy of one grade-level reading passage, preferably all on one page.

Options to Monitor Progress

Conduct weekly curriculum-based measurement probes with oral reading fluency. However, the data should be examined two ways. First, a typical words-read-correctly-per-minute metric can be a strong indicator of reading growth. Second, compute the percentage of words read correctly by dividing the number of words read correctly by the total number of words (words read correctly plus errors), and multiply by 100. Three consecutive data points at or above 93% suggest that the student may be ready to move to a different intervention.

Intervention Steps

1. Provide the student with a grade-level (or appropriate current skill-level) text with enough text to engage in meaningful reading, but not so long as to overwhelm the student. One-page probes work quite well for this task.
2. The student reads the passage orally while the teacher/interventionist follows along.
3. Any word that the student does not read correctly within 2 seconds is verbally provided by the teacher/interventionist by saying, "That word [point to the word] is [pronounce the word]. What word is that?" If the student replies correctly, then the interventionist states "Yes, that word is [state the word]. Good." The error correction procedure is repeated if the student does not correctly state the word.
4. Next, the teacher/interventionist states, "This time we are going to read the passage together. Start at the beginning and you will read the first word, then I'll read the second, and we will alternate back and forth until we read the entire passage. Any questions?"
5. The student reads the first word, the interventionist reads the second, and then they alternate every other word until the passage is complete. The teacher/interventionist should model fluent reading and avoid robotic-sounding speech as much as possible.
6. Any student error is corrected with the standard error correction outlined in Step 3.
7. After completing the passage, the two start over again on the same passage, but this time the teacher/interventionist goes first, followed by the student. Thus every word in the passage is modeled by the teacher/interventionist and read by the student.
8. (Optional) After reading the passage together a second time, the student could be asked to read the passage again independently.

SOURCES

Burns, M. K., Riley-Tillman, T. C., & VanDerHeyden, A. M. (2012). *RTI applications: Vol. 1. Academic and behavioral interventions.* New York: Guilford Press.

Parker, D. C., & Burns, M. K. (2014). Using the instructional level as a criterion to target reading interventions. *Reading and Writing Quarterly, 30,* 79–94.

PRESS Research Group. (2014). *PRESS intervention manual* (2nd ed.). Minneapolis: Minnesota Center for Reading Research.

LISTENING PREVIEWING WITH KEY WORD DISCUSSION

Overview

In Listening Previewing, also termed *passage previewing,* a more-skilled reader reads a passage aloud while a less-skilled reader follows along silently prior to independent reading of the same material. Listening Previewing has been validated as an effective fluency-building strategy across a variety of student populations and settings from elementary through secondary levels. This version promotes vocabulary acquisition and comprehension in addition to fluency by including a discussion of key words prior to reading. In the original study, implemented with five English language learners in a class for students with speech and language impairments, Listening Previewing with key word discussion was more effective in increasing fluency and comprehension than Listening Previewing alone or silent previewing with key word discussion (Rousseau, Tam, & Ramnarain, 1993). This classwide adaptation uses choral responding and a peer-mediated format with a simple error correction procedure to enhance usability and increase students' opportunities for active oral reading practice during the reading instructional period. Two variations are presented: (1) a small-group format for classrooms using a differentiated reading instructional model and (2) a version with a self-monitoring component to enhance motivation. The strategy can be implemented with narrative or expository text in reading, literature, or content-area classes.

Goal

Listening Previewing enhances reading fluency and comprehension by discussing key vocabulary words and providing an opportunity for students to hear what they will read prior to independent reading. Listening Previewing is an acquisition intervention because it facilitates accurate responding. However, it is only appropriate for students who have adequate decoding skills but who also make frequent errors while reading or who have adequate reading fluency but struggle with comprehension.

Intervention Intensity

The intervention should be implemented one-on-one or in small groups, which makes it appropriate as a targeted or intensive intervention.

Materials

1. Stopwatches or watches with second hands, one per student pair.
2. Classroom reading materials, one set per student.
3. Sets of five to eight comprehension questions for each passage, one set per student.
4. Notebooks or folders with sheets of paper, one per student (optional; see Variation 2).

Options to Monitor Progress

1. Using students' regular reading materials, administer curriculum-based oral reading probes with the comprehension option to a group of target students or the entire class.
2. Calculate scores on reading skill sheets, quizzes, or end-of-unit tests for the entire class or a group of target students for 5–10 days or for the previous month.

Intervention Steps

Preparation

Using data collected during the observation period, create Listening Previewing pairs by matching higher performing readers with lower performing readers. Make adjustments as needed to accommodate reading proficiency and student compatibility.

Introduction and Training

1. Explain to the students that they will be working in pairs to practice their reading skills and learn new words. Using yourself as the more proficient reader and a student as the less proficient reader, demonstrate the paired Listening Previewing procedures as follows:
   a. The more proficient reader reads the first paragraph (the first sentence for younger and less skilled students) while the less proficient reader follows along. Then the less proficient reader reads the same paragraph or sentence.
   b. As one student reads, the other corrects four errors: (1) substitutions, (2) omissions, (3) additions, and (4) hesitations of more than 4 seconds. If neither student in the pair knows a word, the students raise their hands to ask for assistance.
2. Assign Listening Previewing partners and have students move to their partner stations (two desks placed together or some similar arrangement). To ensure that higher performing students read first, designate higher performing readers as the "red team" and lower performing students as the "blue team" or some other team names.
3. Conduct a classwide practice session while you move around the room providing encouragement and assistance as needed.

Implementation

1. At the beginning of the reading instructional period, write 10–12 key words from the reading selection on the chalkboard or add them to the word wall. *Key words* are defined as words that may be difficult for students to understand or pronounce, including vocabulary critical to understanding the assignment.
2. Read the first word to the students and have them repeat it chorally. Discuss the word's meaning by means of explanations, gestures, pictures, modeling, or other strategies, including the contexts in which it is used. Ask questions to determine whether students understand the meaning of the word. Repeat this procedure for each of the key words.
3. Then read the selection aloud while students follow along silently. To promote active attention, instruct students to follow along with a finger under each word as you read.
4. After you have finished reading the selection, have students move to their partner stations and take turns reading the same selection, one paragraph at a time, with the higher performing student in each pair reading first.
5. After the student pairs have read the selection, distribute a worksheet with five to eight comprehension questions based on the selection. If desired, have student pairs collaborate in preparing their answers.

6. Review the questions as a whole-class activity and have students correct their own or their partner's papers. Collect the papers to check for scoring accuracy and provide corrective feedback as needed.

Variations

VARIATION 1: LISTENING PREVIEWING IN A SMALL-GROUP FORMAT

Conduct the Listening Previewing and key word discussion during small-group reading instruction. If the group is small enough, have each student read aloud while you listen and provide corrective feedback after the preview. Alternately, have students work in pairs to conduct partner listening previews after the group preview and key word discussion while you move on to the next reading group.

VARIATION 2: LISTENING PREVIEWING WITH SELF-MONITORING

After each student in the pair has read, have partners conduct R-CBMs on a daily or weekly basis, as follows:

1. The higher performing student returns to the beginning of the selection and reads for 1 minute while the lower performing student follows along, tallying errors on a sheet of paper and keeping time. The lower performing student counts the number of words read correctly per minute (WCPM), and the higher performing student graphs his or her results in a reading notebook or folder. The process is repeated for the lower performing student.
2. To help students keep track of errors, teach them to make slash marks on a sheet of paper and to draw a line with a pencil in the passage to mark the last word read in 1 minute.

NOTES

1. Including a self-monitoring component by having students graph their WCPM performance (Variation 2) helps to maintain interest and enhances the effectiveness of this intervention.
2. This intervention also lends itself to implementation in a cross-grade tutoring format or in an after-school tutoring program. Train tutors to conduct the R-CBMs and help their tutees graph their results.

SOURCE

Rousseau, M. K., Tam, B. K., & Ramnarain, R. (1993). Increasing reading proficiency of language-minority students with speech and language impairments. *Education and Treatment of Children, 16,* 254–271.

STORY DETECTIVE

Overview

Story Detective turns the reader into a "detective" by having her or him make predictions about a story as it unfolds through a series of clues. Students are given clues one at a time that so that, when listed in their entirety, they create the outline of a story. The teacher reads one clue, the student then has the opportunity to be the "detective" and make a prediction about where the story is headed, and the teacher follows that prediction by asking the student to explain his or her thoughts. A second clue is then given. The details of this clue may prove or disprove the previous prediction and a new or extended prediction is made. The initial study found that Story Detective increased the reading comprehension of fourth-grade students who were good and poor readers (Hansen & Pearson, 1983).

Goal

Story Detective teaches students to think inductively to comprehend their reading and helps students at any reading level to become more engaged readers. Story Detective allows students (ages 7+) to practice reading comprehension strategies without the added pressures of decoding. Story Detective does not model but instead provides opportunities for practice, which makes it a proficiency intervention.

Intervention Intensity

The intervention could be used as part of instruction with a classroom or small group, but it is best implemented in a smaller group or one-on-one. It is likely most effective for a targeted intervention with small groups of students who need additional support with reading comprehension.

Materials

1. Story Detective can be taught with just about any narrative reading material. It would be best to teach the strategy with reading passages that represent an instructional level for the student or that the student can read fluently and that contain inferences.
2. Story Detective Clue List (teacher created).

Options to Monitor Progress

1. The percentage of comprehension questions answered correctly can be used to monitor progress. Provide the student with 5–10 questions that align with inductive reasoning and ask the student to answer each.
2. Maze data can also be used to monitor progress. Maze tasks require students to read from a passage in which every fifth word is omitted. In place of the omitted word are three choices: the correct word, a word that is somewhat closely related to the correct word (near miss), and a word that is not directly related to the correct word (far miss). Students are asked to read the passage for 3 minutes and to circle the word that is most likely to be the missing word. Maze could show gains in comprehension in general and should probably be administered no more frequently than once per week.

Intervention Steps

Creating Story Detective Clue Lists

1. When first creating a Story Detective Clue List, use a storybook as a guide for writing the clues. This will have to be a story the children are not familiar with.
2. Structure the clue list so that, first, general information is given that leads to subsequent clues that reveal new details, until finally the conclusion of the story is revealed with the last clue.

3. Initial clues should involve general statements about the setting of the story.
4. Middle clues should be less vague and contain new information to discuss.
5. The last sentence always reveals the "mystery."
6. The list should include approximately seven clues (adapt number based on children's age). For example:
   a. The teams arrived eager to enter the arena.
   b. One team was wearing red and white uniforms. The other had on blue and white.
   c. Many of the players wore the same uniform, but one did look a little different.
   d. A whistle blew to begin the game.
   e. Both teams rushed toward the object in the center of the rink.
   f. The crowd cheered as a black disk slid toward the Blue team's end of the rink. A player wearing blue and white dove for the puck but it slid under his body and landed in the goal.
   g. The Red Bird's fans jumped to their feet to congratulate their team on scoring the first goal of the season! The hockey players on the Blue Jays team hung their heads and skated to their bench in disappointment.

Implementing the Story

The Story Detective strategy should be used before the student reads the associated book. After the teacher and student go through the established clues from the list, the student may be encouraged to read back over the story silently. The student who is unable to read could picture walk through the story instead. This poststrategy reading will help the student bridge listening and reading comprehension.

1. The teacher reads the initial clue from a Story Detective Clue List (e.g., "The teams arrived eager to enter the arena!").
2. The student responds by making a prediction or comment about the story and using prior knowledge to reason that prediction (e.g., "The clue said the teams were ready to enter the arena, and I know indoor soccer teams sometimes play in an arena, so the players must be soccer players.").
3. The teacher responds by affirming or redirecting the child's prediction, then reading a second clue (e.g., "So you are thinking this is a story about soccer players because they sometimes play in an arena. Do any other teams play in an arena? Let's read the next clue and see if we find out more about what type of players these are.").
4. The teacher and student are to continue reading clues, recognizing important details, and making connections to prior experiences until the final clue is revealed.

Variation: Writing

Use the think-aloud technique when teaching prewriting strategies. Model the thought process that goes into creating a web or outline. Have students talk about what sentences they may want to include in a story about a given topic before writing begins.

NOTE

Students must have the opportunity to make guesses about a story, *but* those guesses are valid only if they are backed by reasonable deductions from the clues and related back to prior knowledge. The process must be a conversation between a child and an adult in which the adult helps shape the child's responses to include both guesses and the reason behind those guesses. For example:

TEACHER: It was a hot summer day, and Andy was preparing to compete.

STUDENT: He may be getting ready to swim a race.

TEACHER: Why?

STUDENT: The story said it was summertime and swimming is a summer sport.

SOURCES

Burns, M. K., Riley-Tillman, T. C., & VanDerHeyden, A. M. (2012). *RTI applications: Vol. 1. Academic and behavioral interventions.* New York: Guilford Press.

Clark, K., & Graves, M. (2005). Scaffolding students' comprehension of text. *The Reading Teacher, 58,* 570–580.

Hansen, J., & Pearson, P. D. (1983). An instructional study: Improving the inferential comprehension of good and poor fourth-grade readers. *Journal of Educational Psychology, 75,* 821–829.

STORY MAPPING

Overview

Good readers use their knowledge of story structure to analyze, organize, and remember story content across a variety of reading contexts and materials. In contrast, poor readers have a limited understanding of text structure and how to apply it while reading to enhance comprehension. In Story Mapping, students learn to use a graphic framework that focuses their attention on key elements in narrative text, such as character, setting, and outcome, to help them organize and interpret information. Attending to the structural elements of the narrative during the story mapping process helps students to think about the content and relate it to prior knowledge, leading to better reading comprehension. The intervention is delivered in three phases that are designed to increase students' independent use of Story Mapping over time. Story map instruction has been associated with increased ability to identify narrative elements and improvement in literal and inferential comprehension for students with and without disabilities across a range of grade and skill levels (Baumann & Bergeron, 1993; Gurney, Gersten, Dimino, & Carnine, 1990; Mathes, Fuchs, & Fuchs, 1997). Three variations are presented: (1) a version with a self-questioning component, (2) a version with additional visual supports for primary grade students, and (3) a variation with a cooperative learning format.

Goal

Story Mapping improves reading comprehension by providing a visual framework and strategy for analyzing, organizing, and remembering story information. It is a multicomponent intervention that addresses reading comprehension. Although it does not teach comprehension strategies, it does provide a framework to enhance comprehension. Thus it is difficult to place Story Mapping into the learning hierarchy, but it is likely to be acquisition to proficiency because it involves modeling to learn the skill initially.

Intervention Intensity

The intervention could be used as part of instruction with a classroom or small group. Given the discussion nature of the intervention, a group is needed, which makes the intervention most suitable for a small-group targeted intervention for students who need support with reading comprehension.

Materials

1. Paper copies of a story map template appropriate for students' grade level (see *www.adlit. org/strategies/22736* for examples or Google "story maps"), one copy per student per story.
2. Sheet of paper listing story-specific comprehension questions or generic questions such as, Who is the main character? Were there any other important characters in the story? What were they like? When did the story take place? Where did the story take place? What was the problem in the story? How did the characters try to solve the problem? Was there a twist or something that changed the story? What was it? Was the problem solved or not solved? One list per story per student (optional; see Variation 1).
3. Chart with pictures illustrating each story element, such as a picture of a runner breaking the tape for outcome (optional; see Variation 2).
4. Reading notebooks or folders with sheets of paper, one per student (optional; see Variation 3).
5. Story retelling checklist, consisting of a list of the main events and details for two stories.

Additional Materials for Variation 3

Posterboard chart listing leader cues for story mapping steps or 3″ × 5″ index cards with cues, one card per group, as follows:

1. *Tell*—tell the answer for your story part and give evidence to support your answer.
2. *Ask*—ask other group members to share their answers and provide evidence to support their answers.
3. *Discuss*—lead a discussion of your story part and try to reach a consensus. If the group can't agree, the leader has the final say.
4. *Record*—write the group's answer in that section of the story map.
5. *Report*—be ready to report your group's answers to the class.

Options to Monitor Progress

1. Calculate scores on reading classwork, homework, or tests and quizzes for the entire class or a target group of students for the previous month.
2. After the students in a target group have read a story independently, have each one tell you everything he or she can remember about the story from memory. Using a list of the story's main events and details, check off the information recalled as the student retells the story. Calculate the percentage of key events and details recalled per story for each target student.
3. Assign a story to the entire class, a selected reading group, or a group of target students. After reading, have the students complete a set of 10 generic questions (see questions above). Calculate percent-correct scores on the questions for each student. If desired, calculate a classwide or group average percent-correct score by summing the individual scores and dividing by the number of students in the class or group.

Intervention Steps

Introduction and Training

Using reading material from narrative texts selected at the level of the weaker readers in the class, have students read a story silently during the reading instructional period or as a homework assignment. For classes that include very poor readers, create student pairs, consisting of a more proficient and a less proficient reader, and have the pairs read the story aloud together. For younger students, read the story aloud while they follow along.

PHASE 1: MODELING

1. Tell the students that they are going to learn the parts of a story and that this will help them understand and remember more about what they read.
2. Display the transparency with the story map template or draw the template on the chalkboard. Explain the meaning of each element, providing examples of story grammar elements from previously read stories.
3. Help students understand how the elements are interrelated. For example, tell students that identifying the theme requires studying the main character(s), the main problem, and the way in which the main characters solved or did not solve the problem.
4. Using a think-aloud procedure, identify the elements in the story students have just read, filling in the map as you move through the story.

PHASE 2: GUIDED PRACTICE

1. Distribute copies of the story map. Have students read another story and fill in their story maps independently.
2. Then call upon students to identify story map elements as described above. Respond positively to contributions and encourage students to state their opinions, but be clear about why some answers are correct, others are incorrect, and some answers are better than others. Redirect students to the text when necessary.
3. As consensus is reached, record responses on the story map template and have students make any necessary corrections on their individual maps. Have students keep their maps as study aids.

PHASE 3: INDEPENDENT PRACTICE

1. Have students silently read stories and complete their story maps independently. Tell them that they can fill in the maps as they read a story, after they read it, or a combination of both ways.
2. Circulate to provide assistance and feedback as needed, but do not have students respond as a group to story map elements.

Implementation

1. Have students read silently and fill in the maps independently while reading or after reading.
2. Review student responses during a classwide discussion and have students make any necessary corrections on their individual maps.
3. Continue to identify classroom reading assignments to which students could apply the

Story Mapping strategy and ways the strategy could be modified to fit different kinds of tasks.

Variations

VARIATION 1: STORY MAPPING WITH SELF-QUESTIONING

After students have completed their story maps, have them use the maps to answer 10 comprehension questions. If desired, have students work in pairs to complete their maps and answer the questions. Discuss the answers as a classwide activity and have students make corrections to their papers as needed. After students are proficient in the use of the story maps, have them read silently and answer comprehension questions without the maps. If classwide comprehension scores fall below 80% accuracy for 2 consecutive days, reinstate the maps.

VARIATION 2: STORY MAPPING FOR PRIMARY GRADE STUDENTS

For the first training session, display the primary grade story map template on the overhead projector or Smartboard and tell students that a story map is like a road map. Just as a road map guides a traveler from one place to another, a story map leads the reader from the beginning of a story, through the middle of the story, and to the end of the story. Use locations familiar to the students to exemplify the road map analogy. Explain that by learning about and using story maps, students will be able to understand, remember, and enjoy stories more.

Display the chart with pictures illustrating the story elements. Using a story with a simple text structure, such as *The Three Billy Goats Gruff,* begin reading through the story and record the story map elements for *who* and *where* on the template. Call on students to identify the other four parts of the story as you continue reading.

In a second training session, review the story map parts and conduct a classwide practice in mapping, using another story. As you fill in the map, discuss the author's use of description, characterization, the relevance of the story to students' personal experiences, and other features. Distribute copies of the story map template and have students work in pairs or small groups to complete a map for the story currently being read by the class or their reading group.

After students have completed the maps on their own, use the transparency or chalkboard to fill in the story map by calling on students for their responses. Have students correct their own maps as needed.

Implementation

1. Distribute copies of the story map during guided reading activities. Have students complete the maps individually as you proceed through the story.
2. After students are able to complete maps successfully in this format, have them complete the maps on their own during independent story reading for later review during whole-class or small-group instruction.

VARIATION 3: COOPERATIVE STORY MAPPING

Explain to the class that they will be learning a new way of getting more out of what they read by working in teams to complete story maps. Divide the class into teams of four students, including a range of skill levels in each group. Give each student a team assignment for the week, as described in Step 3 below. Guide students through the steps as follows.

Step 1: Reading the Story

All students in the class read the same story. Stories can be read during partner reading sessions, during the reading instructional period, or as homework. For weaker readers who cannot read the same story as the other students, assign a peer to read the story to the student or tape it and have the student listen while following along in the text.

Step 2: Skimming the Story

1. After students have read the story, have them spend 2 minutes skimming the story silently to refamiliarize themselves with the details prior to completing the story maps.
2. Have students determine what they believe are the best answers for all the story elements and note on a sheet of paper where information supporting their answers is located in the story so that they can provide evidence for their answers during the map completion activity with their group.

Step 3: Completing the Story Map

1. Have students move to their groups, give one copy of the story map to each group, and have the groups complete the maps under the direction of a leader. Each student is a leader for one story element and one major event, as follows: (a) main character and first major event, (b) setting and second major event, (c) problem and third major event, and (d) story outcome and fourth major event. For the first few sessions, assign weaker readers to the easier tasks of main character and setting.
2. The student assigned as leader for that element writes the group's answers for that element on the story map, according to the following five steps:
   a. Give your answer for a story part and provide evidence to support your answer.
   b. Ask other students in the group to share their answers and provide evidence in support.
   c. Lead a discussion of the story part.
   d. Reach a consensus and record the group's answer on the map.
   e. Be prepared to report the group's findings to the class.

Step 4: Discussing the Story

1. Lead a classwide discussion of the story elements, focusing on helping students to evaluate whether their answers are correct and to reference portions of the text substantiating their answers.
2. For each story part, ask the leader for that element to report the group answer. Then restate it and ask if another group has a different response. Help students extend their understanding of the story beyond their own group by exploring whether some groups have different answers that may also be correct.
3. Have students make any necessary corrections to their maps and retain them as study aids.

Implementation

1. Have the groups work on their maps collaboratively while reading or after reading.

2. After map completion, conduct a classwide discussion as described above and have students correct their maps as needed.
3. Rotate leadership roles weekly so that students have an opportunity to guide group activities for each story element. Change groupings every few weeks or as needed based on student compatibility and ability levels.

NOTES

1. Training for individual story mapping takes two to four sessions of about 45 minutes each. For Variation 3 (cooperative Story Mapping), two additional sessions are needed, one to explain cooperative learning and review cooperative learning rules (e.g., taking turns to respond, listening to what others are saying, disagreeing in a polite way) and another to demonstrate and practice mapping in the small-group format.
2. To help familiarize students with text structure, initially select texts in which all the story elements are easy to identify. Stories with more complex plot structures, such as abstract problems and unresolved conflicts, can be included as students become more competent in using the strategy.
3. Story maps can also be used to enhance the writing process. Have students create an original story map and write a story using it. Have students take turns reading their stories to each other. This can be conducted as an individual, paired, or small-group activity.

SOURCES

Baumann, J. F., & Bergeron, B. S. (1993). Story map instruction using children's literature: Effects on first graders' comprehension of central narrative elements. *Journal of Reading Behavior, 25,* 407–437.

Gurney, D., Gersten, R., Dimino, J., & Carnine, D. (1990). Story grammar: Effective literature instruction for high school students with learning disabilities. *Journal of Learning Disabilities, 23,* 335–342, 348.

Mathes, P. G., Fuchs, D., & Fuchs, L. S. (1997). Cooperative story mapping. *Remedial and Special Education, 18,* 20–27.

IMPROVING COMPREHENSION WITH A SUMMARIZATION STRATEGY

Overview

Many students have trouble in content-area courses because they lack effective reading strategies, such as identifying main ideas, summarizing information, and monitoring their own learning. Summarization is an especially important strategy for students with poor comprehension skills because it helps them to organize and retain important textual information for use in reading and writing assignments. In this intervention, a three-part instructional sequence—review, modeling, and guided practice—is used to teach a summarization strategy for comprehending science text. A peer review component is included to provide performance feedback and reinforce learning. In the original study, implemented in a summer remedial program with five elementary school students with learning disabilities, the intervention produced substantial increases in science text comprehension and completeness of written summaries for all the participants, with the results maintained at a 4-week follow-up (Nelson, Smith, & Dodd, 1992). Moreover, the students reported that the strategy helped them understand their science texts, and a group of general education elementary school teachers judged the strategy to be effective and easy to implement. Subsequent research successfully used summarization as part of an intervention program for students in late elementary grades who struggled with reading comprehension (Burns, Scholin, & Haegele, 2013). In this adaptation, a second peer-mediated practice component has been added to increase usability and motivation. The intervention can be implemented in any content-area subject to enhance textual comprehension.

Goal

Summarizing improves the comprehension of text using a nine-step summarization strategy with a peer collaboration component. It is designed to help students who read fluently but still struggle with comprehension.

Intervention Intensity

The intervention could be used as part of instruction with a classroom or small group. It could be modified to be part of an intensive intervention program for an individual student, but it would probably work best as a small-group targeted intervention for students who need support with reading comprehension.

Materials

1. A text passage and the Summary Writing Guide (Figure 4.4) that can be projected for the class to see.
2. Paper copies of the Summary Writing Guide, one per student.
3. Short comprehension quizzes, one per training passage (optional).

Options to Monitor Progress

1. Select a passage in the science textbook that students have not read. Develop a list of the most important information items in the passage.
2. Have a group of target students or the entire class read the passage and write a half-page summary of the content.
3. Calculate the percentage of important information items included in each summary by summing the number of important items included, dividing by the total number of important items, and multiplying by 100.
4. Calculate the class average percent-correct score on science quizzes and tests for several weeks or for the previous grading period.

Intervention Steps

Introduction and Training

1. Tell students that they will be learning a summarization strategy to help them understand and remember the information in their science texts.
2. Describe a summary as follows: (a) a summary should contain only important information from what you have read, (b) it should not include personal and unnecessary information, (c) it should combine information when possible, and (d) it should be written in your own words.
3. Describe the cues that help identify the main ideas in a textbook passage, including (a) large type size, (b) italicized and underlined words, (c) words and phrases such as *impor-*

Part I: Identify and Organize the Main Idea and Important Information.

Step 1: Think to yourself, "What was the main idea?"
Write down the main idea.

Step 2: Think to yourself, "What important things did the writer say about the main idea?"
Write down the important things that the writer said.

Step 3: Go back and check to make sure you understood what the main idea was and the important things the writer said about it.

Step 4: Think to yourself, "What is the main idea or topic that I am going to write about?"
Write a topic sentence for your summary.

Step 5: Think to yourself, "How should I group my ideas?"
Put a "1" next to the idea you want to be first, put a "2" next to the idea you want to be second, and so on.

Step 6: Think to yourself, "Is there any important information that I left out? Or is there any unimportant information than I can take out?"
Revise your summary if necessary.

Step 7: Write a summary of what you have read.

Part II: Clarify and Revise the Summary.

Step 8: Read your summary and think to yourself, "Is there anything that is not clear?"
Rewrite your summary if necessary.

Step 9: Ask a classmate to read your summary and tell you if there is anything that is not clear.
Rewrite your summary if necessary.

FIGURE 4.4. Summary Writing Guide for improving comprehension of science text with a summary skills strategy. Adapted from Nelson, Smith, and Dodd (1992).

tant, relevant, and *the purpose is,* (d) pictures and tables, (e) introductory and summary sentences, and (f) repeated words and sentences.

4. Display the Summary Writing Guide on the projector or Smartboard. Review each step in the strategy, including a rationale for its inclusion (see Figure 4.4).

5. Have students follow along in their textbooks as you read through a selected passage and model how to use the Summary Writing Guide. If desired, select a passage that students have read the night before as part of a homework assignment so that they are familiar with the content.

6. Work through the nine steps, using a think-aloud format and including self-instruction statements, such as "What is it I have to do? I need to. . . . " As you fill in the guide, call on students to help you identify cues to the main ideas that can help in writing the summary.

7. During a second training session, model completing the guide for another passage as described above, but have students fill in their guides as you fill in each step on the transparency or chalkboard. Then have students use their completed guides to write a summary of the passage.

8. When students have completed their summaries, have them work in pairs to share their summaries and give each other feedback. Allow time for students to revise their summaries based on their partners' feedback.

9. Have several students read their summaries aloud, and provide praise and corrective

feedback as needed. Conduct a brief discussion reviewing elements of the most effective summaries, and allow time for students to revise their summaries based on the discussion.

10. If desired, administer a short comprehension test based on the target passage, and have students exchange and score each other's papers while you go over the answers. Remind students that using the summarization strategy can help them improve their performance on tests and quizzes.

11. Conduct several more practice sessions until students are proficient in the strategy, as demonstrated by the ability to state the nine steps in order and use the guides to complete summaries of assigned passages with at least 90% accuracy and completeness.

Implementation

1. Continue to have students use the guides to write summaries of passages read in class or as homework assignments. For passages read in class, have students work in pairs to provide each other with feedback on the completeness and accuracy of their summaries.

2. Begin by having students write summaries of a few paragraphs at a time and gradually increase the length of the passages and summaries as students become proficient in the use of the strategy.

3. Gradually fade the use of the guides and summaries as an in-class activity, but encourage students to continue to apply the strategy while reading their textbooks at home and to retain their guides and summaries as study aids for tests.

NOTE

In the original study, the teacher used two overhead projectors simultaneously during training, one to display the training passage and one to display the Summary Writing Guide.

SOURCES

Burns, M. K., Scholin, S., & Haegele, K. M. (2013). A small-group reading comprehension intervention for fourth- and fifth-grade students. *School Psychology Forum: Research into Practice, 7*(2), 40–49.

Nelson, J. R., Smith, D. J., & Dodd, J. M. (1992). The effects of teaching a summary skills strategy to students identified as learning disabled on their comprehension of science text. *Education and Treatment of Children, 15,* 228–243.

PARTNER READING

Overview

Classwide interventions for reading often involve Partner Reading, in which stronger readers are paired with weaker readers, and each takes a turn reading the same passage for 5 minutes while the other follows along and provides error correction. The Partner Reading intervention also involves paragraph shrinking as a comprehension technique in which students identify the main idea of the text in 10 or fewer words. Partner Reading has been consistently shown to improve reading fluency skills in classrooms that contain a high number of struggling learners (Burns et al., 2015; Fuchs, Fuchs, & Burish, 2000).

Goal

Partner Reading can be used to improve reading fluency and comprehension among a classroom of students. Partner Reading with paragraph shrinking is usually implemented when a large percentage of students in one classroom score low on benchmark screening measures of reading. It is a reading fluency and comprehension intervention that is designed to increase proficiency.

Intervention Intensity

Partner Reading is a classwide intervention that could be used when a large number of students within one classroom experience reading difficulties. It could be modified to be part of a small-group intervention, but it has more potential as a classwide intervention.

Materials

Each dyad of students will have a folder that will contain the rules for the activity, a reminder about error correction procedures, and a set of reading passages written at the weaker reader's instructional level.

Options to Monitor Progress

Partner Reading is probably best monitored with curriculum-based measures of oral reading fluency with one 1-minute probe. Each student would be assessed before and after the intervention in order to examine growth.

Intervention Steps

Introduction and Training

1. Explain to the students that they will be reading as buddies (early elementary) or partners (later elementary and up) to practice reading with fluency and understanding.
2. Organize students into pairs by ordering them from the highest score to the lowest score and matching the top reader in the upper half of the group with the top reader in the lower half of the group, the second reader in the upper half with the second reader in the lower half, and so on.
3. Students are trained on how to conduct partner reading for days 1 and 2. The classroom teacher or some other interventionist also model procedures for setup, partner reading, and standard error correction. During the first 2 training days, students practice all procedures as modeled by the teacher. Set-up procedures consist of having the dyads move to the designated area in the classroom and getting ready all materials needed for partner reading.
4. Error correction consists of having the partner stop the reader when he or she makes a mistake. The partner provides the correct word, asks the reader to say the word aloud, and then instructs the reader to reread the sentence. During days 3 through 10, students work in their reciprocal partnerships, taking turns reading text aloud and providing appropriate error correction as needed for their partners.

Implementation

1. Partner dyads meet for 15 minutes each day for 2 weeks.

2. Start by reviewing the rules and procedures and model error correction procedures with instructor guidance before the intervention begins.
3. Students work in reciprocal pairs to read text. The stronger reader reads one passage, written at the weaker reader's instructional level, aloud for 5 minutes, during which time the weaker reader follows along and provides standardized error correction as needed. If neither student knows the word, then the dyad raises their hands and the teacher comes to provide error correction.
4. After 5 minutes, the partners switch roles, and the weaker reader reads the same text aloud for 5 minutes while the stronger reader follows along and provides error correction.
5. Following the partner read, each student engages in paragraph shrinking for the section read. Paragraph shrinking involves having the students restate, or summarize, the main idea of what they had read in 10 words or less. The students state the "who," "what," and "why" of the passage; they are told to put a finger down for each word of their summary, and they stop after placing down 10 fingers. Paragraph shrinking procedures should be modeled each day at the beginning of the lesson.

SOURCES

Burns, M. K., Karich, A. C., Maki, K. E., Anderson, A., Pulles, S. M., Ittner, A., et al. (2015). Identifying classwide problems in reading with screening data. *Journal of Evidence Based Practices for Schools, 14,* 186–204.

Fuchs, D., Fuchs, L. S., & Burish, P. (2000). Peer-assisted learning strategies: An evidence-based practice to promote reading achievement. *Learning Disabilities Research and Practice, 15,* 85–91.

ADDITIONAL RESOURCES

Burns, M. K., Riley-Tillman, T. C., & VanDerHeyden, A. M. (2012). *RTI applications: Vol. 1. Academic and behavioral interventions.* New York: Guilford Press.

Burns, M. K., Pulles, S. M., Helman, L., & McComas, J. J. (2016). Intervention-based assessment frameworks: An example of a Tier 1 reading intervention in an urban school. In S. L. Graves & J. Blake (Eds.), *Psychoeducational assessment and intervention for ethnic minority children: Evidence-based approaches* (pp. 165–182). Washington, DC: American Psychological Association.

PRESS Research Group. (2014). *PRESS intervention manual* (2nd ed.). Minneapolis: Minnesota Center for Reading Research.

PEER TUTORING IN VOCABULARY

Overview

Maximizing the amount of active academic responding in the classroom has been demonstrated to be an effective method of increasing student achievement. In this Peer Tutoring strategy, pairs of students practice vocabulary words together, with rewards contingent upon the combined academic performance of both students. Because the intervention takes only about 20 minutes to complete after students have prepared their vocabulary flashcards for the week, it can be easily incorporated within the reading instructional period, using either a single list of vocabulary words for all students or different lists for small, skill-based instructional groups. Implemented in two seventh- and eighth-grade reading classes in the original study, it produced significant increases in vocabulary quiz scores compared with traditional vocabulary instruction (Malone & McLaughlin, 1997). Peer tutoring has consistently been shown to be an effective intervention for vocabulary (Hughes & Fredrick, 2006).

Four variations are presented, including one for reading classes that use a differentiated instructional format. This strategy is also ideal for implementation in social studies and science, with paired vocabulary practice serving as an introductory and/or review activity for a unit or chapter.

Goal

Peer tutoring to improve reading vocabulary uses increased opportunities for students to practice academic material in the context of an interdependent group contingency to address vocabulary. Vocabulary is important for reading comprehension to occur. The intervention is designed to support students after initial instruction in the concepts. Therefore, peer tutoring in vocabulary is a proficiency intervention that will support practice with vocabulary.

Intervention Intensity

Peer tutoring in vocabulary is a classwide intervention that could be used when a large number of students within one classroom experience reading comprehension difficulties. It could be modified to be part of a small-group intervention, but it has more potential as a classwide intervention.

Materials

1. List of vocabulary words, one per student.
2. Vocabulary quizzes, consisting of one brief quiz per tutoring session and one more comprehensive quiz per week.
3. 3" × 5" index cards, 10 to 20 per student per week.
4. Dictionaries, one per student.
5. Posterboard chart or section of the chalkboard listing student names, with columns for posting stars or checks (see Variations 1 and 2).
6. Small and large gold stars (optional; see Variation 3).

Options to Monitor Progress

1. Calculate percent-correct scores on weekly vocabulary quizzes for a target group of students or the entire class for several weeks or for the previous grading period. If desired, calculate the class average percent-correct score by summing individual scores and dividing by the number of students.
2. Administer curriculum-based vocabulary-matching probes (VM-CBM) to the entire class. Calculate percent-correct scores for each student and, if desired, calculate the class average percent-correct score by summing individual scores and dividing by the number of students.

Intervention Steps

Introduction and Training

1. Explain to the students that they will be working in pairs to help them learn and remember more vocabulary words. Tell them that they will have an opportunity to earn homework passes that can be used for any daily assignment in the target subject (or some other reward).
2. Conduct a training session using the procedures below. Allow about 30 minutes for the initial session, with 20 minutes for demonstration and modeling and 10 minutes for class-wide practice. Be sure to model appropriate voice levels for students during practice sessions.

Implementation

1. On Monday, distribute the list of vocabulary words and assign tutoring partners. Pairs remain the same during the entire week. If students are grouped for reading instruction, pair members of the same group for tutoring (see Variation 4).
2. Begin by asking students to move to their tutoring stations (paired desks or a similar arrangement). Designate one student in each pair to serve as the first tutor. Distribute the new vocabulary list, index cards, and dictionaries.
3. Have students prepare individual sets of flashcards by looking up the vocabulary words in a dictionary and copying the word on one side of an index card and the definition on the other. Have tutoring partners check each other's definitions to ensure that they are accurate, complete, and legible while you circulate and provide assistance as needed.
4. On Tuesday, conduct a brief whole-class review of the definitions and provide corrective feedback as needed.
5. Have the tutoring pairs practice vocabulary definitions for 20 minutes, using the following procedures.
   a. For the first 10 minutes, the tutor shows the tutee a vocabulary card and asks the tutee to define it.
   b. If the definition is correct, the tutor praises the tutee, turns the card face down, and proceeds to the next card.
   c. If the tutee fails to define the word correctly, the tutor reads the definition from the back of the card and has the tutee repeat it. The tutor then inserts the missed card back into the stack of cards near the beginning and returns to it in a short period of time.
   d. After the tutor has gone through the stack of vocabulary cards, he or she starts over from the beginning and presents the words as many times as possible during the 10 minutes.
   e. After 10 minutes, call time and have students switch roles.
6. During tutoring, walk around the room, supervising and praising appropriate tutoring behavior and voice levels.
7. At the end of the tutoring session, administer a vocabulary quiz on the current words, as well as a few words drawn from earlier chapters or lessons.
8. Collect the papers for grading. Alternatively, have students exchange papers, correct each other's answers as you go over each item, and write the percentage of words correctly defined at the top of the paper.

9. Check over all test papers. Provide feedback to the class for scoring errors and adjust pair scores accordingly. (This may need to occur on the following day.)
10. When quizzes have been graded, put stars or checks on the chart to indicate which students have received scores of 90% or higher.
11. When both students in the tutoring pair receive three consecutive quiz scores of 90% or above, award a homework pass or the agreed-upon reward to each student.
12. Conduct one or two additional vocabulary tutoring sessions during the week, as needed, based on the first set of scores. Administer a more comprehensive vocabulary quiz on Friday.
13. After most student pairs have earned the reward once, administer vocabulary quizzes on a weekly rather than a daily basis.

Variations

VARIATION 1: SELF-MONITORING

Have students record their vocabulary scores in their reading notebooks and request homework passes as they are earned. Verify the reported scores in your grade book and award passes accordingly.

VARIATION 2: PUBLIC POSTING VARIATION

Award checks or stars to student pairs who meet the 90% criterion, but do not provide any tangible rewards.

VARIATION 3: WHOLE-CLASS CONTINGENCY VARIATION

Provide a classwide reward, such as extra recess, music time, or a pizza party, if all tutoring pairs achieve the 90% criterion on the weekly quiz.

VARIATION 4: DIFFERENTIATED INSTRUCTION VARIATION

This variation is designed for reading classes using a small-group instructional format. Provide separate vocabulary lists and quizzes for each group and pair students according to their group placement. Teachers could move through each group in turn, administering a quiz to one group while the students in the other groups engage in peer tutoring.

NOTES

1. For greatest benefit, tutoring sessions should be held at least three times a week.
2. To reduce preparation and grading time, use short-answer or item-matching formats on the daily quizzes, and have students check each other's papers under your guidance. If you detect cheating, do not permit students to check their partners' papers.

SOURCES

Hughes, T. A., & Fredrick, L. D. (2006). Teaching vocabulary with students with learning disabilities using classwide peer tutoring and constant time delay. *Journal of Behavioral Education, 15,* 1–23.

Malone, R. A., & McLaughlin, T. F. (1997). The effects of reciprocal peer tutoring with a group contingency on quiz performance in vocabulary with seventh- and eighth-grade students. *Behavioral Interventions, 12,* 27–40.

PARENTS AS READING TUTORS

Overview

Parents often ask how they can help their children become more competent and confident readers. Parents as Reading Tutors (PART) is a simple but effective home-based intervention designed to increase the amount of time in which students actively engage in reading. Unlike many tutoring procedures that require students to struggle through a reading passage until they have completed it, PART provides the opportunity to read material to the point of mastery. Parents are trained in a two-step procedure. Each parent provides, first, 4 minutes of tutoring using a simple error correction procedure and, second, 6 minutes of repeated reading of the tutored material. PART also includes an assessment component so that parent and child can monitor progress from session to session. In the original study (Duvall, Delquadri, Elliott, & Hall, 1992) with four elementary school children, three of whom had learning disabilities, mothers tutored their children daily during the summer, using materials that students would encounter at the beginning of the fall semester. All the target students displayed significant gains on standardized reading tests and immediate pronounced increases in reading rate that generalized to untutored passages at home, as well as to more difficult material in school texts. In this adaptation, a comprehension check is added to each session. More recent meta-analytic research found that parents were more effective partners with schools when they implemented a specific tutoring model than when they engaged in reading with their children (Sénéchal & Young, 2008). Because PART requires little training and relies on the student's regular classroom materials, it can be easily implemented with parents and perhaps even adapted for use by volunteers or community-based tutors in after-school supplementary instructional programs.

Goal

PART is used to improve reading fluency with a simple tutoring procedure that can be delivered by parents. PART should be a proficiency intervention that helps students become more fluent with their reading. The error correction procedures could make it an acquisition intervention, but there should not be a large amount of error correction. If the student makes too many errors (e.g., reading 15% or more of the words incorrectly), then a different intervention should probably be used.

Intervention Intensity

PART can be used as a targeted intervention for students who need additional support with reading fluency. It could be part of an intensive intervention program for individual students, but it should not be the only component of the intervention.

Materials

1. Reading texts or copies of classroom reading materials, one set per parent–child pair.
2. Timer or watch with sound device, one per parent–child pair.
3. Notebook or folder with sheets of paper, one per parent–child pair.

4. Scratch paper, one sheet per tutoring session.
5. Home reading survey, consisting of a sheet of paper listing the following five questions: (a) "How much do you enjoy reading?"; (b) "How often do you read at home?"; (c) "When do you read at home?"; (d) "Do you read with your parents?"; and (e) "If so, how often do you read with your parents?" (optional, one per student; see Options to Monitor Progress 3).
6. Home tutoring log, consisting of a sheet of paper listing days and times for parent tutoring, one per student per week (optional).
7. Small rewards, such as stickers, wrapped candy, and decorated erasers or pencils (optional).

Options to Monitor Progress

1. Administer R-CBM to a group of target students, using both the fluency and comprehension options.
2. Calculate percent-correct scores on reading skill sheets, quizzes, or end-of-unit tests for a group of target students or the entire class for the previous grading period.
3. Administer the home reading survey to a group of target students or to the entire class.

Intervention Steps

Parent–Child Training

1. Parent training can be conducted in an individual, small-group, or large-group format (no more than 20 parents per session). Encourage parents to bring their children to the training session. If children are unable to attend the training, have parents take turns playing the roles of parent and child in the tutoring pairs.
2. Using a volunteer parent or a colleague to take the part of the child, train the parents in the procedures described below.
   a. Select a passage from the materials sent from school. Sit beside the child so that you can both see the passage, set the timer for 10 minutes, and ask the child to begin reading.
   b. When the child makes an error, stop the child, point to the location of the error in the text, correctly pronounce the error word(s), ask the child to pronounce the error word(s) correctly, and then have the child reread the sentence. Errors are defined as (1) substitutions, (2) omissions, (3) additions, and (4) hesitations lasting longer than 4 seconds.
   c. After the child has reread the entire sentence that previously involved one or more errors, praise him or her.
   d. After tutoring for 4 minutes, mark the passage to indicate the farthest point of progress and have the child return to the beginning of the selection and continue reading between the beginning point and the end mark for the remaining 6 minutes. If desired, ask comprehension questions, such as Who?, What?, When?, Where?, and Why? for 3 or 4 additional minutes at the end of the session.
   e. Set the timer for 1 minute and take a "parent check" by having the child read from the beginning point in the passage for 1 minute. Tally errors on a scratch sheet of paper while the child reads but do not correct any errors. At the end of 1 minute, count the total number of words between the beginning and ending points and subtract the number of errors from the total number of words to obtain a words-read-correctly-per-minute (WCPM) score. Help the child graph his or her WCPM score in the notebook or folder.

3. After the demonstration, distribute reading materials at the appropriate level for each participating student and have the parent–child or parent–parent pairs practice while you move among the room to provide encouragement and corrective feedback as needed.

Implementation

1. Each Monday, send home a set of tutoring materials with each target student for use during the week. Ask parents to use the procedure for 4 days a week, 10 minutes per session (plus 3 or 4 minutes for the comprehension option and 2 or 3 minutes for the timed assessment and graphing).
2. If desired, also send home a tutoring log and ask parents to return the completed log on the following Monday. To enhance motivation for both parents and children, provide small classroom-based rewards for students returning the completed logs, such as stickers, wrapped candy, and decorated erasers or pencils.

Variation: Parent Tutoring with Classroom Generalization Check

To determine whether the student's reading gains are generalizing to unfamiliar material, conduct a weekly 1-minute assessment using material from a passage that is one or two pages ahead of the tutored material. Parents can conduct these assessments if the teacher provides the appropriate materials.

NOTE

In the original study, parents were taught to record reading rate (words read per minute) and reading errors on separate graphs. This adaptation uses the standard CBM metric of words read correctly per minute (WCPM) to simplify data recording and facilitate comparisons with Dynamic Indicators of Basic Early Literacy Skills (DIBELS) benchmarks (available on the DIBELS website at *http://dibels.uoregon.edu*).

SOURCES

Duvall, S. F., Delquadri, J. C., Elliott, M., & Hall, R. V. (1992). Parent-tutoring procedures: Experimental analysis and validation of generalization in oral reading across passages, settings, and time. *Journal of Behavioral Education, 2,* 281–303.

Sénéchal, M., & Young, L. (2008). The effect of family literacy interventions on children's acquisition of reading from kindergarten to grade 3: A meta-analytic review. *Review of Educational Research, 78,* 880–907.

ADDITIONAL RESOURCES

Duvall, S. F., Delquadri, J. C., & Hall, R. V. (1996). *Parents as reading tutors.* Longmont, CO: Sopris West.

Designed for volunteers and paraprofessionals as well as parents, this handbook describes the PART procedures in detail and includes materials for graphing children's progress.

Interventions to Improve Mathematics Performance

Much as with reading, early proficiency in mathematics predicts later academic achievement (Duncan et al., 2007) and is closely linked to post–high school success (Ketterlin-Geller, Chard, & Fien, 2008). The National Mathematics Advisory Panel (2008) found that completion of Algebra 2 in high school greatly increased the likelihood of graduating from college and identified three foundational clusters of skills that are essential to developing proficiency with algebra: fluency with whole numbers (e.g., number sense, basic operations, computing problems), fluency with fractions, and geometry and measurement. The National Council of Teachers of Mathematics (NCTM, 2000) identified five components, or strands, for what constitutes mathematics proficiency: (1) conceptual understanding, (2) procedural fluency, (3) adaptive reasoning, (4) strategic competence, and (5) productive disposition.

The different strands or areas of mathematics proficiency listed above are interwoven, and mathematics interventions should address as many as possible. Some interventions focus on one aspect of mathematics proficiency, which is important as long as the interventionist is certain that the student lacks in that particular area. For example, *Part–Part–Whole* is a strong intervention to teach conceptual understanding for students who do not understand the underlying ideas, but *Taped Problems* is a fluency-building activity most closely aligned with procedural fluency, and *Fast Draw* is for solving problems. Again, these interventions have applications across multiple age levels and levels of intensity.

CONCRETE–REPRESENTATIONAL–ABSTRACT

Overview

Concrete–Representational–Abstract (CRA) is an approach to teaching mathematics. It is more of an instructional approach than an intervention, and almost all topics in mathematics can be taught using CRA. With CRA, students work with hands-on materials that represent mathematics problems (concrete), pictorial representations of mathematics problems (representational), and mathematics problems with numbers and symbols (abstract; Peterson, Mercer, & O'Shea, 1988). The interventionist uses a gradual release of learning through a model–lead–test approach. CRA has consistently been shown to be an effective approach to teach mathematics over several studies and meta-analyses (Hattie, 2009). It has been used to successfully teach computation (Mancl, Miller, & Kennedy, 2012) and algebraic concepts to secondary students (Strickland & Maccini, 2013).

Goal

CRA is a method to initially teach mathematical concepts. It is also appropriate as an intervention for students who need additional remediation in a specific concept. Therefore, it is an acquisition intervention because it relies heavily on modeling and immediate feedback to teach a new skill.

Intervention Intensity

CRA should be part of core instruction for classrooms, but it could also be used as part of a targeted intervention for small groups or part of an intensive intervention package for individual students.

Materials

1. Hands-on materials that can be purchased from teacher stores or mathematics manipulatives companies, but materials can also be common objects such as pennies, beans, paper clips, cups, and so forth.
2. Pictorial representations that can be made with cards or on paper. Each pictorial representation should include a number of objects that represents the ideas and the signs, symbols, and numbers that accompany them.
3. An erasable whiteboard and marker (optional).

Options to Monitor Progress

1. Create three math tests with sets of computational problems related to the math facts currently being taught. For 3 consecutive days, distribute one of the tests and give students 1 minute to complete as many problems as possible. Calculate a percent-correct score to yield a problems-correct-per-minute score for each student on each test. At the end of the 3 days, obtain an average problems-correct-per-minute score for each student by dividing by 3. If desired, calculate a classwide problems-correct-per-minute score by summing individual student average problems-correct-per-minute scores and dividing by the number of students in the class.
2. Calculate problems-correct-per-minute scores on math daily worksheets for a target group of students or the entire class for 5–10 days by dividing the number of problems worked correctly by the number of minutes students are given to work. For example, if students have 15 minutes available to work and a student completes 18 problems correctly, the problems-correct-per-minute rate for that student is 1.2.
3. Administer curriculum-based mathematics probes (M-CBM) to the entire class or a selected group of students.
4. Ask the student to draw a representation of a problem and to explain how the drawing aligns with the written problem.

Intervention Steps

1. The interventionist explains the skill being taught and why it is important.
2. Review the basic prerequisite skills (e.g., addition without regrouping for multidigit addition with regrouping).
3. **Concrete.** Write the new (target) problem on the whiteboard and use the manipulative items to demonstrate the problem to the student. Use the same number of items to show the problem in different ways (e.g., $3 \times 4 = 12$ could be $6 \times 2 = 12$). Give the student a second problem and ask him or her to represent it with the items while you provide support. After the student completes the new problem successfully with support, give him or her five problems to complete independently.
4. **Representational.** Write a new (target) problem on the whiteboard and draw the problem with pictures while explaining your drawing as you go. After modeling it for the student, then provide the student with a second problem and ask him or her to draw it on the whiteboard while you give support and immediate corrective feedback. After the student completes the new problem successfully with support, give him or her five problems to complete independently.
5. **Abstract.** Write a new (target) problem on the whiteboard and draw it out, but use numbers instead of objects. For example, instead of having three circles with four objects in each of them (3×4), you could write 4 three times. Another example is to use columns to show place value, but write numbers (e.g., for $55 + 28$, you could have a Tens and Ones

column that had a 5 and 2 in the Tens column and a 5 and 8 in the Ones column. Give the student a second problem and ask him or her to represent it with numbers. After the student completes the new problem successfully with support, give him or her five problems to complete independently.

NOTES

1. Teachers must choose appropriate hands-on materials and pictorial representations to represent the abstract problems and should provide appropriate instruction on using the hands-on materials as needed.
2. Teachers should ensure that students have established prerequisite skills whenever introducing a new skill.

SOURCES

Mancl, D. B., Miller, S. P., & Kennedy, M. (2012). Using the Concrete–Representational–Abstract sequence with integrated strategy instruction to teach subtraction with regrouping to students with learning disabilities. *Learning Disabilities Research and Practice, 27,* 152–166.

Peterson, S. K., Mercer, C. D., & O'Shea, L. (1988). Teaching learning disabled students place value using the concrete to abstract sequence. *Learning Disabilities Research, 4,* 52–56.

Strickland, T. K., & Maccini, P. (2012). Effects of Concrete–Representational–Abstract integration on the ability of students with learning disabilities to multiply linear expressions within area problems. *Remedial and Special Education, 34,* 142–153.

MATH CONCEPTS: PART–PART–WHOLE

Overview

When it comes to mathematics computation, students must understand the underlying concept in order to be successful. Students can complete basic computation without conceptual understanding but cannot generalize the skill to problem solving without understanding the underlying concept. Mathematics conceptual interventions are often conducted without using written numbers, which are abstract and arbitrary—for example: Why does "4" equal • • • •? Because we say it does. There is literally no other reason. Computation is simply putting together or separating sets. This can be modeled with manipulative objects by grouping or dividing them. The following procedures focus on addition, but it could be done with multiplication, subtraction, and division with only minor modifications.

Goal

Part–part–whole helps the student visualize the concept for computation. It is appropriate for students who have number sense but who do not understand the concept of the given computation operation. It is designed to support accuracy and initial learning, which makes it an acquisition intervention.

Intervention Intensity

Part–part–whole could be part of core instruction for classrooms, but it could also be used as part of a targeted intervention for small groups or part of an intensive intervention package for individual students who struggle to understand the underlying concepts for computation.

Materials

The intervention requires a group of small objects that come in different colors (e.g., checker pieces, painted lima beans, rocks, colored paper clips, Legos, or bingo chips).

Options to Monitor Progress

Use regularly administered computation probes. However, be sure to assess the accuracy with which the problems are completed.

Intervention Steps

1. Start by saying, "Today we are going to learn how to [add, subtract, multiply, or divide]."
2. Place a number of objects in front of the student that represent the desired sum.
3. Say "I'm going to take these [name of objects] and place them into two groups." Then count the number of objects in each group and state the resulting equation while calling it a number sentence (e.g., "These 3 objects and these 7 objects make 10 objects. That is a number sentence: 3 plus 7 equals 10").
4. Ask "What is the number sentence?" Praise a correct response and correct an incorrect one.
5. Ask the student to make two different groups, count how many are in each group, and say aloud how many objects are in each group. Then say, "Let's say the number sentence together; _____ plus _____ equals _____." Give corrective feedback and verbal praise as appropriate.
6. Next, give the student the same total of objects of two different colors and ask him or her to separate them into two different groups. After separating them, ask the student to count the objects and say the appropriate number sentence, giving praise and corrective feedback as appropriate.
7. Once the student can complete the previous step correctly, then give him or her a different total number of objects of two colors (e.g., four blue checkers and seven red checkers) and ask him or her to separate them into groups and state the number sentence. Praise and give corrective feedback as needed.
8. Finally, give the student a larger set of objects that are all one color and ask him or her to create two groups with the objects while saying the number sentence. Give corrective feedback for incorrect responses and return to Step 4. Praise correct responses and restate the numbers sentence to the student.
9. Have the student continue to create different sets with the same number of objects while stating the number sentence until he or she does so correctly three consecutive times.

NOTE

This intervention is appropriate *only* for conceptual understanding. Once the concept has been learned, then the student should be taught the abstract symbols that correspond to it and the procedure for completing it. Providing manipulative items as a tool to solve the problem after the student understands the concept usually slows the student's computation down and often does not improve student skill or performance. Make the activity fun by using objects that appeal to the students or by grouping them in a fun way. The games Connect Four or Moncala work well.

SOURCES

Burns, M. K., Riley-Tillman, T. C., & VanDerHeyden, A. M. (2012). *RTI applications: Vol. 1. Academic and behavioral interventions.* New York: Guilford Press.

VanDeWalle, J. A., Karp, K. S., & Bay-Williams, J. M. (2010). *Elementary and middle school mathematics: Teaching developmentally* (7th ed.). Boston: Allyn & Bacon.

TAPED PROBLEMS

Overview

Taped Problems is an intervention to build fluency with basic facts. The student listens to a recorded math fact and writes the answer on a worksheet before hearing the answer on the recording. If the student answers incorrectly or does not produce an answer before hearing the answer, the student writes the correct answer on the worksheet when hearing it. Taped Problems has been used to increase student learning for individual students with severe needs (McCallum & Schmitt, 2011), but it has also been effectively adapted for classwide implementation with students in third grade (Poncy, Skinner, & McCallum, 2012).

Goal

The student should demonstrate conceptual understanding of the problem being practiced before implementing the Taped Problems intervention. Given that it focuses on increased fluency after initial learning, Taped Problems is a proficiency intervention.

Intervention Intensity

Taped Problems can be used for entire classrooms and for small groups. It is probably not appropriate to use as an intensive intervention for individual students because it does not provide adequate repetition. Interventionists should consider a different intervention, such as Incremental Rehearsal (IR), for a more intensive intervention for individual students.

Materials

1. Taped Problems worksheet.
2. A device to create the taped-problems recording.
3. Pencil.

Options to Monitor Progress

1. Create three math tests with sets of computational problems related to the math facts currently being taught. For 3 consecutive days, distribute one of the tests and give students 1 minute to complete as many problems as possible. Calculate a percent-correct score to yield a problems-correct-per-minute score for each student on each test. At the end of the 3 days, obtain an average problems-correct-per-minute score for each student by dividing by 3. If desired, calculate a classwide problems-correct-per-minute score by summing individual student average problems-correct-per-minute scores and dividing by the number of students in the class.
2. Calculate problems-correct-per-minute scores on math daily worksheets for a target group of students or the entire class for 5–10 days by dividing the number of problems worked

correctly by the number of minutes students are given to work. For example, if students have 15 minutes available to work and a student completes 18 problems correctly, the problems-correct-per-minute rate for that student is 1.2.

3. Administer curriculum-based mathematics probes (M-CBM) to the entire class or a selected group of students.

Intervention Steps

1. The teacher creates a worksheet for the student. Typically, a sheet contains 12–24 problems.
2. The teacher creates the recording by reading each problem one at a time and pausing for 1–5 seconds before saying the answer. The length of time depends on the skill being practiced. Single-digit facts for any operation could be shorter (e.g., 2 seconds), but multidigit problems such as addition with and without regrouping would require a longer delay (e.g., 5 seconds).
3. The student listens to a recording of a fact (e.g., "7 times 4 equals . . . ").
4. The student tries to "beat the tape" by writing the correct answer before hearing the answer (e.g., "28").
5. If the student answers incorrectly or does not answer, then he or she writes the correct answer on the sheet.

NOTES

1. The student continues working until the recording ends. Students could listen to the same recording multiple times during the same session to better build fluency.
2. Teachers should select problems that represent an instructional level for the student.
3. Students should practice the procedure for using taped-problems recordings and worksheets.
4. The intervention could easily be adapted to small groups or even the whole class by creating worksheets for each student.

SOURCES

Evidence-Based Intervention Network (n.d.). Taped problems intervention. Available at *http://ebi. missouri.edu/?cat=36&paged=2*.

McCallum, E., & Schmitt, A. J. (2011). The Taped Problems intervention: Increasing the math fact fluency of a student with an intellectual disability. *International Journal of Special Education, 26,* 276–284.

Poncy, B. C., Skinner, C. H., & McCallum, E. (2012). A comparison of class-wide Taped Problems and Cover, Copy, and Compare for enhancing mathematics fluency. *Psychology in the Schools, 49,* 744–755.

TIMED TRIALS

Overview

Timed Trials have been used in education for decades. As an intervention, Timed Trials is versatile and can be used to build fluency for tasks that require multiple steps, such as more involved mathematics computations. However, Timed Trials can also be used to build fluency for simpler operations, such as math facts. It requires approximately 7 minutes each day. Previous research found positive effects for Timed Trials in math at the grade/classroom (VanDerHeyden et al., 2012). Moreover, timed practices of math facts led to better retention and application among elementary-age students with math difficulties than did interventions that used mnemonic strategies (Nelson, Burns, Kanive, & Ysseldyke, 2013) or conceptual understanding (Kanive, Nelson, Burns, & Ysseldyke, 2014).

Goal

Timed Trials is designed to build math operation fluency, but it can easily be adapted to work on spelling, reading, or writing skills. Timed Trials is designed to increase the fluency with which tasks are completed, which makes it a proficiency intervention.

Intervention Intensity

The intervention is appropriate for classwide applications when a large number of students in one classroom struggle with math fact fluency. It could be adapted to use as a targeted intervention with small groups of students, but it likely is not appropriate as an intensive intervention for individual students.

Materials

1. Five math probes (i.e., worksheets containing math problems for the problem skill).
2. Timer.
3. Monitoring chart.

Options to Monitor Progress

1. Calculate the class average on weekly quizzes and/or chapter tests for a selected subject for the previous month by summing individual student scores and dividing by the total number of students.
2. Using a sheet of paper with a list of student names or a copy of a seating chart attached to a clipboard, record the number of times one or more target students respond to a question by hand raising during a selected instructional period for 4–7 days.
3. Calculate the percentage of students with grades of D or F in a selected subject for the current grading period or for the school year thus far.
4. Use single-skill CBM probes of the skill being practiced. The probes could be administered as often as needed, but probably should be given at least once each week.

Intervention Steps (to Be Followed Every Day).

1. Get out materials.
2. Tell students to write their names and the date on math sheet.
3. Have them work all the problems above the line on the worksheet with your or their tutors' help.
4. Set the timer for 2 minutes. Tell students to cover the practice problems above the line.
5. Have students work problems below the practice line for 2 minutes.
6. When timer rings, students should stop working.
7. Ask the students to score their papers with the answer key or with your help.

8. The students should count the number of problems they answered correctly and write the correct answers for the problems they missed.
9. Have them write their scores at the top of the math sheets.
10. The students should write their scores on their monitoring charts.
11. Ask the students, "Did you beat your score? Circle yes or no on the monitoring chart."
12. Say, "If you beat your score, choose a reward from your reward menu."

SOURCES

Burns, M. K., Riley-Tillman, T. C., & VanDerHeyden, A. M. (2012). *RTI applications: Vol. 1. Academic and behavioral interventions*. New York: Guilford Press.

Kanive, R., Nelson, P. M., Burns, M. K., & Ysseldyke, J. (2014). Comparison of the effects of computer-based practice and conceptual understanding interventions on mathematics fact retention and generalization. *Journal of Educational Research, 107,* 83–89.

Nelson, P. M., Burns, M. K., Kanive, R., & Ysseldyke, J. E. (2013). Comparison of a math fact rehearsal and a mnemonic strategy approach for improving math fact fluency. *Journal of School Psychology, 51,* 659–667.

VanDerHeyden, A., McLaughlin, T., Algina, J., & Snyder, P. (2012). Randomized evaluation of a supplemental grade-wide mathematics intervention. *American Educational Research Journal, 49*(6), 1251–1284.

IMPROVING MATH FLUENCY WITH A MULTICOMPONENT INTERVENTION

Overview

Developing fluency with math facts is an important competency for students. Students with limited fluency in computational skills are at a severe disadvantage because they cannot keep up with the pace of classroom instruction, which can lead to failure in the mathematics curriculum. Moreover, students with adequate fluency are more successful in applying their skills to new math tasks and are able to stay academically engaged for longer periods of time. Although increasing opportunities for practice and providing immediate response evaluation and error correction can improve math fluency, it can be difficult for teachers to build in supplementary instructional time or provide individualized feedback. This intervention includes several validated components for building fluency, including explicit timing, positive practice overcorrection, and performance feedback, without increasing instructional time or teacher supervision by embedding them within a peer tutoring structure that requires less than 10 minutes per session. In the original study, implemented with four low-performing fourth graders, the strategy was successful in improving fluency in multiplication facts for all participants (Rhymer, Dittmer, Skinner, & Jackson, 2000). In this version, tutoring and assessment materials are prepared on a whole-class rather than on an individualized basis for usability purposes, with public posting of class performance added to enhance motivation. Also presented is a variation with classwide timing for tutoring and assessments that is especially appropriate for younger students. The intervention can be implemented in any subject area to provide additional opportunities for students to practice basic skills and facts.

Goal

The goal of the multicomponent intervention is to improve speed and accuracy with math facts with a peer tutoring procedure that combines explicit timing, immediate response feedback, and overcorrection. It is designed to increase fluency of math facts, which makes it a proficiency intervention, and it should be used only if the student understands the basic underlying ideas of the math facts being taught.

Intervention Intensity

The intervention is appropriate for classwide applications when a large number of students in one classroom struggle with math fact fluency. It could be adapted to use as a targeted intervention with small groups of students, but it is likely not appropriate as an intensive intervention for individual students.

Materials

1. Stopwatches, one per student pair and one per teacher.
2. Math flashcards, consisting of 3" × 5" index cards with two or three same-factor problems (e.g., 4 × 4 = _____) on one side and the problem with the answer on the other side (e.g., 4 × 4 = 16), one set per student pair.
3. Red and green felt or construction paper circles, approximately 4" in diameter, one of each color per student pair.
4. Assessment sheets, consisting of 8½" × 11" sheets of paper listing the same problems as those on the flashcards, presented in random order, one sheet per student.
5. Assessment answer keys, consisting of 8½" × 11" sheets of paper listing the same problems on the flashcards presented in random order, including the answers, one sheet per student (optional).
6. Red marking pens, one per student.
7. Scratch paper, one or two sheets per student.
8. Posterboard chart labeled "We're on the Fast Track!" and displaying a racetrack divided into segments for displaying the class average number of correctly completed problems per minute.
9. Math folders containing sheets of graph paper, one per student (optional).

Options to Monitor Progress

1. Create three math tests with sets of computational problems related to the math facts currently being taught. For 3 consecutive days, distribute one of the tests and give students 1 minute to complete as many problems as possible. Calculate a percent-correct score to yield a problems-correct-per-minute score for each student on each test. At the end of the 3 days, obtain an average problems-correct-per-minute score for each student by dividing by 3. If desired, calculate a classwide problems-correct-per-minute score by summing individual student average problems-correct-per-minute scores and dividing by the number of students in the class.
2. Calculate problems-correct-per-minute scores on math daily worksheets for a target group of students or the entire class for 5–10 days by dividing the number of problems worked correctly by the number of minutes students are given to work. For example, if students have 15 minutes available to work and a student completes 18 problems correctly, the problems-correct-per-minute rate for that student is 1.2.
3. Administer curriculum-based mathematics probes (M-CBM) to the entire class or a selected group of students.

Intervention Steps

Introduction and Training

1. Explain to the class that they will be learning to work together in pairs to improve their math skills. Display the chart with the racetrack and explain that they will be able to see their progress as a class in solving math problems quickly and accurately.

2. Using a student as a tutee, demonstrate the tutoring procedures described below, including timing and error correction.

   a. Each tutoring pair receives a stack of flashcards, a red and a green circle, and two assessment sheets.

   b. At your signal, each tutor sets the stopwatch for 2 minutes and begins showing flashcards to the tutee while the tutee verbally responds.

   c. If the answer is correct, the tutor responds, "Correct," places the card on the green ("Go—Correct") circle, and presents the next flashcard in the stack.

   d. If the answer is incorrect, the tutor responds, "Incorrect, the answer is _____," places the card on the red ("Stop—Incorrect") circle, and the tutee writes the problem and the correct answer three times on scratch paper. After the tutee has completed this correction process, the tutor presents the next flashcard and continues with the procedure until the 2 minutes have expired. If tutors run out of flashcards before the 2 minutes have elapsed, they go through the Stop cards again.

   e. Students then exchange roles and participate in another 2-minute tutoring session.

   f. When both tutoring sessions have been completed, the students set their stopwatches for 1 minute and work independently to complete as many problems as possible on their assessment sheets.

   g. The students in each pair exchange papers and, using their red pens, score the assessments by referring to the answer sheets. Alternatively, wait until all tutoring pairs have completed their sessions and assessments and call out the answers while students check their partners' papers.

3. Select two more students and guide them through the procedures, while the other students observe and you provide encouragement and corrective feedback as needed.

4. Then conduct a classwide practice tutoring session, using sets of addition flashcards. Have students practice until every pair can perform each step accurately for both tutee and tutor roles with 10 flashcards.

Implementation

1. Divide the class into pairs and designate one student in each pair to serve as tutor first. Students remain as partners for a week at a time but change initial roles for each session.

2. At the beginning of the period, conduct a brief review session of the math computational skills being taught that week.

3. Have students work in tutoring pairs, as described above.

4. Collect the assessment sheets to verify scoring accuracy and compute a class average problems-correct-per-minute score by summing individual student scores and dividing by the number of students in the class.

5. After the initial session, begin each session by distributing the previous session's assignment sheets (corrected for accuracy, if necessary) and providing a minute or two for the pairs to review their progress. Have students record their scores on a bar graph in their math folders, if desired.

6. Report the class average problems-correct-per-minute score, and select a student to fill

in that number on the racetrack chart. Praise the students for their efforts and remind them to encourage each other during tutoring sessions. If desired, deliver a group activity reward, such as a math game time using board or web-based games (see Additional Resources below), when the score reaches a certain criterion.

Variation: Classwide Timing

Using a stopwatch, signal all students to begin the 2-minute tutoring session at the same time. At the end of 2 minutes, call time and allow a minute or two for tutors to count up the number of correctly answered flashcards and praise their tutees. Then have students switch roles and repeat the procedures while you keep time. After each student has served in both roles, conduct the 1-minute assessment as described above.

NOTE

Training requires two 30-minute sessions over a 2-day period.

SOURCE

Rhymer, K. N., Dittmer, K. I., Skinner, C. H., & Jackson, B. (2000). Effectiveness of a multi-component treatment for improving mathematics fluency. *School Psychology Quarterly, 15,* 40–51.

ADDITIONAL RESOURCES

Printable math flashcards and online math flashcard games are available on numerous websites, including *www.coolmath4kids.com, www.funbrain.com/math,* and *www.aplusmath.com.*

Premade and customized math worksheets with computation problems and keys for grades 1–4 are available at *www.mathfactcafe.com* and for elementary through high school mathematics at *www.edhelper.com.*

FAST DRAW: IMPROVING MATH WORD PROBLEM SOLVING WITH STRATEGY INSTRUCTION

Overview

Many students, especially those with learning disabilities, perform reasonably well on low-level math skills, such as calculation, but have difficulty with the higher level skills needed for problem solving and applications. To solve word problems successfully, students must not only be able to perform the necessary computations but must also understand the questions that are being asked, identify the relevant information within the problem, and determine the specific operations needed to solve the problem. In this multicomponent intervention, students learn an eight-step strategy for solving math word problems, along with self-regulation procedures to assist them in completing the strategy successfully.

The strategy is taught in a series of stages, and the mnemonic FAST DRAW is used to help students remember the eight strategy steps. In the original study with four elementary-grade students, two with learning disabilities and two with mild mental retardation, math word problem–solving performance improved significantly for all participants, with gains maintained at 6- and 8-week follow-ups (Cassel & Reid, 1996). Moreover, students' attitudes toward word problems became much more positive during the intervention period. The problem types taught in the intervention address four basic problem types (change, equalize, combine, and compare). Originally delivered in a one-to-one format, the strategy is adapted here for classwide application using a peer tutoring format.

Goal

To increase students' ability to solve math word problems using self-regulated strategy instruction. FAST DRAW is for students who struggle with application of math skills, which makes it a strategy to enhance generalization.

Intervention Intensity

FAST DRAW was studied as an intensive intervention for students with severe difficulties applying math skills. Thus it is appropriate as part of an intervention package for individual students if the interventionist is certain that the student has acquired the prerequisite skills. It could be modified to serve as a targeted intervention for small groups of students who have the basic prerequisite skills but still struggle to solve word problems. Finally, it could be used as a classwide intervention as well.

Materials

1. Math folders containing sheets of paper, one folder per student.
2. Math manipulatives.
3. Prompt cards, consisting of 3″ × 5″ index cards listing the strategy steps and FAST DRAW mnemonic, one per student (see Intervention Steps, Stage 3).
4. Self-monitoring strategy checkoff sheet, one per student (see Intervention Steps, Stage 3).
5. Math word problem worksheets, one per student.
6. Colored marking pens and highlighters, one each per student.
7. Overhead projector and transparencies of math word problems and the strategy steps and mnemonic (optional).

Options to Monitor Progress

1. Administer to the entire class a 20-problem math test consisting of 10 problems involving addition and subtraction facts and problems with regrouping and 10 one-step word problems involving application of knowledge about basic facts and regrouping in addition or subtraction. For example: "The fifth grade class has nine goldfish. The fourth grade class has seven goldfish. How many goldfish does the fifth grade need to give away to have as many as the fourth grade?" Calculate a word problem–solving percent-accuracy score for each student by dividing the number of problems worked correctly by the total number of problems. If desired, calculate a class average word problem–solving percent-accuracy score by summing scores for individual students and dividing by the number of students in the class.
2. Calculate grades on math quizzes and tests for a group of target students or all of the students in the class for the previous several weeks or the current marking period.

Intervention Steps

Stage 1: Introduction and Initial Group Conferencing

1. Explain to the students that they will be learning a strategy called "FAST DRAW" that will help them be more successful in solving math word problems. Tell them that they will have an opportunity to work in pairs while they are learning the strategy.
2. Lead a discussion of the reasons why it is important to know how to solve math word problems in terms of being a future consumer, worker, and citizen, and list the reasons on the chalkboard.
3. Distribute to students their individual results on the 20-item math test administered during the observation period or a list of their grades on math quizzes and tests for the previous several weeks. Using the chalkboard or an overhead projector, demonstrate how to construct a bar graph of percent-correct scores. Then help students construct bar graphs in their math folders, using their performance on the pretest or on previous math assessments as initial data. Explain that they can use the bar graphs to monitor their own progress in solving word problems.

Stage 2: Preskill Development

1. Use manipulatives and simple computation problems to demonstrate the following relationships found in addition and subtraction problems:
    a. The relationship of addition and subtraction to the action implied in a word problem (i.e., for addition, objects are put together; for subtraction, they are separated or removed).
    b. The relationship of addition and subtraction to the size of an answer (i.e., for addition, the largest number in the problem will get larger; for subtraction, it will get smaller).
2. Conduct a classwide practice with each concept that will be taught until students reach an 80% mastery criterion (four out of five problems correct) for each concept.

*Stage 3: Discussion of the FAST DRAW Strategy
and Self-Regulation Procedures*

1. Give each student a prompt card listing the eight strategy steps and the FAST DRAW mnemonic for remembering the steps, as follows:
    F: Find and highlight the question, and then write the label (e.g., addition—change).
    A: Ask what the parts of the problem are and then circle the numbers needed to solve it.
    S: Set up the problem by writing and labeling the numbers.
    T: Tie down the sign by rereading the problem (i.e., decide whether addition or subtraction should be used).
    D: Discover the sign by rechecking the operation.
    R: Read the number problem.
    A: Answer the number problem.
    W: Write the answer and check to see if it makes sense.
2. Discuss how and why each step is used in solving word problems, using examples displayed on the chalkboard or overhead projector.
3. Discuss the importance of using self-statements while applying each step, such as:
    a. A: "To find the question, look for the sentence ending with a question mark."
    b. S: "When setting up the problem, remember to write the larger number on top."

c. *T*: "To tie down the sign, ask, 'Am I putting together?'—so the answer will be larger than the other numbers [if yes, use addition]—or 'Am I taking apart?'—so the answer will be smaller than the largest number [if yes, use subtraction]."

4. Show students how these self-statements can be used to create a self-monitoring checkoff sheet for use during word problem solving. Guide students in generating their own self-statements for using the strategy and have them record them on checkoff sheets in their math folders.

Stage 4: Modeling

1. Model the use of the strategy using the following six self-instructions:
   a. *Problem definition*: "What is it I have to do?"
   b. *Planning*: "How can I solve the problem?"
   c. *Strategy use*: "FAST DRAW will help me remember all the things I need to do to solve a word problem successfully."
   d. *Self-monitoring*: "I can check off the steps of the strategy as I complete them so I can remember what I've done."
   e. *Self-evaluation*: "How am I doing? Does what I'm doing make sense? Did I complete all the steps?"
   f. *Self-reinforcement*: "Great, I'm halfway through the strategy!" or "Oops, I made a mistake, but that's OK because I can fix it. Yay, I did it!"
   g. Have students record examples of statements for each of the six categories on their self-monitoring strategy checkoff sheets. Stress that self-instructional statements do not have to be verbalized aloud; once they are learned, they can be whispered or said to oneself.

Stage 5: Mastery of the Strategy Steps

Divide the class into pairs and have students work together to rehearse the strategy until they have memorized all eight steps, including the FAST DRAW mnemonic, and several positive self-statements about solving math word problems.

Stage 6: Collaborative Practice with Self-Instructions

1. Distribute a worksheet with a set of 7–10 problems of the first problem type to be taught (i.e., addition–change problems).
2. As students work in pairs, move around the room and provide assistance in the correct use of the strategy steps and self-instructions by asking questions and referring to the prompt cards and checkoff sheets. Encourage students to verbalize their self-statements softly to each other and then silently to themselves.
3. After all of the pairs have completed the worksheet, have the students exchange papers and go over the answers as a class. Have students graph the number of items they answered correctly on the bar graphs in their math folders.
4. Continue collaborative practice sessions until students meet a criterion of five out of six problems correct for that problem type.

Stage 7: Independent Performance

1. During the math instructional period, remind students to use the strategy and self-instructions for addition–change problems, but do not provide assistance for that problem type.

If students experience difficulty, return to the collaborative practice stage until they demonstrate mastery again.

2. Return to the collaborative practice stage for the next problem type (subtraction–change problems). Continue introducing word problem types sequentially, alternating collaborative practice and independent performance stages until students are performing at the criterion level on change and equalize problem types in both addition and subtraction. Then follow the same procedure for combine and compare problem types.

SOURCE

Cassel, J., & Reid, R. (1996). Use of a self-regulated strategy intervention to improve word problem–solving skills of students with mild disabilities. *Journal of Behavioral Education, 6,* 153–172.

COGNITIVE ROUTINE FOR MATH PROBLEM SOLVING

Overview

This problem-solving strategy was developed by Montague and Bos (1986) to address self-regulation within cognitive strategy instruction for math problem solving. It is a seven-phase model that has consistently been shown to improve problem-solving skills among students with learning difficulties (Montague, 2008). Students with learning difficulties tend to struggle with recall and do not use consistent strategies to solve problems. Thus the cognitive routine strategy described below provides explicit instruction in selecting the appropriate strategy and includes procedures for generalizing the skill to different settings and problems.

Goal

This intervention is appropriate for students who understand the computation and concepts involved in each problem but who struggle in determining how to apply them. Therefore, the strategy approach described below facilitates generalization.

Intervention Intensity

Cognitive routines could be part of core instruction for classrooms but could also serve as a targeted intervention for small groups of students who have the basic prerequisite skills but still struggle to solve word problems.

Materials

1. Problem-solving problems that apply concepts and computations that the student understands.
2. The steps written out so that you can refer to them during initial modeling, or a cue card as needed (optional).

Options to Monitor Progress

1. Administer to the entire class a 20-problem math test consisting of 10 problems involving basic facts and 10 one-step word problems involving application of knowledge about the

basic facts. Calculate a word problem–solving percent-accuracy score for each student by dividing the number of problems worked correctly by the total number of problems. If desired, calculate a class average word problem–solving percent-accuracy score by summing scores for individual students and dividing by the number of students in the class.

2. Calculate grades on math quizzes and tests for a group of target students or all of the students in the class for the past several weeks or the current marking period.

Intervention Steps

1. Provide the student with a math application/problem-solving item to model the process. As is the case with just about any intervention, the strategy must be modeled first. This is especially important for a metacognitive strategy.

2. Start by saying, "I am going to *read* the problem first to see if I understand it." Then read the problem orally and say "Now I will think to myself—do I understand the problem? If not, then I will read it again."

3. Next, *paraphrase* the problem by saying, "After I'm sure that I understand the problem, I will say it to myself using my own words while I underline the important information. Does the information that I've underlined go with the problem? What question am I trying to answer?"

4. *Visualize* by drawing a picture or diagram to go with the problem that clearly demonstrates the relationship among the parts of the problem. After you have done that, ask "Does the picture fit the problem? Did I show all of the relationships?"

5. *Hypothesize* by deciding what steps and operations are needed to complete the problem and write out the operation symbols.

6. *Estimate* by rounding the numbers and completing the problem in your head. Be sure to explain what you are doing.

7. *Compute* the problem and compare your answer with the estimate that you completed. Say out loud "Does my answer make sense? Is it close to my estimate? Do I have all of the decimal points and signs (e.g., money signs) correct?"

8. *Check* your work to make sure that both the plan and the computation are correct. Ask yourself orally, "Have I checked every step? Is my answer right?"

9. After modeling the process, work through a second problem by stating every step in the sequence as it is needed, but have the student complete the step as you give feedback.

10. Work with the student to practice the sequence until he or she can do it independently. The previous research required the student to memorize the strategy, but perhaps the following could be put on a cue card:
   Read—for understanding.
   Paraphrase—put it in your own words.
   Visualize—draw a picture or diagram.
   Hypothesize—develop a plan to solve the problem.
   Estimate—round and predict your answer.
   Compute—do the computations.
   Check—make sure everything is right.

NOTE

In order for this intervention to work, the student must understand each step and be able to implement each independently. Because this is a cognitive strategy, the interventionist needs to "think aloud" as she or he models the strategy and to encourage the student to also do so during guided practice.

SOURCES

Burns, M. K., Riley-Tillman, T. C., & VanDerHeyden, A. M. (2012). *RTI applications: Vol. 1. Academic and behavioral interventions.* New York: Guilford Press.

Montague, M. (2008). Self-regulation strategies to improve mathematical problem-solving for students with learning disabilities. *Learning Disability Quarterly, 31,* 37–44.

Montague, M., & Bos, C. S. (1986). The effect of cognitive strategy training on verbal math problem solving performance of learning disabled adolescents. *Journal of Learning Disabilities, 19,* 26–33.

Interventions to Improve Writing Performance

Writing is a crucial skill for school success because it is a fundamental way of communicating ideas and demonstrating knowledge in the content areas. The National Commission on Writing (2003, 2004) underscored the importance of writing proficiency to academic success and participation in today's global economy. However, students frequently graduate from U.S. high schools unable to write at the level required by colleges or future employers (Pinkus, 2006). Writing problems are also characteristic of most students with learning disabilities, who have deficits in basic writing skills, such as handwriting, spelling, capitalization, and sentence formation (Graham, Harris, MacArthur, & Schwartz, 1991); have difficulty sustaining effort during writing (Graham, 1990); and produce compositions that are typically brief, poorly organized, and impoverished in both content and development (De La Paz & Graham, 1997; Graham, Harris, & Larsen, 2001).

The pervasiveness of writing problems in the general student population, as well as among students with learning disabilities, suggests that poor writing achievement is related less to internal student disabilities than to inadequate writing instruction. Although there is a growing body of research on effective writing strategies (see Graham & Harris, 2006; Graham & Perin, 2007, for reviews), the myth that writing develops naturally and that good writing cannot be taught has had a negative impact on typical classroom instruction. Despite a greater emphasis in recent years on providing classroom writing experiences for students, informal approaches are still prevalent. Unfortunately, simply increasing the amount of writing students engage in each day is insufficient to improve writing performance, especially for less skilled writers (Graham & Harris, 1997). Similarly, teachers often fail to provide students with high-quality writing assignments and tend to deliver feedback that focuses primarily on improving the surface features of writing rather than on enhancing organization or content (Matsumura, Patthey-Chavez, Valdés, & Garnier, 2002). Research also demonstrates that teachers have difficulty differentiating writing instruction to meet individual student needs. A recent national survey of primary grade teachers (Graham, Harris, Fink-Chorzempa, & MacArthur, 2003) found that nearly half of the teachers made few or no adaptations for struggling writers, and approximately one-sixth of classroom adaptations limited student participation or decision making in some way rather than providing additional learning opportunities. Writing instruction for students with learning disabilities is especially likely to be inadequate. Instruction focuses largely on lower level writing skills, such as spelling and handwriting, with students spending most of their time completing worksheets and copying single words rather than practicing compositional aspects, such as planning, text production, and editing (Graham & Harris, 1997).

Although there is still much less research on effective writing practices compared with reading practices, recent federal initiatives, such as the National Commission on Writing for America's Families, Schools, and Colleges, established in 2002 by the College Board (*www.writingcommission.org*), and the growing use of statewide writing assessments have generated interest in interventions that can enhance the writing skills of all students, as well as students with disabilities. This section includes interventions targeting two aspects of writing: spelling and written expression. Helping students to attain an adequate level of competence in basic writing mechanics so that mechanical difficulties do not interfere with higher order writing processes is an essential goal of writing instruction (Graham, Harris, & MacArthur, 1993). Students also need carefully designed composition instruction focusing on the important ideas of writing, such as the writing process, text structures, and writing for an audience (Stein, Dixon, & Isaacson, 1994).

INTERVENTIONS TO IMPROVE SPELLING PERFORMANCE

Spelling is a critical component of written communication. Without adequate spelling skills, students have difficulty communicating in written form and demonstrating what they have learned. Spelling problems are not common only among students with learning disabilities (Darch, Kim, Johnson, & James, 2000; Fulk & Stormont-Spurgin, 1995); they are widespread in the general student population. In a year-long study of six elementary classrooms (Morris, Blanton, Blanton, & Perney, 1995), only two-thirds of the students observed could spell 86% of a curriculum-based list correctly, and the lowest third could spell only 46% of that list correctly. Moreover, students taught using spelling textbooks varied greatly in their mastery of grade-level spelling patterns. Spelling problems exert detrimental effects on writing in several ways. First, having to focus on spelling interferes with higher order writing processes, such as planning, generating text, and revising (Graham & Santangelo, 2014). Spelling skills account for a sizable proportion of the variance in compositional fluency (66%) and quality (42%) throughout the elementary grades (Graham, Berninger, Abbott, Abbott, & Whitaker, 1997). Second, misspelled words not only interfere with the message the writer is trying to convey but may also influence perceptions of the student's competency as a writer (Graham, Harris, & Chorzempa, 2002). Third, spelling problems may lead students to avoid writing and ultimately to develop the belief that they cannot write, limiting not only their literacy development but also their performance in a wide variety of subject areas (Graham, 1999).

Despite frequent calls to incorporate evidence-based practices into spelling instruction (Fresch, 2003; Graham & Harris, 2006), many teachers appear to lack the knowledge and resources needed to teach spelling effectively. Teachers persist in using traditional but unvalidated activities, such as assigning weekly spelling lists, administering weekly tests, and having students write words multiple times or use them in sentences (Fresch, 2003). Unfortunately, these practices provide insufficient opportunities to improve spelling, especially for poor spellers and students with disabilities. Moreover, some students may be able to score satisfactorily on weekly tests by memorizing the words on the list, only to misspell the same words later because they have not learned the underlying spelling patterns (Templeton & Morris, 1999). Similarly, although current spelling textbooks provide lists of grade-appropriate words, they often fail to emphasize empirically validated strategies for learning the words, such as instruction based on functional spelling units (Berninger et al., 1998). Spelling instruction has also been complicated by the fact that many districts have replaced textbook-based instruction with instruction that is integrated within language arts and content-area subjects. With this approach, words for spelling tests are drawn from a number of nonstandardized sources. Unfortunately, this method not only fails to accommodate the wide range of spelling abilities and spelling problems within most classrooms but also introduces variability in terms of what students are taught at each grade level. At the middle school and high school levels, teachers rarely provide direct instruction in effective spelling strategies, perhaps because they believe that spelling is less important in the curriculum or that students have already acquired—or should have already acquired—spelling techniques in the elementary grades (Fulk & Stormont-Spurgin, 1995). Fortunately, researchers have focused more attention on spelling interventions in recent years (see Wanzek et al., 2006, for a review), based on evidence that targeted spelling instruction can not only improve writing fluency and expressive writing skills (Baker, Gersten, & Graham, 2003) but also facilitate the acquisition of foundational literacy skills, such as word recognition and sentence writing, by at-risk students (Graham & Harris, 2006).

WHAT SPELLING WORDS SHOULD BE TAUGHT?

When spelling instruction is integrated into the curriculum rather than based on a separate textbook or set of materials, teachers often wonder how to select words to teach their students. One approach to spelling instruction in these circumstances is to teach the words that students at each grade level are most likely to use in their writing. This method has the advantage of reducing the number of preassigned words so that, although all students study the most common grade-specific words, teachers can also help students select their own spelling words from the vocabularies in reading, language arts, and content-area classes. Including a subset of student-chosen words not only links spelling instruction to classroom reading and writing activities but also permits students to study words that are of personal interest. Graham and his colleagues have developed two high-frequency graded spelling word lists for use in selecting words to teach: (1) the *Basic Spelling Vocabulary List,* consisting of 850 high-frequency words for students in grades 1–5 (Graham, Harris, & Loynachan, 1993), and (2) the *Spelling for Writing List,* consisting of the 335 words most commonly used in writing by students in grades 1–3 (Graham, Harris, & Loynachan, 1994).

WRITING: LETTER FORMATION

Overview

Many students who struggle with writing have difficulty forming the letters. Moreover, research has consistently linked rapid and correct formation of letters to better writing composition. The current intervention is essentially explicit instruction in letter formation that relies on high modeling. Explicit instruction in letter formation is an important early skill for writing. It falls under the broad category of mechanics of writing, which is often an area in which students who do not enjoy writing struggle. Research has shown that the intervention increased correct letter formation among early elementary-age students (Burns, Ganuza, & London, 2009).

Goal

The goal of explicit instruction in letter formation is to help students learn how to form letters and write more legibly. This intervention is especially useful for students with poor penmanship, especially those in early elementary school. It is designed to increase the accuracy with which students form letters, which makes it an acquisition intervention.

Intervention Intensity

Explicit instruction can be used with large and small groups, but this intervention is ideally suited for individual students with intense needs.

Materials

1. Samples of the student's writing.
2. Paper on which the student can trace letters.
3. Writing paper to practice the letters. Use the same paper that is used to teach penmanship in class.
4. A pencil for the student and a dark marker to write the letter dark enough to be traced. There is no research to support the idea that larger pencils are better for teaching handwriting to young children, so a normal pencil will be fine. However, using larger pencils is acceptable, too.
5. Reinforcers as needed.

Options to Monitor Progress

Letter formation is best measured through curriculum-based measures for written expression using age-appropriate story starters. Allow the students 1 minute to plan and 3 to write. The passage is then scored by computing the percentage of target letters that are correctly formed. A letter is correctly formed if is judged to be visually similar to a standardized example of the kind currently utilized in schools.

Intervention Steps

1. Use five samples of the student's writing to determine letters that the student does not correctly form. It is best to use existing samples of writing as a more authentic assessment. Letters that are incorrectly formed in writing three times are good candidates for intervention.
2. Practice the letters one at a time.
3. Write the letter only slightly larger than usual. Present it to the student and state the name of the letter. Ask the student to restate the letter name and reinforce correct answers (e.g., "Good, that letter is *t*") or correct incorrect replies.
4. Have the student lay a piece of paper over the model and trace it.
5. Cover both the model and the traced letter and ask the student to write the letter from memory.
6. Compare the freehand letter with the original model. If the student correctly wrote the letter, then reinforce him or her and move on to Step 7. If he or she did not form the letter correctly, then go back to Step 3.
7. After the student has correctly formed the letter from memory, have him or her write the letter five more times, with the model being left in view.

NOTE

Although correctly forming letters is important, practicing doing so may not be an inherently enjoyable activity. Many students enjoy being successful, so be sure to heavily verbally reinforce the desired behavior. Frequently say "Good job," "Great," "Excellent," and so forth. After completing the above sequence, immediately provide an opportunity for the student to write something meaningful and fun (a letter to a relative or someone famous, a story, etc.) so that he or she can practice using the letter in context.

SOURCES

Burns, M. K., Ganuza, Z., & London, R. (2009). Brief experimental analysis of written letter formation: A case demonstration. *Journal of Behavioral Education, 18*, 20–34.

Burns, M. K., Riley-Tillman, T. C., & VanDerHeyden, A. M. (2012). *RTI applications: Vol. 1. Academic and behavioral interventions.* New York: Guilford Press.

INCREMENTAL REHEARSAL FOR SPELLING

Overview

As mentioned previously, IR (Tucker, 1989) can be used with students with varying difficulties, for different age groups, and for various skills. We discussed the use of IR to teach words, letters, and math facts, but we include it here for spelling because the procedures are different. IR has been consistently used to increase retention (MacQuarrie, Tucker, Burns, & Hartman, 2002; Burns & Sterling-Turner, 2010) and generalization (Burns, 2007; Nist & Joseph, 2008) of various stimuli.

Goal

IR is generally used after a skill or stimulus has been initially taught. For spelling, IR would be used after the word was taught through whatever approach the school uses, including phonetic decoding. The intervention is described here for use with spelling and is designed to help students retain spelling words, which would make it a maintenance intervention.

Intervention Intensity

IR is an intensive intervention and should only be used for students who really struggle with retaining and using newly learned information. Therefore, it is a one-on-one intervention for students with severe needs.

Materials

1. A dry-erase whiteboard with erasable marker and eraser.
2. A list of known and unknown items.
3. Reinforcers as needed.

Options to Monitor Progress

1. Calculate percent-correct scores on weekly spelling tests for the entire class or a group of target students for several weeks or the previous month.
2. Give a spelling test to the student with only the words that he or she did not know 1, 2, or 7 days after teaching the unknown words.

Intervention Steps

1. Individually present each spelling word to the student in random order to assess whether it is known or unknown. Ask the student to spell each word on a small portable whiteboard after you orally state the word. Words correctly spelled within a reasonable time are considered known. Because the response is written, it is difficult to judge whether a slow or fast response accurately represents automaticity. However, a student who correctly spells the word in, say, 25 seconds likely cannot spell the word effortlessly enough to use in context, and it should be considered an unknown.

2. Record the words that the student correctly spelled in a reasonable time (knowns) and those that were incorrectly spelled or required an excessive length of time (unknowns).

3. Write down the first unknown word on the whiteboard and orally read it to the student while pointing at the individual letters.

4. Ask the student to use the word in a sentence. If the word is used grammatically and semantically correctly, even if the sentence is simplistic, then reinforce the child and move to Step 5. If the word is not correctly used, then provide a short definition or synonym and use the word in a sentence. Next, ask the child to make up a different sentence with the word in it and move to the next step if he or she does so correctly. Words not used correctly at this point should be removed and instructed in more depth.

5. Have the student copy the word by tracing it while saying the letters orally.

6. Cover the word and ask the student to spell the word from memory.

7. Remove the cover and have the student compare her or his spelling to the model. If it is correct, then say, "Good job" and proceed to the next step. If the word is not correct, then repeat steps 6 and 7 until it is spelled correctly.

8. Erase the model and what the student wrote, and rehearse the unknown word with the following sequence and ask the student to state the word every time it is presented:
   a. Orally state the first unknown word and ask him or her to spell it and then spell the first known word. Erase the writing.
   b. Orally state the first unknown word and ask him or her to spell it, spell the first known word, and spell the second known word. Erase the writing.
   c. Orally state the first unknown word and ask him or her to spell it, spell the first known word, spell the second known word, and spell the third known word. Erase the writing.
   d. Orally state the first unknown word and ask him or her to spell it, spell the first known word, spell the second known word, spell the third known word, and spell the fourth known word. Erase the writing.
   e. Orally state the first unknown word and ask him or her to spell it, spell the first known word, spell the second known word, spell the third known word, spell the fourth known word, and spell the fifth known word. Erase the writing.

9. After completing the rehearsal sequence with the first word, that first unknown word is then treated as the first known, the previous eighth known is removed, and a new unknown word is introduced. Thus the number of words always remains six.

10. Continue individually rehearsing unknown words until three errors occur while rehearsing one word. Errors need not occur only on the word currently being rehearsed.

NOTE

The critical component of IR is the high repetition (Szadokierski & Burns, 2008), but the high percentage of known items also allows the student to be successful during the intervention. If the student makes errors on the known words, then replace them. Sometimes very easy known words are used, or you may even ask the student to write a number or draw a shape.

ADDITIONAL RESOURCES

Burns, M. K., Riley-Tillman, T. C., & VanDerHeyden, A. M. (2012). *RTI applications: Vol. 1. Academic and behavioral interventions.* New York: Guilford Press.

Burns, M. K., & Sterling-Turner, H. (2010). Comparison of efficiency measures for academic interventions based on acquisition and maintenance of the skill. *Psychology in the Schools, 47,* 126–134.

MacQuarrie, L. L, Tucker, J. A., Burns, M. K., & Hartman, B. (2002). Comparison of retention rates using traditional drill sandwich, and incremental rehearsal flash card methods. *School Psychology Review, 31,* 584–595.

Nist, L. & Joseph, L. M. (2008). Effectiveness and efficiency of flashcard drill instructional methods on urban first-graders' word recognition, acquisition, maintenance, and generalization. *School Psychology Review, 37,* 294–308.

Tucker, J. A. (1989). *Basic flashcard technique when vocabulary is the goal.* Unpublished teaching materials, University of Chattanooga, School of Education, Chattanooga, TN.

PARTNER SPELLING

Overview

Teachers are increasingly encountering a wider range of spelling abilities among their students. In this game-like intervention, students work in mixed-ability triads to provide each other with active spelling practice and immediate corrective feedback in a 20-minute three-step tutoring routine. The structure of the Partner Spelling strategy permits teachers to incorporate a variety of accommodations and adaptations to meet individual learning needs, including individualizing spelling lists based on students' individualized objectives and previous spelling performance. In the original study, implemented in one fourth- and two fifth-grade general education classrooms, each of which included a student with severe disabilities, the strategy resulted in substantial gains in spelling accuracy for all three students with special needs without negatively affecting the performance of three normally achieving comparison peers (McDonnell, Thorson, Allen, & Mathot-Buckner, 2000). Partner Spelling also increased rates of academic responding and reduced rates of competing behavior for five of the six target students, compared with traditional spelling instruction. Participating teachers rated the strategy highly and reported that it helped their low-performing students became more confident spellers. A variation for classrooms using a differentiated spelling instructional model is also presented.

Goal

The goal of Partner Spelling is to improve spelling performance with a collaborative learning format designed to accommodate students with a wide range of spelling skills. It is for students who struggle with spelling and is designed to increase accuracy with immediate feedback and modeling as needed. Thus it is an acquisition intervention.

Intervention Intensity

Spelling Wizards is used with classrooms with a large number of students who struggle with spelling. It could be modified to use as a targeted intervention with a small group, but it is not intensive enough for interventions with individual students.

Materials

1. List of 20 spelling words drawn from the regular spelling curriculum or grade-level word lists, one per student triad.
2. List of 5–20 spelling words for students with very poor spelling skills. The words for students with disabilities should be selected jointly by the general education teacher and the special education teacher to be consistent with students' goals and objectives.
3. Sheets of lined paper, one per student.

Options to Monitor Progress

1. Calculate percent-correct scores on weekly spelling tests for the entire class or a group of target students for several weeks or the previous month.
2. Using a Classwide Scanning Form with a 3-, 5-, or 10-minute interval, scan the room, starting with the front and ending with the back, and tally the number of students who are exhibiting academic responding and competing behaviors, as defined here.
   a. *Academic responding* is defined as working on the task at hand, looking at the teacher during presentations, engaging in verbal behaviors related to the academic task, and any other behavior relevant to the lesson.
   b. *Competing behavior* is defined as playing with nonlesson materials, failing to look at the teacher during presentations, talking about subjects unrelated to the task, failing to comply with teacher directions, and any other behavior not relevant to the lesson.
3. Conduct these observations during the spelling period for 30–45 minutes for 4–7 days.

Intervention Steps

1. Divide the class into triads consisting of students with a range of spelling performance levels. If the class includes students with disabilities or very poor spelling skills, include no more than one student with a disability or one very low performing student in each triad.
2. Tell the students that they will be working in teams of three so everyone can have more fun and get the most out of the spelling lesson. Explain that students will take turns serving in one of three roles: (a) the "word wizard," who writes and orally spells words; (b) the "word conjurer," who presents the words and gives feedback; and (c) the "word keeper," who checks the word wizard's spelling.
3. Select three students to demonstrate the strategy while the rest of the class observes. Guide the students through the steps described below, emphasizing the roles played by each member of the team.
   a. The word conjurer randomly selects a word from the appropriate spelling list (the general word list for students without disabilities or an individualized list for a poor speller or student with disabilities), and says, "Spell _____" to the word wizard. If the word conjurer cannot read the word to be spelled, the word keeper supplies the word or raises his or her hand to ask for assistance.
   b. The word wizard has 5 seconds to write the word and spell it aloud.
   c. The word conjurer and the word keeper jointly check the spelling accuracy of the

response. The word conjurer then provides feedback to the word wizard by saying, "I agree" or "I disagree." If the word wizard did not spell the word correctly, the word keeper shows him or her the word on the list, and the steps are repeated until the word wizard spells the word correctly.

    d. After the word wizard has had an opportunity to spell all of the words on his or her list, the roles are rotated until each student has had an opportunity to serve as word wizard. Students should receive at least one trial on each word on their list during partner spelling sessions.

4. Conduct one more demonstration, using another student triad. Then have the entire class practice the procedures while you circulate, giving praise for appropriate tutoring and corrective feedback as needed. Also point out examples of cooperative and helpful tutoring behaviors as you move around the room.

5. Conduct partner spelling for 20 minutes twice a week during the regularly scheduled spelling instructional period, or more frequently if desired.

Variation: Differentiated Instructional Format

Form student triads based on spelling groups and provide each triad with a list appropriate for that group.

NOTE

Because triads that include very low performing students or students with disabilities may proceed through the tutoring routine at a slower pace than the rest of the groups, even with individualized lists, have enrichment spelling activities available for early finishers.

SOURCE

McDonnell, J., Thorson, N., Allen, C., & Mathot-Buckner, C. (2000). The effects of partner learning during spelling for students with severe disabilities and their peers. *Journal of Behavioral Education, 10,* 107–121.

ADD-A-WORD FOR SPELLING SUCCESS

Overview

In many classrooms, the typical spelling program consists of assigning the same list of words to the entire class on Monday, having students complete various spelling activities during the week, and administering a test on Friday. Unfortunately, such a program is ineffective for many students, especially students with disabilities, because it fails to provide sufficient practice or accommodate individual rates of progress. In this intervention, students learn a five-step self-managed procedure for daily spelling practice, using words from individual "flow lists" that are adjusted based on performance on daily tests. Words must be spelled correctly for 2 consecutive days before they are dropped from the list and a new word added. Correctly spelled words are retested at two later dates to assess retention and mastery, after which they are dropped from the student's list. The Add-a-Word procedure has resulted in improved spelling achievement for poor spellers, normally progressing students, and students with disabilities in elementary and middle school settings, with improvements generalizing to creative writing assignments (Schermerhorn & McLaughlin, 1997; Struthers, Bartalamay, Bell, & McLaughlin, 1994).

In this adaptation, spelling practice and assessments occur in a partner learning format to reduce teacher preparation and testing time and permit students to receive feedback more promptly. A variation with a public posting component to enhance motivation is also presented.

Goal

Add-a-Word is used to improve spelling performance with individualized spelling lists, daily practice sessions with a structured error correction procedure, and daily progress monitoring. The intervention is a proficiency intervention because it is an effective method to practice spelling words after they are initially taught.

Intervention Intensity

The Add-a-Word intervention was researched with students with severe spelling difficulties. It is probably most appropriate for use as a targeted intervention with small groups of students, but it could likely be modified to work with larger groups or even as an intensive intervention with individual students.

Materials

1. List of spelling words drawn from the regular spelling curriculum, grade-level word lists, and/or errors in the student's creative writing or other written productions, one per student with the student's name and date on it. Use lists of 5–10 words for primary grade students and 10–18 words for elementary to middle school students; you will need to prepare new lists each day, based on students' performance on the previous day.
2. Individual master spelling lists, consisting of words consistently spelled correctly, one per student.
3. Spelling notebooks or folders containing an index card and sheets of lined paper, one per student.
4. Spelling practice sheet, one per student.
5. Posterboard chart with a list of student names or student pairs on the left-hand side and columns for the days of the week on the right-hand side (optional; see Variation).

Options to Monitor Progress

1. Calculate percent-correct scores on weekly spelling tests for the entire class or a group of target students for several weeks or for the previous month.
2. Calculate the percentage of students in the entire class who score 90% or better on weekly spelling tests for several weeks or the previous month.
3. Administer curriculum-based spelling probes to a target group of students.

Intervention Steps

Introduction and Training

1. Using information obtained during the observation period, create student pairs by matching students with similar spelling skills. Rotate spelling pairs every 3 or 4 weeks.

2. Tell the students that they will be working in pairs to become better spellers, using a method called "Add-a-Word." Explain that they will be practicing and taking daily tests on their own individual spelling lists. The results of the daily tests will be used to create a master list consisting of words they have learned to spell. Once a word has been spelled correctly on 2 consecutive days, it will be dropped from the daily practice list and placed on the master list, and a new word will be added to the daily list. After 5 days, any words that have been removed from the list will be placed on the list again as review words and retested. If spelled correctly, the word or words will be placed on the list again in 1 month. If a word is misspelled at any time, it will be returned to the list.

3. Using the chalkboard or the overhead projector, demonstrate the steps in the procedure as described below.

   a. *Step 1: Study.* The student softly pronounces the first word on his or her list and looks closely at its spelling features.

   b. *Step 2: Copy.* The student copies the word from the list onto the spelling practice sheet and checks the original list to see that the word has been correctly copied.

   c. *Step 3: Cover.* The student covers the word with an index card and writes the word from memory next to the covered word.

   d. *Step 4: Compare.* The student uncovers the word and compares his or her second spelling of the word with the spelling on the list to determine correctness. If the word is spelled correctly, the student goes on to the next word. If the word is misspelled, the student erases the word and repeats the Copy, Cover, and Compare (CCC) procedure with that word until the word is written correctly.

4. Assign pairs and have the students move to partner spelling stations (paired desks or some other arrangement). Distribute the spelling folders and spelling lists and conduct a classwide practice session while you circulate to provide encouragement and assistance, as needed.

5. When both students in the pair have written each word on their list correctly from memory twice, have them exchange lists and use their partner's list to administer spelling tests to each other in their spelling notebooks.

6. Using the original lists, have the partners correct each other's tests, while you circulate to provide assistance as needed.

Implementation

1. At the end of each spelling period, collect the notebooks and spelling lists and review the tests for accuracy. Use the results to prepare a new list for each student for the following day based on his or her performance. Also update students' master lists as needed.

2. For best results, implement the Add-a-Word strategy three or four times a week.

Variation: Add-A-Word with Public Posting

For public posting based on individual performance, list student names in alphabetical order on the chart. Each day that a student achieves 80% correct or better (or some other criterion) on his or her list, give that student a gold star to place on the chart beside his or her name. Alternately, have students post color-coded stars to indicate improvement (red star) and perfect performance (blue star) rather than a specific accuracy criterion.

For public posting based on team performance, list the names of students by assigned pairs on the chart. Permit a team to post a gold star if both partners meet the accuracy criterion or a red or blue star if both partners achieve an improved or perfect performance, respectively. If one partner earns a red star and the other earns a blue star on the same day, the pair may choose which star they prefer to post.

NOTE

Allow two sessions of about 30–45 minutes for training, the first for demonstrating the individual practice procedures and the second for reviewing the procedures and demonstrating test administration, scoring, and recording procedures in the paired format.

SOURCES

Schermerhorn, P. K., & McLaughlin, T. F. (1997). Effects of the add-a-word spelling program on test accuracy, grades, and retention of spelling words with fifth and sixth grade regular education students. *Child and Family Behavior Therapy, 19*, 23–35.

Struthers, J. P., Bartalamay, H., Bell, S., & McLaughlin, T. F. (1994). An analysis of the add-a-word spelling program and public posting across three categories of children with special needs. *Reading Improvement, 31*, 28–36.

STRATEGY INSTRUCTION IN STORY WRITING

Overview

Self-Regulated Strategy Development (SRSD) is an instructional approach that teaches students a multistep strategy for planning, writing, and revising in the context of a set of self-regulation procedures, including goal setting, self-instruction, and self-reinforcement. In this classwide version, students learn a five-step strategy for composing stories, as well as strategies for regulating the writing process in a series of mini-lessons. Paired and small-group activities are included at several steps to provide opportunities for feedback and collaborative practice without direct teacher supervision. Students also learn a mnemonic to help them remember the story grammar elements taught in the strategy lessons. In the original study, implemented in two fifth-grade classrooms and one fourth-grade classroom, each of which included a student with learning disabilities, the story-writing strategy resulted in longer, more complete, and higher quality stories for the students with learning disabilities and their normally achieving peers (Danoff, Harris, & Graham, 1993). Moreover, the improvements in story structure and quality were maintained and generalized to other story-writing tasks for the majority of students. A variation that extends partner learning opportunities to additional stages of the training is also included. Meta-analytic research of writing interventions found that SRSD was the most effective intervention for students in grades 4–12 (Graham & Perin, 2007).

Goal

The goal of SRSD is to improve narrative writing performance with a self-regulated story grammar strategy. Strategy instruction writing is designed to facilitate writing after initial instruction. Thus it facilitates fluent application of the skill, which makes it a proficiency intervention.

Intervention Intensity

SRSD has been shown to work well with groups of students and with students with severe writing needs. Therefore, it seems most appropriate as a small-group intervention or for individual students. Aspects of it could be incorporated into core writing instruction.

Materials

1. Posterboard chart listing the five strategy steps and the mnemonic for remembering the seven story parts (see Intervention Steps, Stage 3).
2. Strategy cue cards, consisting of index cards listing the five steps and mnemonic, one each per student.
3. Previously written stories or typed sets of sample stories, two or three per student.
4. Writing portfolios or notebooks containing sheets of lined paper and, if desired, graph paper, one per student.
5. Story starters (e.g., "When Martina walked into her homeroom Friday morning, she noticed right away that something had changed.").

Options to Monitor Progress

1. Select a picture that would be interesting to your students and easy to write about, and display it so that the entire class can see it. Give the following instructions:

   "Look at this picture and write a story to go with it in your writing notebook. Do your best."

2. Score the stories for each of the following seven elements: (a) main character(s), (b) location, (c) time, (d) characters' goal(s), (e) action to achieve the goals, (f) resolution, and (g) characters' reaction, as follows: 0 points = element is not present; 1 point = element is present; 2 points = element is highly developed. Award 1 additional point for each of the following characteristics: (a) the story contains two or more goals, (b) the story contains more than one well-defined episode, and (c) story events happen in a logical manner (total of 17 possible points per story).
3. Evaluate two or three previously written stories for a group of target students or the entire class according to the following 4-point rating scale: 1 = poor, 2 = fair, 3 = good, 4 = excellent. Consider organization, sentence structure, grammar, vocabulary, spelling, and imaginative content in evaluating overall story quality.

Intervention Steps

Stage 1: Initial Conference

1. Tell the students that they will be learning a strategy to help them write better stories and to have more fun doing it.
2. Lead a discussion of story writing that includes the following: (a) the seven common parts of a story (see Intervention Steps, Stage 3); (b) the goal for learning the composition strategy, that is, to write stories that are more fun to write and more fun for others to read; and (c) the role of story parts in improving story quality.

Stage 2: Preskill Development

1. Discuss the parts commonly included in the two major components of a story: (a) *setting*, including main character(s), time, and place; and (b) *episode*, including the characters' goals, actions to achieve goals, resolution, and the characters' reactions.
2. Guide students in identifying examples of the seven story elements in literature the class is currently reading and discuss the different ways that writers develop and expand story parts.
3. Using sample story starters or writing prompts, have the class practice generating ideas for story parts.

4. Have students select two or three previously written stories from their portfolios or provide handouts of two or three sample stories and have them determine which story parts are present in each story.
5. Using an overhead projector or the chalkboard, demonstrate how to create a bar graph recording the number of parts in a story. Explain that students can use graphing to monitor their own use of story parts and their progress in learning the composition strategy.

Stage 3: Discussion of the Composition Strategy

1. Display the chart and distribute the cue cards listing the five strategy steps and the story part reminder (mnemonic), as follows:

THE COMPOSITION STRATEGY

> *Step 1*: Think of a story you would like to share with others.
> *Step 2*: Let your mind be free.
> *Step 3*: Write down the story part reminder: W(ho)–W(hen)–W(here); What = 2; How = 2.
> *Step 4*: Write down ideas for each part.
> *Step 5*: Write your story, using good story parts and making sure your story makes sense.

THE STORY PART REMINDER

> Who is the main character? Who else is in the story?
> When does the story take place?
> Where does the story take place?
> *What* does the main character do or want to do? What do other characters do or want to do?
> *What* happens when the main character does it or tries to do it? What happens with other characters?
> *How* does the story end?
> *How* does the main character feel? How do other characters feel?

2. Discuss the rationale for each of the five steps of the composition strategy.
3. Explain the procedures for learning the strategy, stressing students' roles as collaborators and the importance of effort in mastering the strategy.
4. Provide models of self-statements that can help students generate good ideas and story parts when writing. Invite students to volunteer self-statements they find useful ("Slow down, I can take my time"; "I can do it"; etc.). Then have students generate three creativity self-statements and record them in their writing portfolios.

Stage 4: Modeling

1. Share a story idea with the class and model how to use the strategy to develop the idea further while "thinking aloud."
2. Call on students for assistance as you plan and make notes for each story part on the chalkboard and write a first draft of the story.
3. While composing the story, model five types of self-statements: (a) problem definition ("What do I need to do?"), (b) planning ("First, I need to think of a story to share"), (c) self-evaluation ("Does this part make sense?"), (d) self-reinforcement ("People are going to like this part!"), and (e) coping ("I can write good stories!").

4. When the story is completed, lead a discussion of the importance of what we say to ourselves during the creative process, and identify the types of self-statements you have used. Have students review their previously recorded self-statements and revise them as desired.

Stage 5: Memorization of the Strategy and Mnemonic

1. Divide the class into pairs and have students work together to memorize the five-step strategy, the mnemonic, and several positive self-statements about writing.
2. Have the pairs review the story parts in one or more of their own previously written stories or sample stories and graph the number of parts in their writing portfolios. Circulate to provide encouragement and assistance, as needed.

Stage 6: Collaborative Practice

1. Have students work in pairs to plan stories collaboratively. Remind students that the goal is to include all seven of the story parts in each story. For students who typically use all or nearly all of the story parts, discuss how they can improve their parts with more detail, elaboration, and action.
2. Circulate to make sure students are using the strategy steps and mnemonic appropriately. Encourage students to use their self-statements covertly, if they are not already doing so.
3. When students complete a story, have them work with their partners to identify the story parts, compare their counts of the parts, fill in their graphs, and compare the numbers to the goal of seven parts per story.
4. Lead a class discussion of the ways students can maintain the strategy and generalize it to other experiences and tasks (e.g., when reading stories in English class or when writing outlines).

Stage 7: Independent Performance

1. Allow students to continue to refer to their strategy cue cards and self-statements if they wish to do so, but encourage them to try writing without them.
2. Encourage students to continue using the graphing process for two more stories and then tell them that future graphing is up to them.

Variation: Partner Learning Format

Divide the class into dyads by pairing a higher performing student with a lower performing student. Have students work in pairs beginning in Stage 2 to determine the number of parts in their previously written stories or the sample stories. This variation is especially useful for classrooms containing students with disabilities or very diverse writing skills.

NOTES

1. Between one and three collaborative writing experiences (see Stage 6) are typically needed before students are ready to use the strategy independently.
2. Because SRSD in writing targets only selected aspects of the writing process, it should be integrated into existing programs or combined with other approaches to provide a comprehensive writing program. For example, SRSD can be implemented during writer's workshop in a program that uses a process approach to writing.

SOURCES

Danoff, B., Harris, K. R., & Graham, S. (1993). Incorporating strategy instruction within the writing process in the regular classroom: Effects on the writing of students with and without learning disabilities. *Journal of Reading Behavior, 25,* 295–322.

Graham, S., & Perin, D. (2007). A meta-analysis of writing instruction for adolescent students. *Journal of Educational Psychology, 99,* 445–476.

WRITING POWER: COGNITIVE STRATEGY INSTRUCTION IN EXPOSITORY WRITING

Overview

Effective expository writing requires metacognitive knowledge of the processes of planning, drafting, and revising, as well as the ability to use text structure to organize and improve compositions. Unfortunately, many students, especially those with learning disabilities, have a limited understanding of the processes involved in writing expository material and have difficulty using text structures to produce well-organized compositions. This multicomponent intervention teaches expository writing strategies and text structure processes in a four-stage instructional sequence: (1) text analysis, (2) modeling of the writing process, (3) guided practice, and (4) independent strategy use. A series of "think sheets" linked to different aspects of the writing process prompt students to engage in self-questions or self-instructional statements that promote the development of the inner language critical to planning and composing (Raphael & Englert, 1990). The acronym POWER is used to help students remember the five subprocesses in the writing process (Plan, Organize, Write, Edit/Editor, and Review). In the original study, conducted with 183 fourth and fifth graders from 12 schools in high-poverty neighborhoods, students with and without learning disabilities demonstrated significant gains in writing ability for two text structures taught during the intervention and a text structure on which they were not instructed (Englert, Raphael, Anderson, Anthony, & Stevens, 1991).

Goal

The goal of the POWER strategy is to improve students' expository writing skills with multistage strategy instruction, written prompts, self-editing, and peer collaboration. It is designed to facilitate writing after initial instruction. Thus it facilitates fluent application of the skill, which makes it a proficiency intervention.

Intervention Intensity

The POWER strategy is designed for small groups. Aspects of it address good core instruction in writing and could be used for an entire classroom, and the intervention could be intensified through increased dosage, but it probably works best with small groups.

Materials

1. Four passages taken from student writing examples from the previous year or mock examples illustrating one or more types of expository text structures (explanation, compare/contrast, problem/solution, expert, etc.) and varying in quality from poor to good.
2. Copies of six "think sheets," one copy of each think sheet per student, as follows:
   a. *Plan* think sheet (see Figure 4.5 for an example).

Name: _____ Date: _____

Topic: _____

Who: For whom am I writing?

Why: Why am I writing this?

What: What do I already know about the topic?

How: How do I group my ideas?

First main idea:	*Second main idea:*
Point 1:	Point 1:
Point 2:	Point 2:
Point 3:	Point 3:
Third main idea:	*Fourth main idea:*
Point 1:	Point 1:
Point 2:	Point 2:
Point 3:	Point 3:

FIGURE 4.5. Plan Think Sheet. Adapted from Raphael and Englert (1990). Copyright 1990 by Wiley. Adapted by permission.

   b. *Organize* think sheet, consisting of a text structure map or set of questions related to the target text structure. For example, an explanation think sheet would list questions such as "What is being explained?"; "What materials/things do I need?"; "What is the setting?"; and "What are the steps?"

   c. *Write* think sheet, consisting of lined sheets of paper for translating ideas from the Plan and Organize think sheets into a first draft.

   d. *Edit* think sheet, listing questions such as "What do I like best?"; "Why?"; "What parts are not clear?"; "Why not?"; "What do I need to add?"; and "What questions do I have for my editor?"

   e. *Editor* think sheet, with a list of instructions parallel to the questions on the Edit think sheet, such as "Read your classmate's paper"; "Star the parts you liked best"; "Place question marks by places that are not clear"; "List your suggestions about what needs to be added."

   f. *Revise* think sheet, consisting of a sheet of lined paper for listing the suggestions made by the author and reader during the editing step.

3. Posterboard chart displaying the acronym POWER (Plan, Organize, Write, Edit/Editor, Review) for the strategy steps.

Options to Monitor Progress

1. Have a group of target students or the entire class write a composition comparing and contrasting two people, places, or things (comparison–contrast text structure). Empha-

size that they should write their papers for someone who does not know anything about their subject. Score the papers for each of five traits: (a) identification of the two things being compared and contrasted; (b) description of how the two things are alike; (c) explanation of how the two things are different; (d) use of key words (e.g., *alike, different, but*); and (e) adherence to comparison–contrast text structure (i.e., introduction sentence, similarities/differences, conclusion). For each trait, award a score of "0" if the trait is not present, "1" if the trait is present, and "2" if the trait is highly developed (maximum score = 10 points).

2. Have a group of target students or the entire class write papers explaining how to do something (explanation text structure). Emphasize that they should write their papers for someone who does not know anything about their subject. Score the papers for each of four traits: (a) introduction to the topic being explained; (b) inclusion of a comprehensive sequence of steps; (c) inclusion of key or signal words (e.g., *first, second, third, finally*); and (d) adherence to explanation text structure (i.e., introduction, logical sequence of steps, and closure). For each trait, award a score of "0" if the trait is not present, "1" if the trait is present, and "2" if the trait is highly developed (maximum score = 8 points).

3. Have the entire class write comparison–contrast or explanation papers, as described above. Score the papers according to the following 5-point holistic scale to indicate the overall appeal of the paper and the extent to which the student accomplished the purpose of writing a comparison–contrast or explanation paper: 1 = unacceptable quality, 2 = poor quality, 3 = fair quality, 4 = average quality, 5 = high quality.

Intervention Steps

Stage 1: Text Analysis

1. Explain to the students that they will be learning a set of strategies for planning and writing that can help them write better compositions. Explain that they will have the opportunity to practice the strategies in pairs so that they can give and receive feedback from their classmates on their compositions.

2. Display the chart and tell the students that they can remember the strategies by using the acronym "POWER," which stands for the five subprocesses in the writing process: *plan, organize, write, edit/editor,* and *revise.* Encourage the students to memorize the subprocesses, using the acronym.

3. Display a transparency of a student writing example or mock example of the first target text structure on the overhead projector while you lead a think-aloud discussion of the features of the text structure and the quality of the writing sample.

4. For example, for an explanation text structure, discuss the text aids to comprehension (e.g., key words such as *first* and *second* that indicate the location of steps) and the kinds of questions the text was intended to answer (e.g., did the writer address "What is being explained?"; "Who or what materials are involved?"; "Where does it take place?"; and "What are the steps?").

5. Also think aloud about your own problems in understanding the example and invite students to discuss the type of additional information that would answer readers' questions.

6. Using additional examples of varying quality, invite students to participate in the text analysis process themselves by identifying signal words, asking text structure questions, and posing readers' questions.

Stage 2: Modeling the Writing Process

1. Using the overhead projector and transparency, introduce the *plan* think sheet. Explain to students that it will help them remember ideas from their own knowledge and experiences, consider strategies related to identifying their audience and purpose for writing, and develop a plan for grouping their ideas into categories. Stress that all of the think sheets are simply note-taking tools to help them record their ideas for later reference.

Stage 3: Guided and Collaborative Practice

1. Invite students to participate in a dialogue about the writing process as you use the *plan* think sheet to construct a class paper on a topic related to the target text structure (comparison–contrast, explanation, or expert).
2. As instruction proceeds, have students assume increasing responsibility for self-questions and planning strategies, while you act as scribe to record students' ideas on the *plan* think sheet and guide students' strategy use and assumption of the writing dialogue.
3. Introduce the other think sheets in a similar way by modeling and thinking aloud while performing the writing process. For example, demonstrate how the *organize* think sheet can help students organize their ideas into text structure categories and use the target text structure as a map to plan their compositions.

Stage 4: Collaborative and Independent Practice

1. Have students develop plans for individual papers involving the same text structure as the modeled paper.
2. After students have planned their individual papers, divide the class into pairs and have partners share their plans, including their *plan* think sheets, to elicit feedback, questions, and advice from each other.
3. Display examples of strategy use and problems encountered by students on overhead transparencies to guide the writing discussion.
4. Continue to provide modeling and feedback on the strategies as students develop more independence in writing. If desired, have students prepare independently a paper for publication in a class book.
5. Repeat these stages for each of the targeted text structures.

NOTES

1. Allow one training session per think sheet. Teachers should individualize think sheets according to their own preferences, the types of texts students are writing, and the individual needs of students.
2. To avoid embarrassing students by displaying their low-quality written productions, select examples saved from the previous year, create sample papers, or retype student papers on a word processor and edit them until the authors cannot be recognized.

SOURCES

Englert, C. S., Raphael, T. E., Anderson, L. M., Anthony, H. M., & Stevens, D. D. (1991). Making writing strategies and self-talk visible: Writing instruction in regular and special education classrooms. *American Educational Research Journal, 28,* 337–372.

Raphael, T. E., & Englert, C. S. (1990). Writing and reading: Partners in constructing meaning. *The Reading Teacher, 43,* 388–400.

PLAN AND WRITE: SRSD FOR ESSAY WRITING

Overview

Writing essays is a frequent requirement in the middle and high school curriculum and, increasingly, on high-stakes assessments. In this intervention, students learn to plan and write expository essays using the SRSD model of instruction. Six instructional stages provide a framework for strategy development and can be combined, reordered, repeated, or modified, depending on teacher preference and student needs. In the original investigations, implemented with seventh and eighth graders in six regular education and three inclusive classrooms, the strategy had positive effects on essay length, quality, and completeness for all of the target students, including low-achieving, average, and high-achieving writers, as well as students with learning disabilities (De La Paz, 1999; De La Paz, Owen, Harris, & Graham, 2000). Moreover, the positive changes in writing performance and writing behaviors, such as planning, were maintained over a 1-month follow-up. Teachers and students alike were enthusiastic about the effects of the intervention, and the seventh-grade participants in one study reported that they applied the strategy on their high-stakes competency examination. A variation for enhancing vocabulary and spelling is also presented.

Goal

PLAN and WRITE is designed to teach students a strategy for planning, writing, and revising expository essays, as well as a set of strategies for regulating their own writing behavior. It is a self-regulation strategy that facilitates writing after initial instruction. Thus it facilitates fluent application of the skill, which makes it a proficiency intervention.

Intervention Intensity

The PLAN and WRITE SRSD has been shown to work well with groups of students and with students with severe writing needs. Therefore, it seems most appropriate as a small-group intervention or for individual students. Aspects of it could be incorporated into core writing instruction.

Materials

1. Posterboard chart listing the PLAN (*P*ay attention to prompt, *L*ist main ideas, *A*dd supporting ideas, *N*umber your ideas) and WRITE (*W*ork from your plan to develop your thesis statement, *R*emember your goals, *I*nclude transition words for each paragraph, *T*ry to use different kinds of sentences, *E*xciting words in your essay) strategy steps.
2. Cue cards, consisting of index cards listing the strategy steps, one per student.
3. Projected and print copies of several student essay examples from the previous year or mock examples, one copy of each example per student.
4. Brainstorming sheet, consisting of a sheet of paper for identifying possible responses to a writing prompt and outlining main and supporting ideas, one per student.
5. Essay sheet, consisting of a sheet of paper with a space at the top for writing the thesis statement and preprinted subheadings, such as "introductory paragraph"; "body paragraphs one, two, and three"; and "conclusion," one per student.

6. Highlighters, one per student.
7. Copies of essay prompts, one per student; prompts should elicit expository text, such as:
   a. "Choose a country you would like to visit. Write an essay explaining why you would like to visit this country."
   b. "Think about how students can improve their grades. Write an essay explaining why getting good grades is important and what students can do to improve their grades."
   c. "Think about rules you believe are unfair. Write an essay stating the rules you think should be changed and explaining why you think so."
8. Copies of the classroom rubric or standards for grading essays or the state assessment scoring rubric (optional; see Intervention Steps, Stage 3).
9. Quiz with questions about strategy use in essay writing (optional; see Intervention Steps, Stage 6).
10. Posterboard chart or section of the chalkboard listing "Million Dollar Words" (optional; see Variation).

Options to Monitor Progress

1. Distribute copies of an essay prompt to the entire class. Have students write an essay based on the prompt within a 35-minute time limit, a period equivalent to the requirements of your state's writing assessment, or another appropriate time frame. Note that the essays obtained in this or the next option can be used as baseline essays in the individual student conferences conducted in Stage 3 of the Intervention Steps.
2. For each essay, count the number of functional essay elements as follows: (a) *premise*, defined as a statement specifying the writer's position on the topic; (b) *reasons*, defined as explanations to support or refute a position; (c) *conclusion*, defined as a closing statement summing up an individual paragraph or the overall premise of the essay; and (d) *elaborations*, defined as a unit of text that expands on a premise, reason, or conclusion in terms of emphasis, examples, or other functional content.
3. Administer an essay prompt to a group of target students or the entire class as described above. Rate each essay on a holistic scale from 1–7 based on the quality of the ideas, development and organization, coherence, mechanics, and quality of vocabulary as follows: 1 = unacceptable, 2 = poor, 3 = fair, 4 = average, 5 = good, 6 = very good, 7 = outstanding.

Intervention Steps

Stage 1: Overview of Purpose

1. Tell students that they are going to learn a writing strategy for composing expository essays that will help them be more capable and confident writers.
2. Set the goal of learning, such as preparing for the writing proficiency essay on the state assessment, improving essay writing ability for use in content-area classes, and so on.
3. Discuss how writers use planning strategies when they write and the benefits of using those strategies.
4. Using the chart, present the PLAN and WRITE strategy and the rationale for each step.

Stage 2: Activating Background Knowledge

1. For the first session in this stage, display a sample essay on the overhead projector and have students read it collaboratively. Ask them to identify the introductory, body, and

concluding paragraphs. Help them to determine whether the sample essay contains a good thesis statement and to identify transition words in each paragraph.

2. Have students search the essay for different sentence types in terms of form (simple, compound, and complex) and function (declarative, imperative, exclamatory, and question). Have students take notes during the discussion and incorporate their suggestions for revision on the transparency.

3. During a second session, conduct a similar review of the same essay with the primary focus on the writer's use of vocabulary. Help student identify "million dollar words," that is, words they consider to be exciting, interesting, and unique. Have them make suggestions for changes in vocabulary that would improve the essay.

Stage 3: Review of Students' Initial Writing Abilities

1. Explain the classroom rubrics or standards for grading essays or the scoring rubric used in the state assessment, if appropriate.

2. Distribute copies of an essay prompt, and have students practice Step 1 of the PLAN and WRITE strategy while you conduct brief individual conferences reviewing students' performance on their most recent baseline essay.

3. If desired, give students individual copies of the classroom or state assessment scoring rubric and identify one or two features in need of improvement. Encourage students to select one or two writing goals to address the identified weaknesses, such as keeping on topic, using mature vocabulary, having few or no errors in grammar, and making the essay lively and fun to read.

Stage 4: Modeling the Planning Strategy

1. Using the projector, display another essay prompt and model the use of the PLAN and WRITE strategy by thinking aloud through the planning and writing process. Include a variety of self-instructions to show students how to manage the process (e.g., "OK, I've decided to write my thesis statement first, so it goes at the beginning of my introductory paragraph").

2. Identify the essential components of the prompt and model the use of the brainstorming sheet to record and organize your ideas. Also demonstrate how to use the essay sheet to write the thesis statement and decide whether to place it as the first or last sentence in the introductory paragraph.

3. Distribute cue cards to students and demonstrate how to use them as reminders of what each paragraph should include.

4. Throughout the demonstration, emphasize how good writers use the processes and procedures several times during planning and composition. For example, during the last two steps of WRITE, revise sentence types and vocabulary as you model writing the paper.

Stage 5: Collaborative Practice

1. Display an essay prompt on the projector, and help students use the PLAN and WRITE strategy to plan and compose an essay on a classwide basis.

2. Divide students into dyads or triads. Distribute copies of another essay prompt, and have the students collaborate in planning and composing a second essay. Discuss and model expected behaviors for collaborative writing practice. Circulate to monitor behavior and provide assistance as needed. As you circulate, write brief positive comments on students' papers and note where revisions would be helpful.

3. After students have composed their essays, conduct a whole-class discussion about various essay components, such as the relationship between introductory and concluding paragraphs, different sentence types and forms, and examples of mature vocabulary in student essays.
4. Have students work again in dyads or triads to give each other feedback and suggestions for revision. Give students highlighters and a list of criteria to search for in their partners' papers (e.g., appropriate content, focus on the topic, use of transition words, use of mature vocabulary words). Allow time for students to revise their papers and circulate to answer questions, prompt, and provide assistance as needed.

Stage 6: Independent Practice

1. Explain to students that their goal is to be able to use the strategy without relying on the procedural supports (cue cards and brainstorming and essay sheets) to generate an essay within class or state assessment time limits and to demonstrate mastery of at least one of their self-selected goals.
2. Distribute an essay prompt and have students use the strategy to write an essay. Provide assistance as needed but gradually fade prompting and the use of the procedural supports as students become more proficient in using the strategy.
3. During independent practice sessions, conduct a second set of individual conferences to assess students' mastery of the strategy. Ask students to recall each strategy step, provide examples of transition words, provide a word and a synonym for that word, and state how they plan to write an introductory paragraph. Alternately, administer a quiz requiring students to respond to these questions in writing and lead a classwide discussion of the results afterward.
4. Have students select one of their essays for inclusion in a class writing portfolio.

Variation: PLAN and WRITE with Million-Dollar Word Search

As part of Stage 5, have students search each other's papers for "million-dollar words" and highlight the words they identify. Have students add their million-dollar words to a list posted at the front of the classroom or written on the chalkboard. As the words accumulate, group them in sets of 5–10 to create weekly vocabulary and spelling lists or use them as bonus words in the regular weekly spelling test.

NOTES

1. In the original studies, teachers taught the strategy over periods ranging from 2 weeks (De La Paz et al., 2000) to 4–6 weeks (De La Paz, 1999). Several sessions are needed for each of Stages 2, 4, 5, and 6.
2. This strategy allows for paired or small-group collaborative learning during many aspects of the writing process. Change pairs or groupings each week so that students have an opportunity to work with peers with a variety of writing abilities.

SOURCES

De La Paz, S. (1999). Self-regulated strategy instruction in regular education settings: Improving outcomes for students with and without learning disabilities. *Learning Disabilities Research and Practice, 14,* 92–106.

De La Paz, S., Owen, B., Harris, K. R., & Graham, S. (2000). Riding Elvis' motorcycle: Using self-regulated strategy development to PLAN and WRITE for a state writing exam. *Learning Disabilities Research and Practice, 15,* 101–109.

ADDITIONAL RESOURCES

The Center on Accelerating Student Learning (CASL) website (*www.kc.vanderbilt.edu/casl/srsd. html*) provides links to sample lesson plans for writing interventions based on the SRSI model, including strategies for story writing and early opinion essays.

PLANNING AND STORY-WRITING STRATEGY

Overview

It seems that very little triggers concerns about a student's writing skills more than poor penmanship, but good composition is what truly defines good writers. Moreover, it is often difficult to get struggling writers to write enough so that their writing skills can be assessed. Strategies for enhancing writing skills have consistently led to improved composition and overall skill in writing. The planning and story-writing strategy is an intervention that involves having the student Pick an idea, Organize her or his thoughts (i.e., develop a writing plan) and Write and say more, which is remembered by the acronym *POW*. Research has consistently demonstrated that the POW intervention has increased composition skills for struggling writers in elementary school (Lienemann, Graham, Leader-Janssen, & Reid, 2006).

Goal

The goal of the POW strategy is to help students organize their thoughts to help make writing a step-by-step process rather than an overwhelming idea. The writing strategy is designed to facilitate writing after initial instruction. Thus it facilitates fluent application of the skill, which makes it a proficiency intervention.

Intervention Intensity

Most of the research with POW has been done with individual students who are struggling writers. Therefore, POW is appropriate for use as an intensive intervention for individual students, but it could also be adapted for use with small groups or even for classwide applications.

Materials

1. Writing paper.
2. A pencil for the student.
3. Reinforcers as needed.

Options to Monitor Progress

1. Perhaps the most straightforward way to assess the effects of the intervention is to examine the writing that the student completes within classroom instruction.
2. Teachers could also conduct curriculum-based measures for written expression using age-appropriate story starters. For each assessment, be sure to provide 1 minute to plan and

3 minutes to write. The resulting writing could be scored with words written per minute, which is a measure of production. It would also be helpful to use a rubric that examines the organization of the writing sample.

Intervention Steps

1. Start by having the student brainstorm ideas. It usually helps to provide parameters from which to pick (e.g., "Today we are going to write about summer").
2. The teacher/interventionist should first model thinking out loud and brainstorming for a different but related topic.
3. Have the student brainstorm a list of topics and ask questions or give cues (e.g., "it is OK to take your time and pick a really good idea") as needed to keep the brainstorming going.
4. Have the student cross off any ideas that are less appealing and then select a topic from those that are left.
5. Model how to organize thoughts into an outline or framework. Do not use a typical outline format with its confusing Roman numbers, just list three main ideas—one at the top of the page, one in the middle, and one at the end. Then write indented supporting ideas underneath each one.
6. After modeling how to organize one's thoughts, ask the student to organize his or her thoughts in the same manner. Be sure to give feedback as you go so that the student uses the correct process, and be sure to give frequent verbal reinforcement.
7. The last phase of the strategy is difficult to model because it involves actually writing. The interventionist would then describe his or her thought processes and would discuss how he or she could answer *who, what, where, when, why,* and *how* for the writing assignment. He or she would also model how to decide whether the writing makes sense and is complete.
8. The student would then start writing while the interventionist provides liberal and immediate feedback that focuses on content rather than penmanship, spelling, or punctuation. She or he should also make encouraging statements and comments about how much fun writing can be when you know what to do.
9. Provide the student with a cue card that contains the acronym POW and what each letter stands for. During the very next writing assignment, work with the student again, but do not provide any modeling; just give immediate corrective and encouraging feedback. Repeat steps above as needed.

Implementation

Although a different aspect of writing from forming letters, composition may be a frustrating task for students who struggle with writing. Thus, provide frequent encouraging statements and reinforcement. Successful writing can be enjoyable, so be sure to reduce reinforcement as the student learns the skill. Additionally, the thought processes involved in writing are not observable but are extremely important. Therefore, interventionists need to explicitly and frequently model what they are thinking.

ADDITIONAL RESOURCES

Burns, M. K., Riley-Tillman, T. C., & VanDerHeyden, A. M. (2012). *RTI applications: Vol. 1. Academic and behavioral interventions.* New York: Guilford Press.

Harris, K. R., Graham, S., & Mason, L. H. (2003). Self-regulated strategy development in the classroom: Part of a balanced approach to writing instruction for students with disabilities. *Focus on Exceptional Children, 35*(7), 1–16.

Harris, K. R., Graham, S., Mason, L. H., & Friedlander, B. (2008). *POWERFUL writing strategies for all students.* Baltimore: Brookes.

Lienemann, T. O., Graham, S., Leader-Janssen, B., & Reid, R. (2006). Improving the writing performance of struggling writers in second grade. *Journal of Special Education, 40,* 66–78.

PEER EDITING FOR EFFECTIVE REVISION

Overview

Learning to revise is an important component skill in the writing process. To revise successfully, students must reflect on what they have written, develop criteria for evaluating their work, and implement the revisions. Compared with more proficient writers, less skilled writers make fewer revisions, and the changes they do make are usually attempts to correct mechanical errors that have little impact on overall quality. In this intervention, students work in pairs to help each other revise written productions, using a nine-step strategy that incorporates word processing in the composing and revising stages. In the original study, implemented with six seventh graders with learning disabilities in a school computer laboratory, the peer editing intervention was successful not only in increasing the number and quality of revisions for all target students but also in increasing overall writing quality in terms of content, organization, and style (Stoddard & MacArthur, 1993). Subsequent research has consistently demonstrated the effects of peer editing both for the student receiving the feedback and for the student who is editing someone else's writing (Lundstrom & Baker, 2008). The strategy can be easily adapted for students of diverse writing abilities and for a variety of writing instructional goals. Two variations are presented: a paper-and-pencil version and a version for elementary-grade students.

Goal

Peer editing improves writing performance by integrating strategy instruction in the writing process, peer collaboration, and word processing. Given that it is designed to facilitate writing after initial instruction, peer editing supports the fluent application of the skill, which makes it a proficiency intervention.

Intervention Intensity

Peer editing was designed to work with groups of students. Thus it could be incorporated into core instruction, but it could also be used as a targeted intervention for small groups of students.

Materials

1. Computers and software word processing programs.
2. Prompt sheets, consisting of printed copies of the nine steps in the peer editing strategy (see Introduction and Training, Step 5), one per student.
3. Eight to 10 writing prompts on computer disks, memory sticks, or in a computer file; prompts should be designed to elicit personal narratives, such as, "Think about a time

when you were surprised by something. What happened and why were you surprised? Write a story for your friends to read about the time when you were surprised."

4. Printed copies of sample personal narratives, one per student.
5. Projected sample personal narrative (optional).
6. Writing portfolios or notebooks with lined paper, one per student (see Variation 1).
7. Paper copies of writing prompts, one per student (see Variation 1).

Options to Monitor Progress

1. Have a group of target students or the entire class write and revise between one and three stories according to the following procedures:
   a. In an initial session using computers, have students call up the class file with a writing prompt printed at the top. Tell them to take a minute to read the prompt and plan their composition. Explain that they will have a chance to make revisions later. Have students compose their stories at the computers, save them, and print hard copies.
   b. In a second session, give students printed copies of their stories and tell them to think about changes they can make to improve their stories and to make notes on the first draft with a pencil or pen. Then have them make revisions on the computer and print a final draft.
   c. Score student compositions using one or more of the following measures:
      • Number of words, counting each word that is recognizable as a word.
      • Proportion of mechanical errors, defined as the number of errors in spelling, capitalization, and punctuation, divided by the total number of words.
      • Number of appropriate revisions, including changes in mechanics, organization, vocabulary, and other features that improve the quality of the composition.
      • Overall quality on a scale from 1 to 7, as follows: 1 = unsatisfactory, 2 = poor, 3 = fair, 4 = average, 5 = good, 6 = very good, 7 = excellent.
      • Quality change from first to second draft on a 5-point scale, as follows: –2 = second draft much worse than first, –1 = second draft worse than first, 0 = second draft same quality as first, +1 = second draft better than first, +2 = second draft much better than first.
2. Have a group of target students or the entire class write and revise between one and three stories, using a paper-and-pencil format. Rate the revised stories on a 3-point scale, as follows: –1 = worse than the first draft, 0 = no change, +1 = better than the first draft.

Intervention Steps

Introduction and Training

1. Tell students that they are going to work in pairs to learn a strategy for improving their written compositions. Explain that the class will be focusing on writing personal narratives and using computers to make the task easier and more fun.
2. If necessary, conduct a training session on the use of the computers and the word processing program that will be used for the intervention. Conduct the initial peer editing training session in the classroom rather than in a computer laboratory, however.
3. Discuss with students the characteristics of a personal narrative—for example: "A personal narrative is a true story about you that describes something that happened to you so clearly that readers feel as if they had been there."
4. Give each student copies of a sample personal narrative and the peer editing procedures. Lead a discussion of the importance of revision in the overall writing process.

5. Explain each step of the peer editing strategy, as described below. If desired, use an overhead projector with a transparency of the sample narrative to demonstrate the revision procedures. Explain that both students in a pair complete the first two steps in turn. Then each student works independently on the other student's paper as a peer editor, after which the partners take turns discussing the two papers.

   Step 1: Listen carefully and follow along as the author reads the first draft of his or her composition aloud.

   Step 2: Tell the author what you liked best.

   Step 3: Reread your peer editor's paper to yourself.

   Step 4: Ask yourself the four key revision questions about the composition:

   Parts? Does it have a good beginning, middle, and ending?

   Order? Does it follow a logical sequence?

   Details? Where could the writer add more details?

   Clarity? Is there any part that is hard to understand?

   Step 5: Make notes on your peer editor's draft based on the revision questions.

   Step 6: Discuss your suggestions with the author.

   Step 7: Work independently at the computer to revise your own paper.

   Step 8: Meet again with your partner to discuss the revisions you each have made and to check each other's papers for mechanical errors.

   Step 9: Work independently at the computer to make final revisions and print out your composition.

6. Guide a pair of students through a demonstration of the strategy in a paper-and-pencil format, using the same sample narrative. Be sure to discuss the importance of positive peer support during the demonstration.

7. Assign partners, distribute copies of a second sample personal narrative, and conduct a classwide practice. Circulate to provide assistance and encourage appropriate peer editing behaviors, as needed.

8. Using another sample narrative or students' own compositions from the observation period, conduct at least one more training session in the classroom with a paper-and-pencil format.

Implementation

1. Using a prepared prompt, have students compose a personal narrative on computers and then work in pairs to apply the peer editing strategy. Encourage students to refer to their prompt sheets and to memorize the four key words in the revision questions. Circulate to provide assistance and prompt positive peer editing behaviors, as needed.

2. In a second session, have students make the final revisions to their drafts on computers and print out hard copies. Change pairs every few weeks to give students an opportunity to work with peer editors with a range of writing abilities.

Variations

VARIATION 1: PAPER AND PENCIL

Teach the strategy using a paper-and-pencil format, with printed copies of writing prompts. After the peer editing pairs make notes about suggested changes on each other's first drafts, have students recopy their own stories, incorporating the revisions.

VARIATION 2: ELEMENTARY-GRADE VARIATION

Initially teach the strategy using a paper-and-pencil format as described in Variation 1. Include only two revision questions in Step 4 of the peer editing process: (1) Clarity? Is there anything that is not clear? (2) Details? Where could more information be added? When most of the students are demonstrating improvement in their revisions, introduce the word processing composition and revision format.

NOTES

1. In the original study, students made more revisions with handwriting than with word processing, both before and after implementation. The authors suggest that the greater number of revisions for handwritten narratives was due to incidental revisions made during recopying, whereas revisions made with the word processor were intentional.
2. Allow two sessions for writing and revising each composition.

SOURCES

Lundstrom, K., & Baker, W. (2009). To give is better than to receive: The benefits of peer review to the reviewer's own writing. *Journal of Second Language Writing, 18,* 30–43.

Stoddard, B., & MacArthur, C. A. (1993). A peer editor strategy: Guiding learning-disabled students in response and revision. *Research in the Teaching of English, 27,* 76–103.

Interventions to Improve Content-Area Performance

Intervention efforts often ignore content areas (e.g., social studies, science), which is problematic given that much of secondary instruction occurs in content areas and success in content areas involves reading and comprehending expository text while demonstrating advanced understanding on diverse assessments (Wexler, Reed, Mitchell, Doyle, & Clancy, 2015). Although there are specific skills for enhancing success in content areas, how to best instruct in them continues to be an area of debate (Brozo, Moorman, Meyer, & Stewart, 2013). *Collaborative Strategic Reading* and other reading comprehension interventions can be helpful for content areas, but the interventions described here are specifically for this important and often-overlooked area.

CONCEPT MAPPING TO IMPROVE COMPREHENSION

Overview

Concept maps, also called *cognitive maps* or *graphic organizers,* use lines, arrows, figures, and diagrams to show how key ideas in textual material are organized and related. Concept mapping facilitates both teaching and learning in the content areas by translating textbook information into a visual display that serves as a blueprint for organizing a reading assignment or a written report based on that reading. Moreover, in contrast to a traditional lecture format, in which students listen passively to teacher-delivered instruction, concept mapping increases academic engagement by requiring students to analyze and organize relevant textual information. In this intervention, students learn to use concept maps displaying the connections between major and minor concepts in science lessons.

In the original study, conducted with 124 low-achieving, predominantly Hispanic, inner-city seventh graders, concept mapping instruction improved comprehension scores on an end-of-unit test by approximately six standard deviations over traditional read-and-discuss science instruction (Guastello, Beasley, & Sinatra, 2000). Meta-analytic research with 55 studies found large effects for increasing student retention of material (Nesbit & Adesope, 2006). The strategy can be used to enhance comprehension in any subject in which students must understand and remember textual material. A variation with text reading at home that permits more rapid coverage of the curriculum is also included.

Goal

Concept maps help students understand, categorize, and remember content when they are used during whole-class instruction. Concept mapping facilitates initial learning, but the intervention focuses more on remembering the material and understanding it to better generalize it.

Intervention Intensity

Concept mapping works with classrooms of students and could be used within content-area instruction. Concept maps are also appropriate for small groups of students or even as part of an intensive intervention program for individual students.

Materials

1. Content-area curricular materials, including a teacher's guide and student textbooks or materials, one textbook or set of materials per student.
2. Copy of a sample concept map for a previously taught chapter or unit of study that can be presented to the entire class. See *www.eduplace.com/graphicorganizer* for examples, or type "graphic organizer" into a search engine.
3. Two concept maps for each unit of study to be targeted (one completed map as a key and one blank map per student).

Options to Monitor Progress

1. Calculate the class average percent-correct score on science quizzes and tests for several weeks or for the previous grading period.
2. Calculate the number of students with grades of D or F in science for the current marking period or the school year thus far.
3. Administer curriculum-based vocabulary-matching probes to the entire class or a group of target students.

Intervention Steps

1. Explain to the students that they will be learning a new way of analyzing and organizing information in their science textbooks so that they can understand and remember the material better and do better on tests and quizzes.
2. Introduce the unit of study by asking questions to assess students' prior knowledge of the

content. Also ask students what they would like to learn about the topic and help them to make predictions about the topic.

3. Give a global overview of the unit and introduce the main unit objectives. For example, for a unit on the circulatory system, the main objectives are: (a) understanding the three main parts of the circulatory system, (b) identifying the subcategories of the circulatory system, and (c) describing the subcategory characteristics and functions.
4. Display the concept map based on familiar material on a transparency or Smartboard. Explain how the map depicts the main concept and graphically illustrates how the subordinate ideas and details in the material are related to the main concept. Explain that you will be helping them construct concept maps for the new material to be covered.
5. At the beginning of the unit, display the blank map. During each lesson, continue constructing the map as you read through the unit with the students section by section. As you fill in the map, call on students to help you locate the information to be included.
6. After each section has been read, conduct a discussion of the key ideas, and have students fill in the relevant parts of their own concept maps.
7. Continue discussing the material in the unit and helping students to map each major component and specific details under each of the subheadings. Repeat this process until you have completed the entire unit and students have completed their concept maps.
8. Have students take the concept maps home as study guides for the unit test.
9. As students become more proficient in constructing the maps, have them work in pairs to map an assignment independently, using a concept map template previously introduced in class. Then have the student pairs construct concept maps on their own for a section in a unit. Review the maps as a whole-class activity, and have students modify their maps as needed.

Variation: Concept Mapping with Home Prereading

Have students read sections of the target unit as homework the night before you conduct concept mapping instruction with that content. This variation permits more rapid coverage of the curriculum, but it is not recommended for classes with large numbers of very poor readers.

SOURCES

Guastello, E. F., Beasley, T. M., & Sinatra, R. C. (2000). Concept mapping effects on science content comprehension of low-achieving inner-city seventh graders. *Remedial and Special Education, 21,* 356–365.

Nesbit, J. C., & Adesope, O. O. (2006). Learning with concept and knowledge maps: A meta-analysis. *Review of Educational Research, 76,* 413–448.

Novak, J. D., & Canas, A. J. (2006). *The theory underlying concept maps and how to construct them.* Pensacola: Florida Institute for Human and Machine Cognition. Available at *http:// cmap.ihmc.us/Publications/researchPapers/theorycmaps/TheoryUnderlyingConceptMaps. bck-11-01-06.htm.*

ADDITIONAL RESOURCES

Concept map templates and concept map generation programs are available for free download on numerous websites, including the University of Oregon's Computer-Based Study Strategies (*http://*

cbss.uoregon.edu/clearing/index.html), Soft Schools concept map maker (*www.softschools.com/ teacher_resources/concept_map_maker*), Teach-nology (*www.teach-nology.com*), and Intervention Central (*http://interventioncentral.com/sites/default/files/pdfs/pdfs_interventions/advanced_ story_map_worksheet.pdf*).

COLLABORATIVE STRATEGIC READING

Overview

Many students perform poorly in content-area subjects because they lack the metacognitive skills necessary to monitor their reading comprehension, as well as strategies to improve their understanding when they have difficulty. Collaborative strategic reading (CSR) combines reading comprehension strategy instruction with cooperative learning to enhance students' understanding of expository textual material. Students learn four strategies through direct instruction and teacher modeling: (1) *Preview* (previewing and predicting), (2) *Click and Clunk* (monitoring for understanding and vocabulary knowledge), (3) *Get the Gist* (identifying the main idea), and (4) *Wrap Up* (self-questioning for understanding). After students have become proficient in applying the strategies during teacher-directed activities, they work in groups to implement the strategies collaboratively, with each student performing a designated role. Originally developed to enhance comprehension and content knowledge acquisition for students with learning disabilities and low-achieving students, CSR has also yielded positive outcomes for English language learners and average- and high-achieving students across a range of grade levels, including elementary, middle, and high school (Klingner, Vaughn, & Schumm, 1998; Vaughn & Klingner, 1999). CSR can be used to enhance comprehension and domain knowledge in any content-area subject or with narrative textual material.

Goal

CSR improves reading comprehension, increases conceptual learning, and promotes active student involvement in content-area classes by teaching comprehension strategies within a collaborative peer context. The intervention involves explicit instruction of comprehension strategies, which makes it an acquisition intervention.

Intervention Intensity

CSR works with classrooms of students and could be used within content-area instruction but is also appropriate for use as a targeted intervention with small groups of students.

Materials

1. "Cue cards," consisting of index cards listing the responsibilities for each group member, one set of cards per group.
2. "Learning logs," consisting of preprinted sheets of paper, one per student.
3. Three-hole binders or folders with sheets of lined paper and pockets for learning logs, one per student.
4. Posterboard charts or projected learning log form and CSR plan.
5. Curricular materials, such as content-area textbooks and student newspapers or magazines.
6. Timers or watches with second hands, one per group (optional).

Options to Monitor Progress

1. Calculate scores on homework, quizzes, or unit tests in the selected content-area subject for the entire class or a target group of students for the grading period to date.
2. Administer curriculum-based vocabulary-matching (VM-CBM) probes to the entire class or a group of target students.
3. Using a Classwide Scanning Form to conduct observations for 30–45 minutes for 4–7 days during the selected content-area class. Use a 3- or 5-minute interval, scan the room at the end of each interval, starting with the front of the room and ending with the back, and tally the number of students in each of the following behavior categories:
   a. *On-task behavior,* defined as asking or answering lesson-oriented questions, writing when requested, looking at the teacher during presentations, and any other behavior relevant to the lesson.
   b. *Off-task behavior,* defined as sitting without appropriate materials, looking at nonlesson materials, or failing to work after assignments have been made.
   c. *Disruptive behavior,* defined as any behavior interfering with instruction or the on-task behavior of other students, such as talking without permission, getting out of one's seat, or making noises.

Intervention Steps

Introduction and Training

1. Explain to students that they will be learning a set of strategies to help them understand and remember what they read. These are strategies that good readers use automatically when they read, but everyone can learn them. After students learn the strategies, they will be working in groups to apply them.
2. Display the Plan for Strategic Reading Chart (see Table 4.1). Explain that the *Preview* and *Wrap-Up* strategies are used only once per reading selection (*Preview* before reading the

TABLE 4.1. Steps to Preview Reading

Before reading

Step 1: Preview—List everything that you already know about the topic, predict what you will learn by reading, and read the first paragraph.

During reading

Step 2: Click and Clunk—Were there any parts that were hard to understand (clunks)? How can you fix the clunks? Use fix-up strategies.

   a. Reread the sentence with the clunk and the sentences before and after the clunk looking for clues.
   b. Reread the sentence without the clunk. Think about what would make sense.
   c. Look for a prefix or suffix in the clunk that might help.
   d. Break the clunk apart and look for smaller words you already know.

Step 3: Get the Gist—What is the most important *who* or *what*? What is the most important idea about the who or what? Do Steps 2 and 3 again with all the paragraphs or sections in the passage.

After reading

Step 4: Wrap Up—What questions would show that you understand the most important information? What did you learn?

entire passage for that session—typically 12–14 paragraphs—and *Wrap Up* after reading the entire passage), whereas the *Click and Clunk* and *Get the Gist* strategies are used after each paragraph or two.

3. Using a selection from a student magazine or newspaper, model the strategies described below, using a think-aloud procedure. Verbalize your thoughts to make explicit why, how, and when you apply each of the strategies while reading. As you model the strategies, display the learning log form on a chart or overhead projector. Explain that learning logs can be used for recording ideas while applying each strategy or for writing down "clunks" (unfamiliar words and concepts) and "gists" (main ideas).

STEP 1: PREVIEW

1. *Preview* is designed to generate interest and questions about the material, stimulate background knowledge and associations, and assist in predictions. When students have little background information about a topic, conduct this step as a whole-class activity prior to small-group work.
2. Using the selected passage, model the Preview steps as follows: (a) read the title; (b) examine the visual clues, such as pictures, tables, charts, and graphs; (c) read the headings and predict what they mean; (d) look for key words, as indicated by highlighting, underlining, and italics; (e) read the first and last paragraphs of the selection; and (f) predict what you think you will learn from the selection.
3. Using another selection, conduct a whole-class practice of the Preview step and provide feedback and assistance as needed.

STEP 2: CLICK AND CLUNK

1. Tell students that this step will help them think about what they do and don't understand about what they are reading. A "click" occurs when readers identify something they know—it clicks because it makes sense. A "clunk" is a word or concept that readers don't understand—it's like a running into a brick wall.
2. Display the learning log form and explain that learning logs can be used to record ideas while applying each strategy or to write down clunks.
3. Tell students that readers can "de-clunk" words by using "fix-up strategies," such as consulting a dictionary, rereading, or asking a classmate or the teacher. Refer to the fix-up strategies on the Plan for Strategic Reading chart, and tell students that these strategies can help them de-clunk difficult words and ideas.
4. Using the same selection as in Step 1, model the Click and Clunk process. Then have students read another short selection and practice clicking and clunking. Provide photocopies of the selection, so that students can mark their clicks and clunks in the margins of the text.

STEP 3: GET THE GIST

1. Explain that "getting the gist" means identifying the main idea or most critical information in a section of text (one or two paragraphs) and rephrasing it in one's own words.
2. Have students read two paragraphs in their text, think of a gist (a sentence of no more than 12 words summarizing the main idea), and write it on a sheet of paper. Call on students to share their gists and ask them to provide evidence to support them. Then have the students vote as a class on which gist is the best and why.

STEP 4: WRAP UP

1. Tell students that *Wrap Up* is an opportunity to review what they have read by asking themselves questions about the passage and thinking about the most important ideas.
2. Model a series of literal and inferential questions about the passage, such as: (a) "How would you . . . ?", (b) "How were _____ and _____ the same or different?", and (c) "How would you interpret . . . ?"
3. After modeling questions for the selection, help students generate their own questions.

Implementation

1. After conducting whole-class training and practice sessions for each step, divide the class into groups of four or five. Be sure that each group includes students with a variety of reading levels and at least one student with leadership skills.
2. Assign the following roles in each group and explain the tasks for each role as follows:
   a. *Leader*: Focuses the group on the four strategies by saying what to read next and what strategy to apply next. The leader also asks the teacher for assistance, if necessary.
   b. *Clunk expert*: Reminds the group of fix-up strategies for figuring out difficult words or concepts.
   c. *Gist expert*: Helps the group remember the steps in figuring out the main idea and makes sure that the main idea includes the key ideas without unnecessary details.
   d. *Announcer*: Calls on group members to read or share ideas and represents the group during whole-class group reporting.
   e. *Encourager* (if there is a fifth student in a group): Encourages all group members to participate, gives feedback to members, evaluates how well the group has worked together, and provides suggestions for improvement.
3. Initially, the clunk expert records the clunks and the gist expert records the gists. As students become more skillful in performing their roles, introduce the learning logs so that each student can record his or her own clunks and gists.
4. Give each group a set of cue cards. Explain that the cue cards are reminders of the steps each student in the group should follow. Rotate roles each week so that each student has an opportunity to practice all the functions.
5. Assign a selection from the textbook, and have the groups practice applying the four strategies. Initially, have the leader select group members to read the text aloud, two paragraphs at a time. Specify time limits for each of the steps, depending on the length of the instructional period, and call time for each step. If desired, have group members share their gists orally to save time as they work through the material. As the groups work, circulate to clarify difficult words, model strategy use, and provide positive feedback or redirection as needed.
6. After the group sessions, conduct a whole-class debriefing, during which you invite the groups to share their gists, clunks, and effective fix-up strategies.
7. Have the students work in CSR groups several times a week with expository text until they can use the strategies effectively (about 2–3 weeks for elementary school students or 1 week for middle and high school students). After students have reached proficiency, substitute CSR two or three times a week for whole-class textbook reading sessions.
8. Discontinue the cue cards as students become more proficient in using the strategies and carrying out their roles. Gradually discontinue whole-class timing, or have the groups serve as their own timekeepers.

Variation: Group-Prepared Learning Logs

Have students prepare learning logs as a collaborative rather than an individual activity. Assign one student per group to serve as recorder, and have the groups refer to their logs during whole-class discussions.

NOTES

1. Training takes about 4 days. For the first day of training, model the entire CSR plan to help students get the big picture. On subsequent days, provide instruction in how to implement each of the CSR strategies. Starting with the fourth day, teach students how to work in groups to implement the strategies on a collaborative basis.
2. When beginning CSR, use short selections from high-interest nonfiction publications, such as student news magazines or community-based newspapers, rather than from a textbook.

SOURCES

Klingner, J. K., Vaughn, S., & Schumm, J. S. (1998). Collaborative strategic reading during social studies in heterogeneous fourth-grade classrooms. *Elementary School Journal, 99,* 3–22.

Vaughn, S., & Klingner, J. K. (1999). Teaching reading comprehension through collaborative strategic reading. *Intervention in School and Clinic, 34,* 284–292.

ADDITIONAL RESOURCES

Resources for implementing Collaborative Strategic Reading are available at the website of the Vaughn Gross Center for Reading and Language Arts, University of Texas at Austin (*www. texasreading.org/utcrla*). A variety of CSR forms is also available at the International Reading Association's Read Write Think website (*www.readwritethink.org/lessons/lesson_view. asp?id=95*). A commercially published version of CSR is available from Sopris West (*www. sopriswest.com*).

USING CRITICAL THINKING MAPS TO IMPROVE CONTENT-AREA COMPREHENSION

Overview

Students often make poor grades in content-area subjects because they have difficulty comprehending their textbooks. Although they may have adequate word recognition skills, they have trouble learning and remembering textual information because they lack strategies for thinking critically about what they are reading and are unfamiliar with expository text structures. This intervention uses a model–lead–test format to teach students a mapping strategy that provides a framework for guiding their thinking processes as they read. In the original study, conducted with six high school students, four in a remedial reading program and two in a special education program for students with mild retardation, use of critical thinking maps was associated with significant increases on standardized vocabulary and comprehension tests and comprehension of lesson material, with improvement generalizing to similar content (Idol, 1987). In this adaptation, the one-to-one instructional format has been modified for classwide implementation. Critical thinking maps can be used in any subject that requires students to read expository text. Also included is a variation with a self-monitoring component to enhance motivation and task persistence.

Goal

Critical thinking maps improve comprehension of social studies textual material by teaching students to use a five-component graphic organizer during reading. It is designed to address comprehension of content-area text. However, the intervention teaches a specific approach to comprehension (critical thinking map), which makes it an acquisition intervention.

Intervention Intensity

Critical thinking maps work with classrooms of students and could be used within content-area instruction. Thinking maps are also appropriate for small groups of students or even as part of an intensive intervention program for individual students.

Materials

1. Printed copies of critical thinking maps, one per student.
2. Copies of generic comprehension questions, one per student. Include questions such as, "What was the main idea?"; "What were the most important steps?"; "What were some other points of view?"; "Was there something that you thought should have been mentioned and wasn't?"; "What do you think after reading this?"; "How is this related to something in the world today?"
3. Red pens for checking papers, one per student.
4. Social studies folders with paper for graphing scores on comprehension questions (see Variation).

Options to Monitor Progress

1. Administer a five-question generic comprehension quiz to the entire class after students have read the social studies lesson for the day. Score each question using the following 5-point rating scale: 0 = no response or completely wrong, 1 = poor response, 2 = partially correct but incomplete response, 3 = satisfactory response, 4 = excellent response (total possible points = 20). Record comprehension scores for 4–7 days. If desired, calculate a class daily average score by summing individual scores and dividing by the number of students in the class.
2. Calculate grades on weekly or end-of-unit social studies quizzes and tests for the entire class for several weeks.
3. Have a group of target students respond orally or in writing to the following question: "What do you do to help yourself understand and remember what you read?" Tally the number of acceptable strategies reported by each student. Acceptable strategies include paying attention to the text, reading slower, repeated reading, skimming for main ideas, using section headings and illustrations, self-questioning, and so on. If desired, calculate a group average number of acceptable strategies by dividing the total number of strategies by the number of students in the group.

Intervention Steps

Stage 1: Modeling Phase

1. Visually display (with Smartboard or overhead projector) the critical thinking map or reproduce it on the chalkboard. Explain to the students that they will be learning to use the map to get more out of reading their social studies textbooks.

2. Explain each of the map components as follows:
   a. *Important events*: Important events, points, or steps that lead to the main intent or idea of the lesson, such as the positive and negative attributes of an issue or the causal and/or temporal points.
   b. *Main idea*: The most important message conveyed by the author, whether explicit or implicit, reflecting the author's attitudes toward the information presented in the text.
   c. *Other viewpoints/opinions*: The reader's own perspective and opinions about what has been read, including the background information and knowledge the reader has already acquired about the topic.
   d. *Reader's conclusions*: The reader's final conclusions about the passage and reasons to support them, based on information from all of the preceding map components.
   e. *Relevance to today*: The reader's comparisons between the historical lesson and present-day events and ideas about what today's individuals can learn from past events.
3. Note the number of pages in the lesson to be read. Then read the passage aloud, pausing as you encounter answers to map components in the text. Fill in the map components on the transparency or chalkboard as you identify answers to them in the lesson.
4. After you have read through the entire lesson, read the map components aloud or call on students to do so. Guide the class in checking what you have written for accuracy and completeness, and add more information as necessary.
5. Distribute copies of the five generic comprehension questions and have students silently read the questions and write down their responses without referring back to the text.
6. Review the answers to the questions and have students correct their responses using red pens.
7. Continue this modeling phase for two more lessons or until most students are achieving ratings of "3" (satisfactory) or higher on four of the five questions.

Stage 2: Lead Phase

1. Distribute copies of the map and instruct the students to read the lesson silently.
2. Demonstrating with the overhead projector or on the chalkboard, help students reexamine the lesson for answers to map components and complete their maps.
3. Have students take turns orally rereading the contents of the map components, checking for accuracy, and adding more information if necessary.
4. Collect the maps, distribute the comprehension questions, and have students complete them.
5. Have students correct their papers with red pens while you review answers to the questions and discuss any discrepancies between incorrect comprehension answers and correct map information. Have students rewrite any incorrect answers.

Stage 3: Test Phase

1. As students become successful in completing the map components, discontinue classwide demonstrations and provide individual help as needed.
2. When the majority of students are obtaining satisfactory ratings on all five of the comprehension questions with little or no assistance, discontinue use of the map.
3. If desired, discontinue the use of the comprehension questions. Instead, have students read the lesson silently and then write a paragraph pertaining to each of the map components during class time or as a homework assignment.

Variation: Critical Thinking Maps with a Self-Monitoring Component

Have students monitor their own progress by graphing their scores on the comprehension quizzes in their social studies folders.

NOTES

1. This intervention lends itself readily to a collaborative learning format. After students work in pairs or small groups to complete their maps, have the pairs or groups help you as you complete a map on the chalkboard or a transparency. Provide time for students to correct their maps if necessary so that they can use them as study aids.
2. To save instructional time, have students read the lesson as homework and conduct a brief review prior to map completion (see Stage 2, Step 2).

SOURCE

Idol, L. (1987). A critical thinking map to improve content area comprehension of poor readers. *Remedial and Special Education, 8,* 28–40.

DISSECT: THE WORD IDENTIFICATION STRATEGY

Overview

As students progress through school, the ability to read, understand, and recall information from texts becomes increasingly important to academic success. Because middle school and secondary school texts are written at reading levels well above those of low-achieving students or students with reading disabilities, these students have great difficulty learning information presented in print form. The problem is especially acute in social studies and science classes, where assignments require students to decode and understand complex unfamiliar words in their textbooks and to cover large amounts of material independently. Even if these less skilled readers have learned basic sound–symbol relationships and have acquired a small sight vocabulary, their inability to apply structural analysis skills to identify new content-specific vocabulary can lead to academic failure.

   This intervention trains students in a general problem-solving strategy that uses specific substrategies to identify difficult words rapidly. A mnemonic device (DISSECT), formed by the key words in each strategy step, helps students remember the procedure. In the original study, conducted with 12 seventh-, eighth-, and ninth-grade students with learning disabilities, the DISSECT strategy was effective in improving reading accuracy for all of the target students in both ability-level and grade-level material and in improving comprehension for the majority of the students (Lenz & Hughes, 1990). A study with more than 600 students in sixth and ninth grades implemented a learning strategies curriculum that included DISSECT, which resulted in better reading comprehension for the treatment group over the control group for students in sixth grade (Cantrell, Almasi, Carter, Rintamaa, & Madden, 2010).

Goal

DISSECT improves word identification skills in content-area textbooks with a strategy for pronouncing and recognizing complex multisyllabic words. The intervention supports students' ability to read words in context so that they can better understand their reading. It does not teach initial skill and does not provide practice. Therefore, it could be considered a generalization intervention that is appropriate to support students' comprehension of text.

Intervention Intensity

The intervention is likely most appropriate for small groups of students who require targeted support for reading comprehension.

Materials

1. Social studies or science textbooks or current classroom reading material in the content areas.
2. Posterboard chart listing common prefixes and suffixes.
3. Posterboard chart listing the DISSECT steps.
4. Sheet of paper listing common prefixes and suffixes (optional; one per student).
5. Classroom dictionaries, one per student.

Options to Monitor Progress

1. Have a group of target students read aloud a short passage (about 400 words) from the social studies or science textbook on an individual basis. Calculate a reading accuracy percentage score for each student by dividing the total number of words read correctly (total number of words in the passage minus the number of words missed) by the total number of words in the passage.
2. Calculate average grades on content-area quizzes or tests for a group of target students or the entire class for the previous month or marking period. If desired, calculate a group or classwide quiz or test average by dividing the sum of individual student scores by the total number of students in the group or class.
3. Using generic passages or passages from students' social studies or science textbooks, administer curriculum-based measures of oral reading fluency to a group of target students, using both the fluency and comprehension options.

Intervention Steps

Introduction and Training

1. Display the list of DISSECT steps and the list of prefixes and suffixes. If desired, give students individual copies of these materials to consult during classwork and/or homework assignments.
2. Conduct a general discussion of the importance of good reading skills to success in the targeted subject. If desired, have students calculate their averages on content-area quizzes and tests for the current marking period or provide them with their averages.
3. Tell the students that they will be learning a seven-step strategy that will help them read and remember difficult words. Explain that the word *dissect*—"to separate into parts"— will help them remember the steps of the strategy.
4. Using the DISSECT chart and the chalkboard, describe and demonstrate the seven strategy steps to use when encountering a difficult word, as follows:
   a. *D—Discover the Context.* Skip the difficult word, read to the end of the sentence, and use the meaning of the sentence to make your best guess as to a word that fits in the

place of the unfamiliar word. If the guessed word does not match the difficult word, proceed to the next step.

   b. *I—Isolate the Prefix*. Using the list of prefixes, look at the beginning of the word to see if the first several letters form a prefix that you can pronounce. If so, box it off by drawing a line between the prefix and the rest of the word.

   c. *S—Separate the Suffix*. Using the list of suffixes, look at the end of the word to see if the last several letters form a suffix that you can pronounce. If so, box it off by drawing a line between the suffix and the rest of the word.

   d. *S—Say the Stem*. If you recognize the *stem* (the part of the word that remains after the prefix and the suffix have been boxed off), pronounce the prefix, stem, and suffix together. If you cannot recognize the stem, proceed to the next step.

   e. *E—Examine the Stem*. Break the stem into short two- to three-word parts and read each part. For example, with the word *exponent, ex* is the prefix and *nent* is the suffix. The word would be broken into *ex /po/ nent. Alternative* would be *al/ter/na/ tive*.

   f. *C—Check with Someone*. If you still cannot pronounce the word, ask someone (teacher, parent, or a better reader) in an appropriate way to help you. If someone is not available, go to the next step. (Model or have students model examples and non-examples of appropriate ways to seek assistance.)

   g. *T—Try the Dictionary*. Look up the word in the dictionary, use the pronunciation guide to pronounce the word, and read the definition if you don't know the meaning of the word.

5. Discuss situations in which students can apply the strategy (e.g., homework assignments, leisure time reading of newspapers and magazines) and the benefits students can expect if they learn and use the strategy, such as improved grades, more rewarding reading experiences, and greater knowledge of world and community events.

6. Write a multisyllabic word from a current reading assignment on the chalkboard and use it to demonstrate the entire strategy, using a think-aloud procedure so that students can observe all of the processes involved.

7. Write other multisyllabic words on the chalkboard and select students to demonstrate the strategy. Prompt students to think aloud as they go through the steps, and provide support and corrective feedback as needed.

Implementation

1. During social studies or science lessons, review the strategy when introducing new vocabulary. Select students to demonstrate the strategy on several words.

2. Provide time for students to apply the strategy during class assignments. If desired, divide the class into pairs and have the pairs work together to apply the strategy to a section of the text or reading materials while you circulate to provide assistance.

NOTES

1. For the purposes of this intervention, *prefix* and *suffix* are defined as any recognizable group of letters at the beginning or end of a word, respectively, that students can identify and pronounce correctly.

2. The strategy is most effective on reading assignments that follow teachers' discussion of the content in class.

3. The first five steps of the strategy usually will not work with vocabulary words to which the students have not been introduced.

4. Students should learn the strategy so thoroughly that they can complete the first five steps in no more than 10 seconds.

SOURCES

Cantrell, S. C., Almasi, J. F., Carter, J. C., Rintamaa, M., & Madden, A. (2010). The impact of a strategy-based intervention on the comprehension and strategy use of struggling adolescent readers. *Journal of Educational Psychology, 102*, 257–280.

Lenz, B. K., & Hughes, C. A. (1990). A word identification strategy for adolescents with learning disabilities. *Journal of Learning Disabilities, 23*, 149–158, 163.

ADMIRALS AND GENERALS: IMPROVING CONTENT-AREA PERFORMANCE WITH STRATEGY INSTRUCTION AND PEER TUTORING

Overview

For success in the content areas of social studies and science, students must be able to read the textbook, organize and remember content, retrieve important facts and concepts for tests, and express themselves in written form on classroom tasks and assessments. In this intervention, which combines comprehension strategy instruction with peer tutoring, students work in pairs to read textbook passages aloud, apply summarization strategies to the material, and tutor each other using the summary fact sheets they have prepared. During the oral reading portion, the higher performing student reads first to provide a more effective reading model before the lower performing student reads the same material. Originally implemented with middle and high school students with disabilities in history and social studies classes, the strategy was successful in improving student summarization skills and performance on tests and quizzes, as well as increasing on-task behavior, compared with traditional instruction or a guided-notes condition (Mastropieri, Scruggs, Spencer, & Fontana, 2003; Spencer, Scruggs, & Mastropieri, 2003). Moreover, teachers and students alike rated the strategy highly. A variation that permits more rapid content coverage is also presented.

Goal

This strategy is intended to improve performance in social studies and history classes by teaching students a summarization strategy in the context of a peer tutoring format.

Intervention Intensity

Admirals and Generals was developed to support struggling readers in content-area courses. Therefore, it is probably appropriate as a targeted intervention with small groups of children or as part of an intensive intervention program for individual students. A stronger reader is always needed to serve as a model for the struggling reader.

Materials

1. Social studies or history textbook, one per student.
2. Posterboard charts listing (a) the rules for peer tutoring, (b) procedures for identifying and correcting oral reading errors, and (c) questions included on the summarization sheets.

3. Cue cards, consisting of index cards listing the same information as the charts, one card per student.
4. Review sheets listing key points and vocabulary terms from the target chapter, one review sheet per student per week.
5. 10-item multiple-choice or short-answer quizzes covering the content on the review sheets, one quiz per student per week.
6. Manila folders containing sheets of lined paper (for summaries), review sheets, and cue cards, one folder per student.

Options to Monitor Progress

1. Have the entire class or a group of target students silently read a paragraph from the social studies or history textbook. Then have the students write a 10- to 15-word sentence summarizing the paragraph they have just read. Score summary sentences on a 5-point scale for completeness and accuracy as follows: 1 = very poor, 2 = fair, 3 = average, 4 = good, and 5 = excellent. If desired, calculate a class average summarization score by summing individual scores and dividing by the number of students in the class.
2. Calculate the class average percent-correct score on social studies or history tests for the previous grading period.
3. Using a Classwide Scanning Form with a 3- or 5-minute interval, scan the room at the end of each interval, starting with the front of the room and ending with the back, and tally the number of students in each of the following behavior categories:
   a. *Active engagement,* defined as writing when requested, looking at the teacher, reading aloud from or following along in the textbook, responding to teacher-delivered questions, or any other behavior relevant to the lesson.
   b. *Passive off-task behavior,* defined as sitting quietly but not attending to the lesson.
   c. *Disruptive behavior,* defined as making noises, getting out of seat, calling out, or any other behavior that interferes with instruction or the on-task behavior of other students.
   Conduct these observations for 30–45 minutes for 4–7 days during the social studies or history instructional period.

Intervention Steps

Introduction and Training

1. Using grades, standardized tests, and/or teacher judgment, divide the class into pairs, each consisting of one higher performing and one lower performing student.
2. Explain to the students that they will be working together in pairs to help them learn and remember the information in their textbooks. Tell them that one student in the pair (the higher performing reader) is the admiral and the other (lower performing reader) is the general. (Admirals always read first so that the lower performing student has a more fluent model prior to reading independently.)
3. Demonstrate the rules and procedures for partner reading as described below, using a student as the tutee. Then distribute the folders containing the cue cards and other materials, have students move to their tutoring stations (i.e., paired desks), and conduct a classwide practice while you circulate to provide assistance and support as needed.

Implementation

1. Begin with a brief whole-class review of the information covered the previous day. Then present key new concepts to activate students' prior knowledge and build background knowledge of the content to be covered.
2. Distribute the folders and have students work in pairs to apply the following procedures to each assigned paragraph in the textbook or curricular materials:
   a. The admirals (readers) read one paragraph while the generals (tutors) follow along and listen. If the reader misreads a word, omits a word, or pauses for more than 4 seconds, the tutor stops the reader, indicates which error has been made, and asks him or her to correct it. If the reader cannot correct the error, the tutor prompts, corrects the error, or asks for teacher assistance if the word is unfamiliar. The reader then rereads the sentence and continues.
   b. Then students reverse roles, with the generals reading the same paragraph a second time and the admirals correcting reading errors and prompting, as described above.
   c. After reading each paragraph, students ask each other the following three questions in order: (1) "Who or what is the section about?"; (2) "What is happening to the who or what?"; and (3) "What is the summary sentence (in 10 to 15 words)?"
3. Students work with their partners to develop answers to the three questions but record their answers independently on their own summarization sheets.
4. After completing the summarization sheets, students use the review sheets to take turns asking each other questions from the chapter.
5. During tutoring sessions, circulate to answer questions and assist students in generating correct answers and summary sentences as needed. Tutoring sessions should last about 35 minutes. If a pair completes the assigned reading before the allotted time is up, have them quiz each other on additional material from the chapter.
6. When about 10 minutes remain in the period, conduct a whole-class review session. Using the chalkboard, whiteboard, Smartboard, or overhead projector, call on students to supply their responses to the three questions. Discuss responses that differ and encourage students to modify their own answers to reflect information based on the classwide discussion.
7. As students become more proficient in the summarization strategy, have the pairs read three paragraphs at a time and then answer the questions for those three paragraphs.

Variation: Peer Tutoring without Listening Previewing

Rather than having the generals read the passages previously read by the admirals, have students read successive paragraphs during tutoring sessions. This variation permits greater content coverage and may be more acceptable to students. In the original studies, some of the students complained about having to read material previously read by their partners. Monitor students' progress carefully, however, and reinstitute the repeated reading if the class shows signs of struggling.

NOTES

1. Training takes three to four sessions. Introduce the rules and procedures for partner reading and error correction in the first one or two sessions. In subsequent sessions, introduce the summarization strategies and the review sheet activity.
2. To assist students in decoding and understanding unfamiliar terms and proper names during

oral reading, review key vocabulary terms, including people and places in the text, as part of the whole-class discussion prior to each peer tutoring session.
3. Teachers in the original investigations commented that careful partner pairing was critical to keeping students on task and maintaining a positive learning environment.

SOURCES

Mastropieri, M. A., Scruggs, T. E., Spencer, V., & Fontana, J. (2003). Promoting success in high school world history: Peer tutoring versus guided notes. *Learning Disabilities Research and Practice, 18*, 52–65.

Spencer, V. G., Scruggs, T. E., & Mastropieri, M. A. (2003). Content area learning in middle school social studies classrooms and students with emotional or behavioral disorders: A comparison of strategies. *Behavioral Disorders, 28*, 77–93.

Interventions to Improve Homework Completion and Accuracy

TEAM UP FOR HOMEWORK SUCCESS

Overview

Helping students assume responsibility for their own homework assignments can be challenging for teachers and students alike. This intervention package combines self-management strategies with interdependent group contingencies, public posting, and collaborative learning to help students monitor their own homework completion and accuracy. Teams of four students meet in structured sessions to monitor assignments, review effective homework strategies, and complete team scorecards. Three of the team roles incorporate research-based self-management strategies, including self-monitoring, self-instruction, and self-evaluation, while a fourth team member serves as a replacement if needed. Students of teams that meet a weekly criterion for homework accuracy have access to a classroom raffle. In the original study with 16 low-performing sixth graders, participants demonstrated substantial increases in homework completion rates in mathematics and scores on standardized math tests and curriculum-based measures (Olympia, Sheridan, Jenson, & Andrews, 1994). In addition, parents reported significantly fewer problems related to homework completion. Variations with whole-team rewards and randomized homework accuracy goals are also presented.

Goal

Team Up for Homework Success improves daily homework completion and accuracy with peer-mediated self-management procedures and a classwide raffle. The intervention should increase accuracy, but it is primarily designed to support independent practice through homework, which is a proficiency intervention.

Intervention Intensity

Team Up for Homework Success could be used with classrooms of students, but it could also be modified for use as a targeted intervention for small groups of students.

Materials

1. Daily homework assignment in the selected academic subject.
2. Answer sheets corresponding to homework assignments, one per team.
3. "Team scorecards," consisting of 3″ × 5″ index cards listing team members' names down the left-hand side, with columns headed "Daily Score" and "Yes/No" (for goal completion rating), one per team per week.
4. Posterboard chart listing the duties for each team role.
5. "League scorecard," consisting of a posterboard chart with team names and five columns, labeled with the days of the school week, for posting "win" stickers.
6. Stickers or stars.
7. Shoebox labeled "Raffle Tickets" and containing slips of paper with student or team names.
8. Opaque jar labeled "Homework Goals" and containing 16 slips of paper listing a variety of accuracy criteria, such as four "80%" slips, four "85%" slips, four "90%" slips, and four "95%" slips (optional; see Variation 2).
9. Raffle prizes, consisting of fast food cards, video game tokens, school supplies, wrapped candy, and so forth.

Options to Monitor Progress

1. Calculate homework completion rates in a selected subject for each student or a target group of students for 1–3 weeks by counting the number of days that homework is returned and expressing this number as a percentage. For example, if a student returns homework assignments on 9 out of 15 days, that student's homework completion rate is 60%. If desired, calculate the percentage of students in the entire class whose homework completion rate is below 80% in the selected subject by summing the number of students with completion rates below 80% and dividing by the number of students in the class.
2. Calculate homework accuracy rates in a selected subject for each student or a group of target students for 5–10 days by counting the number of correct problems completed, dividing by the number of problems assigned, and multiplying that number by 100%. For example, if a student answers 12 of 20 problems correctly, that student's homework accuracy rate is 60%. If desired, calculate the percentage of students in the entire class whose homework accuracy rate is below 80% in the selected subject by summing the number of students with accuracy rates below 80% and dividing by the number of students in the class.

Intervention Steps

Introduction and Training

1. Explain to students that they will be playing a game to help them get more out of their homework assignments in the selected subject. Tell them that the game has teams like baseball (football, hockey, etc.), with each player on the team playing a special role in the group effort.
2. Explain that teams consist of four members: (a) "coach," (b) "scorekeeper," (c) "manager," and (d) "pinch hitter." Explain that the pinch hitter's role is to attend team meetings and take the role of other team members when they are absent. Assign students to teams and to roles within each team.
3. Review the steps in the team process and the team members' roles, as described below. Then conduct a demonstration of a team meeting, using four students to model the roles.

THE COACH

a. Prompts and directs team functions.

b. Assembles the team, reminds members of the weekly accuracy goal, and reviews homework completion strategies as needed.

c. Reminds team members of the goal for the next day's homework and encourages team members to reach it.

THE SCOREKEEPER

a. Counts the number of assignments turned in by team members and grades them according to the answer sheet supplied by the teacher.

b. Determines each member's homework accuracy score and records it on each member's paper.

c. Fills in each member's homework accuracy score on the team scorecard and checks "Yes" or No" to indicate whether or not all members obtained the weekly accuracy goal.

THE MANAGER

a. Reviews the team scorecard and declares a "win" or "loss" depending on whether team performance met or exceeded the weekly accuracy goal.

b. Posts a "win" sticker on the league scorecard if the team met or exceeded the goal.

Implementation

1. Have each team select a team name and discuss strategies for increasing homework accuracy and completion. Each student performs the assigned role for 3 days, after which roles are reassigned so that eventually each student has an opportunity to perform all team functions. Change teams every 4 weeks.

2. Each week, set an accuracy goal (e.g., 85% accuracy) on homework assignments to determine eligibility to participate in the raffle and post the goal on the chalkboard. Team averages for the week must equal or exceed the goal for students to be eligible for the raffle.

3. Conduct team meetings daily (or each day that a homework assignment is due) at the beginning of the instructional period. Meetings should last 10–15 minutes, after which students hand in their corrected homework to you for review and managers return team scorecards until the next session.

4. Check homework papers for accuracy. If students have calculated homework scores incorrectly, rescore the papers and remind scorekeepers to check accurately.

5. On Fridays, have each manager check the weekly average for his or her team to determine whether the team has met the goal. Distribute raffle tickets to managers of teams that have met the weekly goal for distribution to team members.

6. Have members of winning teams write their names on slips of paper and place their raffle tickets in the Raffle Ticket Box. Draw three or four tickets (or a number corresponding to about 10–15% of the number of students in the class) and deliver rewards to the students whose names are drawn.

7. As homework performance improves, gradually raise the accuracy criterion or require that all students on a team meet the criterion in order for team members to be eligible for the raffle.

Variations

VARIATION 1: HOMEWORK TEAMS WITH WHOLE-TEAM REWARDS

Set a daily rather than a weekly criterion for homework accuracy. Have the manager of each team meeting the criterion place a raffle ticket with the team's name on it in the box. On Friday, draw a single ticket and deliver rewards to each member of the team whose name is drawn.

VARIATION 2: HOMEWORK TEAMS WITH RANDOMIZED GOALS

Display the Homework Goals Jar and review the contents as described in the Materials section. Explain that you will draw a slip of paper from the jar each day during the team session to determine the goal for the day. Students of teams with averages that meet or exceed the selected goal may place a raffle ticket in the box. Conduct the raffle on Friday as described above and deliver rewards to students whose names are drawn. Alternately, implement whole-team rewards as indicated in Variation 1 and deliver rewards to each member of the team whose name is drawn.

NOTES

1. This intervention works best in a subject with homework assignments that can be easily scored using an answer key, such as mathematics, or with assignments that are dichotomously scored (i.e., true–false, multiple choice).
2. In the original study, there were only negligible differences in homework accuracy rates between treatment and control groups despite significant gains in homework completion rates and on other criterion measures for target students. As with any academic intervention, carefully assessing students for the presence of academic skills deficits versus performance deficits is critical to success.

SOURCE

Olympia, D. E., Sheridan, S. M., Jenson, W. R., & Andrews, D. (1994). Using student-managed interventions to increase homework completion and accuracy. *Journal of Applied Behavior Analysis, 27,* 85–99.

PROJECT BEST: SEVEN STEPS TO SUCCESSFUL HOMEWORK COMPLETION

Overview

Homework can provide students with additional opportunities to learn new content and practice new skills, but only if they complete their assignments with care and accuracy. Unfortunately, many students, especially those with disabilities, have difficulties mastering the complex sequence of behaviors required for homework completion, including recording assignments quickly and correctly, developing a plan for completing assignments, and following assignments through to completion. This intervention teaches students a seven-step strategy for managing homework assignments, as well as a set of metacognitive behaviors supporting effective homework practices, such as self-monitoring, self-instruction, and self-evaluation. The first letters of the major steps and the substeps of the strategy form the words *project* and *best*, respectively, which serve as mnemonic devices to guide students during the self-instruction process. As students work through the steps, they complete three forms: (1) a monthly calendar for long-range planning, (2) a weekly study schedule, and (3) an assignment sheet specifically designed for students with writing problems. First implemented with nine middle school students with learning disabilities enrolled in general education classes, the intervention had positive effects on homework completion rates, teacher ratings of the quality of completed homework assignments, and quarterly grades for eight of the nine target students (Hughes, Ruhl, Schumaker, & Deshler, 2002). Moreover, the students maintained improvements in homework performance after strategy instruction was discontinued.

Goal

Project Best improves homework accuracy and completion rates using a seven-step self-management strategy. The strategy focuses on homework completion. Although the intervention also increases accuracy, it is a proficiency intervention because it facilitates independent practice.

Intervention Intensity

Project Best works with classrooms of students, but it could also be used as a targeted intervention for small groups of students who struggle to complete homework. It could also be used as part of an intensive intervention program for individual students.

Materials

1. Posterboard chart labeled "Seven Steps to Successful Homework Completion" and displaying the PROJECT steps and the BEST substeps, as described below.
2. Homework assignment sheets, one per student per week (see below).
3. Weekly study schedule, consisting of an 8½″ × 11″ sheet of paper with eight columns, the first listing times in 30-minute increments and another seven columns for the days of the week, one per student per week.
4. Monthly planners, consisting of purchased homework planners or sheets of paper with dated blocks for each day of the month, one per student per month.
5. Manila folders, one per student.
6. Samples of the homework assignment sheet, study schedule, and planner pages that can be projected for the class to see (optional).

Options to Monitor Progress

1. Calculate the percentage of completed homework assignments for a target group of students or the entire class in one or more subjects for 5–10 days or several weeks.
2. Calculate the percentage of homework assignments completed with 80% or above accuracy for a target group of students or the entire class in one or more subjects for 5–10 days or several weeks.
3. Using report card grades, calculate quarterly grade point averages for a group of target students by associating each letter grade with a number (i.e., A = 4, B = 3, C = 2, D = 1, F = 0), summing the numbers, and dividing by the total number of academic subjects.

Intervention Steps

Introduction and Training

1. Tell students that they are going to learn an effective strategy that will help them complete their homework and make better grades in school.
2. Display the folders, the chart with the PROJECT and BEST strategy steps, and examples of the monthly planner, weekly study schedule, and assignment sheet. Review the assignment completion steps as presented below, including where, when, why, and how the strategy can be used. Have students take notes about the strategy steps during the training.

STEP 1: PREPARE YOUR FORMS.

    a. *Prepare the monthly planners.* Fill in numbers corresponding to the days of the current and subsequent month on two monthly planning sheets. Note special events, such as holidays, athletic games, and so forth, so that you can plan study time on those days and on surrounding days.

    b. *Prepare the weekly study schedule.* Write in the date for each day of the week and block out time periods during each day when homework cannot be done (e.g., eating, sleeping, attending soccer practice, practicing the piano).

STEP 2: RECORD AND ASK.

    a. *Record assignments.* As soon as a teacher gives an assignment, record it on the assignment sheet, using abbreviations such as "SS" for social studies or "E" for English and circling words printed on the sheet instead of writing them. For example, if the assignment is to read Chapter 3 and answer questions 1 through 10, circle the words *read* and *answer* and then write the rest of the assignment on the lines provided. Also note the due date. If the assignment is due in a different week from the current one, record the assignment and due date on the monthly planner. Remember to check the monthly planner each night to monitor upcoming due dates.

    b. *Ask questions.* Think about the instructions the teacher has given and ask about anything that is unclear immediately, after school, or at another appropriate time. Record any additional information learned on the assignment sheet.

STEP 3: ORGANIZE. (THIS STEP OCCURS AT THE END OF THE DAY
AFTER ALL ASSIGNMENTS HAVE BEEN RECORDED.)

    a. *Break the assignment down into parts.* Break each task into parts and list each part on a piece of scrap paper. For example, for a book report, list the following parts: (1) selecting a book, (2) reading the book, (3) making notes, (4) completing a first draft, and (5) executing a final draft. Count each part and record that number next to "# of parts" on the assignment sheet.

    b. *Estimate the number of study sessions.* Estimate the number of study sessions, defined as a 30-minute block of time, required to complete the assignment and write this number on the assignment sheet next to "# of study sessions."

    c. *Schedule the sessions.* Write the abbreviation of the assignment (e.g., BK RPT for "book report") in a box on the weekly study schedule corresponding to the days and times you will work on the assignment. Remember to schedule study sessions far enough in advance that you can complete the assignment on time.

d. *Take materials home.* Put all materials needed to complete each assignment that evening or weekend in your backpack and carry them home.

STEP 4: JUMP TO IT

Get out the materials you need, tell yourself you're going to do a good job, and check the requirements for each assignment.

STEP 5: ENGAGE IN THE WORK

Engage in the activities required to complete the assignment. If you have any problems doing the homework, seek assistance from your parents or a study partner from class (if permitted by your teacher).

STEP 6: CHECK YOUR WORK

Evaluate the quality of your work, based on your assessment of its neatness, completeness, and the effort you have put into it. Make any necessary corrections and circle a "quality grade" on the assignment sheet. Place the assignment in your homework folder.

STEP 7: TURN IN YOUR WORK

a. Put the assignment folder in a designated location so that you can find it easily.

b. The next day, take the folder to school, check the monthly planner and assignment sheet to ensure that all due homework is turned in, and hand in the assignments.

c. When the assignment has been turned in, record the date on the assignment sheet next to "Done" and give yourself a pat on the back for sticking to the plan and completing the work.

3. Model the use of all the steps of the strategy, using transparencies of the forms, if desired. Speak your thoughts aloud while showing the students how to perform each step and substep of the strategy—for example:

"Now I need to schedule my study sessions for the homework assignments I got today. I'll start with the ones that are due tomorrow so I have time to get them done tonight." (Check the assignment sheet and monthly planner.)

"I have a math assignment and a Spanish assignment. I think math will take one session and Spanish will probably take two sessions. So I need three sessions for this evening." (Get out weekly study schedule.)

"When I look at my weekly study schedule, I see that I have time open between 5:00 P.M. and 6:30 P.M. So I'll write 'math' in the first box and 'Spanish' in the next two boxes in that time slot." (Write the subject names in the appropriate boxes.)

"Then I'll have dinner and still have time for guitar practice."

4. Ask questions about each step and substep until students have memorized the strategy and can answer questions about the steps and substeps fluently.

5. Distribute the manila folders with copies of the three forms, including a homework planner or two monthly planning sheets, and have students practice using the first three steps of the strategy with simulated assignments. Move around the room to provide assistance and corrective feedback as needed.

Implementation

1. Give each student an assignment sheet each Friday for the coming week. Distribute two monthly planning sheets every other month if students are not using their own planners.
2. Instruct students to take the assignment sheet to each class and write the next day's assignments on the sheet.
3. Conduct periodic classwide reviews of the strategy as needed.

NOTE

In the original study, strategy instruction was conducted in a resource room setting four times a week for about 30 minutes per session. For classwide implementation, training takes about three 30-minute sessions, with reviews after holidays and vacations.

SOURCE

Hughes, C. A., Ruhl, K. L., Schumaker, J. B., & Deshler, D. D. (2002). Effects of instruction in an assignment completion strategy on the homework performance of students with learning disabilities in general education class. *Learning Disabilities Research and Practice, 17,* 1–18.

CHAPTER FIVE

Interventions to
Improve Social Behavior

In the past two decades, there has been a significant amount of discussion about the seriousness of social behavior issues in schools (Hoagwood & Erwin, 1997; National Research Council and Institute of Medicine, 2009; Osius & Rosenthal, 2009; Public Agenda, 2004; Rose & Gallup, 2005; U.S. Department of Education, 2000; U.S. Surgeon General, 1999). Despite this discussion, teachers still receive less than adequate training focusing on classroom management and working with children who display problematic social behavior in their classrooms or the school in general. In this chapter, we present a variety of interventions that have been designed to improve social behavior in a variety of settings and locations.

The interventions in this chapter have been grouped into four general categories: classroom, individual, academic behavior, and nonclassroom settings. In the classroom intervention section, strategies are presented that are designed to be used with a group of children and a target teacher. For example, the *Good Behavior Game* was designed for a teacher to use with his or her class to reduce disruptive behavior (Barrish, Saunders, & Wolf, 1969). For the most part, these interventions are designed to help raise the general level of engagement and reduce the amount of disruption across a group of students. Although such intervention can be useful with students who have more serious behavior issues, as they can support higher quality social behavior in academic environments, they are not specifically designed to address the more intense issues. The next grouping of interventions is focused on directly addressing cases in which individual students exhibit significant behavior issues. For example, *Noncontingent Reinforcement* was designed to help students who misbehave in order to get teacher attention (Carr, Severtson, & Lepper, 2009). This intervention has been used with a broad range of students, from those with intensive needs to those with minor issues. The section on academic behavior includes interventions that were designed to increase academic engagement. Lastly, interventions that have been developed for use in schools outside of the classroom are discussed in the final section. For example, an adaptation of the *Good Behavior Game* developed for use in a physical education class has been included (Patrick, Ward, & Crouch, 1998).

It is important to note that most behavior interventions can be adapted to be used in a different setting. Pragmatically, each intervention is based on the general idea that most student behavior issues are related to acquisition issues or behavioral fluency issues. Specifically, children who have not learned appropriate behavior will need interventions that assist in establishing the desired behavior and helping the student understand when to perform the behavior. Behavioral fluency issues are considered as two types, depending on whether the misbehavior helps the student either to get something (e.g., teacher or peer attention) or to escape something (e.g., an uncomfortable social situation or academic task demands). Interventions designed in each general category can often be adjusted to work in different settings (e.g., classroom, hallway, lunchroom) or with students with different levels of intensity of the problem behavior. In the end, each of these interventions is simply a way of supporting the appropriate behavior in a thoughtful manner; they can only be considered evidence based when they are implemented and documented to be successful for the specific case.

Classroom Behavior Interventions

THE CLASSROOM CHECK-UP

Overview

The Classroom Check-Up (CCU) is a classwide intervention targeting current and future student problem behavior through classroom teaching practices (Reinke, Herman, & Sprick, 2011). This consultation model is designed to increase behavior management while focusing on changing the entire classroom ecology, addressing the need for classroom-level support while minimizing treatment integrity problems common to school-based consultation. Classroom management has a direct link to levels of student involvement and academic achievement, making it a critical component of teaching. Furthermore, a nationwide survey of teachers across all grade levels indicated that teachers feel a strong need for additional training and support in classroom management (Coalition for Psychology in Schools and Education, 2006). Effective classroom management can help to decrease disruptive classroom behaviors and increase student engagement in academic tasks (Reinke & Herman, 2002). School-based consultation is one promising method of supporting teacher implementation of effective classroom behavior management practices. Supporting teachers' competency are effective practices for managing classroom variables that have been shown to be influential to student outcomes, such as use and type of praise, reprimands, and opportunities for students to respond. Overall, classroom consultation can create meaningful, lasting teacher and student behavior change at the classroom level. The CCU's consultation model has been shown effective as a tool to increase teacher behaviors through feedback and support.

Goal

Although there is sufficient evidence to support the need for school-based consultation for classroom management, one-time consultation training is not enough to effectively create sustainable change. Therefore, consultants should provide teachers with continuous support throughout the various stages listed below.

Intervention Intensity

The intervention can be used for a variety of classrooms with appropriate adaptions for age, topic, and intensity of problem behavior.

Options to Monitor Progress

The CCU has developed an assessment framework to measure the progress of the teacher in key areas. See the Additional Resources section below for information about where to access this information.

Intervention Steps

The CCU utilizes a motivational interviewing (MI) framework (see Figure 5.1) for implementation purposes. MI is a collaborative style for strengthening a person's own motivation and commitment to change. The goal of MI is to elicit language that conveys a teacher's desire, ability, reasons, need, and/or commitment to make a change. Within the CCU model, four processes of MI are implemented:

1. *Collaboration*—Establishing a trusting relationship and involving the client in talking about issues.
2. *Evocation*—Narrowing the conversation to patterns of the behavior that the client wants to change.
3. *Evoking*—Eliciting the client's motivation for change by increasing her or his confidence and readiness for change.
4. *Planning*—Developing the practical steps the client wants to use to achieve the change she or he desires.

Step 1. Assess the Classroom.

Step 1 of the CCU is assessing the classroom environment through direct observation, completion of a teacher interview, and a brief classroom ecology checklist by the consultant. The purpose of the teacher interview is to establish rapport and to discover areas of strength and weakness (self-identified by the teacher) within the current classroom management system. The questions work to identify the client's values and motivations for teaching while addressing current and past classroom management strategies. The classroom ecology checklist is used to collect information about the instructional and behavior management systems of the

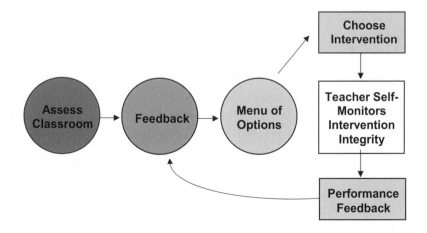

FIGURE 5.1. Classroom Checkup Model.

classroom, routines and expectations, and the physical layout of the classroom. In addition, observing the classroom in the natural environment is critical.

Step 2. Provide Feedback.

After this comprehensive classroom evaluation, the consultant meets with the teacher to convey the findings. This includes a summary of the data and specific visual and verbal feedback addressing the teacher's strengths and weaknesses.

Step 3. Develop a Menu of Options.

Using the feedback, predominantly attending to identified areas of concern, the consultant and the teacher work together to develop a menu of potential intervention strategies to implement in the classroom, striving for positive classroom outcomes. This menu should be built by the consultant's knowledge of research and address the teacher's vision while building on his or her strengths.

Step 4. Choose the Intervention.

In collaboration, the consultant and teacher should select one or two interventions from the menu stage. This intervention should be tailored to the needs of the classroom, and a corresponding action plan for implementation should be developed.

Step 5. Teacher Self-Monitors Treatment Integrity.

This step of the CCU begins on the first day of implementation of the individualized classroom intervention. During this stage, the teachers monitor daily implementation of the chosen intervention using an intervention procedural checklist. Teachers monitor whether or not they successfully complete each component of the intervention. Each day the teachers check off the number of steps to the intervention that they completed.

Step 6. Provide Ongoing Monitoring.

During Step 6, the coach conducts ongoing classroom observations and provides performance feedback. Teacher and coach then review and revise implementation practices as needed.

Critical Components for Successful Implementation

1. *Performance feedback and action planning.* The consultant must be given access to the classroom in order to assess current classroom management practices, to provide valuable performance feedback, and to produce a menu of options and ultimately an appropriate evidence-based intervention.
2. *MI and collaborative partnership.* The consultant must encourage personal responsibility for decision making while giving direct advice if asked and must support teacher self-efficacy by identifying existing strengths.
3. *Systemic support.* Utilizing Steps 5 and 6, teacher self-monitoring of treatment integrity and ongoing monitoring from the consultant can significantly increase integrity of intervention implementation and the likelihood of future classroom management success.

Critical Assumptions/Problem-Solving Questions

Providing coaching for effective classroom management practices typically holds the assumption that teachers welcome evaluation and feedback; however, many times teachers are in positions in which this partnership may not be received well or is perhaps not voluntary. The CCU consultation model has a unique component of MI that addresses a client's current stage of change and provides support accordingly.

NOTE

The Classroom Check-Up brief was developed by Lauren Henry for the EBI Network.

SOURCES

Coalition for Psychology in Schools and Education. (2006, August). *Report on the Teacher Needs Survey*. Washington, DC: American Psychological Association, Center for Psychology in Schools and Education.

Reinke, W. M., Herman, K. C., & Sprick, R. (2011). *Motivational interviewing for effective classroom management: The Classroom Check-Up*. New York: Guilford Press.

Reinke, W. M., Lewis-Palmer, T., & Merrell, K. (2008). The Classroom Check-Up: A classwide teacher consultation model for increasing praise and decreasing disruptive behavior. *School Psychology Review, 37*(3), 315–332.

Sprick, R., Knight, J., Reinke, W. M., & McKale, T. (2006). *Coaching classroom management: Strategies and tolls for administrators and coaches*. Eugene, OR: Pacific Northwest.

ADDITIONAL RESOURCES

The CCU website (*theclassroomcheckup.com*) can provide imperative support to the CCU process. Providing essential information and resources for the consultant and teacher, this site makes each step feasible for schools where physical ongoing coach support is limited.

ACTIVE TEACHING OF CLASSROOM RULES

Overview

Simply listing classroom rules on a chart or the chalkboard is not sufficient to develop and maintain appropriate student behavior. In contrast, actively teaching classroom rules not only communicates to students exactly what is expected but also provides teachers with opportunities to reinforce behavior consistent with the rules. This proactive intervention teaches classroom rules as a lesson with feedback and examples and includes a brief daily review and rehearsal to reinforce learning. As noted in the review of the evidence base for classroom management strategies by Simonsen, Fairbanks, Briesch, Myers, and Sugai (2008), there have been a number of studies that support the use of this general intervention (Greenwood, Hops, Delquadri, & Guild, 1974; McNamara, Evans, & Hill, 1986; Rosenberg, 1986; Sharpe, Brown, & Crider, 1995). In one classic study, conducted in a seventh-grade mathematics class referred as a group for problem behavior, active rule teaching and review resulted in a significant reduction in disruptive behavior and a corresponding increase in academic engagement (Johnson, Stoner, & Green, 1996). Moreover, the rules strategy was more effective than two other interventions implemented with the same group of students in two other classes: a self-monitoring intervention implemented in reading class and an intervention consisting of a weekly class syllabus and individual student conferences implemented in language arts class. A variation with a parent involvement component is also presented.

Goal

The purpose of this intervention is to help create and maintain a productive, disruption-free classroom by explicitly teaching and regularly reviewing classroom rules. This intervention is designed for students who need assistance in learning appropriate social skills and who need to be supported in the use of the skills in learning environments.

Intervention Intensity

The intervention can be used for a variety of students in classrooms with appropriate adaptations for age, topic, and intensity of problem behavior.

Materials

1. Posterboard chart with a list of classroom rules, such as:
   a. Be prepared for class every day.
   b. Be considerate of others.
   c. Be on time to class.
   d. Do what you are asked to do the first time you are asked.
   e. Follow directions.
2. 8½″ × 11″ sheets of paper listing the rules, one per student.

Options to Monitor Progress

1. Measure the student's academic engagement and disruptive behavior with Direct Behavior Rating (DBR). These data can be collected in each period in which the intervention is active and graphed for analysis. Conduct observations for 3–5 days prior to the start of the intervention to establish a baseline and then in each instructional period in which the intervention is used.
2. Using a *Classwide Scanning Form* with a 5-minute interval, scan the room beginning with the left side and tally the number of students displaying each of the three categories of behavior listed below:
   a. *Disruptive behavior,* defined as behavior that produces observable physical changes in the classroom environment and interferes with assignment completion for oneself or other students (e.g., talking without permission, making noises, throwing paper).
   b. *Inappropriately engaged behavior,* defined as directing attention toward or engaging in nonlesson activities or materials (e.g., writing and passing notes, gazing into space, looking at unengaged classmates, playing with nonlesson materials).
   c. *Appropriately engaged behavior,* defined as directing attention toward or engaging in assigned tasks and activities (e.g., raising hand, participating in class discussions, writing on worksheets).
3. Conduct these observations for 30–45 minutes during a selected instructional period for 4–7 days.
4. Using a *Group Event Recording Form,* record the number of disruptive behaviors as defined above during a selected instructional period for 4–7 days.

Intervention Steps

Introduction and Training

1. During the selected instructional period, display the classroom rules on the chart and give each student a handout listing the rules.
2. Spend about 10 minutes discussing the rules, the rationale for each rule, and the importance of rules in creating a classroom environment in which every student feels free to learn. Provide specific examples for each rule and invite students to offer their own examples.
3. Tell students that you will be observing them at various times during the lesson to see if they are following the rules.

Implementation

1. During the lesson, provide behavior-specific praise and feedback at least three times for individual students and groups of students who are following one or more of the rules—for example: "I appreciate how Row 3 students are following directions."
2. After the first day, spend about 3 minutes reteaching one or two rules at the beginning of each class period. During the lesson, deliver specific praise to students as individuals and groups for following the rules.

Variation: Rule Review with Parent Involvement

Have students take home their copies of the classroom rules, discuss them with their parents, and return them signed.

NOTE

This intervention was originally implemented with an intact group of students who were taught by different teachers in different classrooms. For self-contained classroom groups, reteach the rules at the beginning of the school day.

SOURCES

Greenwood, C. R., Hops, H., Delquadri, J., & Guild, J. (1974). Group contingencies for group consequences in classroom management: A further analysis. *Journal of Applied Behavior Analysis, 7*(3), 413–425.

Johnson, T. C., Stoner, G., & Green, S. K. (1996). Demonstrating the experimenting society model with classwide behavior management interventions. *School Psychology Review, 25,* 199–214.

McNamara, E., Evans, M., & Hill, W. (1986). The reduction of disruptive behaviour in two secondary school classes. *British Journal of Educational Psychology, 56,* 209–215.

Rosenberg, M. S. (1986). Maximizing the effectiveness of structured classroom management programs: Implementing rule-review procedures with disruptive and distractible students. *Behavior Disorders, 11*(4), 239–248.

Sharpe, T., Brown, M., & Crider, K. (1995). The effects of a sportsmanship curriculum intervention on generalized positive social behavior of urban elementary school students. *Journal of Applied Behavior Analysis, 28*(4), 401–416.

Simonsen, B., Fairbanks, S., Briesch, A., Myers, D., & Sugai, G. (2008). Evidence-based practices in classroom management: Considerations for research to practice. *Education and Treatment of Children, 31,* 351–380.

DECREASING INAPPROPRIATE VERBALIZATIONS WITH A PEER-MONITORED SELF-MANAGEMENT PROGRAM

Overview

Inappropriate verbalizations, such as calling out, talking to peers, and making noises, can be a serious impediment to ongoing instruction. Moreover, unwanted verbalizations often lead to other off-task behaviors and more serious problem behavior, such as student-to-student aggression. In this strategy, students work collaboratively to monitor and evaluate their own verbalizations in the context of a group contingency to reduce inappropriate verbalizations. First implemented in a third-grade classroom that included four students diagnosed with ADHD, the intervention substantially decreased talking out in all four target students, along with their matched controls (Davies & Witte, 2000). In the original study, students also recorded their behavior on individual self-monitoring forms so that researchers could assess the number of inappropriate verbalizations per student, as well as differences between student self-monitoring and teacher monitoring. Because the individual self-monitoring component increases intervention complexity and did not appear to enhance self-monitoring accuracy, it is included here as a variation. A variation with an additional contingency to encourage accurate self-monitoring is also presented.

Goal

The purpose of this intervention is to reduce inappropriate verbalizations and classroom rule infractions by using a peer-monitored self-management procedure with a group contingency. This intervention is designed for students who need help to fluently display appropriate classroom behavior.

Intervention Intensity

The intervention can be used for a variety of students in classrooms with appropriate adaptations for age, topic, and intensity of problem behavior.

Materials

1. Posterboard chart listing the class rules, such as:
   a. Talk only when you have permission from the teacher.
   b. Use polite and kind words when talking with others.
   c. Follow all teacher instructions the first time they are given.
   d. Do your work so others can do their work.
2. "Group behavior charts," consisting of 9″ × 12″ sheets of laminated construction paper divided into three sections (one-half green, one-fourth blue, and one-fourth red), one chart per table or desk cluster.
3. Circles of black laminated construction paper, the size of a 50-cent piece, attached to group behavior charts with Velcro tabs, five circles per chart (or a number reflecting data collected during the observation period).
4. A reinforcement menus for each student that contains a list of reinforcers from which to select (optional).

5. Paper bag containing small tangible reinforcers, such as stickers, wrapped candy, and inexpensive school supplies (optional).

6. "Individual behavior charts," consisting of 8½″ × 11″ sheets of paper, with two columns, labeled "I caught myself!" and "Teacher moved my dot," respectively, one per student (optional, see Variation 1).

Options to Monitor Progress

1. Using a sheet of paper attached to a clipboard, record the number of inappropriate verbalizations for the entire class or a target group of students during a selected instructional period. *Inappropriate verbalizations* are defined as student verbalizations made without teacher permission, such as calling out, making noises, or talking to peers. Conduct these observations for 4–7 days. If desired, use these data to determine the criterion for the maximum of inappropriate verbalizations allowed for the groups to obtain the reward (i.e., the number of circles on each chart).

2. Using a *Classwide Scanning Form* with a 3- or 5-minute interval, scan the room at the end of each interval, starting with the front of the room and ending with the back, and tally the number of students in each of the following behavior categories:
   a. *Appropriate classroom behavior,* defined as behavior that does not interfere with ongoing instruction or the learning of other students and does not include any inappropriate behavior as defined below.
   b. *Inappropriate classroom behavior,* defined as talking without permission, getting out of seat without permission, making noises, or any other verbal or motor behavior that disrupts ongoing instruction or the on-task behavior of other students.
   Conduct these observations for 30–45 minutes for 4–7 days.

3. Measure classwide disruptive behavior and respectful behavior with DBR. These data can be collected in each period in which the intervention is active and graphed for analysis. Data on target individual children can be collected when the goal of the intervention is a single student. Conduct observations for 3–5 days prior to the start of the intervention to establish a baseline and then in each instructional period in which the intervention is used.

Intervention Steps

Introduction and Training

1. This intervention requires students to be seated in groups of four or five. If the classroom has individual desks rather than tables, arrange desks in clusters of four. Be sure to disperse the most talkative and disruptive students among the groups.

2. Explain to the students that they will be playing a game that will help remind them to work quietly without talking out and disturbing others.

3. Using *Say, Show, Check: Teaching Classroom Procedures* (described later in this chapter) and the rules chart, review the classroom rules and provide examples and nonexamples of the target behavior (talking without permission). Conduct role plays and provide corrective feedback until you are certain that students understand when talking is permitted and when it is not.

4. Place one chart with the black circles in the green section in the middle of each table or desk cluster within easy reach of each group member. Explain that if a student forgets the rule and talks out (or breaks another of the regular classroom rules), that student must move one dot from the green section to the blue section. If the student fails to do so, a group member should remind him or her. After 10 seconds, you will move the dot to the red section yourself.

5. Caution the class that you will not tolerate any negative behavior toward students who are responsible for having a dot moved. Tell the class that if you observe any negative behavior directed toward a student who has caused the group to have a dot moved, you will move another dot for that group.

6. Tell students that all groups with at least one dot left in the green section of their charts at the end of the intervention period will receive a reward. Explain that you will provide time for a brief daily meeting to give group members an opportunity to brainstorm strategies for earning the reward. If desired, have students select a group name.

7. If desired, distribute the *Reinforcement Menus* and help students identify rewards that each group would like to earn. Alternatively, describe the available activity rewards (game time, free time, extra recess, etc.) or tangible rewards (wrapped candy, decorated pencils, erasers, etc.).

8. Conduct a demonstration in which you model moving a dot and reacting appropriately. Then have students work with their groups to practice the self-monitoring process, including responding to members whose behavior results in dots being moved.

Implementation

1. For the first 5 minutes of each intervention period, have each group conduct a meeting to discuss its performance on the previous day (e.g., "What did we do well? What can we do better? How can we help each other if someone is having a bad day?").

2. During the intervention period, monitor the groups to ensure that students are moving their dots from the green section into the blue section when they make inappropriate verbalizations or break other classroom rules. If a student makes an inappropriate verbalization and no one in the group moves the dot to the blue section within 10 seconds, go over to that group and move the dot to the red section yourself without comment. If any group members argue or display a negative reaction, quietly move another dot.

3. At the end of the intervention period, circulate to determine which groups have at least one dot remaining in the green section and to evaluate the difference between student and teacher monitoring (the difference between the number of dots placed in the blue and the red sections, respectively). Deliver the reward to winning groups or record the names of the winning groups on the chalkboard and deliver the reward at the end of the day.

Variations

VARIATION 1: GROUP PLUS INDIVIDUAL SELF-MONITORING

1. Distribute individual behavior sheets to students along with the group charts at the beginning of the intervention period. Tell students that they are responsible not only for monitoring and recording talk-outs as a team but also for recording their own talk-outs.

2. Instruct students to put a check in the appropriate column for every inappropriate verbalization they make, depending on whether they or you first observe a talk-out. That is, they should put a check in the "I caught myself" column when they observe that they talked out and a check in the "Teacher moved my dot" column when you have to move the dot for them.

3. Collect the sheets at the end of each intervention period for use in monitoring inappropriate verbalization rates for individual students and groups and evaluating the accuracy of student self-monitoring.

4. Fade the individual behavior sheets as inappropriate verbalizations decrease and student self-monitoring becomes more accurate.

VARIATION 2: SELF-MONITORING ACCURACY-BASED GROUP CONTINGENCY

1. To encourage accurate self-monitoring, require teams to have only one dot in the red section in order to receive the reward, even if they have only one dot or none in the blue section. During the original study, researchers found that students did not always monitor their own performance accurately. In fact, there was no measurable difference between the number of times the teacher moved the dots and the number of times students "caught themselves."

NOTES

1. Although the original study did not report any negative peer interactions when group dots were moved, peer harassment is a potential side effect of any interdependent group contingency. To minimize this possibility, stress team cooperation, model appropriate responses to the moving of dots, and remove additional dots if a group displays negative behavior toward a member who must move a dot.
2. This intervention is also ideal for targeting negative peer-to-peer verbalizations, such as derogatory remarks, arguing, or teasing.

SOURCE

Davies, S., & Witte, R. (2000). Self-management and peer-monitoring within a group contingency to decrease uncontrolled verbalizations of children with attention-deficit/hyperactivity disorder. *Psychology in the Schools, 37,* 135–147.

THE GOOD BEHAVIOR GAME

Overview

The Good Behavior Game (GBG) is a simple but effective intervention that uses team competitiveness and group incentives to reduce disruptive behavior in the classroom (Barrish, Saunders, & Wolf, 1969; Kellam, Ling, Merisca, Brown, & Ialongo, 1998). Student teams compete for rewards or privileges, which are awarded to teams not exceeding a specific number of rule violations. In case all teams meet the criteria, each team gets the reward. The critical components in the game's effectiveness include positive peer pressure, specific performance criteria for winning, immediate behavior feedback, and group-based reinforcement. The GBG has been proven to be effective in reducing disruptive and aggressive behavior in elementary and middle school classrooms with regular education, at-risk, and special needs student populations. Moreover, longitudinal research demonstrates that enrollment in GBG classrooms in first and second grade significantly reduces aggressive and disruptive behavior among at-risk students at the end of first and second grade and at entry to middle school. In this book, three variations are presented: (1) a response-cost version, in which points are deducted for rule infractions; (2) a version with unpredictable rewards; and (3) a version with positive behavior incentives for teams that have exceeded the day's limit for rule infractions. The Good Behavior Game Plus Merit, a variation in which bonus points are awarded for positive academic or social behavior to offset demerits, is presented as a separate intervention.

Goal

The purpose of this intervention is to increase on-task behavior and reduce inappropriate and disruptive behavior with team-based contingencies. This intervention is designed for students who have acquired the requisite skills for appropriate classroom behavior but need reinforcement to do so fluently.

Intervention Intensity

The intervention can be used for a variety of students in classrooms with appropriate adaptations for age, topic, and intensity of problem behavior.

Materials

1. Posterboard chart displaying the classroom rules, such as:
   a. Talk only when you have the teacher's permission.
   b. Stay in your seat unless you have permission to get up.
   c. Be polite and kind to others.
   d. Follow the teacher's instructions the first time they are given.
2. Posterboard chart or section of the chalkboard divided into two parts labeled "Team 1," "Team 2,"and so on (or labeled with team names) and listing team members' names, if desired, with a column for each day of the week.
3. Victory tags, consisting of "winner" stickers or circles of colored construction paper with "winner" stickers affixed to them and threaded with yarn, to be worn around the neck (optional, for early primary grade students).
4. Manila envelope with a question mark on it, containing a slip of paper describing a tangible reward (e.g., "Draw from the candy jar"; "Homework pass") or an activity-based reward (e.g., "10 minutes of music time"; "5 minutes of extra recess"; "Line up first for lunch") (optional, see Variation 2).
5. Small rewards, such as stickers, wrapped candy, and decorated pencils and erasers (optional).

Options to Monitor Progress

1. Using a *Classwide Scanning Form* with a 3- or 5-minute interval, scan the room at the end of each interval, starting with the front of the room and ending with the back, and tally the number of students in each of the following behavior categories:
   a. *On-task behavior*, defined as asking or answering lesson-oriented questions, writing when requested, looking at the teacher during presentations, and any other behavior relevant to the lesson.
   b. *Off-task behavior*, defined as sitting without having appropriate materials at hand, looking at nonlesson materials, and looking around the room after assignments have been made.
   c. *Disruptive behavior*, defined as any behavior disrupting instruction or the on-task behavior of other students, such as inappropriate verbal or motor behavior, failing to follow directions, and aggression.

Conduct these observations during a selected instructional period for 30–45 minutes for 4–7 days.

2. Using a *Group Event Recording Form,* record the frequencies of three or four disruptive behaviors, such as getting out of seat, name-calling, talking out, and failing to follow directions during a selected instructional period for a target group of students or the entire class for 4–7 days. Use these baseline data to set a demerit criterion at a value that is approximately half of the average number of disruptive behaviors. For example, if students display an average of 30 disruptive behaviors during the selected period, set the initial criterion at 15.

3. Using a sheet of paper attached to a clipboard, record the number of classroom rule infractions during a selected instructional period for the entire class for 4–7 days. Use these baseline data to set the demerit criterion at a value that is approximately half of the average number of rule infractions. For example, if students display an average of 20 rule infractions during the selected period, set the initial criterion at 10.

4. Measure classwide academic engagement with DBR. These data can be collected in each period in which the intervention is active and graphed for analysis. Conduct observations for 3–5 days prior to the start of the intervention to establish a baseline and then in each instructional period in which the intervention is used.

Intervention Steps

Introduction and Training

1. Select a time for implementation, such as the morning work period or an instructional period when students are especially unproductive and disruptive. Tell the students that they will be playing a game to help everyone get more out of the period during which the game will be played. Explain the times when the game will be played and post the times on the chalkboard.

2. Divide the class into two or three teams. Be sure that teams contain approximately equal numbers of male and female students and that students with problem behavior are divided equally among teams. To facilitate monitoring behavior and delivering rewards, use rows or desk groupings to assign teams or change seating arrangements to reflect team membership. Allowing teams to select names fosters team spirit and makes it easier to encourage or reprimand teams.

3. Write the team names or numbers and names of team members if desired on the chalkboard, with a column for each day of the week.

4. Explain the game's procedures as described below, including the criterion for the maximum number of demerits permitted to earn the reward. Also describe the rewards for the winning team(s), such as wearing victory tags for the rest of the day, lining up first for lunch, getting to pack up first at the end of the day, or small tangible rewards. If all the teams win, possible rewards include a video or DVD, 15 minutes of free time, or a special art activity at the end of the day.

5. Review the classroom rules and demonstrate the process of giving demerits for rule infractions as described below. Be sure to model how students should respond to receiving a demerit and explain that arguing or other inappropriate reactions will result in an additional demerit.

Implementation

1. At the beginning of the intervention period, conduct a brief review of the classroom rules and the GBG criterion (e.g., no more than 10 demerits for the period).

2. During the intervention period, record a demerit beside the team name each time a student on that team breaks a rule. As you record the demerit, state the reason. For example, say, "Anthony, that's an 'out of seat,' " while putting a check mark under the appropriate team's name. If you have listed individual team members' names on the chart or chalkboard, put the check mark next to the name of the student who committed the infraction.

3. Tally demerits at the end of the intervention period and determine which, if any, teams have met the criterion. If none of the teams exceeds the predetermined limit, all teams are winners and receive the reward.

4. Begin by playing the GBG three times a week for 15 minutes or during the selected instructional period. Gradually increase the duration by approximately 10 minutes per intervention period every 3 weeks, up to a maximum of 3 hours, or three or four instructional periods per day.

5. If necessary, adjust the criterion slightly to reflect the longer periods of implementation, but gradually lower the limit for demerits to no more than four or five infractions per day.

6. Initially, announce the game period and deliver the rewards immediately afterward or as soon as possible. As students become more familiar with the procedure, initiate the game period without prior notice at different times of the day and during different activities and routines, such as walking down the hall to the cafeteria. Delay rewards until the end of the school day.

7. After several weeks of implementation, fade the rewards to once a week. Record the number of daily demerits for each team and deliver the reward on Fridays to teams meeting the criterion on 4 out of 5 days.

Variations

VARIATION 1: THE GOOD BEHAVIOR GAME WITH RESPONSE COST

1. Begin the intervention period by awarding each team a fixed number of credits, such as 10 credits. Set a minimum criterion for winning, such as five credits remaining at the end of the intervention period.

2. Remove one credit each time a member of a team breaks a rule.

3. Deliver the reward to teams that meet or exceed the criterion. If all teams meet or exceed the criterion, all teams are winners.

VARIATION 2: THE GOOD BEHAVIOR GAME WITH MYSTERY MOTIVATORS

1. Implement the standard GBG or the GBG as described above in Variation 1.

2. Display a manila envelope with a question mark written on the front of it and containing a slip of paper describing a reward on a desk or table where all students can see it. Explain that winning teams will receive the reward written on the hidden slip of paper.

3. At the end of the day, open the envelope and deliver the reward to teams that meet the criterion.

VARIATION 3: THE GOOD BEHAVIOR GAME WITH A "BETTER BEHAVIOR BOOSTER"

1. This variation helps to prevent the number of rule infractions from increasing if students perceive that their team has exceeded the limit on a particular day and can no longer obtain the daily reward.

2. Provide a larger group reward, such as 15 minutes of free time, at the end of the week to teams with five or less "extra" rule infractions (i.e., demerits exceeding the daily crite-

rion). Record the extra marks on bar graphs drawn on the chalkboard and labeled with team names so that teams can monitor their progress during the week. Deliver the reward at the end of the week to teams meeting this criterion.

NOTES

1. Occasionally, chronically defiant and disruptive students will declare that they do not want to play the game and will deliberately violate the rules to incur penalty points for their team. If this occurs, explain to the class that it is not fair to penalize an entire team because a few students will not control their behavior. Create another team consisting of the problem student(s) and add a negative contingency, such as requiring losing teams to have a "silent lunch" or deducting 5 minutes of recess for each mark scored over the criterion. If the problem persists, conduct a *Debriefing* session to help identify factors contributing to the problem and support the student(s) in displaying acceptable replacement behaviors (see *Debriefing: Helping Students Solve Their Own Behavior Problems* later in this chapter).
2. Teachers sometimes express concern about monitoring only inappropriate behavior. In that case, the *Good Behavior Game Plus Merit*, which provides bonuses for appropriate behavior, can be substituted (see below).
3. Field testing suggests that the response-cost variation (Variation 1) is more effective than the original procedure of recording demerits. Moreover, teachers have consistently preferred the response-cost version to the original.

SOURCES

Barrish, H. H., Saunders, M., & Wolf, M. M. (1969). Good Behavior Game: Effects of individual contingencies for group consequences on disruptive behavior in a classroom. *Journal of Applied Behavior Analysis, 2*, 119–124.

Kellam, S. G., Ling, X., Merisca, R., Brown, C. H., & Ialongo, N. (1998). The effect of the level of aggression in the first grade classroom on the course and malleability of aggressive behavior into middle school. *Development and Psychopathology, 10*, 165–185.

THE GOOD BEHAVIOR GAME PLUS MERIT

Overview

It has been noted that the GBG really is all about "bad" behavior. This variation of the GBG combines group contingencies for reducing disruptive behavior with a bonus for positive academic behavior (Darveaux, 1984). As in the GBG, teams receive a reward if the number of demerits they accumulate for rule infractions remains below a fixed criterion. In contrast to the original, however, the Good Behavior Game Plus Merit permits students to compensate for inappropriate behavior by earning credits for improvement in academic performance. It is especially useful with students who become argumentative or unproductive when corrected because the opportunity to remove demerits and regain access to rewards is built into the procedure. In the original study, the strategy was successful not only in reducing disruptive behavior for two students with behavior disorders in a second-grade classroom but also in improving assignment completion and increasing active participation for both targeted and nontargeted students. Two variations are presented: (1) a response-cost variation in which teams are awarded a fixed number of credits that are deducted for rule infractions and (2) a variation awarding merit points for exemplary behavior, as well as for academic improvement.

Goal

The purpose of this intervention is to increase on-task behavior and academic productivity and reduce disruptive behavior with positive team competitions. This intervention is designed for students who have acquired the requisite skills for appropriate classroom behavior but need reinforcement to do so fluently.

Intervention Intensity

The intervention can be used for a variety of students in classrooms with appropriate adaptations for age, topic, and intensity of problem behavior.

Materials

1. Posterboard chart with a list of classroom rules, such as:
   a. Raise your hand and wait to be recognized when you want to talk.
   b. Keep from making too much noise.
   c. Stay in your seat unless you have permission to get up.
   d. Keep from tattling on other students.
   e. Follow teacher directions the first time they are given.
2. Posterboard chart listing the ways students can earn merit points, such as:
   a. Earn a score of 80% or better on your classwork.
   b. Participate actively in class discussions.
   c. Be especially polite and helpful to others (see Variation 2).
3. 3" × 5" index cards with the words "One Merit" written on each; the number of cards should equal the number of students in the class (optional).

Options to Monitor Progress

1. Record percent-correct scores on classwork assignments for the entire class or a target group of students during a selected instructional period for 5–10 days or for several weeks.
2. Using a sheet of paper attached to a clipboard, record the frequency of active classroom participation for the entire class or a target group of students during a selected instructional period for 4–7 days. *Active classroom participation* is defined as responding appropriately to a teacher-delivered question or contributing an appropriate statement or question to class discussion.
3. Using a *Classwide Scanning Form* with a 3-, 5-, or 10-minute interval, scan the room, starting with the front and ending with the back, and tally the number of students exhibiting on-task, off-task, and disruptive behavior, as defined below.
   a. *On-task behavior*: working on the task at hand, looking at the teacher during presentations, and any other behavior relevant to the lesson.
   b. *Off-task behavior*: sitting without having appropriate materials at hand, looking at noninstructional materials, and looking around the room after assignments have been made.
   c. *Disruptive behavior*: any behavior disrupting the on-task behavior of other students, such as inappropriate verbal or motor behaviors.
   Conduct these observations during a selected instructional period for 30–45 minutes for 4–7 days.
4. Measure classwide academic engagement with DBR. These data can be collected in each period in which the intervention is active and graphed for analysis.

Intervention Steps

Introduction and Training

1. Select an instructional period for implementation, such as the period when students are most disruptive, least productive, and/or participate least often in class discussions. Explain to the students that they will be playing a game during the period to help everyone get the most out of that subject.
2. Divide the class into two or three teams. Be sure to distribute students with problem behavior between teams. If desired, have the teams select their own names.
3. On a section of the chalkboard visible to all students, write "Team 1," "Team 2,"and so on (or the names of the teams), with a column for each day of the week. If desired, list names of team members under each team name.
4. Set a criterion for winning the game, such as no more than five demerits during the intervention period. Also describe the rewards for the winning team(s), such as 10 minutes of free time, 10 minutes of computer time, homework passes, extra recess, lining up first to go home, and so forth. All teams can win or lose.
5. Demonstrate the process of giving demerits, as described below. Model how students should respond to receiving a demerit and explain that arguing or other inappropriate reactions will result in an additional demerit for the team.
6. Using the charts, review the classroom rules and the ways students can earn merit points.

Implementation

1. During the selected period, record a demerit beside the team name each time a student breaks a rule. State the reason for the demerit as you record it. For example, say, "Sonya, you didn't follow directions" while putting a check mark under the appropriate team's name and a check mark next to the student's name, if listed.
2. During the intervention period, give merit cards to students who display the designated positive academic and/or social behaviors. Alternately, record merit points in the form of plus (+) marks on the chalkboard next to team names and, if desired, student names.
3. At the end of the period, have students hold up their merit cards for you to count or tally the number of pluses per team. Erase one demerit for every five merit points earned by a team. Collect the merit cards, if used.
4. At the end of the period or the end of the day, deliver rewards to teams not exceeding the criterion.
5. As student behavior improves, post the winning team(s) for an entire week and deliver a reward to teams meeting the criterion on 4 out of 5 days.

Variations

VARIATION 1: GOOD BEHAVIOR GAME PLUS MERIT WITH RESPONSE COST

1. Begin the period with a certain number of credits per team, such as 10. Set a minimum criterion for winning, such as five credits. Remove one credit each time a member of a team breaks a rule. Restore one credit for every five merit points earned by members of that team.
2. Deliver rewards to teams with the designated number of credits remaining at the end of the intervention period. If both teams meet or exceed the criterion, both teams are winners.

VARIATION 2: GOOD BEHAVIOR GAME PLUS MERIT FOR BEHAVIOR IMPROVEMENT

Award merit points for prosocial behavior, as well as for improved academic performance. For example, if you observe a student being especially helpful, cooperative, or kind, publicly identify the student and the prosocial behavior and award a merit point to that team.

NOTES

1. This has been one of the most popular interventions in the field testing. Teachers find it very easy to use and often develop their own variations. Most teachers prefer to record merit points on the chalkboard rather than to distribute merit cards.
2. As with the GBG, the response-cost variation (Variation 1) appears to be more effective and more acceptable to teachers than the original.

SOURCE

Darveaux, D. X. (1984). The good behavior game plus merit: Controlling disruptive behavior and improving student motivation. *School Psychology Review, 13,* 510–514.

CLASSWIDE FUNCTION-RELATED INTERVENTION TEAMS

Overview

Classwide Function-Related Intervention Teams (CW-FIT) is a behavioral intervention designed to explicitly teach and reinforce appropriate social behaviors through the use of a game-like activity that can be implemented within the general education classroom setting (Kamps et al., 2011, 2015; Wills, Iwaszuk, Kamps, & Shumate, 2014; Wills et al., 2010).

This intervention can be strategically implemented during "problem" times of the day to decrease problem behavior. CW-FIT incorporates multiple research-based behavioral strategies, including direct instruction of skills, self- and peer management, extinction by removing reinforcement (i.e., withholding attention when problem behaviors occur), differential reinforcement of alternative behaviors through dependent group contingencies, token economy, and teacher praise.

Goal

This intervention addresses behavioral problems that are occurring across a group of students or classwide. CW-FIT has dual functionality, first, by incorporating explicit direct instruction so students can learn the appropriate behaviors and, second, by providing positive reinforcement in a systematic way so that the students can increase fluency in demonstrating the desired behaviors. This intervention is designed to address problem behaviors that are maintained by receiving attention from adults and peers by teaching and reinforcing appropriate alternative behaviors that can replace the problem behaviors.

Intervention Intensity

The intervention can be used for a variety of students in classrooms with appropriate adaptations for age, topic, and intensity of problem behavior.

Options to Monitor Progress

Measure classwide academic engagement and disruptive behavior with DBR. These data can be collected in each period in which the intervention is active and graphed for analysis. Conduct observations for 3–5 days prior to the start of the intervention to establish a baseline and then in each instructional period in which the intervention is used.

Intervention Steps

1. Select the target behaviors to be taught. Typical behaviors taught in CW-FIT include the following:
   a. Gaining the teacher's attention
      - Look at the teacher.
      - Raise your hand.
      - Wait for the teacher to call on you.
      - Ask your question or give your answer.
   b. Following directions
      - Look at the person and listen.
      - Say "OK."
      - Do it.
      - Check back (if needed).
   c. Ignoring inappropriate behaviors
      - Keep a pleasant face.
      - Look away from the person.
      - Keep a quiet mouth.
      - Pretend you are not listening.
      - Follow directions—do your work.
2. Teaching component
   a. Define each target behavior by describing the steps listed above. It can be helpful to create posters that can serve as prompts for the students.
   b. Model the behavior by showing the students what the activity looks like. You can show examples as well as nonexamples of the behavior.
   c. Practice with the students by having them role-play with you and their peers to further demonstrate to the class.
   d. Provide specific feedback to students during practice opportunities.
3. Divide the class into teams of 2–5 students and assign them a team name/number.
4. Write the team names on the board—it is where you will be tallying each team's points.
5. Explain the criteria for the game.
   a. Remind students of those appropriate target behaviors.
   b. Explain the procedures for the game, which consists of teams receiving points every 2–3 minutes when all students are displaying the behavioral skills at the beep.
   c. Tell the students how long they are playing the game (during math class, after lunch, whole day, etc.)
   d. Set a point goal and discuss with the class what reward they want if they win the game. The reward is given at the end of the class period to all groups who met the goal.
6. Initiate the game with the class by starting the timer with 2–3 minute intervals set.
7. Keep track of points during the game and provide behavior-specific praise to students demonstrating appropriate skills. During this game, provide minimal attention to any inappropriate behaviors.
8. Reward and praise the teams who meet their behavioral goal using specific praise.

Critical Components for Successful Implementation

The reward should be something that students will prefer and that will serve as a powerful motivator. The behavioral expectations should be clearly taught and prompts displayed so that students understand what they should be doing. The points and rewards need to be given consistently to those meeting expectations and not given to those who aren't showing appropriate behaviors. Specific praise should be used with high frequency to provide feedback to students.

NOTE

The CW-FIT brief was developed by Amanda Allen for the EBI Network.

SOURCES

Kamps, D., Wills, H., Dawson-Bannister, H., Heitzman-Powell, L., Kottwitz, E., Hansen, B., et al. (2015). Class-wide function-related intervention teams "CW-FIT" efficacy trial outcomes. *Journal of Positive Behavior Interventions, 17*(3), 134–145.

Kamps, D., Wills, H. P., Heitzman-Powell, L., Laylin, J., Szoke, C., Petrillo, T., & Culey, A. (2011). Class-wide function-related intervention teams: Effects of group contingency programs in urban classrooms. *Journal of Positive Behavior Interventions, 13*, 154–167.

Wills, H. P., Iwaszuk, W. M., Kamps, D., & Shumate, E. (2014). CW-FIT: Group contingency effects across the day. *Education and Treatment of Children, 37*(2), 191–210.

Wills, H. P., Kamps, D., Hansen, B. D., Conklin, C., Bellinger, S., Neaderhiser, J. & Nsubuga, B. (2010). The Class-wide Function-based Intervention Team (CW-FIT) program. *Preventing School Failure, 54*, 164–171.

USING BANKING TIME TO BUILD POSITIVE TEACHER–STUDENT RELATIONSHIPS

Overview

Positive teacher–student relationships are critical not only to children's academic and social development but also to effective classroom management, because student cooperation is essential to a productive, disruption-free classroom. In the *Banking Time* (BT) intervention, teachers provide brief sessions of focused, nondirective interactions that convey messages of safety, predictability, and support for exploration rather than evaluation of performance. First developed to improve teachers' relationships with individual children at risk for behavior disorders and to help prevent teacher burnout, the strategy is called "Banking Time" because the sessions are designed to help teachers and students "invest" positive interactions to "draw on" during stressful times, so that the teacher–child relationship can survive conflict without resuming the negative cycle of interactions. BT has also been validated as a classroom-level intervention by incorporating sessions into a small-group activity format (Pianta, 1999). By rotating through groups of five or six students, teachers can conduct BT sessions with each student two or three times a week. The original individual-student format is included as a variation. As a final note, this intervention is consistent with the principles of noncontingent reinforcement, which has a significant evidence base.

Goal

The purpose of this intervention is to promote positive teacher–student relationships and create a supportive climate for learning, with regular sessions of nondirective teacher–student interactions. This intervention is useful for students who have learned the desired behaviors but need support in displaying them fluently.

Intervention Intensity

The intervention can be used for a variety of students in classrooms with appropriate adaptations for age, topic, and intensity of problem behavior.

Materials

None.

Options to Monitor Progress

1. Using a *Group Event Recording Form,* record the frequency of one or more inappropriate and disruptive behaviors, such as call-outs, making noises, arguing, and being out of seat, for a target student, a group of target students, or the entire class. Conduct these observations for 30–45 minutes during a selected instructional period for 4–7 days.
2. On a sheet of paper attached to a clipboard, record the number of reprimands you deliver to a target student, a group of target students, or the entire class during a selected instructional period for 4–7 days.
3. Using a sheet of paper attached to a clipboard, record the frequency of negative student verbalizations made by the entire class or a group of target students. *Negative verbalizations* are defined as teasing, name-calling, threatening, or any other unfriendly or aggressive verbalization. Conduct these observations for 30–45 minutes during one or more selected instructional periods or transitions for 4–7 days.
4. Measure classwide academic engagement and disruptive behavior with DBR. These data can be collected in each period in which the intervention is active and graphed for analysis. Conduct observations for 3–5 days prior to the start of the intervention to establish a baseline and then in each instructional period in which the intervention is used.

Intervention Steps

Preparation

1. Select a time during the school day when students are already working in small groups or when small-group activities can be readily implemented so that BT sessions can occur predictably. For example, BT can be included during cooperative learning activities, center time, or end-of-day activities.
2. Decide how long BT sessions can be (between 5 and 15 minutes) during the selected period. For example, if the time allotted for cooperative learning is 40 minutes, you can provide an 8-minute BT session for each of five groups during that period.
3. Identify no more than three primary BT messages that emphasize the caring and helpful aspects of your role as teacher. If possible, select these messages on the basis of observations of current teacher–student relationships made by a consultant (see Note 2). Messages should be designed to disconfirm students' negative expectations of or beliefs about the teacher and to promote positive expectations of and beliefs about the teacher. Sample BT messages include the following:
   a. "I am interested in you."
   b. "I accept you."
   c. "I am a helper when you need me or ask me."

   d. "I will try to be fair and available."
   e. "I can help you solve problems."

Introduction and Training

1. Tell the students that you have selected a regular part of the classroom routine (e.g., cooperative learning time, center time) during which you will be spending time with them in a different way.
2. Explain what the small-group activities will be and when they will occur. Write the weekly schedule for BT on the chalkboard where all the students can see it.
3. Explain to students that you will be spending time with them rather than teaching them during that period, but that the rules for behavior are the same as during other classroom time. That is, if a student breaks a classroom rule during a BT session, you will deliver the usual consequence after the session.

Implementation

1. Conduct BT sessions at the appointed time each week. As much as possible, permit students to direct the small-group activities or to be engaged with the learning or play materials within the limits established.
2. During BT sessions for small groups or individual students, keep your behavior and verbalizations as neutral and objective as possible. Observations of student behavior should not focus on skill performance. Try to refrain from teaching, directing, and offering reinforcement during sessions.
3. If a student breaks a rule during BT, do not terminate the BT session for that group or child. Instead, try to use the session as a way of understanding the problem behavior and affirming the messages of consistency, helpfulness, and caring. At the conclusion of the session, administer the usual consequence.
4. Between BT sessions, use the same relationship-theme messages to communicate consistency, helpfulness, and caring during routine classroom interactions, such as teacher requests for compliance and student requests for assistance. For examples, during small-group instruction, say, "I need help from everyone in using quiet voices so that I can hear the students in the reading circle." During center time or independent seatwork, say, "I wonder if you need help with that. I'm here to help."

Variation: Banking Time with Individual Students

To implement BT with one or more individual target students, provide 5-minute one-to-one sessions two or three times a week during independent seatwork, center time, collaborative learning time, or at the end of the day during the "packing up" period. Keep your comments and interactions as low key and unobtrusive as possible while other students continue with the regular classroom routine. Incorporating BT into the last moments of the school day can help mend relationships that have become strained during the course of the day's events.

NOTES

1. BT must not be contingent on student behavior (e.g., "Class, you have really earned your Banking Time today" or "Jeremy, I'm sorry, but your behavior has been so bad that you've lost your Banking Time today"). Adhering to this guideline can be very difficult for teachers

who believe that paying attention to misbehaving students will reinforce the problem behavior. According to the researcher, this is the case only when teacher attention is contingent on the misbehavior, that is, when it occurs immediately after and in the same situation as the misbehavior. Because BT sessions are scheduled beforehand, teacher attention during BT sessions should not serve as a reinforcer for inappropriate behavior.

2. Having a consultant observe the class to help select specific BT messages is strongly recommended, especially if teacher–student relationships have already deteriorated.

3. Role-playing BT with a consultant or colleague who can provide supportive feedback is a key aspect in successful implementation. This type of adult–child interaction does not come easily to many educators, who are accustomed to delivering instructional and managerial statements rather than nondirective, nonevaluative messages.

SOURCE

Pianta, R. C. (1999). *Enhancing relationships between children and teachers*. Washington, DC: American Psychological Association.

ADDITIONAL RESOURCE

Banking Time is a component in *Students, Teachers, and Relationship Support* (STARS), a classroom intervention program developed by Robert Pianta and Bridget Hamre and available from Psychological Assessment Resources, Inc.

A MULTICOMPONENT INTERVENTION TO REDUCE DISRUPTIVE BEHAVIOR

Overview

Aggressive, defiant, and disruptive students reduce opportunities to learn for themselves and their fellow students. The more time teachers must spend dealing with disruptive behavior, the greater the impact on student achievement. Interventions targeting disruptive behavior should not only be effective in reducing the problem behaviors but also time-efficient and capable of being easily integrated into the daily classroom routine. This highly usable intervention combines public posting of classroom rules with a response-cost token economy and unpredictable rewards (Mottram, Bray, Kehle, Broudy, & Jenson, 2002). After students accumulate a predetermined number of points within the token economy, they earn access to a "mystery motivator," a reward or description of a reward placed in an envelope and publicly displayed. Originally implemented with three second graders with behavior disorders, the strategy produced an immediate, pronounced decrease in disruptive behaviors for all three students. Moreover, disruptive behavior rates for target students were consistently lower than rates for a peer control group during the intervention period and a 3-week follow-up phase. The teacher reported that the intervention was easy to implement, and the target students awarded it high satisfaction ratings. Here the strategy is adapted for classwide application with an interdependent group contingency. Two variations are also presented: the original version targeting individual students and a team-based version.

Goal

The purpose of this intervention is to reduce disruptive behavior with a multicomponent intervention consisting of publicly posted classroom rules, a token economy with response cost, and mystery motivators.

Intervention Intensity

The intervention can be used for a variety of students in classrooms with appropriate adaptations for age, topic, and intensity of problem behavior.

Materials

1. Posterboard chart listing the class rules, such as:
   a. Do what the teacher tells you to do.
   b. Stay in your seat unless the teacher gives you permission to leave it.
   c. Keep your eyes on the teacher or your work during instruction.
   d. Talk only when you have been called on after raising your hand.
2. "Points chart" consisting of a chart drawn on the chalkboard, with one column for each day of the week; for Variation 2, divide each column into two, and label the columns "Team 1" and "Team 2."
3. "Mystery Motivator envelope," consisting of a large manila envelope with a large question mark drawn on it (for Variation 1, one envelope per target student).
4. Index cards listing activity rewards, such as extra recess, indoor games, or music time or describing access to small tangible rewards, such as "candy for everyone" to indicate that each student may have a piece of wrapped candy.
5. Small tangible rewards, such as stickers, wrapped candy, bubble gum, pencils, and sports cards (optional; see Variation 1).
6. *Reinforcement Menus*, one per student (optional).
7. Red marking pen (optional; see Variation 1).

Options to Monitor Progress

1. Using a *Group Event Recording Form*, tally the number of disruptive behaviors for the entire class or a group of target students during the selected instructional period. *Disruptive behaviors* are defined as failing to follow teacher directions, getting out of one's seat without permission, talking or making noises, playing with nonlesson materials, or any other behavior interfering with instruction. Conduct these observations for 30–45 minutes for 4–7 days.
2. Using a *Group Interval Recording Form* with a 15-second interval, code the behavior of each student in the class or each target student in turn during the selected instructional period as on task (+) or disruptive (–), beginning at the left side of the room. Place a minus (–) if the student being observed displays one or more disruptive behaviors during the interval, as defined above. Conduct these observations for 30–45 minutes for 4–7 days.
3. Using a sheet of paper attached to a clipboard, record the number of classroom rule infractions during a selected instructional period for the entire class or a target group of students for 4–7 days.
4. Measure classwide disruptive behavior and respectful behavior with DBR. These data should be collected in each period in which the intervention is active and graphed for analysis. Data can be collected on the classroom, a small group, or an individual child based on the focus of the intervention. Conduct observations for 3–5 days prior to the start of the intervention to establish a baseline and then in each instructional period in which the intervention is used.

Intervention Steps

Introduction and Training

1. Tell the class that they will have an opportunity to earn rewards for following the class-room rules and helping everyone get the most out of instruction during a selected period or intervention interval, such as the morning instructional block.
2. Using the rules chart and *Say, Show, Check: Teaching Classroom Procedures,* review the classroom rules. Post the rules chart where it is visible to everyone.
3. Display the index cards and the Mystery Motivator envelope, and place one card in the envelope. Explain to the students that they will have an opportunity to earn the reward written on the card if they follow the class rules during the entire period. Place the envelope on your desk where all students can see it.
4. Review the available rewards, or, if desired, distribute copies of a *Reinforcement Menu* and guide the students in selecting a set of rewards.
5. Referring to the points chart on the chalkboard, explain that you will award one point for every 15 minutes (or some other interval) that students follow all the rules. Explain that you will erase a point if any student breaks a rule and/or displays inappropriate behavior at any time. Caution the class that you will deduct an additional point if a student argues or displays inappropriate behavior in response to point removal.
6. Explain that if there are five points remaining at the end of the intervention period, you will select a student to open the Mystery Motivator envelope and identify the reward written on the card.

Implementation

1. At the beginning of the intervention period, place one of the index cards in the Mystery Motivator envelope. To increase the suspense, have the students watch while you shuffle the cards and randomly select a card to be placed in the envelope.
2. Place a check on the chalkboard for each 15 minutes (or the predetermined reinforcement interval) that there are no rule infractions and praise students for their good behavior—for example, "Great job, class! You earned your point!"
3. If a student breaks a rule, calmly state the student's name and the rule infraction, and erase one point. If the student argues, complains, or responds in some other negative way, deduct another point.
4. At the end of the intervention period, review the point totals on the chalkboard. If there are at least five points remaining, praise the class and permit a randomly selected student to open the Mystery Motivator envelope and read what is written on the index card. Deliver the reward to the class immediately or at the end of the day.
5. As behavior improves, gradually increase the length of the interval and the number of points needed to earn the reward. Then substitute praise for tangible reinforcers and deduct 5 minutes of recess time for each rule infraction or incident of disruptive behavior.

Variations

VARIATION 1: INDIVIDUAL OR SMALL-GROUP VARIATION

1. Using a *Reinforcement Menu,* help each target student select a set of possible rewards. Write the name of each target student and a question mark on a manila envelope. Place a small reward or an index card describing an activity reward (e.g., extra computer time,

first to line up for lunch, lunch with the teacher) in each envelope and place the envelopes on your desk.

2. Tape an index card to the top of the desk of each target student. Explain to the target students that if they retain at least five points at the end of the intervention period, they will receive the reward in the envelope.

3. During the intervention period, use a red marking pen to mark a point on the index card of each target student who follows the rules for the prescribed interval. If a student breaks a rule, deduct one point.

4. At the end of the period or school day, deliver the reward in the envelope to target students who have retained at least five points. Activity and social rewards can be delivered on the following day when time permits.

5. As behavior improves, require the target students to earn more points over a longer period of time in order to earn a reward.

VARIATION 2: TEAM-BASED VARIATION

1. Divide the class into two teams, based on seating arrangements. Make sure that disruptive students are distributed approximately equally across the two teams.

2. Place an index card describing an identical small tangible reward or activity reward in each of two manila envelopes and place the envelopes in a prominent position on your desk.

3. Record points on the chalkboard at the prescribed interval for teams that are following the classroom rules, and deduct one point from team scores for every rule infraction by a team member, as described above.

4. Tally points at the end of the intervention period and deliver the reward to any team(s) with at least five points. If both teams win, a more valued group activity reward can be delivered.

5. As behavior improves, require teams to meet the criterion on 4 out of 5 days and deliver the reward on Friday.

NOTES

1. It is important for students to accrue points for positive behavior as rapidly as possible when the intervention is first implemented. If the class accumulates too many penalty points in the beginning, students may become discouraged and stop attempting to behave positively. To avoid this possible pitfall, begin each intervention period with a brief review of the classroom rules and the potential rewards to enhance students' awareness of the target behaviors and increase anticipation of the reward. Similarly, keep reinforcement intervals relatively short (10–15 minutes) during initial implementation.

2. If a student deliberately misbehaves so as to prevent the class or team from winning, place that student on an independent (i.e., individual) contingency.

SOURCE

Mottram, L. M., Bray, M. A., Kehle, T. J., Broudy, M., & Jenson, W. R. (2002). A classroom-based intervention to reduce disruptive behavior. *Journal of Applied School Psychology, 19,* 65–74.

REDUCING DISRUPTIVE BEHAVIOR WITH RANDOMIZED GROUP CONTINGENCIES

Overview

Although group contingencies can be effective in increasing appropriate behavior and are easier to deliver than individual reinforcers, it can be difficult to identify rewards that are not only practical for teachers but also reinforcing for every student. If some students do not value the reinforcers, group contingency procedures may not alter their behavior in the desired direction. This intervention addresses this limitation by randomizing reinforcements so that students cannot determine which reward is available for displaying the desired behavior. Similarly, randomizing the targeted behaviors and the criteria for earning rewards can encourage students to maintain appropriate behavior throughout the intervention period because they are unsure of the behavior that will be selected or the exact criteria for reinforcement. In the original studies, interventions with randomized group contingency components produced immediate dramatic improvement in the behavior of elementary students in regular education classes and secondary students with emotional disorders in a self-contained special education classroom (Kelshaw-Levering, Sterling-Turner, Henry, & Skinner, 2000). Two variations are presented: one randomizing rewards and the criteria for receiving them and another randomizing two additional group contingency components.

Goal

The purpose of this intervention is to reduce disruptive behavior and increase appropriate behavior with a randomized group contingency program. This intervention is designed for students who have acquired the requisite skills for appropriate classroom behavior but need reinforcement to do so fluently.

Intervention Intensity

The intervention can be used for a variety of students in classrooms with appropriate adaptations for age, topic, and intensity of problem behavior.

Materials

1. "Rules chart," consisting of a posterboard chart listing the class rules, such as:
    a. Stay in your seat unless you have permission to be out of it.
    b. Raise your hand before speaking.
    c. Keep from talking to others unless given permission.
    d. Pay attention when the teacher is talking.
    e. Do what the teacher tells you to do at once.
2. One opaque glass or plastic jar with slips of paper (two jars for Variation 1 and four jars for Variation 2).
3. List of student names attached to a clipboard (for Variations 1 and 2; also label five columns corresponding to the target behaviors—i.e., infractions of each of the classroom rules).
4. "Rewards chart," consisting of a posterboard chart listing a variety of activity and social rewards.

Options to Monitor Progress

1. Using a sheet of paper attached to a clipboard, tally the number of rule infractions for the entire class during a selected instructional period or a fixed interval, such as the first third of the day, for 4–7 days. Calculate the average number of rule infractions per period or interval and use that number to set the initial criterion (see Intervention Step 5) at about half that number.
2. Using a *Group Interval Recording Form* with a 10-second interval, code the behavior of each student in turn as on task (+) or off-task/disruptive (–), beginning at the left side of the room. Record a minus (–) if the student is off task or disruptive at any time during the interval, as defined below.
   a. *On-task behavior* is defined as attending to the teacher or the assignment, participating in class discussions, and any other lesson-related behavior.
   b. *Off-task/disruptive behavior* is defined as failing to follow teacher instructions; calling out; talking without permission; being out of one's seat without permission; looking at something other than the teacher, participating peers, or classwork; or any other behavior interfering with one's own learning or that of others.
   Conduct these observations for 30 to 45 minutes during a selected instructional period for 4–7 days.
3. Measure classwide academic engagement and disruptive behavior with DBR. These data can be collected in each period in which the intervention is active and graphed for analysis. Conduct observations for 3–5 days prior to the start of the intervention to establish a baseline and then in each instructional period in which the intervention is used.

Intervention Steps

Preparation

Label the first jar "Rewards." On 15–20 slips of paper, write a variety of activity and social rewards, such as intervals for extra recess (e.g., 5 minutes, 10 minutes), intervals of free time (e.g., 5 minutes, 10 minutes, 15 minutes), special snacks (e.g., peanut butter cups, lollipops), and "party points" (points ranging from 1 to 5, with a total of 45 needed for a class party). Place the slips of paper in the jar.

ADDITIONAL PREPARATION FOR VARIATION 1

Label the second jar "Behavior." Place in the jar 15–20 slips of paper listing either (a) a target behavior corresponding to the classroom rules (e.g., out-of-seat, call-out, talk-out, or off-task behavior or noncompliance) and a number ranging from 0 to the criterion number (e.g., off task–3), or (b) the word *all* and a number (e.g., all–5). The number represents the number of times the target behavior(s) can occur during a given interval. *All* indicates that you will evaluate all of the target behaviors, that is, the total number of marks across behaviors.

ADDITIONAL PREPARATION FOR VARIATION 3

Label the third and fourth jars as "Whole Class or Individual Student" and "Names." Place 10–15 slips of paper labeled "Whole Class" and "Individual Student" in the jar with that label. Put a slip of paper with the name of each individual student in the jar labeled "Names." Alternatively, to reduce preparation time and enhance motivation, have students write their names on the slips of papers and place them in the jar.

Introduction and Training

1. Using the Rules chart, review the classroom rules with the students and post the chart where it is visible to everyone. Explain to the students that they will be able to earn certain privileges or treats by following the rules.
2. Display the clipboard with the list of students' names and explain that you will put a check beside the name of any student who breaks a classroom rule.
3. Explain that you have divided the school day into three intervals during which students can earn rewards. Set the intervals to accommodate regular breaks in the day for ease of reinforcement delivery. For implementation within a single instructional period, explain that students can earn rewards at the end of the period.
4. Display the Rewards chart and the Rewards jar and slips of paper, and review the available reinforcers.
5. State the criterion for earning rewards—for example: "If our class has less than 15 checks [or some value approximately half of the baseline rate] for breaking the rules, I will choose someone to draw a reward from the jar."

Implementation

1. If a student breaks a rule, state the student's name and the infraction, and place a mark on the checklist next to the student's name—for example, "Heather, that's a talk-out."
2. Halfway through each of the three daily intervals (or halfway through the instructional period), remind students that they are working to try to earn a reward at the end of the interval or period. Deliver this reminder regardless of the frequency of target behaviors. Do not comment on the appropriateness or inappropriateness of student behavior at this time or the number of checks earned by individual students or the class as a whole.
3. At the end of the interval, consult the checklist to determine whether students have met the criterion. If the class has met the criterion, praise the class and permit a randomly selected student to draw a slip of paper from the Rewards jar and hand it to you without reading what is written on it. Identify the reward and deliver it to the class as soon as possible.
4. As student behavior improves, gradually increase the length of the interval until you are drawing from the jar and delivering rewards once a day. Then conduct the drawing and reward delivery on a weekly basis. If you are implementing the intervention within a single period, gradually increase the number of consecutive days on which students must meet the criterion to receive a reward until you are delivering a reward for 4 consecutive days of successful behavior.

Variations

VARIATION 1: RANDOMIZED REINFORCEMENTS AND RANDOMIZED CRITERIA

1. Display the Rewards chart and jar and discuss the available rewards as described above.
2. Display the Behavior jar and the slips of paper and review their contents, as described above. Explain that students will not know the criterion for reinforcement or what the reward may be. Instead, the reward and criterion may change from period to period, depending on what is drawn from the jar.
3. During the intervention period, use the checklist to record rule infractions by student name and rule. Halfway through each of the three daily intervals (or halfway through the instructional period), remind students that they are working for a chance to earn a reward at the end of the interval.

4. At the end of the interval, draw a slip of paper from the Behavior jar. State the target behavior(s) and the number that have been drawn.
5. Consult the checklist to determine whether the class has met the criterion.
   a. *Example 1*: If you draw a slip of paper with "Noncompliance–9" on it, there must be no more than 9 checks" in the noncompliance column for that interval for the class to meet the criterion.
   b. *Example 2*: If you draw a slip of paper with "All–12" on it, there must be no more than 12 marks across all behaviors for that interval for the class to meet the criterion.
6. If the class has met the criterion corresponding to the slip of paper that has been drawn, randomly select a student to draw a slip of paper from the Rewards jar. Identify the reward and deliver it to the class as soon as possible.

VARIATION 2: RANDOMIZED REINFORCEMENTS, CRITERIA, BEHAVIORS, AND TARGET STUDENTS

1. Display the first two jars and the rewards as described above. Explain that students will not know the criterion for earning reinforcement or what the reward may be. Instead, the reward and criterion may change from period to period, depending on what is drawn from the jar.
2. Display the Whole Class or Individual Student jar and the Names jar. Review their contents as described in the Materials section above. Explain that students will not know whether the behavior of the entire class or an individual student will be evaluated according to the criterion that is drawn.
3. Use the checklist to record rule infractions by student name and rule and provide the prompt halfway through each of the intervals as described above for Variation 1.
4. At the end of the interval, draw a slip of paper from each of the four jars in the following order:
   a. First, draw a slip of paper from the Behavior jar. State the target behavior(s) and the number that have been drawn.
   b. Second, draw a slip of paper from the Whole Class or Individual Student jar to determine whether to evaluate the behavior of the entire class or an individual student in terms of the slip of paper that has been drawn from the Behavior jar.
   c. If you draw an "Individual Student" slip, draw a slip from the Names jar. Consult the checklist to determine whether that student has met the selected criterion for that behavior during the interval. If that student has met the criterion for that target behavior, announce the target behavior and the criterion and permit that student to draw a slip of paper from the Rewards jar. If the individual student did not meet the criterion, tell the class they have failed to meet the criterion and return the slips of papers to their respective jars without announcing the name of the student. For example, if you draw a "Noncompliance–5" slip of paper from the Behavior jar and an "Individual Student" slip of paper from the Whole Class or Individual Student jar, the student whose name has been drawn must have received no more than five checks for noncompliance during that interval to meet the criterion.
   d. If you draw a "Whole Class" slip, consult the checklist to determine whether the class as a whole has met the selected criterion for that behavior during the interval. If the class has met the criterion, announce the criterion and select a student to draw a slip of paper from the Rewards jar. If not, state that the class has failed to meet the criterion and return the slips of papers to their respective jars without announcing the specifics of the contingency you have drawn. For example, if you draw an "All–15" slip of

paper, there must be no more than 15 marks on the checklist for the class to meet the criterion.

NOTES

1. In the original study, the version with all components randomized (Variation 2) was implemented after the first version (randomized reinforcers only) and appeared to be slightly more effective.
2. According to the authors, the teacher prompt during the interval (see Implementation Step 2) is a critical component in intervention effectiveness.
3. In the case of students who continue to exhibit unacceptable levels of inappropriate behavior, the checklist can provide information for use in parent–teacher conferences, functional behavioral assessments, and/or behavior support plans.

SOURCE

Kelshaw-Levering, K., Sterling-Turner, H. E., Henry, J. R., & Skinner, C. H. (2000). Randomized interdependent group contingencies: Group reinforcement with a twist. *Psychology in the Schools, 37,* 523–533.

POSITIVE PEER REPORTING

Overview

Students who provoke other students or fail to cooperate with their classmates during instruction and group activities are at risk for poor peer relationships and other negative academic and social outcomes. Moreover, efforts to deal with these students can be time-consuming and stressful for teachers, reducing instructional time and creating a negative classroom environment. *Positive Peer Reporting* (PPR) is a strategy that targets not only students who engage in negative interactions with their peers but also socially rejected students. Students earn points toward group rewards by praising their classmates' prosocial behaviors during brief daily compliment sessions, thereby giving individuals with poor social skills an incentive to display appropriate behavior in order to gain positive peer attention and nontargeted students an incentive to focus on the positive rather than negative aspects of their classmates' behavior. PPR has been demonstrated to be effective in improving the social interactions, peer acceptance, and social involvement of socially rejected or isolated elementary and middle school students in regular education, special education, and residential settings (Moroz & Jones, 2002). Moreover, PPR helps to create a positive classroom atmosphere that encourages cooperation and promotes learning. Two variations are presented: (1) a version with a randomization component to enhance motivation to observe and report prosocial behavior and (2) a version with a cumulative-point reward system.

Goal

The purpose of this intervention is to enhance prosocial behavior and positive peer relationships and reduce inappropriate social behaviors by systematically encouraging and reinforcing peer compliments. This intervention is designed for students who have acquired the requisite skills for appropriate classroom behavior but need reinforcement to do so fluently. In this intervention, peer attention must function as a reinforcer for it to be effective.

Intervention Intensity

The intervention can be used for a variety of students in classrooms with appropriate adaptations for age, topic, and intensity of problem behavior.

Materials

1. "Points chart," consisting of a posterboard chart displaying the number of points needed to earn the group reward and the number of points earned per day; if desired, make a bar graph in the form of a thermometer and color in the points earned each day with a different colored marker.
2. "Compliments chart," consisting of a posterboard chart listing the steps in providing compliments and examples, as follows:

Four Steps in Giving Compliments

     a. Look at the person.
     b. Smile.
     c. Report something positive the person did or said during the day.
     d. Then make a positive comment, such as, "Good job!" or "Way to go!"

Examples of Compliments

     a. "Phoebe told me my new headband looked nice."
     b. "Kevin gave me a pencil to borrow when I couldn't find mine."
     c. "Joy had a great idea during our group project."
     d. "Mario helped me log on during computer time."
3. Glass or see-through plastic jar, labeled "Honey Pot," and cotton balls (optional; see Variation 2).

Options to Monitor Progress

1. Using a *Group Event Recording Form,* record the number of negative and positive social interactions displayed by the entire class or a group of target students during recess, a major transition (such as packing up at the end of the day), or an instructional period that includes classwide discussions or cooperative learning activities.
     a. *Negative social interactions* are defined as incidents of negative verbal behavior (e.g., arguing, teasing, yelling), negative physical behavior (e.g., hitting, pushing, taking materials), or any other unfriendly or uncooperative behavior.
     b. *Positive social interactions* are defined as incidents of appropriate peer–peer interactions, including working or playing cooperatively, giving or offering assistance, talking or listening in a pleasant manner, or any other friendly or cooperative interaction.
     Conduct these observations during the targeted period for 4–7 days. If desired, use these data to help set a criterion for the number of points (compliments) needed to earn the reward (see Intervention Steps/Introduction and Training, Step 4).
2. Create a sociometric rating scale by writing student names in alphabetical order on a sheet of paper, with a 5-point Likert-type scale (1 = "not at all," 2 = "a little," 3 = "some," 4 = "a lot," 5 = "very much") beside each name. Distribute copies of the rating scale and ask students to circle the number that best describes how much they would like to work on a project with each of their classmates (for younger students, ask how much they would like

to play with each of their classmates). Collect the completed scales and calculate the average score for each student. Use these data to help identify the group of target students.

3. Measure classwide disruptive behavior and respectful behavior with DBR. These data should be collected in each period in which the intervention is active and graphed for analysis. Data can be collected on the classroom, a small group, or an individual child based on the focus of the intervention. Conduct observations for 3–5 days prior to the start of the intervention to establish a baseline and then in each instructional period in which the intervention is used.

Intervention Steps

Introduction and Training

1. Tell the students that they are going to have an opportunity to help create a friendlier classroom atmosphere and earn group rewards by participating in a new activity. Each day, three or four students (or an appropriate number, based on class size) will have a chance to be the class "stars," and everyone will have a chance to praise the stars' friendly and helpful behavior that has contributed to making the classroom a good place to learn and have fun.

2. Using the compliments chart, conduct a 20-minute training session in which you teach students how to give compliments. Provide examples and nonexamples of compliments, have students offer their own examples, and give praise and corrective feedback as needed. For example, if students give vague praise ("I want to compliment Allison. She was nice today"), ask, "What nice things did you see Allison do?"

3. Tell students that during the "star time" (e.g., at the end of the morning instructional period, during afternoon homeroom period, during circle/advisory time), you will review the list of stars for the day and invite other students to raise their hands to offer compliments about each of those students.

4. Explain that if you call on a student and he or she is able to offer a sincere, appropriate compliment about one of the class stars, the class will earn a point toward a group reward (e.g., classroom game, special snack, popcorn party, video, music time, extra recess). Set a criterion for the number of points required to earn the reward, using data obtained during the observation period, if desired.

Implementation

1. At the beginning of the day or intervention period, select two or three students at random, as well as one or two of the target students.

2. Announce the list of names, remind the students that they will be asked to provide compliments for each star at the end of the intervention period, and write the names in alphabetical order on the chalkboard.

3. At the end of the intervention period, ask students to raise their hands if they have an appropriate compliment for the first student on the list. Use group rather than individual prompts to encourage praise statements—for example: "Would anyone else like to say anything?" not "Does anyone else have a compliment for Maria?"

4. Once the first student has received two or three appropriate compliments, give that star an opportunity to praise another star, if desired. Then move to the next name on the list.

5. After all of the stars have received compliments, tally the number of appropriate compliments and add that number of points to the points chart. The PPR session should last between 5 and 7 minutes.

6. Deliver the reward when the criterion has been reached. Praise the students for their positive and cooperative behavior and begin a new points chart.

Variations

VARIATION 1: POSITIVE PEER REPORTING WITH MYSTERY STARS

On selected days, tell the students that they will need to observe each other's friendly and helpful behaviors very carefully that day because you will not be announcing the names of the stars until the end of the intervention period or the end of the school day. At the end of the intervention period or day, announce the names of the stars, write their names on the chalkboard, and conduct the PPR session as described above.

VARIATION 2: POSITIVE PEER REPORTING WITH A "HONEY POT"

During PPR sessions, place a cotton ball ("honey") in a jar ("Honey Pot") for each appropriate compliment. When the Honey Pot is full of honey (i.e., the jar is full of cotton balls), deliver the reward.

NOTES

1. Do not place the same names on the list every day, even for the most rejected students, because this may embarrass them and lead to greater ostracism by the rest of the class.
2. If a student offers a sarcastic remark rather than a compliment, tell that individual that you will not award points for any comments that may be embarrassing or hurtful to a fellow student, even if they are presented as a compliment. Follow up by talking with the student privately about the purpose of the peer compliments and helping the student formulate appropriate compliments for the next PPR session. If the problem persists, deliver a consequence (e.g., loss of recess) and have the student complete a *Debriefing* form (see *Debriefing: Helping Students Solve Their Own Behavior Problems* later in this chapter).
3. During field testing, teachers observed that some students occasionally reacted negatively (by pouting, arguing, etc.) when their names were not on the daily list of stars, especially during the initial stages of implementation. To address this problem, remind students prior to the announcement of the star list that everyone will have a chance to be a star for the day and model appropriate responses during the star list posting.

SOURCE

Moroz, K. B., & Jones, K. M. (2002). The effects of positive peer reporting on children's social involvement. *School Psychology Review, 31,* 235–245.

DELIVERING EFFECTIVE PRAISE

Overview

Teacher-delivered praise is an integral part of a comprehensive classroom management program and a key component in many intervention packages targeting academic achievement or behavior (Houghton, Wheldall, Jukes, & Sharpe, 1990; Kamins & Dweck, 1999; Sutherland, Wehby, & Copeland, 2000). Praise also helps to create a positive classroom climate and can enhance student motivation and persistence with challenging tasks. Despite its potentially positive impact, however, praise is often ineffective in improving academic performance or social behavior because it lacks specificity and contingency. Similarly, praise that emphasizes ability can lead to impaired performance and reduced motivation and resilience in the face of setbacks, whereas praise that focuses on the processes students use when performing a task, including effort and strategies, enhances performance, task persistence, and interest in learning. In this intervention, these three dimensions—specificity, contingency, and process focus—are combined to maximize the impact of teacher-delivered positive attention. Privacy is included as an optional component for older students because of evidence that middle school and high school students respond more positively to praise delivered privately rather than publicly.

Goal

The purpose of this intervention is to improve on-task behavior, academic achievement, and motivation with systematic teacher-delivered praise.

Intervention Intensity

The intervention can be used for a variety of students in classrooms with appropriate adaptations for age, topic, and intensity of problem behavior.

Materials

None.

Options to Monitor Progress

1. Measure classwide academic engagement and disruptive behavior with DBR. These data can be collected in each period in which the intervention is active and graphed for analysis. Conduct observations for 3–5 days prior to the start of the intervention to establish a baseline and then in each instructional period in which the intervention is used.
2. Using a *Classwide Scanning Form* with a 5-minute interval, tally the number of students in each of the categories below during the selected instructional period, beginning with the left side of the room:
   a. *On-task behavior,* defined as looking at the textbook or lesson materials, writing on worksheets, raising one's hand to ask task-related questions, and looking at the teacher during instruction.
   b. *Off-task behavior,* defined as sitting without appropriate materials, looking at or playing with nonlesson materials, gazing around the room after assignments have been made, or failing to attend to the teacher during instruction.
   c. *Disruptive behavior,* defined as behavior that interferes with the learning of others, such as making noises, calling out, or verbal or physical aggression.
   Conduct these observations for 30–45 minutes for 4–7 days.
3. Select an instructional period during which students are especially unproductive or disruptive. Divide the class by eye into four groups of approximately equal numbers of students. Using a *Group Time Sampling Form,* observe the students in the first group for 4 seconds. If all of the students in the group are on task for all 4 seconds, code that group as on task. If any of the students are off task for any of the 4 seconds, code the group as off task. Repeat these observations for the second and third group and then return to the first group. Calculate the classwide percentage of on-task behavior by summing the num-

ber of on-task intervals and dividing by the total number of observations. Conduct these observations for 30–45 minutes for 4–7 days.

4. Select a small group of students who are frequently unproductive or disruptive during instruction or independent seatwork. For each student, calculate the percent-accuracy and completion rate on one or more class assignments during the selected period by dividing the number of correctly completed problems by the total number of problems assigned. Conduct these observations for 4–7 days.

Intervention Steps

1. Select an instructional period during which students are especially off task and unproductive.

2. When a student performs a desired behavior, move close to the student, obtain eye contact if possible, and deliver a specific, contingent, and process-focused praise statement as follows:

   a. *Specific*. Using the student's name, describe the approved behavior in specific terms— for example: "Joshua, you're really working hard on those math problems today," not "Good job!" or "That's nice."

   b. *Contingent*. Deliver the praise as soon as possible after you observe the desired behavior.

   c. *Process-oriented*. Focus the praise on the student's effort and/or strategies, rather than on his or her ability or the outcome.
      - *Effort example*: "Wow, Joshua, you did really well on your spelling! You must have studied really hard!" not "Wow, Joshua, you did really well on your spelling! You're so smart!"
      - *Strategy example*: "Joshua, it looks like you've figured out how to set up equations with two unknowns! That's really using your head," not "See, Joshua, you can do it if you try!"

   d. *Private*. For middle and high school students, move close to the student, obtain eye contact if possible, and deliver the praise so quietly that it is audible only to the target student.

3. Try to deliver at least 10–15 praise statements per instructional period. Also try to deliver at least five classwide praise statements per instructional period—for example: "Seventh grade, you are really working hard on your group projects! I'm so proud of your efforts!"

4. Remember to provide praise contingent upon prosocial as well as academic behavior.
   - *Public example*: "Class, I'm really impressed with the way you're working so well together as teams on your history timelines!"
   - *Private example*: "Stephanie, I've been noticing how kind you've been to Tamara today and how you've been showing her how we do things. It's not easy to be a new student, and you're being a big help."

NOTE

Delivering private praise can be difficult during whole-class instruction if teachers spend most of their time in one area of the classroom. Circulating periodically around the room during whole-class instruction not only facilitates praise delivery but also helps to prevent minor incidents of inappropriate behavior from escalating.

SOURCES

Houghton, S., Wheldall, K., Jukes, R., & Sharpe, A. (1990). The effects of limited private reprimands and increased private praise on classroom behaviour in four British secondary school classes. *British Journal of Educational Psychology, 60,* 255–265.

Kamins, M. L., & Dweck, C. S. (1999). Person versus process praise and criticism: Implications for contingent self-worth and coping. *Developmental Psychology, 35,* 835–847.

Sutherland, K. S., Wehby, J. H., & Copeland, S. R. (2000). Effect of varying rates of behavior-specific praise on the on-task behavior of students with EBD. *Journal of Emotional and Behavioral Disorders, 8*(1), 2–8, 26.

DELIVERING EFFECTIVE REPRIMANDS

Overview

Teachers use reprimands more frequently than any other behavior management strategy and much more often than praise in both regular and special education classrooms (Van Acker & Grant, 1996; Wehby, Dodge, & Valente, 1993; Wehby, Symons, & Shores, 1995). Although reprimands can help to reduce inappropriate behavior (Abramowitz & O'Leary, 1990; Acker & O'Leary, 1987) and, in some cases, improve academic productivity as well (Abramowitz, O'Leary, & Futtersak, 1988), there are several problems associated with the use—or, rather, the overuse and misuse—of reprimands. For example:

- Reprimands can be highly disruptive to ongoing instruction, especially when they are long, loud, and delivered at a distance from the misbehaving student.

- Although reprimands may temporarily suppress inappropriate behavior, they lose their effectiveness if they are used excessively. Students rapidly habituate to frequent reprimands, so that teachers must increase the frequency and volume of their reprimands to obtain the same results, leading to an escalating cycle of student misbehavior followed by teacher reprimands of greater intensity but diminishing effectiveness.

- Peer attention can sustain student misbehavior, even in the context of teacher reprimands. In fact, by providing teacher attention for misbehavior, frequent reprimands can actually reinforce the very behaviors they are designed to reduce, especially for students who are at risk for aggression (Maag, 2001; Van Acker & Grant, 1996).

While, ideally, teachers focus on delivering praise and increasing specific statements, we understand that reprimands will continued to be utilized. Research on teacher–student communications has identified seven dimensions that enhance reprimand effectiveness: (1) promptness, (2) brevity, (3) softness, (4) proximity, (5) calmness, (6) eye contact, and (7) touch. *Promptness* is the single most important parameter in reprimand delivery. To be effective, reprimands should be delivered as soon as possible after the inappropriate behavior has occurred. Because peer attention serves as a competing reinforcer for misbehavior, even a 2-minute delay after the onset of off-task behavior can render reprimands ineffective (Abramowitz, Eckstrand, O'Leary, & Dulcan, 1992; Abramowitz & O'Leary, 1990). Second, short reprimands consisting of the student's name and no more than two other words are more effective than long reprimands, probably because short reprimands provide less attention for inappropriate behavior and are less likely to elicit arguments from misbehaving students (Abramowitz et al., 1988). Third, soft, private reprimands that are audible only to the target student can have a dramatic positive effect on behavior (Houghton et al.,

1990), whereas loud, public reprimands are not only ineffective but can precipitate a cycle of misbehavior, followed by louder reprimands, followed by more disruptive behavior (Rosén, O'Leary, Joyce, Conway, & Pfiffner, 1984). Fourth, reprimands have little effect when delivered from a distance but produce a marked reduction in disruptive behavior when delivered close to (within 1 meter of) the misbehaving student (Van Houten, Nau, MacKenzie-Keating, Sameoto, & Colavecchia, 1982). Fifth, maintaining a calm, consistent tone of voice and keeping from becoming emotionally upset are critical to reprimand effectiveness (Rosén et al., 1984). Finally, the effectiveness of verbal reprimands is enhanced by eye contact (Everett, Olmi, Edwards, & Tingstrom, 2005; Hamlet, Axelrod, & Kuerschener, 1984), as well as by physical contact, such as a firm grasp of the student's shoulder (Van Houten et al., 1982). The following intervention combines the first six dimensions to maximize the effectiveness of this form of teacher–student communication as a classroom management strategy. Because some students may misinterpret or respond negatively to any type of physical contact, touch is included only as a variation.

Goal

To reduce off-task and disruptive behavior with systematic teacher-delivered reprimands.

Intervention Intensity

The intervention can be used for a variety of students in classrooms with appropriate adaptations for age, topic, and intensity of problem behavior.

Materials

None.

Options to Monitor Progress

1. Measure classwide academic engagement and disruptive behavior with DBR. These data can be collected in each period in which the intervention is active and graphed for analysis. Conduct observations for 3–5 days prior to the start of the intervention to establish a baseline and then in each instructional period in which the intervention is used.
2. Select an instructional period during which students are most disruptive and unproductive. Using a *Classwide Scanning Form,* scan the room every 3–5 minutes from left to right and tally the number of students in each of the following behavior categories:
   a. *On-task behavior,* defined as answering or asking lesson-oriented questions, looking at the teacher during instruction, sitting quietly and waiting for directions, or any other behavior consistent with the ongoing lesson or activity.
   b. *Off-task behavior,* defined as sitting without appropriate materials, looking at nonlesson materials, or looking around the room after assignments have been made.
   c. *Disruptive behavior,* defined as any behavior that disrupts the academic performance of another student, including making noises, calling out, and physical aggression.
   Record these behaviors for 30–45 minutes for 4–7 days.
3. Select a small group of students who frequently exhibit off-task or disruptive behavior during a selected instructional period. Using a *Group Interval Recording Form,* glance at a target student every 5 seconds and record the student's behavior at that instant as on-task, off-task, or disruptive as defined above. Record behavior for each target student in turn for 30–45 minutes for 4–7 days.

4. Calculate the class average percent-correct score for classwork during the selected instructional period for 5–10 days by summing individual student percent-correct scores and dividing by the total number of students.
5. Using a sheet of paper attached to a clipboard, record the number of reprimands you deliver to the entire class or a target group of students during a selected instructional period for 4–7 days.

Intervention Steps

1. If this intervention is primarily directed toward a small group of students, move them near the front of the classroom or to an area that you can reach rapidly.
2. When a student exhibits an undesired behavior, immediately move to within touching distance, obtain eye contact if possible, and deliver a reprimand as described below.
   a. *Prompt*: Deliver the reprimand as soon as possible after you observe the inappropriate behavior.
   b. *Short*: Use a firm tone and deliver the reprimand in statement form with as few words as possible in addition to the student's name. For example: "Sam, stop talking!"
   c. *Soft*: Deliver the reprimand so that it is audible only to the student being reprimanded.
   d. *Close*: Deliver the reprimand near enough to the student to be able to obtain eye contact and within touching distance.
   e. *Calm*: Maintain emotional control. Use a calm, consistent tone of voice.
3. Tell the student what he or she should be doing at that time and ask whether he or she needs help with the activity.
4. Try to catch the reprimanded student behaving appropriately within the next few minutes so you can provide praise for positive academic or social behavior.

Variation: Reprimands with Touch

If the student is off task, gently lay a hand on the student's upper arm or shoulder for the duration of the reprimand (3–4 seconds). Do not use this variation if the student is exhibiting disruptive or aggressive behavior, if the student has a history of negative responses to physical touch, or if school policy discourages or forbids any form of physical contact with students.

NOTES

1. Even if this intervention is directed primarily at one student or a small group of unproductive or disruptive students, effective reprimands should be used with all of the students in the class because of evidence of positive "spillover" effects. That is, class peers seated near target students receiving effective reprimands also show improvement in on-task behavior and productivity (Van Houten et al., 1982).
2. Because reprimand efficacy is most strongly related to promptness, this procedure requires frequent scanning of the room to detect potential problems.
3. Attempt to obtain eye contact when delivering reprimands, but do not force the student to look at you. Forcing eye contact may be shaming for some students and may provoke a confrontation. Moreover, if obtaining eye contact prolongs the length of the reprimand, the reprimand will be less effective.
4. Although maintaining emotional control can be very difficult when dealing with a provocative or chronically disruptive student, a calm demeanor and an even, consistent tone of voice are critical to reprimand effectiveness. Managing one's emotions prevents a power struggle,

provides a model of self-control, and avoids damaging the teacher–student relationship. More-over, field testing indicates that the ability to evoke a negative emotional reaction from a teacher can be highly reinforcing for certain students.

SOURCES

Abramowitz, A. J., Eckstrand, D., O'Leary, S. G., & Dulcan, M. K. (1992). ADHD children's responses to stimulant medication and two intensities of a behavioral intervention. *Behavior Modification, 16,* 193–203.

Abramowitz, A. J., & O'Leary, S. G. (1990). Effectiveness of delayed punishment in an applied setting. *Behavior Therapy, 21,* 231–239.

Abramowitz, A. J., O'Leary, S. G., & Futtersak, M. W. (1988). The relative impact of long and short reprimands on children's off-task behavior in the classroom. *Behavior Therapy, 19,* 243–247.

Acker, M. M., & O'Leary, S. G. (1987). Effects of reprimands and praise on appropriate behavior in the classroom. *Journal of Abnormal Child Psychology, 15,* 549–557.

Everett, G. E., Olmi, D. J., Edwards, R. P., & Tingstrom, D. H. (2005). The contributions of eye contact and contingent praise to effective instruction delivery in compliance training. *Education and Treatment of Children, 28,* 48–62.

Hamlet, C. C., Axelrod, S., & Kuerschener, S. (1984). Eye contact as an antecedent to compliant behavior. *Journal of Applied Behavior Analysis, 17,* 553–557.

Houghton, S., Wheldall, K., Jukes, R., & Sharpe, A. (1990). The effects of limited private reprimands and increased private praise on classroom behaviour in four British secondary school classes. *British Journal of Educational Psychology, 60,* 255–265.

Maag, J. W. (2001). Rewarded by punishment: Reflections on the disuse of positive reinforcement in schools. *Exceptional Children, 67,* 173–186.

Rosén, L. A., O'Leary, S. G., Joyce, S. A., Conway, G., & Pfiffner, L. J. (1984). The importance of prudent negative consequences for maintaining the appropriate behavior of hyperactive students. *Journal of Abnormal Child Psychology, 12,* 581–604.

Van Houten, R., Nau, P. A., MacKenzie-Keating, S. E., Sameoto, D., & Colavecchia, B. (1982). An analysis of some variables influencing the effectiveness of reprimands. *Journal of Applied Behavior Analysis, 15,* 65–83.

Van Acker, R., & Grant, S. H. (1996). Teacher and student behavior as a function of risk for aggression. *Education and Treatment of Children, 19,* 316–334.

Wehby, J. H., Dodge, K. A., & Valente, E. (1993). School behavior of first grade children identi-fied as at-risk for development of conduct problems. *Behavioral Disorders, 19,* 67–78.

Wehby, J. H., Symons, F. J., Canale, J. A., & Go, F. J. (1998). Teaching practices in classrooms for students with emotional and behavioral disorders: Discrepancies between recommendations and observations. *Behavioral Disorders, 24,* 51–56.

TOOTLING: ENHANCING STUDENT RELATIONSHIPS WITH PEER REPORTING, PUBLIC POSTING, AND GROUP CONTINGENCIES

Overview

Many important social skills are acquired and mastered during day-to-day interactions with peers, that is, through incidental learning. Unfortunately, classroom environments are typi-cally structured to prevent incidental negative behavior rather than to encourage incidental prosocial behavior, with rule systems that identify inappropriate behaviors and the aversive consequences that will follow them. Students often participate in these punishment-focused programs by "tattling" (monitoring and reporting their classmates' negative behaviors) and fail to notice their classmates' positive social interactions. In contrast, "tootling" (a combination of "tattling" and "tooting your own horn") is designed to improve the quality of student–student interactions in the classroom by encouraging students to focus on each other's prosocial behaviors (Cashwell, Skinner, & Smith, 2001). Tootling includes three components: (1) direct instruction in peer monitoring of prosocial behaviors, (2) an interdependent group contingency to reinforce peer reporting of these behaviors, and (3) public posting of the number of tootles (Skinner, Cashwell, & Skinner, 2000). Studies in elementary classrooms demonstrate that students can learn to report peer prosocial rather than antisocial behaviors and that group rewards and publicly posted progress feedback increase positive peer reporting rates. By encouraging students to attend to their classmates' positive rather than negative social behaviors, tootling has the potential not only to increase prosocial behaviors but also to enhance positive peer relationships and the classroom climate. Tootling is especially helpful in classrooms in schools with high student turnover rates and classrooms that include students with emotional or behavior disorders, who are at high risk for social rejection and isolation.

Goal

The purpose of this intervention is to promote positive peer relationships and a warm, collaborative classroom environment with peer reporting of prosocial behaviors, public posting, and group rewards. This intervention is designed for students who need assistance both in learning appropriate social skills and in being supported in the skills use in learning environments.

Intervention Intensity

The intervention can be used for a variety of students in classrooms with appropriate adaptations for age, topic, and intensity of problem behavior.

Materials

1. 3″ × 5″ index cards, three to five per student per day.
2. Shoe box with a slot cut in the top and wrapped in bright wrapping paper.
3. "Tootling Progress Chart," consisting of a posterboard chart with a ladder drawn on it and removable cardboard icons to indicate progress, such as a smiley face, foot, or stick figure.
4. Tape (optional).

Options to Monitor Progress (Select One or More)

1. Using a sheet of paper attached to a clipboard, record the number of tattling behaviors during recess, center time, the cooperative learning period, or the morning instructional period for 4–7 days. *Tattling behaviors* are defined as any student complaints about the verbal or physical behavior of a classmate.
2. Using a sheet of paper attached to a clipboard, record the frequency of negative verbalizations emitted by the entire class during a selected instructional period or for the morning instructional period for 4–7 days. *Negative verbalizations* are defined as verbalizations with unpleasant content directed toward oneself or peers, such as making self-derogatory comments, teasing or verbally threatening peers, or making inappropriate comments that disrupt instruction. Calculate the number of negative verbalizations per minute by divid-

ing the number of negative verbalizations by the number of minutes in the observation period.

3. Measure classwide academic engagement and disruptive behavior with DBR. These data can be collected in each period in which the intervention is active and graphed for analysis. Conduct observations for 3–5 days prior to the start of the intervention to establish a baseline and then in each instructional period in which the intervention is used.

Intervention Steps

Introduction and Training

1. Tell the class that that they will be playing a "tootling" game that will give them a chance to name a classmate who has been friendly or helpful to them during the school day.
2. Explain the difference between *tattling* and *tooling* as follows: *Tattling* involves telling the teacher when a classmate does something wrong. *Tootling* involves telling the teacher when a classmate does something helpful for you or another classmate.
3. Review the criteria for tootling as follows:
   a. The behavior observed must be that of another classmate (not teacher behavior or behavior of students from other classrooms).
   b. Students can only report instances in which a classmate was friendly to or helped them or other students—not the teacher or other adults.
   c. The behavior has to occur at school.
4. Provide examples of tootling, such as helping others to pick up their books, lending a student a pencil, greeting a new student pleasantly, encouraging another student in a game at recess, and showing a student how to solve a math problem.
5. Invite the students to provide their own examples. Praise the examples that fit the criteria for tootling and provide corrective feedback if students give examples that do not fit the criteria.
6. Demonstrate on the chalkboard how to record tootles, as follows: who (name of classmate) did what (friendly or helpful behavior) and for whom (name of classmate who was the recipient of the prosocial behavior).
7. Give each student an index card and ask everyone to write down one tootle.
8. Collect the cards and read the examples aloud. Commend examples that fit the definition of tootling and offer corrective feedback for examples that do not.
9. Display the Tootling Progress Chart and explain that when the class cumulative total of tootles reaches 100, the entire class will earn a 30-minute extra recess period (or another group activity reward).

Implementation

1. At the beginning of the following day, give each student an index card or, for early primary grade students, tape a card to each desk. Place the shoe box and a stack of index cards on your desk or a table.
2. Ask the students to observe their classmates for friendly and helpful behaviors during the day and write down all the tootles they observe. When students fill out a card, they are to place it in the box and take another index card from the stack next to the shoe box.
3. At the end of each day, open the shoe box and count the number of tootles. Only count

tootles in which students identify who, did what, and for whom. If more than one student reports the same instance, count all instances.

4. At the beginning of each day, announce how many tootles the class made the previous day. Read examples that fit the criteria, as well as one or two that do not fit the criteria.

5. Tape the cardboard icon on the ladder at the appropriate rung to indicate the number of tootles earned toward the goal (cumulative total). Praise the students for being good observers and encourage them to continue reporting their peers' prosocial behaviors.

6. When the class meets the goal, praise the students and tell them they have a day off from tootling. Provide the extra recess or group activity reward on the day students reach the goal, if possible.

7. On the following day, set a new, higher goal (e.g., 150 tootles) and indicate a new group activity reinforcer, such as 30 minutes of time in the school gym, access to a special play area, or an opportunity to choose a video or DVD to watch in the classroom.

Variation: Tootling with Verbal Reporting

For students with limited writing skills, such as younger students and students with disabilities, tootles can be reported verbally. Schedule a specific time for tootling each day, such as 10 minutes after recess or at the end of the day. Praise students for tootles that meet the criteria and provide feedback when errors are made. Keep a running total of tootles that meet the criteria, announce the total at the end of the tootling session, and tape the icon on the ladder at the appropriate rung, as described above.

NOTE

Some students may engage in a competition to see who can write the most cards, with an emphasis on depositing cards in the box rather than observing prosocial behaviors. In that case, limit students to three to five cards per day and remind them that the purpose of the activity is to notice their peers' positive behaviors, not to write the most cards.

SOURCES

Cashwell, T. H., Skinner, C. H., & Smith, E. S. (2001). Increasing second-grade students' reports of peers' prosocial behaviors via direct instruction, group reinforcement, and progress feedback: A replication and extension. *Education and Treatment of Children, 24,* 161–175.

Skinner, C. H., Cashwell, T. H., & Skinner, A. L. (2000). Increasing tootling: The effects of a peer-monitored group contingency program on students' reports of peers' prosocial behaviors. *Psychology in the Schools, 37,* 263–270.

Evidence-Based Classroom/Small-Group Interventions

CLASSWIDE ANTECEDENT MODIFICATIONS

Overview

The context of the environment in which behaviors occur is not usually considered when analyzing a child's behavior. Instead, more attention is typically given to the consequences following that particular behavior (especially when it is a disruptive behavior being analyzed). While consequences of behaviors matter, what occurred *before* the problem behavior should also be considered when creating an intervention. Altering the antecedent of the target behavior has the substantial advantage of being proactive. As such, with appropriate modifications of the antecedents, a problem behavior (e.g. disruptive behavior or task demand refusal) can be avoided. This brief presents a series of classwide antecedent alterations that will change typical antecedents of problem behaviors to antecedents that prompt appropriate behaviors. See Kern and Clemens (2007) for an excellent, thorough review of this class of intervention.

Goal

This classwide intervention is appropriate for settings in which classwide behavior problems occur (e.g., disruptive behavior or task refusal). In such settings, antecedents that typically produce problem behaviors (e.g., academic task demands that are too difficult result in students "acting out" and refusing to do academic activities) are altered and transformed into antecedents that produce appropriate behavior (e.g., appropriate academic task demands or choice of task sequence = increase of time on task) will greatly reduce problem behavior and increase academic engagement.

Intervention Intensity

The intervention can be used for a variety of students with appropriate adaptations for age, topic, and intensity of problem behavior.

Materials

Reinforcers as necessary.

Options to Monitor Progress

Measure the student's academic engagement and disruptive behavior with DBR. These data can be collected in each period in which the intervention is active and graphed for analysis. Conduct observations for 3–5 days prior to the start of the intervention to establish a baseline and then in each instructional period in which the intervention is used.

Intervention Steps

1. Set classroom rules.
   a. Develop, model, and post clear classroom rules. If some children don't have the skill to follow a rule, try using direct instruction to teach the skill.
   b. Reinforce (e.g., with praise or token) appropriate behavior as quickly as possible; minimize reinforcement (e.g. remove attention) for inappropriate behavior.
   c. Have a consistent classroom schedule.
2. Set appropriate task demands. All instructional material should be appropriate for the student's current level.
3. Structure the class to increase interest.
   a. Use a brisk pace with ample opportunity for student response. Consider a classwide response system such as choral responding or response cards to increase classwide response opportunities.

    b. Include easy tasks among more difficult tasks.

    c. Allow student choice.

    d. Use high-interest materials/topics.

Critical Components for Successful Intervention

1. Clear development of classroom rules.
2. Identification of student instructional level.
3. Appropriate task demands.
4. Accurate selection of reinforcer(s) and high-interest material.

Evaluation

Compare DBR results in the baseline phase and in the intervention phase.

SOURCES

Burns, M. K., Riley-Tillman, T. C., & VanDerHeyden, A. M. (2012). *RTI applications: Vol. 1. Academic and behavioral interventions.* New York: Guilford Press.

Kern, L., & Clemens, N. H. (2007). Antecedent strategies to promote appropriate classroom behavior. *Psychology in the Schools, 44,* 65–75.

CHOICE MAKING

Overview

This intervention has the potential to be effective with children who can do a task but are deciding not to do so. The purpose of choice-making interventions is to promote engagement by providing the opportunity for student decision making and agency with regard to assignment choice and/or order. A review of 13 choice-making intervention studies by Shogren, Faggella-Luby, Bae, and Wehmeyer (2004) found that it was consistently effective in reducing the frequency of problem behaviors. A secondary benefit of this intervention is that it promotes self-determination, which may be particularly useful for students with disabilities, given that their opportunities for decision making are often restricted.

Goal

A choice-making intervention provides a method for reducing undesirable behaviors by allowing student choice in at least one of two areas: assignment selection or the order of assignment completion. With the first option, the teacher provides the student with two or more assignments with comparable content, and the student is allowed to choose which assignment to complete. With the latter option, the student is provided with multiple assignments and given the opportunity to decide the order of assignment completion. The two approaches can be combined, and students can be given the opportunity to both choose the assignments themselves and the order of assignment completion.

Intervention Intensity

The intervention can be used for a variety of students with appropriate adaptations for age, topic, and intensity of problem behavior.

Options to Monitor Progress

Measure the student's academic engagement and disruptive behavior with DBR. These data can be collected in each period in which the intervention is active and graphed for analysis. Conduct observations for 3–5 days prior to the start of the intervention to establish a baseline and then in each instructional period in which the intervention is used.

Intervention Steps

Assignment Selection

1. Instead of providing a single assignment option to promote the acquisition of learning material from a given lesson, provide two or more assignment options that satisfy the same instructional objectives.
2. Describe the assignment options to the target student and require him or her to select one of the available options.

Choice of Assignment Order

1. Communicate clear expectations to the target student regarding which assignments must be completed.
2. Provide the student with the option of choosing the order of assignments to be completed.

Critical Components for Successful Intervention

1. While providing the target student with choices, maintain consistent expectations regarding work completion in relation to student decisions.
2. Insure that there is an appropriate match between student academic skills and assignment difficulty.
3. Set a time limit for assignment completion.
4. Provide positive reinforcement (verbal or material) for on-task behavior and assignment completion and ignore off-task behaviors.

Evaluation

Compare DBR results in the baseline phase and in the intervention phase.

NOTE

The choice-making intervention was developed by Daniel Cohen, MPH, for the EBI Network.

SOURCE

Shogren, K. A., Faggella-Luby, M. N., Bae, S., & Wehmeyer, M. L. (2004). The effect of choice-making as an intervention for problem behavior: A meta-analysis. *Journal of Positive Behavior Interventions, 6,* 228–237.

Evidence-Based Individual Behavioral Proficiency Interventions

DIFFERENTIAL REINFORCEMENT OF AN INCOMPATIBLE OR ALTERNATIVE BEHAVIOR

Overview

Children will continue to engage in problem behaviors that are reinforced. Therefore, it is important to minimize reinforcement for disruptive behavior to reduce disruptive behavior. Unfortunately, simply removing reinforcement often results in an "extinction burst." Data tell us that about 40% of the time, when an adult makes adjustments to the environment to stop reinforcement for a problem behavior (e.g., ignoring disruptive behavior that the child has been exhibiting to obtain adult attention), the child will escalate disruptive behavior in an attempt to bring back the reinforcement. This escalated frequency, magnitude, and duration of the disruptive behavior is called an "extinction burst." Extinction bursts are very problematic in classroom environments. As such, differential reinforcement (DR) interventions have been developed to concurrently remove or reduce reinforcement for the problem behavior while reinforcing a functionally similar replacement behavior. Thus the problem behavior diminishes while the child is provided with an alternative (more acceptable) means to access the desired reinforcement. To understand DR interventions, consider a child who calls out inappropriately in class for teacher attention. It is understood that the calling-out behavior is maintained by the resulting teacher attention. Using DR procedures, the teacher would ignore the calling-out behavior and call on the child only when his or her hand is raised (an alternative behavior). Over time, the DR procedures will result in higher rates of hand raising and lower rates of calling out. In the end, the child is trained to exhibit the desired behavior when he or she wants teacher attention. This section provides a simple guide to DR procedures focusing on DR of incompatible or alternative behaviors (DRI and DRA, respectively). A DRA example involves providing reinforcement for an alternative behavior (hand raising in the above example). DRI is a version of DR that selects an incompatible behavior as the replacement behavior. For example, in-seat behavior is incompatible with out-of-seat behavior. Selecting an incompatible behavior as the replacement behavior minimizes the risk of inadvertently reinforcing the problematic behavior. For example, it is possible that the child may raise his or her hand while also calling out. Because hand raising is reinforced with teacher attention, the reinforcer is provided even though the problematic behavior also occurred and is similarly reinforced. If an incompatible behavior cannot be identified, then an alternative behavior will suffice (see Intervention Step 4 below).

Goal

This intervention was designed to increase rates of appropriate behavior and decrease rates of problem behavior by selectively providing reinforcement only to the desired behavior. There have been many empirical demonstrations of the effectiveness of DR interventions (Cooper, Heron, & Heward, 2007; Vollmer, Iwata, Zarcone, Smith, & Mazaleki, 1993).

Intervention Intensity

The intervention can be used universally in schools with appropriate adaptations for age, topic, and intensity of problem behavior.

Options to Monitor Progress

Measure the student's academic engagement and disruptive behavior with DBR. These data can be collected in each period in which the intervention is active and graphed for analysis. Conduct observations for 3–5 days prior to the start of the intervention to establish a baseline and then in each instructional period in which the intervention is used.

Intervention Steps

1. Identify the consequence that is reinforcing the inappropriate behavior (e.g., verbal praise, escape).
2. Identify an incompatible or alternative behavior that can produce the same consequence. Note that identification of an incompatible appropriate behavior is preferred.
3. Begin with a continuous fixed ratio (CFR) DR schedule. The goal of this step is to ensure that the child is reinforced for the alternative behavior in the initial stages of the DR intervention.
4. Once the DR schedule has been initiated, the teacher is instructed not to respond to the target problem behavior if it is presented. If the teacher is using a DRA procedure and the child exhibits both the problem and alternative behaviors concurrently, it is suggested that the teacher reinforce the child but note that the reinforcement is due to the alternative behavior.
5. After a number of intervention days or sessions (e.g., 5 days, or 20–25 sessions for more severe cases) applying the DR, if a marked reduction has occurred in the problem behavior, start to fade the reinforcement schedule. Note that after the intervention period is complete, the desired behavior should continue to be reinforced at an appropriate level for the child and the environment. If the desired behavior is not reinforced, the child will return to the problem behavior (or some new behavior) to receive the desired reinforcement.

Critical Components for Successful Intervention

1. Successful identification of the reinforcer for the problematic behavior.
2. Identification of an appropriate incompatible or alternative behavior that the child is capable of doing.
3. An initial schedule of DR that ensures that the child will be reinforced when he or she exhibits the desired behavior. A CFR schedule is preferred whereby the student receives reinforcement each time the alternative behavior occurs.
4. The problem behavior should be ignored once the DR schedule is initiated.
5. A fading process of the DR schedule that is gradual enough so that the child does not reengage in the problem behavior. One way to accomplish this is to make the reinforcement intermittent (i.e., every so many occurrences of the desired behavior are reinforced) and unpredictable or variable such that the child knows that the alternative behavior will be reinforced periodically but is not sure exactly which instance of the desirable behavior will occasion reinforcement.

Critical Assumptions/Problem-Solving Questions

DR interventions have a number of known limitations, as outlined by Vollmer and colleagues (1993).

1. DR interventions are not considered the most effective approach for very severe behavior cases. NCR procedures should be considered for such cases.
2. DR interventions can result in an extinction burst with associated issues.
3. DR interventions can be cumbersome for teachers. Care should be taken when designing the intervention to consider feasibility issues.

SOURCES

Burns, M. K., Riley-Tillman, T. C., & VanDerHeyden, A. M. (2012). *RTI applications: Vol. 1. Academic and behavioral interventions.* New York: Guilford Press.

Cooper, J. O., Heron, T. E. & Heward, W. L. (2007). *Applied behavior analysis* (2nd ed). Columbus, OH: Prentice Hall.

Vollmer, T. R., Iwata, B. A., Zarcone, J. R., Smith, R. G., & Mazaleki, J. L. (1993). The role of attention in the treatment of attention-maintained self-injurious behavior: Noncontingent reinforcement and differential reinforcement of other behavior. *Journal of Applied Behavior Analysis, 26,* 9–21.

MYSTERY MOTIVATOR

Overview

Whereas many students will engage in appropriate academic and behavior task demands without systematic reinforcement plans, others will need additional behavioral supports. The Mystery Motivator intervention was designed to increase the proficiency of any academic or behavioral task demand by providing a "mystery" reinforcement using a random schedule (Jenson, Rhode, & Reavis, 1994). Assuming that the reinforcer pool has some reinforcing value, the lure of a mystery reinforcer should additionally motivate students to engage in the academic task, even when the task is difficult. It can be difficult for teachers to develop a deep enough pool of interventions that retain value for the whole school year. Adding a surprise component to the reinforcer pool helps keep the process fun and exciting. Mystery Motivators can be used in a variety of content areas, including reading, math, social studies, science, writing, and homework completion, as well as social behavior compliance. They can also be contingent on a variety of outcome-based criteria (e.g., high test averages, classroom participation, rule adherence). This intervention can be used to shape the behavior of an entire class or be tailored to work for one individual. There have been a number of empirical demonstrations of the effectiveness of the Mystery Motivator interventions (e.g., Madaus, Kehle, Madaus, & Bray, 2003; Moore, Waguespack, Wickstrom, Witt, & Gaydos, 1994).

Goal

This intervention was developed to increase fluency through the application of positive reinforcement.

Intervention Intensity

The intervention can be used for a variety of students with appropriate adaptations for age, topic, and intensity of problem behavior.

Materials

1. Preferred reinforcing stimuli list.
2. Reinforcers.
3. Mystery Motivator chart.
4. Note cards.

Options to Monitor Progress

Measure the student's academic engagement and disruptive behavior with DBR. These data can be collected in each period in which the intervention is active and graphed for analysis. Conduct observations for 3–5 days prior to the start of the intervention to establish a baseline and then in each instructional period in which the intervention is used.

Intervention Steps

1. Make reinforcement chart.
2. Construct a motivation chart for the entire class with all the student names and days of the week.
   a. Randomly place some letter on a few days of the week beside each student's name. For example Jenson and colleagues (1994) suggest using an *M* to designate a Mystery Motivator day. Be sure to place more motivators on the calendar during the initial stages of the intervention so that children are more likely to earn a Mystery Motivator. Each child should have different placement of the mystery *M*.
   b. Cover up all of the days using a note card.
   c. For each note card placed over the *M*, place the name of the motivator on the back.
3. Define goal (e.g., 100% homework completion in all subject areas, 80% accuracy on test grades in math).
4. If the criterion is met, have the child remove the note card on that particular day. It is important to make this activity exciting. If the *M* is located on that day, the reinforcer should be given as soon as possible.
5. When there is not an *M* behind the note card, be sure to encourage students that there will be other opportunities to earn the Mystery Motivator.

Critical Components for Successful Intervention

1. Place many *M*s on the calendar during the teaching (initial) phase of the intervention.
2. After the initial phase of the intervention, place reinforcements randomly. A child should not be able to determine a pattern of when it is more likely that there will be an *M*.
3. All goals should be clearly noted in a manner that students fully understand. Students must know what they are expected to do in order to earn the chance to receive a mystery reinforcer for this intervention to be successful.
4. Select a goal that is easy to attain during the initial stages of the intervention. This will increase the likelihood that the initial intervention implementation will be a success.
5. Reinforcers should be given as soon as possible.

Critical Assumptions/Problem-Solving Questions

1. It is important to know whether or not the students are performing their academic tasks at grade level and whether or not they are capable of performing the assigned tasks suc-

cessfully. If not, a skill-based acquisition-level intervention should be selected in order to teach the academic/behavioral skill first.

2. Students have to desire the Mystery Motivators; otherwise the intervention will be unsuccessful.

3. Students in lower grades or with lower cognitive functioning may need more consistent reinforcement in order for them to understand the connection between the demonstration of an appropriate behavior and receipt of the Mystery Motivator. In such cases, each day can have an *M,* but with a different reinforcer on each day. In this case, the type of reinforcer is the surprise.

4. Tangible motivators may be more enticing for younger students or students who are functioning at a lower cognitive level.

SOURCES

Burns, M. K., Riley-Tillman, T. C., & VanDerHeyden, A. M. (2012). *RTI applications: Vol. 1. Academic and behavioral interventions.* New York: Guilford Press.

Jenson, W. R., Rhode, G., & Revis, H. K. (1994). *The tough kid tool box.* Longmont, CO: Sopris West.

Madaus, M. M. R., Kehle, T. J., Madaus, J., & Bray, M. A. (2003). Mystery motivator as an intervention to promote homework completion and accuracy. *School Psychology International, 24,* 369–377.

Moore, L. A., Waguespack, A. M., Wickstrom, K. F., Witt, J. C., & Gaydos G. R. (1994). Mystery motivator: An effective and time-efficient intervention. *School Psychology Review, 23,* 106–118.

THE RESPONSE COST RAFFLE

Overview

The Response Cost Raffle is an intervention that begins with giving a class or target student a number of tokens or raffle tickets at the start of the intervention period. The response-cost procedure involves removing a specific amount of positive reinforcement—usually in the form of a token—contingent upon an act of undesirable behavior. This simple but innovative intervention combines response cost with a classroom raffle system to reduce disruptive behavior. Moreover, removing "raffle tickets" for lack of progress on classroom assignments and emphasizing to students that they must complete classroom tasks can have positive effects on academic productivity. One of the most usable behavioral strategies in this book, it requires very little teacher training, takes only a few minutes to prepare each day, and is highly acceptable to teachers and students alike. This intervention has strong support in the literature (e.g., Witt & Ellott, 1982; Proctor & Morgan, 1991). In a study with four junior high school students with behavior problems who were receiving part-time services in a special education resource room, the raffle was highly effective in increasing appropriate behavior and academic performance and decreasing disruptive behavior (Proctor & Morgan, 1991). Here the strategy has been adapted for classwide use. Two variations are presented, including a team-based version that incorporates peer influence for positive behavior and the original version for use with individual students or a small target group.

Goal

This intervention was designed to decrease the frequency of inappropriate behavior for a target student or group of students using a response-cost procedure and a classroom lottery.

This intervention is most appropriate for children who have acquired appropriate social behavior skills for the environment but need help displaying the correct behavior consistently.

Intervention Intensity

The intervention can be used for a variety of students with appropriate adaptations for age, topic, and intensity of problem behavior.

Materials

1. *Reinforcement Menus,* one per student (optional).
2. "Raffle prize list," consisting of a posterboard chart with a list of rewards or "raffle prizes."
3. "Target behavior chart," consisting of a posterboard chart listing four or five target negative behaviors and alternative positive behaviors, such as:
   a. *Don't* call out. *Do* raise your hand.
   b. *Don't* fail to follow directions. *Do* follow directions the first time they are given.
   c. *Don't* get up without permission. *Do* stay in your seat unless you have permission to get up.
   d. *Don't* use inappropriate language. *Do* use kind and polite words.
4. "Raffle tickets," consisting of slips of paper, five per student per intervention period.
5. "Raffle ticket box," consisting of a shoe box with a top.
6. Tape.
7. "Raffle prizes," consisting of small individual rewards, such as miniature candy bars, bubble gum, homework passes, fast-food certificates, and inexpensive school supplies.
8. Slips of colored construction paper, five per student table, with a different color for each table (see Variation 2).
9. Plastic or paper cups, one per student table (see Variation 2).

Options to Monitor Progress

1. Using a *Group Event Recording Form,* record the frequency of three or four disruptive behaviors that occur during a selected instructional period for the entire class or a group of target students for 4–7 days. For example, record the frequency of the following behaviors: (a) calling out, (b) being out of seat, (c) arguing with the teacher or a classmate, and (d) failing to follow teacher's directions the first time they are given.
2. Calculate the average percentage of classwork completed by the entire class during a selected instructional period for 5–10 days by calculating the percentage completion rate for each student, summing those rates, and then dividing by the total number of students.
3. Measure classwide academic engagement with DBR. These data can be collected in each period in which the intervention is active and graphed for analysis. Conduct observations for 3–5 days prior to the start of the intervention to establish a baseline and then in each instructional period in which the intervention is used.

Intervention Steps

Introduction and Training

1. Explain to students that they will have a chance to participate in a classroom raffle and win prizes by earning points for good behavior during a selected instructional period.

2. Display the raffle prize list and discuss the individual prizes with the students. Also review a set of group prizes that will be available if you draw a "group" ticket from the box (see Implementation Step 6), such as a video or DVD, 15 minutes of free time, extra recess, and so forth. Alternately, distribute copies of a reinforcement menu and help the class select a set of prizes from among the reinforcers you have listed. List these rewards on the chart and post it at the front of the classroom.

3. Display the target behavior chart. Using *Say, Show, Check: Teaching Classroom Procedures,* demonstrate the target negative behaviors that you wish to decrease (calling out, failing to follow directions, etc.) and the positive behaviors you wish to increase (raising a hand to speak, following directions when first given, etc.).

4. Display the slips of paper and explain that they represent raffle tickets. Tell the class that everyone will receive five tickets at the beginning of the period. Any time that a student displays a target negative behavior during the period, you will remove a ticket from that student's desk. Any remaining tickets will be placed in the raffle ticket box. On Friday, you will hold a drawing, and the student whose slip of paper is drawn will be able to select a reward from the rewards list. Remind the class that students who are able to retain more tickets during the week have a better chance of winning the raffle and receiving a prize.

5. Demonstrate how students should behave when a raffle ticket is removed. Explain that if students argue or respond negatively to ticket removal, they will lose more tickets. Guide several students through a role play of ticket removal to ensure that everyone understands the behavioral expectations.

Implementation

1. At the beginning of the intervention period, give each student five raffle tickets. Have students write their names on the tickets and tape the tickets to the front edge of their desks.

2. Remind students that they are playing the game to help them get more out of the lesson. Whenever a student engages in a negative target behavior, briefly state what the behavior violation is, remove the ticket, and continue with the lesson—for example: "Ronnice, you didn't follow directions, so you lose a ticket."

3. If a student argues or responds negatively to the removal of a ticket, quietly remove another ticket. Do this as long as the student responds inappropriately. If the student continues to behave inappropriately and has no tickets left, deliver a preplanned negative consequence, such as taking away recess for that day or requiring the student to complete a *Debriefing* form (see *Debriefing: Helping Students Solve Their Own Behavior Problems* later in this chapter).

4. Five minutes before the end of the period, collect all tickets remaining on students' desks. Write "group" on two of the tickets and tell the students that the entire class will win a prize if one of these tickets is chosen. Place all of the tickets in the raffle ticket box.

5. On Friday of each week, conduct the raffle by drawing one ticket from the box and declaring the winner. Have the winner select a prize from the list of available rewards. If the class is large, you may wish to draw two tickets and award two prizes.

6. If a group ticket is drawn, the winning student selects from the list of whole-class prizes, such as a classroom game, popcorn party, music time, free time, or a video.

7. Discard the rest of the tickets and begin the raffle procedure again the following Monday during the selected instructional period.

8. As behavior improves, gradually raise the criterion by reducing the number of tickets students receive during each intervention period.

Variations

VARIATION 1: INDIVIDUAL OR SMALL-GROUP VARIATION

1. To implement the raffle with an individual student or a small group of target students, use reinforcement menus to help students select their own rewards.
2. Using a different color of paper for each student's tickets, tape the tickets to the front of the student's desk or slip them inside the subject area folder or notebook, with half of each ticket showing. Remove a ticket for each rule infraction as described above.
3. At the end of the intervention period, collect any remaining tickets and place them in the raffle ticket box. Conduct the drawing as unobtrusively as possible at the end of the week and deliver the prize as the student is leaving for the day.
4. If a student is displaying very high negative behavior rates, conduct the raffle on a daily rather than a weekly basis initially to enhance motivation. As behavior improves, gradually increase the reward delivery interval from daily to weekly.

VARIATION 2: TEAM-BASED VARIATION

1. Divide the class into teams, based on seating arrangements. For students seated at tables or desk clusters, place a plastic or paper cup containing five colored tickets on each table or on one of the desks, with a different color for each group. Use different colors to prevent students from taking other teams' tickets to replace their own.
2. Remove a ticket for each incident of negative behavior as described above.
3. At the end of the intervention period, place all remaining tickets in the raffle ticket box and add two tickets of a different color to serve as group tickets. Taking care not to look at the box so as to avoid seeing the ticket colors, draw a ticket.
4. Deliver a reward to all members of the team whose ticket is drawn or to the entire class, if one of the group tickets is drawn.

NOTES

1. For this intervention to be effective, teachers must respond to inappropriate behavior immediately (i.e., removing a ticket for an infraction as soon as the infraction occurs). In the Proctor and Morgan (1991) study, researchers observed that teachers were inconsistent in response and often removed tickets only for blatant rule violations.
2. Although the researchers did not report negative student reactions to the withdrawal of tickets, negative student responses were occasionally observed during field testing. During training, and thereafter as needed, model appropriate responses to ticket removal and review the consequences for inappropriate reactions.
3. During field testing, some teachers expressed concern about publicly posting examples of negative behavior. In that case, substitute a chart of the classroom rules, stated in positive terms, for the target behavior chart.

SOURCES

Proctor, M. A., & Morgan, D. (1991). Effectiveness of a response cost raffle procedure on the disruptive classroom behavior of adolescents with behavior problems. *School Psychology Review, 20,* 97–109.

Witt, J. C., & Elliott, S. N. (1982). The response cost lottery: A time efficient and effective classroom intervention. *Journal of School Psychology, 20*(2), 155–161.

SAY, SHOW, CHECK: TEACHING CLASSROOM PROCEDURES

Overview

Socializing students to the rule-based environment of the school is a critical component of proactive classroom management. This keystone strategy maximizes instructional time and minimizes opportunities for disruptive behavior by providing direct instruction in how students should behave during classroom routines and activities. Using a three-step lesson format, the teacher shows the rule visually, checks student understanding by exhibiting the incorrect action, and then models the correct behavior again (Wolfgang & Wolfgang, 1995). The core components of this strategy have been documented to be effective in a number of studies (e.g., Lewis, Colvin, & Sugai, 2000). Knowledge of rules builds students' sense of security in the classroom, permits them to be ready for instruction, and prevents them from having to discover the rules by accidentally misbehaving and being reprimanded.

Goal

The purpose of this intervention is to teach classroom rules and procedures through explicit instruction, guided practice, and performance feedback.

Intervention Intensity

The intervention can be used universally in schools with appropriate adaptations for age, topic, and intensity of problem behavior.

Materials

None.

Options to Monitor Progress

1. Measure the student's academic engagement and disruptive behavior with DBR. These data can be collected in each period in which the intervention is active and graphed for analysis. Conduct observations for 3–5 days prior to the start of the intervention to establish a baseline and then in each instructional period in which the intervention is used.
2. Using a sheet of paper attached to a clipboard, record the number of reprimands you deliver during selected classroom routines, such as class discussions, lining up for lunch and specials, or cooperative learning activities, for 4–7 days.
3. Using a *Group Event Recording Form,* tally the number of inappropriate behaviors during one or more classroom routines for 4–7 days. *Inappropriate behaviors* are defined as any behaviors that interfere with the completion of classroom routines, such as dawdling, failing to follow directions, and verbal or physical aggression.

Intervention Steps

Step 1: Say

1. Introduce the rule to be taught and the rationale for its use:

    "Today we are going to learn how to participate in class discussions. Following the rules for class discussions makes it easier for everyone to have a chance to take part."
2. Use words to verbally encode the motor or procedural rule:

    "We raise our hands when we want to participate in class discussions."

Step 2: Show

Show the rule visually by having a student model the correct behavior or do it yourself: "Serena, show the class how we raise our hands and wait to be called on to participate in discussions." After the student demonstrates, say, "That's right!"

Step 3: Check

1. Check students' understanding by exhibiting the incorrect behavior while asking them to watch for a mistake: Call out, "I know, I know!" while wildly waving your hand. Then ask, "Class, did I ask to participate correctly?"
2. Demonstrate the correct behavior or ask a student to demonstrate it, and have students respond as to the correctness of the behavior: "Randy, show us how we raise our hands and wait to be called on to participate." After the student demonstrates, ask, "Was that correct, class?"
3. Praise the student for demonstrating the behavior correctly and the rest of the class for watching attentively.

Variation: Small-Group Demonstration with Classwide Feedback

To reinforce learning, add a small-group practice component to the *Show* and *Check* stages. After you guide an individual student through a role play of the correct behavior, invite a group of students seated in a row or at a desk cluster or table to show the appropriate behavior and have the rest of the class evaluate the correctness of the demonstration.

NOTES

1. When using this strategy with upper elementary or middle school groups, demonstrate the incorrect behavior (see Intervention Step 3) cautiously, if at all. Demonstrating the incorrect behavior or having a student demonstrate it can result in temporary increases in incorrect responding in an effort to attract peer attention.
2. Teachers report that this is one of the most useful strategies in the entire book in helping to establish and maintain an orderly classroom environment.

SOURCES

Lewis, T., Colvin, G., & Sugai, G. (2000). The effects of pre-correction and active supervision on the recess behavior of elementary students. *Education and Treatment of Children, 23*(2), 109–121.

Wolfgang, C. H., & Wolfgang, M. E. (1995). *The three faces of discipline for early childhood: Empowering teachers and students* (pp. 223–225). Boston: Allyn & Bacon.

USING THE COUPON SYSTEM TO DECREASE INAPPROPRIATE REQUESTS FOR TEACHER ASSISTANCE

Overview

Students' excessive or inappropriate requests for teacher assistance can disrupt ongoing instruction and reduce opportunities for learning in both whole-class and small-group settings. This simple, cost-effective intervention uses a response-cost token system to encourage independent effort and reduce unnecessary requests for help. Originally implemented with a second grader with learning disabilities in a regular education classroom, the strategy produced an immediate, marked decrease in inappropriate attention-seeking behaviors (Salend & Henry, 1981). Adapted here for classwide application by using peer monitoring and a group contingency within a team format, it is especially useful when the teacher is delivering small-group instruction while the rest of the class is performing independent seatwork. Two variations are included: (1) a classwide teacher-mediated response-cost system and (2) the original individualized format.

Goal

This intervention is designed to decrease inappropriate requests for teacher assistance with a peer-monitored response-cost token system.

Materials

1. Coupons, consisting of 1″ × 2″ strips of colored construction paper, a specific number per team or target student, with different colors for each team.
2. Paper or plastic cups, one per team.
3. Tape (optional; see Variation 2).
4. Small material rewards, such as stickers, school supplies, and wrapped candy (optional).

Options to Monitor Progress

1. Measure the student's academic engagement and disruptive behavior with DBR. These data can be collected in each period in which the intervention is active and graphed for analysis. Conduct observations for 3–5 days prior to the start of the intervention to establish a baseline and then in each instructional period in which the intervention is used.
2. Select an instructional period that includes independent seatwork. Using a sheet of paper attached to a clipboard, tally the number of requests for unnecessary assistance made by the entire class or a group of target students for 4–7 days. These data will help you determine how many requests for assistance to permit at the beginning of the intervention.
3. Using a sheet of paper attached to a clipboard, record the frequency of disruptive behaviors displayed by the entire class or a group of target students during a selected instructional period for 4–7 days. *Disruptive behaviors* are defined as any student behaviors that interfere with ongoing instruction or the on-task behavior of another student, such as calling out, being out of one's seat without permission, or talking loudly.

Intervention Steps

Introduction and Training

1. Explain to the students that they will be playing a game to help them learn to work more independently during the selected instructional period.
2. Using *Say, Show, Check: Teaching Classroom Procedures,* discuss and demonstrate appropriate and inappropriate requests for assistance. Explain that asking for help when it is not really needed reduces the amount of time you have to teach and students have to learn.
3. Divide the class into teams according to rows, tables, or desk clusters and assign a "team captain" for the week.

4. Place a paper or plastic cup containing the predetermined number of strips of construction paper on the captain's desk or in the center of the table or cluster. Distribute one more coupon per team than the permitted number of requests for assistance (e.g., six coupons for five requests).

5. Explain that the strips of paper are "coupons" that can be redeemed for various privileges, such as lunch with the teacher, computer time, a special art activity, or extra recess time, or for small material rewards, such as stickers, school supplies, and wrapped candy.

6. Explain that each time a student requests your help during the target period, you will assess the student's ability to understand and complete the task. If the student again seeks assistance after you have informed him or her not to do so by saying, "I think you understand what to do," you will instruct the captain of that student's team to remove one coupon and return it to you.

7. At the end of the period, the captains will count and report the number of remaining coupons. All teams with at least one coupon left at the end of the period will receive the reward.

8. Using a group of students seated at a row, table, or desk cluster, demonstrate the procedures, including responding appropriately to the removal of a coupon, counting the remaining coupons, and reporting the results.

Implementation

1. At the beginning of the intervention period, distribute the specified number of coupons to each team. Be sure to use different colored strips for each team to prevent students from supplementing their coupons with coupons taken from other teams. At your direction, have captains remove coupons for inappropriate requests for help, as described above.

2. At the end of the period, have the captains report the number of coupons remaining for their teams. Deliver the reward immediately or at the end of the school day to all members of winning teams. Encourage losing teams to try harder the next day. If all teams are winners, provide a bonus group activity reward, if desired.

3. As students make fewer inappropriate requests for help, decrease the number of coupons distributed per team or increase the length of the intervention period.

Variations

VARIATION 1: CLASSWIDE COUPON SYSTEM

1. For implementation as a whole-class rather than a team-based strategy, place a predetermined number of coupons in a plastic or paper cup on your desk or at the table where you are conducting small-group instruction.

2. When a student makes an inappropriate request for help, remove a coupon and announce your action, as well as the number of remaining coupons—for example: "Tamira, I think you understand what to do. That's one coupon lost. Class, you have four coupons left."

3. If at least one coupon remains at the end of the period, deliver the reward to the entire class.

VARIATION 2: SINGLE-STUDENT OR SMALL-GROUP COUPON SYSTEM

For implementation with a single student or a small group of target students, tape a predetermined number of coupons on the desk of each target student and remove them for inappropriate requests for help (or instruct the student to bring them to you). Deliver a reward if the student has at least one coupon remaining at the end of the period.

NOTES

1. If the intervention targets only a few students rather than the entire class, it is important to use social and activity reinforcers (e.g., eating lunch with the teacher, helping the teacher prepare materials, positive school–home notes) rather than material reinforcers so that the rest of the class is not deprived of the opportunity to earn tangible rewards.
2. Because asking for assistance is appropriate when students do not understand their assignments or lack the skills necessary to complete them, providing explicit instructions for completing seatwork assignments and assessing students' competence to perform the assigned tasks are essential to the success of this strategy.
3. This intervention can also be used to reduce disruptive behavior, such as inappropriate verbalizations (e.g., calling out without permission, talking to other students who are trying to work). In the original investigation, a second experiment produced an immediate and substantial reduction in the inappropriate verbalizations of a fifth grader with learning disabilities during the reading instructional period in a regular classroom.

SOURCE

Salend, S. J., & Henry, K. (1981). Response cost in mainstreamed settings. *Journal of School Psychology, 19*, 242–249.

Individual Behavior Interventions

NONCONTINGENT REINFORCEMENT

Overview

Understanding that children will engage in problem behaviors if they are reinforced, one strategy to minimize the utility of the behavior is to saturate the environment with the reinforcer *prior* to the demonstration of the disruptive behavior. To understand why this intervention would be effective, think about a child who desires teacher attention who has found that calling out in class consistently results in the teacher focusing attention on him or her (albeit not in a positive manner). A noncontingent reinforcement (NCR) intervention directs the teacher to provide him or her attention (in this case a more positive version) prior to the child's "asking" with the problem behavior. As such, the child has no need to be disruptive and will, hopefully, in time, prefer positive attention on a leaner schedule than negative attention on a more consistent schedule. This intervention brief has been developed to present a fixed-time NCR delivery with extinction and schedule thinning, as this version of NCR was found by Carr and colleagues (2009) to have a well-established evidence base.

NCR is a powerful method to reduce problematic behavior. NCR involves giving the student access to a reinforcer frequently enough that he or she is no longer motivated to exhibit disruptive behavior to obtain that same reinforcer. A classic example of NCR is a teacher placing a child on his or her lap during group instruction such that the child has no motivation to seek the teacher's attention while the teacher is conducting story time with the class. There have been many empirical demonstrations of the effectiveness of the NCR interventions, with a comprehensive demonstration of the evidence base by Carr and colleagues in 2009. In addition to being demonstrated effective in reducing problem behavior, NCR interventions have the distinct advantage of reducing problem behavior with less of a chance of an extinction burst period. Because the child is already receiving as much of the reinforcer as he or she could want, there is no brief increase in disruption that commonly follows treatments that involve withholding reinforcement from a child. There is a rich literature base on use of NCR. Two cautions are worth noting. When thinning the NCR schedule (i.e., reducing the amount of reinforcement the student gets), disruptive behavior may reoccur, necessitating the use of extinction procedures. Second, reinforcer substitution may occur, meaning that the student may continue to exhibit disruptive behavior to obtain other reinforcers.

Goal

The purpose of this intervention is to reduce inappropriate behavior by providing reinforcement prior to a child's misbehaving for attention. This intervention is most appropriate for children who have acquired social behavior skills necessary for the environment but need help displaying the correct behavior consistently.

Intervention Intensity

The intervention can be used universally in schools with appropriate adaptations for age, topic, and intensity of problem behavior.

Options to Monitor Progress

Measure the students' academic engagement and disruptive behavior with DBR. These data can be collected in each period in which the intervention is active and graphed for analysis. Conduct observations for 3–5 days prior to the start of the intervention to establish a baseline and then in each instructional period in which the intervention is used.

Intervention Steps

1. Identify the reinforcer for the inappropriate behavior (e.g. verbal praise, escape).
2. Develop a fixed schedule to apply the NCR for the target child. The goal of this step is to develop an initial schedule that is likely to catch the child before he or she engages in the problem behavior, thereby making the disruptive behavior unnecessary. Adapt the schedule based on the age, developmental level, and severity of the behavior problem. For young children, or those with severe behavior problems, the initial NCR schedule will need to be very dense (e.g., once every 30 seconds). For higher functioning children with more mainstream behavior difficulties, the NCR schedule can be initially less ambitious (e.g., once every 15 minutes). Implementers can easily determine how dense it should be by examining the frequency of disruptive behavior that is followed by reinforcement in the classroom at baseline and ensuring that the schedule delivers reinforcement more frequently at first. So, for example, if talking out occurs once every 5 minutes on average in the classroom, then NCR should be delivered in less than 5-minute intervals.
3. When initially applying the NCR, do not refer to the problem behavior or note that the child is behaving appropriately.
4. Once the NCR schedule has been initiated, do not respond to the target problem behavior if and when it occurs.
5. After applying the NCR for a number of intervention days or sessions (for more severe cases; e.g., 5 days or 20–25 sessions), if a marked reduction in the problem behavior occurs, start to thin out the reinforcement schedule. Thinning the schedule means reducing the frequency with which the child is provided reinforcement when NCR is in effect.

It is important to make gradual adjustments to the schedule to minimize the chances of a burst in disruptive behavior. When thinning the schedule, the problem behavior will likely reoccur. When it does, research suggests that withholding reinforcement (i.e., extinction) or delivering a mild consequence such as response cost can effectively mitigate the reoccurrence. The value of NCR is that the extinction period is often less pronounced because the disruption has been reduced to zero levels.

Critical Components for Successful Implementation

1. Successful identification of the reinforcer for the problem behavior. This step is essential. NCR will not work if the function of disruption is unknown. This strategy is not the same as simply providing rewards on a very dense schedule.
2. An initial schedule of NCR that minimizes the likelihood that the child will need to engage in the problem behavior to get the desired reinforcement.
3. Problem behavior is ignored once the NCR schedule is initiated.
4. A fading process that is gradual enough to minimize the degree to which the child reengages in the problem behavior.

SOURCES

Burns, M. K., Riley-Tillman, T. C., & VanDerHeyden, A. M. (2012). *RTI applications: Vol. 1. Academic and behavioral interventions.* New York: Guilford Press.

Carr, J. E., Severtson, J.M., & Lepper, T. L. (2009). Noncontingent reinforcement is an empirically supported treatment for problem behavior exhibited by individuals with developmental disabilities. *Research in Developmental Disabilities, 30*(1), 44–57.

CONTINGENT OBSERVATION

Overview

This classic intervention was designed to provide a simple method to aid a child in the acquisition of desired behavior through observing other children behave appropriately (Porterfield, Herbert-Jackson, & Risley, 1976; White & Bailey, 1990). Specifically, using a modified time-out procedure, the student is removed from an activity and instructed both why they were removed and what the appropriate behavior would have been. Then the child is instructed to observe appropriate behavior for a short time prior to reengaging in the activity. Finally, when the child behaves appropriately, he or she is immediately praised. This intervention can be used as a follow-up to the "active teaching of classroom rules" intervention, also found in this book.

Goal

The goal of the intervention is to assist a child acquire a desired behavior.

Intervention Intensity

The intervention can be used for a variety of students with appropriate adaptations for age, topic, and intensity of problem behavior.

Materials

1. A "Sit and Watch" space placed within view of group activities.
2. A "Quiet Place" within the classroom (or elsewhere), but as far away from the group as possible.
3. A classroom rules chart clearly displayed.

Options to Monitor Progress

Measure the student's academic engagement and disruptive behavior with DBR. This data can be collected in each period in which the intervention is active and graphed for analysis. Conduct observations for 3–5 days prior to the start of the intervention to establish a baseline and then in each instructional period in which the intervention is used.

Intervention Steps

1. When a child displays an inappropriate behavior, describe it to him or her: "Josh, do not push other children when you want to take a turn at the computer." In addition, describe the appropriate behavior: "Josh, when you want a turn you need to ask the other children, and then wait for them to finish up. Remember to keep your hands in your personal space."
2. Next, direct the child to go to the periphery of the activity and instruct him or her to observe other children behaving appropriately, "Josh, please take a turn in the Sit and Watch chair and see how Luke asks Steve to take a turn at the computer and then waits nicely for Steve to finish up."
3. After a brief amount of time (approximately 1–3 minutes), ask if the child is ready to rejoin the group. "Josh, are you ready to try to ask to take a turn at the computers? Remember how Luke asked and then waited nicely for Steve to finish up. Remember to keep your hands in your personal space." If the student indicates that he or she is ready to return and behave appropriately, allow him or her to do so. If the student does not respond or says he or she is not ready, allow him or her to continue to observe. For example, "Josh, sit here and watch until you think that you can ask for a turn properly while keeping your hands in your personal space."
4. When the student returns to the group and displays the appropriate behavior, give praise or some other positive reinforcement as soon as possible "Josh, I like how you asked to use the computer while keeping your hands to yourself."

Additional Procedures

If the child cries for an extended period of time or continues to disrupt the group while in the Sit and Watch space, move him or her to a designated "Quiet Place." This can be in the same room or elsewhere, as long as the child is unable to make contact with the group. Allow the child to remain in the "Quiet Place" until he or she calms down and is able to return to the group. "Josh, since you are not sitting and watching, you are going to the Quiet Place to practice sitting quietly." When he or she is calm, return the child to the Sit and Watch space and proceed through the steps described above.

Critical Components for Successful Intervention

1. A clear set of rules and desired behaviors must be established prior to implementing this intervention.

2. Students should be explicitly taught the purpose of the Sit and Watch procedure. Role-playing a situation in which Sit and Watch would be used is helpful. Each of the procedures should be implemented in order for this intervention to be successful.
3. A child or children who can demonstrate the appropriate behavior.

Critical Assumptions/Problem-Solving Questions

1. *Assumptions*: The student is able to demonstrate the ability to perform the desired behavior. Other students are modeling the desired behavior.
2. *Limitations*: Children who are unable to recognize desired social behaviors in others may not benefit from this intervention.

SOURCES

Burns, M. K., Riley-Tillman, T. C., & VanDerHeyden, A. M. (2012). *RTI applications: Vol. 1. Academic and behavioral interventions*. New York: Guilford Press.
Porterfield, J. K., Herbert-Jackson, E., & Risley, T. R. (1976). Contingent observation: An effective and acceptable procedure for reducing disruptive behavior of young children in a group setting. *Journal of Applied Behavior Analysis, 9*, 55–64.
White, A. G., & Bailey, J. S. (1990). Reducing disruptive behaviors of elementary physical education students with sit and watch. *Journal of Applied Behavior Analysis, 23*, 353–359.

SIT AND WATCH: TEACHING PROSOCIAL BEHAVIORS

Overview

Children often misbehave because they have not learned the appropriate skills in social situations or have not been held accountable for their behavior. This keystone intervention uses *contingent observation*, which combines instruction with a brief time-out, to teach students prosocial behaviors they are not presently displaying. As a proactive classroom management strategy, it not only increases instructional opportunities for disruptive students and their classmates by minimizing the time needed for behavior sanctioning but also helps to prevent inappropriate behavior from escalating by avoiding punitive strategies that can provoke arguments and confrontations (Porterfield et al., 1976). The procedure has been validated with preschool and elementary-grade students in regular and special education classrooms (White & Bailey, 1990). Teachers in the preschool and early primary grades indicate that successful use of this strategy is critical in creating an orderly classroom. Two variations are included in this presentation: one with a self-management component that reduces the amount of teacher monitoring needed and one for physical education classes and/or the playground.

Goal

To teach children appropriate social behaviors with guided observation and a brief time-out.

Intervention Intensity

The intervention can be used universally in schools with appropriate adaptations for age, topic, and intensity of problem behavior.

Materials

1. "Sit and Watch chair," placed on the edge of classroom activities (e.g., in a corner but facing the class rather than the wall) with or without a "Sit and Watch Chair" label affixed to it.
2. "Quiet Place" in the classroom, consisting of a comfortable chair or pillow on a rug placed as far away as possible from the center of classroom activity.
3. Backup "Quiet Place" in another classroom or the school office, consisting of a comfortable chair placed as far away as possible from the center of activity but still observable.
4. Posterboard chart listing the classroom rules, such as:
   a. Follow the teacher's directions.
   b. Be polite and kind to others.
   c. Finish all your work.
   d. Respect others and their property.

Materials for Variation 2

1. Posterboard chart listing the rules for physical education or recess, such as:
   a. Follow the teacher's and aide's directions.
   b. Line up promptly when you are called.
   c. Use equipment safely.
   d. Play so that everyone can have fun.
2. Two or three kitchen timers (optional).

Options to Monitor Progress

1. Using a *Group Event Recording Form,* tally the number of disruptive behaviors for the entire class or a group of target students during a selected instructional period or interval, such as the first 2 hours of the day, for 4–7 days. *Disruptive behaviors* are defined as aggression, crying or whining, having tantrums, damaging toys or classroom materials, and interfering with the task-related behavior of other students.
2. Using a sheet of paper attached to a clipboard, record the number of reprimands you deliver to the entire class or to one or more target students during a selected instructional period or interval for 4–7 days.
3. Measure academic engagement, disruptive behavior, and/or respectful behavior with DBR. These data can be collected in each period in which the intervention is active and graphed for analysis. Conduct observations for 3–5 days prior to the start of the intervention to establish a baseline and then in each instructional period in which the intervention is used.

Intervention Steps

Introduction and Training

1. Display the chart with the classroom rules and discuss the rationale for each rule. For young students, use a chart with pictured rules.
2. Point out the Sit and Watch chair and explain that you will be telling students who forget to follow the classroom rules to sit in the chair for a short time and watch the other students behaving appropriately.
3. Also point out the Quiet Place and explain that this is a place for students who have trouble sitting in the Sit and Watch chair.

4. Teach the Sit and Watch procedures as described below, using *Say, Show, Check: Teaching Classroom Procedures*.

5. Then guide a student who typically displays appropriate behavior through a role play of the procedures while the other students observe. Select a second student and include a visit to the Quiet Place as part of the role play.

Implementation

1. When inappropriate behavior occurs, first describe it to the misbehaving student:

   "Andy, don't hit other children at your table."

2. Then describe what would have been appropriate behavior in the situation:

   "Keep your hands to yourself when you are doing your work."

3. Tell the student to go to the Sit and Watch chair (escort preschoolers to the chair until they are accustomed to the routine). Tell him or her to observe the appropriate social behavior of the other students:

   "Go to the Sit and Watch chair and watch how the other children work without hitting."

4. When the student has been watching quietly for a brief period (about 1 minute for preschoolers, 3 minutes for older children), ask if he or she is ready to rejoin the activity and display the appropriate behavior:

   "Do you know how to work without hitting now?"

5. If the student indicates by nodding or verbalizing readiness to return, allow him or her to do so. If the student does not respond or responds negatively, tell him or her to sit and watch until ready to perform the appropriate behavior:

   "Sit here and watch the children until you think you can do your work without hitting others."

6. When the student has been sitting quietly for another brief period, return to the student and repeat Steps 4 and 5.

7. When the student returns to the group, give positive attention for appropriate behavior as soon as possible:

   "Good, you're doing your work without hitting others."

8. If the student cries for more than a few minutes or refuses to sit quietly so that other children's activities are disturbed, take him or her to the Quiet Place in the classroom. Explain the reason for the removal by saying:

   "Since you can't sit quietly here, you need to go to the Quiet Place and practice sitting quietly."

9. When the student is calm and is sitting quietly in the Quiet Place, ask if he or she is ready to sit quietly and watch. Return the student to the Sit and Watch chair after a positive response and continue from Step 3. If the student continues to be disruptive or gives a negative response, tell him or her to continue to sit quietly:

   "Practice sitting quietly and I will ask you again in a few minutes if you're ready to return to the group."

10. If the student continues to be very distressed or disruptive after another query, implement the backup Quiet Place as described above.

Variations

VARIATION 1: SIT AND WATCH WITH SELF-MANAGEMENT COMPONENT

Instead of approaching students in the Sit and Watch chair and asking them if they are ready to return to the group, teach them to raise their hands to indicate their readiness to return. With this variation, the teacher does not need to interrupt instruction to interact with the student.

VARIATION 2: SIT AND WATCH IN PHYSICAL EDUCATION CLASSES OR ON THE PLAYGROUND

1. At the beginning of the physical education period or in the classroom before recess, explain to students that they will be learning a new way of helping everyone have more fun during physical education or recess.
2. Display the chart with the rules for physical education or recess and discuss the purpose of each rule.
3. Designate a Sit and Watch location, such as against one wall of the gymnasium or on one side of the playground.
4. Demonstrate the Sit and Watch procedures, and have several students role-play going to the Sit and Watch area. If you will be using timers, teach students how to set them for 3 minutes.
5. When a student breaks a rule or engages in unsafe or inappropriate behavior, send the student to the Sit and Watch area. If you are using timers, the student must sit down, set the timer to ring in 3 minutes, and stay in the area until the timer has rung. Otherwise, the student must sit down in the Sit and Watch area until you signal that he or she may rejoin the group. Release the student after he or she has been sitting quietly for about 3 minutes. Continue to observe the student so that you can provide praise for appropriate behavior as soon as possible.
6. Be sure to monitor the student in the Sit and Watch area and not to place children too closely together when more than one child is removed from the group.
7. Students who are sent to Sit and Watch twice in one period must remain in the Sit and Watch area for 6 minutes on the second occasion.
8. If students are sent to Sit and Watch three times in one period, they must remain in the Sit and Watch location for the rest of the physical education or recess period.
9. Students who tattle on others or talk to a student in Sit and Watch must go to Sit and Watch.

NOTES

1. Field testing indicates that additional positive behavior support may be needed to help very defiant and/or undercontrolled young children respond appropriately to the Sit and Watch procedures. Conduct an individual role play with the target student prior to implementation and praise the student for compliance during the rehearsal. If the student is subsequently sent to Sit and Watch and either resists going to the chair or attempts to get out of it before being released, deliver a *Precision Command* at eye level (e.g., "You need to sit in the Sit and Watch chair and watch the other students playing without hitting until I tell you that you can get up"). Then stand near the chair so that you can return the student promptly to the chair if needed.
2. Providing a backup Quiet Place in another location, such as a nearby classroom or the prin-

cipal's office, is essential to the success of this strategy. In these cases, arrange for the student to be escorted to the other classroom or the office by a teacher's aide or another staff member. Practice the entire procedure with the target student and the participating staff members and discuss it with the student's parents. Ask staff members to interact with the student as little as possible during the Quiet Place time. These out-of-class time-outs should last no longer than 15 minutes, depending on the age of the child, and should be followed in the classroom by returning the child to the Quiet Place and continuing from Step 8.

SOURCES

Porterfield, J. K., Herbert-Jackson, E., & Risley, T. R. (1976). Contingent observation: An effective and acceptable procedure for reducing disruptive behavior of young children in a group setting. *Journal of Applied Behavior Analysis, 9,* 55–64.

White, A. G., & Bailey, J. S. (1990). Reducing disruptive behaviors of elementary physical education students with sit and watch. *Journal of Applied Behavior Analysis, 23,* 353–359.

DEBRIEFING: HELPING STUDENTS SOLVE THEIR OWN BEHAVIOR PROBLEMS

Overview

When problem behavior occurs, the consequences typically available to teachers may be only temporarily effective in modifying the inappropriate behavior, especially in the case of chronically unproductive or noncompliant students. If a student persists in behaving ineffectively, teachers are likely to deliver more punitive consequences, creating an escalating cycle of problem behavior and negative teacher response that damages the teacher–student relationship and reduces learning opportunities for all students. Debriefing consists of a set of structured teacher–student interactions that follow the application of consequences for problem behavior and are designed to help students identify and use socially acceptable behaviors when they confront challenging situations (Sugai & Colvin, 1997). Debriefing comprises three basic steps: (1) identifying the circumstances triggering the problem behavior, (2) reminding the student of a socially acceptable replacement response (or teaching it if the behavior has not been acquired), and (3) preparing the student to resume the classroom routine. As part of the debriefing strategy, the student completes a written form that serves as a plan for the alternative prosocial behavior. Debriefing not only reduces misbehavior by teaching appropriate replacement behaviors, but it also improves the teacher–student relationship by interrupting the misbehavior–punishment cycle. Often implemented in special education settings and by school disciplinary staff in the context of an office referral, debriefing can also be conducted by regular classroom teachers in one-to-one or small-group formats. Three variations are included: (1) a teacher-delivered version with a delayed debriefing session, (2) a teacher-delivered version without a writing component for minor rule infractions, and (3) a version for implementation by office disciplinary personnel.

Goal

The purpose of this intervention is to help chronically disruptive or unproductive students develop and use positive alternative behaviors by means of structured problem-solving conferences. This intervention is particularly useful for students who have learned the target social behavior but need assistance in displaying the behavior consistently and appropriately.

Intervention Intensity

The intervention can be used for a variety of students with appropriate adaptations for age, topic, and intensity of problem behavior.

Materials

Debriefing Form (see Figure 5.2).

Options to Monitor Progress

1. Using a *Group Event Recording Form,* record the frequency of one or more problem behaviors for one or more target students during a selected instructional period. For example, tally the number of call-outs, out-of-seats, or acts of noncompliance for 4–7 days.
2. On a sheet of paper attached to a clipboard, record the number of reprimands you deliver to one or more target students during a selected instructional period for 4–7 days.
3. Calculate the number of office disciplinary referrals for a target student, a group of target students, or the entire class for the previous month.

Intervention Steps

1. When an incident of problem behavior occurs, call the student displaying the problem behavior to your desk or an area of the classroom where conversation can be as private as possible. Quickly and quietly administer or assign the usual consequence for the rule infraction (e.g., points lost from behavior chart, office referral, lunchtime detention).
2. After the student has completed the consequence, talk with the student briefly about the factors that may have contributed to the problem and how the student might manage the situation more appropriately the next time.
3. Give the student a Debriefing Form (see Figure 5.2), and allow time for the student to complete it at his or her desk. If time does not permit, have the student return the completed form the following day and review it with him or her as described below.
4. When the student has completed the form, ask him or her to read it aloud and elaborate upon the written response. Praise efforts to identify alternative prosocial behaviors and provide corrective feedback and suggestions as needed. Make sure the form is legible.
5. To underscore the importance of the Debriefing Form and problem-solving process, have the student sign the form. Make copies of the form for the student, office disciplinary staff, and yourself, and send a copy home for the parent or guardian to sign and return with the student.
6. To help determine whether the student is prepared to cooperate with adult directives and participate appropriately in the normal classroom routine, ask the student what he or she is expected to do at this time and whether he or she is ready to rejoin the class activity. If time and circumstances permit, have the student role-play more appropriate ways of responding.
7. If the student does not appear ready to resume the normal classroom routine, administer a modified time-out (e.g., sitting quietly with or without head down on the desk for 2 minutes), and then visit with the student again to assess readiness for a successful transition.
8. Arrange for the student to experience success as soon as possible in the classroom and provide positive attention for prosocial behaviors.

Student: _____

Teacher: _____

Date: _____

What was the problem behavior? _____
_____

When, where, and why did the behavior happen? _____
_____
_____

What can you do differently next time? _____
_____
_____

What should you do now? _____
_____
_____

Do you need help now? _____
_____
_____

Student Signature: _____

Teacher Signature: _____

Parent/Guardian Signature: _____

FIGURE 5.2. Sample Debriefing Form.

9. Talk with the student again in the next few days to review his or her progress in responding appropriately to the problem situation and other circumstances previously associated with ineffective behavior and provide support for acceptable alternative responses.

Variations

VARIATION 1: DELAYED DEBRIEFING

Although debriefing is most effective when it is conducted immediately after the student has served the consequence and before he or she resumes the regular classroom routine, teacher-conducted sessions must sometimes be postponed until there is an opportunity for conferencing (e.g., lunchtime, recess, packing up to go home, homeroom advisory period).

In this event, give the Debriefing Form to the student after the consequence has been served, have the student complete the form and return it, and conduct the debriefing session as soon as circumstances permit.

VARIATION 2: DEBRIEFING WITHOUT A WRITTEN PLAN

1. In situations in which the problem behavior is less serious, administer an in-seat time-out and omit the writing requirement. For example, if a student crumples up a paper and throws it on the floor when told to correct the paper, quietly direct the student to fold his or her arms and put his or her head down on the desk for 30 seconds. Tell the student that you will talk with him or her later about solving the problem.
2. After the student has completed the time-out and after an interval of about 10 minutes, move to the student's desk and in a quiet, calm tone of voice, indicate the following: (a) a more appropriate manner of responding in the same situation and (b) the consequence if the behavior continues (e.g., the student will have to miss recess or have an office disciplinary referral). Also provide support for successfully resuming the classroom routine (e.g., indicate how to get started in correcting the paper).
3. Be sure to praise the student when he or she begins displaying the appropriate behavior.

VARIATION 3: DEBRIEFING BY OFFICE DISCIPLINARY STAFF

For implementation by office staff, conduct the debriefing session as described above but outside of the classroom. Give a copy of the completed Debriefing Form to the student's teacher and ask the teacher to review it within 24 hours and talk with the student about what he or she will do differently the next time the problem circumstances arise. Teachers should avoid dwelling on the misbehavior in favor of reintegrating the student into the classroom and arranging success experiences as soon as possible.

NOTES

1. The key to successful implementation of this strategy is maintaining the focus on helping the student to acquire appropriate prosocial behaviors rather than using the debriefing session to recall previous rule infractions. Role-playing with a colleague or consultant prior to implementation can be very helpful in avoiding a resumption of the misbehavior–punishment cycle.
2. Have students complete the Debriefing Form themselves only if they are willing to do so and have the necessary writing skills. For students who are very distressed, are young, or have limited reading or writing skills, completing the form may be difficult or aversive and may lead to an escalation of the inappropriate behavior. In that case, the teacher or staff member should read the questions to the student and write in the responses. Alternately, implement Variation 2, especially if the problem behavior is not severe.
3. If a small group of students displays a pattern of disruptive behaviors in the classroom (e.g., excessive socializing, arguing), conducting a debriefing session with the entire group can both be productive and time-efficient. Debriefing interviews with groups of more than three students are not recommended, however, because of the possibility of peer reinforcement for negative behaviors.
4. The Debriefing Form can serve as a written record of the behavior incident for inclusion in the student's file or for use in a teacher–parent–student conference. As in the debriefing session, the conference should focus on encouraging home support for prosocial alternative behaviors rather than simply discussing previous incidents of inappropriate behavior. If the problem persists, a functional behavioral assessment (FBA) should be conducted to develop an individual-

ized behavior support plan that specifies an acceptable replacement response for the problem behavior and arranges the classroom environment to maximize opportunities for the student to display the prosocial rather than the problem behavior.

SOURCE

Sugai, G., & Colvin, G. (1997). Debriefing: A transition step for promoting acceptable behavior. *Education and Treatment of Children, 20*, 209–221.

THREE STEPS TO SELF-MANAGED BEHAVIOR

Overview

Helping students learn to manage their own behavior is an important goal for teachers at any level. Self-management of behavior increases student independence and self-reliance and helps ensure that newly acquired competencies will transfer to other settings and situations. In this intervention, a three-component self-monitoring procedure is paired with a token economy to reduce inappropriate behavior and improve academic productivity. Implemented with two eighth graders with learning disabilities and behavior problems in two general education classes and a study hall class, the self-management package was successful in decreasing off-task and disruptive behavior and increasing academic performance and assignment completion rates in all targeted classes (Dalton, Martella, & Marchand-Martella, 1999). Moreover, all of the participating teachers indicated that they would use the strategy again to reduce unwanted behaviors. In this classwide adaptation, data collection measures for the three self-monitoring components have been combined into a single form, and a team-based format with a dependent group contingency has been substituted for an individualized matching and reward system. Two variations are presented: one with a single overall behavior self-rating scale and another with a classwide group contingency.

Goal

The purpose of this intervention is to reduce disruptive behavior and increase academic productivity with self-monitoring and interdependent group contingencies. This intervention is designed to increase academic engagement and appropriate behavior for students who have acquired the requisite skills but need help with self-monitoring and reinforcement to do so fluently.

Intervention Intensity

The intervention can be used universally in schools with appropriate adaptations for age, topic, and intensity of problem behavior.

Materials

1. Self-Monitoring Form (see Figure 5.3), one form per student.
2. *Reinforcement Menu,* one per student.
3. Classroom clock, large enough to be visible to all students.
4. Overhead projector and transparency of the Self-Monitoring Form (optional).
5. Posterboard chart with a list of classroom rules, such as:
   a. "Stay in your seat unless you have permission to get up."

    b. "Raise your hand and wait to be called on to speak."
    c. "Use appropriate language."
    d. "Follow the teacher's directions at all times."
    e. "Do your best on all assignments."
4. Posterboard chart listing the rating criteria for the point system, as described below (see Intervention Step 5).
5. Section of the chalkboard divided into two parts labeled "Team 1" and "Team 2" (or labeled with team names), with a column for each day of the week.
6. Small tangible reinforcers, such as stickers, wrapped candy, decorated pencils and erasers, and so forth.
7. Red felt-tip pen or marker.

Options to Monitor Progress

1. Select an instructional period during which students are especially disruptive or unproductive. Using a *Group Interval Recording Form* with a 30-second interval and beginning at the left side of the room, glance at each student in turn at 30-second intervals. Record a plus (+) if the student is off task at any time during the interval until one rating is made for each student. When you have rated all students, begin again at the left side of the room.
    a. *Off-task behavior* is defined as being out of one's seat, talking with classmates without permission, playing with nonlesson materials, and engaging in any other behavior interfering with task completion for oneself or others.
    b. Conduct these observations for 30–45 minutes during the selected instructional period for 4–7 days.
2. Using a sheet of paper attached to a clipboard, tally the number of classroom rule infractions during the selected instructional period for the entire class or a target group of students for 4–7 days.
3. Measure academic engagement and disruptive behavior with DBR. These data can be collected in each period in which the intervention is active and graphed for analysis.

Intervention Steps

Introduction and Training

1. Explain to the students that they will be learning a new way of managing their own behavior so that they can get more out of each lesson. Also explain that they will be able to earn points toward rewards for positive behavior as part of the self-management process.
2. Using the rules chart, review the classroom rules, including the rationale for each rule.
3. Using the *Reinforcement Menus*, help students develop a set of rewards, including group activity rewards.
4. Using *Say, Show, Check: Teaching Classroom Procedures,* sit at a student desk near the chalkboard and have the class observe while you demonstrate examples of on-task and off-task behavior. Have students indicate if your behavior is on task or off task by responding chorally or giving a thumbs-up for on-task behavior and a thumbs-down for off-task behavior. Praise students when they evaluate your behavior accurately. If they respond incorrectly to an example, demonstrate the behavior again and ask, "Is this on-task or off-task behavior?"
5. Using the ratings chart, review the following criteria for the overall behavior rating scale (see Figure 5.3):

Student: _____

Teacher: _____

Date: _____

Before Class

I have my class materials.	Yes	No
I have my homework completed (if assigned).	Yes	No
I am in class on time.	Yes	No
I am sitting and ready to work.	Yes	No

During Class

I am participating in the class activity (check every 5 minutes and circle Y for Yes or N for No).

5	10	15	20	25	30	35	40	45	50
Y N	Y N	Y N	Y N	Y N	Y N	Y N	Y N	Y N	Y N

After Class

I followed all directions.	Yes	No
I worked for the whole class as directed.	Yes	No
I have homework tonight.	Yes	No

My overall behavior in this class was:

1	2	3	4	5
Poor		OK		Great

My overall behavior in this class was (teacher rating):

1	2	3	4	5
Poor		OK		Great

Form Completed (if yes, 5 points): _____

Teacher rating (if 3–5): _____

Total Points: _____

FIGURE 5.3. Sample Self-Monitoring Form: Class To-Do Checklist.

a. 5 = great: working on the assignment and following the rules throughout the period.

b. 4 = good: working on the assignment and following the rules throughout the period, with one minor infraction, such as talking without permission.

c. 3 = OK: working on the assignment and following the rules for more than half of the period, with one or two behavior reminders.

d. 2 = needs improvement: working on the assignment and following the rules for less than half of the period, with more than two behavior reminders.

e. 1 = poor: off task for most of the period, failing to follow the rules, and more than two behavior reminders.

6. Divide the class into two teams, based on seating arrangements. If necessary, change the seating arrangement so that students with attention and/or behavior problems are approximately equally distributed between the teams.

7. Distribute copies of the Self-Monitoring Form, and lead students through the three sections of the form, using the overhead projector and transparency, if desired, as follows:

    a. At the beginning of class, respond to the three questions in the Before Class section by circling "Yes" or "No."

    b. During the period, glance at the classroom clock every 5 minutes and ask yourself, "Am I working?" Circle "Yes" if you are on task and "No" if you are off task.

    c. At the end of the period, respond to the five questions in the After Class section by circling "Yes" or "No."

    d. Then rate your overall behavior by circling one of the numbers at the bottom of the form.

8. Tell students that during the last few minutes of the period, you will collect the Self-Monitoring Forms by team. Randomly select one form from each team, review the forms, give an overall behavior rating to that student, and award points as follows:

    a. 5 points = all of the components completed correctly.

    b. Additional 5 points = teacher rating of 4 or 5.

9. Explain that when a team receives a total of 10 points for 4 consecutive days, all of the members of that team will receive a reward.

10. Conduct a training session during which students practice using the Self-Monitoring Forms and rating themselves. Provide feedback on the completeness of the forms and the accuracy of their self-ratings.

Implementation

1. At the beginning of the instructional period, distribute the Self-Monitoring Forms and remind students to check the classroom clock at the appropriate interval.

2. Near the end of the period, instruct students to mark the After Class section and the overall rating scale.

3. Collect the forms by team and randomly draw one form from each team. Do not reveal the identity of the students whose forms have been drawn.

4. Review the forms, award points as appropriate, and announce to the class when a team has achieved the criterion. Have a team member write the points total on the chalkboard under the team number or name.

5. When a team earns a total of 10 points for 4 consecutive days, deliver a reward to all of the members of that team. If both teams earn 10 points for 4 consecutive days, deliver a classwide activity reward, such as a popcorn party, 15 minutes of music time, or some other reward.

6. When most students are receiving teacher ratings of 3 or above, increase the length of the During Class self-monitoring interval to 15 minutes. When most students are receiving teacher ratings of 4 or 5, implement the overall behavior rating scale as the sole component (see Variation 1).

Variations

VARIATION 1: SINGLE BEHAVIOR RATING SCALE VERSION

Implement the 5-point overall behavior rating scale as the sole component (see Note 2) and modify the Self-Monitoring Form accordingly. Award points and deliver rewards as described above. Because only one match is required per student, this version can be easily implemented on an individualized basis with one student or a small group of students.

VARIATION 2: CLASSWIDE VERSION

Implement the intervention as described above but do not divide the class into teams. After the class period, have students turn in their forms. Randomly select a single form and rate it, without revealing the identity of the student. Award points as described above and record earned points on the chalkboard each day. Deliver a group activity reward or small tangible rewards to each student when the class has earned 10 points on 4 consecutive days.

NOTES

1. If the intervention is implemented with an individual student or a small group of students, have students keep their Self-Monitoring Forms inside their subject-area folders to make the procedure less intrusive. At the end of the period, have them bring their forms to be matched or go to their desks to conduct the teacher–student matching. Rewards should be social in nature (lunch with the teacher, a day as classroom messenger, etc.) rather than tangible so that other students do not feel deprived of the opportunity to earn reinforcement.
2. In the original study, teachers and students alike selected the overall behavior rating scale as the most effective of the three components in the self-monitoring system.

SOURCE

Dalton, T., Martella, R. C., & Marchand-Martella, N. E. (1999). The effects of a self-management program in reducing off-task behavior. *Journal of Behavioral Education, 9,* 157–176.

Academic Behavior Interventions

USING MYSTERY MOTIVATORS TO SUPPORT HOMEWORK COMPLETION

Overview

Although proficient homework completion is associated with academic success for students of every ability level, many students lack the motivation to complete their homework assignments. This strategy targets performance deficits in homework with a game-like intervention permitting access to an unknown reinforcer for students achieving a specific homework criterion (Madaus, Kehle, Madaus, & Bray, 2003; Moore, Waguespack, Wickstrom, Witt, & Gaydos, 1994). This "Mystery Motivator" is an unpredictable reward represented by a manila envelope with a question mark written on it, which is prominently displayed on the teacher's desk. Inside the envelope is a card indicating what the class will win if students attain the homework goal. The "mystery" part of this intervention helps to make common rewards more effective. Pragmatically, even if some students might not like one or two of the rewards, students will not know whether they are getting less preferred or more preferred rewards. This is essential for group interventions in which different students may have different responses to each reward option. In addition, each day it is not known whether the class will get a reward or not; the total number of rewards given thus decreases. Essentially, the uncovering of the Mystery Motivator acts as a reinforcer in itself. The Mystery Motivator intervention has been demonstrated to have powerful effects on homework completion and accuracy for elementary school students and is highly rated by both students and teachers. In the original studies, target students received individual Mystery Motivator charts and earned rewards for their individual performances. Here the strategy is adapted for classwide application, with a single Mystery Motivator chart and an interdependent group contingency to capitalize on peer support for homework productivity. A variation with publicly posted rewards is also presented.

Goal

This intervention is designed to increase homework accuracy and completion for students who have acquired the requisite skills for homework completion but need reinforcement to do so fluently. It employs group contingencies that involve unknown rewards.

Intervention Intensity

The intervention can be used universally in schools with appropriate adaptations for age, topic, and intensity of problem behavior.

Materials

1. "Mystery Motivator Chart," consisting of a posterboard chart divided into boxes labeled with the 5 days of the school week. For younger students, use a novel format, such as a rocket ship divided into five parts to represent the days of the week.
2. Squares of construction paper and Scotch tape or a set of "invisible ink" and developer ink pens.
3. Manila envelope with a large question mark drawn on it with a black marker.
4. 3" × 5" index cards listing group activity rewards, such as extra recess, indoor games, and music time, or describing access to small tangible rewards, such as "candy for everyone" to indicate that each student may select a piece of wrapped candy from a jar.
5. Small tangible rewards, such as wrapped candy, stickers, colorful erasers, and so forth.
6. *Reinforcement Menus,* one per student (optional; see Variation).

Options to Monitor Progress

1. Calculate homework completion rates in one or more subjects for each student or a target group of students for 5–10 days or the previous marking period. *Homework completion rates* are defined as the number of completed assignments divided by the number of assignments given.
2. Calculate homework accuracy rates in one or more subjects for each student or a target group of students for 5–10 days or the previous marking period. *Homework accuracy rates* are defined as the number of correct items divided by the total number of items.
3. Calculate the percentage of students completing all homework assignments with at least 80% accuracy in one or more subjects for 5–10 days or the previous marking period.
4. Calculate grades in one or more subjects, such as those in which achievement is poorest, for the entire class or a target group of students for the marking period to date.

Intervention Steps

Preparation

1. Write the letter *M* (for Mystery Motivator) in the boxes on the Mystery Motivator Chart corresponding to the number of days that the reward is available (see Implementation Step 1 below). Then tape a square over each box so that the squares conceal which days are labeled with an *M* and which are blank.
2. Alternately, use the invisible ink marker to write an *M* in the squares corresponding to the days on which the reward is available.

Introduction and Training

1. Explain to the students that they will have an opportunity to earn rewards for good homework performance in the selected subject(s).
2. Display the manila envelope with the question mark on it. Explain that every day that all students turn in all assigned homework in the selected subject(s) with at least 80% accuracy (or some other criterion), you will choose someone to remove the tape and lift the tab on the Mystery Motivator Chart for that day or to color over the square with a developer pen. If an *M* appears beneath the tab or is revealed when the developer pen is applied, the class will earn the reward in the envelope.

Implementation

1. Begin by making the reward available (signaled by the *M*) for at least 3 of 5 days each week. Be sure to make the *M*s random, so that students cannot predict on which days the reward will be available (e.g., not every other day).
2. Each day, check each student's homework in the target subject(s) to see if it is complete and to record a percent-accuracy score. As soon as you are able to determine whether the class has met the goal (which will probably be the following day after you have checked papers), announce the results. If the class has met the criterion, select a student to lift up the tab or apply the developer pen to color the square marking the day on which the goal was met. If an *M* appears on the square, open the envelope and announce the reward. Provide the reward immediately or as soon as possible (e.g., extra recess at the regular recess time).
3. If no *M* appears, lead the class in applauding their excellent homework performance and remind them that they will have another chance to earn a Mystery Motivator the next day. Remember that the uncovering of the tab should be an event, so it is important to make it fun and exciting.
4. If the class did not meet the criterion, encourage the students to try harder the next day.
5. After the class has met the original criterion for at least 3 of 5 days for several weeks, reduce the number of days per week on which the Mystery Motivator is available and/or raise the criterion (e.g., 85% accuracy).

Variation: Mystery Motivators with Publicly Posted Reward Menu

1. Distribute *Reinforcement Menus* and have students mark their preferences. Also invite students to add any favorite classroom activities not on the list. Based on student responses and classroom resources, develop a classwide reward menu and post it in the classroom

when the Mystery Motivator intervention is in effect. When the *M* appears on the chart, permit students to vote on a reward from the menu and deliver it as soon as possible.
2. Alternately, number the rewards on the posted menu. Each day, place a slip of paper with a number on it corresponding to a reward in the envelope. If the *M* appears on the chart, deliver the reward matching that number.

NOTES

1. To reduce the temptation for students to look under the tab on the chart, inform the class that if anyone turns up a tab without permission, the class will forfeit its chance to earn a reward that day.
2. Invisible and developer markers such as Crayola Changeables are available at office and school supply stores and at *www.crayola.com.*

SOURCES

Madaus, M. M. R., Kehle, T. J., Madaus, J., & Bray, M. A. (2003). Mystery motivator as an intervention to promote homework completion and accuracy. *School Psychology International, 24,* 369–377.
Moore, L. A., Waguespack, A. M., Wickstrom, K. F., Witt, J. C., & Gaydos, G. R. (1994). Mystery motivator: An effective and time-efficient intervention. *School Psychology Review, 23,* 106–118.

GUIDED NOTES

Overview

Guided Notes provide premade notes that include blank spaces for writing down components from the lesson of the day. Using Guided Notes allows the student to have opportunities to demonstrate his or her ability to actively engage and increase his or her time on task while a lesson is being taught (Konrad, Joseph, & Eveleigh, 2009). After the lesson has been completed, notes are reviewed by the teacher. In order to reinforce the student, the teacher should reviews the notes with excitement, praise, and other forms of positive reinforcement for each blank completed correctly. This intervention can be used with students in regular education settings (especially with those in grades 4–12) or with students receiving additional educational services. Guided Notes is a flexible intervention that can be adapted for any instructional level and altered for students with specific skill deficits. Guided Notes are inexpensive and efficient, allow teachers to exhibit their own styles, and are often preferred over "regular" notes by both teachers and students. In addition, the sheets provide prompts for students to actively listen and engage in the learning process.

Goal

Guided Notes can provide appropriate attending prompts for students so that they may engage in on-task academic behavior and will allow the student to be rewarded for listening to instruction (e.g., listening to the teacher instead of counting the number of tiles on the ceiling). Having the students engage in the appropriate attending behaviors will reduce the likelihood that they will engage in inappropriate behaviors (e.g., talking without permission, walking around the room). Guided notes, if implemented with integrity, will allow students to receive positive reinforcement for their appropriate attending behavior.

Intervention Intensity

The intervention can be used across a variety of subjects but is typically used with individual students or small groups working on the same material.

Options to Monitor Progress

Measure the student's academic engagement with DBR. These data can be collected in each period in which the intervention is active and graphed for analysis. Conduct observations for 3–5 days prior to the start of the intervention to establish a baseline and then in each instructional period in which the intervention is used.

Materials

1. Guided Notes (see Figure 5.4).
2. Presentation software/overheads.
3. Response cards (if utilizing a supplemental strategy).
4. Reinforcers valuable to students (if utilizing a lottery incentive).

Intervention Steps

1. Make a lesson outline using a form of presentation software or overheads, concentrating on major concepts and facts to be learned.
2. Make a student handout from the lesson outline. Leave blank spaces for the student to fill in that correspond to the most important concepts in the lesson plan. Blank spaces may be short (one to three words) or long (four to eight words) depending on the students' instructional level.
3. Lead a training activity to teach the students how to use Guided Notes while listening to instructions and looking at presentation materials (e.g. PowerPoint slides, transparencies). First, explain to the students how the notes work. Next, provide an example and model the way in which the students need to fill out the notes. Finally, hold a practice session with feedback so that the students will know whether or not they are filling them out correctly.
4. Teach the planned lesson utilizing the presentation software/overheads that go along with students' Guided Notes. Include prompts and/or questions while teaching the lesson if it seems necessary or if it will aid in student learning.
5. Review the students' notes in order to provide positive reinforcement. This can be done by collecting, grading, and returning the notes to the students or, more preferably, by checking the notes in front of the students so that you can provide positive praise and specific feedback.
6. Supplemental strategies may be added to the Guided Notes intervention to further promote student success and responding.

Supplemental Strategies

1. Use Guided Notes as an intervention for the entire class.
2. Combine Guided Notes with unison responding, a lottery incentive, or response cards.
3. Quiz students on the material from the Guided Notes after a lesson.
4. Offer extra credit to those who accurately fill out Guided Notes.
5. Use with an entire class, a small group of students, or an individual student.

Guided Notes—Second-Grade Social Studies

1. We elect a new president every _____ years.
2. Presidential candidates must be citizens of the _____.
3. Presidential candidates must be at least _____ years old.
4. They must have lived in the USA for at least _____ years.
5. Candidates campaign by traveling all over the USA and _____ as many people as they can.

Guided Notes—Fifth-Grade Writing

1. A _____ is a group of _____ that tell about one _____.
2. The _____ in a paragraph usually comes _____ and tells the main idea of the paragraph.
3. Sometimes, though, the topic sentence can come at the _____ or in the _____ of a paragraph.
4. When looking for a _____ sentence, try to find the one that tells the _____ of the paragraph.
5. _____ follow the topic sentence and provide details about the topic.

Guided Notes—Eighth-Grade Math

1. When two figures are _____, you can slide, flip, or _____ one so it fits exactly on the other one.
2. The _____ of the angles of any triangle is _____. The _____ of the angles of any quadrilateral is _____.
3. In the expression 6^3, six is the _____ and three is the _____. The problem would be solved by multiplying (_____) (_____) (_____) = _____.
4. To divide numbers or _____ with the same base, _____.
5. Whatever you do to one side of an equation, you must do to the other side of the equation in order to keep it _____ or _____.

FIGURE 5.4. Examples of Guided Notes. Examples were produced with the Guided-Notes Maker on the Intervention Central website (*http://rti2.org/rti2/guided_notes*).

Critical Components for Successful Intervention

1. The Guided Notes instruction and lesson plans/materials must match each students' instructional level.
2. Students must have demonstrated that they are capable of completing Guided Notes.
3. Training the students in how to use Guided Notes is necessary; otherwise, the intervention will likely fail.
4. Guided Notes should be reviewed by the teacher and/or turned in and handed back as soon as possible so that students may receive specific feedback about their performance, along with positive reinforcement.
5. Guided Notes must contain enough blank spaces to give students an adequate amount of opportunities to respond.
6. If Guided Notes is used as a classwide intervention, make sure that the criterion for earning a reinforcer is set at a level at which all students will be capable (intellectually, physically, etc.) of earning their reward.

NOTE

The lead student developer on the brief was Lindsey Long, a graduate of the MA/CAS School Psychology Program at East Carolina University in Greenville, North Carolina.

SOURCES

Burns, M. K., Riley-Tillman, T. C., & VanDerHeyden, A. M. (2012). *RTI applications: Vol. 1. Academic and behavioral interventions.* New York: Guilford Press.

Konrad, M., Joseph, L. M., & Eveleigh, E. (2009). A meta-analytic review of guided notes. *Education and Treatment of Children, 32,* 421–444.

THE REWARDS BOX: ENHANCING ACADEMIC PERFORMANCE WITH RANDOMIZED GROUP CONTINGENCIES

Overview

Interdependent group contingencies are reward systems based on the performance of all the students in the classroom. This approach can be an efficient method for teachers to support academic behavior because every student has an opportunity to earn reinforcement. One problem with group contingencies is that they are limited by the fact that the rewards may be reinforcing for some students but neutral or even aversive for others. Moreover, if students perceive that they cannot meet the criterion for the reward after an initially poor performance, they have little incentive to engage in appropriate behavior for the rest of the intervention period. This intervention solves these problems by randomizing both the rewards and the performance criteria to target academic productivity and performance in a particular subject area. The teacher randomly selects a group criterion (classwide average percent-correct score on daily assignments of 75%, 80%, 85%, etc.) and provides a group-oriented reward if the weekly class average meets that goal. First implemented in a self-contained classroom with five middle school students with emotional disorders, the intervention produced large, educationally meaningful gains in spelling, mathematics, and English for all participants (Popkin & Skinner, 2003). In the original study, the three academic subjects were targeted in succession. This adaptation targets a single academic subject, with the multiple-subject implementation included as a variation. Reward delivery has also been reduced from a daily to a weekly basis for usability purposes, with a daily reward system presented as a variation. Another highly usable variation that requires teachers to evaluate only a single student's performance is included, as are variations targeting homework and quiz or test performance.

Goal

This intervention is designed to increase academic performance in one or more academic subjects for students who have acquired the requisite skills for academic engagement but need reinforcement to do so fluently. It employs a randomized interdependent group contingency system.

Intervention Intensity

The intervention can be used universally in schools with appropriate adaptations for age, topic, and intensity of problem behavior.

Materials

1. *Reinforcement Menu*, optional.
2. Three shoe boxes, labeled "Rewards," "Goals," and "Suggestions," respectively.
3. Thirty 3″ × 5″ index cards, listing the criteria for student performance (e.g., one index card with "50%," three with "60%," three with "70%," four with "80%," four with "85%," five with "90%," five with "95%," and five with "100%"); 20–30 blank index cards.
4. Red pens, one per student (optional; see Note).
5. Shoe box containing slips of paper with the name of each student in the class, labeled "Student Names" (optional; see Variation 5).
6. Rewards, such as wrapped candy, school supplies, and stickers (optional).

Options to Monitor Progress

1. Calculate percent-correct scores for each student on daily assignments in a selected academic subject for the past several weeks. Then calculate a class average percent-correct score by summing individual student scores and dividing by the total number of students.
2. Calculate the class average percent-correct score on weekly quizzes and/or chapter tests in the selected academic subject for the previous month by summing individual student scores and dividing by the total number of students.
3. Measure classwide academic engagement with DBR. These data can be collected in each period in which the intervention is active and graphed for analysis.

Intervention Steps

Introduction and Training

1. Explain to the class that they will have a chance to earn rewards if they meet certain goals on their in-class assignments for Monday through Thursday in the selected subject. If the class meets the specified goal, you will randomly select a reward from a set of rewards on Fridays, and everyone will receive it.
2. Administer a *Reinforcement Menu* or conduct a discussion in which you give examples of group rewards (e.g., 15 minutes of computer time, 10 minutes of music, homework passes, 20 minutes of free time) and invite students to suggest other rewards. Write acceptable rewards on the chalkboard during the discussion.
3. Using this list, write each reward on an index card and put the cards in the Rewards box. Place the Suggestions box and the blank index cards on a table accessible to all students and tell them that they may put suggestions for other group rewards in the box. Explain that you will add their suggestions to the rewards if you believe that they are appropriate.
4. Next, display the Goals box and explain that you will also randomly select a goal for group academic performance. Demonstrate by randomly selecting a card and reading the criterion (e.g., class average of 90% in the selected subject). Explain that if the class had met or exceeded this goal for their weekly average score, you would have randomly selected a card from the Rewards box and given all students the reward or permitted all students to participate in the activity.
5. Tell the students that if they do not meet the selected goal, you will not draw a reward from the Rewards box on Friday, but they will have an opportunity to earn a reward the following week.
6. Tell students the number of cards with each criterion in the Goals box and answer any questions about the procedures. Place the Goals box and the Rewards box on your desk.

Implementation

1. Each Friday, randomly select a card from the Goals box. Check your grade book to determine the class's average percent-correct score for the target subject, announce the criterion, and announce whether the class has met it.
2. If the class has met the criterion, randomly select a card from the Rewards box and announce which reward has been drawn and when it will be delivered.
3. Return the goal and reward cards to their respective boxes so that they can be selected again at the next drawing.

Variations

VARIATION 1: THE DAILY REWARDS BOX

1. To provide rewards on a daily basis, calculate percent-correct scores on the daily assignment in the targeted subject area for each student in the class. Calculate the class average percent-correct score by summing individual scores and dividing by the number of students in class that day. Use this score to determine whether the class has met the performance criterion drawn from the Goals box.
2. At the end of the day, randomly select a card from the Goals box, check your grade book, announce the criterion, and announce whether the class has met the criterion. If so, randomly select a card from the Rewards box.
3. If possible, provide the reward at the end of the day. If not, deliver the reward as soon as possible the following day. Note that this version requires evaluating each student's performance before the end of the day; however, depending on the criterion drawn, the class average can be estimated. For example, if the goal selected is 80% and all students score above 90%, there is no need to calculate the exact average.

VARIATION 2: THE REWARDS BOX FOR MULTIPLE SUBJECT AREAS

1. After 2 weeks of implementation in one subject, tell students that you are adding goals for another subject to the Goals box. Explain that the class will need to work hard in both subjects in order to increase their chances of earning a reward.
2. Add 30 more index cards with subject-specific goals to the Goals box, for a total of 60 cards. To distinguish the two sets of goals, write the name of the subject, as well as the goal, on each card (e.g., Mathematics—70%; Spelling—85%).
3. Note that you must now evaluate and record each student's performance in two subjects by the end of the week so that you can calculate or estimate the class average score on both sets of assignments.
4. If desired, add a third subject after 2 weeks of two-subject implementation, using the same procedures. This version requires 90 cards in the Goals box.

VARIATION 3: THE REWARDS BOX FOR HOMEWORK PERFORMANCE

1. Explain to the class that they will have a chance to earn rewards if they achieve a certain average score on their daily homework in the selected subject (e.g., a class average of 85% for complete, accurate homework). Grade homework each night so that students can potentially receive a reward the following day.
2. After several weeks, require the class to achieve a specified weekly rather than daily homework average in order to receive the reward.

VARIATION 4: THE REWARDS BOX FOR QUIZ OR TEST PERFORMANCE

Tell the students that they will have a chance to earn rewards if they achieve a certain average score on their quizzes or tests in the selected subject (e.g., a class average of 85% or better on the next four weekly quizzes). This variation enhances maintenance and generalization of academic gains because it requires students to achieve the same level of performance over a longer period of time to receive the reinforcement. However, because students are not eligible for rewards for several weeks or longer, depending on the quiz or test schedule, do not implement this variation until students have responded positively to the daily assignment version.

VARIATION 5: THE REWARDS BOX WITH SINGLE-STUDENT PERFORMANCE EVALUATION

1. After the classwide intervention has been implemented for several weeks, announce that you will now be randomly selecting one student and determining whether that student's weekly average on daily assignments meets the randomly selected criterion.
2. Each Friday, randomly select a slip of paper from the Student Names box and a card from the Goals box. Check your grade book to determine the student's average daily assignment score, announce the criterion you have drawn, and announce whether the student has met this criterion. Be sure not to identify the student by name and to return the paper to the Student Names box immediately.
3. If the student has met the criterion, randomly select a card from the Rewards box and announce which reward has been drawn and when it will be delivered.
4. Note that this variation is easier to implement than the original version and the other variations because you must evaluate only one student's performance.

NOTE

For maximum usability, select subjects that have easy-to-grade daily assignments, such as spelling and mathematics. To speed up grading, have students exchange papers and use red pens to grade each other's papers while you go over the answers. Monitor students carefully during the grading process, and if you detect cheating, do not deliver any rewards that day.

SOURCE

Popkin, J., & Skinner, C. H. (2003). Enhancing academic performance in a classroom serving students with serious emotional disturbance: Interdependent group contingencies with randomly selected components. *School Psychology Review, 32,* 282–295.

Behavior Interventions for Use in Nonclassroom Settings

THE TIMELY TRANSITIONS GAME: REDUCING ROOM-TO-ROOM TRANSITION TIME

Overview

Although room-to-room transitions are a necessary part of the school day, they take up time that could be available for learning. Room-to-room transitions are also likely scenarios for inappropriate and disruptive behavior because students are physically closer to each other, the situation is less structured, and teachers have more difficulty monitoring behavior. Attempts to address student misbehavior can further extend transition time, such as when the teacher requires the entire class to wait in the hall until every student is quiet before entering the classroom. This game-like intervention encourages students to make rapid, disruption-free transitions with a combination of overt timing, publicly posted feedback, and an interdependent group contingency with randomly selected transitions and time criteria. Randomizing transitions and time criteria provides a powerful incentive for appropriate behavior because the class can still earn a reward after a poor transition, given that any of the targeted transitions may be selected at the end of the day and used to determine whether the randomly selected criterion has been met. In two investigations, the first with a second-grade classroom and the second with a sixth-grade classroom, the *Timely Transitions Game* produced immediate, large, and sustained decreases in transition times, with the average weekly transition time reduced by approximately 2 hours in the first study and by 1.5 hours in the second study (Campbell & Skinner, 2004; Yarbrough, Skinner, Lee, & Lemmons, 2004). Teachers also reported that inappropriate transition behaviors decreased in frequency and intensity. A variation targeting a single transition rather than multiple transitions is also presented.

Goal

The purpose of the intervention is to facilitate rapid, disruption-free room-to-room transitions by means of a transition game combining explicit timing, public posting, and a group contingency with randomized elements.

Intervention Intensity

The intervention can be used for a variety of students with appropriate adaptations for age, topic, and intensity of problem behavior.

Materials

1. Stopwatch or watch with second hand.
2. Two plastic containers, with press-on paper labels and slips of paper, as follows:
   a. Label the first container "Transitions." Place in the container six slips of paper with one of the following phrases written on each slip: "Going to recess," "Returning from recess," "Going to lunch," "Returning from lunch," "Going to specials," "Returning from specials." (Modify the descriptions to reflect the targeted transitions. Skip this step if you are implementing the variation.)
   b. Label the second container "What It Takes to Win." Place in the container 13 slips of paper with a range of acceptable transition times, using data obtained during the observation period to help select the time criteria.
3. "Timely Transitions Feedback Chart," consisting of a posterboard chart or section of the chalkboard.
4. Brightly colored construction paper letters (optional).
5. Materials for a class party, such as popcorn, videos, DVDs, or music CDs.

Options to Monitor Progress

1. Select one or more room-to-room transitions, such as to and from recess, to and from the cafeteria, and to and from specials. Using a stopwatch or watch with a second hand and a sheet of paper attached to a clipboard, record the number of seconds required for students

to complete the selected transitions for 4–7 days. For transitions that involve leaving the classroom, begin timing when you give the signal to line up and stop timing when the last student exits the classroom. For transitions that involve returning to class, begin timing when students cross the threshold of the classroom and stop timing when all students have been seated quietly for 5 seconds.

2. Using a sheet of paper attached to a clipboard, tally the number of inappropriate behaviors that occur during one or more room-to-room transitions for 4–7 days. *Inappropriate behaviors* are defined as talking without permission, touching or pushing other students, getting out of line, and failing to follow directions.

Intervention Steps

Introduction and Training

1. Explain to the students that they will be learning a game that will help them get to recess, lunch, and specials faster and will give them a chance to earn a class party for appropriate behavior.
2. Guide students through the transition procedures, as described below.

STEP 1: REVIEW APPROPRIATE TRANSITION BEHAVIOR.

1. Review appropriate ready-to-line-up behavior as follows: (a) clear your desks, (b) sit in your seats quietly, and (c) wait for your row or table to be called.
2. Review appropriate in-line behavior as follows: (a) get in line promptly when your row or table is called; (b) stand quietly, facing forward; (c) keep your hands and feet to yourself; and (d) wait for directions.

STEP 2: DEMONSTRATE THE TIMING PROCEDURE AND CONDUCT A PRACTICE TRANSITION.

1. Tell the students that they will have a chance to practice making effective transitions by going to and from the specials room (or some other destination).
2. Display the stopwatch and tell the students that you will start it when the transition begins and let it run until they are ready to leave the classroom.
3. Say, "It is time to line up now to go to the specials room," and start the stopwatch. When all of the students are displaying ready-to-line-up behavior, have them line up by rows, tables, or some other arrangement. When all of the students are exhibiting appropriate in-line behavior, stop the stopwatch and direct them to file out of the classroom and walk toward the destination room.
4. If students misbehave at any time while they are in the hallway during the transition, stop the class and start the stopwatch again. When students are again displaying appropriate in-line behavior, stop the stopwatch and instruct them to continue transitioning. The transition is over when the last student crosses the threshold of the destination room. Record the transition time on a slip of paper or a sheet of paper attached to a clipboard.
5. Conduct another practice transition back to the classroom. As before, start the stopwatch after you direct students to line up and stop it when they are exhibiting appropriate in-line behavior. If students exhibit inappropriate behavior during the transition, stop the class and start the stopwatch. When students are behaving appropriately again, stop the stopwatch and resume the transition.
6. When you reach the classroom, start the stopwatch again when the first student crosses

the threshold and stop it when all students are in their seats and have been sitting quietly for 5 seconds.

7. Tell students what their transition times were going to and from the destination room and record those times on the chalkboard.

STEP 3: EXPLAIN THE GROUP REWARD PROCEDURE.

1. Display the "Transitions" and "What It Takes to Win" containers. Explain that you will write the date and each targeted transition time on the Timely Transitions Feedback Chart each day. At the end of the day, you will draw a slip of paper from the "Transitions" container to select the transition time that will be used to determine whether the class meets the criterion for earning the reward.

2. Show the students the slips of paper with the criterion times and list the times on the chalkboard. To ensure that students understand the times, write times over 1 minute in minutes and seconds.

3. Explain that you will select a criterion time from the "What It Takes to Win" container and compare it with the students' actual time for the transition you have drawn. The class will earn a letter in the word P–A–R–T–Y if their time is less than the criterion time drawn from the container. If the actual time is greater than the criterion, you will put a dash on the chart to indicate that no letter was earned. After the word *party* is spelled, the class will celebrate with a popcorn party (or some other type of party).

Implementation

1. Remind students about the Timely Transitions Game at the start of each school day.

2. Using the stopwatch or watch with a second hand, record transition times for each targeted transition. When students return from a destination room or area, announce the number of seconds required to go to and return from the destination and record the two transition times on the Timely Transitions Feedback Chart. Repeat this process throughout the school day.

3. At the end of the day, draw a slip of paper from the "Transition" container to indicate the selected transition and put a star beside that time on the chart (or have a student do this).

4. Then draw or have another student draw a slip of paper from the "What It Takes to Win" container and record the selected time in the eighth column on the chart. If the actual time for the selected transition is less than the criterion, record a letter in the last column and praise the class. If desired, tape a large construction paper letter (e.g., P, A) to the top of the chalkboard each day that the class met the criterion.

5. If the actual time is greater than the criterion, enter a dash in the last column on the chart and encourage the class to do better the next day.

6. Deliver the group reward when the word *party* is spelled out on the chart.

Variation: Single-Transition Version

Select a single problematic transition, such as entering the classroom and settling down after lunch or recess. Prepare a "What It Takes to Win" container holding slips of paper with a range of acceptable times. Record the amount of time needed to complete the selected transition and write it on the chalkboard. At the end of the day, draw a slip of paper from the container and record a letter on the Timely Transitions Feedback Chart if the class time beats the time you have drawn.

NOTES

1. To maintain student motivation, vary the reinforcers after the class earns each reward. Other rewards used in the original studies included listening to music during independent seatwork (M–U–S–I–C), going outside for lunch (P–I–C–N–I–C), watching a brief video (M–O–V–I–E), and eating treats brought by students (C–U–P–C–A–K–E–S).
2. As students become more successful in making rapid transitions, use longer words or phrases to represent rewards, such as F–I–E–L–D–T–R–I–P–T–O–Z–O–O, and replace longer times in the time criteria pool with shorter times.

SOURCES

Campbell, S., & Skinner, C. H. (2004). Combining explicit timing with an interdependent group contingency program to decrease transition times: An investigation of the timely transitions game. *Journal of Applied School Psychology, 20,* 11–27.

Yarbrough, J. L., Skinner, C. H., Lee, Y. J., & Lemmons, C. (2004). Decreasing transition times in a second grade classroom: Scientific support for the timely transitions game. *Journal of Applied School Psychology, 20,* 85–107.

SIX STEPS TO EFFECTIVE CLASSROOM TRANSITIONS

Overview

Rapid, orderly transitions are an essential component of proactive classroom management. Because transitions occur frequently during the school day, teachers have multiple opportunities to increase academic learning time and promote prosocial behaviors by managing transitions efficiently. This multicomponent intervention targets transitions with a combination of explicit instruction, active supervision, goal setting, timing, and performance feedback in a game-like format. In an early study, in a class of preschool students, a version of this intervention reduced transition time related to cleaning up from 11.6 minutes to 4.3 minutes (Wurtele & Drabman, 1984). In a second study, implemented in four elementary school classrooms, transition times were reduced to 4 minutes or less across all four classrooms (LaFleur, Witt, Naquin, Harwell, & Gilbertson, 1998). Three variations are included: one for preschoolers, one with a response-cost contingency, and one with a class-wide incentive.

Goal

The purpose of this intervention is to promote quick, orderly transitions using a six-step instructional sequence in a game-like format.

Intervention Intensity

The intervention can be used for a variety of students with appropriate adaptations for age, topic, and intensity of problem behavior.

Materials

Timer with audible bell or stopwatch with audible signal.

Options to Monitor Progress

1. Using a sheet of paper attached to a clipboard, record the number of minutes required for students to complete one or more transitions for 4–7 days.
2. Using a sheet of paper attached to a clipboard, tally the number of disruptive behaviors that occur during one or more transitions for 4–7 days. *Disruptive behaviors* are defined as behaviors that interfere with the orderly completion of a transition, such as dawdling, failing to follow directions, getting out of line, pushing, and arguing.
3. Measure classwide academic engagement and disruptive behavior with DBR. These data can be collected in each period in which the intervention is active and graphed for analysis. Conduct observations for 3–5 days prior to the start of the intervention to establish a baseline and then in each instructional period in which the intervention is used.

Intervention Steps

Introduction and Training

1. Explain to the students that they will be learning to make faster transitions so that you have more time to teach and they have more time to learn and have fun at school.
2. Demonstrate the signal that you will use to indicate that the transition is beginning (e.g., clapping hands, switching off the lights, executing a clapping pattern that students must repeat).
3. Guide students through the six-step transition process, as described below.

STEP 1: SIGNAL TO OBTAIN STUDENT ATTENTION.

Give the transition signal to focus student attention on you—for example, clap your hands three times.

STEP 2: COMMUNICATE YOUR EXPECTATIONS FOR ACADEMIC AND SOCIAL BEHAVIOR.

1. Give academic directions: tell students what they need to do to get ready for the next activity:

   "Put your social studies books away and get out your math homework."
2. Give behavior directions: remind students how they should behave during transitions and how they should look so you know they are ready to begin the next activity:

   "Remember, change your materials without making too much noise with them and without talking. Then show me you're ready for math by sitting quietly with your math homework on your desk."

STEP 3: SPECIFY THE TIME LIMIT FOR THE TRANSITION.

Tell students the amount of time they have to get ready for the next activity, set the timer for that amount of time, and encourage them to "beat the buzzer":

   "You have 2 minutes to get ready for math. [Display the timer or stopwatch.] Ready? Try to beat the buzzer!" [Set the timer or stopwatch for the specified time.]

STEP 4: MONITOR FOR COMPLIANCE.

1. Walk around the room and observe students as they perform the transition.
2. Praise students who are following the academic and behavior directions and redirect or give a specific prompt for noncompliant students.

STEP 5: SIGNAL THE END OF THE TRANSITION BY BEGINNING THE NEXT ACTIVITY.

Begin the next lesson promptly.

STEP 6: PROVIDE PERFORMANCE FEEDBACK ON THE SUCCESS OF THE TRANSITION.

1. Tell the students whether they beat the buzzer or whether the time required for the transition exceeded the criterion. Remind them that every student must have completed the transition within the time limit for the criterion to be met.
2. Praise the class if they met the criterion. If the time exceeded the criterion, tell the students that you are disappointed they did not beat the buzzer but that they will have another opportunity to beat the buzzer later that day.

Implementation

1. Use the timer or stopwatch to monitor times for targeted transitions throughout the day.
2. Provide praise and corrective feedback as needed after each transition.

Variations

VARIATION 1: BEAT THE BUZZER

1. For preschoolers or early primary grade students, modify the directions as follows:

> "Boys and girls, today we are going to play a game. I am going to give you _____ minutes on this timer, and I want to see if you can [move from first activity to second activity] before the time is up. All your materials from [first activity] must be put away, and you must be ready for [second activity] when the time is up. [Hold up the stopwatch or display the timer.] Get ready to beat the buzzer! . . . Go!"

2. As students become more successful in making rapid transitions, gradually reduce the number of minutes permitted for the targeted transitions.

VARIATION 2: TRANSITIONING WITH RESPONSE COST

Write the permitted amount of time for the target transition(s) on the chalkboard and take away 5 minutes of recess that day or the next day for each 1 minute over the criterion.

VARIATION 3: ALL-DAY TRANSITIONING WITH INCENTIVES

1. Select two to five key transitions throughout the school day. Draw bar graphs on the chalkboard to represent the number of minutes required for students to complete each of these transitions and label each graph (e.g., "Getting Ready for Lunch," "Preparing for Dismissal").
2. Using data collected during the observation period, set a criterion for the total time permitted to complete all of the targeted transitions.

3. Time each targeted transition as it occurs and record the number of minutes required for completion on the appropriate graph. Near the end of the day, sum the total number of minutes spent in transitioning and announce whether the class has met the criterion. If the criterion has been met, provide an end-of-day activity reward, such as extra outdoor recess or a classroom game session. As the class becomes more successful in meeting the daily criterion, require students to meet the criterion on 4 out of 5 days in order to earn the reward.

NOTES

1. Using a stopwatch rather than a timer does not appear to reduce the effectiveness of the strategy and is more acceptable to older students.
2. In the study by LaFleur and her colleagues (1998), the authors set a criterion of 4 minutes for transitions. Because other studies have demonstrated that in-class transitions can be completed in less than 4 minutes (e.g., Campbell & Skinner, 2004; Yarbrough et al., 2004), teachers should adjust criterion times to reflect baseline data and their goals for student performance.

SOURCES

LaFleur, L., Witt, J. C., Naquin, G., Harwell, V., & Gilbertson, D. M. (1998). Use of coaching to enhance proactive classroom management by improvement of student transitioning between classroom activities. *Effective School Practices, 17,* 70–82.

Wurtele, S. K., & Drabman, R. S. (1984). "Beat the buzzer" for classroom dawdling: A one-year trial. *Behavior Therapy, 15,* 403–409.

REDUCING HALLWAY NOISE WITH SOUND-LEVEL MONITORING AND GROUP CONTINGENCIES: A SCHOOLWIDE INTERVENTION

Overview

Noise in school hallways during transitions is a perennial problem for teachers and administrators and can be accompanied by disruptive behavior fueled by peer attention. Excessive hallway noise not only interferes with ongoing instruction in classrooms not transitioning but also decreases the quality of a school's social climate. This schoolwide intervention targets transitions to and from the lunchroom with a combination of student-directed components (active teaching, peer modeling, guided practice, and group rewards) and environmental modifications (manipulating hall lights). Implemented in a rural middle school with 525 students in grades 6–8, the intervention resulted in a substantial reduction in the level and variability of noise during lunchtime transitions compared with the previous strategy of verbal reminders and detentions (Kartub, Taylor-Greene, March, & Horner, 2000). Hall monitors and teachers also observed peer social support for appropriate behavior, with students prompting their classmates to be quiet when they entered the hallway. The faculty continued the intervention into the following year, during which both new and returning students maintained low levels of hallway noise. In the original study, researchers used a sound-level meter to assess noise levels. In this adaptation, qualitative ratings of noise levels have been substituted, with the sound-level meter version included as a variation. A variation designed for implementation by individual classroom teachers is also presented.

Goal

The goal of this intervention is to reduce excessive hallway noise and encourage appropriate behavior during lunchtime transitions with a schoolwide intervention package. This intervention is designed for students who have acquired the requisite skills but need reinforcement to do so fluently.

Intervention Intensity

The intervention can be used universally in schools with appropriate adaptations for age, topic, and intensity of problem behavior.

Materials

1. Sound-level meter (optional; see Option 3 and Note 2).
2. Rating scale with indices of noise (optional; see Option 1).

Options to Monitor Progress

1. Create a noise-level rating scale with ratings ranging from 1 (very low) to 5 (very high). Using the scale, rate the perceived level of hallway noise during one or more targeted transitions for 4–7 days. If desired, graph the ratings.
2. Using a sheet of paper attached to a clipboard, record the number of verbal reminders (e.g., "Walk quietly," "Don't yell," "Don't push") delivered by teachers or hall monitors to students during one or more targeted transitions for 4–7 days.
3. Using a sound-level meter, assess peak noise levels at five 1-minute intervals during one or more targeted transitions and use the median (middle) level as a noise index. Conduct these assessments for 4–7 days.

Intervention Steps

Introduction and Training

FACULTY TRAINING

1. At a whole-faculty meeting, obtain a consensus as to appropriate hall behavior and acceptable noise levels for students during the targeted transition(s).
2. Demonstrate the sound-level meter or distribute copies of the noise-level rating scale and explain the intervention procedures, as described below.

STUDENT TRAINING

1. Adjust the school schedule temporarily to allow a 7-minute training session for each lunch period. If another transition is targeted (e.g., entering or exiting the school), have teachers conduct a training session in their classrooms close to the time of the selected transition.
2. During the training session, review appropriate hallway behavior, such as moving quickly and quietly, keeping from talking or talking very quietly, not disturbing other classrooms that are still working, and following teacher and staff instructions.
3. Ask for volunteers or select a small group of students to serve as peer models. Coach the students in demonstrating appropriate noise levels (silence or quiet talking) versus inappropriate levels of noise while walking in the hall.

4. If possible, reduce hall lighting or add a blinking light to provide a visual contrast for times when quiet is required. Teach students a motto to help them remember the rules, such as "Lights low, voices go" or "When you see the light, lips stay tight."

5. Have the student volunteers demonstrate walking through the hall and emitting appropriate and inappropriate levels of noise. Have the rest of the students observe and rate the behavior of the peer models as appropriate or inappropriate with a "thumbs up" or "thumbs down" signal.

6. Tell students that they will receive 5 minutes of extra lunchtime for every 3 days with acceptable levels of noise during lunchtime transitions.

7. Later that day, have each teacher conduct a practice lunchtime transition (or other targeted transition) and provide praise and corrective feedback as needed.

Implementation

1. Have a designated staff member evaluate noise levels using the rating scale or sound meter during the lunchtime transition or the targeted transition. Alternately, assign one teacher or hall monitor to conduct the noise ratings.

2. Announce on the intercom system at the conclusion of each lunchtime transition whether the students in that lunch period have met the noise-level criterion. If another transition is targeted, make the announcement at the end of the school day. Praise the students if they have met the criterion and encourage them to try harder the next day if they failed to do so.

3. When a lunch period group has made quiet hallway transitions for 3 consecutive days, award the extra lunchtime to the classes in that group.

4. Conduct a follow-up whole-faculty meeting 1 week after initial implementation to monitor effectiveness and make modifications as needed.

5. Gradually fade the visual signal as students become successful in making quiet, disruption-free transitions.

Variation: Individual Classroom Version

1. To implement the intervention with a single classroom group, flip the classroom lights on and off to signal the beginning of the lunchroom transition and carry the rating scale during the transition period to record noise levels.

2. If desired, create a bar graph on the chalkboard to record the occasions on which students earn the extra lunchtime reward. Provide a group activity reward, such as a popcorn or ice cream party after lunch, when the class has earned the reward for a specified number of days.

NOTES

1. The extra lunchtime reinforcer is designed to provide the same reward that supports excessive noise in the hallway, that is, peer attention.

2. Sound-level monitors beginning at about $60.00 are available from a variety of sources, including *www.reliabilitycheck.com* and *www.testequipmentdept.com*.

SOURCE

Kartub, D. T., Taylor-Greene, S., March, R. E., & Horner, R. H. (2000). Reducing hallway noise: A systems approach. *Journal of Positive Behavior Interventions, 2,* 179–182.

THE GOOD BEHAVIOR GAME PLUS MERIT—PHYSICAL EDUCATION VERSION

Overview

The Good Behavior Game (GBG) is a classic intervention first developed by Barrish, Saunders, and Wolf (1969). The goal of the GBG is to reduce problem behavior through group contingencies. The core of the intervention is based on breaking a class into two groups who are competing with each other to be the most well behaved. The side with the least amount of problem behavior wins the competition.

This example of the GBG by Patrick, Ward, and Crouch (1998) is focused on a unique application in physical education class. Although physical education classes provide an ideal context for helping students to acquire important social competencies, such as the principles of fair play and good sportsmanship, they also provide opportunities for inappropriate behavior, such as verbal and physical aggression, noncompliance, and attention seeking. This variation of the *Good Behavior Game Plus Merit* is designed to reduce inappropriate behavior and encourage prosocial behavior in the context of playing games. The intervention consists of four components: (1) daily goal setting by the teacher, (2) public posting of student performance, (3) a daily special activity for teams meeting the goal, and (4) an end-of-unit activity for teams consistently meeting the goal. To encourage students to be supportive of each other, teams compete not against each other but against a daily criterion, with all teams meeting the criterion receiving access to reinforcement. First conducted in three physical education classes with fourth-, fifth-, and sixth-grade students during a volleyball unit, the strategy produced immediate reductions in inappropriate behavior and concomitant increases in appropriate social behavior.

Goal

This intervention is intended to promote appropriate social behaviors, especially those related to game playing, using public posting and a group contingency with response cost. It is designed to increase appropriate behavior and decrease disruptive behavior for a group of students who need help to fluently display appropriate behavior in the classroom.

Intervention Intensity

The intervention can be used for a variety of students with appropriate adaptations for age, topic, and intensity of problem behavior.

Materials

1. Posterboard chart listing the rules for physical education class, such as:
   a. "Follow the teacher's directions."
   b. "Line up promptly when you are called."
   c. "Use equipment safely."
   d. "Do your best to participate in every activity."
   e. "Play so that everyone can have fun."
2. Portable chalkboard or whiteboard divided into columns, one column per team, and labeled "Team 1," "Team 2," etc. (or labeled with student-selected team names).
3. Colored chalk or dry-erase markers, one color per team (optional).
4. "Points sheet," consisting of a sheet of paper attached to a clipboard divided into columns, one column per team and labeled as described above.
5. Colored tags or badges to distinguish between teams, one set per team (optional; see Variation).

Options to Monitor Progress (Select One or Both)

1. Using a sheet of paper attached to a clipboard or a *Group Event Recording Form,* tally the number of appropriate and inappropriate social behaviors and false acts that occur during a 30- to 45-minute observation or during the entire physical education period for 4–7 days.

   a. *Appropriate social behaviors* are defined as (1) physical contacts or gestures that are supportive or responses to good play (e.g., pat on the back, high five, handshake, thumbs up, raising hands in the air, or clapping hands); and (2) encouraging and supportive verbal statements (e.g., "You can do it," "Good job," "Nice try," "Way to go").

   b. *Inappropriate social behaviors* are defined as (1) physical contact that is combative in nature (e.g., pushing, hitting) or behavior that interferes with the ongoing activity (e.g., damaging equipment, using equipment inappropriately, leaving the game, or refusing to participate); (2) discouraging or offensive gestural behavior (e.g., making faces or clapping hands after a poor performance); and (3) discouraging or offensive verbal statements (e.g., ridiculing others, arguing, laughing at others' mistakes, or telling others to "shut up").

   c. *False acts* are defined as appropriate social behaviors emitted in the absence of any play for the purpose of earning points (e.g., saying, "Great job!" to a student during a break in the game and in the proximity of the teacher).

   If desired, calculate a classwide daily average number of appropriate behaviors by dividing the number of appropriate behaviors by the number of observation days and use this number to set the first daily criterion for winning (see Intervention Steps, Implementation Step 1 below).

2. Using a sheet of paper attached to a clipboard, record the number of reprimands delivered during a 30- to 45-minute observational period or during the entire physical education period. Conduct these observations for 4–7 days.

Intervention Steps

Preparation

Divide the class into teams of five to six students, depending on the current activity schedule. Be sure to divide disruptive and aggressive students among the teams. Schedule game play so that teams play against each other on a rotated schedule.

Introduction and Training

1. Explain to the students that they will be playing a game designed to help them remember to be good sports so that everyone can have more fun in physical education class.

2. Display the poster listing the rules for behavior during physical education class and review them with the students, including a discussion of the rationale for each rule.

3. Display the chalkboard or whiteboard with the team names and the clipboard. Explain that you will be awarding points to each team when its members demonstrate good sportsmanship and removing points from the team score if you observe inappropriate behavior.

4. Explain that only genuine instances of good sportsmanship can earn points. Give examples of "false acts" as defined above and explain that you will deduct points for any false acts by team members because these behaviors do not involve good sportsmanship.

5. Announce the teams and, if desired, permit students to select a team name and write it on

the points chart. Explain that the winning team(s) will receive 3 minutes of extra game play or a special activity at the end of each lesson.

6. Remind students that being a good loser is part of good sportsmanship. Explain that if any student displays inappropriate behavior in response to not achieving the daily goal, you will deduct a point from that team's total the next day.

7. Conduct a brief game to serve as a classwide practice during which you award points for appropriate behavior and provide feedback and redirection as needed.

Implementation

1. At the beginning of each class, announce the daily criterion. For example, begin with a criterion that is 10 times the class average for appropriate social behaviors prior to intervention (see Options to Monitor Progress, Option 1). Thereafter, require teams to meet or exceed the previous day's performance.

2. Record pluses for appropriate behavior and minuses for inappropriate behavior under team columns on the points sheet during game playing. Record a minus if a student commits a false act.

3. During scheduled breaks in the game, select a student from each team to record points awarded for appropriate behavior and/or deducted for inappropriate behavior on the chalkboard or whiteboard under the team name. If desired, have the teams record their points in different colored chalk or markers to discourage cheating.

4. At the end of the game period, have students total their team scores. Announce the winner(s) (teams meeting the criterion) and deliver the special activity reward. Teams not meeting the criterion do not receive the special game time and must sit quietly on the sidelines.

5. After the first day of the intervention, teams must meet or exceed the previous day's performance (or another criterion established in the event that teams earned an exceptionally large number of points on the previous day).

6. At the end of the unit, provide a special lunchtime game for the two teams (or more, if equal) in the class that met the daily criterion most frequently.

7. Rotate team membership throughout the year so that students have an opportunity to be on teams with all of their classmates.

8. Gradually fade the public posting of team points to occur only once, at the end of the game period.

Variation: Whole-Class Version

For physical education classes that primarily involve whole-class activities rather than team-based games, divide the class into two teams for use in awarding points. Have students wear colored tags or badges during the activities so that you can distinguish the members of each team and award points as described above.

NOTES

1. Contrary to the researchers' prediction, the intervention had no effect on students' volleyball skills.

2. Allowing students to select team names fosters team spirit and facilitates praising or reprimanding the teams.

SOURCES

Barrish, H. H., Saunders, M., & Wolf, M. M. (1969). Good behavior game: Effects of individual contingencies for group consequences on disruptive behavior in a classroom. *Journal of Applied Behavior Analysis, 2*(2), 119–124.

Patrick, C. A., Ward, P., & Crouch, D. W. (1998). Effects of holding students accountable for social behaviors during volleyball games in elementary physical education. *Journal of Teaching in Physical Education, 17,* 143–156.

POSITIVE BEHAVIOR SUPPORTS ON THE PLAYGROUND: A SCHOOLWIDE INTERVENTION

Overview

Although recess occurs daily or several times a week for most students at the elementary level, problems often occur because of the large numbers of students, too few or inadequately trained supervisors, and the inherent difficulty in monitoring a large, unstructured environment. Rules and routines may also vary from supervisor to supervisor, exacerbating the problem because students are unsure of expectations for behavior or consequences for misbehavior. This schoolwide intervention combines classroom instruction and playground practice in appropriate recess behavior, a time-out procedure, and rewards for classrooms displaying appropriate behavior (Lewis, Powers, Kelk, & Newcomer, 2002). Implemented in an elementary school of 450 students with a 50% turnover rate and a high percentage of pupils from impoverished backgrounds, the strategy was effective in reducing the frequency of problem behavior across all three targeted recess periods. The strategy can also be implemented with a subset of classrooms or grades that share a common playground time or on an individual classroom basis when the teacher also serves as the recess supervisor.

Goal

The goal of this intervention is to reduce inappropriate and aggressive behavior on the playground with social skills lessons, guided practice, active monitoring and supervision, and group incentives. This intervention is designed for students who need help to fluently display appropriate behavior on the playground.

Intervention Intensity

The intervention can be used for a variety of students with appropriate adaptations for age, topic, and intensity of problem behavior.

Materials

1. Lessons in playground social skills and games, one lesson per targeted game, activity, and behavior (see Preparation section below).
2. "Good Behavior Coupons," consisting of wrist-size brightly colored elastic loops, 20 to 30 loops per playground supervisor per recess period (depending on the number of students on the playground at one time).
3. Cans or jars, one per classroom.
4. Posterboard chart listing playground rules, one per classroom (optional).
5. Small edible rewards, such as wrapped candy (optional).

Options to Monitor Progress

1. Calculate the number of office disciplinary referrals for recess rule infractions for the previous month.
2. Using a sheet of paper attached to a clipboard, tally the number of disruptive behaviors demonstrated by students during one or more recess periods for 4–7 days. *Disruptive behaviors* are defined as aggressive actions against others (e.g., hitting, pushing, kicking); misuse of equipment (e.g., jumping off the top of climbing equipment, throwing kickballs at others); and disrupting ongoing games (e.g., grabbing the ball, jumping into line, making verbal or physical threats, arguing). If desired, calculate the rate of disruptive behaviors per minute by dividing the total number of disruptive behaviors per period by the number of minutes in the period. For example, if 45 disruptive behaviors occur during a 20-minute recess period, the rate of disruptive behaviors is 2.25 per minute.
3. Using a sheet of paper attached to a clipboard, record the number of time-outs served by students during one or more recess periods for 4–7 days. A *time-out* is defined as 5 minutes of standing in a designated time-out location on the playground for a recess rule infraction.

Intervention Steps

Preparation

1. In collaboration with physical education teachers and the schoolwide behavior support team or intervention assistance team, develop a set of brief lessons addressing rules and routines for playground games, such as basketball, four square, kickball, jump rope, and soccer. Lessons should include (a) a definition of the rule, (b) examples of the rule, and (c) modeling of the expected behavior. Lessons should be no more than 20–30 minutes each.
2. Develop three additional lessons addressing the following playground social skills: (a) how to join a game, (b) how to win and lose a game, and (c) how to line up to reenter the building when the bell rings.

Introduction and Training

FACULTY TRAINING

1. Conduct a whole-faculty meeting, including paraprofessionals involved in playground supervision, in which the staff develops schoolwide rules for playground behavior, such as:
   a. "Keep your hands and feet to yourself."
   b. "Use equipment appropriately."
   c. "Follow the rules for joining games (wait in line or ask)."
   d. "Use appropriate language."
   e. "Show respect for everyone."
   f. "Do what the recess supervisors tell you to do, the first time they tell you."
2. Designate a location on the playground to serve as a time-out area, such as a corner or portion of the playground fence marked with tape or chalk.
3. After the social skills lessons have been developed, conduct another whole-faculty meeting to review the lessons and demonstrate sample lessons.

PLAYGROUND SUPERVISOR TRAINING

1. Conduct two training sessions with all faculty and staff playground supervisors to include one 15-minute meeting and one 10-minute follow-up meeting. Training should focus on

three supervisor behaviors: (a) moving around the playground area; (b) scanning the entire playground area; and (c) interacting with students to have brief, pleasant conversations, deliver rule reminders, and award Good Behavior Coupons, as described below.

2. If needed, include training in organizing and supervising common playground games.

STUDENT TRAINING

1. Teachers introduce the intervention to the students by reviewing the playground behavior rules, using a chart listing the rules, if desired. Teachers model the appropriate behaviors for each rule and have students practice them in the classroom.

2. After the classroom rule review, teachers conduct a playground practice in which they again model appropriate behavior for each rule and have students participate in role plays of appropriate behavior for various games and playground situations.

3. Over the next 2 weeks, teachers deliver the series of social skills lessons in their classrooms. In addition, teachers review and practice the skills with their students at least twice on the playground during nonrecess periods.

Implementation

1. For the first few weeks, teachers conduct a brief review of playground rules before each recess period.

2. During recess periods, playground supervisors organize and supervise group games and activities as needed and review the specific rules briefly with students beforehand.

3. During the recess period, playground supervisors provide specific praise and distribute Good Behavior Coupons to students who are following the behavior rules and exhibiting the targeted social skills—for example: "Trent, you're doing a great job taking turns in kickball. You've earned a coupon!" Students can place the loops on their wrists to avoid losing them.

4. If a student breaks a rule, the supervisor delivers a warning–for example: "Ayesha, one of our playground rules is, *Show respect for everyone.* That means no pushing. This is a warning."

5. If the student breaks the rule again, the supervisor sends the student to the designated time-out area for a 5-minute time-out.

6. If a student exhibits aggression or unsafe behavior, no warning is given, and the student serves a 5-minute time-out before being allowed to resume playing.

7. When the students return to the classroom, they place their loops in the can on the teacher's desk. As students place the loops in the can, the teacher asks them why they earned the loop and delivers additional praise. Teachers keep a running total of the number of coupons earned on the chalkboard.

8. When the can is full (or the class has earned a specified number of coupons), the class receives a reward, such as a pizza party, an extra recess period, or a video or DVD with popcorn. If desired, teachers may offer a choice of rewards and let the class vote.

NOTES

1. Encourage supervisors to organize cooperative games rather than having students organize their own games or play randomly. Participation in cooperative games at recess is associated with decreases in aggressive behaviors compared with participation in competitive games (Heck, Collins, & Peterson, 2001).

2. Regardless of whether implementation is on a schoolwide, grade/classroom cluster, or indi-

vidual classroom basis, training all personnel serving as supervisors for a specific playground period and providing performance feedback during initial implementation is essential to the success of this intervention.

3. Although the original study did not provide for a backup time-out procedure, field testing indicates that some kind of negative consequence is important in maintaining appropriate playground behavior, even in the context of a token reinforcement program.

4. The strategy can be easily adapted to target appropriate lunchroom behavior if student seating is based on classroom assignment.

SOURCE

Heck, A., Collins, J., & Peterson, L. (2001). Decreasing children's risk taking on the playground. *Journal of Applied Behavior Analysis, 34,* 349–352.

Lewis, T. J., Powers, L. J., Kelk, M. J., & Newcomer, L. L. (2002). Reducing problem behaviors on the playground: An investigation of the application of schoolwide positive behavior supports. *Psychology in the Schools, 39,* 181–190.

IMPROVING BUS-RIDING BEHAVIOR WITH A SCHOOLWIDE INTERVENTION

Overview

Disruptive behavior on the school bus can create a dangerous situation by distracting the driver or leading to student-to-student aggression. Student conflicts that arise during bus rides can also spill over into the classroom, fueling additional disruption and interfering with instruction. This schoolwide intervention targets bus-riding behavior with training for students in bus rules, training for drivers in rewarding appropriate student behavior, and a weekly lottery available to students receiving good behavior cards from bus drivers. Originally implemented in an elementary school serving 624 students in kindergarten through grade 5 in a high-poverty urban setting, the strategy was highly successful in decreasing disruptive bus behaviors, as measured by bus discipline referrals and bus suspensions (Putnam, Handler, Ramirez-Platt, & Luiselli, 2003). Moreover, these positive outcomes were maintained during a follow-up period, with school personnel assuming full responsibility for implementation without ongoing consultation.

Goal

This intervention is intended to improve bus-riding behavior with explicit instruction for students, training for bus drivers, and a schoolwide lottery for students displaying good bus-riding behavior. It is designed to decrease disruptive behavior for students who need help to fluently display appropriate behavior on buses.

Intervention Intensity

The intervention can be used universally with appropriate adaptations for age, topic, and intensity of problem behavior.

Materials

"Safe Bus Riding Chart," consisting of a posterboard displaying schoolwide bus rules and consequences, one per classroom, such as:

Rules for Safe Bus Riding

1. Stay in your seat while the bus is moving.
2. Keep hands and objects inside at all times.
3. Do not eat on the bus.
4. Follow the driver's instructions at all times.
5. Be respectful of the driver, other students, and school property.
6. Use appropriate language.

Negative Consequences

1. Failure to follow any of the bus rules = office referral.
2. Endangering the safety of other students or staff, interfering with the operation of the bus, or accumulating _____ (predetermined number of) office disciplinary referrals = bus suspension.

Positive Consequences

1. "Catch-Them-Being-Good" cards, consisting of 3″ × 5″ index cards or slips of paper with space for recording instances of positive student bus behavior.
2. Rewards, such as fast food certificates, CDs, school supplies, candy bars, and so forth.

Options to Monitor Progress

1. Calculate the number of office disciplinary referrals for inappropriate bus behavior for the previous month or marking period.
2. Calculate the number of bus suspensions for the previous month or marking period.

Intervention Steps

Introduction and Training

FACULTY TRAINING

1. During a whole-faculty meeting that includes bus driver representatives, develop a list of safe bus-riding behaviors and consequences for failure to follow the rules. Use the list of rules and consequences to prepare one Safe Bus Riding Chart for each classroom.
2. Review procedures for rewarding positive student behavior with the "Catch-Them-Being-Good" (CTBG) cards and the weekly lottery system as described below.
3. Discuss the types of prizes that students would value and teachers would find acceptable and arrange to obtain or purchase them (see Note 1). Also, develop a list of activity privileges, such as extra gym time, an extended lunch period, early lunchtime release, lunch off campus, 15 minutes of basketball practice with the coach, and so on.

STUDENT TRAINING

1. Teachers use the charts to discuss the safe bus-riding behaviors with students during the homeroom or advisory period. Teachers select students to demonstrate appropriate behavior during role plays and provide praise and corrective feedback as needed.
2. Teachers display the CTBG cards and explain the schoolwide lottery system as follows:
   a. Bus drivers will be observing students to "catch them being good," that is, to catch students who are following the bus-riding rules.

b. Each day, drivers will award CTBG cards to students who are following the safe bus-riding rules.

c. Students receiving cards will turn them in to their teachers, who will enter them into a weekly school lottery.

d. Each Friday, the principal (or some designated staff member) will draw five cards (or some appropriate number, based on the total student population) and announce the winners over the intercom. In addition, the school bus with the fewest office referrals and suspensions will be recognized as "bus of the week."

BUS DRIVER TRAINING

1. Conduct a training session with all drivers during which you review how to monitor students during transportation and how to provide positive reinforcement by "catching students being good."
2. Display the CTBG cards and explain that drivers are to give the cards to students who are displaying appropriate or exemplary behavior.
3. Collaborate with the drivers to determine a specific number of CTBG cards to be awarded each day (such as one or two cards per bus), depending on the number of buses and students.

Implementation

1. Initiate the intervention on a Monday, if possible. Have teachers hand in the CTBG cards for their homerooms or advisories to the designated staff member on Friday.
2. Conduct the drawing and announce the winners, including the bus of the week.
3. Designate a staff member with bus supervisory responsibility to provide brief updates to bus drivers on student bus behavior and review any problems or concerns. Have the staff member distribute additional CTBG cards during these updates.
4. Provide opportunities for bus representatives to attend faculty meetings periodically to enhance collaboration between school staff and drivers in supporting safe bus behavior.

Variation: Bus of the Year

Maintain a record of which buses earn the bus of the week award and acknowledge a bus of the year during the final week of school. If desired, post a notice or plaque in the school main hall identifying the number and driver of the winning bus.

NOTES

1. In the original study, local merchants donated the majority of tangible prizes, and school-sponsored activity privileges were scheduled during school hours.
2. The researchers noted that surveillance cameras, which had been installed in all of the buses to monitor student activity, were permanently removed during the intervention period.

SOURCE

Putnam, R. F., Handler, M. W., Ramirez-Platt, C. M., & Luiselli, J. K. (2003). Improving student bus-riding behavior through a whole-school intervention. *Journal of Applied Behavior Analysis, 36,* 583–590.

IMPROVING BEHAVIOR IN TRANSITION SETTINGS WITH ACTIVE SUPERVISION AND PRECORRECTION: A SCHOOLWIDE INTERVENTION

Overview

Room-to-room transitions, such as leaving the classroom to go to the lunchroom or entering or leaving the school building, are frequent settings for problem behavior. Moreover, if problem behavior occurs during these transitions, it is likely to spill over into the next setting, reducing valuable instructional time. This schoolwide intervention uses two antecedent-based strategies—active supervision and precorrection—to target three critical transitions: (1) entering the school building at the beginning of the day, (2) leaving the classroom and entering the cafeteria, and (3) leaving the classroom and exiting from the school building at the end of the day (Colvin, Sugai, Good, & Young-Yon, 1997). In this intervention, supervisors remind students of the expected behaviors before they enter transition areas (precorrection) and move around, visually scan the areas, and interact with students during transitions (active supervision). This intervention requires a single training session for teachers and supervisors, along with a few reminders at staff meetings, and no supplementary materials or resources. In the original study, conducted in an elementary school with 475 students in kindergarten through grade 5, the intervention resulted in a dramatic reduction in the frequency of problem behavior in all three transition settings. This intervention is highly consistent with schoolwide positive behavior supports and interventions (PBIS) and is a way to introduce PBIS to schools without adopting the whole model.

Goal

The purpose of this intervention is to reduce problem behavior during major transitions by means of a schoolwide effective transition program. This intervention is most appropriate for students who need help to fluently display appropriate hallway/transition behavior.

Intervention Intensity

The intervention can be used universally in schools with appropriate adaptations for age, topic, and intensity of problem behavior.

Materials

Posterboard charts, one per classroom, one in the hall near the main door, and one near the cafeteria (optional), labeled "How to Make a Great Transition," and listing the transition rules, such as:

1. "Walk when you enter and leave the school and in the hall."
2. "Keep your hands and feet to yourself."
3. "Use a quiet voice."

Options to Monitor Progress

1. Calculate the number of office disciplinary referrals (ODRs) for inappropriate behavior during beginning-of-day, lunchtime, and end-of-day transitions for the entire student body or for students in selected grades for the previous month or the school year to date.
2. Using a *Group Event Recording Form,* record the number of problem behaviors displayed by students during one or more targeted transitions for 4–7 days. *Problem behav-*

iors are defined as running, pushing, shouting, hitting, yelling, entering prohibited areas (e.g., gardens and shrubbery areas), and failing to follow supervisor instructions.

3. Measure hallway disruptive behavior and respectful behavior with DBR. These data can be collected in each transition in which the intervention is active and graphed for analysis. Data on targeted individual children can be collected when the goal of the intervention is a single student. Conduct observations for 3–5 days prior to the start of the intervention to establish a baseline and then in each instructional period in which the intervention is used.

Intervention Steps

Introduction and Training

FACULTY TRAINING

1. During a whole-faculty meeting, have staff members identify major problem behaviors exhibited by students in the targeted transitions and the appropriate behaviors students are expected to display in those settings. Include all teaching staff and transition area supervisors in the meeting. If supervisors are not available during faculty meeting times, conduct another training meeting.

2. Define *precorrections* as reminders of transition rules. Explain that precorrections or rule reminders help prevent disruptions from occurring by letting students know exactly what behaviors are expected in the transition settings.

3. Ask all staff to deliver three rule reminders to students just before they enter the transition areas: (a) walk, (b) keep your hands and feet to yourself, and (c) use a quiet voice.

4. Model delivery of rule reminders—for example: "OK, students, I want you to remember our three rules for leaving the classroom to go home: walk, keep your hands and feet to yourself, and use a quiet voice."

5. Define the three supervisor behaviors that constitute *active supervision* as follows:
   a. *Move around*: Vary your position physically, avoid standing in one place, and remain standing.
   b. *Look around*: Visually scan all areas, especially distant areas.
   c. *Interact with the students*: Greet students by smiling or waving; chat briefly with students about items of interest; gesture to indicate appropriate behavior; comment on good behavior; inform students when they are breaking the rules; praise students who are following the rules; avoid long conversations with individual students.

6. If a student breaks a rule, state the rule that was broken and send the student back to the starting point to begin the transition again.

7. Conduct role plays to show examples and nonexamples of each active supervision component.
   a. *Example*: To demonstrate moving around, have two supervisors move constantly around an area of the room.
   b. *Nonexample*: Have one supervisor sit down and chat with another supervisor.

STUDENT TRAINING (OPTIONAL)

Have teachers use the transition rules charts to discuss appropriate transition behaviors with students during the homeroom or advisory period. Have teachers select students to role-play appropriate transition behaviors and provide praise and corrective feedback as needed.

Implementation

1. At the beginning of the school day, have supervisors direct students to line up at the front doors of the building and remind them of the three transition rules before they are allowed to enter the school. Continue this strategy for the entering-school transition.

2. On a daily basis for the first week and on an intermittent basis for the next 2 weeks, have the principal make the following announcement over the public address system prior to the beginning of the first lunch period: "Excuse me, teachers. I would like you to remind students of the three rules for going to the cafeteria." Near the end of the school day, have the principal make the following announcement: "Excuse me, teachers. I would like you to remind students of the three rules for leaving the school." Have the principal continue to make the announcements on the schedule described above.

3. Have classroom teachers remind students of the three rules just prior to exiting the classroom to go to the cafeteria and just prior to leaving for the day, after the principal's requests.

4. Have teachers continue these reminders even when the principal does not make the announcements.

5. Provide brief (3–5 minute) reminders about active supervision behaviors and precorrections at staff meetings twice a month or more, if needed.

NOTES

1. In the original study, the only direct student training consisted of brief rule reminders by teachers prior to going to the cafeteria and prior to leaving at the end of the day. The optional rule review in classrooms is presented here as an additional precorrection procedure.

2. The researchers determined that activeness of supervisor behaviors was more important than the number of supervisors in reducing inappropriate behavior during implementation. The number of supervisory staff, which varied from one to six, was unrelated to improvement in student transition behaviors.

SOURCE

Colvin, G., Sugai, G., Good, R. H., III, & Young-Yon, L. (1997). Using active supervision and precorrection to improve transition behaviors in an elementary school. *School Psychology Quarterly, 12,* 344–363.

CHAPTER SIX

Interventions to Improve Outcomes for Preschool Children

Recent federal and state initiatives have led to an exponential increase in programs designed to promote children's school readiness, with states spending nearly $1 billion on preschool education (Barnett, Hustedt, Hawkinson, & Robin, 2006) and as many as 43 states currently offering prekindergarten programs (Early et al., 2005). In 2005, 57% of preprimary children ages 3–5 were attending center-based early childhood care and education programs, including 43% of 3-year-olds (National Center for Education Statistics, 2007). IDEA 2004 permits school districts to use up to 15% of their federal funds to develop and implement early intervention services, including training for teachers in scientifically based academic instruction and behavioral interventions for children who require additional academic and behavioral support but have not been identified as needing special education (20 U.S.C. § 1413[f][1][2]). The growth in early childhood educational programs has also been fueled by concerns related to the rising numbers of young children entering day care and preschool settings with multiple risk factors and the recognition that early intervention is most effective in changing children's developmental trajectories (Good Start, Grow Smart Interagency Workgroup, 2005; VanDerHeyden & Snyder, 2006). Currently, 43% of children under the age of 6 live in low-income households, and 22% live in households below the poverty line (less than $20,000 for a family of four in 2006), and the proportion is rising. Between 2000 and 2005, the percentage of children in low-income families increased by 11%, and the percentage living below the poverty level increased by 16% (National Center for Children in Poverty, 2006). In addition, the preschool population includes a growing number of children who have been identified with special needs even before school entry (Early et al., 2005). With the move toward full inclusion in the field of early childhood special education, preschool teachers are encountering more children with developmental delays, challenging behaviors, and other significant learning and behavioral needs. In a large national sample of kindergarten teachers, respondents reported that 16% of the children in their classrooms had serious difficulty making the transition to kindergarten. In addition, up to 46% of teachers reported that half or more of their students had specific learning-related problems, such as difficulty following directions, academic skill deficiencies, and difficulty working independently (Rimm-Kaufman, Pianta, & Cox, 2000).

The importance of high-quality early educational programs, especially for children from at-risk backgrounds, is documented by a large body of evidence attesting to the powerful and long-term effects of classroom practices in early childhood environments on children's cognitive and social competence (e.g., Burchinal & Cryer, 2003, Burchinal, Peisner-Feinberg, Pianta, & Howes, 2002; Magnuson, Ruhm, & Waldfogel, 2007). Unfortunately, not all young children are being served by high-quality programs. According to two major studies of state-funded prekindergarten programs by the National Center for Early Development and Learning (NCEDL; Early et al., 2005), many preschoolers, especially those from low-income families, are enrolled in low-quality programs. Although the prekindergarten classrooms in the NCEDL studies typically had a warm, inviting atmosphere, instructional quality was highly variable and often poor. On average, children were engaged in meaningful learning or play activities less than half of the time (42%), with nearly a quarter (22%) of the time occupied by transitions and routines, such as waiting between activities, standing in line, and toileting. Adult–child interactions were infrequent, and when they did occur, they were not at a level that would support the development of higher order language or thinking skills. Especially alarming was the finding that the poorest quality classrooms were also those serving the highest proportion of at-risk children, including children living in poverty, children from minority backgrounds, and children in families with lower levels of parental education—precisely the children who were most in need of high-quality educational experiences (LoCasale-Crouch et al., 2007; Pianta et al., 2005).

Language competence plays a critical role in children's socialization, interactions with others, and ability to access educational experiences. Unfortunately, a substantial number of children are entering kindergarten with low levels of the oral language skills that are critical to future academic success (Lonigan & Whitehurst, 1998; Whitehurst et al., 1999). Hart and Risley (1992, 1995) documented the profound differences in the quantity and quality of language experiences for young children from different socioeconomic statuses (SES). Hart and Risley estimate that by age 3, the spoken vocabularies of children of families living in urban poverty are only half the size of the vocabularies of children in middle-class families (500 vs. 1,100 unique words). Moreover, children in higher SES families hear many more questions (up to 45% of parent utterances) and more repetitions and elaborations of their own topics (up to 5% of parent utterances) compared with children in lower SES families, where a significant portion of parent utterances (up to 20%) consist of prohibitions.

There are also tremendous disparities in children's picture book reading experiences and access to resources for literacy development across SES levels. There are striking differences between low-income and middle-income families in terms of the quality and quantity of print resources in the home. In a study of four neighborhoods in the same city (two low-income and two middle-income neighborhoods), Neuman and Celano (2001) found inequities at all levels of analysis, including signage, public places for reading, and the number and quality of books in childcare centers, school libraries, and public libraries.

Children with poorly developed oral language skills are at high risk for negative outcomes in academic and social domains. Although the exact nature of the relationship is unclear, behavior problems are common among children with language difficulties (Qi & Kaiser, 2003; Tomblin, Zhang, Buckwalter, & Catts, 2000), and preschoolers with language impairments are at significantly greater risk for behavior disorders (Beitchman et al., 2001; Benasich, Curtiss, & Tallal, 1993; McCabe, 2005). Language difficulties place children at risk for academic problems and learning disabilities, even after controlling for intelligence (Catts, Fey, Zhang, & Tomblin, 1999; Larrivee & Catts, 1999; Lewis, Freebairn, & Taylor, 2000), as well as for a range of social, emotional, and behavioral problems, especially in the case of boys (Brownlie et al., 2004). Despite the importance of oral language skills in helping children make a successful transition to kindergarten, many at-risk preschoolers are not receiving the kinds of language-enhancing experiences they need. Most classrooms offered a poor instructional climate for promoting language and literacy development, with children spending only 7% of their time in teacher-directed language development activities (Early et al., 2005). The interventions described here can support can support those development activities.

PROMOTING INDEPENDENT IN-CLASS TRANSITIONS
WITH SELF-ASSESSMENT AND CONTINGENT PRAISE

Overview

Transitions from one activity to another occupy a significant proportion of the time in preschool classrooms—as much as 30% of the day. This innovative self-management intervention package is designed not only to minimize the amount of time spent on in-class transitions but also to increase students' ability to perform transitions independently, a critical skill for all preschoolers, especially those in early childhood special education environments who will be moving into inclusive classrooms. Unlike many self-management procedures that involve time-consuming one-to-one matches between teacher and student, this intervention requires only one structured teacher–student interaction—a choral-response-based self-assessment— so that learning time is minimally disrupted. In a study with three classrooms of preschoolers with developmental delays, the duration of targeted transitions significantly decreased across all three classrooms (Connell, Carta, Lutz, Randall, & Wilson, 1993). Moreover, all three randomly selected target students demonstrated significant increases in appropriate transition behaviors and accompanying decreases in competing behavior and teacher prompting, with behavioral gains maintained after the strategy was withdrawn. The intervention has also been demonstrated to increase on-task behavior and compliance in free play and small-group instructional settings (Miller, Strain, Boyd, Jarzynka, & McFetridge, 1993). A variation with an individual matching procedure for children who do not respond to the classwide self-assessment is also presented.

Goal

This intervention is intended to reduce the duration of in-class transition times and promote independent transition skills with explicit instruction, self-assessment, and contingent praise. The focus is to help students learn the process and implement it independently, which makes it a fluency or generalization intervention.

Intervention Intensity

Using self-assessment with praise for transitions works with classrooms of students, but it could be modified for small groups. It is probably not intense enough to be an intervention for individual students.

Materials

1. "Good Behavior Chart," consisting of a posterboard chart with photographs of students in the classroom modeling transition behaviors for a targeted transition, such as:
   a. Starting to clean up (represented by a picture of a student with a hand on the light switch).

    b. Putting materials where they belong (represented by a picture of a student placing a toy on a shelf).

    c. Coming to the carpet for circle time (represented by a picture of a student sitting on a rug).

    d. Listening quietly (represented by a child sitting with mouth closed).

2. Sheet of paper with a list of student names down the left-hand side and a column on the right-hand side for recording a plus or minus (optional).

3. Hand stamps or stickers (optional).

4. Additional charts depicting appropriate behaviors for other transitions or activities, such as free play (with photographs of students using materials appropriately in solitary or small-group play) or small-group instruction (with photographs of students listening attentively and participating actively; optional).

Options to Monitor Progress

1. Using a sheet of paper attached to a clipboard, record the number of teacher prompts and reprimands delivered during one or more selected in-class transitions for a group of target students or the entire class for 4–7 days.

2. Using a list of student names attached to a clipboard, record a plus (+) for appropriate transition behavior or a minus (–) for inappropriate transition behavior for each student during the targeted in-class transition(s), as defined below:

    a. *Appropriate transition behavior* is defined as behavior related to the transition, such as picking up toys, moving to the next activity, getting in line, sitting or standing quietly, and waiting for directions.

    b. *Inappropriate transition behavior* is defined as any behavior that interferes with the transition, such as continuing to play after the cue to clean up or move to another activity has been given, interfering with others cleaning up or transitioning, wandering around the classroom, and failing to comply with a teacher directive.

Calculate the classwide percentage of students with appropriate transition behavior by dividing the number of pluses by the number of students in the class. Conduct these observations during the targeted transition(s) for 4–7 days.

3. Using a stopwatch or watch with a second hand and a sheet of paper attached to a clipboard, record in minutes and seconds the interval from the time that you give the cue for one or more selected in-class transitions to the time that all students have completed the transition. Conduct these observations during one or more in-class transitions for 4–7 days.

Intervention Steps

Introduction and Training

1. Select a problematic in-class transition, such as the transition between cleaning up from free play and getting ready for the opening circle time.

2. Tell the children that they are going to learn to how to make transitions quickly and quietly so that everyone can learn more and have more fun at school.

3. Using the Good Behavior Chart, teach appropriate behaviors for the targeted transition as follows:

    a. Select a student to flash the lights and say, "It's time to clean up and come to the carpet for circle time."

    b. Using *Say, Show, Check: Teaching Classroom Procedures*, discuss appropriate and inappropriate examples of transitioning—for example: "Does starting to clean up when told mean that when we flash the light and say, 'It's time to clean up,' we can keep on playing? No. We stop playing and put our things away, don't we?"

   c. First model and then lead students in practicing the appropriate transition behaviors, such as putting toys away, moving to the circle, and sitting on the carpet and waiting quietly for directions.

4. Teach the self-assessment procedure by having students raise their hands or give a thumbs-up/thumbs-down to indicate whether they think they have displayed appropriate transition behaviors.

5. Guide a student through a demonstration of each of the targeted transition skills and the self-assessment procedure. Then conduct a classwide practice and provide feedback on behavior and self-assessment accuracy as needed.

Implementation

1. Prior to the targeted transition, use the Good Behavior Chart to review the rules for transitioning and remind students of the behaviors they will be self-monitoring.

2. During the transition, provide praise for appropriate behavior. If desired, use the list of student names to record a plus (+) for appropriate transition behaviors and a minus (−) for inappropriate transition behaviors so that you can refer to it during the teacher–student matching process.

3. After the students have completed the transition and are ready for the next activity, display the Good Behavior Chart and ask the children to indicate by raising their hands above their heads or giving a thumbs-up if they thought they performed the targeted behaviors during the previous transition. If you have used the checklist to record transition behavior, refer to it at this time to evaluate the accuracy of student self-ratings.

4. During teacher–student matching, provide praise for appropriate behavior and accurate self-assessment. For example: "Heather, you have your hand in the air. I agree, you did a great job of putting your toys away and coming quickly to circle time." If desired, also give a sticker or hand stamp to each child who made a successful transition and self-assessed accurately.

5. Provide corrective feedback for inappropriate transition behavior and/or inaccurate self-assessment. For example: "Devon, you have a thumbs-up, but I don't agree. I saw you playing with toys after you were told to come to the carpet. Let's work harder on that next time."

6. After students are making the targeted transition successfully, fade the self-assessment procedure to twice a week and then to once a week.

7. If desired, use the procedure to target another transition or another setting, such as free play or small-group instruction, using a chart with pictured rules appropriate for that context.

Variation: Individual Self-Assessment Format

1. If a student fails to respond to the group self-assessment procedure, conduct a brief (30-second) individual assessment after the targeted transition by asking the student if he or she displayed the appropriate behaviors. For example: "Tanya, did you start to clean up when the lights flashed? Show me a thumbs-up or thumbs-down."

2. Provide praise for successful performance and accurate self-assessment or corrective feedback as needed. Then continue with the group self-assessment procedure as described above.

NOTES

1. Although hand raising makes it easier to see each child's self-rating, teachers in the Miller et al. study (1993) observed that children enjoyed making the thumbs-up/thumbs-down gesture and used it to rate their own performances and those of their peers in nontargeted situations. If you use the thumbs-up/thumbs-down format, teach students to raise their hands above their heads when making the signal and keep them up until you have matched their self-rating.
2. For classrooms served by a teacher and an instructional assistant, divide the class into two groups and conduct the self-assessment procedure simultaneously in two sections of the room.

SOURCES

Connell, M. C., Carta, J. J., Lutz, S., Randall, C., & Wilson, J. (1993). Building independence during in-class transitions: Teaching in-class transition skills to preschoolers with developmental delays through choral-response-based self-assessment and contingent praise. *Education and Treatment of Children, 16,* 160–174.

Miller, L. J., Strain, P. S., Boyd, K., Jarzynka, J., & McFetridge, M. (1993). The effects of classwide self-assessment on preschool children's engagement in transition, free play, and small-group instruction. *Early Education and Development, 4,* 162–181.

SIX STEPS TO EFFECTIVE SMALL-GROUP INSTRUCTION

Overview

Learning how to listen and respond appropriately during small-group instruction is a keystone competency for preschool children. Unfortunately, teachers often rely on lengthy verbal directions and fail to include modeling and guided practice when attempting to teach children a learning activity. Moreover, although teachers may be trained in the use of isolated behavior management strategies, such as praise and redirection, they may not have learned how to apply the strategies throughout an instructional activity to maintain attention and ensure task completion. As a result, students have low levels of engagement during learning activities and require constant prompting to pay attention and sustain effort on tasks. This six-step sequence of managerial and instructional strategies, which includes demanding eye contact, step-by-step directions, modeling, praise, corrective feedback, and redirectives, structures teachers' interactions to help children successfully complete an activity. Time limits are given for each step in the sequence to ensure a brisk instructional pace. In the original study, with four teachers in two day care classrooms and a total of 14 target students with behavior problems, the direct-instruction sequence was associated not only with significant increases in attention to instruction and time on task for all of the target children but also with more positive teacher–student interactions (Hiralall & Martens, 1998).

Goal

This intervention is designed to promote active student engagement and task completion during small-group activities with a structured instructional and managerial sequence.

Intervention Intensity

The six steps for small-group instruction intervention are designed to work with any small group, including small classrooms, small-group instruction within a classroom, or a small-group intervention. It probably has little utility as an intervention for individual students.

Materials

None.

Options to Monitor Progress

1. Using a *Group Interval Recording Form* with a 10-second interval, glance at each student participating in a small-group instructional setting and record the student's behavior at that instant as on task (+) or off task (–), as defined below.
   a. *On-task behavior* is defined as having one's head and eyes oriented toward the teacher while the teacher is talking, actively working on the assigned task, or having head and eyes oriented toward the task.
   b. *Off-task behavior* is defined as looking around the room, being out of seat, playing with objects unrelated to the task, arguing with classmates, or any other behavior not related to the activity.

   Conduct these observations for 15–20 minutes during a small-group instructional period for a group of target students or the entire class for 4–7 days. If you observe the entire class, rotate observations from group to group.
2. Using a sheet of paper attached to a clipboard, record the number of redirectives and reprimands delivered to a group of target students after instructions for a small-group activity have been given. *Redirectives* and *reprimands* are defined as statements used to modify or correct a child's behavior once instructions have been given. Conduct these observations for 15–20 minutes during a small-group instructional period for 4–7 days.

Intervention Steps

Step 1: Demand Eye Contact and Attention (1 Minute).

Begin the activity by asking for eye contact and attention. Include a "teaser" statement to heighten children's interest in the activity:

> "Look at me and listen. Our activity today is making a holiday card. We are going to learn to make something very special that you can take home to show your family!"

Step 2: Model the Steps in the Task (4–5 Minutes).

1. Be sure the children are looking at you while you deliver clear oral directions for the activity in a step-by-step format. After you give each direction, model the relevant step:

   > "The first thing you have to do is to cut out the card. Now, look at me and watch how I do it. [Demonstrate cutting out the card.]"
2. If any of the children in the group are not paying attention, demand eye contact:

   > "Ross, look at me and listen."
3. Repeat this format for every step in the task.

Step 3: Provide Individual Praise to Appropriately Behaving Students (2 Minutes).

Deliver specific individual praise to each child who is behaving appropriately. Praise statements should include the child's name and the appropriate action he or she is performing:

> "Anne, you are doing a wonderful job gluing sparkles on your card."

Step 4: Provide Individual Corrective Feedback as Needed (3 Minutes).

1. If any children are off task, demand eye contact and redirect that child individually with a single directive statement:

    "Stefan, look at me, stop playing with the glitter, and please cut out your card."

2. If necessary, provide additional modeling or instruction:

    "Stefan, watch me while I cut out the card."

3. Once the off-task child begins to engage in appropriate behavior, deliver praise as described above.

Step 5: Provide Additional Individual Praise to On-Task Students (2 Minutes).

Deliver individual praise to each child who is on task, as described in Step 3.

Step 6: Redirect Off-Task Students as Needed (3 Minutes).

As needed, provide individual redirection to any child who is off task, as indicated in Step 4. Provide praise once the child begins to engage in on-task behavior.

NOTES

Praise statements should be delivered briskly in order to maintain an appropriate instructional pace and prevent other students from becoming off task. As students' task engagement increases, praise statements can be shortened.

SOURCE

Hiralall, A. S., & Martens, B. K. (1998). Teaching classroom management skills to preschool staff: The effects of scripted instructional sequences on teacher and student behavior. *School Psychology Quarterly, 13,* 94–115.

ENHANCING EMERGENT LITERACY SKILLS WITH DIALOGIC READING

Overview

In the typical picture book reading in preschool classrooms, the teacher reads while the children listen. In dialogic reading, the teacher assumes the role of an active listener, asking specific types of questions and encouraging children's responses to the book so that the children become the storytellers. As the dialogue progresses, the teacher encourages more linguistically complex responses by expanding children's utterances and posing more challenging questions. The acronyms CROWD and PEER are used to help teachers remember the interactional reading strategies. Dialogic reading has a significant positive impact on children's oral language abilities and emergent literacy skills across a wide variety of preschool populations, including English language learners, children with language delays, and educationally at-risk children and is superior to regular parent- or teacher-led book reading (Hargrave & Sénéchal, 2000). For best results, dialogic reading should be conducted for about 10 minutes per day, three to five times a week, with groups of no more than eight children. Because some studies indicate that the effects on language development are nearly doubled when children participate in dialogic reading at home and at school (Reese, Sparks, & Leyva, 2010), a parent-led version is included as a variation.

Goal

This intervention is intended to improve oral language and emergent literacy skills through a structured picture book reading procedure that involves children as active participants in the reading process. This is a fluency intervention because it does not directly teach skills but increases positive experience with the material.

Intervention Intensity

Dialogic reading can be used with students as part of core instruction or to provide additional support for students who struggle. It is probably not intensive enough to be the only intervention for individual students who are experiencing significant learning difficulties, but it could certainly be part of the intervention program.

Materials

Attractive illustrated books appropriate for preschoolers, selected according to the following criteria:

1. Books should contain colorful, attractive illustrations so that the story can be told through the illustrations alone and without having to rely completely on the text.
2. Books should include vocabulary in the illustrations and text that is potentially novel to the children.
3. Books should be relatively short in order to increase reader–child interactions.
4. Books should be appropriate for the entire age range of children in the classroom.
5. Books should not consist of rhyme or word books, which tend to limit the range of questions that can be asked.
6. Books should not be specific to particular holidays (e.g., Christmas books in March).
7. Books should not have been previously shared with children in the classroom.

Options to Monitor Progress

1. Read through an unfamiliar book with a group of target students. After reading the book, return to the beginning and ask open-ended questions of each child in turn as you proceed through the book a second time (e.g., "Mary Anne, tell me about this page").
2. As each child responds, tally on a sheet of paper the number of words or the number of different nouns produced. Calculate an average verbal production score for the target group by summing individual scores and dividing by the number of children in the group.
3. Administer the Picture Naming task on the *Individual Growth and Development Indicators* (IGDIs) to a group of target students or to the entire class. If desired, calculate a group or classwide average by summing individual scores and dividing by the number of children in the group or class.
4. Create a list of 20 nouns from the first 10 books you will be using during dialogic reading sessions. Make photocopies (color, if possible) of pictures of the 20 nouns from the books. Show the 20 pictures to a group of target students or to the entire class in a one-to-one assessment setting and ask each child to label them. Record a picture-naming percent-accuracy score for each student assessed. If you test the entire class, calculate a classwide

picture-naming percent-accuracy score by summing the total number of pictures accurately named and dividing by the number of children in the class.

Intervention Steps

Preparation

1. Select a picture book, using the criteria listed above.
2. Divide the class into groups of five to eight students. If you share dialogic reading with another person (see Note 1), you can provide daily 10-minute sessions for every student in a class of 20 children (with a ratio of 1 reader to 5 children), for a total of 20 minutes of dialogic reading per school day.

Implementation

1. Have the group sit next to you so that all the children can see the book. Introduce the picture book by displaying the cover and asking the children what they think the book will be about.
2. Have children take turns responding to questions but have the entire group repeat new vocabulary words and phrases. Don't let one child dominate the session, and don't let children interrupt each other.
3. Follow correct answers by asking children to say more or by asking another question. Provide assistance in answering when needed. Convey encouragement for children's responses and your own interest and enthusiasm for the story and the reading process.
4. As you read through the book with the group, ask CROWD questions and use PEER strategies, as follows:

CROWD QUESTION TYPES

   a. *Completion prompts*: Questions that require children to provide a missing word to complete a sentence—for example: "When they went outside to play, they put on their _____."
   b. *Recall prompts*: Questions that require children to remember events in the story—for example: "Can you remember some of the games that the children played?"
   c. *Open-ended prompts*: Statements that encourage children to respond to the story in their own words—for example: "Now it's your turn to tell what's happening on this page. Let's start with Miguel. Miguel, tell us what's happening here."
   d. *Wh-prompts*: *Who*, *what*, *where*, *which*, and *why* questions—for example: "Where did the children go to play after school?"
   e. *Distancing prompts*: Questions that require children to relate the story content to their own experiences—for example: "Has anyone ever gone to a park like Lorenzo and Maria did?"

PEER STRATEGIES

   a. *Prompt*: Prompt children to label objects in the book and talk about the story—for example: "Who knows the name for this kind of animal?"
   b. *Evaluate*: Evaluate children's responses by praising correct responses and offering alternative object labels or providing answers for incorrect responses—for example:

   TEACHER: What did Sammy decide to do after school?

   CHILD: Baseball!

TEACHER: Well, Sammy might have wanted to play baseball, but remember that he ended up playing soccer with Mike.

  c. *Expand*: Expand children's verbalizations by repeating what they have said and adding information—for example:

TEACHER: What is happening in this picture?

CHILD: He wet!

TEACHER: That's right, Anna, the boy is soaking wet because he got caught in the rain.

  d. *Repeat*: Encourage children to repeat the expanded utterances—for example:

TEACHER: What kind of animal is this?

CHILD: Doggie!

TEACHER: Yes, that's a dog. That kind of dog is called a *beagle*. Let's all say "beagle!"

CHILDREN: Beagle!

5. During the course of the week, read each book twice to each group.

Variation: Parent-Led Dialogic Reading

1. To train parents in dialogic reading, plan for a 1-hour session, with 30 minutes for demonstration and discussion and 30 minutes for parents to practice the strategies, either with their own children or with other parents in role-play situations. For parent-led dialogic reading, a one-to-one reading format replaces the small-group format, but the basic approach, CROWD questions, and PEER strategies are identical.

2. After the training session, provide parents with a picture book each Monday afternoon. Ask parents to read the book to their child for a minimum of 10 minutes at least five times during the week and to return the book the following Monday. Provide another book every week during the course of the intervention.

3. Consider videotaping an adult implementing the intervention with a child for use in the parent training session. As always, be sure to obtain signed consent from the adult participant and also parental consent for the child to participate in the videotaped session and for the videotape to be used for training purposes.

NOTES

1. Dialogic reading can be delivered by trained paraprofessionals, parents or community volunteers, or secondary-level students with appropriate monitoring and supervision.

2. Practicing the techniques with a consultant or fellow teacher prior to implementation is very helpful in developing effective dialogic reading skills.

SOURCES

Hargrave, A. C., & Sénéchal, M. (2000). A book reading intervention with preschool children who have limited vocabularies: The benefits of regular reading and dialogic reading. *Early Childhood Research Quarterly, 15,* 75–90.

Reese, E., Sparks, A., & Leyva, D. (2010). A review of parent interventions for preschool children's language and emergent literacy. *Journal of Early Childhood Literacy, 10,* 97–117.

ADDITIONAL RESOURCES

Read Together, Talk Together (Pearson Early Learning, 2002), a commercially published version of dialogic reading, is available at *www.pearsonearlylearning.com*. There are two kits—one for ages 2 and 3 and one for ages 4 and 5—each of which includes 20 books, teacher–parent notes for each book, a program handbook, a teacher training video, and a parent training video.

BUILDING VOCABULARY SKILLS WITH INTERACTIVE BOOK READING

Overview

Shared picture book reading provides opportunities for enhancing early literacy and language development by introducing children to new vocabulary, print conventions and functions, and the syntactic structure of language. For many young children living in poverty, out-of-home environments are the primary place where they experience shared reading. This intervention adapts one-to-one book reading strategies validated in home settings to a whole-group classroom format to enhance the vocabulary skills of children with limited book exposure and underdeveloped literacy and language skills. Presented in a 4-day instructional sequence, the strategy has three key elements: (1) presenting target vocabulary words multiple times and in multiple contexts, (2) providing concrete representations of target words, and (3) using reading strategies that emphasize open-ended questioning and dialoguing. A unique component of this intervention is the use of center time activities linked to story content to reinforce vocabulary. In the original study, conducted in eight classrooms of 4-year-olds from low-income families in a Title I early learning center, children in the intervention classrooms scored significantly better than children in control classrooms on a standardized receptive vocabulary test and on receptive and expressive book vocabulary measures (Wasik & Bond, 2001). Interactive picture book reading has consistently been shown to increase vocabulary and print knowledge (Mol, Bus, & de Jong, 2009), even among children with delays (Pollard-Durodola et al., 2011).

Goal

This intervention is intended to promote preschoolers' vocabulary development by combining interactive book reading with multiple opportunities to hear and use target vocabulary in a meaningful context. Therefore, the intervention does not teach vocabulary but supports use and generalization.

Intervention Intensity

Interactive picture book reading can be used with students as part of core instruction or to provide additional support for students who struggle. It is probably not intensive enough to be the only intervention for individual students who are experiencing significant learning difficulties, but it could certainly be part of the intervention program.

Materials

1. Age-appropriate picture books related to common preschool themes, such as "gardening," "welcome to school," "clothing," and "the seasons," and containing similar vocabulary words, two books per theme.

2. "Story prop box," consisting of a box containing objects representing the target vocabulary words, one set of objects per theme; for example, for books related to a gardening theme, objects could include seeds; a miniature shovel, rake, and garden hose; plastic flowers; a carrot; an ear of corn; and plastic insects.

3. List of target vocabulary words selected from the books; target words should be common words that are likely to be unfamiliar to the children but are necessary for understanding the stories.

4. Picture cards depicting target vocabulary words (see Note 3).

5. One large blank book or sheets of paper on a flipchart.

6. Small blank books, one per student (optional).

7. Materials for center time activities related to the target vocabulary (see the Preparation section).

Options to Monitor Progress

1. Show each child in a target group or in the entire class one picture at a time from the picture card set and ask him or her to name the object in the picture. Using a sheet of paper attached to a clipboard, calculate a picture-naming percent-accuracy score for each child by tallying the number of correct responses and dividing by the total number of pictures presented. If desired, calculate a group or classwide median (middle) picture-naming percent-accuracy score.

2. Display the first set of story props to a group of target children or every child in the class, one at a time, and ask each child to name the objects (to measure expressive vocabulary). Alternatively, display the box with all of the objects in it, name each object, and ask the child to locate it in the box (to measure receptive vocabulary). Using a sheet of paper attached to a clipboard, record the number and percentage of objects named and/or recognized correctly by each child.

Intervention Steps

Preparation

1. Using the picture cards, make a big book of pictures of the target vocabulary words in the two theme-related books or attach the pictures to sheets of paper on a flipchart. If desired, make the same book in a smaller form, one book per child.

2. Develop one or more center time activities related to the vocabulary and concepts in the books. For example, for a garden theme, activities could include arts and crafts (e.g., painting a garden picture or making a paper plate garden), science activities (e.g., planting carrot seeds), and cooking activities (e.g., making a vegetable platter for snack time).

Implementation

1. This intervention requires reading one of the two theme-related books twice and the second book once, according to the following schedule:

   a. *Day 1*: Have the children identify the story props and read the first book using the interactive reading strategies described below. Between interactive reading sessions, place the story props in an area of the classroom where the children can play and interact with them.

   b. *Day 2*: Have children identify the story props and read the same book again. Then have children work in small groups in center activities related to the vocabulary.

c. *Day 3*: Read the second book and have children label the props.

d. *Day 4*: Have children work in small groups in center activities related to the vocabulary. Read the big book containing pictures of vocabulary words and engage the children in a discussion of the words. If you have created small versions of the big book for students, have them follow along in their books as you "read."

2. When reading the books, use the following interactive reading procedures:

BEFORE READING

1. After a child names an object, ask what he or she can do with the object. Introduce the target vocabulary by holding up a story prop and asking, "What is this?" or "What do you call this?" Provide praise for accurate naming and give the correct label if the children are unable to identify an object.

2. Then ask open-ended questions about the object, such as "What can I do with this _____?" or "Tell me what you know about this _____." Provide praise or corrective feedback as needed. Continue the naming and discussion until all the story props have been presented.

3. Introduce the first of the two books as follows:

"Today we are going to read a book about [theme of book]. The name of the book is [title] by [author(s)]. In this book, we will find many of the words for the objects we have just seen. Let's look at the cover of the book to see what we think the book is about. What does it look like this book is about? [Select three or four children to make predictions about the book.]"

DURING READING

1. During reading, ask open-ended questions that promote discussion and involve the children in the story—for example:

"Tell me more about what is happening on this page."

"What do you think will happen next?"

"Why do you think [character] did that?"

"How did [character] feel about . . . ?"

2. As children respond, refer to the objects in the prop box as appropriate.

AFTER READING

1. After reading, review the story by asking reflection questions—for example:

"Let's think about the story we just read. How did the boy decide what he would plant?"

"What part of the book did you like the best?"

"Tell me why you think the boy was so sure the carrot would grow."

2. Make connections between the vocabulary and concepts in the story and the center activity—for example:

"The boy watched his plants grow just like we have been watching our plants grow. Our plants are growing because we watered them and put them in the sun. Now you will have a chance during center time to plant some more seeds."

NOTES

1. In the original study, classroom size ranged from 12 to 15 children.

2. To maximize children's ability to attend to the book reading sessions, use *Say, Show, Check: Teaching Classroom Procedures* to demonstrate appropriate listening and participation skills (e.g., raise your hand to speak, listen to others when they are talking) prior to implementation. Conduct periodic reviews at the beginning of sessions as needed.
3. Picture libraries are available from many educational publishers and can often be found in preschool and elementary school media centers.

SOURCES

Mol, S. E., Bus, A. G., & de Jong, M. T. (2009). Interactive book reading in early education: A tool to stimulate print knowledge as well as oral language. *Review of Educational Research, 79*, 979–1007.

Pollard-Durodola, S. D., Gonzalez, J. E., Simmons, D. C., Kwok, O., Taylor, A. B., Davis, M. J., et al. (2011). The effects of an intensive shared book-reading intervention for preschool children at risk for vocabulary delay. *Exceptional Children, 77*, 161–183.

Wasik, B. A., & Bond, M. A. (2001). Beyond the pages of a book: Interactive book reading and language development in preschool classrooms. *Journal of Educational Psychology, 93*, 243–250.

IMPROVING COMPLIANCE WITH PRECISION REQUESTS AND A TIME-OUT PROCEDURE

Overview

Learning to comply with adult directives is an important social competency for preschoolers and is essential to children's success in school. This simple intervention package promotes compliance with a combination of precision requests and a time-out procedure in the form of a happy-face chart. Happy-face cards, signaling the availability of reinforcement, are posted beside children's names as long as they comply with teacher requests and are removed for failure to comply, with a brief in-class time-out as a backup contingency. In the original study, conducted in a self-contained preschool special education classroom, the combination of precision requests and the time-out procedure dramatically improved compliance for a target student and was more effective than the time-out alone (Yeager & McLaughlin, 1995). Although all seven students in the classroom received reinforcement each time they complied with a teacher request, reward delivery is delayed in this adaptation until the end of an activity to increase usability and enhance maintenance of appropriate behaviors by lengthening the schedule of reinforcement. Subsequent research has consistently found that time-outs with signals for availability of reinforcement reduced inappropriate behavior (Kostewicz, 2010). A variation for implementation with individual target children is also included.

Goal

This intervention is intended to improve compliance and reduce disruptive behavior by means of precision requests and a time-out procedure. It does not teach skills but reinforces the student for using them, which is a fluency intervention.

Intervention Intensity

The intervention improves compliant behavior for students experiencing behavioral difficulties as either a targeted intervention or as part of an intensive intervention package for students experiencing severe behavior problems.

Materials

1. "Classroom Rules Chart," consisting of a posterboard listing the classroom rules, with a picture representing each rule, such as:
   a. "Do what you are told, the first time you are told."
   b. "Do your best on all your work."
   c. "Be kind and helpful to others."
   d. "Keep your hands and feet to yourself."
2. "Happy Face Chart," consisting of a posterboard chart listing student names, with a happy-face card or sticker attached to the chart beside each name.
3. Small tangible reinforcers, such as stickers and hand stamps, or small edible rewards, such as pretzels, marshmallows, jelly beans, and wrapped candy.

Options to Monitor Progress

1. Using a sheet of paper attached to a clipboard, tally the number of reprimands delivered to a target group of students or the entire class during a selected activity period for 4–7 days.
2. Using a sheet of paper attached to a clipboard, record the number of teacher requests delivered during a selected activity period to a group of target students or the entire class. For each request, record a plus (+) if the student complies within 5 seconds and a minus (–) if the student fails to comply within 5 seconds. Calculate group or classwide compliance rates by dividing the number of teacher requests by the number of times students complied with teacher directives within 5 seconds and multiply the result by 100. For example, if there are 30 teacher requests, and students comply within 5 seconds on 15 of the 30 occasions, the compliance rate is 50%. Conduct these observations for 20–30 minutes during the selected activity period for 4–7 days.

Intervention Steps

Introduction and Training

1. Display the Happy Face Chart and explain to the students that they will be able to earn a reward at the end of an activity (e.g., free play, small-group instruction, and circle time) as long as they follow your directions. The happy-face cards will be posted beside their names as long as they follow your directions to let them know that they are able to earn rewards. Post the chart at the front of the classroom where it is visible and accessible to all students.
2. Move a chair to the periphery of classroom activity but not so far away that you cannot easily monitor a student seated in it. Explain to the class that this is the time-out chair. If a student does not follow directions, the student will need to sit in the time-out chair and observe the other children following directions. Be sure that the chair is turned toward, not away from, classroom activities.

Implementation

1. At the beginning of the day, review the classroom rules, using specific examples and modeling appropriate compliance behaviors for each rule. Also point out the Happy Face Chart and encourage the students to follow directions so that they can keep their happy-face cards and be eligible for rewards.

2. If a student does not comply with a request, tell the student to take down his or her happy face from the chart or take it down yourself.

3. Then move close to the student, obtain eye contact, if possible, and make the request again, beginning with the prompt "Please." Make the request in the form of a statement and use a firm but quiet tone:

   "Juan, please put the toy away and get in line."

4. If the student complies with the request within 5 seconds, provide praise, referring to the act of compliance or the specific requested behavior.

   "Very good, Juan, you followed directions about getting in line quickly! Thank you for getting in line and helping us get to recess on time."

   Restore the happy-face card to the chart or let the student put it back.

5. If the student does not comply within 5 seconds, repeat the request using the prompt "I need you to . . . ":

   "Juan, you need to put the toy away and get in line right now."

   Use the same distance, eye contact, and tone of voice as in the first request.

6. If the student complies with this request within 5 seconds, praise the student and restore the happy-face card, as in Step 4. If the student still does not comply within 5–10 seconds of the second request, send him or her to the time-out chair for 4 minutes.

7. Repeat this process until the student complies, but do not interact with the student during the time-out period.

8. At the end of the activity, deliver rewards to students whose happy-face cards are displayed on the Happy Face Chart and praise them for following your directions. Tell students who did not earn a reward that they will have a chance to follow directions and earn a reward during the next activity or intervention period.

9. Restore happy-face cards for all students to the chart at the beginning of each activity or intervention period. Gradually lengthen the intervention period, and replace tangible rewards with social rewards (e.g., lead the class in applauding their own good behavior, giving a class cheer or thumbs up).

Variation: Individualized Time-Out

1. For implementation with one student or a small group of students, give each target student a small adhesive happy-face sticker to wear at the beginning of each activity. Remove stickers for noncompliance and restore them for compliance, as described above for the happy-face cards.

2. At the end of the activity period, deliver a small reward to target students still wearing their stickers. As student compliance improves, lengthen the interval between reward delivery (e.g., successful completion of two activities) and substitute social rewards.

SOURCES

Kostewicz, D. E. (2010). A review of timeout ribbons. *Behavior Analyst Today, 11*, 95–104.

Yeager, C., & McLaughlin, T. F. (1995). The use of a time-out ribbon and precision requests to improve child compliance in the classroom: A case study. *Child and Family Behavior Therapy, 17*, 1–9.

BUTTON, BUTTON, WHO'S GOT THE BUTTON?: REDUCING DISRUPTIVE BEHAVIOR WITH RESPONSE COST

Overview

Inattentiveness, impulsivity, or excessive activity in young children can limit their own opportunities to learn and those of their classmates in preschool settings. This intervention is designed to increase on-task behavior and reduce off-task and disruptive behavior in preschoolers with a developmentally appropriate version of response cost. Buttons posted beside each child's name on a chart are removed for each rule infraction, with rewards available if children retain a specific number of buttons at the end of each activity. Response cost has consistently been shown to improve behavioral difficulties of preschool children with attention difficulties (Rajwan, Chacko, & Moeller, 2012). More specifically, when implemented in three general education preschool classrooms with four preschoolers with ADHD, the response-cost intervention was associated with marked reductions in disruptive behavior among the targeted students to a level commensurate with that of their peers, as measured by behavioral observations and teacher ratings at the end of treatment and at a 2- or 3-week follow-up (McGoey & DuPaul, 2000). Teachers and students alike judged the intervention to be highly acceptable, and teachers continued to use the strategy after the investigation was withdrawn. Two variations are provided, one substituting an interdependent group contingency for individual rewards and one targeting transitions.

Goal

This intervention is designed to increase on-task behavior and reduce inattentive and disruptive behavior in preschoolers with a response-cost procedure. It does not teach skills but reinforces children for using them, which is a fluency intervention.

Intervention Intensity

Response cost can be used for students experiencing behavioral difficulties as either a targeted intervention or as part of an intensive intervention package for students experiencing severe behavior problems.

Materials

1. "Happy Face Chart," consisting of a posterboard chart with space or slots for posting student name cards; write each student's name on the chart or cards; the chart should be large enough to display five small Velcro buttons and one large Velcro button beside each student's name for each activity or intervention period during the day.
2. Five small Velcro buttons and three large Velcro buttons per student per activity or intervention period.
3. Circles of green construction paper and tape, 10 small circles and 1 large circle per activity or intervention period (optional; see Variation).
4. "Surprise Box," consisting of a cardboard box containing small rewards, such as wrapped candy, colored pencils, action figures, small toys, stickers, and so forth.
5. "Classroom Rules Chart," consisting of a posterboard chart listing the classroom rules, with a drawing or photograph of a student to illustrate each rule, such as:
   a. "Stay in the activity area."
   b. "Keep your hands and feet to yourself."

   c. "Listen quietly when the teacher is talking."
   d. "Finish your work."
   e. "Raise your hand to talk during circle and meeting time."

Options to Monitor Progress

1. Using a *Group Event Recording Form,* record the number of inappropriate social behaviors during an activity period. *Inappropriate social behaviors* are defined as engaging in negative verbal or physical interactions with adults and/or peers, off-task behavior (looking away from the activity or the teacher for at least 3 seconds), disobeying classroom rules, and displaying tantrums (yelling, kicking, and/or sulking after interacting with an adult or peer). Conduct these observations for a group of target students or the entire class for 20–30 minutes during a selected activity period for 4–7 days. If you are implementing the variation, use these data to help determine the classwide criterion for reinforcement.
2. Using a sheet of paper attached to a clipboard, record the number of time-outs served by the entire class or a group of target students during a selected activity or the morning or afternoon session for 4–7 days. A *time-out* is defined as 3 minutes of sitting in a time-out chair or in the time-out area as a consequence for disruptive behavior.

Intervention Steps

Introduction and Training

1. Post the Happy Face Chart at the front of the classroom. Explain to the students that they will have a chance to see how well they are behaving in school every day. They will also have a chance to pick a prize from the Surprise Box if they remember to follow the rules for good behavior.
2. Using the Classroom Rules Chart, review behavior expectations for the class. Help the students provide examples and nonexamples of the expected behaviors. Also model appropriate behavior in response to the removal of a button for a rule infraction.
3. Point out the Velcro buttons on the Happy Face Chart to the students and explain that the buttons will help them follow the classroom rules so that everyone can have fun at school. Tell them that they will lose a small button if they break a rule. If they have three small buttons left at the end of the activity, they will earn a large button. Everyone with three big buttons at the end of the school day will be able to draw a prize from the Surprise Box.

Implementation

1. If a student breaks one of the rules, remove one of the small buttons from the chart next to the child's name, and state the reason for the removal—for example: "Jason, you lost a button for not listening to my directions."
2. At the end of the activity, review the chart with the class to determine which students have enough buttons (three) to retain the large button on the chart. Remove the large button for any students with fewer than three buttons left and encourage them to try harder during the next activity.
3. At the end of the day, allow students who have retained three large buttons on the chart to draw a prize from the Surprise Box. Encourage those who did not meet the criterion to try harder the next day.

Variation: Interdependent Group Contingency Response Cost

1. At the beginning of each activity period, tape 10 small green ("GO") circles (or some other number based on the observational data) and three large circles on the wall where all students can see them.

2. Inform the class of the criterion for reinforcement (the number of circles that must remain at the end of the activity period), and remove one small circle for each rule infraction.

3. If the specified number of circles remains at the end of the activity, praise the class and indicate that they have retained their "GO" button (a large green circle). If the class has not met the criterion, remove the large circle and encourage them to do better during the next activity.

4. Continue this procedure for each activity, and leave the large circles posted on the wall when students meet the criterion. Deliver a reward to each student if three large circles remain at the end of the day.

NOTES

1. Establishing clear, specific rules for instructional activities and reviewing them with students at the beginning of each school day and/or prior to each activity are essential to the success of this intervention.

2. In the original study, an individual token reinforcement system in which students earned buttons for following the rules was also effective in reducing disruptive behavior. Teachers indicated that it was difficult to observe and reward positive behaviors on a consistent basis, however, and preferred the response-cost procedure.

SOURCES

McGoey, K. E., & DuPaul, G. J. (2000). Token reinforcement and response cost procedures: Reducing the disruptive behavior of preschool children with attention-deficit/hyperactivity disorder. *School Psychology Quarterly, 15,* 330–343.

Rajwan, E., Chacko, A., & Moeller, M. (2012). Nonpharmacological interventions for preschool ADHD: State of the evidence and implications for practice. *Professional Psychology: Research and Practice, 43,* 520–526.

RED LIGHT/GREEN LIGHT

Overview

For young children, the ability to adjust to classroom behavior standards and expectations, such as following teacher directives, relating positively to peers, attending to instruction, and managing negative emotions, is essential to future school success. This adaptation of the *Good Behavior Game* provides continuous visual cues and immediate performance feedback in the context of a group-oriented contingency to encourage appropriate academic and social behavior. Providing visual signals for behavior is especially helpful for young children, who often have difficulty attending to oral directions. Moreover, the ongoing visual feedback encourages children to monitor and regulate their own behavior. Field testing indicated that the strategy was easy to implement and was effective in increasing on-task behavior and academic productivity and reducing off-task and disruptive behavior in prekindergarten and early primary grade classrooms (Barrish, Saunders, & Wolf, 1969). More recent research found that visual feedback increased self-regulation among children with a deficit in this area (Tominey & McClelland, 2011). Two variations are presented, one targeting transitions and one with classwide rather than team-based contingencies for maximum usability.

Goal

This intervention is designed to reduce off-task and disruptive behavior by combining a visual feedback system for appropriate classroom behavior with team-based rewards. The intervention can teach self-regulation, which makes it an acquisition intervention.

Intervention Intensity

The intervention could serve two purposes. First, it could be used to reinforce behavior for a group of students, and, second, it could also be used as part of a more intensive intervention package for students experiencing severe behavior problems.

Materials

1. Posterboard chart with a list of classroom rules, such as:
   a. "Listen when the teacher is talking."
   b. "Stay in your seat or area unless you have permission to move."
   c. "Be kind and helpful to others."
   d. "Use inside voices during center time."
   e. "Do what the teacher tells you to do, the first time you are told."
2. "Stoplights," consisting of posterboard or flannel cutouts in the shape of a stoplight, with three vertical circles to which paper or flannel circles can be affixed and labeled with team names or numbers, one stoplight per team (one stoplight for Variation 2).
3. Red, yellow, and green flannel or paper circles with tape, three sets per team (one set for Variation 2).
4. "Team badges," consisting of colored adhesive tags, color-coded by team, one badge per student.
5. Stickers, hand stamps, "good day" certificates, or "victory tags" consisting of circles of brightly colored construction paper with or without "winner" or gold star stickers and hung around the neck with yarn.

Options to Monitor Progress

1. Using a *Group Interval Recording Form* and beginning at the left side of the room, glance at each student every 10 seconds and record that student's behavior at that instant as on task, off task, or disruptive, as defined below. When you have rated all the students, begin again at the left side of the room.
   a. *On-task behavior* is defined as working on the task at hand, looking at the teacher during instruction, and any other behavior relevant to the lesson or activity.
   b. *Off-task behavior* is defined as sitting without having appropriate materials at hand, playing with nonlesson materials, failing to look at the teacher during instruction, or failing to begin an activity or task after directions have been given.
   c. *Disruptive behavior* is defined as calling out, being out of one's seat without permission, verbal or physical aggression, failing to comply with teacher directives, and

any other behavior interfering with instruction or the on-task behavior of another student.

Conduct these observations for 20–30 minutes during a selected instructional period for 4–7 days.

2. Using a *Group Event Recording Form,* tally the number of disruptive behaviors during one or more instructional periods for the entire class or a group of target students for 3–5 days. *Disruptive behaviors* are defined as verbal or physical aggression, noncompliance, or any other behaviors that interfere with instruction or the on-task behavior of other students.

3. Using a list of student names attached to a clipboard, tally the number of times you issue a directive and a student fails to comply within 5 seconds of the directive during a selected activity or instructional period. Conduct these observations for 20–30 minutes for a group of target students or the entire class for 4–7 days.

Intervention Steps

Introduction and Training

1. Select a time for implementation, such as center time or an instructional period when students are especially unproductive and disruptive.

2. Divide the class into two or more teams. If the students are seated at tables, use tables as teams. Be sure to distribute the most disruptive students and male and female students among teams. Help each team select a name, if desired, and have each student wear a team badge so that you can easily identify team membership as students move from one activity to another.

3. Explain to the students that they will be playing a game during that period to help everyone get the most out of the activity or lesson.

4. Using *Say, Show, Check: Teaching Classroom Procedures,* display the list of classroom rules and review each rule.

5. Explain that you will be observing the teams and using the stoplights to show them how well they are following the rules during the activity, as follows:
   a. Teams following the rules receive a green light ("GO"), indicating that they should continue their good behavior.
   b. Teams that break a rule receive a yellow light ("WARNING"), indicating that they are being warned to stop the inappropriate behavior.
   c. Teams that continue to break a rule after a warning or display any aggressive behaviors receive a red light ("STOP").
   d. Teams ending the rating period on green are winners. All teams can win or lose.

6. Display the stoplights and demonstrate the use of the circles to rate student behavior. Model appropriate student responses to changing the circles from green to yellow or yellow to red.

Implementation

1. At the beginning of the intervention period, attach a green circle to each stoplight.

2. Every 20–30 minutes or at the end of each activity, rate each team's behavior by attaching a circle to the team's stoplight. Briefly state why each team is receiving that particular rating. If the rating is unchanged from the previous rating interval, state why the rating is the same.

3. If a team member displays any aggressive or highly disruptive behavior before the regular rating time, immediately change that team's rating to red. If any team member responds inappropriately (argues, sulks, etc.) when you change a rating from green to yellow, then immediately change that team's rating to red.
4. Deliver rewards to any teams ending the intervention period on green. As behavior improves, increase the length of the interval between rewards until you are delivering rewards at the end of the morning and/or afternoon session or at the end of the school day.

Variations

1. To encourage rapid, orderly transitions between activities, add a rule about transitions (e.g., "Make quick and quiet transitions") and rate teams on transition-related behaviors as well.
2. Implement the strategy as a classwide intervention and use only one stoplight. Rate behavior every 20–30 minutes (or once per activity) as described above and deliver individual rewards or a group activity-based reward, such as music time or a classroom game, if the class ends the rating period on green.

NOTES

1. Victory tags are especially valued as reinforcers by young children and make practical rewards because they can be reused.
2. In the case of a persistently noncompliant or aggressive child who does not respond to the team or group format, make an individual stoplight for the child to wear (similar to a victory tag)—in effect, making the student a team of one.

SOURCES

Barrish, H. H., Saunders, M., & Wolf, M. M. (1969). Good behavior game: Effects of individual contingencies for group consequences on disruptive behavior in a classroom. *Journal of Applied Behavior Analysis, 2*(2), 119–124.

Tominey, S. L., & McClelland, M. M. (2011). Red light, purple light: Findings from a randomized trial using circle time games to improve behavioral self-regulation in preschool. *Early Education and Development, 22*, 489–519.

ADDITIONAL PRINT RESOURCES

Barnett, D. W., Bell, S. H., & Carey, K. T. (1999). *Designing preschool interventions: A practitioner's guide.* New York: Guilford Press.

Written from an ecobehavioral perspective, this book presents a framework for designing individualized interventions for children ages 2–5 with learning or behavior difficulties. Emphasis is placed on evidence-based interventions that can be used in natural settings with individuals or small groups of children.

VanDerHeyden, A., Snyder, P., & Hojnoski, R. (Eds.). (2006). Integrating frameworks from early childhood intervention and school psychology to accelerate growth for all young children [Special series]. *School Psychology Review, 35*(4).

This special series includes articles addressing critical components of response-to-intervention (RTI) approaches with young children, including barriers to effective implementation and decision making, progress monitoring tools for quantifying child outcomes, strategies for helping children with extremely challenging behaviors, models for differentiating academic from language deficits, and multi-tiered behavioral intervention programs.

ADDITIONAL WEBSITE RESOURCES

Center for Evidence-Based Practice: Young Children with Challenging Behavior
http://challengingbehaviorfmhi.usf.edu

Funded by the U.S. Department of Education's Office of Special Education Programs, the center focuses on developing a database on evidence-based practices to address the needs of young children who are displaying, or are at risk for, problem behavior.

Get It Got It Go!
http://ggg.umn.edu

Funded by the U.S. Department of Education and part of the Center for Early Education Development at the University of Minnesota, Get It Got It Go! provides a free online management system to help practitioners learn to use the *Individual Growth and Development Indicators* (IGDIs), download the IGDI measures, and manage children's scores, including generating graphical progress reports. The site also offers links to resources for preschool teachers, including a lesson bank and fund of language and early literacy activities (*http://ggg.umn.edu/go/go_teacherideas.html*).

Get Ready to Read
http://getreadytoread.org

Launched by the National Center for Learning Disabilities in 2001, Get Ready to Read is a nationwide campaign to provide early childhood care providers and parents with an understanding of the skills and knowledge 4-year-old children need in order to be ready to learn to read in kindergarten. The site offers a 20-item research-based screening instrument assessing print knowledge, emergent writing, and linguistic awareness.

National Center for Early Development and Learning
www.ncedl.org

The National Center for Early Development and Learning (NCEDL) is an early childhood research project sponsored by the U.S. Department of Education's Institute for Educational Sciences (IES). NCEDL focuses on enhancing the cognitive, social, and emotional development of children from birth through age 8 and provides an online journal.

Recognition and Response
www.recognitionandresponse.org

Managed by the National Center for Learning Disabilities, the Recognition and Response system provides information on the use of the RTI approach with preschoolers and is designed to help parents and teachers respond to learning difficulties in young children who may be at risk for learning disabilities before they are referred for formal assessment and placement in special education. Current efforts include the development of an observational assessment called the *Recognition and Response Observation and Rating System* (RRORS) for use with other screening and progress monitoring measures.

References

Abramowitz, A. J., Eckstrand, D., O'Leary, S. G., & Dulcan, M. K. (1992). ADHD children's responses to stimulant medication and two intensities of a behavioral intervention. *Behavior Modification, 16,* 193–203.

Abramowitz, A. J., & O'Leary, S. G. (1990). Effectiveness of delayed punishment in an applied setting. *Behavior Therapy, 21,* 231–239.

Abramowitz, A. J., O'Leary, S. G., & Futtersak, M. W. (1988). The relative impact of long and short reprimands on children's off-task behavior in the classroom. *Behavior Therapy, 19,* 243–247.

Acker, M. M., & O'Leary, S. G. (1987). Effects of reprimands and praise on appropriate behavior in the classroom. *Journal of Abnormal Child Psychology, 15,* 549–557.

Adams, M. J., Foorman, B. R., Lundberg, I., & Beeler, T. (1998). *Phonemic awareness in young children: A classroom curriculum.* Baltimore: Brookes.

Aimsweb. (2010). *Curriculum-based measurement national norms.* Bloomington, MN: Pearson.

Allen, S. J., & Blackston, A. R. (2003). Training preservice teachers in collaborative problem solving: An investigation of the impact on teacher and student behavior change in real-world settings. *School Psychology Quarterly, 18,* 22–51.

Allinder, R. M., & Oats, R. G. (1997). Effects of acceptability on teachers' implementation of curriculum-based measurement and student achievement in mathematical computation. *Remedial and Special Education, 18,* 113–120.

Alvermann, D., & Earle, J. (2003). Comprehension instruction. In A. P. Sweet & C. Snow (Eds.), *Rethinking reading comprehension* (pp. 12–30). New York: Guilford Press.

American Psychological Association. (2010). *Ethical principles of psychologists and code of conduct.* Washington, DC: Author.

Ardoin, S. P., Witt, J. C., Suldo, S. M., & Connell, J. E. (2004). Examining the incremental benefits of administering a maze and three versus one curriculum-based measurement reading probes when conducting universal screening. *School Psychology Review, 33,* 218–233.

Athanasiou, M. S., Geil, M., Hazel, C. E., & Copeland, E. P. (2002). A look inside school-based consultation: A qualitative study of the beliefs and practices of school psychologists and teachers. *School Psychology Quarterly, 17,* 258–298.

Bahr, M. W., Fuchs, D., Fuchs, L. S., Fernstrom, P., & Stecker, P. M. (1993). Effectiveness of student versus teacher monitoring during prereferral intervention. *Exceptionality, 4,* 17–30.

Bahr, M. W., Walker, K., Hampton, E. M., Buddle, B. S., Freeman, T., Ruschman, N., et al. (2006). Creative problem solving for general education intervention teams: A two-year evaluation study. *Remedial and Special Education, 27,* 27–41.

Bahr, M. W., Whitten, E., Dieker, L., Kocarek, C. E., & Manson, D. (1999). A comparison of school-based intervention teams: Implications for educational and legal reform. *Exceptional Children, 66,* 67–83.

Baker, S., Gersten, R., & Graham, S. (2003). Teaching expressive writing to students with learning disabilities research-based applications and examples. *Journal of Learning Disabilities, 36,* 109–123.

Barnett, D. W., Bauer, A. M., Ehrhardt, K. E., Lentz, F. E., & Stollar, S. A. (1996). Keystone targets for change: Planning for widespread positive consequences. *School Psychology Quarterly, 11,* 95–117.

Barnett, D. W., Bell, S. H., & Carey, K. T. (2002). *Designing preschool interventions: A practitioner's guide.* New York: Guilford Press.

Barnett, D. W., Bell, S. H., Gilkey, C. M., Lentz, F.

E., Graden, J. L., Stone, C. M., et al. (1999). The promise of meaningful eligibility determination: Functional intervention-based multifactored preschool evaluation. *Journal of Special Education, 33*, 112–124.

Barnett, D. W., Collins, R., Coulter, C., Curtis, M. J., Ehrhardt, K., Glaser, A., et al. (1995). Ethnic validity and school psychology: Concepts and practices associated with cross-cultural professional competence. *Journal of School Psychology, 33*, 219–234.

Barnett, D. W., Daly, E. J., Jones, K. M., & Lentz, F. E. (2004). Response to intervention: Empirically based special service decisions from single-case designs of increasing and decreasing intensity. *Journal of Special Education, 38*, 66–79.

Barnett, W. S., Hustedt, J. T., Hawkinson, L. E., & Robin, K. B. (2007). *The state of preschool 2006: State preschool yearbook*. New Brunswick, NJ: National Institute for Early Education Research, Rutgers University.

Barrish, H. H., Saunders, M., & Wolf, M. M. (1969). Good behavior game: Effects of individual contingencies for group consequences on disruptive behavior in a classroom. *Journal of Applied Behavior Analysis, 2*, 119–124.

Barth, J. M., Dunlap, S. T., Dane, H., Lochman, J. E., & Wells, K. C. (2004). Classroom environment influences on aggression, peer relations, and academic focus. *Journal of School Psychology, 42*, 115–133.

Baumann, J. F., & Bergeron, B. S. (1993). Story map instruction using children's literature: Effects on first graders' comprehension of central narrative elements. *Journal of Reading Behavior, 25*, 407–437.

Bear, G. G. (2013). Teacher resistance to frequent rewards and praise: Lack of skill or a wise decision? *Journal of Educational and Psychological Consultation, 23*, 318–340.

Beck, M., Burns, M. K., & Lau, M. (2009). The effect of preteaching reading skills on the on-task behavior of children identified with behavioral disorders. *Behavioral Disorders, 34*(2), 91–99.

Becker, K. D., Bradshaw, C. P., Domitrovich, C., & Ialongo, N. S. (2013). Coaching teachers to improve implementation of the Good Behavior Game. *Administration and Policy in Mental Health and Mental Health Services Research, 40*, 482–493.

Begeny, J., Upright, J., Easton, J., Ehrenbock, C., & Tunstall, K. (2013). Validity estimates and functionality of materials and procedures used to monitor the implementation integrity of a reading intervention. *Journal of Applied School Psychology, 29*, 284–304.

Beitchman, J. H., Wilson, B., Johnson, C. J., Atkinson, L., Young, A., Adlaf, E., et al. (2001). Fourteen-year follow-up of speech/language-impaired and control children: Psychiatric outcome. *Journal of the American Academy of Child and Adolescent Psychiatry, 40*, 75–82.

Benasich, A. A., Curtiss, S., & Tallal, P. (1993). Language, learning, and behavioral disturbances in childhood: A longitudinal perspective. *Journal of the American Academy of Child and Adolescent Psychiatry, 32*, 585–594.

Bergan, J. R., & Kratochwill, T. R. (1990). *Behavioral consultation and therapy*. New York: Plenum Press.

Berger, J., Yiu, H. L., Nelson, D., Vaganek, M., Rosenfield, S., Gravois, T., et al. (2014). Teacher utilization of instructional consultation teams. *Journal of Educational and Psychological Consultation, 24*, 211–238.

Berkowitz, M. J., & Martens, B. K. (2001). Assessing teachers' and students' preferences for school-based reinforcers: Agreement across methods and different effort requirements. *Journal of Developmental and Physical Disabilities, 13*, 373–387.

Berninger, V. W., Vaughan, K., Abbott, R. D., Brooks, A., Abbott, S. P., Rogan, L., et al. (1998). Early intervention for spelling problems: Teaching functional spelling units of varying size with a multiple-connections framework. *Journal of Educational Psychology, 90*, 587–605.

Bhattacharya, A., & Ehri, L. C. (2004). Graphosyllabic analysis helps adolescent struggling readers read and spell words. *Journal of Learning Disabilities, 37*, 331–348.

Binder, C. (1996). Behavioral fluency: Evolution of a new paradigm. *Behavior Analyst, 19*, 163–197.

Boardman, A. G., Argüelles, M. E., Vaughn, S., Hughes, M. T., & Klingner, J. (2005). Special education teachers' views of research-based practices. *Journal of Special Education, 39*, 168–180.

Bowman-Perrott, L., Davis, H., Vannest, K., Williams, L., Greenwood, C., & Parker, R. (2013). Academic benefits of peer tutoring: A meta-analytic review of single-case research. *School Psychology Review, 42*, 39–55.

Bradley-Klug, K. L., Shapiro, E. S., Lutz, J. G., & DuPaul, G. J. (1998). Evaluation of oral reading rate as a curriculum-based measure within literature-based curriculum. *Journal of School Psychology, 36*, 183–197.

Bramlett, R. K., Murphy, J. J., Johnson, J., Wallingford, L., & Hall, L. D. (2002). Contemporary practices in school psychology: A national survey of roles and referral problems. *Psychology in the Schools, 39*, 327–335.

Brantley, D. C., & Webster, R. E. (1993). Use of an independent group contingency management system in a regular classroom setting. *Psychology in the Schools, 30*, 60–66.

Bridgeland, J. M., Dilulio, J. J., Jr., & Morison, K. B. (2006). *The silent epidemic: Perspectives of high school dropouts*. Washington, DC: Vivic Enterprises.

Briesch, A. M., Chafouleas, S. M., & Riley-Tillman,

T. C. (2010). Generalizability and dependability of behavioral assessment methods: A comparison of systematic direct observation and Direct Behavior Rating. *School Psychology Review, 39,* 408–421.

Briesch, A. M., Chafouleas, S. M., Riley-Tillman, T. C., & Contributors. (2016). *Direct Behavior Rating: Linking assessment, communication and intervention.* New York: Guilford Press.

Brown-Chidsey, R., Steege, M. W., & Mace, F. C. (2008). Best practices in evaluating the effectiveness of interventions using case study data. In A. Thomas & J. Grimes (Eds.), *Best practices in school psychology V* (pp. 2177–2191). Bethesda, MD: National Association of School Psychologists.

Brownlie, E. B., Beitchman, J. H., Escobar, M., Young, A., Atkinson, L., Johnson, C., et al. (2004). Early language impairment and young adult delinquent and aggressive behavior. *Journal of Abnormal Child Psychology, 32,* 453–467.

Brozo, W. G., Moorman, G., Meyer, C., & Stewart, T. (2013). Content area reading and disciplinary literacy: A case for the radical center. *Journal of Adolescent and Adult Literacy, 56,* 353–357.

Buck, G. H., Polloway, E. A., Smith-Thomas, A., & Cook, K. W. (2003). Prereferral intervention processes: A survey of state practices. *Exceptional Children, 69,* 349–360.

Burchinal, M. R., & Cryer, D. (2003). Diversity, child care quality and developmental outcomes. *Early Childhood Research Quarterly, 18,* 401–426.

Burchinal, M. R., Peisner-Feinberg, E., Pianta, R., & Howes, C. (2002). Development of academic skills from preschool through second grade: Family and classroom predictors of developmental trajectories. *Journal of School Psychology, 40,* 415–436.

Burks, M. (2004). Effects of classwide peer tutoring on the number of words spelled correctly by students with LD. *Intervention in School and Clinic, 39,* 301–304.

Burns, M. K. (1999). Effectiveness of special education personnel in the intervention assistance team model. *Journal of Educational Research, 92,* 354–356.

Burns, M. K. (2002). Utilizing a comprehensive system of assessment to intervention using curriculum-based assessments. *Intervention in School and Clinic, 38,* 8–13.

Burns, M. K. (2007). Reading at the instructional level with children identified as learning disabled: Potential implications for response-to-intervention. *School Psychology Quarterly, 22,* 297–313.

Burns, M. K., Appleton, J. J., & Stehouwer, J. D. (2005). Meta-analytic review of responsiveness-to-intervention research: Examining field-based and research-implemented models. *Journal of Psychoeducational Assessment, 23,* 381–394.

Burns, M. K., Codding, R. S., Boice, C. H., &

Lukito, G. (2010). Meta-analysis of acquisition and fluency math interventions with instructional and frustration level skills: Evidence for a skill-by-treatment interaction. *School Psychology Review, 39*(1), 69–83.

Burns, M. K., & Gibbons, K. (2013). *Implementing response-to-intervention in elementary and secondary schools: Procedures to assure scientific-based practices* (2nd ed.). New York: Routledge.

Burns, M. K., Hodgson, J., Parker, D. C., & Fremont, K. (2011). Comparison of the effectiveness and efficiency of text previewing and preteaching keywords as small-group reading comprehension strategies with middle school students. *Literacy Research and Instruction, 50,* 241–252.

Burns, M. K., Karich, A. C., Maki, K. E., Anderson, A., Pulles, S. M., Ittner, A., et al. (2015). Identifying classwide problems in reading with screening data. *Journal of Evidence-Based Practices for Schools, 14,* 186–204.

Burns, M. K., & Mosack, J. (2005). Criterion-referenced validity of measuring acquisition rates with curriculum-based assessment. *Journal of Psychoeducational Assessment, 25,* 216–224.

Burns, M. K., & Parker, D. C. (2014). *Curriculum-based assessment for instructional design: Using data to individualize instruction.* New York: Guilford Press.

Burns, M. K., Peters, R., & Noell, G. H. (2008). Using performance feedback to enhance implementation fidelity of the problem-solving team process. *Journal of School Psychology, 46,* 537–550.

Burns, M. K., Pulles, S. M., Helman, L., & McComas, J. J. (2016). Intervention-based assessment frameworks: An example of a tier 1 reading intervention in an urban school. In S. L. Graves & J. Blake (Eds.), *Psychoeducational assessment and intervention for ethnic minority children: Evidence-based approaches* (pp. 165–182). Washington, DC: American Psychological Association.

Burns, M. K., Riley-Tillman, T. C., & VanDerHeyden, A. M. (2012). *RTI applications: Vol. 1. Academic and behavioral interventions.* New York: Guilford Press.

Burns, M. K., Scholin, S., & Haegele, K. M. (2013). A small-group reading comprehension intervention for fourth- and fifth-grade students. *School Psychology Forum: Research into Practice, 7*(2), 40–49.

Burns, M. K., & Senesac, B. V. (2005). Comparison of dual discrepancy criteria to assess response to intervention. *Journal of School Psychology, 43,* 393–406.

Burns, M. K., & Sterling-Turner, H. (2010). Comparison of efficiency measures for academic interventions based on acquisition and maintenance of the skill. *Psychology in the Schools, 47,* 126–134.

Burns, M. K., & Symington, T. (2002). A meta-analysis of prereferral intervention teams: Student and systemic outcomes. *Journal of School Psychology,* *40,* 437–447.

Burns, M. K., Tucker, J. A., Frame, J., Foley, S., & Hauser, A. (2000). Interscorer, alternateform, internal consistency, and test–retest reliability of Gickling's model of curriculumbased assessment for reading. *Journal of Psychoeducational Assessment, 18,* 353–360.

Burns, M. K., VanDerHeyden, A. M., & Jiban, C. (2006). Assessing the instructional level for mathematics: A comparison of methods. *School Psychology Review, 35,* 401–418.

Burns, M. K., & Wagner, D. (2008). Determining an effective intervention within a brief experimental analysis for reading: A meta-analytic review. *School Psychology Review, 37,* 126–136.

Burns, M. K., Wiley, H. I., & Viglietta, E. (2008). Best practices in implementing effective problem-solving teams. In A. Thomas & J. Grimes (Eds.), *Best practices in school psychology V* (pp. 1633–1644). Bethesda, MD: National Association of School Psychologists.

Burns, M. K., & Ysseldyke, J. E. (2009). Reported prevalence of evidence-based instructional practices in special education. *Journal of Special Education, 43,* 3–11.

Burns, M. K., Zaslofsky, A. F., Kanive, R., & Parker, D. C. (2012). Meta-analysis of incremental rehearsal using phi coefficients to compare single-case and group designs. *Journal of Behavioral Education, 21,* 185–202.

Busch, T. W., & Espin, C. A. (2003). Using curriculum-based measurement to prevent failure and assess learning in the content areas. *Assessment for Effective Intervention, 28*(3–4), 49–58.

Callahan, K., Rademacher, J. A., & Hildreth, B. L. (1998). The effect of parent participation in strategies to improve the homework performance of students who are at risk. *Remedial and Special Education, 19,* 131–141.

Cameron, J., & Pierce, W. D. (1994). Reinforcement, reward, and intrinsic motivation: A meta-analysis. *Review of Educational Research, 64,* 363–423.

Cameron, J., Pierce, W. D., Banko, K. M., & Gear, A. (2005). Achievement-based rewards and intrinsic motivation: A test of cognitive mediators. *Journal of Educational Psychology, 97,* 641–655.

Campbell, S., & Skinner, C. H. (2004). Combining explicit timing with an interdependent group contingency program to decrease transition times: An investigation of the Timely Transitions Game. *Journal of Applied School Psychology, 20,* 11–27.

Cantrell, S. C., Almasi, J. F., Carter, J. C., Rintamaa, M., & Madden, A. (2010). The impact of a strategy-based intervention on the comprehension and strategy use of struggling adolescent readers. *Journal of Educational Psychology, 102,* 257–280.

Carr, J. E., Severtson, J. M., & Lepper, T. L. (2009). Noncontingent reinforcement is an empirically supported treatment for problem behavior exhib-

ited by individuals with developmental disabilities. *Research in Developmental Disabilities, 30,* 44–57.

Cashwell, T. H., Skinner, C. H., & Smith, E. S. (2001). Increasing second-grade students' reports of peers' prosocial behaviors via direct instruction, group reinforcement, and progress feedback: A replication and extension. *Education and Treatment of Children, 24,* 161–175.

Cassel, J., & Reid, R. (1996). Use of a self-regulated strategy intervention to improve word problem-solving skills of students with mild disabilities. *Journal of Behavioral Education, 6,* 153–172.

Catts, H. W., Fey, M. E., Zhang, X., & Tomblin, J. B. (1999). Language basis of reading and reading disabilities: Evidence from a longitudinal investigation. *Scientific Studies of Reading, 3,* 331–361.

Chafouleas, S. M., Briesch, A. M., Neugebauer, S. R., & Riley-Tillman, T. C. (2011). *Usage Rating Profile—Intervention, Revised.* Storrs: University of Connecticut.

Chafouleas, S. M., Briesch, A. M., Riley-Tillman, T. C., Christ, T. J., & Kilgus, S. G. (2010). An investigation of the generalizability and dependability of direct behavior ratings (DBRs) to measure engagement and disruptive behavior of middle school students. *Journal of School Psychology, 48,* 219–246.

Chafouleas, S. M., Christ, T., Riley-Tillman, T. C., Briesch, A. M., & Chanese, J. (2007). Generalizability and dependability of direct behavior ratings to measure social behavior of preschoolers. *School Psychology Review, 36,* 63–79.

Chafouleas, S. M., Hagermoser Sanetti, L. M., Jaffery, R., & Fallon, L. M. (2012). An evaluation of a classwide intervention package involving self-management and a group contingency on classroom behavior of middle school students. *Journal of Behavioral Education, 21,* 34–57.

Chafouleas, S. M., Jaffery, R., Riley-Tillman, T. C., Christ, T. J., & Sen, R. (2013). The impact of target, wording, and duration on rating accuracy for direct behavior rating. *Assessment for Effective Intervention, 39,* 39–53.

Chafouleas, S. M., Kilgus, S. P., Riley-Tillman, T. C., Jaffery, R., & Harrison, S. (2012). Preliminary evaluation of various training components on accuracy of direct behavior ratings. *Journal of School Psychology, 50,* 317–334.

Chafouleas, S. M., Martens, B. K., Dobson, R. L., Weinstein, K. S., & Gardner, K. B. (2004). Fluent reading as the improvement of stimulus control: Additive effects of performance-based interventions to repeated reading on students' reading and error rates. *Journal of Behavioral Education, 13,* 67–81.

Chafouleas, S. M., Riley-Tillman, R. W., Christ, T. J., & Sugai, G. (2009). DBR Standard Form. Retrieved from *www.directbehaviorratings.org.*

Chafouleas, S. M., Riley-Tillman, T. C., & Sassu, K.

A. (2006). Acceptability and reported use of daily behavior report cards among teachers. *Journal of Positive Behavior Interventions, 8,* 174–182.

Chafouleas, S. M., Riley-Tillman, T. C., & Sugai, G. (2007). *School-based behavior assessment and monitoring for informing instruction and intervention.* New York: Guilford Press.

Chard, D. J., Clarke, B., Baker, S., Otterstedt, J., Braun, D., & Katz, R. (2005). Using measures of number sense to screen for difficulties in mathematics: Preliminary findings. *Assessment for Effective Intervention, 30,* 3–14.

Christ, T. J., Riley-Tillman, T. C., & Chafouleas, S. M. (2009). Foundation for the development and use of direct behavior rating (DBR) to assess and evaluate student behavior. *Assessment for Effective Intervention, 34,* 201–213.

Christ, T. J., Riley-Tillman, T. C., Chafouleas, S., & Jaffery, R. (2011). Direct Behavior Rating: An evaluation of alternate definitions to assess classroom behaviors. *School Psychology Review, 40,* 181–199.

Christie, C. A., & Schuster, J. W. (2003). The effects of using response cards on student participation, academic achievement, and on-task behavior during whole-class, math instruction. *Journal of Behavioral Education, 12,* 147–165.

Clark, K., & Graves, M. (2005). Scaffolding students' comprehension of text. *The Reading Teacher, 58,* 570–580.

Clarke, B., & Shinn, M. R. (2004). A preliminary investigation into the identification and development of early mathematics curriculum-based measurement. *School Psychology Review, 33,* 234–248.

Coalition for Psychology in Schools and Education. (2006, August). *Report on the Teacher Needs Survey.* Washington, DC: American Psychological Association, Center for Psychology in Schools and Education.

Codding, R. S., Archer, J., & Connell, J. (2010). A systematic replication and extension of using incremental rehearsal to improve multiplication skills: An investigation of generalization. *Journal of Behavioral Education, 19,* 93–105.

Cohen, J. (1988). *Statistical power analysis for the social sciences.* Hillsdale, NJ: Erlbaum.

Collins, S., Higbee, T. S., Salzberg, C. L., & Carr, J. (2009). The effects of video modeling on staff implementation of a problem-solving intervention with adults with developmental disabilities. *Journal of Applied Behavior Analysis, 42,* 849–854.

Colvin, G., Sugai, G., Good, R. H., III, & Young-Yon, L. (1997). Using active supervision and precorrection to improve transition behaviors in an elementary school. *School Psychology Quarterly, 12,* 344–363.

Conley, C. M., Derby, K. M., Roberts-Gwinn, M., Weber, K. P., & McLaughlin, T. F. (2004). An analysis of initial acquisition and maintenance of sight words following picture matching and copy, cover, and compare teaching methods. *Journal of Applied Behavior Analysis, 37,* 339–350.

Connell, M. C., Carta, J. J., Lutz, S., Randall, C., & Wilson, J. (1993). Building independence during in-class transitions: Teaching in-class transition skills to preschoolers with developmental delays through choral-response-based self-assessment and contingent praise. *Education and Treatment of Children, 16,* 160–174.

Conoley, J. C., & Conoley, C. W. (1992). *School consultation: Practice and training.* New York: Pearson College Division.

Cooper, H., Valentine, J. C., & Charlton, K. (2000). The methodology of meta-analysis. In R. Gersten, E. P. Schiller, & S. R. Vaughn (Eds.), *Contemporary special education research: Syntheses of the knowledge base on critical instructional issues* (pp. 263–280). New York: Routledge.

Cooper, J. O., Heron, T. E., & Heward, W. L. (2007). *Applied behavior analysis* (2nd ed.). Columbus, OH: Prentice Hall.

Coulter, W. A. (1988). Curriculum-based assessment: What's in a name? *Communiqué, 18*(3), 13.

Cowan, R. J., & Sheridan, S. M. (2003). Investigating the acceptability of behavioral interventions in applied conjoint behavioral consultation: Moving from analog conditions to naturalistic settings. *School Psychology Quarterly, 18,* 1–21.

Dalton, T., Martella, R. C., & Marchand-Martella, N. E. (1999). The effects of a self-management program in reducing off-task behavior. *Journal of Behavioral Education, 9,* 157–176.

Daly, E. J., III, Andersen, M., Gortmaker, V., & Turner, A. (2006). Using experimental analysis to identify reading fluency interventions: Connecting the dots. *Behavior Analyst Today, 7,* 133–150.

Daly, E. J., III, Martens, B. K., Dool, E. J., & Hintze, J. M. (1998). Using brief functional analysis to select interventions for oral reading. *Journal of Behavioral Education, 8,* 203–218.

Daly, E. J., III, Martens, B. K., Hamler, K. R., Dool, E. J., & Eckert, T. L. (1999). A brief experimental analysis for identifying instructional components needed to improve oral reading fluency. *Journal of Applied Behavior Analysis, 32,* 83–94.

Daly, E. J., III, Persampieri, M., McCurdy, M., & Gortmaker, V. (2005). Generating reading interventions through experimental analysis of academic skills: Demonstration and empirical evaluation. *School Psychology Review, 34,* 395–414.

Danoff, B., Harris, K. R., & Graham, S. (1993). Incorporating strategy instruction within the writing process in the regular classroom: Effects on the writing of students with and without learning disabilities. *Journal of Reading Behavior, 25,* 295–322.

Darch, C., Kim, S., Johnson, S., & James, H. (2000). The strategic spelling skills of students with learning disabilities: The results of two studies. *Journal of Instructional Psychology, 27,* 15–26.

Darney, D., Reinke, W. M., Herman, K. C., Stormont, M., & Ialongo, N. S. (2013). Children with co-occurring academic and behavior problems in first grade: Distal outcomes in twelfth grade. *Journal of School Psychology, 51,* 117–128.

Darveaux, D. X. (1984). The Good Behavior Game Plus Merit: Controlling disruptive behavior and improving student motivation. *School Psychology Review, 13,* 510–514.

Davies, S., & Witte, R. (2000). Self-management and peer-monitoring within a group contingency to decrease uncontrolled verbalizations of children with attention-deficit/hyperactivity disorder. *Psychology in the Schools, 37,* 135–147.

De La Paz, S. (1999). Self-regulated strategy instruction in regular education settings: Improving outcomes for students with and without learning disabilities. *Learning Disabilities Research and Practice, 14,* 92–106.

De La Paz, S., & Graham, S. (1997). Strategy instruction in planning: Effects on the writing performance and behavior of students with learning difficulties. *Exceptional Children, 63,* 167–181.

De La Paz, S., Owen, B., Harris, K. R., & Graham, S. (2000). Riding Elvis' motorcycle: Using self-regulated strategy development to PLAN and WRITE for a state writing exam. *Learning Disabilities Research and Practice, 15,* 101–109.

Deno, S. L. (1985). Curriculum-based measurement: The emerging alternative. *Exceptional Children, 52,* 219–232.

Deno, S. L. (1986). Formative evaluation of individual student programs: A new role for school psychologists. *School Psychology Review, 15,* 358–374.

Deno, S. L., Fuchs, L. S., Marston, D., & Shin, J. (2001). Using curriculum-based measurements to establish growth standards for students with learning disabilities. *School Psychology Review, 30,* 507–524.

Deno, S. L., & Mirkin, P. K. (1977). *Data-based program modification: A manual.* Reston, VA: Council for Exceptional Children.

DiGennaro-Reed, F. D., Codding, R., Catania, C. N., & Maguire, H. (2010). Effects of video modeling on treatment integrity of behavioral interventions. *Journal of Applied Behavior Analysis, 43,* 291–295.

Diliberto, J. A., Beattie, J. R., Flowers, C. P., & Algozzine, R. F. (2008). Effects of teaching syllable skills instruction on reading achievement in struggling middle school readers. *Literacy Research and Instruction, 48,* 14–27.

Doll, B., Haack, K., Kosse, S., Osterloh, M., Siemers, E., & Pray, B. (2005). The dilemma of pragmatics: Why schools don't use quality team consultation practices. *Journal of Educational and Psychological Consultation, 16,* 127–155.

Doughty, S. S., & Anderson, C. M. (2006). Effects of noncontingent reinforcement and functional communication training on problem behavior and mands. *Education and Treatment of Children, 29*(1), 23–50.

DuFour, R., & Eaker, R. (1998). *Professional learning communities at work: Best practices for enhancing student achievement.* Bloomington, IN: Solution Tree.

DuFour, R., Eaker, R., & DuFour, R. (2005). *On common ground.* Bloomington, IN: National Educational Service.

Duncan, G. J., Dowsett, C. J., Claessens, A., Magnuson, K., Huston, A. C., Klebanov, P., et al. (2007). School readiness and later achievement. *Developmental Psychology, 43,* 1428–1446.

Dunst, C. J., & Raab, M. (2010). Practitioners' self-evaluations of contrasting types of professional development. *Journal of Early Intervention, 32,* 239–254.

Duvall, S. F., Delquadri, J. C., Elliott, M., & Hall, R. V. (1992). Parent-tutoring procedures: Experimental analysis and validation of generalization in oral reading across passages, settings, and time. *Journal of Behavioral Education, 2,* 281–303.

Early, D., Barbarin, O., Bryant, D., Burchinal, M., Chang, F., Clifford, R., et al. (2005). *Pre-kindergarten in eleven states: NCEDL's multi-state study of pre-kindergarten and study of State-Wide Early Education Programs (SWEEP): Preliminary descriptive report.* Chapel Hill: University of North Carolina, Frank Porter Graham Child Development Institute, National Center for Early Development and Learning. Retrieved November 27, 2006, from *www.fpg.unc.edu/~NCEDL.*

Eckert, T. L., & Hintze, J. M. (2000). Behavioral conceptions and applications of acceptability: Issues related to service delivery and research methodology. *School Psychology Quarterly, 15,* 123–148.

Elkonin, D. B. (1973). U.S.S.R. In J. Downing (Ed.), *Comparative reading* (pp. 551–579). New York: Macmillan.

Elliott, S. N., Turco, T. L., & Gresham, F. M. (1987). Consumers' and clients' pretreatment acceptability ratings of classroom group contingencies. *Journal of School Psychology, 25,* 145–153.

Elliott, S. N., Witt, J. C., Kratochwill, T. R., & Stoiber, K. C. (2002). Selecting and evaluating classroom interventions. In M. R. Shinn, H. M. Walker, & G. Stoner (Eds.), *Interventions for academic and behavior problems: II. Preventive and remedial approaches* (pp. 243–294). Bethesda, MD: National Association of School Psychologists.

Englert, C. S., Raphael, T. E., Anderson, L. M., Anthony, H. M., & Stevens, D. D. (1991). Making writing strategies and self-talk visible: Writing instruction in regular and special education classrooms. *American Educational Research Journal, 28*, 337–372.

Erchul, W. P., & Martens, B. K. (2002). *School consultation: Conceptual and empirical bases of practice* (2nd ed.). New York: Kluwer Academic/Plenum.

Espin, C. A., Busch, T. W., Shin, J., & Kruschwitz, R. (2001). Curriculum-based measurement in the content areas: Validity of vocabulary-matching as an indicator of performance in social studies. *Learning Disabilities Research and Practice, 16*, 142–151.

Espin, C. A., Shin, J., & Busch, T. W. (2005). Curriculum-based measurement in the content areas: Vocabulary matching as an indicator of progress in social studies learning. *Journal of Learning Disabilities, 38*, 353–363.

Espin, C. A., & Tindal, G. (1998). Curriculum-based measurement for secondary students. In M. R. Shinn (Ed.), *Advanced applications of curriculum-based measurement* (pp. 214–253). New York: Guilford Press.

Esquivel, S. L., Ryan, C. S., & Bonner, M. (2008). Involved parents' perceptions of their experiences in school-based team meetings. *Journal of Educational and Psychological Consultation, 18*, 234–258.

Evans, J. H., Valleley, R. J., & Allen, K. D. (2002). Parent implementation of an oral reading intervention: A case study. *Child and Family Behavior Therapy, 24*(4), 39–50.

Everett, G. E., Olmi, D. J., Edwards, R. P., & Tingstrom, D. H. (2005). The contributions of eye contact and contingent praise to effective instruction delivery in compliance training. *Education and Treatment of Children, 28*, 48–62.

Evidence-Based Intervention Network. (n.d.). Taped Problems intervention. Available at *http://ebi.missouri.edu/?page_id=805*.

Figueroa, R. A., & Newsome, P. (2006). The diagnosis of LD in English learners: Is it nondiscriminatory? *Journal of Learning Disabilities, 39*, 206–214.

Flugum, K. R., & Reschly, D. J. (1994). Prereferral interventions: Quality indices and outcomes. *Journal of School Psychology, 32*, 1–14.

Forman, S. G., Shapiro, E. S., Codding, R. S., Gonzales, J. E., Reddy, L. A., Rosenfield, S. A., et al. (2013). Implementation science and school psychology. *School Psychology Quarterly, 28*, 77–100.

Fresch, M. J. (2003). A national survey of spelling instruction: Investigating teachers' beliefs and practice. *Journal of Literacy Research, 35*, 819–848.

Fuchs, D., Fuchs, L. S., & Burish, P. (2000). Peer-assisted learning strategies: An evidence-based practice to promote reading achievement. *Learning Disabilities Research and Practice, 15*, 85–91.

Fuchs, L. S. (2003). Assessing intervention responsiveness: Conceptual and technical issues. *Learning Disabilities Research and Practice, 18*, 172–186.

Fuchs, L. S., & Deno, S. L. (1994). Must instructionally useful performance assessment be based in the curriculum? *Exceptional Children, 61*, 15–24.

Fuchs, L. S., Fuchs, D., Hamlett, C. L., & Allinder, R. M. (1991). The contribution of skills analysis to curriculum-based measurement in spelling. *Exceptional Children, 57*, 443–452.

Fuchs, L. S., Fuchs, D., Hamlett, C. L., Walz, L., & Germann, G. (1993). Formative evaluation of academic progress: How much growth can we expect? *School Psychology Review, 22*, 27–48.

Fuchs, L. S., Fuchs, D., Hosp, M. K., & Jenkins, J. R. (2001). Oral reading fluency as an indicator of reading competence: A theoretical, empirical, and historical analysis. *Scientific Studies of Reading, 5*, 239–256.

Fuchs, L. S., Fuchs, D., Karns, K., Hamlett, C. L., & Katzaroff, M. (1999). Mathematics performance assessment in the classroom: Effects on teacher planning and student problem solving. *American Educational Research Journal, 36*, 609–646.

Fuchs, L. S., Fuchs, D., & Speece, D. L. (2002). Treatment validity as a unifying construct for identifying learning disabilities. *Learning Disability Quarterly, 25*, 33–45.

Fulk, B. M., & Stormont-Spurgin, M. (1995). Spelling interventions for students with disabilities: A review. *The Journal of Special Education, 28*, 488–513.

Gansle, K. A., Noell, G. H., VanDerHeyden, A. M., Naquin, G. M., & Slider, N. J. (2002). Moving beyond total words written: The reliability, criterion validity, and time cost of alternate measures for curriculum-based measurement in writing. *School Psychology Review, 31*, 477–497.

Gersten, R., Chard, D., & Baker, S. (2000). Factors enhancing sustained use of research-based instructional practices. *Journal of Learning Disabilities, 33*, 445–457.

Gersten, R., Fuchs, L. S., Williams, J. P., & Baker, S. (2001). Teaching reading comprehension strategies to students with learning disabilities: A review of research. *Review of Educational Research, 71*, 279–320.

Ghaith, G., & Yaghi, H. (1997). Relationships among experience, teacher efficacy, and attitudes toward the implementation of instructional innovation. *Teaching and Teacher Education, 13*, 451–458.

Gickling, E. E., & Armstrong, D. L. (1978). Levels of instructional difficulty as related to on-task behavior, task completion, and comprehension. *Journal of Learning Disabilities, 11*, 559–566.

Gickling, E. E., Shane, R. L., & Croskery, K. M. (1989). Developing math skills in low-achieving high school students through curriculum-based assessment. *School Psychology Review, 18*, 344–356.

Good, R. H., & Kaminski, R. A. (2002). *Dynamic Indicators of Basic Early Literacy Skills*. Eugene, OR: Institute for the Development of Educational Achievement.

Good Start, Grow Smart Interagency Workgroup. (2005, December). *Good Start, Grow Smart: A guide to Good Start, Grow Smart and other federal early learning initiatives*. Washington DC: Child Care Bureau, Administration for Children and Families, U.S. Department of Health and Human Services.

Goyette, R., Dore, R., & Dion, E. (2000). Pupils' misbehaviors and the reactions and causal attributions of physical education student teachers: A sequential analysis. *Journal of Teaching in Physical Education, 20*, 3–14.

Graden, J. L., Casey, A., & Christenson, S. L. (1985). Implementing a prereferral intervention system: Part I. The model. *Exceptional Children, 51*, 377–384.

Graham, S. (1990). The role of production factors in learning disabled students' compositions. *Journal of Educational Psychology, 82*, 781–791.

Graham, S., Berninger, V. W., Abbott, R. D., Abbott, S. P., & Whitaker, D. (1997). Role of mechanics in composing of elementary school students: A new methodological approach. *Journal of Educational Psychology, 89*, 170–182.

Graham, S., & Harris, K. R. (1997). It can be taught, but it does not develop naturally: Myths and realities in writing instruction. *School Psychology Review, 26*, 412–424.

Graham, S., & Harris, K. R. (2006). Strategy instruction and the teaching of writing. In C. A. MacArthur, S. Graham, & J. Fitzgerald (Eds.), *Handbook of writing research* (pp. 187–207). New York: Guilford Press.

Graham, S., Harris, K. R., & Chorzempa, B. F. (2002). Contribution of spelling instruction to the spelling, writing, and reading of poor spellers. *Journal of Educational Psychology, 94*, 669–686.

Graham, S., Harris, K. R., Fink-Chorzempa, B., & MacArthur, C. (2003). Primary grade teachers' instructional adaptations for struggling writers: A national survey. *Journal of Educational Psychology, 95*, 279–292.

Graham, S., Harris, K. R., & Larsen, L. (2001). Prevention and intervention of writing difficulties for students with learning disabilities. *Learning Disabilities Research and Practice, 16*, 74–84.

Graham, S., Harris, K. R., & Loynachan, C. (1993). The basic spelling vocabulary list. *The Journal of Educational Research, 86*, 363–368.

Graham, S., Harris, K. R., & Loynachan, C. (1994). The spelling for writing list. *Journal of Learning Disabilities, 27*, 210–214.

Graham, S., Harris, K. R., & MacArthur, C. A. (1993). Improving the writing of students with learning disabilities: Self-regulated strategy development. *School Psychology Review, 22*, 656–670.

Graham, S., Harris, K. R., MacArthur, C. A., & Schwartz, S. (1991). Writing and writing instruction for students with learning disabilities: Review of a research program. *Learning Disability Quarterly, 14*, 89–114.

Graham, S., & Perin, D. (2007). A meta-analysis of writing instruction for adolescent students. *Journal of Educational Psychology, 99*, 445–476.

Graham, S., & Santangelo, T. (2014). Does spelling instruction make students better spellers, readers, and writers?: A meta-analytic review. *Reading and Writing, 27*, 1703–1743.

Gravois, T. A., & Gickling, E. E. (2002). Best practices in curriculum-based assessment. In A. Thomas & J. Grimes (Eds.), *Best practices in school psychology IV* (pp. 885–898). Bethesda, MD: National Association of School Psychologists.

Gray, C. L., Gutkin, T. B., & Riley, T. R. (2001). Acceptability of rewards among high school teachers, parents, students, and administrators: Ecological implications for consultation at the high school level. *Journal of Educational and Psychological Consultation, 12*, 25–43.

Greenwood, C. R., Arreaga-Mayer, C., Utley, C. A., Gavin, K. M., & Terry, B. J. (2001). Classwide Peer Tutoring Learning Management System: Applications with elementary-level English language learners. *Remedial and Special Education, 22*, 34–47.

Greenwood, C. R., Carta, J. J., Kamps, D., Terry, B., & Delquadri, J. (1994). Development and validation of standard classroom observation systems for school practitioners: Ecobehavioral Assessment Systems Software (EBASS). *Exceptional Children, 61*, 197–210.

Greenwood, C. R., Hops, H., Delquadri, J., & Guild, J. (1974). Group contingencies for group consequences in classroom management: A further analysis. *Journal of Applied Behavior Analysis, 7*, 413–425.

Gresham, F. M., MacMillan, D. L., Beebe-Frankenberger, M. E., & Bocian, K. M. (2000). Treatment integrity in learning disabilities intervention research: Do we really know how treatments are implemented? *Learning Disabilities Research and Practice, 15*, 198–205.

Guastello, E. F., Beasley, T. M., & Sinatra, R. C. (2000). Concept mapping effects on science content comprehension of low-achieving inner-city seventh graders. *Remedial and Special Education, 21*, 356–365.

Gunter, P. L., Hummel, J. H., & Conroy, M. A. (1998). Increasing correct academic responding: An effective intervention strategy to decrease behavior problems. *Effective School Practices, 17*(2), 55–62.

Gurney, D., Gersten, R., Dimino, J., & Carnine, D. (1990). Story grammar: Effective literature instruction for high school students with learning disabilities. *Journal of Learning Disabilities, 23,* 335–342, 348.

Gutkin, T. B., & Curtis, M. J. (1999). School-based consultation theory and practice: The art and science of indirect service delivery. In C. R. Reynolds & T. B. Gutkin (Eds.), *The handbook of school psychology* (3rd ed., pp. 598–637). New York: Wiley.

Haager, D., & Windmueller, M. P. (2001). Early reading intervention for English language learners at-risk for learning disabilities: Student and teacher outcomes in an urban school. *Learning Disability Quarterly, 24,* 235–250.

Hagermoser Sanetti, L. M., & DiGennaro Reed, F. D. (2012). Barriers to implementing treatment integrity procedures in school psychology research: Survey of treatment outcome researchers. *Assessment for Effective Intervention, 37,* 195–202.

Hagermoser Sanetti, L. M., Gritter, K. L., & Dobey, L. M. (2011). Treatment integrity of interventions with children in the school psychology literature from 1995 to 2008. *School Psychology Review, 40,* 72–84.

Hagermoser Sanetti, L. M., Luiselli, J. K., & Handler, M. W. (2007). Effects of verbal and graphic performance feedback on behavior support plan implementation in a public elementary school. *Behavior Modification, 31,* 454–465.

Hamlet, C. C., Axelrod, S., & Kuerschener, S. (1984). Eye contact as an antecedent to compliant behavior. *Journal of Applied Behavior Analysis, 17,* 553–557.

Hamre, B. K., & Pianta, R. C. (2001). Early teacher–child relationships and the trajectory of children's school outcomes through eighth grade. *Child Development, 72,* 625–638.

Hansen, J., & Pearson, P.D. (1983). An instructional study: Improving the inferential comprehension of good and poor fourth-grade readers. *Journal of Educational Psychology, 75,* 821–829.

Hargrave, A. C., & Sénéchal, M. (2000). A book reading intervention with preschool children who have limited vocabularies: The benefits of regular reading and dialogic reading. *Early Childhood Research Quarterly, 15,* 75–90.

Haring, N. G., & Eaton, M. D. (1978). Systematic instructional technology: An instructional hierarchy. In N. G. Haring, T. C. Lovitt, M. D. Eaton, & C. L. Hansen (Eds.), *The fourth R: Research in the classroom* (pp. 93–126). Columbus, OH: Merrill.

Harn, B., Parisi, D., & Stoolmiller, M. (2013). Balancing fidelity with flexibility and fit: What do we really know about fidelity of implementation in schools? *Exceptional Children, 79,* 181–193.

Harris, A. J., & Jacobson, M. D. (1972). *Basic elementary reading vocabularies.* New York: Macmillan.

Harris, K. R., Graham, S., & Mason, L. H. (2003). Self-regulated strategy development in the classroom: Part of a balanced approach to writing instruction for students with disabilities. *Focus on Exceptional Children, 35*(7), 1–16.

Harris, K. R., Graham, S., Mason, L. H., & Friedlander, B. (2008). *POWERFUL writing strategies for all students.* Baltimore: Brookes.

Harrison, S. E., Riley-Tillman, T. C., & Chafouleas, S. M. (2014). Direct behavior ratings: Considerations for rater accuracy. *Canadian Journal of School Psychology, 29,* 3–20.

Hart, B., & Risley, T. R. (1992). American parenting of language-learning children: Persisting differences in family–child interactions observed in natural home environments. *Developmental Psychology, 28,* 1096–1105.

Hart, B., & Risley, T. R. (1995). *Meaningful differences in the everyday experience of young American children.* Baltimore: Brookes.

Hasbrouck, J., & Tindal, G. A. (2006). Oral reading fluency norms: A valuable assessment tool for reading teachers. *The Reading Teacher, 59,* 636–644.

Hattie, J. A. C. (2009). *Visible learning: A synthesis of 800+ meta-analyses on achievement.* New York: Routledge.

Hawkins, R. O., Morrison, J. Q., Musti-Rao, S., & Hawkins, J. A. (2008). Treatment integrity for academic interventions in real-world settings. *School Psychology Forum, 2*(3), 1–15.

Hawkins, S. M., & Heflin, L. J. (2010). Increasing secondary teachers' behavior-specific praise using a video self-modeling and visual performance feedback intervention. *Journal of Positive Behavior Interventions, 13,* 97–108.

Heck, A., Collins, J., & Peterson, L. (2001). Decreasing children's risk taking on the playground. *Journal of Applied Behavior Analysis, 34,* 349–352.

Henderlong, J., & Lepper, M. R. (2002). The effects of praise on children's intrinsic motivation: A review and synthesis. *Psychological Bulletin, 128,* 774–795.

Hintze, J. M., & Christ, T. J. (2004). An examination of variability as a function of passage variance in CBM progress monitoring. *School Psychology Review, 33,* 204–217.

Hiralall, A. S., & Martens, B. K. (1998). Teaching classroom management skills to preschool staff: The effects of scripted instructional sequences on teacher and student behavior. *School Psychology Quarterly, 13,* 94–115.

Hixson, M. D., Christ, T. J., & Bruni, T. (2014). Best practices in the analysis of progress monitoring data and decision making. In P. L. Harrison & A. Thomas (Eds.), *Best practices in school psychology: Foundations* (pp. 343–354). Bethesda, MD: National Association of School Psychologists.

Hoagwood, K., & Erwin, H. D. (1997). Effectiveness of school-based mental health services for children: A 10-year research review. *Journal of Child and Family Studies, 6*(4), 435–451.

Horn, C. (2010). Response cards: An effective intervention for students with disabilities. *Education and Training in Autism and Developmental Disabilities, 45*(1), 116–123.

Horner, R. H., Sugai, G., & Anderson, C. M. (2010). Examining the evidence base for school-wide positive behavior support. *Focus on Exceptional Children, 42*, 1–14.

Hosp, J. L. (2008). Best practices in aligning academic assessment with instruction. In A. Thomas & J. Grimes (Eds.), *Best practices in school psychology V* (pp. 363–376). Bethesda, MD: National Association of School Psychologists.

Hosp, J. L., & Reschly, D. J. (2004). Disproportionate representation of minority students in special education: Academic, demographic, and economic predictors. *Exceptional Children, 70*, 185–199.

Hosp, M. K., Hosp, J. L, & Howell, K. W. (2016). *The ABCs of CBM: A practical guide to curriculum-based measurement* (2nd ed.). New York: Guilford Press.

Houghton, S., Wheldall, K., Jukes, R., & Sharpe, A. (1990). The effects of limited private reprimands and increased private praise on classroom behaviour in four British secondary school classes. *British Journal of Educational Psychology, 60*, 255–265.

Hughes, C. A., Ruhl, K. L., Schumaker, J. B., & Deshler, D. D. (2002). Effects of instruction in an assignment completion strategy on the homework performance of students with learning disabilities in general education class. *Learning Disabilities Research and Practice, 17*, 1–18.

Hughes, T. A., & Fredrick, L. D. (2006). Teaching vocabulary with students with learning disabilities using classwide peer tutoring and constant time delay. *Journal of Behavioral Education, 15*, 1–23.

Hylander, I. (2012). Conceptual change through consultee-centered consultation: A theoretical model. *Consulting Psychology Journal: Practice and Research, 64*, 29–45.

Idol, L. (1987). A critical thinking map to improve content area comprehension of poor readers. *Remedial and Special Education, 8*, 28–40.

Jacob, S., & Decker, D. M. (2010). *Ethics and law for school psychologists* (5th ed.). New York: Wiley.

Jenson, W. R., Rhode, G., & Revis, H. K. (1994). *The Tough Kid Tool Box*. Longmont, CO: Sopris West.

Jewell, J., & Malecki, C. K. (2005). The utility of CBM written language indices: An investigation of production-dependent, production-independent, and accurate-production scores. *School Psychology Review, 34*, 27–44.

Jeynes, W. (2012). A meta-analysis of the efficacy of different types of parental involvement programs for urban students. *Urban Education, 47*, 706–742.

Johnson, T. C., Stoner, G., & Green, S. K. (1996).

Demonstrating the experimenting society model with classwide behavior management interventions. *School Psychology Review, 25*, 199–214.

Jones, K. M., & Wickstrom, K. F. (2002). Done in sixty seconds: Further analysis of the assessment model for academic problems. *School Psychology Review, 31*, 554–568.

Jones, K. M., Wickstrom, K. F., Noltemeyer, A. L., Brown, S. M. Schuka, J. R., & Therrien, W. J. (2009). An experimental analysis of reading fluency. *Journal of Behavioral Education, 18*, 35–55.

Joseph, L. M. (2000a). Developing first graders' phonemic awareness, word identification, and spelling: A comparison of two contemporary phonic instructional approaches. *Reading Research and Instruction, 39*(2), 160–169.

Joseph, L. M. (2000b). Using word boxes as a large group phonics approach in a first grade classroom. *Reading Horizons, 41*(2), 117–127.

Kahle, A. L., & Kelley, M. L. (1994). Children's homework problems: A comparison of goal setting and parent training. *Behavior Therapy, 25*, 275–290.

Kamins, M. L., & Dweck, C. S. (1999). Person versus process praise and criticism: Implications for contingent self-worth and coping. *Developmental Psychology, 35*, 835–847.

Kaminski, R. A., & Good, R. H., III. (1996). Toward a technology for assessing basic early literacy skills. *School Psychology Review, 25*, 215–227.

Kamps, D., Wills, H., Dawson-Bannister, H., Heitzman-Powell, L., Kottwitz, E., Hansen, B., et al. (2015). Class-wide function-related intervention teams "CW-FIT" efficacy trial outcomes. *Journal of Positive Behavior Interventions, 17*, 134–145.

Kamps, D., Wills, H. P., Heitzman-Powell, L., Laylin, J., Szoke, C., Petrillo, T., et al. (2011). Class-wide function-related intervention teams: Effects of group contingency programs in urban classrooms. *Journal of Positive Behavior Interventions, 13*, 154–167.

Kanive, R., Nelson, P. M., Burns, M. K., & Ysseldyke, J. (2014). Comparison of the effects of computer-based practice and conceptual understanding interventions on mathematics fact retention and generalization. *Journal of Educational Research, 107*, 83–89.

Kartub, D. T., Taylor-Greene, S., March, R. E., & Horner, R. H. (2000). Reducing hallway noise: A systems approach. *Journal of Positive Behavior Interventions, 2*, 179–182.

Kellam, S. G., Ling, X., Merisca, R., Brown, C. H., & Ialongo, N. (1998). The effect of the level of aggression in the first grade classroom on the course and malleability of aggressive behavior into middle school. *Development and Psychopathology, 10*, 165–185.

Kelshaw-Levering, K., Sterling-Turner, H. E., Henry, J. R., & Skinner, C. H. (2000). Randomized interdependent group contingencies: Group reinforcement with a twist. *Psychology in the Schools, 37,* 523–533.

Kern, L., & Clemens, N. H. (2007). Antecedent strategies to promote appropriate classroom behavior. *Psychology in the Schools, 44,* 65–75.

Ketterlin-Geller, L. R., Chard, D. J., & Fien, H. (2008). Making connections in mathematics: Conceptual mathematics intervention for low-performing students. *Remedial and Special Education, 29,* 33–45.

Kettler, R. J., Glover, T. A., Albers, C. A., & Feeney-Kettler, K. A. (2014). *Universal screening in educational settings: Evidence-based decision making for schools.* Washington, DC: American Psychological Association.

Kilgus, S. P., Chafouleas, S. M., Riley-Tillman, T. C., & Welsh, M. (2012). Direct behavior rating scales as screeners: A preliminary investigation of diagnostic accuracy in elementary schools. *School Psychology Quarterly, 27,* 41–50.

Kilgus, S. P., Riley-Tillman, T. C., Chafouleas, S. M., Christ, T. J., & Welsh, M. E. (2014). Direct behavior rating as a school-based behavior universal screener: Replication across sites. *Journal of School Psychology, 52,* 63–82.

Killion, J. (2009). Coaches' roles, responsibilities, and reach. In J. Knight (Ed.), *Coaching approaches and perspectives* (pp. 7–28). Thousand Oaks, CA: Corwin Press.

Klingner, J., & Artiles, A. J. (2006). English language learners struggling to learn to read: Emergent scholarship on linguistic differences and learning disabilities. *Journal of Learning Disabilities, 39,* 386–389.

Klingner, J. K., Ahwee, S., Pilonieta, P., & Menendez, R. (2003). Barriers and facilitators in scaling up research-based practices. *Exceptional Children, 69,* 411–429.

Klingner, J. K., & Harry, B. (2006). The special education referral and decision-making process for English language learners: Child study team meetings and placement conferences. *Teachers College Record, 108*(11), 2247–2281.

Klingner, J. K., Vaughn, S., Hughes, M. T., & Arguelles, M. E. (1999). Sustaining research-based practices in reading: A 3-year follow-up. *Remedial and Special Education, 20,* 263–287.

Klingner, J. K., Vaughn, S., & Schumm, J. S. (1998). Collaborative strategic reading during social studies in heterogeneous fourth-grade classrooms. *Elementary School Journal, 99,* 3–22.

Konrad, M., Joseph, L. M., & Eveleigh, E. (2009). A meta-analytic review of guided notes. *Education and Treatment of Children, 32,* 421–444.

Kostewicz, D. E. (2010). A review of timeout ribbons. *Behavior Analyst Today, 11,* 95–104.

Kovaleski, J. F. (2002). Best practices in operating pre-referral intervention teams. In A. Thomas & J. Grimes (Eds.) *Best practices in school psychology IV* (pp. 645–655). Bethesda, MD: National Association of School Psychologists.

Kovaleski, J. F., Gickling, E. E., & Morrow, H., & Swank, P. (1999). High versus low implementation of instructional support teams: A case for maintaining program fidelity. *Remedial and Special Education, 20,* 170–183.

Kovaleski, J. F., Tucker, J. A., & Stevens, L. J. (1996). Bridging special and regular education: The Pennsylvania Initiative. *Educational Leadership, 53,* 44–47.

Kratochwill, T. R., & Shernoff, E. S. (2004). Evidence-based practice: Promoting evidence-based interventions in school psychology. *School Psychology Review, 33,* 34–48.

Kratochwill, T. R., & Stoiber, K. C. (2000). Empirically supported interventions and school psychology: Conceptual and practice issues: Part II. *School Psychology Quarterly, 15,* 233–253.

Kretlow, A. G., Cooke, N. L., & Wood, C. L. (2012). Using in-service and coaching to increase teachers' accurate use of research-based strategies. *Remedial and Special Education, 33,* 348–361.

Kruger, L. J., Struzziero, J., Watts, R., & Vacca, D. (1995). The relationship between organizational support and satisfaction with teacher assistance teams. *Remedial and Special Education, 16,* 203–211.

LaFleur, L., Witt, J. C., Naquin, G., Harwell, V., & Gilbertson, D. M. (1998). Use of coaching to enhance proactive classroom management by improvement of student transitioning between classroom activities. *Effective School Practices, 17,* 70–82.

Lane, K. L., Mahdavi, J. N., & Borthwick-Duffy, S. (2003). Teacher perceptions of the prereferral intervention process: A call for assistance with school-based interventions. *Preventing School Failure: Alternative Education for Children and Youth, 47,* 148–155.

Lane, K. L., O'Shaughnessy, T. E., Lambros, K. M., Gresham, F. M., & Beebe-Frankenberger, M. E. (2001). The efficacy of phonological awareness training with first-grade students who have behavior problems and reading difficulties. *Journal of Emotional and Behavioral Disorders, 9,* 219–231.

Larabee, K. M., Burns, M. K., & McComas, J. J. (2014). Effects of an iPad-supported phonics intervention on decoding performance and time on-task. *Journal of Behavioral Education, 23,* 449–469.

Larrivee, L. S., & Catts, H. W. (1999). Early reading achievement in children with expressive phonological disorders. *American Journal of Speech–Language Pathology, 8,* 118–128.

Lembke, E., Deno, S. L., & Hall, K. (2003). Identifying an indicator of growth in early writing proficiency for elementary school students. *Assessment for Effective Intervention, 28,* 23–36.

Lentz, F. E., Jr., Allen, S. J., & Ehrhardt, K. E. (1996).

The conceptual elements of strong interventions in school settings. *School Psychology Quarterly, 11,* 118–136.

Lenz, B. K., & Hughes, C. A. (1990). A word identification strategy for adolescents with learning disabilities. *Journal of Learning Disabilities, 23,* 149–158, 163.

Lewis, B. A., Freebairn, L. A., & Taylor, H. G. (2000). Academic outcomes in children with histories of speech sound disorders. *Journal of Communication Disorders, 33,* 11–30.

Lewis, T., Colvin, G., & Sugai, G. (2000). The effects of pre-correction and active supervision on the recess behavior of elementary students. *Education and Treatment of Children, 23*(2), 109–121.

Lewis, T. J., Powers, L. J., Kelk, M. J., & Newcomer, L. L. (2002). Reducing problem behaviors on the playground: An investigation of the application of schoolwide positive behavior supports. *Psychology in the Schools, 39,* 181–190.

Lienemann, T. O., Graham, S., Leader-Janssen, B., & Reid, R. (2006). Improving the writing performance of struggling writers in second grade. *Journal of Special Education, 40,* 66–78.

Lindo, E. J. (2006). The African American presence in reading intervention experiments. *Remedial and Special Education, 27,* 148–153.

Little, E., Hudson, A., & Wilks, R. (2002). The efficacy of written teacher advice (tip sheets) for managing classroom behaviour problems. *Educational Psychology, 22,* 251–266.

LoCasale-Crouch, J., Konold, T., Pianta, R., Howes, C., Burchinal, M., Bryant, D., et al. (2007). Observed classroom quality profiles in state-funded pre-kindergarten programs and associations with teacher, program, and classroom characteristics. *Early Childhood Research Quarterly, 22,* 3–17.

Lonigan, C. J., & Whitehurst, G. J. (1998). Relative efficacy of parent and teacher involvement in a shared-reading intervention for preschool children from low-income backgrounds. *Early Childhood Research Quarterly, 13,* 263–290.

Love, N. (2009). *Using data to improve learning for all: A collaborative inquiry approach.* Thousand Oaks, CA: Corwin Press.

Lundstrom, K., & Baker, W. (2009). To give is better than to receive: The benefits of peer review to the reviewer's own writing. *Journal of Second Language Writing, 18,* 30–43.

Maag, J. W. (2001). Rewarded by punishment: Reflections on the disuse of positive reinforcement in schools. *Exceptional Children, 67,* 173–186.

MacQuarrie, L. L., Tucker, J. A., Burns, M. K., & Hartman, B. (2002). Comparison of retention rates using traditional drill sandwich, and incremental rehearsal flash card methods. *School Psychology Review, 31,* 584–595.

Madaus, M. M. R., Kehle, T. J., Madaus, J., & Bray, M. A. (2003). Mystery motivator as an intervention to promote homework completion and accuracy. *School Psychology International, 24,* 369–377.

Magnuson, K. A., Ruhm, C., & Waldfogel, J. (2007). The persistence of preschool effects: Do subsequent classroom experiences matter? *Early Childhood Research Quarterly, 22,* 18–38.

Malecki, C. K., & Jewell, J. (2003). Developmental, gender, and practical considerations in scoring curriculum-based measurement writing probes. *Psychology in the Schools, 40,* 379–390.

Malone, R. A., & McLaughlin, T. F. (1997). The effects of reciprocal peer tutoring with a group contingency on quiz performance in vocabulary with seventh- and eighth-grade students. *Behavioral Interventions, 12,* 27–40.

Mancl, D. B., Miller, S. P., & Kennedy, M. (2012). Using the Concrete–Representational–Abstract sequence with integrated strategy instruction to teach subtraction with regrouping to students with learning disabilities. *Learning Disabilities Research and Practice, 27,* 152–166.

Martens, B. K., & Witt, J. C. (2004). Competence, persistence, and success: The positive psychology of behavioral skill instruction. *Psychology in the Schools, 41,* 19–30.

Mastropieri, M. A., Scruggs, T. E., Spencer, V., & Fontana, J. (2003). Promoting success in high school world history: Peer tutoring versus guided notes. *Learning Disabilities Research and Practice, 18,* 52–65.

Mathes, P. G., Fuchs, D., & Fuchs, L. S. (1997). Cooperative story mapping. *Remedial and Special Education, 18,* 20–27.

Mathes, P. G., Howard, J. K., Allen, S. H., & Fuchs, D. (1998). Peer-assisted learning strategies for first-grade readers: Responding to the needs of diverse learners. *Reading Research Quarterly, 33*(1), 62–94.

Matsumura, L. C., Patthey-Chavez, G. G., Valdés, R., & Garnier, H. (2002). Teacher feedback, writing assignment quality, and third-grade students' revision in lower- and higher-achieving urban schools. *Elementary School Journal, 103*(1), 3–25.

McCabe, P. C. (2005). Social and behavioral correlates of preschoolers with specific language impairment. *Psychology in the Schools, 42,* 373–387.

McCallum, E., & Schmitt, A. J. (2011). The Taped Problems intervention: Increasing the math fact fluency of a student with an intellectual disability. *International Journal of Special Education, 26,* 276–284.

McCandliss, B., Beck, I. L., Sandak, R., & Perfetti, C. (2003). Focusing attention on decoding for children with poor reading skills: Design and preliminary tests of the word building intervention. *Scientific Studies of Reading, 7,* 75–104.

McDonnell, J., Thorson, N., Allen, C., & Mathot-Buckner, C. (2000). The effects of partner learning during spelling for students with severe disabilities and their peers. *Journal of Behavioral Education, 10*, 107–121.

McDougal, J. L., Moody Clonan, S., & Martens, B. K. (2000). Using organizational change procedures to promote the acceptability of prereferral intervention services: The school-based intervention team project. *School Psychology Quarterly, 15*, 149–171.

McGlinchey, M. T., & Hixson, M. D. (2004). Using curriculum-based measurement to predict performance on state assessments in reading. *School Psychology Review, 33*, 193–203.

McGoey, K. E., & DuPaul, G. J. (2000). Token reinforcement and response cost procedures: Reducing the disruptive behavior of preschool children with attention-deficit/hyperactivity disorder. *School Psychology Quarterly, 15*, 330–343.

McLane, K. (n.d.). *Student progress monitoring: What this means for your child.* Washington, DC: National Center on Student Progress Monitoring.

McNamara, E., Evans, M., & Hill, W. (1986). The reduction of disruptive behaviour in two secondary school classes. *British Journal of Educational Psychology, 56*(2), 209–215.

McNamara, K., & Hollinger, C. (2003). Intervention-based assessment: Evaluation rates and eligibility findings. *Exceptional Children, 69*, 181–193.

Meyers, B., Valentino, C. T., Meyers, J., Boretti, M., & Brent, D. (1996). Implementing prereferral intervention teams as an approach to school-based consultation in an urban school system. *Journal of Educational and Psychological Consultation, 7*, 119–149.

Miller, F. G., Chafouleas, S. M., Riley-Tillman, T. C., & Fabiano, G. A. (2014). Teacher perceptions of the usability of school-based behavior assessments. *Behavioral Disorders, 39*, 201–210.

Miller, F. G., Cohen, D., Chafouleas, S. M., Riley-Tillman, T. C., Welsh, M. E., & Fabiano, G. A. (2015). A comparison of measures to screen for social, emotional, and behavioral risk. *School Psychology Quarterly, 30*(2), 184–192.

Miller, L. J., Strain, P. S., Boyd, K., Jarzynka, J., & McFetridge, M. (1993). The effects of classwide self-assessment on preschool children's engagement in transition, free play, and small-group instruction. *Early Education and Development, 4*, 162–181.

Mitchell, R. R., Tingstrom, D. H., Dufrene, B. A., Ford, W. B., & Sterling, H. E. (2015). The effects of the Good Behavior Game with general-education high school students. *School Psychology Review, 44*, 191–207.

Mol, S. E., Bus, A. G., & de Jong, M. T. (2009). Interactive book reading in early education: A tool to stimulate print knowledge as well as oral language. *Review of Educational Research, 79*, 979–1007.

Montague, M. (2008). Self-regulation strategies to improve mathematical problem-solving for students with learning disabilities. *Learning Disability Quarterly, 31*, 37–44.

Montague, M., & Bos, C. S. (1986). The effect of cognitive strategy training on verbal math problem solving performance of learning disabled adolescents. *Journal of Learning Disabilities, 19*, 26–33.

Moore, L. A., Waguespack, A. M., Wickstrom, K. F., Witt, J. C., & Gaydos, G. R. (1994). Mystery Motivator: An effective and time-efficient intervention. *School Psychology Review, 23*, 106–118.

Moroz, K. B., & Jones, K. M. (2002). The effects of Positive Peer Reporting on children's social involvement. *School Psychology Review, 31*, 235–245.

Morris, D., Blanton, L., Blanton, W. E., & Perney, J. (1995). Spelling instruction and achievement in six classrooms. *Elementary School Journal, 96*, 145–162.

Mottram, L. M., Bray, M. A., Kehle, T. J., Broudy, M., & Jenson, W. R. (2002). A classroom-based intervention to reduce disruptive behavior. *Journal of Applied School Psychology, 19*, 65–74.

National Association of School Psychologists. (2010). *Principles for professional ethics.* Bethesda, MD: Author.

National Center for Children in Poverty. (2006). *Basic facts about low-income children: Birth to age 6.* New York: Columbia University Mailman School of Public Health, National Center for Children in Poverty. Retrieved November 26, 2006, from *www.nccp.org/pub_ycp06b.html.*

National Center for Education Statistics. (2007). *The condition of education 2005* (NCES 2007-064). Washington, DC: U.S. Department of Education, Institute of Education Sciences. Retrieved June 1, 2007, from *http://nces.ed.gov/programs/coe.*

National Center for Education Statistics. (2015). *Condition of education.* Washington, DC: U.S. Department of Education.

National Center for Education Statistics. (2016). *Digest of education statistics, 2014.* Washington, DC: U.S. Department of Education.

National Commission on Writing. (2003, April). *The neglected R: The need for a writing revolution.* Available at *www.collegeboard.com.*

National Commission on Writing. (2004, September). *Writing: A ticket to work . . . or a ticket out: A survey of business leaders.* Available at *www.collegeboard.com.*

National Council of Teachers of Mathematics. (2000). *Principles and standards for school mathematics* (Vol. 1). Reston, VA: Author.

National Mathematics Advisory Panel. (2008). *Foundations for success: The final report of the National Mathematics Advisory Panel.* Washington, DC: U.S. Department of Education.

National Reading Panel. (2000). *Report of the*

national reading panel: Teaching children to read: An evidence-based assessment of the scientific research literature on reading and its implications for reading instruction: Reports of the subgroups. Washington, DC: National Institute of Child Health and Human Development, National Institutes of Health.

National Research Council & Institute of Medicine. (2009). Preventing mental, emotional, and behavioral disorders among young people: Progress and possibilities (M. E. O'Connell, T. Boat, & K. E. Warner, Eds.). Washington, DC: National Academies Press.

Nelson, J. M., & Machek, G. R. (2007). A survey of training, practice, and competence in reading assessment and intervention. School Psychology Review, 36, 311–327.

Nelson, J. R., Smith, D. J., & Dodd, J. M. (1992). The effects of teaching a summary skills strategy to students identified as learning disabled on their comprehension of science text. Education and Treatment of Children, 15, 228–243.

Nelson, P. M., Burns, M. K., Kanive, R., & Ysseldyke, J. E. (2013). Comparison of a math fact rehearsal and a mnemonic strategy approach for improving math fact fluency. Journal of School Psychology, 51, 659–667.

Nesbit, J. C., & Adesope, O. O. (2006). Learning with concept and knowledge maps: A meta-analysis. Review of Educational Research, 76, 413–448.

Neuman, S. B., & Celano, D. (2001). Access to print in low-income and middle?income communities: An ecological study of four neighborhoods. Reading Research Quarterly, 36, 8–26.

Nist, L., & Joseph, L. M. (2008). Effectiveness and efficiency of flashcard drill instructional methods on urban first-graders' word recognition, acquisition, maintenance, and generalization. School Psychology Review, 37, 294–308.

Northup, J. (2000). Further evaluation of the accuracy of reinforcer surveys: A systematic replication. Journal of Applied Behavior Analysis, 33, 335–338.

Novak, J. D., & Canas, A. J. (2006). The theory underlying concept maps and how to construct them. Pensacola: Florida Institute for Human and Machine Cognition. Available at http://cmap.ihmc.us/Publications/researchPapers/theorycmaps/TheoryUnderlyingConceptMaps.bck-11-01-06.htm.

Olympia, D. E., Sheridan, S. M., Jenson, W. R., & Andrews, D. (1994). Using student-managed interventions to increase homework completion and accuracy. Journal of Applied Behavior Analysis, 27, 85–99.

Ortiz, A. A., Wilkinson, C. Y., Robertson-Courtney, P., & Kushner, M. I. (2006). Considerations in implementing intervention assistance teams to support English language learners. Remedial and Special Education, 27, 53–63.

Osius, E., & Rosenthal, J. (2009). The National Research Council/Institute of Medicine's adolescent health services: Highlights and considerations for state health policymakers. Washington, DC: National Academy for State Health Policy.

Parker, D. C., & Burns, M. K. (2014). Using the instructional level as a criterion to target reading interventions. Reading and Writing Quarterly, 30, 79–94.

Parker, D. C., McMaster, K. L., & Burns, M. K. (2011). Determining an instructional level for beginning writing skills. School Psychology Review, 40, 158–167.

Patrick, C. A., Ward, P., & Crouch, D. W. (1998). Effects of holding students accountable for social behaviors during volleyball games in elementary physical education. Journal of Teaching in Physical Education, 17, 143–156.

Pelco, L. E., & Reed-Victor, E. (2007). Self-regulation and learning-related social skills: Intervention ideas for elementary school students. Preventing School Failure: Alternative Education for Children and Youth, 51, 36–42.

Perry, K. E., Donohue, K. M., & Weinstein, R. S. (2007). Teaching practices and the promotion of achievement and adjustment in first grade. Journal of School Psychology, 45, 269–292.

Persampieri, M., Gortmaker, V., Daly, E. J., Sheridan, S. M., & McCurdy, M. (2006). Promoting parent use of empirically supported reading interventions: Two experimental investigations of child outcomes. Behavioral Interventions, 21, 31–57.

Peterson, S. K., Mercer, C. D., & O'Shea, L. (1988). Teaching learning disabled students place value using the concrete to abstract sequence. Learning Disabilities Research, 4, 52–56.

Petursdottir, A. L., McMaster, K., McComas, J. J., Bradfield, T., Braganza, V., Koch-McDonald, J., et al. (2009). Brief experimental analysis of early reading interventions. Journal of School Psychology, 47, 215–243.

Phillips, K. J., & Mudford, O. C. (2011). Effects of noncontingent reinforcement and choice of activity on aggressive behavior maintained by attention. Behavioral Interventions, 26, 147–160.

Pianta, R. C. (1999). Enhancing relationships between children and teachers. Washington, DC: American Psychological Association.

Pianta, R. C., Howes, C., Burchinal, M., Bryant, D., Clifford, R., Early, D., et al. (2005). Features of pre-kindergarten programs, classrooms, and teacher: Do they predict observed classroom quality and child–teacher interactions? Applied Developmental Science, 9, 144–159.

Pinkus, L. (2006). Who's counted? Who's counting? Understanding high school graduation rates. Washington, DC: Alliance for Excellent Education.

Polanin, J. R., & Espelage, D. L. (2015). Using a

meta-analytic technique to assess the relationship between treatment intensity and program effects in a cluster-randomized trial. *Journal of Behavioral Education, 24,* 133–151.

Pollard-Durodola, S. D., Gonzalez, J. E., Simmons, D. C., Kwok, O., Taylor, A. B., Davis, M. J., et al. (2011). The effects of an intensive shared book-reading intervention for preschool children at risk for vocabulary delay. *Exceptional Children, 77,* 161–183.

Poncy, B. C., Skinner, C. H., & McCallum, E. (2012). A comparison of class?wide Taped Problems and Cover, Copy, and Compare for enhancing mathematics fluency. *Psychology in the Schools, 49,* 744–755.

Popkin, J., & Skinner, C. H. (2003). Enhancing academic performance in a classroom serving students with serious emotional disturbance: Interdependent group contingencies with randomly selected components. *School Psychology Review, 32,* 282–295.

Porterfield, J. K., Herbert-Jackson, E., & Risley, T. R. (1976). Contingent observation: An effective and acceptable procedure for reducing disruptive behavior of young children in a group setting. *Journal of Applied Behavior Analysis, 9,* 55–64.

PRESS Research Group. (2014). *PRESS intervention manual* (2nd ed.). Minneapolis: Minnesota Center for Reading Research.

Proctor, M. A., & Morgan, D. (1991). Effectiveness of a response-cost raffle procedure on the disruptive classroom behavior of adolescents with behavior problems. *School Psychology Review, 20,* 97–109.

Public Agenda. (2004). Teaching interrupted: Do discipline policies in today's public schools foster the common good? Available at *www.publicagenda. org/files/teaching_interrupted.pdf.*

Putnam, R. F., Handler, M. W., Ramirez-Platt, C. M., & Luiselli, J. K. (2003). Improving student bus-riding behavior through a whole-school intervention. *Journal of Applied Behavior Analysis, 36,* 583–590.

Qi, C. H., & Kaiser, A. P. (2003). Behavior problems of preschool children from low-income families: Review of the literature. *Topics in Early Childhood Special Education, 23,* 188–216.

Rajwan, E., Chacko, A., & Moeller, M. (2012). Nonpharmacological interventions for preschool ADHD: State of the evidence and implications for practice. *Professional Psychology: Research and Practice, 43,* 520–526.

Raphael, T. E., & Englert, C. S. (1990). Writing and reading: Partners in constructing meaning. *The Reading Teacher, 43,* 388–400.

Rathvon, N. (1999). *Effective school interventions: Strategies for enhancing academic achievement and social competence.* New York: Guilford Press.

Reese, E., Sparks, A., & Leyva, D. (2010). A review of parent interventions for preschool children's language and emergent literacy. *Journal of Early Childhood Literacy, 10,* 97–117.

Reinke, W. M., & Herman, K. C. (2002). Creating school environments that deter antisocial behaviors in youth. *Psychology in the Schools, 39,* 549–559.

Reinke, W. M., Herman, K. C., & Sprick, R. (2011). *Motivational interviewing for effective classroom management: The Classroom Check-Up.* New York: Guilford Press.

Reinke, W. M., Lewis-Palmer, T., & Merrell, K. (2008). The Classroom Check-Up: A classwide teacher consultation model for increasing praise and decreasing disruptive behavior. *School Psychology Review, 37,* 315–332.

Rhymer, K. N., Dittmer, K. I., Skinner, C. H., & Jackson, B. (2000). Effectiveness of a multi-component treatment for improving mathematics fluency. *School Psychology Quarterly, 15,* 40–51.

Riley-Tillman, T. C., Burns, M. K., & Gibbons, K. (2013). *RTI applications: Vol. 2. Assessment, design and decision making.* New York: Guilford Press.

Riley-Tillman, T. C., Chafouleas, S. M., & Briesch, A. M. (2007). A school practitioner's guide to using Daily Behavior Report Cards to monitor interventions. *Psychology in the Schools, 44,* 77–89.

Riley-Tillman, T. C., Chafouleas, S. M., & Eckert, T. (2008). Daily Behavior Report Cards and Systematic Direct Observation: An investigation of the acceptability, reported training and use, and decision reliability among school psychologists. *Journal of Behavioral Education. 17,* 313–327.

Riley-Tillman, T. C., Methe, S. A., & Weegar, K. (2009). Examining the use of direct behavior rating methodology on classwide formative assessment: A case study. *Assessment for Effective Intervention, 34,* 224–230.

Rimm-Kaufman, S. E., Fan, X., Chiu, Y. J., & You, W. (2007). The contribution of the Responsive Classroom Approach on children's academic achievement: Results from a three-year longitudinal study. *Journal of School Psychology, 45,* 401–421.

Rimm-Kaufman, S. E., Pianta, R. C., & Cox, M. J. (2000). Teachers' judgments of problems in the transition to kindergarten. *Early Childhood Research Quarterly, 15,* 147–166.

Roberts, M. L., & Shapiro, E. S. (1996). Effects of instructional ratios on students' reading performance in a regular education program. *Journal of School Psychology, 34,* 73–91.

Rock, M. L. (2005). Use of strategic self-monitoring to enhance academic engagement, productivity, and accuracy of students with and without exceptionalities. *Journal of Positive Behavior Interventions, 7,* 3–17.

Rose, L. C., & Gallup, A. M. (2005). The 37th annual Phi Delta Kappa/Gallup Poll of the public's attitudes toward the public schools. *Phi Delta Kappan, 87,* 41–57.

Rosén, L. A., O'Leary, S. G., Joyce, S. A., Conway, G., & Pfiffner, L. J. (1984). The importance of prudent negative consequences for maintaining the appropriate behavior of hyperactive students. *Journal of Abnormal Child Psychology, 12,* 581–604.

Rosenberg, M. S. (1986). Maximizing the effectiveness of structured classroom management programs: Implementing rule-review procedures with disruptive and distractible students. *Behavioral Disorders, 11,* 239–248.

Rousseau, M. K., Tam, B. K., & Ramnarain, R. (1993). Increasing reading proficiency of language-minority students with speech and language impairments. *Education and Treatment of Children, 16,* 254–271.

Rubinson, F. (2002). Lessons learned from implementing problem-solving teams in urban high schools. *Journal of Educational and Psychological Consultation, 13,* 185–217.

Salend, S. J., & Henry, K. (1981). Response cost in mainstreamed settings. *Journal of School Psychology, 19,* 242–249.

Scheeler, M. C., Congdon, M., & Stansbery, S. (2010). Providing immediate feedback to co-teachers through bug-in-ear technology: An effective method of peer coaching in inclusion classrooms. *Teacher Education and Special Education, 33,* 83–96.

Scheeler, M. C., & Lee, D. L. (2002). Using technology to deliver immediate corrective feedback to preservice teachers. *Journal of Behavioral Education, 11,* 231–241.

Schermerhorn, P. K., & McLaughlin, T. F. (1997). Effects of the Add-a-Word spelling program on test accuracy, grades, and retention of spelling words with fifth- and sixth-grade regular education students. *Child and Family Behavior Therapy, 19,* 23–35.

Schreder, S. J., Hupp, S. D. A., Everett, G. E., & Krohn, E. (2012). Targeting reading fluency through brief experimental analysis and parental intervention over the summer. *Journal of Applied School Psychology, 28,* 200–220.

Scott, T. M., McIntyre, J., Liaupsin, C., Nelson, C. M., Conroy, M., & Payne, L. D. (2005). An examination of the relation between functional behavior assessment and selected intervention strategies with school-based teams. *Journal of Positive Behavior Interventions, 7,* 205–215.

Sénéchal, M., & Young, L. (2008). The effect of family literacy interventions on children's acquisition of reading from kindergarten to grade 3: A meta-analytic review. *Review of Educational Research, 78,* 880–907.

Shapiro, E. S. (2011). *Academic skills problems: Direct assessment and intervention* (4th ed.). New York: Guilford Press.

Shapiro, E. S., & Gebhardt, S. N. (2012). Comparing computer-adaptive and curriculum-based measurement methods of assessment. *School Psychology Review, 41,* 295–305.

Shapiro, E. S., Keller, M. A., Lutz, J. G., Santoro, L. E., & Hintze, J. M. (2006). Curriculum-based measures and performance on state assessment and standardized tests: Reading and math performance in Pennsylvania. *Journal of Psychoeducational Assessment, 24,* 19–35.

Sharpe, T., Brown, M., & Crider, K. (1995). The effects of a sportsmanship curriculum intervention on generalized positive social behavior of urban elementary school students. *Journal of Applied Behavior Analysis, 28*(4), 401–416.

Sheridan, S. M. (2000). Considerations of multiculturalism and diversity in behavioral consultation with parents and teachers. *School Psychology Review, 29,* 344–353.

Sheridan, S. M., Rispoli, K. M., & Holmes, S. R. (2014). Treatment integrity in conjoint behavioral consultation: Active ingredients and potential pathways of influence. In L. M. H. Sanetti & T. R. Kratochwill (Eds.), *Treatment integrity: A foundation for evidence-based practice in applied psychology* (pp. 255–278). Washington, DC: American Psychological Association.

Shin, J., Deno, S. L., & Espin, C. (2000). Technical adequacy of the maze task for curriculum-based measurement of reading growth. *Journal of Special Education, 34,* 164–172.

Shinn, M. R., Ysseldyke, J. E., Deno, S. L., & Tindal, G. A. (1986). A comparison of differences between students labeled learning disabled and low achieving on measures of classroom performance. *Journal of Learning Disabilities, 19,* 545–552.

Shogren, K. A., Faggella-Luby, M. N., Bae, S., & Wehmeyer, M. L. (2004). The effect of choice-making as an intervention for problem behavior: A meta-analysis. *Journal of Positive Behavior Interventions, 6,* 228–237.

Simonsen, B., Fairbanks, S., Briesch, A., Myers, D., & Sugai, G. (2008). Evidence-based practices in classroom management: Considerations for research to practice. *Education and Treatment of Children, 31,* 351–380.

Sindelar, P. T., Griffin, C. C., Smith, S. W., & Watanabe, A. K. (1992). Prereferral intervention: Encouraging notes on preliminary findings. *Elementary School Journal, 92*(3), 245–259.

Skiba, R. J., Horner, R. H., Chung, C. G., Rausch, M. K., May, S. L., & Tobin, T. (2011). Race is not neutral: A national investigation of African American and Latino disproportionality in school discipline. *School Psychology Review, 40,* 85–107.

Skinner, C. H., Cashwell, T. H., & Skinner, A. L. (2000). Increasing tooting: The effects of a peer-monitored group contingency program on students' reports of peers' prosocial behaviors. *Psychology in the Schools, 37,* 263–270.

Skinner, C. H., McLaughlin, T. F., & Logan, P. (1997). Cover, Copy, and Compare: A self-managed academic intervention effective across skills, students, and settings. *Journal of Behavioral Education, 7*, 295–306.

Slonski-Fowler, K. E., & Truscott, S. D. (2004). General education teachers' perceptions of the prereferral intervention team process. *Journal of Educational and Psychological Consultation, 15*, 1–39.

Snow, C. E., Burns, M. S., & Griffin, P. (Eds.). (1998). *Preventing reading difficulties in young children.* Washington, DC: National Academies Press.

Solomon, B. G., Klein, S. A., & Politylo, B. C. (2012). The effect of performance feedback on teachers' treatment integrity: A meta-analysis of the single-case literature. *School Psychology Review, 41*, 160–175.

Southam-Gerow, M. A., & McLeod, B. D. (2013). Advances in applying treatment integrity research for dissemination and implementation science: Introduction to special issue. *Clinical Psychology: Science and Practice, 20*, 1–13.

Spencer, V. G., Scruggs, T. E., & Mastropieri, M. A. (2003). Content area learning in middle school social studies classrooms and students with emotional or behavioral disorders: A comparison of strategies. *Behavioral Disorders, 28*, 77–93.

Sprick, R., Knight, J., Reinke, W. M., & McKale, T. (2006). *Coaching classroom management: Strategies and tools for administrators and coaches.* Eugene, OR: Pacific Northwest.

Stage, S. A., & Quiroz, D. R. (1997). A meta-analysis of interventions to decrease disruptive classroom behavior in public education settings. *School Psychology Review, 26*, 333–368.

Stecker, P. M., Fuchs, L. S., & Fuchs, D. (2005). Using curriculum-based measurement to improve student achievement: Review of research. *Psychology in the Schools, 42*, 795–819.

Stein, M., Dixon, R. C., & Isaacson, S. (1994). Effective writing instruction for diverse learners. *School Psychology Review, 23*, 392–405.

Sterling-Turner, H. E., Watson, T. S., Wildmon, M., Watkins, C., & Little, E. (2001). Investigating the relationship between training type and treatment integrity. *School Psychology Quarterly, 16*, 56–67.

Stewart, L. H., & Silberglitt, B. (2008). Best practices in developing academic local norms. In A. Thomas & J. Grimes (Eds.), *Best practices in school psychology* (V, pp. 225–242). Bethesda, MD: National Association of School Psychologists.

Stoddard, B., & MacArthur, C. A. (1993). A peer editor strategy: Guiding learning-disabled students in response and revision. *Research in the Teaching of English, 27*, 76–103.

Stoiber, K. C., & Kratochwill, T. R. (2000). Empirically supported interventions and school psychology: Rationale and methodological issues—Part I. *School Psychology Quarterly, 15*, 75–105.

Stokes, T. F., & Baer, D. M. (1977). An implicit technology of generalization. *Journal of Applied Behavior Analysis, 10*, 349–367.

Stoner, G., Scarpati, S. E., Phaneuf, R. L., & Hintze, J. M. (2002). Using curriculum-based measurement to evaluate intervention efficacy. *Child and Family Behavior Therapy, 24*(1–2), 101–112.

Strickland, T. K., & Maccini, P. (2012). Effects of Concrete–Representational–Abstract integration on the ability of students with learning disabilities to multiply linear expressions within area problems. *Remedial and Special Education, 34*, 142–153.

Struthers, J. P., Bartalamay, H., Bell, S., & McLaughlin, T. F. (1994). An analysis of the add-a-word spelling program and public posting across three categories of children with special needs. *Reading Improvement, 31*, 28–36.

Sugai, G., & Colvin, G. (1997). Debriefing: A transition step for promoting acceptable behavior. *Education and Treatment of Children, 20*, 209–221.

Sugai, G., Horner, R. H., & Gresham, F. M. (2002). Behaviorally effective school environments. In M. R. Shinn, H. M. Walker, & G. Stoner (Eds.), *Interventions for academic and behavior problems: II. Preventive and remedial approaches* (pp. 315–350). Bethesda, MD: National Association of School Psychologists.

Sullivan, A. L. (2011). Disproportionality in special education identification and placement of English language learners. *Exceptional Children, 77*, 317–334.

Sutherland, K. S., Wehby, J. H., & Copeland, S. R. (2000). Effect of varying rates of behavior-specific praise on the on-task behavior of students with EBD. *Journal of Emotional and Behavioral Disorders, 8*(1), 2–8, 26.

Szadokierski, I., & Burns, M. K. (2008). Analogue evaluation of the effects of opportunities to respond and ratios of known items within drill rehearsal of Esperanto words. *Journal of School Psychology, 46*, 593–609.

Telzrow, C. F., McNamara, K., & Hollinger, C. L. (2000). Fidelity of problem-solving implementation and relationship to student performance. *School Psychology Review, 29*, 443–461.

Templeton, S., & Morris, D. (1999). Questions teachers ask about spelling. *Reading Research Quarterly, 34*, 102–112.

Theodore, L. A., Bray, M. A., Kehle, T. J., & Jenson, W. R. (2001). Randomization of group contingencies and reinforcers to reduce classroom disruptive behavior. *Journal of School Psychology, 39*, 267–277.

Thurber, R. S., Shinn, M. R., & Smolkowski, K. (2002). What is measured in mathematics tests?: Construct validity of curriculum-based mathematics measures. *School Psychology Review, 31,* 498–513.

Tomblin, J. B., Zhang, X., Buckwalter, P., & Catts, H. (2000). The association of reading disability, behavioral disorders, and language impairment among second-grade children. *Journal of Child Psychology and Psychiatry and Allied Disciplines, 41,* 473–482.

Tominey, S. L., & McClelland, M. M. (2011). Red light, purple light: Findings from a randomized trial using circle time games to improve behavioral self-regulation in preschool. *Early Education and Development, 22,* 489–519.

Treptow, M. A., Burns, M. K., & McComas, J. J. (2007). Reading at the frustration, instructional, and independent levels: The effects on students' reading comprehension and time on task. *School Psychology Review, 36*(1), 159–166.

Truscott, S. D., Cosgrove, G., Meyers, J., & Eidle-Barkman, K. A. (2000). The acceptability of organizational consultation with prereferral intervention teams. *School Psychology Quarterly, 15,* 172–206.

Tucker, J. A. (1988). *Basic flashcard technique when vocabulary is the goal.* Unpublished teaching materials, University of Chattanooga, School of Education, Chattanooga, TN.

Turan, Y., & Erbaş, D. (2010). Social validation in special education. *Journal of International Social Research, 3,* 605–612.

Turco, T. L., & Elliott, S. N. (1986). Assessment of students' acceptability ratings of teacher-initiated interventions for classroom misbehavior. *Journal of School Psychology, 24,* 277–283.

U.S. Department of Education. (2000). *Annual report to Congress on the implementation of the Individuals with Disabilities Act.* Washington, DC: Office of Special Education and Rehabilitative Services.

U.S. Surgeon General. (1999). Mental health: A report of the Surgeon General. Retrieved June 27, 2016, from *www.surgeongeneral.gov/library/mentalhealth/home.html.*

Van Acker, R., & Grant, S. H. (1996). Teacher and student behavior as a function of risk for aggression. *Education and Treatment of Children, 19,* 316–334.

Van Houten, R., Nau, P. A., MacKenzie-Keating, S. E., Sameoto, D., & Colavecchia, B. (1982). An analysis of some variables influencing the effectiveness of reprimands. *Journal of Applied Behavior Analysis, 15,* 65–83.

VanDerHeyden, A. M., & Burns, M. K. (2005). Using curriculum-based assessment and curriculum-based measurement to guide elementary mathematics instruction: Effect on individual and group accountability scores. *Assessment for Effective Intervention, 30*(3), 15–31.

VanDerHeyden, A. M., McLaughlin, T., Algina, J., & Snyder, P. (2012). Randomized evaluation of a supplemental grade-wide mathematics intervention. *American Educational Research Journal, 49*(6), 1251–1284.

VanDerHeyden, A. M., & Snyder, P. (2006). Integrating frameworks from early childhood intervention and school psychology to accelerate growth for all young children. *School Psychology Review, 35,* 519.

VanDerHeyden, A., Snyder, P., & Hojnoski, R. (Eds.). (2006). Integrating frameworks from early childhood intervention and school psychology to accelerate growth for all young children [Special series]. *School Psychology Review, 35*(4).

VanDeWalle, J. A., Karp, K. S., & Bay-Williams, J. M. (2010). *Elementary and middle school mathematics: Teaching developmentally* (7th ed.). Boston: Allyn & Bacon.

Vaughn, S., & Coleman, M. (2004). The role of mentoring in promoting use of research-based practices in reading. *Remedial and Special Education, 25,* 25–38.

Vaughn, S., & Klingner, J. K. (1999). Teaching reading comprehension through collaborative strategic reading. *Intervention in School and Clinic, 34,* 284–292.

Vollmer, T. R., Iwata, B. A., Zarcone, J. R., Smith, R. G., & Mazaleki, J. L. (1993). The role of attention in the treatment of attention-maintained self-injurious behavior: Noncontingent reinforcement and differential reinforcement of other behavior. *Journal of Applied Behavior Analysis, 26,* 9–21.

Volpe, R. J., Burns, M. K., DuBois, M., & Zaslofsky, A. F. (2011). Computer-assisted tutoring: Teaching letter sounds to kindergarten students using incremental rehearsal. *Psychology in the Schools, 48,* 332–342.

Von Brock, M. B., & Elliott, S. N. (1987). Influence of treatment effectiveness information on the acceptability of classroom interventions. *Journal of School Psychology, 25,* 131–144.

Wagner, M., Newman, L., Cameto, R., Garza, N., & Levine, P. (2005). *After high school: A first look at the postschool experiences of youth with disabilities. A report from the National Longitudinal Transition Study–2.* Menlo Park, CA: SRI International.

Wanzek, J., Vaughn, S., Wexler, J., Swanson, E. A., Edmonds, M., & Kim, A. H. (2006). A synthesis of spelling and reading interventions and their effects on the spelling outcomes of students with LD. *Journal of Learning Disabilities, 39,* 528–543.

Wasik, B. A., & Bond, M. A. (2001). Beyond the pages of a book: Interactive book reading and language development in preschool classrooms. *Journal of Educational Psychology, 93,* 243–250.

Watkinson, J. T., & Lee, S. W. (1992). Curriculum-based measures of written expression for learning-disabled and nondisabled students. *Psychology in the Schools, 29,* 184–191.

Wayman, M. M., Wallace, T., Wiley, H. I., Tichá, R., & Espin, C. A. (2007). Literature synthesis on curriculum-based measurement in reading. *Journal of Special Education, 41*, 85–120.

Wehby, J. H., Dodge, K. A., & Valente, E. (1993). School behavior of first grade children identified as at-risk for development of conduct problems. *Behavioral Disorders, 19*, 67–78.

Wehby, J. H., Symons, F. J., Canale, J. A., & Go, F. J. (1998). Teaching practices in classrooms for students with emotional and behavioral disorders: Discrepancies between recommendations and observations. *Behavioral Disorders, 24*, 51–56.

Weissenburger, J. W., & Espin, C. (2005). Curriculum-based measures of writing across grade levels. *Journal of School Psychology, 43*, 153–169.

Wexler, J., Reed, D. K., Mitchell, M., Doyle, B., & Clancy, E. (2015). Implementing an evidence-based instructional routine to enhance comprehension of expository text. *Intervention in School and Clinic, 50*, 142–149.

White, A. G., & Bailey, J. S. (1990). Reducing disruptive behaviors of elementary physical education students with Sit and Watch. *Journal of Applied Behavior Analysis, 23*, 353–359.

Whitehurst, G. J., Zevenbergen, A. A., Crone, D. A., Schultz, M. D., Velting, O. N., & Fischel, J. E. (1999). Outcomes of an emergent literacy intervention from Head Start through second grade. *Journal of Educational Psychology, 92*, 261–272.

Wickstrom, K. F., Jones, K. M., LaFleur, L. H., & Witt, J. C. (1998). An analysis of treatment integrity in school-based behavioral consultation. *School Psychology Quarterly, 13*, 141–154.

Wilkinson, C. Y., Ortiz, A. A., Robertson, P. M., & Kushner, M. I. (2006). English language learners with reading-related LD: Linking data from multiple sources to make eligibility determinations. *Journal of Learning Disabilities, 39*, 129–141.

Wilkinson, L. A. (2005). Bridging the research-to-practice gap in school-based consultation: An example using case studies. *Journal of Educational and Psychological Consultation, 16*, 175–200.

Wills, H. P., Iwaszuk, W. M., Kamps, D., & Shumate, E. (2014). CW-FIT: Group contingency effects across the day. *Education and Treatment of Children, 37*, 191–210.

Wills, H. P., Kamps, D., Hansen, B. D., Conklin, C., Bellinger, S., Neaderhiser, J., & Nsubuga, B. (2010). The Class-wide Function-based Intervention Team (CW-FIT) program. *Preventing School Failure, 54*, 164–171.

Witt, J. C., & Elliott, S. N. (1982). The response-cost lottery: A time efficient and effective classroom intervention. *Journal of School Psychology, 20*(2), 155–161.

Witt, J. C., & Elliott, S. N. (1985). Acceptability of classroom intervention strategies. In T. R. Kratochwill (Ed.), *Advances in school psychology* (pp. 251–288). New York: Routledge.

Witzel, B. S., & Mercer, C. D. (2003). Using rewards to teach students with disabilities: Implications for motivation. *Remedial and Special Education, 24*, 88–96.

Wolfe, V. V., Boyd, L. A., & Wolfe, D. A. (1983). Teaching cooperative play to behavior problem preschool children. *Education and Treatment of Children, 6*, 1–9.

Wolfgang, C. H., & Wolfgang, M. E. (1995). *The three faces of discipline for early childhood: Empowering teachers and students* (pp. 223–225). Boston: Allyn & Bacon.

Wood, S. J., Murdock, J. Y., Cronin, M. E., Dawson, N. M., & Kirby, P. C. (1998). Effects of self-monitoring on on-task behaviors of at-risk middle school students. *Journal of Behavioral Education, 8*, 263–279.

Wurtele, S. K., & Drabman, R. S. (1984). "Beat the buzzer" for classroom dawdling: A one-year trial. *Behavior Therapy, 15*, 403–409.

Yarbrough, J. L., Skinner, C. H., Lee, Y. J., & Lemmons, C. (2004). Decreasing transition times in a second grade classroom: Scientific support for the Timely Transitions Game. *Journal of Applied School Psychology, 20*, 85–107.

Yeager, C., & McLaughlin, T. F. (1995). The use of a time-out ribbon and precision requests to improve child compliance in the classroom: A case study. *Child and Family Behavior Therapy, 17*, 1–9.

Yell, M. L., Shriner, J. G., & Katsiyannis, A. (2006). Individuals with Disabilities Education Improvement Act of 2004 and IDEA regulations of 2006: Implications for educators, administrators, and teacher trainers. *Focus on Exceptional Children, 39*(1), 1–24.

Index

Note. "f " or "t" following a page number indicates a figure or a table.